MILTON'S CENTURY

Borgo Press Books by MICHAEL R. COLLINGS

All Calm, All Bright: Christmas Offerings
The Art and Craft of Poetry: Twenty Exercises Toward Mastery
BlueRose and Other Chapbooks
Brian Aldiss
Dark Transformations: Deadly Visions of Change
Devil's Plague: A Mystery Novel
The Films of Stephen King
GemLore: An Introduction to Precious and Semi-Precious Gemstones
The House Beyond the Hill: A Novel of Horror
In Endless Morn of Light: Moral Freedom in Milton's Universe
In the Void: Poems of Science Fiction, Myth and Fantasy, & Horror
Lines from Collings Hill, by Nellie Hunt Collings (editor)
The Many Facets of Stephen King
Matrix: Echoes of Growing Up West
Milton in Context
Milton's Century: A Timeline of the Literary, Political, Religious, and Social Context of John Milton's Life
Naked to the Sun: Dark Visions of Apocalypse
The Nephiad: An Epic Poem in XII Books
Piers Anthony
Scaring Us to Death: The Impact of Stephen King on Popular Culture
Shadow Valley: A Novel of Horror
Singer of Lies: A Science Fantasy Novel
The Slab: A Novel of Horror
Static! A Novel of Horror
Tales Through Time: Poems, Revised and Enlarged Edition
Three Tales of Omne: A Companion to Wordsmith
Toward Other Worlds: Perspectives on John Milton, C. S. Lewis, Stephen King, Orson Scott Card, and Others
Wer *Means* Man *and Other Tales of Wonder and Terror*
Whole Wheat for Food Storage (with Judith Collings)
Wordsmith, Part One: The Veil of Heaven
Wordsmith, Part Two: The Thousand Eyes of Flame

MILTON'S CENTURY

A TIMELINE OF THE LITERARY, POLITICAL, RELIGIOUS, AND SOCIAL CONTEXT OF JOHN MILTON'S LIFE

MICHAEL R. COLLINGS

THE BORGO PRESS
MMXIII

Borgo Literary Guides
ISSN 0891-9623
Number Fifteen

MILTON'S CENTURY

Copyright © 2013 by Michael R. Collings

FIRST EDITION

Published by Wildside Press LLC

www.wildsidebooks.com

DEDICATION

To four scholars of the Renaissance
who stimulated my interest
in things Miltonic:

Dr. John Steadman
UNIVERSITY OF CALIFORNIA, RIVERSIDE
and THE HUNTINGTON LIBRARY

Dr. William Geiger
WHITTIER COLLEGE

Dr. Gilbert McEwen
WHITTIER COLLEGE

Dr. Stanley Stewart
UNIVERSITY OF CALIFORNIA, RIVERSIDE

And
In memory of a Historian
who taught me how:

Dr. Harry Nerhood
WHITTIER COLLEGE

CONTENTS

INTRODUCTION 9
DECADE ONE: 1600-1609. 12
DECADE TWO: 1610-1619. 78
DECADE THREE: 1620-1629 137
DECADE FOUR: 1630-1639 191
DECADE FIVE: 1640-1649 238
DECADE SIX: 1650-1659 333
DECADE SEVEN: 1660-1669 393
DECADE EIGHT: 1670-1679. 460
DECADE NINE: 1680-1689 499
DECADE TEN: 1690-1700. 537
AND BEYOND.... 573
APPENDIX ONE: GENEALOGICAL TABLES 576
SOURCES AND RESOURCES 589
ABOUT THE AUTHOR 609

INTRODUCTION

No artist creates in a vacuum. Beyond the conscious influence of books read, artwork seen, minds probed through conversation or exchange of letters, artists are in no small part products of everything that surrounds them—people, places, things, events.

Milton's Century is designed to place one particular genius—John Milton, arguable the finest poet the English nation (perhaps even Western civilization) has produced—in the context of his time. And what a remarkable time it was. The seventeenth century elicited perhaps more memorable writers than any other, beginning as it did with William Shakespeare, whose artistic career was drawing to a climax as the century opened; and ending with the first growths of such minds as Alexander Pope and Jonathan Swift.

The seventeenth century is marked by the most radical turning points of any time in English history. Within a span of years, an anointed King was executed as a common criminal by the people he believed God had given him to rule; and shortly thereafter, large congregations of those same people waited with breathless expectation for the descent of King Jesus Himself to sit upon the vacant throne. A decade later, a pleasure-loving King was returned to his earthly throne, only to see it ravaged by plague and by fire. And within another few years, the entire framework of monarchy was fundamentally altered as government shifted irrevocably from the one to the many.

The century began with a "noble and puissant nation rousing

herself like a strong man after sleep" from the superstition and mystery of what we now call the Dark Ages and almost overnight, it sometimes seems, inventing new ways to study and perceive the universe around them. It began in the final vestiges of the Middle Ages, and ends looking resolutely toward a new Cosmos, a new Age of Reason, of science and mathematics, of machines and inventions…in a word, toward *our* world.

Milton's Century proposes to show Milton as a person of his time, to re-create through words and dates the literary, political, religious, social climate that helped elicit *Paradise Lost*, *Paradise Regained*, and a host of other masterpieces of English literature and letters from his pen and from the pen of scores of other writers. A day-by-day accounting of a full century would be inordinately large—bulky, unwieldy, so full of information as to be virtually useless. Even a week-by-week accounting is beyond the scope of this project.

At times, however, this book will proceed day by day, week by week, watching events large and small unfold, observing from a distance the ebb and flow of ideas as revealed in works equally great and small…soul-stirring tragedies played out on stages meant to represent the entire world, and light, sometimes even silly ballads and songs sung from roughly printed broadsheets nailed to doors. From these rhythms, these currents of thought and belief, emerges an image of a remarkable century, peopled by remarkable minds who singly and as a culture altered the course of human history.

The format is straightforward. For each year of the seventeenth century, the timeline begins with literary productions, often undated and undatable; then moves to key historical moments—births and deaths, appointments to offices of state. Then the information is broken down into months and days, as far as such precise information is available to modern researchers.

Intertwining through it all are the moments—signaled by **boldface type**—when Milton's life rises to the surface: births and deaths within his family; key decisions made at times of social and cultural crisis that helped bring him to the fore; responses to and consequences of his work, his thought, his words.

I have spent much of my academic and creative career imaginatively immersed in Milton's Century. I hope you find it as fascinating and compelling as I have.

—Michael R. Collings
Malibu, CA and Meridian, ID
1995-2011

DECADE ONE: 1600-1609
THE BIRTH OF A PRINCE AND
THE DEATH OF A QUEEN

1600

John Milton, Sr., m. Sara Jefferay (1599-1600?)[1]
The Paradise of the Senses in Eden, anonymous engraving
Robert Armin, *Fool upon Fool*, jestbook, published
John Bodenham, ed., *England's Helicon*[2]
Sir William Cornwallis, *Essayes*, collection of 25 essays
Thomas Dekker, *The Shoemaker's Holiday*, printed; *Old Fortunatus*, printed
Robert Devereux, 2nd Earl of Essex, *Apology, against those which falsely taxe him to be the only hinderer of the peace*, defense of his actions in Cadiz, published without his authorization; suppressed by ecclesiastical authorities
John Dowland, *Second Book of Songs or Ayres*, published, lute music
England's Parnassus, includes poems by Ben Jonson
Edward Fairfax, *Godfrey of Bulloigne, or The Recoverie of Jerusalem. Done into English heroicall verse...*, translation of Torquato Tasso, *Gerusalemme Liberata*[3]

---

1. John Milton, Sr., was born in the Parish of Stanton St. John, near Oxford, in 1563, the son of Richard Milton and Elizabeth Haughton; Sara Jefferay (also spelled *Jeffrey* or *Jefferays*) was born about 1572, the daughter of Paul Jeffrey of Stanton St. John, and his wife Helen or Ellen.

2. According to H. R. Woudhuysen, this one book constitutes the single most important collection of Elizabethan lyrics published (Penguin Book, 786).

3. Torquato Tasso (1544-1595), wrote not only the *Jerusalem Delivered*, known to Milton as *Il Goffredo*, but also a number of critical works, including the multi-volume *Discourses on the Heroic Poem*, which Edmund

William Gilbert, *De Magnete, Magneticisque Corporibus, et de Magno Magnete Tellure* (On the Magnet and Magnetic Bodies, and on the Great Magnet the Earth), scientific treatise

Fulke Greville, 1st Lord Brooke, *Alaham*, produced

Richard Hakluyt, *Principal Navigations, Voyages, Traffiques, and Discoveries of the English Nation*, 3 volumes (1598-1600)

Robert Jones, *First Booke of Songs and Ayres*, published, lute-music

Christopher Marlowe, *Hero and Leander: begun by Christopher Marloe; and finished by George Chapman*, 2nd edition[4] reprinted (further reprints 1606, 1609, 1613, 1616, 1617, 1622, 1629, 1637); *Lucans First Book Translated Line by Line*, published by Thomas Thorpe

Thomas Middleton[5], *The Ghost of Lucrece*

Thomas Morley, *The First Booke of Ayres*

Sir Walter Raleigh, "The Lie," circulating in manuscript

Samuel Rowlands, *The Letting of Humours Blood in the Headvein*, rudimentary prose Characters

Cyril Tourneur, *The Transformed Metamorphosis*, printed

John Weever, *Faunus and Melliflora*, brief Ovidian epic

Thomas Wilson, *The State of England*, treatise upon the Succession

Woodforde family diaries begin[6]

Spenser, John Milton, and other key poets of the late English Renaissance considered useful guides to the theory and practice of Epic.

4. The second edition of the poem first appeared in 1598, with Marlowe's verses divided into sestiads and augmented by four sestiads written by George Chapman. The ten editions between 1600 and 1640 testify to the enduring popularity of the work during the period.

5. Middleton is associated with some two dozen plays.

6. "No collector of English diaries can escape the Woodforde family. It is probably that between 1600 and 1820 there can hardly have been a day on which one Woodforde or another did not note down what he ate for dinner, or what the weather was like, or that the harvest was carried, or

Giordano Bruno[7] executed (b. 1548)
Richard Hooker d. (b. 1553
John Earle b. (?)
Peter Heylyn b.
Elizabeth Hooten[8] b
Henry Lawrence b.
Herman Mylius b., in Oldenburg
Leonard Philaras b. (1590?), in Athens
William Prynne b. (?)
Leo van Aitzema b., in Doccum
William Walwyn b. (?)
George Chapman, arrested for debt
Samuel Rowlands, *The Letting of Humour's Blood* and *A Merry Meeting: or, 'Tis Merry when Knaves Meet*, satires, publicly burned
John Selden, completes education at Magdalen College, Oxford
The Children of the Chapel (theatrical company) revived; the Children of Paul's revived the previous year, 1599

Jan 6—TWELFTH NIGHT — William Shakespeare, *Twelfth Night*, performed at Whitehall
Jan 7 — Amelia Lanier's[9] last visit to Simon Forman for astro-

---

that the tailor overcharged him for mending a waistcoat." Kate O'Brien, in Elizabeth Bowen, and others, *The Heritage of British Literature*, p. 182-183.

7. For connections between Bruno and the seventeenth century, see Frances A. Yates, *Giordano Bruno and the Hermetic Tradition* and her other studies.

8. Hooten has been called the first Quaker, leading a separatist congregation calling itself Friends some time before she became acquainted with George Fox (Hugh Barbour and J. William Frost, *The Quakers*, p. 331).

9. Her name is variously spelled as Amelia, Emilia, Aemilia, or Æmilia Lanier or Lanyer—a apparent confusion that is typical of most names, and of spelling in general, during the period. Sir Walter Raleigh (to use the modern preference) wrote Rauley early in his career, then settled on Ralegh; similarly, Ben Jonson persisted in spelling his name without the usual medial 'h' even though many of his contemporaries chose not to do so.

logical readings noted in his journal

Jan 8 — Philip Henslowe and Peter Streete, contract signed for the erection of The Fortune Theater, home-stage for the Lord Admiral's Men; The Globe open the previous year, 1599

Jan 15 — Luce Morgan[10] committed to Bridewell Prison

Feb 2 — CANDLEMAS DAY

Feb 24 — Edmund Calamy baptized

Feb 27 — John Milton, Sr., admitted to the Company of Scriveners

Mar — Margaret Stuart, d. (b. 1598), Linlithgow Palace, Scotland (daughter of James I)

— Thomas Deloney d. (b. 1540-1545?)

Mar 6 — Shakespeare's company performs *Henry IV, Part I*, at the Lord Chamberlain's House, before ambassadors from the Spanish Netherlands

Mar 15 — Simon Forman records seeing a performance of Michael Drayton, Anthony Munday, and others, *Sir John Oldcastle*, a play suggested by the success of William Shakespeare's Falstaff

Mar 20 — Robert Devereux, 2nd Earl of Essex, returns to his own house after enforced residence at York House but is not allowed his freedom

Mar 25 — LADY DAY (honoring the Feast of the Annunciation)—official New Year's Day until 1752

Mar 28 — Thomas Dekker, with Henry Chettle and Thomas Haughton, *The pleasant comodie of Patient Grissill*, SR, play

Apr — Will Kemp, *Nine Dayes wonder*, with "Kempes humble request to the impudent generation of Ballad-makers and their coherents, that it would please their Rascalities, to pity his pains in the great journey he pretends; and not fill the country with lies of his never-done-acts, as they did in his

---

10. Luce Morgan is Leslie Hotson's candidate for Shakespeare's 'Dark Lady" (see Mr. W. H., 238-255); she seems not as appealing as Amelia Lanier, perhaps, but Hotson asserts that she nevertheless fits the criteria required by the Sonnets.

late Morrice to Norwich. To the tune of Thomas Deloney's Epitaph," published

Apr 8 — Ben Jonson, *Every Man out of His Humour*, SR[11] by William Holme

Apr 23 — St. George's Day

Apr 25 — St. Mark's Day

May 10 — Archbishop John Whitgift confiscates unlicensed copies of Essex's *Apology*, at Essex's request[12]

Jun 5 — Robert Devereaux, 2nd Earl of Essex, tried at York House on charges of disobedience to Elizabeth I; Francis Bacon appointed to prosecute his former patron

Jun 11 — St. Barnabas' Day

Jun 14 — Lord Keeper Sir Thomas Egerton addresses the Star Chamber concerning "libellers who by tongue and pen did not spare to censure states, &c. And such of late had slandered her Majesty's officers by libels," a further attack on satirists[13]

Jun 22 — The Privy Council limits the number of theaters in London to two and allows only two performances per week

Jun 25 — The Stationers' Company orders *The Wanton Wife of Bath* recalled and burned as a "disorderly ballad"; five subsequent editions of the ballad recorded by 1700

Jul — John Heyward questioned and subsequently imprisoned in the Tower for connections between his *The first part of the life and raigne of King Henrie the IIII* (1599) and Essex's

---

11. "SR": Entered for publication in the *Register* of the Worshipful Company of Stationers, England's official guild for printers and publishers. Entry in the *Register* is valuable in that it provides an approximate date for the appearance of books, tracts, pamphlets, ballads, plays, and other printed materials. In some instances, actual publication followed several weeks, months, occasionally even years after entry in the *Register*, but for the most part the entry provides the most accurate and authoritative publication information. Most of the *Stationers' Register* information incorporated in this Chronology is drawn from a research data-base constructed by Cyndia Clegg.

12. Cyndia Susan Clegg, *Press Censorship*, p. 209.

13. Cyndia Susan Clegg, *Press Censorship*, p. 215.

Rebellion[14]

Jul 25 — FEAST OF ST. JAMES

Fall — Ben Jonson, *The Fountains of Self-Love; or, Cynthia's Revels*, performed by the Chapel Children in Blackfriars Theater

Aug 5 — Tuesday: The Gowrie Conspiracy against King James VI, in Scotland[15]

Aug 14 — Thomas Deloney, *The fyrste parte of the Gentill Craft*, SR

— William Shakespeare, *The Chronicle History of Henry V...*, SR

Aug 23 — William Shakespeare, *Much Adoe About Nothing...*, SR by Andrew Wise

Aug 26 — Robert Devereux, 2nd Earl of Essex, allowed his freedom but forbidden access to the Court; since Elizabeth I has revoked his monopolies, deeply in debt[16]

— Sir Walter Raleigh, chief opponent of Essex at court, appointed Governor of Jersey by Elizabeth I

Sep — The Fortune Theater, built in a square rather than in the circle of The Globe, opens

Sep 2 — Samuel Rowlands, *Tis mery metinge or tis mery when knaves meet*, satire (authorized in spite of the putative ban against satires from 1599), SR

Sep 29 — MICHAELMAS

Oct 2 — Robert Devereux, 2nd Earl of Essex, returns to Essex House in London

---

14. Cyndia Susan Clegg gives extensive background to the connections between text and political action in *Press Censorship in Elizabethan England* p. 203ff.

15. Historians are still uncertain whether the "Gowrie Conspiracy" represented a legitimate plot against James's monarchy and his life, or whether James (who could be as Machiavellian as any monarch of the time) purposely manipulated the 'conspiracy' in order to rid himself of two troublesome nobles.

16. Son of Walter Devereux (d. 1576) and Lettice Knollys, who later married Robert Dudley, Earl of Leicester and long-time favorite of ElizabethI.

Oct 6 — Samuel Rowlands, *Tis mery metinge and The letting of Humours blood...*, burned by order of the Stationers' Company [17]

Oct 16 — Samuel Rowlands, *The letting of Humours blood in the Headvaine*, satire (authorized in spite of the putative ban against satires from 1599), SR

Oct 20 — Sir Thomas Egerton, Lord Chancellor Ellesmere, m. Lady Alice Spenser, Dowager Countess of Derby

Oct 28 — William Shakespeare, *The Most Excellent Historie of the Merchant of Venice...*, quarto, SR by Thomas Hayes

After Oct — **Richard Milton** d.

Nov 1 — ALL SAINTS' DAY

— Posthumous trial of the Earl of Gowrie and his brother

Nov 2 — ALL SOULS' DAY

Nov 18 — The Scottish Parliament orders the bodies of the Earl of Gowrie and his brother, Alexander Ruthven hanged, drawn and quartered, concluding the "Gowrie Conspiracy"

Nov 19 — Charles, Duke of Albany (afterward King Charles I) b. at Dumfermline Castle, Fife, Scotland to James VI of Scotland and Anne of Denmark[18]

Dec (?) — John Donne m. Anne More, niece and ward of Sir Thomas Egerton, Lord Chancellor Ellesmere

Dec 23 — Prince Charles chr., Edinburgh, Scotland, by David Lindsay, Bishop of Ross

---

17. "Apparently the burning of this book as a sufficient advertisement to make it worth reprinting, for on 4 Mar. 1601 and again on 1 Mar. 1602 Stationers were fined 2s 6d a piece 'for their disorders in buyinge of the books of humours letting blood in the vayne being newe printed after yt was first forbydden and burnt'...In all twenty-nine booksellers were fined..." (cited in Clegg, *Press Censorship*, p. 216-217).

18. From a letter written by George Nicolson, English Ambassador to Scotland, to Sir Robert Cecil: "This night at 11 of the clock the queen was delivered of a son and word thereof this night at about 3 hours brought to the King. Whereon the King this morning is gone to the Queen and 3 pieces of ordnance shot by this castle in joy of the same" (cited in Pauline Gregg, *King Charles I*, p. 3) A sickly child who was unable to stand or walk unaided well past the age of four, Charles was not expected to survive.

1601

John Milton, Sr., several musical pieces published in Thomas Morley, *Madrigales, The Triumphes of Oriana*, a collection of musical tributes to Elizabeth I by England's finest composers[19]

Nicholas Breton, *No whipping, nor tripping: but a kinde friendly Snipping*, pamphlet criticizing satirists for attacking individuals

Thomas Campion, The Songs from *Rossiter's Book of Ayres*, published

Robert Chester, *Love's Martyr: or Rosalins complaint. Allegorically shadowing the truth of love, in the constant fate of the phoenix and the turtle*, published, includes William Shakespeare, "The Phoenix and the Turtle,"[20] and works by Ben Jonson, John Marston, and George Chapman

Sir William Cornwallis, *Discourses upon Seneca the Tragedian; and Essayes*, a further collection of 24 essays

Samuel Daniel, *The Works of Samuel Daniel Newly Augmented*

Thomas Dekker, *Satiriomastix, or the Untrussing of the Humorous Poet*; attacks Ben Jonson's comedies of humors

Thomas Deloney, *Strange Histories, or Songes and Sonets, of Kings, Prince, Dukes, Lordes, Ladyes, Knights, and Gentlemen*, 1st and 2nd printings

---

19. Esmore Jones states that music by John Milton, Sr., was still popular enough to be sung some years after the old man's death (*Milton*, p. 4).

20. Blakemore Evans suggests that the poem was written specifically for Chester's collection. (*Riverside Shakespeare*, p. 53.)

Arthur Dent, *The Plaine Mans Path-way to Heaven; Wherein every man may clearly see whether he shall be saued or damned. Set forth Dialogue-wise for the better understanding of the simple...*, published in Amsterdam (25th edition, 1640)[21]

Bishop Francis Godwin, *A Catalogue of the Bishops of England*

Richard Greenham, *The Workes of...Richard Greenham*, 3rd edition, Puritan treatises

Hugo Grotius, *Adamus Exul*, Latin drama on the Fall of Man, published at The Hague; possible influence on **John Milton's Paradise Lost**

Edward Guilpin, *The Whipper of the Satyre his pennance in a white sheet*, pamphlet criticizing satirists

Ben Jonson, *Cynthias Revels; Poetaster; Every Man in His Humor* (written 1598), printed

John Lyly, *Love's Metamorphosis*

John Marston, *Antonio's Revenge*, written; *What You Will*

Christopher Marlowe, *The Massacre at Paris*, published

Thomas Morley, *Madrigales, The Triumphes of Oriana*, edited collection of musical tributes to Elizabeth I, one manifestation of the cult of Elizabeth, by England's finest composers

Philip Rossiter, *A Booke of Ayres*, set foorth to be song, published

William Shakespeare, *Twelfth Night*, printed

John Weever, *The whipping of the Satyre*, pamphlet critiquing satirists, published[22]; *The Mirror of Martyrs, or the Life and Death of That Thrice Valiant Captain and Most Godly Martyr, Sir John Oldcastle, Lord Cobham*, published

Thomas Nashe d. (b. 1567)

Pierre (Peter) du Moulin b

John Geree b

---

21. The text became one of John Bunyan's favorite books. By the early 18th century, Dent's spiritual treatise had sold in excess of 100,000 copies.

22. Cyndia Susan Clegg points out that a number of such pamphlets appeared in 1601 as responses to the "Bishops' Ban" and burning of specific satires in 1599 (*Press Censorship*, p. 212)

Ben Jonson's first daughter, Mary, b.; dies later the same year

Joseph Hall (afterward Bishop of Exeter and Norwich) enters the ministry

Jan 19 — Henry Herbert, 2nd Earl of Pembroke, d. (b. 1534?)

Feb 3 — Conspirators in the Essex rebellion, except for the Earl himself, meet at the house of the Earl of Southampton to discuss their plans

Feb 7 — William Shakespeare, *Richard II*, performed at the express request of Robert Devereux, 2nd Earl of Essex[23]

Feb 8 — Sunday — Essex' Rebellion; Robert Devereux, 2nd Earl of Essex, enters the City of London

Feb 19 — Robert Devereux, 2nd Earl of Essex, Henry Wriothesley, Earl of Southampton, and other conspirators, arraigned for treason at Westminster Hall

Feb 25 — Ash Wednesday — Robert Devereux, 2nd Earl of Essex; Edward Russell, 3rd Earl of Bedford, fined and exiled from court[24]

Feb (?) — Fulke Greville destroys one of his plays following the Essex Rebellion, fearing that it might be "construed or strained to a personification of vices in the present governors and government"[25]

Mar 5 — Other co-conspirators in the Essex Rebellion—including Sir Christopher Blunt, Sir Charles Davers, Sir Gelly Merrick and Henry Cuffe—tried and subsequently executed

Apr 14 — Francis Bacon, *Declaration of the Practices and*

---

23. The performance was seen as quasi-treasonous, particularly in light of Elizabeth's awareness of parallels between her reign and that of Richard II. The spectacle of the deposition of a reigning monarch would have especially pained the aging Elizabeth, who had already been long pressured to settle the sticky matter of her own successor.

24. Bedford remained estranged from the court; his wife, Lucy, Countess of Bedford, on the other hand, became one of the key literary patrons of the time.

25. Cited in Christopher Hill, *A Nation of Change*, p. 208.

Treasons attempted and committed by Robert late earl of Essex and his Complices, completed and sent to the Queen's printer

Apr 11 — Magdalene Newport Herbert, mother of the poets Edward and George Herbert establishes her family—ten children, a total of 26 individuals—at Charing Cross, Westminster

— John Gorse, steward of the household, begins keeping his *Kitchin Booke*, a daily account of life in the Herbert establishment in Charing Cross

Apr 27 — Marriage of John Donne and Anne More formally declared valid by the Archbishop of Canterbury's court

May 1 — William Shakespeare purchases New Place in Stratford and grazing rights to common pastures

May 9 — William Laud (later Archbishop of Canterbury) advanced to senior fellow, St. John's College, Oxford

May 12 — **Burial of John and Sara Jefferay Milton's oldest son or daughter, name and sex unknown**

May 17 — Anthony Bacon d. (b. 1559), brother of Francis and key intelligence operator for the Earl of Essex[26]

Summer — Anne of Denmark, Queen of Scotland and later Queen of England; letter to Pope Clement VIII reassuring him of her devotion to the Roman Church

Jul 4 — Lancelot Andrewes becomes Dean of Westminster Abbey

Aug 16 — John Donne, *The Progress of the Soul*

Sep 23 — ST. MATTHEW'S DAY — Don Juan d'Aquila, at the head of a Spanish army, lands in Ireland, formally deprives Elizabeth of her crown by Papal edict, and absolves her subjects of allegiance to her

Sep 27 — Louis, Dauphin of France, (afterward, Louis XIII,

---

26. Although Anthony Bacon was acknowledged as an intimate member of the household, he was never charged with complicity in the Earl of Essex's Rebellion; Francis Bacon's reputation was subsequently (and remains) tainted with hints of venality—that he effectively turned against his patron in order, at least in part, to save his brother.

King of France), b. to Henry IV and Marie de Medici

Oct 8 — Philip Henslowe, Diary, entry indicating that work has begun on the play of Six Clothiers, from Thomas Deloney's *Thomas of Reading*[27]

Oct 27 — Elizabeth I opens Parliament; its attention focused on the crisis in Ireland

— John Donne, M.P. for Brackley in Elizabeth I's last Parliament

Dec 24 — CHRISTMAS EVE — Charles Blount, Lord Mountjoy defeats the Irish rebel Hugh O'Neill, Earl of Tyrone, and a portion of the Spanish army in Ireland

---

27. The play is not extant.

1602

John and Sara Milton's daughter Anne Milton b.
Francis Beaumont, *Salmacis and Hermaphroditus*
Sir John Beaumont, *Metamorphosis of Tobacco*
Tommaso Campanella, *Civitas Solis* (City of the Sun), utopian treatise, begun
Thomas Campion, *Observations in the Art of English Poesy*
Jean de Beau Chesne and John Baildon, *A Booke containing Divers Sortes of Hands*, 3rd issue (originally published 1570), first English manual of handwriting.
Thomas Churchyard, *A True Discourse Historicall, of the succeeding Governors in the Netherlands*, published
John Davies of Hereford, *Microcosmos*
John Dee, *Monas Hieroglyphica*, included in *Theatrum Chemicum*, edited by L. Zetzner; alchemical treatise, published in Germany
Thomas Dekker, *Satiriomastix, or the Untrussing of the Humorous Poet*, performed
Thomas Deloney, *Strange Histories. Of Kings, Princes, Dukes, Earles, Lords, Ladies, Knights, and Gentlemen. With the great troubles and miseries of the Duches of Suffolke...*, published, ballads; Battista Guarini, *Il Pastor Fido* [The Faithful Shepherd], translated into English
Mary Sidney Herbert, Countess of Pembroke, *A Dialogue between two shepherds, Thenot and Piers, in praise of Astrea*
Josias Nichols, *The Plea of the Innocent*, treatise defining

    Dissenters' beliefs
Thomas Pavier *The Spanish Tragedy…Newly Corrected, Amended, and Enlarged with New Additions of the Painter's Part, and Others, As It Hath of Late Been Divers Times Acted*, reprint of Thomas Kyd's tragedy with possible additions by Ben Jonson
A Poetical Rhapsody
Samuel Rowlands, *Tis Merrie when Gossips Meete,* possibly influenced by Geoffrey Chaucer, *The Canterbury Tales*
William Shakespeare, *Troilus and Cressida* performed (?)
'W. S.,' Thomas, *Lord Cromwell*, published, later (Third Folio) attributed to William Shakespeare
Robert Southwell, *Saint Peters Complaint. Newlie augmented with other poems*, published[28]
Thomas Speght, 2nd edition of Geoffrey Chaucer's works (first edition, 1598)[29]
Elizabeth Jane Weston, *Poemata*, published in Frankfurt
William Perkins d.
Joseph Caryl b.
William Chillingworth b.
Mildmay Fane, 2nd Earl of Westmorland, b.
Owen Feltham b. (?)
Shakerley Marmion b.
William Strode b.
George Thomason b.
The Bodleian Library, founded by Sir Thomas Bodley, opens at Oxford
Philip Massinger admitted to St. Alban Hall, Oxford
John Ford admitted to the Middle Temple

---

  28. Southwell, a Jesuit priest, had been executed at Tyburn in 1595.

  29. Speght included among his critical comments the suggestion that Chaucer's poetry might be capable of scansion, a point largely ignored during the century and later derided by John Dryden in his "Preface to Fables Ancient and Modern." On the whole, Chaucer attracted little interest among the readers and poets of the early seventeenth-century. (Raphael Falco, *Conceived Presences*, p. 13-14)

John Webster begins writing for the stage, collaborating with Anthony Munday, Michael Drayton, Thomas Middleton, Thomas Dekker, and others.

Jan 18 — Robert, Duke of Kintyre, b. (son of James I)
— William Shakespeare, *Merry Wives of Windsor*, SR by John Busby and Arthur Johnson[30]
Feb 2 — William Shakespeare, *Twelfth Night; or, What You Will*, performed at the Middle Temple
Apr 19 — Thomas Deloney, *A booke called Thomas of Reading*, SR, transferring ownership from Thomas Middleton to Thomas Pavier
May 1 — William Lilly b. (astrologer)
May 27 — Robert, Duke of Kintyre, d. (son of James I)
Jul — William Laud, B. D., St. John's College, Oxford; thesis on infant baptism and the need for Bishops in the church
— Pope Clement VIII urges the conversion of James VI of Scotland (later King James I)
Jul 26 — William Shakespeare, *The Tragicall Historie of Hamlet Prince of Denmarke*, SR by James Robertes[31] Jul 28 and 29
— John Lyly, *The Entertainment at Chiswick*, staged, for Elizabeth I
Dec — Anthony Munday, *The Set at Tennis*, performed
Dec 10 — John Bradshaw baptized
Dec 18 — Sir Simonds D'Ewes b.
Dec 22 — Hugh O'Neill, Earl of Tyrone, leader of the Irish Rebellion, submits to Elizabeth I

---

30. The title-page indicates that the play had been "Acted before Her Majesty and elsewhere."

31. "A booke called 'the revenge of Hamlett Prince (of) Denmarke' as yt was latelie Acted by the Lord Chamberleyne his servantes." Oscar James Campbell, *Shakespeare's Hamlet*, p. 6.

1603

John Milton, Sr., established in Bread Street, London[32]

Sir Francis Bacon, *Apology in certain imputations concerning the Earl of Essex*, sold in St. Paul's Churchyard as an open letter to the Earl of Devonshire; *Valerius Terminus*

Henoch Clapham, *An Epistle Discoursing on the Present Pestilence*, Puritan tract arguing that the Plague stuck only those who sinned

Henry Crosse, *Virtues Common-wealth*, prose, suggesting Theophrastan characters

Thomas Dekker, *The Wonderful Year, 1603*, prose description of an outbreak of the Plague in London

Thomas Dekker and Thomas Middleton, *The Magnificent*

---

32. Elbert Hubbard writes: "The Miltons lived in Bread Street, and out of the back garret window of their house could catch a glimpse of the Globe Theatre.

"The father of John Milton might have known Shakespeare—might have dined with him at the 'Mermaid,' played skittles with him on Hampstead Heath, fished with him from the same boat in the river at Richmond; and then John Milton, the lawyer, might have discreetly schemed for passes to the 'Globe' and gone with his boy John, Junior, to see 'As You Like It' played with the Master himself in the role of old Adam.

"Bread Street was just off Cheapside, where the Mermaid Tavern stood, and where Beaumont, Fletcher, Ben Jonson and other roysterers often lingered and made the midnight echo with their mirth. In all probability, John Milton, senior, father of John Milton, junior, knew Shakespeare well." (Elbert Hubbard, *John Milton*, p. 99)

In spite of the colloquial tone of the passage, Hubbard seems accurate in his description of the Milton's Bread Street house and its propinquity to the literary center of London at the time.

Entertainment Given to King James
Michael Drayton, *The Barrons Warres*[33]
John Florio, *Essayes on Morall, Politike, and Millitarie Discourses of Lo. Michaell de Montaigne*, translation of Michel de Montaigne,[34] with dedications to Lucy, Countess of Bedford and others
Arthur Golding, *The XV Bookes of P. Ouidius Naso, entytled Metamorphosis, translated oute of Latin into English meter*, reprinted (original edition 1567)
Fulke Greville, 1st Lord Brooke, *Mustapha*, produced (as late as 1608?)
Thomas Heywood, *A Woman Killed with Kindness*
Ben Jonson, *Sejanus His Fall*
Thomas Lodge, *Treatise of the Plague*, a defense of himself and fellow-doctors for leaving plague-stricken London for the safety of the country
Elizabeth Melville, Lady Culross, *Ane Godlie Dreame*
Thomas Robinson, *The Schoole of Musicke, the perfect method of true fingering of the Lute, Pandora, Opharion, and Viol da Gamba*, published
William Shakespeare, *Hamlet*, "bad" quarto[35] published
Ercole and Torquato Tasso, *15 Joyes of Marriage*, reprint of book banned and burned in 1599, ordered by Archbishop John Whitgift and Richard Bancroft to the Stationers' Company
Edward Benlowes b.

---

33. A revision of Drayton's earlier *Mortimeriados*, a title that suggests a rather more extensive sense of epic than does the later, more prosaic title.

34. Michel de Montaigne (1533-1592) essentially developed the essay as a literary form; his example was quickly emulated by Sir Francis Bacon and others in England

35. I.e., a text derived from printer's copy in turn reproduced from memory by a spectator of a performance or from a surreptitious shorthand transcription made during a performance. A "good quarto," considered more reliable and authentic, derives from a prompt copy or the dramatist's own manuscript. Oscar James Campbell, *Shakespeare's Hamlet*, p. 7; citing Alfred W. Pollard, *Shakespeare Folios and Quartos* (London, 1909).

Roger Williams b. (?)

Outbreak of Plague kills more than 30,000 in London, including Ben Jonson's son[36]

Jacobus Arminius appointed to a post at the University of Leiden

Without a degree, Simon Forman is licensed as a physician by Cambridge University[37]

Thomas Hobbes attends Magdalen Hall, Oxford University

Jan 14 — An ailing Elizabeth I leaves Whitehall for the last time for one of her favorite residences, her "warm box," Richmond Palace

Feb — George Chapman, *Old Joiner of Aldgate*, played by the Children of Paul's

Feb 7 — William Shakespeare, *Troilus and Cressida*, SR

— *The Manner to dye well*, religious treatise, SR

Feb 21 — John Dowland, *The Third Booke of Songs*, published, lute-music, SR

Mar 3 — Arthur Dent, *Pastyme for Parents*, SR

Mar 16 — Samuel Harsnett, *Declaration of Egregious Popishe Impostures*,[38] SR

---

36. See Ben Jonson's poem, "On My First Son" for a suggestion as to how deeply the continuing tragedy of recurrent plague affected seventeenth-century writers and how they coped with loss and grief. Until after the Great Plague of 1665, death by plague haunts the pens and imaginations of writer after writer.

37. Forman notes in his journals—and later in his responses to the Royal College of Physicians—that he had remained in London during the Plague, administering to the sick, while the physicians fled to the much safer countryside. A. L. Rowse argues that Forman, who relied on herbs and generally avoided bleeding and leeching as standard treatments for a variety of illnesses, probably did no more harm and quite possibly much more good than the physicians themselves (*Sex and Society*, pp. 9-10). Any discussion of seventeenth-century medical procedures would bear out Rowse's conclusions, since those who survived afflictions quite often did so in spite of rather than because of the ministrations of doctors.

38   William Shakespeare's use of the book as a source in writing *King*

Mar 22 — Elizabeth I persuaded by her Chamberlain to take to her bed

Mar 23 — Elizabeth I summons the Archbishop of Canterbury to pray for her[39]

Mar 24 — Elizabeth I, England's last Tudor monarch, d., after a reign of 44 years and 5 months[40]

— James VI, King of Scotland,[41] succeeds to the throne as James I of England; publicly proclaimed in London at 10:00 AM

— The Privy Council orders all theaters closed because of the Plague

— Thereafter: Joseph Hall, *The King's Prophecy; or, Weeping Joy*, poem in praise of James I

Mar 28 — James I, *Basilicon Doron* (The King's Gift)[42], treatise on kingship; revised edition (privately published, 1598-99; reprints 1616, 1620

Lear suggests that the play was written after this date. Kenneth Muir, *King Lear*, p. xx.

39. "In early March 1603 Elizabeth was suddenly overtaken by a series of maladies—'imposthumation in her head, aches in her bones, and continual cold in her legs, besides a notable decay of judgment, insomuch as she cannot abide discourses of government and state, but delighteth to hear old *Canterbury Tales* to which she is very attentive'" (quoted in Lisa Jardine and Alan Stewart, *Hostage*, 259-260

40. She was reported to have died "mildly like a lamb, easily as a ripe apple from the tree" (John Winton, *Sir Walter Raleigh*, p. 239)

41. James VI and I (b. 1566) was the only son of Mary, Queen of Scots, who in turn had been imprisoned and ultimately executed by order of Elizabeth I. The Stuart claim to the English throne descended through Margaret Tudor (d. 1541), the sister of Henry VIII; Margaret had first married James IV, King of Scotland, then Archibald Douglas Earl of Angus. James VI of Scotland was the great-grandson of James IV and Margaret Tudor through his mother, Mary, Queen of Scots; and the great-grandson of Margaret Tudor and Archibald Douglas through his father, Henry Stuart, Lord Darnley—thus receiving, as it were, a double dose of Tudor royal blood.

42. Even for a reigning monarch, James enjoyed remarkable success with this book; it went through no less than seven editions in 1603.

Mar 29 — *King James Proclaimed*, SR
Mar 31 — James officially proclaimed King of England, Scotland, France, and Ireland at the Market Cross in Edinburgh
Apr 1 — *Bills of such as dye this yere of plague.* SR
— *Ditty for New crowned King.* SR
— *London's Lamentacion for her former synnes.* SR
— *Panegyricus viz Jacobus...Anagrammatizetai.* SR
— *Preservative from the Plage.* SR
— *Song of Joye for the Kinges coronaicon.* SR
— *Triumphant song in honor of the Kings coronation.* SR
Apr 3 — James I bids public farewell to Scotland at St. Giles
— James I, *Dæmonologie, a dialogue*, entered on the Stationers' Register; *True Lawes of free monarchies.* SR
— Robert Pricket, *A Souldiours Wysshe to his Sovereign James I*, SR
Apr 5 — James I leaves Scotland for London; shortly after his departure, his distraught Queen Anne suffers a miscarriage
Apr 6 — *Confirming the just title of James VI to England.* SR
Apr 8 — *England's Welcome to James.* SR
Apr 10 — Toby Matthew, Bishop of Durham, preaches before James I at Newcastle
Apr 12 — James I, *Lepanto*, SR
— Anthony Nixon, *Elizaes Memoriall, James Arrival, Romes Downfall*, SR
Apr 14 — John Hayward, *Life and Raigne of King Henry IV*, political tract, SR[43]
Apr 15 — Richard Mulcaster (?), *Elegy upon the Death...of Lady Elizabeth*, elegy for Elizabeth I, SR
— *Perfume against the noysome pestilence prescrybed.* SR
Apr 16 — T. Greene, *Poets Vision & Princes Glory*, political treatise, SR
— [Samuel Rowlands], *Ave Caesar*, political treatise, SR

---

43. The tract had been written several years earlier but publication withheld because of its treatment of Richard II and Elizabeth I's fury at references to the deposed king. The tract had in fact been deeply involved as evidence against Robert Devereux, 2nd Earl of Essex, during his trial for treason

Apr 18 — *Remedy Against the Plague*, SR
Apr 22 — George Downame, *Lectures against Antechrist*, SR
Apr 23 — James I knights Sir Everard Digby[44]
May — Sir Walter Raleigh, *A Discourse Touching a War with Spain*
May 3 — James I arrives at Theobalds, the estate of Sir Robert Cecil
May 9 — [T. M.], *The True Narration of the Entertainment of His Royal Majesty, from the time of his departure from Edinburgh till his receiving at London...together with The names of those Gentlemen whom His Majesty honoured with Knighthood*,[45] SR, even though it contains materials relating to events a week later
May 11 — James I enters the Tower of London by the King's Stairs
May 14 — John Savile, *King James entertainment at Theobaldes*, SR
May 17 — Nine actors, including William Shakespeare, receive a Royal Patent from James I, authorizing them to present plays at the Globe
May 18 — *Upon the Death of Robert Devereux 17 February 1602*, ballad, SR
May 30 — Samuel Daniel, *Panegyricke to the King*; with *Defence of Rhyme*, response to Edmund Campion's *Observations*; both SR
Late May-Early June — Francis Bacon, *A Brief Discourse Touching the Happy Union of the Kingdoms of England and Scotland*, published
Jun — John Savile, *King James his Entertainment at Theobalds. With his welcome to London, together with a Salutary Poem,*

---

44. Digby, considered by many if not most to represent the model of knighthood for his generation, was the father of Sir Kenelm Digby...and the thirteenth and last conspirator to join the Gunpowder Plot in 1605.

45. The pamphlet lists the names of 303 men raised to Knighthoods during James' progress to London; during his reign, he made a total of 2,323 Knights

published

Jun 1 — Gabriel Powel, *Catholickes Supplication for Toleration*, SR

Jun 2 — Queen Anne and Prince Henry Frederick[46] (b 1594) leave Scotland for London; Princess Elizabeth (b. 1596) and Prince Charles remain behind

Jun 15 — William Thorne, *Kennyng Glasse for a Christian King*, SR

Jun 20 — Ben Jonson, *Particular Entertainment of the Queen and Prince Their Highnesses at Althorpe*[47]

Jun 24 — William Watson's abortive anti-Jesuit, pro-Papist plot to capture King James and insure Catholic equality

Jun 25 — Ben Jonson, *The Satyr*, performed before Queen Anne at Althorp, Northamptonshire

— Christopher Muriell, *Answere unto "The Catholique Supplication to James,"* SR

Jul — Claudio Aquaviva, General of the Jesuits in Rome, warns Father Henry Garnet, Superior of the Jesuits in England, against any acts of violence

Jul 2 — Prince Henry invested as Knight of the Garter at Windsor

Jul 3 — Sir Francis Bacon, letter to Sir Robert Cecil, indicating Bacon's willingness to accept one of James' (debased) knighthoods, since he planned on marrying; Alice Barnham is at this time eleven years old

Jul 4 — Sir William Leighton, *Vertue Triumphant dedicated to His Majestie*, SR

---

46. Prince Henry was, from birth, a sturdy and healthy child, who was accordingly trained in the ways of kingship, on the logical assumption that he would certainly survive his sickly younger brother. Charles' training, on the other hand, was largely overlooked, especially during his childhood. At this point in his life, the two-and-a-half-year-old Charles suffered intermittent fevers and could neither walk nor talk; in his physical disabilities he clearly resembled his royal father.

47. This masque was probably written shortly after the death of Jonson's son from the Plague.

Jul 11 — Sir Kenelm Digby b.
Jul 12 — Thomas Thayre, *Treatise of the Pestilence, ... All the cures...*, SR
Jul 12-16 — Cobham's Plot against James discovered; a purported attempt to place Lady Arabella Stuart on the English throne, with Spanish complicity
Jul 14 — Francis Herring, *Certain Rules for tyme of Pestilential Contagion*, SR
Jul 17 — Sir Walter Raleigh arrested and committed to the Tower for complicity in Cobham's Plot[48]
Jul 22 — Francis Davidson, *Poeticall Rhapsody*, SR entr
— Henry Holland, *Spiritual Preservation against the Pestilence*, SR
Jul 23 — Sir Francis Bacon knighted by James I at Whitehall, along with some three hundred others; receives patent as King's Counsel Extraordinary
Jul 25 — Coronation of King James I; Anne of Denmark declines to participate in the Protestant rite
Jul 27 — *Relation of many visitations of the Plague*, SR
Aug 5 — James I introduces a day of thanksgiving for his surviving the Gowrie Plot in 1600
Aug 23 — William Shakespeare, *The Second Part of Henrie the Fourth...*, SR by Andrew Wise and William Aspley
Aug-Sep (?) — Francis Bacon, *Certain Considerations Touching the Better Pacification and Edification of the Church of England*, written
Oct — Thomas Morley d. (b. 1557/8)
Oct 15 — **John Milton, Sr., SR for two madrigals in Thomas Bateson, *First Set of English Madrigals***
— Thomas Morley, *Triumphs of Oriana*, SR, includes music by John Milton, Sr.
Nov 12 — Sir Walter Raleigh brought to trial, with Sir Edward

---

48. It has been argued (see Samuel Gardiner, *History*, I, p. 118) that Cobham's Plot, peripherally related to Watson's Plot, was in large measure manipulated by Robert Cecil as a means of discrediting and imprisoning his chief opponent, Sir Walter Raleigh.

Coke, Attorney-General, prosecuting

Nov 15 — Participants in Watson's Plot and Cobham's Plot convicted

Nov 17 — Sir Walter Raleigh[49] convicted and condemned to death on charges of treason against the King for complicity in a plot to replace James I with a his cousin, Lady Arabella Stuart; Raleigh's sentence commuted to incarceration for life in the Tower

Nov 19 — Samuel Rowlands, *Looke to it for Ile stabbe ye*, SR

Nov 22 — William Watson and a companion priest, William Clarke, executed

Nov 29 — William Lily, *Rules Construed*, 9th edition, SR Nov 30

— William Gilbert d. (b. 1544), physician and natural philosopher

Dec 8 — *Kings Majestie his Armes.* SR

Dec 10 — Final three conspirators face execution but are reprieved, still proclaiming Raleigh's guilt

Dec 26 — Henry Petoe, *Whipping of Runnawaies.* SR

---

49. Ralegh was his own preferred spelling of his name; references by other writers also spelled the name Raleigh. With the exception of an expedition to the Orinoco in 1616, he spent the years from 1603 until his execution in 1618 imprisoned in the Tower of London; his execution, though deferred for fifteen years and ultimately the result of Raleigh's subsequent inability to accept James' foreign policy, was marginally legitimized by this 1603 conviction.

1604

James I, *Counterblaste to Tobacco*, published anonymously[50]
Sir Francis Bacon, *Certaine Considerations Touching the Better Pacification and Edification of the Church of England*, published after being privately presented to James I in 1603; *Certain Articles or Considerations touching the Union of the Kingdoms of England and Scotland* (published 1657)
Henoch Clapham. *Henoch Clapham, his Demaundes and Answeres touching the Pestilence*, retraction of Clapham's earlier equation of plague with sinfulness, written while he is imprisoned in The Clink for publishing the earlier book
Book of Common Prayer, revised version
George Chapman, *All Fools*, performed; *The Tragedy of Bussy d'Ambois*, performed
Sir William Cornwallis, *The Miraculous and Happie Union of England and Scotland*, published
William Covell, *A Modest and Reasonable Examination, of Some Things in Use in the Church of England*, anti-Puritan treatise, including "The Censure of a Book called the *Plea of the Innocent*," response to Josias Nichols
Thomas Dekker, *The Honest Whore, Part I*
Michael East, *Madrigales*, including lyrics by Nicholas Breton

---

50. James was vehemently opposed to the practice of smoking tobacco, which was in turn espoused with equal and opposite fervor by one of the great political thorns in James' side through much of his reigh, Sir Walter Raleigh, last survival of the Elizabethan privateers.

Arthur Golding, *A woorke concerning the Trewnesse of the Christian Religion, written in French; Against Atheists, Epicures, Paynims, Iewes, Mahumetists, &c. By Philip of Mornay, Lord of Plessie Marlie*, translation reprinted (original edition 1587

Ben Jonson, *Penates, or a Private Entertainment for the King and Queen*, commissioned by Sir William Cornwallis

Christopher Marlowe, *Dr. Faustus*, published; A-text[51]

Thomas Middleton, *The Phoenix*, performed; *Father Hubbard's Tales*, satire, SR

William Shakespeare, *Hamlet*, "good" quarto published

Anthony Scoloker, *Diaphantus*, published, including Sir Walter Raleigh, "The Passionate Man's Pilgrimage"

John Webster and Thomas Dekker, *Northward Ho!*, written

Owen Feltham b.

Henry Parker b

Roger Williams b. (?)

Peace established with Spain

John Whitgift, Archbishop of Canterbury, d.; Richard Bancroft appointed Archbishop of Canterbury

Charles Leigh commands England's first Jacobean attempt to colonize Guiana; returns within two months

Orlando Gibbons appointed organist to the Chapel Royal

Canon law orders communion tables to placed east-west in the

---

51. Marlowe died (or perhaps did not die, as argued by those who pitch for Marlowe as the author of the Shakespeare plays) in 1593. His major dramatic achievement was thus not published until some two decades after its first performance and after its author's death. For an analogous case, compare the first appearances of a number of Shakespeare's plays in printed form in the Folio of 1632. (It is interesting to note that modern understanding of Marlowe, his career, and his death, has undergone a number of transformations as new data develop. Alfred Noyes' poem on the death of Marlowe, in *Tales of the Mermaid Tavern* [1913], was, for example, written before the discovery of the coroner's report concerning the incident in Deptford; Noyes' account is incorrect in almost every detail, yet represents the level of understanding available at the beginning of this century.)

church or chancel

Jan 4 — Elizabeth Grymeston[52], *Miscelanea, Meditations, Memoratives*, SR

Jan 8 — Samuel Daniel, *Vision of Twelve Goddesses*, performed, masque, first of the Christmas-tide or Twelfth Night masques under the reign of James I; dancers include Queen Anne and Lucy Harington Russell, Countess of Bedford

Jan 11 — James I proclaims his intention to call his first Parliament[53]

Jan 14 — Hampton Court Conference begins; approves an Authorized Translation of the Bible, to be prepared by Lancelot Andrewes and other key scholars

Jan 31 — James I summons his first Parliament

Feb 1 — All properties of Sir Walter Raleigh assigned to trustees; Raleigh considered legally dead

Feb 8 — Michael Drayton, *The Owle*, SR

Feb 12 — Francis Herring, *Modest Defence against ympoisoned Amulettes*, SR

Feb 19 — James I publicly condemns Papism as a detestable superstition

Feb 22 — All Jesuits and Priests ordered to leave England immediately; fines against recusants increased

Mar 15 — James I ceremonially enters London, through nine allegorical triumphal arches designed, and erected by Inigo Jones, Ben Jonson, Thomas Dekker, Stephen Harrison, and others

— Ben Jonson, *King's Entertainment*, performed

— Thereafter: Stephen Harrison, *The Archs of Triumph Erected in Honor of the High and Mighty Prince James...at his Majesties Entrance and Passage through his Honorable City of London*

---

52. Grymeston (before 1563-1601/04) compiled her writing as lessons for her son.

53. This Parliament would sit for six years, from 1604-1610.

— William Shakespeare mentioned by name in the accounts of the Great Wardrobe

Mar 19 — Ben Jonson, *King's Entertainment 15 Mar 1604*, SR

— James I, speech to Parliament denying any intention to tolerate Catholicism

Mar 20 — Michael Drayton, *Pean tryumphant (triuimphall)*, SR

Mar 21 — Nicholas Breton, *I praie be no angrie*, SR

Mar 22 — Francis Trigge, *Petiticion of Church & Commons against Enclosure*, SR

Mar 27 — Gilbert Dugdale, *The Time Triumphant, Declaring in brief the arrival of our Sovereign liege Lord, King James, into England, his coronation at Westminster...*, SR

— Cecil receives reports of 900 recusants brought before the assizes in Yorkshire

Mar 28 — *Triumphs of the Tilt 29 Mar 1604*, ballad, SR

Apr 1 — PALM SUNDAY — Father Thomas Strange, a Jesuit recently returned to England, begins writing a religious manual

Apr 2 — (John?) Dowland, *Seven Teares*, music, SR

— *Monstrous Fishe in forme of a Woman*, SR

Apr 4 — Thomas Churchyard buried. (b. 1520?)

Apr 24 — Bill introduced in Commons to outlaw all Catholics

Apr 30 — William Alexander, *Works*, including *Monarchicke Tragedies, Parenethis...*, SR

May 1 — Ben Jonson, *Private Entertainment of the King and Queen*, performed at the house of Sir William Cornwallis

May 14 — Szegedius, *Antithesis between Christ & the Pope*, translation, SR

— Andrew Willet, *Limbomastix*, SR

May 18 — Sir Francis Bacon, *Apology in certain imputations concerning the Earl of Essex*, SR

May 20 — Robert Catesby, Thomas Wintour, John (Jack) Wright, Thomas Percy, and Guy (Guido) Fawkes meet at the Duck and Drake in London, setting in motion the Powder Treason

May 23 — Father Thomas Strange completes his manual, dedicating it to Robert Catesby

May 24 — Guy Fawkes[54], acting as a servant of Thomas Percy under the name John Johnson, leases house abutting on the House of Parliament

Jun 4 — Dr. John Dee, *To the King's Most Excellent Majesty*, a formal petition that Dee be tried for sorcery in order that he might be proven innocent and thus clear his name[55]

— William Wrednot, *Wisdom's Palace* [*Palladis Palatium*], SR

Jun 4 — W. Terrlo, *Piece of frere Bacon's brazen heads prophecye*, SR

Jun 10 — Nicholas Breton, *Passionate Shepherd*, SR

Jun 11 — Gilbert Dugdale, *Practises of Elizabeth Caldwell and Jeffrey Bown*, SR

Jun 24 — Edward de Vere, 17th Earl of Oxford d. (b. 2 Apr 1550), of the plague[56]

Jun 25 — Michael Drayton, *Moyses A Map of his Miracles*, SR

Jun 27 — W. Willymat, *Loiall Subjectes Looking Glasse*, SR

---

54. Other conspirators included Robert Catesby, who initiated the plot; Thomas Winter, who had urged a Spanish invasion of England during Elizabeth's reign; Thomas Percy, steward to and relative of the 9th Earl of Northumberland; and Christopher Wright

55. James I fully believed in witches and witchcraft and as a result had little sympathy for Elizabeth I's arch-mathematician and astrologer, John Dee (quondam possessor, by the way, of the largest private library of books and manuscripts in England). Dee's petition makes it clear that while Dee believes he can conjure righteous spirits (i.e., angels) he denies any traffic with "Divels, or damned Spirits" (Peter French, *John Dee*, p. 10)

56. Oxford is, along with Francis Bacon, one of the leading candidates among anti-Stratfordians as the author of Shakespeare's plays. His death in 1604—several years before traditional chronologies assume a number of the plays were written—creates a prime objection to his candidacy. John Michell discusses the unaccountable panic created at James' court by Oxford's death (*Who Wrote Shakespeare*, p. 175), implying that the prime objection notwithstanding, there may have been something relating to Oxford that James and his circle did not want known.

Jul — William Shakespeare sues Stratford apothecary over the price of malt

Jul 5 — John Marston, *The Malcontent*, SR

Jul 7 — Parliament adjourns after passing heavy anti-Catholic legislation, intending to assemble on February 7, 1605

Jul 17 — Prince Charles, departs for London from Scotland with servants, attendants, escorts, and trumpeters

Aug 18 — Sir Francis Bacon appointed King's Counsel, with official title of Learned Counsel

Aug 19 — Anglo-Spanish peace officially proclaimed at Cheapside, London

Aug 23 — Francis Pilkington, *Book of Ayres*, with *Tableture for the Lute*, SR

Aug 29 — William Wille[y]mat, *Phisicke againste disperacon*, SR, religious treatise

Aug 31 — Samuel Heiron, *Answere to a Popishe Rime*, SR

Sep 13 — Guillaume de Saluste du Bartas, *Third Dayes Creacon*, translation, SR

Sep 27 — John Davies, *Wittes Pilgrimage (by Poeticall Essaies)...*, SR

Oct — Gunpowder Plotters return to London; Robert Keyes joins the conspiracy

Oct 1 — Nicholas Breton, *Phantaxtix*, SR

Oct 29 — Antony Shirley, *Wittes newe diall*, SR

Oct 30 — *2 Ballets: Ship of fooles, Cry of the Cuntry*, ballads, SR

Nov 1 — William Shakespeare, *Othello*, performed at Court

Nov 2 — Ben Jonson, *Sejanus his Fall*, SR

Nov 5 — Sir Philip Sidney, *Arcadia*, SR

Nov 10 — [William Camde]N., *Reserches of Brittainne*, SR

Nov 12 — John Hayward, *Treatise of Union of England & Scotland*, SR

Nov 22 — Joshua Sylvester, *Bartas His, Devine Weekes & Works of the Worldes*, an incomplete English translation of

Guillaume de Salust du Bartas, *La Sepmaine*[57], SR
Nov 29 — Samuel Daniel, *Philotas*, SR
Dec — Thomas Bates joins the Gunpowder Plot
Dec 4 — John Dove, *Confutation of Atheisme*, SR
Dec 24 — Gunpowder Plotters clear a passageway to the lower walls of Parliament House[58]; shortly thereafter Parliament prorogued until October 3, 1605 because of fears of renewed plague
Dec 26 — William Shakespeare, *Measure for Measure*, performed at Court
— M. Suttcliffe, *Answer to a peticion by Catholics*, SR

---

57. Bartas, especially as mediated by Joshua Sylvester, proved to be one of the most enduring early literary influences on John Milton; six decades later, Du Bartas/Sylvester still constitute a persistent presence in the vocabulary and sentence structures of *Paradise Lost*

58. Antonia Fraser suggests that the digging of this 'mine' was more myth than reality (*Faith and Treason*, p. 110)

1605

Robert Armin, *Fool upon Fool*, 2nd edition, jest-book
William Bradshaw, *English Puritisme*, published in Holland
William Camden,[59] *Remains of a Greater Worke Concerning Britain*
George Chapman, *The Widow's Tears* and *The Tragedy of Caesar and Pompey*, performed (?)
Samuel Daniel, *Certain Small Poems; Philotas*[60], published
Michael Drayton, *Poems*
John Fletcher, *Woman's Prize*, written
Joseph Hall, *Meditations and Vowes*, published, gaining for Hall the attention of Prince Henry and Edward, Lord Denny
Margaret Hoby, unpublished diary for 1599-1605, the earliest extant diary by an English woman (published 1930)
Tobias Hume, *Musical Humors. The First Part of Airs*, published, music and lyrics
Robert Jones, *Ultimum vale, with a triplicity of musicke*, including lyrics by Thomas Campion
Ben Jonson, George Chapman, and John Marston, *Eastward Hoe*
The London Prodigal. As it was Played by the Kings Majesty's servants. By William Shakespeare, London. Printed by T. C.

---

59. Camden, Ben Jonson's teacher at Westminster School, was considered one of the accomplished scholars of his day.

60. *Daniel's Philotas*, a tragedy touching upon Alexander the Great, resulted in Daniel's being summoned to the Privy Council to explain apparent connections between his play and the Essex rebellion.

for Nathanial Butter, published apparently without SR[61]
John Marston, *Sophonisba, Wonder of Women*
John Pilkington, *The First Booke of Songs*, published, lute-music
Sir Thomas Smith, *Voiage and entertainment in Rushia. With the tragicall ends of two Emperors and one empress, within one month of his being there; and the miraculous preservation of the now reigning Emperor, esteemed dead for 19 years*, travel report by the first Governor of the English East India Company
Joshua Sylvester, *Bartas his Devine Weekes and Works*, 1st collection of fragments, Sylvester's translations starting from 1592
John Gauden b.
Theodore Haak b.
Thomas Randolph b. (poet and dramatist)
William Spurstowe b
Thomas Campion, M.D., University of Caen
George Herbert enrolls at Westminster School (until 1608)

Jan 6 — TWELFTH NIGHT — Prince Charles created Duke of York
— Ben Jonson, *Masque of Blackness*, performed with choreography by Inigo Jones; one of the last performances in the Elizabethan Banqueting Hall, shortly to be replaced by Inigo Jones' Palladian-inspired, neo-Classical structure[62]; dancers include Queen Anne and Lucy Harington Russell, Countess of Bedford; the cost ran upwards of £3,000 to mount the masque
Jan 11 — Z. Jones, *A Treatise of Spectres or Strange Sights*,

---

61. Butter also published *King Lear*, a circumstance that lends some weight to the attribution of *The London Prodigal*.

62. Jones' Banqueting Hall remains one of the few architectural remnants of the early seventeenth century in London. The Great Fire of 1665 destroyed much of the inner city, along with its churches and public buildings; in our own century, bombings during World War II accounted for the loss of more.

translation from P. Le Loyer, *Livres des Spectres ou Apparitions*, SR

Feb 8 — *Fayre Maid of Bristoe, as played at Hampton Court by His Majesties players*, SR

— *History of Richard Whittington, as was plaied by the prynces servants*, SR

— Prince Charles in the care of Sir Robert Carey and his wife; Carey reports that the child still cannot stand or walk unaided[63]

Feb 12 — Joseph Hall, *Meditations and vowes divine*, SR

Feb 24 — Pope Clement VIII d. (b. 1536

Feb 28 — *Evorandus, Prince of Denmark*, SR

Mar — Thomas Percy purchases cellar running directly beneath Parliament House; Gunpowder Plotters move forward with their plans

— After opening a doorway, Guy Fawkes moves twenty barrels of gunpowder into the cellar, laying iron bars across the top of them to increase the power of the explosion, and covering the whole with stacks of wood

Mar 2 — Thomas Decker, *Westward Ho*, drama, SR entered then stricken

Mar 5 — John Donne receives official permission to travel abroad with Sir Walter Chute; he returns in 1606

Mar 11 — Thomas Bell, *Dolefull Crye of Rome*, tract, SR

— George Pettie, *Pettie Pallace of Petty his Pleasures*, SR

Mar 21 — Richard Verstegan, *A Restitution of Decayed Intelligence in Antiquities*, dedicated to King James and tracing the King's genealogy back to Brutus and Arthur[64]

---

63. Pauline Gregg suggests that Charles might well have suffered from rickets, a disease endemic in sixteenth-century Britain, and discusses Carey's decision to put the child in iron boots as therapy. (*King Charles I*, p. 12)

64. There is some evidence that Milton at least considered the idea of writing a heroic poem about Arthur; the possibility has, over the centuries, become solidified by references to Milton's proposed but theoretical Arthuriad. Unfortunately for the poet's plans, the Stuart monarchy increasingly

Mar 25 — Robert Wintour, John Grant, and Christopher Wright join the Gunpowder Plot

— Plotters lease a cellar (ground-floor storeroom) in Westminster

Mar 31 — EASTER — Eliza Vaux, letter to Agnes Lady Wenman, a fellow Catholic, indicating that an extraordinary event was in the offing

Apr 5 — John Stow d. (b. 1525); antiquarian author of *Survey of London*

Apr 8 — Philip IV of Spain, b

Apr 9 — Princess Mary, b. to James I and Anne of Denmark, the first of their children born in England[65]

Apr 11 — [Thomas Bell], *The Pope's Funerall*, SR

Apr 27 — Thomas Bell, *Regiment of the Churche*, SR

Apr 30 — *Unlawfulnes & Danger of Toleration*, SR

— Reverend John Wakeman, *Solomon's Exaltation*, sermon preached before James I, implicitly comparing the King to Solomon

May 2 — George Closse, *Prodigious Child Born in Bradford*, SR

— *The Life and Death of Gamaliel Ratsey, famous thiefe hanged*, SR

May 4 — Robert Cecil created 1st Earl of Salisbury[66]

May 8 — [William Shakespeare?], *The True Chronicle history of King Leir*, SR

— Anthony Wooten, *Answer to a Popish Pamphlet*, SR

May 20 — George Salteren, *De Antiquis Britaniae Legibus*, SR

May 29 — Pope Paul V (1550-1621) elected; born Camillo

---

based its mythos on Arthurian traditions; by the time Milton began serious work on his great poem, it would have been impossible for him to celebrate a figure already appropriated as an image of Monarchy.

65. Mary's was the first royal birth in almost seventy years, since the birth of Edward VI to Henry VIII and Jane Seymour in 1537

66. Cecil had previously been ennobled as 1st Baron Cecil of Essendon, then elevated to the peerage as 1st Viscount Cranborne

Borghese

May 31 — *Ratsey's Ghost*, SR

Jun 5 — Thomas Brewer, *Commendation of Porters*, broadsheet ballad, registered

— George Herbert, elected a scholar at Westminster School

Jun 9 — Robert Catesby speaks with Father Henry Garnet in London about theoretical terrorism

Jun 26 — John Marston, *The Dutche Curtizan*, SR

Jun 28 — *Women Will Have Their Will*, ballad, SR

— *Women Will Have Their Will, 2nd Part*, ballad, SR

— Parliament officially prorogued from October 3 to November 5

Jul 3 — *Lamentable Murther in Yorkeshire*, ballad, SR

Jul 5 — Thomas Heywood, *If ye know not me you know no body*, SR

Jul 12 — Charles Howard, *Royal Enterteynment of the Ambassador to Spayne*, SR

Jul 16 — *The Life and Death of Richard Whittington, Lord Maiour of London*, ballad, SR

Jul 24 — William Shakespeare invests in a share of Stratford parish tithes; mentioned in the will of Augustine Phillips, a fellow actor

— Father Henry Garnet hears the confession of Father Oswald Tesimond, who reveals Catesby's confession and details of the Gunpowder Plot (with Catesby's permission)

Jul 26 — Plotters have brought thirty-six barrels of gunpowder into the cellar beneath the House of Lords

Aug 5, Tuesday — *Lamentable Murthers of John Fitz*, ballad, SR

— Public thanksgiving on the anniversary of the Gowrie Plot celebrated

Aug 6 — Ben Jonson, *Sejanus, His Fall*, SR; William Strachey's sonnet, "On Sejanus"

— Bulstrode Whitelock b.

Aug 12 — Fitz, John, *Bloody Murthers by John Ffyghtes*, pamphlet, SR

— *Warning for Churles & drunckardes*, ballad, SR

Aug 19 — Sir Francis Bacon, *The Advancement of Learning Divine and Human*, SR

Aug 27-30 — James I, Anne, and Prince Henry Frederick arrive in Oxford

— Matthew Gwynn, *Tres Sybillæ*, Latin play, produced before James I[67]

Sep 4 — George Chapman, *Eastward Ho*, SR

Sep 12 — *Urano, the Grene Knight & Beroshia*, SR

Sep 13 — *John Fitz, his ghost*, ballad, SR

Sep 16 — *Strange Throughinge of stones in Chicke Lane*, SR

Sep 19 — Sir Francis Bacon, *Advancement of Learning, Book II*, SR

— Anthony Nixon, *Oxfordes Triumph*, royal entertainment, with the King's Oration, SR

— Eclipse of the moon occurs, with concomitant predictions of doom and disaster

Sep 29 — Ambrose Rookwood recruited into the Gunpowder Plot

Oct — Lancelot Andrewes elevated by James I from Dean of Westminster to Bishop of Chichester[68]

Oct 1 — Oliver O[r]merod, *A Picture of a Puritane: Or, A Relation of the Opinions, qualities, and practices of the Anabaptists in Germanie, and of the Puritanes in England*, SR, defense of the Established Church against Puritans

Oct 2 — Eclipse of the sun occurs, with concomitant predictions of doom and disaster

Oct 5 — Theaters closed; Plague in London

Oct 7 — Lucas Ozliander, *Controversies between Protestantes*

---

67. Antonia Fraser suggests that details of Gwynn's Latin performance may have significantly influenced Shakespeare's plot development in *Macbeth*, produced the year following the Gunpowder Plot; William Shakespeare, she notes, "was in Oxford at this time" (*Faith and Treason*, p. 134).

68. Andrewes had twice been offered bishoprics by Elizabeth I but had refused them since both had entailed alienation of episcopal revenues as conditions of appointment.

& *Papistes*, SR

Oct 8 — Samuel Rowlands, *Theatre of Divine Recreation*, SR

Oct 9 — Robert Catesby gives a party at the Irish Boy, with Ben Jonson present

Oct 14 — Francis Tresham recruited into the Gunpowder Plot as the twelfth member, by Robert Catesby

Oct 19 — Sir Thomas Browne b.

Oct 21 — Sir Everard Digby, thirteenth and final plotter, recruited for the Gunpowder Plot

Oct 26 — William Parker, 4th Baron Monteagle, receives a letter warning him not to attend the opening session of Parliament; Monteagle immediately delivers the letter in person to Robert Cecil at Whitehall

Nov 1 — Robert Cecil shows the Monteagle letter to James I

Nov 2 — The Privy Council, alerted by the Monteagle letter, decides to allow the conspiracy to 'ripen'

Nov 3 — Lancelot Andrewes consecrated Bishop of Chichester, appointed Lord High Almoner[69]

Nov 4 — The suspicious cellar searched, but no gunpowder evident

Nov 5 — Gunpowder Plot to assassinate James I and Members of Parliament officially revealed; Guy Fawkes discovered in the storeroom beneath Parliament by Sir Thomas Knyvett, preparing to explode charges of gunpowder[70]; remaining

---

69. As a newly consecrated Bishop, Andrewes would necessarily have been in attendance in the House of Lords at the time of the Gunpowder Plot and, consequently, blown up had the plot succeeded; his subsequent responses to the plot have a distinct sense of personal involvement.

70. Historians disagree as to how much James' ministers and Privy Council knew about the plot beforehand. Interpretations of the event range from seeing it as a legitimate if misguided plot by a handful of disgruntled Catholics, to a carefully stage-managed production firmly under the control of Robert Cecil, James' key minister, with the intent of manipulating an incipient anti-Catholic furor in England. Whatever the truth of the case, reaction by the government was swift, and retribution brutal and severe. For a comprehensive treatment of the affair, see Alan Haynes, *The Gunpowder Plot*.

Plotters attempt to flee

— William Habington b, son of Thomas Habington

Nov 6 — James I allows torture in the questioning of 'John Johnson' (Guy Fawkes)

Nov 7 — The Privy Council summons Ben Jonson, a recent convert to Catholicism, to aid in investigating the Gunpowder Plot

— Arch-priest Father George Blackwell, the Pope's representative in England, publishes statement denouncing the Plot and the plotters

— Francis Bacon, *The Two Books of Francis Bacon: Of the Proficiencie and Advancement of Learning*, published; publication noted in a letter by John Chamberlain

Nov 8 — Party of Plotters surrounded at Holbeach by Sir Richard Walsh and 200 men; Robert Catesby, the ringleader, and Thomas Percy killed[71]

Nov 9 — James I addresses Parliament concerning the Gunpowder Plot

Nov 13 — Guillaume Saluste Du Bartas, *Posthumus Bartas, 3rd Day of Second Week*, translation, SR

Nov 17 — Niccoló Molin, Venetian Ambassador, reports rumors that link Robert Cecil, 1st Earl of Salisbury, with manipulating the Powder Treason to strengthen government policies against Catholics

Nov 26 — George Chapman, *Vincentio and Margaret* [*The Gentleman Usher*], SR

— Samuel Daniel, *The Queenes Arcadia*, SR

Dec 5 — Father Henry Garnet, *A Treatise of Equivocation*, manuscript, dedicated to Robert Southwell, S.J., found in the chambers of one of the Plotters, Tresham

---

71. The conspirators were trapped in a house near Holbeche, in Staffordshire. In a shoot-out that might rival anything the American Old West would later offer, sheriffs surrounded the house and opened fire. Four of the men were killed, Catesby and Percy by a single bullet. Samuel Gardiner's 1883 *History* draws a grimly moral message out of their deaths (Vol. I, 258-264).

— T. M. [Thomas Morton], *Exact Discovery of Romish Doctrine in Conspiracy & Rebellion*, SR
— George Peele, *Jestes of George Peele*, jest-book, SR
Dec 9 — [Thomas Dekker], *Duello, A papist*
— Oliver Ormerod, *Picture of a Papiste*, SR
Dec 11 — Thomas Goad, *Cithara, Octochorda*, on the Gunpowder Plot, SR
Dec 15 — Theaters re-open in London
Dec 16 — *Wifes Newe yeres gift to her husband*, ballad, SR
Dec 26 — William Shakespeare, *King Lear*, performed at Court, with the memory of the Gunpowder Plot still fresh

1606

Richard Alison, *An howres recreation in musicke*, with lyrics by Thomas Campion

Barnabe Barnes, *Offices enabling privat Persons for the special service of all good Princes and Policies*, published

John Carpenter, *Schelomonecham; or, King Solomon his Solace*, dedicated to James I and defining multiple parallels between the two monarchs

John Coprario, *Funeral Teares*, published, lute-music

John Ford, *Fame's Memorial*, elegy

Philemon Holland, translation of Suetonius, *History of Twelve Caesars*

Ben Jonson, *Volpone* (or 1605?), performed at Oxford and Cambridge

John Marston, *The Insatiate Countess* (?)

Thomas Middleton, *A Mad World, My Masters*

Abraham Ortelius, (1527-1598), *Theater of the Whole World*, published, with contemporary engravings of maps

Henry Peacham, *Art of Drawing and Limning in Water-colour*, published, an early handbook

Cyril Tourneur, *The Revenger's Tragedy*, written (?)

Sir Francis Vere, *Commentaries...Being Diverse Pieces of Service, wherein he had command...*, written (published 1657)

Elizabeth Weston, *Parthenicon*, published at Prague

William Dugard b.

Giles Fletcher receives BA, Trinity College, Cambridge; afterward fellow of the university

Esther Inglis begins her residence in England[72] (until 1615)

Jan — Oath of Allegiance passed

Jan 3 — I. H., *Unmaskinge of Murder: on Catholic Treason*, religious tract, SR

Jan 5 — Robert Devereux, 3rd Earl of Essex, m. Lady Frances Howard[73]

— Ben Jonson, *Hymenæi* [*Masque of Hymen*], wedding masque for the fourteen-year-old Robert Devereux, 3rd Earl of Essex, and Lady Frances Howard, thirteen-year-old daughter of the Earl of Suffolk

Jan 6 — TWELFTH NIGHT — Ben Jonson, *Barriers*, second wedding masque for Robert Devereux and Lady Frances Howard.

Jan 9 — Ben Jonson cited for recusancy (not complying with the Church of England)

Jan 10 — George Chapman, *Sir Gyles Goosecap*, SR

Jan 13 — P. S., *Fearfull Thunder & Lightning at Olvesto*

Jan 16 — *Ballet of the Fire in Shoreditch*, ballad, SR

— Nicholas Breton, *Wittes Private Wealth*, SR

— G. Markham, *Countess of Bedfordes Arcadia, where Pembroke's Ends*, SR

Jan 17 — Geoffrey Chaucer, *The Ploughman's Tale, shewing the Pope is Antichrist*, edited with commentary by T. Brampton (or A. Wooton), SR

Jan 20 — William Leigh, *Great Brytayns great Deliverance*

---

72. Inglis, of French Huguenot descent through her parents, who settled in Scotland after the St. Bartholomew's Day Massacre (1572), is the single female calligrapher of the period whose work has survived. Married to Bartholomew Kello, she anglicized her father's name, Langlois, to Inglis and retained it throughout her life. Her volumes were presented to Elizabeth I, James I, Princes Henry and Charles, and assorted Sidneys and Herberts. Thirty years after her death, John Evelyn admired her handiwork on display at the Bodleian Library. Jonathan Goldberg, *Writing Matters*, pp. 146-155.

73. The marriage ended in divorce seven years later because of Howard's ambition to marry Robert Carr, later the Earl of Somerset.

from Gunpowder, tract, SR

Jan 21 — Parliament reassembles

Jan 23 — Sir Edward Montague introduces a bill to make November 5 an annual day of thanksgiving[74]

Jan 25 — Thomas Dekker, *News from Hell; Divelles Let Loose*, prose, SR

Jan 27 — Eight surviving Gunpowder Plotters tried and condemned: Guy Fawkes, Thomas and Robert Wintour, John Grant, Ambrose Rookwood, Sir Everard Digby, and Robert Keyes

Jan 30 — Sir Orlando Bridgeman b.

— Sir Everard Digby, Robert Wintour, John Grant, and Thomas Bates, executed in St. Paul's Churchyard

Jan 31 — Guy Fawkes, Thomas Wintour, Ambrose Rookwood, and Robert Keyes, executed in the Old Palace Yard at Westminster

Feb — *Strange fearful & true newes which happened at Carlstadt, in the Kingdome of Croatia*, pamphlet, recounts eclipses of the sun and moon in terms that suggest William Shakespeare's *King Lear*

— Sir William Davenant[75] b.

Feb 1 — *Traytours Downfall*, ballad, SR

---

74. Montague thus "introduced the concept of a plain and downright English festival which survived in one form or another for nearly four hundred years (Antonia Fraser, *Faith and Treason*, p. 218).

75. Davenant, whose surname also appears as D'Avenant, often claimed to be William Shakespeare's 'godson,' a frequent euphemism for natural son, thus accounting (one assumes that Davenant must have assumed) for his literary skills; at times, he seems more concerned with constructing his hereditary right to literary fame than in branding his mother as unfaithful. Davenant succeeded Ben Jonson as Poet Laureate. (See Raphael Falco, *Conceived Presences*, for a discussion of the importance of literary genealogies—real or imagined, literal or figurative—for the period). The spelling of the poet laureate's name has always been problematical. Records relating to his father, John, include the names 'Devenet,' 'Devnet,' 'Devenett,' 'Davenett,' 'Dabenett,' 'Dennant,' 'Davenaunte,' and 'Davinant.' The poet's own preference was for 'D'Avenant'; most references to him at the time and subsequently have used 'Davenant,' however.

Feb 3 — *Execution of the eight Traytors*, ballad, SR
Feb 4 — Thomas Cooper, *The Romishe Spyder*, religious tract, SR
Feb 5 — Robert Fletcher, *Nine Worthies*, SR
Feb 13 — *Prodigy at Carlstadt*, ballad, SR
— Father Henry Garnet first examined by the Privy Council concerning the Gunpowder Plot
Feb 17 — William Middleton, *Papistomaxtix*, SR
— *The Pope's Escucheon: Heresey, Frenzy & Hipocricy*, ballad, SR
Feb 18 — W. Whitaker, *Anser to Campion's Tenne Reasons in Controversy*, religious tract, SR
Mar 3 — Sir William Davenant, baptized, St. Martin's Church, Carfax
— Edmund Waller b
Mar 12 — John Marston, *The Parasitaster, or the Fawne*, SR
Mar 17 — John Marston, *Sophonisba, the Wonder of Women*, SR
Mar 28 — Father Henry Garnet, tried and condemned for treason in conjunction with the Gunpowder Plot[76] ; Sir Edward Coke presides
Mar 29 — John Bartlet, *A Book of Ayres with a triplicite of Musick*, SR
— Henrie Greenwood, *A treatise of the great and generall daye of judgement: necessary for every Christian...*, religious tract, SR
Mar 31 — *Trimming of Traitors*, ballad, SR
Apr — Royal Charter for the Council of Virginia

---

76. "Soon after the execution, all Catholic Europe was listening with eager credulity to the story of Garnet's straw. It was said that one of the straws used upon the scaffold had a minute likeness of the martyr's head on one of the husks. The miracle was trumpeted abroad...and found its way from common conversation into the pages of grave writers. An inquiry was instituted by the Government, and it was found that some who had seen the straw declared that there was nothing wonderful in the matter at all, and that the drawing could have been easily executed by any artist of moderate skill" (Samuel Gardiner, *History*, I, 282).

— Robert Cecil, 1ˢᵗ Earl of Salisbury, made Knight of the Garter[77]

Apr 5 — Henry Holland, *History of Adam*, SR

Apr 6 — Patent sealed authorizing Richard Hakluyt's first voyage to Virginia

Apr 7 — Father Edward Oldcorne, John Wintour, Humphrey Littleton, and Ralph Ashley executed for complicity in the Gunpowder Plot

Apr 8 — Joseph Hall, *Heaven upon Earth*[78]

Apr 9 — John Danyel, *Book of Songs for the Lute, Viol and Voice*, SR

Apr 14 — *Arraignment & Execucon of the Traytors*, ballad, SR

Apr 19 — Michael Drayton, *Poems Lyric and Pastoral*

Apr 26 — *The Pope's Desperatt Last Will & Testament*, ballad, SR

Apr 28 — W. H., *Reformed Travailer*, moralistic fiction, SR

May 3 — Father Henry Garnet hanged, drawn, and quartered (b. 1555)

— Father John Gerard, S.J., escapes from England in the aftermath of the Gunpowder Plot

May 5 — *Garnett's Araignement; Pope's Looking Glasse*, religious ballad, SR

— *Shamefull Downfall of the Pope's Kingdom*, religious ballad, SR

— *The Pope's Petigree*, SR

May 8 — William Hubbard, *Great Britaynes Thanksgyvinge*,

---

77. Several other Garter Knights, including the King of France and the King of Denmark, objected to such a high honor being given a man of so common a birth as Cecil (Antonia Fraser, *Faith and Treason*, p. 275).

78. Hall is referred to in Thomas Fuller's *The History of the Worthies of England* as "our English Seneca for the pureness, plainness and fulness of his style; not unhappy at controversies, more happy at comments, better in his sermons, best of all in his meditations" (cited in *Milton Encyclopedia*, III, 147). Hall published *Toothless Satyrs* in 1597, referring to himself as the first English satirist, and followed that book the next year with *Three Last Books of Byting Satires*; the latter was burned by the Stationers' in June, 1599, along with satires by John Marston and Christopher Marlowe.

religious tract, SR

May 10 (or 11?) — Sir Francis Bacon m. Alice Barnham (b. 1598); the groom is forty-five, the bride just under fourteen

May 13 — Arthur Golding (b. 1536, death recorded in register of Belchamp St. Paul's

— Joseph Hall, *Meditations Divine & Moral, 3rd Century*, SR

May 26 — George Closse, *Paricide Papiste*, SR

Jun 6 — Pierre Corneille b, dramatist

Jun 21 — Nathaniel Baxter, *Sidney's Ourania: Endymions song & Tragedie*, edited by Sir Philip Sidney's former tutor, SR

Jun 22 — Princess Sophia b. to James I and Anne of Denmark

Jun 23 — Princess Sophia d.

Jun 27 — Henry Percy, 9th Earl of Northumberland, tried by the Court of the Star Chamber for complicity in the Gunpowder Plot; imprisoned in the Tower for life[79]

Jun 29 — Samuel Gardiner, *A Book of Angling*, SR

— John Owen, *Epigrammatum Libri Tres*, SR

— Thomas Williamson, *The Sword of the Spirit Drawen against Papistes*, religious tract, SR

Jul — William Laud, D.D., St. John's College, Oxford

Jul 1 — Peter Fairlambe, *Recantacon of a Brownist*, religious tract, SR

Jul 15 — Rembrandt van Rijn b, Leiden, Netherlands

---

79. Henry Percy was judged guilty of having admitted his kinsman and steward, Thomas Percy, as a Gentleman Pensioner the year before, without first administering the Oath of Supremacy to him, thus providing one of the conspirators physical access to the King's person; for this he was sentenced to forfeiture of all offices, to imprisonment at the King's pleasure, and to an £11,000 fine. Northumberland is perhaps best known as the "Wizard Earl" for his interest in mathematics, astronomy, astrology, alchemy, the cosmology of Giordano Bruno, and other 'occult' sciences. He was associated with the "School of Night" that centered on Sir Walter Raleigh in the 1580s and 1590s, in which Christopher Marlowe participated. While incarcerated in the Tower, he assembled a following of scholars and philosophers, including Thomas Hariot (also a member of the School of Night), Walter Hughes, and Thomas Hughes, all mathematicians, known to contemporaries as the "Three Magi." For a brief discussion of Hariot, see A. L. Rowse, *Christopher Marlowe*, pp. 118-120.

Jul 16 — Richard West, *News from Bartholomue Fayre*, SR
Jul 25 — John Ford, *Honour Triumphant: The King of Denmark's Welcome*, pamphlet, SR
Aug 5 — Lancelot Andrewes, Bishop of Chichester begins his series of nine annual public sermons commemorating the discovery of the Gowrie Plot against James I
Aug 7 — William Shakespeare, *Macbeth*, performed at Court before King Christian of Denmark, Queen Anne's brother[80]
Aug 8 — *The King of Denmark's Welcomme into England*, SR
Aug 12 — William Perkins, *De Predestinacone*, SR
Aug 19 — H. Roberts, *England's Farewell to Christian IV, King of Denmark, with a relacon of such shewes and severall pastymes presented to His Majesty at courte...and other places*, SR
Aug 22 — Ahmad I (1590-1617), *The Great Turk's Letter to all Christian Princes*, SR
Sep — Pope Paul V condemns the Oath of Allegiance
Sep 16 — Samuel Rowlands, *Bloody (Terrible) Battel between Tyme and Death*, SR
Oct 6 — Thomas Dekker, *The Seven Deadly Sins of London*, prose, SR
Oct 11 — T. Windale [Udall], *Weakness of the Grounds of Popery*, religious tract, SR
Oct 13 — *Murther of a Boy of 3*, ballad, SR
Oct 17 — H.P. [Henry Parrot], *The Mouse Trap*, book of epigrams, SR
Oct 23 — Henry Peacham, *The Art of Drawing with a Pen*, SR
Nov — John Lyly d. (b. 1553 or 1554)
Nov 5 — Bishop Lancelot Andrewes begins his series of ten

---

80. Prince Hamlet's disparagement of Danish drinking and carousing at the court of King Claudius receives confirmation in reports of King Christian's behavior while in England, which included having to be carried drunkenly insensate from more than one court banquet. Antonia Fraser notes that the performance date of the play must have been shortly after the trial and execution of Father Henry Garnet, with the public interest in equivocation that both raised (*Faith and Treason*, p. 281n)

annual public sermons commemorating the foiling of the Gunpowder Plot

Nov 8 — Joseph Hall, *Art of Divine Meditation*, religious tract, SR

Nov 11 — John Dove, *Defense of Church Government in England*, religious tract, SR

Nov 24 — [G. Wilson], *Commendacon of coks and cock Fighting*, SR

Dec — Three ships, with 140 men, set sail for Hakluyt's first voyage to Virginia

Dec 5 — Samuel Rowlands, *Diogenes Lanthorne*, SR

Dec 16 — Guillaume Saluste Du Bartas, *Posthumus Bartas, 4th Day of Second Week*, translation, SR

Dec 18 — [George Godwin], *Automachia: Self Conflict of a Christian*, SR

Dec 26 — William Shakespeare, *King Lear*, performed at Court before James I

Dec 31 — John Davies of Hereford, *Summa Totalis, or All in All the Same Forever*, SR

1607

Barnabe Barnes, *Devil's Charter*, play on the life of Pope Alexander VI

James Cleland, *Institution of a Young Nobleman*, educational treatise

Thomas Dekker, *A Knights Conjuring. Done in earnest: Discovered in Jest*, including portions of John Donne's *The Storme*"[81]

Thomas Dekker and John Webster, *The Famous Historie of Sir Thomas Wyatt*

Thomas Deloney, *Strange Histories, or Songes and Sonets, of Kings, Prince, Dukes, Lordes, Ladyes, Knights, and Gentlemen*, 3rd edition, including the earliest printing of John Donne's "A Lame Beggar"

John Fletcher, *The Knight of the Burning Pestle*, written (?)

Sir John Harington, *The Englishmans Doctor: or, the School of Salerne*

S. Harwood, *A Discourse of the Severall Kinds and Causes of Lightning*, treatise discussing lightning as divine punishment for sin

Esther Inglis, *Octonaries Upon the Vanitie and Inconstancie Of the World*

Ben Jonson, *Volpone, or The Foxe*, printed by Thomas Thorppe, with "Amicissimo et Meritissimo Ben Jonson" by John Donne

---

81. This indicates the earliest printing of any part of this poem, and one of the earliest appearances of any poem, by John Donne.

William Russell, *The Report of a Bloudie and Terrible Massacre in the City of Mosco, with a fearfull and tragicall end of Demetrius the last Duke, before him raigning at this present*, translation of a Dutch merchant's account of the reign of Dmitrius (Apr 3-Jun 15, 1605)

William Shakespeare, *Anthony and Cleopatra; Timon of Athens* (probably written 1605-1608)

'W. S.,' *The Puritan*, published, later (Third Folio, 1644) attributed to William Shakespeare

Rev. Edward Topsell, *History of the Four-Footed Beasts*, translations and paraphrases of Konrad Gesner, *Historia Animalium*, a foundation text in modern zoology

Cyril Tourneur, *The Revenger's Tragedy*, published[82]

Arthur Dent d. (b. c.1553)

Robert Chamberlain b.

Jane Savage b. (afterward, Jane Paulet, Marchioness of Winchester)

Princess Sophia, last child of James I and Anne of Denmark, b. and d., buried in Westminster Abbey[83]

William Harvey elected to the Royal College of Physicians

Francis Beaumont and John Fletcher begin their collaboration

Jan 6 — TWELFTH NIGHT — Thomas Campion, *Masque at Whitehall 6 Jan 1607* [*The Lord Hay's Masque*], wedding masque for Honoria Denny and James Lord Hay; presided over by James I; SR Jan 26, 1607

Jan 9 — William Cleuer, *Instruction of children in Latin*, SR

Jan 14 — John Dove, *Bellarmini controversia primi, verbo dei...*, 2nd edition of *Defence of Church Government*, SR

---

82. Entered on the *Stationers' Register* anonymously, *The Revenger's Tragedy* is often associated with Middleton; it also represents a climax of sorts in the tradition of "revenge tragedy" that includes Thomas Kyd's *The Spanish Tragedy* and William Shakespeare's *Hamlet*.

83. Wealth, rank, and status had relatively little to do with children's survival. Only three of James and Anne's seven children survived to adulthood; even then Prince Henry died early, at age eighteen.

Feb 2 — Thomas Cash, *Two Murthers in Lyncolnshire*, SR

Feb 6 — *Report of Fearful Innundations* (in Somerset) *Feb 1607*, tract, SR

Feb 11 — *Overflowing of Waters in Summersett*, ballad, SR

Feb 12 — *News from Monmouthshire...overflowing Waters*, tract, SR

Feb 23 — *God's Warning to England in late over Waters*, ballad, SR

Mar 3 — Gervase Markham, *The English Horsman*, SR

Mar 7 — *Divers Lamentable Fires in Shires*, news pamphlet, SR

Mar 11 — Thomas Ford, *Musicke of Sundry Kyndes*, SR

Mar 21 — R. P. [Robert Pricket], *Popishe Myracles with a Confutacon*, SR

Apr — Thomas Deloney (b. c.1543); contemporary reference to him as having just died

Apr 13 — John Higgins, *Mirror of Magistrates*, "Newly enlarged with a last part," SR; reissue of 1574 edition

Apr 20 — Thomas Dekker, *Whore of Babilon*, SR

Apr 24 — Thomas Heywood, *Fair Maid of the Exchange*, SR

Apr 25 — *Horrible Murders in Jerome Bowes House*, tract, SR

May 2 — Christopher Lever, *Quene Elizabeths Teares*, SR

— Olivier de Serres, *Life of Silkworms and Planting of Mulberry Trees*, SR

May 9 — Thomas Middleton, *The Phoenix*, SR

May 14 — *Miracle upon Miracle: The Great Floodes*, SR

May 15 — Thomas Middleton, *Michaelmas Term*[84]

May 20 — Francis Beaumont and John Fletcher, *The Woman Hater*, drama, SR

Jun 3 — George Chapman, *The Revenge of Bussy D'Ambois* (?)

Jun 25 — *Commons Complaint for the Death of Popham*, political ballad, SR

---

84. The quarter of the year beginning 29 September.

— John Nicholl, *Plantinge of Guiana*, SR
— Sir Francis Bacon named Solicitor-General and Clerk of the Star Chamber[85]
Summer — John Marston, *Entertainment*, in honor of Alice Spenser, Dowager Countess of Derby, at Ashby House
Jul 5 — [Gervase Markham?], *Shape and Proporcon of a Perfect Horse*, SR
Jul 8 — Joseph Hall, *Holy Observations*, SR
Jul 11 — John Donne sends his "La Corona" sonnets, including "To the Lady Magdalen Herbert: of St. Mary's Magdalen," to Magdalene Newport Herbert,[86] his literary patron and the mother of Edward and George Herbert
Jul 13 — Wenceslas Hollar b.
Jul 31 — G. Wilkins, *Misery of Inforced Marriage*, SR
Aug 6 — Thomas Dekker, *Northward Ho*, SR
— John Marston, *What You Will*, SR
— Thomas Middleton, *The Widdow of Watlins Street: The Puritan*, SR
— Cardinal Robert Bellarmine writes to the Catholic Archpriest George Blackwell in England, reaffirming papal condemnation of English Catholics who take the Oath of Allegiance
Sep 5 — William Shakespeare, *Hamlet*, first recorded performance, on the ship *H.M.S. Dragon* at Sierra Leone

---

85. Bacon rose rapidly to political prominence under James I after years of languishing in the service of Elizabeth. A particularly canny judge of character (unlike her successor, James I), Elizabeth seems never to have quite trusted the cunning and wily Bacon, referred to by his more critical biographers as little better than a court toady.

86. Left a widow with a large number of young children, Magdalene Herbert immediately established herself as a figure of strength and character, managing her estates, educating her children, and seeing to it that they had every opportunity for advancement, while retaining the respect (at times almost reverence, it seems) of poets of the caliber of John Donne. Her eldest son Edward served with distinction as an ambassador and became a poet of some note; her younger son, George, became arguably the premier religious poet of the century.

Sep 16 — Princess Mary Stuart, d.
Oct 6 — T. D. (Thomas Dekker?] and George Wilkins, *Jests to Make You Merry, Jest of Cocke Watt*
Oct 7 — Thomas Middleton, *The Revengers Tragedy*, SR; *A Trick to Catch the Old One*, SR
Oct 12 — Michael Drayton, *Legend of Great Cromwell*, SR
— Thomas Middleton, *Family of Love*, acted by the Children of His Majesty's Revels
Oct 14 — *Jesuytes Commedies, Acted at Lyon in France*, SR
Oct 16 — Barnabe Barnes, *Tragedie of Pope Alexander VI*, as played before His Majesty, SR
— Giovanni Croce, *Musica Sacra to Sixe Voyces*, SR
Oct 19 — *Jesuites Commedie or Newes from Lyon*, ballad, SR
Oct 23 — *God's Wrath at Lyon to Jesuit in a Play*, ballad, SR
Oct 24 — Samuel Rowlands, *Dr. Merry Man his medicines against Melancholy*, SR
Nov 20 — Joseph Hall, *Epistles, Volume 1, 2 Decades*, SR
Nov 26 — William Shakespeare, *Historye of King Lear*, SR by Nathaniel Butter
Dec 24 — Sir Robert Carr (later favorite of James I) knighted

1608

Robert Armin, *A Nest of Ninnies*, jest-book
Jacobus Arminius, *Declaration of Sentiments*, published
Sir Francis Bacon, *Commentarius Solatus*, notebook and commonplace book
Francis Davison, *A Poetical Rapsodie*, published
John Donne, *Elegy IX, The Autumnal*[87]
John Fletcher, *The Faithful Shepherdess* (?)
Robert Glover, *Nobilitas Politica vel Civilis*
Arthur Golding, *Epitome of Frossard's Chronicles written in Latin by John Sleydane*, translation
Guazzo, *Compendium Maleficrum*, published
The Merry Devil of Edmonton, published (six quarto editions by 1655), later attributed to William Shakespeare
William Perkins, *Discourse on the Damned Art of Witchcraft*, published (written before 1602)
Ericius Puteanus, *Comus*, dream-vision
William Shakespeare, *Coriolanus* (?); *King Lear*, printed (First Quarto)
'William Shakespeare,' *A Yorkshire Tragedy*, "Acted by his majesty's Players at the Globe," with SR by 'Wylliam Shake-spere'[88]
Thomas Shelton, translation of Miguel de Cervantes, *Don*

---

87. The poem is dedicated to Magdalene Newport Herbert.

88. The anomalous SR entry in the name of the author provides some evidence that in spite of the attribution the play was not in fact by Shakespeare.

Quixote, completed (published 1612); first translation of the work

Joshua Sylvester, complete translation of *Bartas His Devine Weeks & Workes*

Rev. Edward Topsell, *History of Serpents*, translations and paraphrases from Konrad Gesner, *Historia Animalium*

George Wilkins, *The Painful Adventures of Pericles Prince of Tyre*, novel based on Shakespeare's play

John Dee, mathematician and astrologer, d. (b. 1527)

Nathaniel Fiennes, b

Robert Greville, b. (cousin and adopted son to Fulke Greville, 1st Lord Brooke)

John Reeve b.

Proposed union of Scotland and England rejected by Parliament

Protestant Union formed within the Holy Roman Empire, with Frederick V, the young Elector Palatine, as its spearhead

Robert Cecil, Earl of Salisbury, appointed Lord Treasurer

Phineas Fletcher, M.A., King's College, Cambridge

George Herbert elected to Trinity College, Cambridge

Hans Lippershey, a Dutch maker of eyeglasses, offers an early prototype telescope to the government; first person to apply for a patent for the device

James Shirley enters the Merchant Taylors' School

Inigo Jones completes his first known building, the New Exchange in the Strand

Jan 6/10 — TWELFTH NIGHT — Ben Jonson, *Masque of Beauty*, sequel to *Masque of Blackness*

Jan 10 — Thomas Middleton, *Powles Walkes,*[89] *or a gallant Dismasked*, SR

Jan 18 — Guillaume de Saluste du Bartas, *History of Judyth*,

---

[89]. Paul's Walk was the name given to the central corridor at old St. Paul's Cathedral which had, by the early part of the century, become as much a commercial location as a religious one, notorious for drawing not only merchandisers of all sorts, but prostitutes, dissolute gentlemen, cut-purses, and others of equally disreputable reputations..

translation, SR by H. Lownes (first published in Edinburgh, 1584

Feb 1 — William Fulbeck, *Nymphothicnes: Elegie on Lady Jane Grey*, SR

Feb 5 — Thomas Hobbes —, B.A., Oxford University; recommended as tutor to the eldest son of William Cavendish, Baron Hardwick (later 3rd Earl of Devonshire)[90]

Feb 9 — Ben Jonson, *Haddington Masque*, written to celebrate the marriage of Viscount Haddington and Lady Elizabeth Radcliffe

Feb 13 — Elizabeth Cavendish, Countess of Shrewsbury (familiarly known as Bess of Hardwick), grandmother to Lady Arabella Stuart, d. (b. 1518)

Mar 7 — Joseph Hall, *The Second Volume; Characters of Virtues and Vices*[91], SR

Mar 10 — Alexander Gill, the Elder, appointed high master of St. Paul's School

Mar 14 — Thomas Dekker, *The Bellman of London*, SR

Mar 22 — Thomas Middleton, *(Your) Five Wittie Gallantes*, as acted by the Children of the Chapel

Mar 26 — *Adam's Tragedie*, SR

Spring — Magdalene Newport Herbert m. Sir John Danvers, some twenty years her junior

Apr 2 — Henry Peacham, *More the Merrier*, SR

Apr 5 — Thomas Brewer, *The Life & Death of the Merry Devil of Edmonton, with Smugge's Pranks*, prose tract, SR

---

90. Because William Cavendish, the younger, was married, he could not attend the University; hence the need for a tutor for an eighteen-year-old young man.

91. The *Characters* introduce into English the Theophrastan 'character,' or highly literary, prose thumbnail sketch of a personality type, often tinged with wit ranging from gentle probing to caustic satire, just as often providing vehicles for linguistic style and elegance. Hall's *Characters* were also among the first to deal with abstractions rather than human types. Theophrastan characters became increasingly popular during the first decades of the seventeenth century. For a full study of the form, see Benjamin Boyce, *The Theophrastan Character*.

Apr 11 — H. P. [Henry Parrot], *Epigrams or Humores Lottrye*, SR
Apr 12 — John Dram Day, *Humour out of breathe*, SR
Apr 15 — Elizabeth Abbot, *The arraignment, etc., of Elizabeth Abbot*, pamphlet, SR
— Ballad on Elizabeth Abbot, SR
Apr 18 — *Waste done by a sudden fyer in Bury St. Edmonds 12 Apr 1608*, SR
Apr 19 — Thomas Sackville, 1st Earl of Dorset and Lord High Treasurer, d. (b. 1536)
Apr 21 — Ben Jonson, *Characters of Two Royall Maskes*, SR
— R. West, *Wyttes ABC, or Century of Epigrams*, SR
Apr 29 — Thomas Dekker, *Converted Courtisan or honest Whore, II*, SR
May 2 — Thomas Middleton, *A Yorkshire Tragedy*, drama, SR
May 4 — Richard Middleton, *Epigrams and Satyres*, SR
May 13 — Joseph Hall, *Pharisaisme and Christianitie*, SR
May 20 — William Shakespeare, *Anthony and Cleopatra* and *Pericles*, SR entries by Edward Blount
Jun — Sir Richard Fanshawe b.
— Thomas Fuller, b.; clergyman and historian
Jun 3 — Thomas Heywood, *Rape of Lucrece, a Tragedy*, SR
Jun 5 — George Chapman, *Conspiracy and Tragedy of Charles Duke of Byron*, published, in two parts, SR
Jun 7 — Randall Cotgrave, *Dictionary in French and English...*, SR
Jun 10 — Thomas Carew matriculates at Merton College, Oxford University, at age 13
Jun 19 — Sir Thomas Overbury, knighted
Jun 23 — Samuel Rowlands, *Famous History of Guy of Warwick*, SR
Jun 25 — Sir Francis Bacon appointed Solicitor-General
Jun 29 — Joseph Hall, *Vowes & Meditations, 1, 2, & 3 Centuries*, SR
Jul 4 — *The Famous & renowned History of Morindos a King of Spain; Who maryed with Miracolas a Spanish Witch: and*

of their Seven daughters...., prose fiction, SR
Jul 7 — Thomas Dekker, *Ravens Almanacke*, SR
Jul 13 — Ferdinand III, Holy Roman Emperor, b.
Jul 18 — Samuel Hieron, *Answer to a Popish Ryme*, religious tract, SR
Aug 6 — Philippe de Mornay, *Address to the Jews upon the Comminge of Messias*, translation, SR
Aug 13 — W. Bettie, *History of Titana and Theseus*, SR
— John Smith of Jamestown, *A True Relation of Such Occurrences and Accidents of Note as Happened in Virginia*, SR
Aug 23 — *Fearfull Vision in the Ayre over Caen 7 Aug. 1608*, ballad, SR
Aug 28 — Sir Francis Vere d. (b. 1554)
Sep 24 — W. Bailey, *Rumor of Warres among Tymes & Signs of Peace*, SR
Oct 4 — Thomas Middleton, *Mad World My Masters*, play, SR
Oct 17 — Joseph Hall, *Epistles, Volume 2*, SR
Oct 25 — Thomas Dekker, *Lanthorne & Candlelight: The Bellman, II*, SR
Oct 27 — Sir Walter Raleigh's principle estate, Sherbourne, presented by James I to his favorite, Sir Robert Carr, later 1st Earl of Somerset
Nov 25 — Fulke Greville, 1st Lord Brooke, *Mustapha and Zangar*, SR
Dec 1 — Denakol, *No Parliament Powder. But shot and powder for the Pope...*, SR
Dec 5 — Thomas Heywood, *Troia Britannic; or, Great Britain's Troy*, heroic poem of 13,000 lines, SR
Dec 6 — George Monck b.
Dec 8 — Joseph Hall, *Solomon's Divine Arts*, SR
Dec 9 — **John Milton, b., at the sign of the "Spread Eagle," Milton family home in Bread Street, London**; several blocks from old St. Paul's Cathedral and near the Mermaid Tavern, where Ben Jonson would later preside over the "Sons

of Ben"[92]

Dec 15 — John Milton (Mielton), *a Sixefold Politian*, political tract, SR

Dec 20 — **John Milton baptized, All Hallows Church, Bread Street**

— Sir Aston Cockayne baptized

Dec 22 — *Two Monstrous Births in Nov and Dec (1608)*, news pamphlets, SR

---

92. The "Spread Eagle' was the insignia of the scrivener and thus an advertisement for the senior Milton's occupation. For a discussion of the use of sign-boards such as the "Spread Eagle" to designate private homes in seventeenth-century London, see Liza Picard, *Restoration London*, pp. 8-9. Milton was a city-child, who would spend most of his life living within the confines of London.

1609

Robert Armin, *History of the two Maids of More-clacke, with the life and simple maner of John in the Hospitall*, published

Sir Francis Bacon, *De Sapientia Veterum* [*The Wisdom of the Ancients*], published

Francis Beaumont and John Fletcher, *Philaster* and *Coxcomb*, written

Samuel Daniel, *Civil Wars between the Two Houses of Lancaster and Yorke*, in eight books[93]

Thomas Dekker, *The Gull's Hornbook*[94]

John Donne, begins composing the *Holy Sonnets*

Alfonso Ferrabosco, *Ayres*, with the first appearance of John Donne's "The Expiration"

Joseph Hall, *Solomon's Divine Art*, published

Ben Jonson, *Epicoene, or the Silent Woman*, performed by the Children of the Queen's Revels

Thomas Middleton, *Two Gates of Salvation*, SR

Sir Walter Raleigh, *Dialogue Between a Jesuit and a Recusant*

Thomas Ravenscroft, *Pammelia. Musicks miscellanie*, published

William Shakespeare, *Cymbeline; Pericles*, "bad" quarto published

---

93. Daniel's poem originally appeared as *First Fowre Bookes of the Civile Wars between the Two Houses of Lancaster and Yorke*, in 1595.

94. This has been called the "most famous of the Jacobean pamphlets," providing satirical representations of the "gulls," or foolish characters, of the day Edwin Riddell, *Lives of the Stuart Age*, p. 122.

Edmund Spenser, *The Faerie Queene*, 1ˢᵗ folio; complete, with *Mutability Cantos*, printed by H. L. for Matthew Lownes

Tarlton's Jests, published, jest-book⁹⁵

Joseph Wybarne, *The New Age of Old Names* published, including lines from John Donne's *Satyre III*

Charles Diodati b. (?)⁹⁶

Lodowick Muggleton b.

Robert Wild b.

Gerrard Winstanley b.

The Catholic League forms in Europe as a counter-poise to the Protestant Union, laying foundations for the Thirty-Years War for religious and political supremacy

Bishop Lancelot Andrewes transferred to the See of Ely

Robert Harcourt commands the second Jacobean voyage to colonize Guiana; his colony survives until 1613

Galileo Galilei further refines the telescope

Giles Fletcher enrolls at Trinity College, Cambridge (until 1618)

John Marston enters the Church; his writing career had ended in 1607

Ignatius of Loyola⁹⁷, founder of the Jesuit Order, beatified by

---

95. The collection was named for Richard Tarlton (d. 1588), the foremost comic actor of his day.The stories collected around his name perpetuated the legends of his being both a natural comic and Queen Elizabeth's official jester, neither of which was accurate. The books was purportedly published in 1609, although the earliest extant edition is dated 1611. (P. M. Zall, *Nest*, p. 91).

96. Charles' brother was named John; Milton probably knew both of the Diodati boys, but Charles remained his closest childhood friend.

97. More central to the purposes of this study, Loyola was not only excoriated in England as the founder of the Jesuit order but also virtually revered (or at least emulated) as the originator of a sequence of meditation practices; the "Ignatian" meditation, as it was called, provides a key structural element for many of the poems written by John Donne, George Herbert, John Milton, and other poets of the period. It is a rigid system of intellectualization, subdividing the act of meditation into analogues of Memory, Understanding, and Will, corresponding to Composition of Place,

Pope Paul V

Jan 1 — Sir Francis Bacon, *Discourse of the Plantation in Ireland* (published 1657)
Jan 13 — Boethius (c 480-524), *Philosophical Comfort*, new translation of *De Consolatione Philosophiae*, SR
Jan 14 — Thomas Brewer, *A ballad made by Thomas Brew. Of the Twoo monstruous births in Devon and Plymmouth in November last*, SR
Jan 20 — John Dowland, *Ornithoparcus: The Art of Singing*, SR
Jan 26 — Ben Jonson, *His Case is Altered*, play, SR
Jan 28 — William Shakespeare, *Troilus and Cressida*, SR by Richard Bonian and Henry Walley
Feb 1 — Alphons Ferabosco, *Book of Ayres*, music, SR
Feb 2 — Ben Jonson, *Masque of Queenes*, produced, with Lucy Harington Russell, Countess of Bedford among the dancers
Feb 6 — *Murther at Lewes 13 Jan. 1608*, ballad, SR
Feb 10 — Sir John Suckling baptized[98]
Feb 18 — Edward Hyde, b.; afterward 1st Earl of Clarendon and Lord High Chancellor to Charles II
Feb 20 — Thomas Tuke, *Highe Way to Heaven*, religious tract on election, SR
Feb 22 — Ben Jonson, *Masque of Queenes Celebrated*, SR
Feb 27 — John Wilbye, *Second Sett of Madrigalls*, music, SR
Mar — Bishop Lancelot Andrewes, answer to Cardinal Bellarmine's attack on the Oath of Allegiance
Mar 3 — Barnaby Riche, *Survey of Ireland discovering Disobedience*, political tract, SR
Mar 10 — John Mason, *Tragedy of the Turk, with Borgias Death*, SR

Meditation, and Colloquy. See especially Louis L. Martz, *The Poetry of Meditation and The Meditative Poem*.

98. In addition to being a graceful lyric poet, Suckling, an inveterate gambler, invented an early version of the contemporary card game, Cribbage, by some reports while he languished in prison during the Civil Wars.

Mar 18 — R. M., *Profitable Dialogue for Perverted Papists*, religious tract, SR

Apr 21 — William Bradshaw, *Doctrine of Communicating Worthily*, religious tract, SR

Apr 24 — *Have with you to Pimlico*, ballad

Apr 25 — *Birth of Three Monsters in Flaunders*, tract, SR

Apr 29 — *Zenomachia: Against the Plague*, SR

May 3 — Robert Gray, *Good Speed to Virginia*, political tract

— *Sonnets of Mr William Shakespeare*, published by Thomas Thorpe

May 4 — George Chapman, *Tears of Peace*, SR

— Benjamin Whichcote b.[99]

May 5 — George Herbert named as a King's Scholar for Trinity College, Cambridge

May 20 — William Shakespeare, *Sonnets of Mr William Shakespeare*, SR by Thomas Thorp

May 30 — Thomas Middleton, *Travells of Sir Robert Sherley*, SR

By Jun — Bishop Lancelot Andrewes, *Tortura Torti*, controversialist treatise defending James I and the Oath of Allegiance against Cardinal Bellarmine and Pope Paul VI, in press

Jun 2 — A. Barker, *Piracies Ward; Dansker; Turks against English French Dutch and Spanish*, political tracts

Jun 15 — *Collection of Murders Committed in England*, SR

Jun 16 — Anthony Nixon, *Original Ground of the Present Wars of Sweden*, political tract, SR

Jul 3 — Two Ballads: *Pirate Ward* and *Danseker the Dutchman*, SR

Jul 9 — George Webb, *God's Controversy with England: Paul's Cross Sermon 11 Jun. 1609*, SR

Jul 10 (?)— Gerrard Winstanley b.[100]

---

99. Leader of the Cambridge Platonists, Whichcote himself published nothing.

100. Winstanley's birth date remains uncertain, although George Sabine notes a baptismal record for this date; Winstanley's death date remains unknown

Jul 20 — Ben Jonson, *The Case is Altered*, SR adding the name of a third publisher, B. Sutton

Jul 26 — Arthur Dent, *Playne Mans Pathway to Heaven II*, religious tract, SR

Aug 21 — T. Wuedale [Udall], *Reply to BC's reply to the Weake Grounds of Popery*, religious tract, SR

Aug 26 — *Monstrous Child born in Sandwick*, tract, SR

Aug 31 — *Strange News: Monstrous Child*, ballad, SR

Sep — Lancelot Andrewes elevated to Bishop of Ely

Sep 1 — Stephen Hobbes, *Margarita Chirurgica*, medical tract, SR

Sep 9 — *Bill of Prices: Mercerye and Silke Wares*, SR

Oct 6 — Nicholas Morgan, *Perfection of Horsmanship*, SR

Oct 10 — Gerrard Winstanley baptized

Oct 12 — T. R. [Thomas Ravenscroft], *Deuteromelia: Songs of Myrth or Freeman's Songs*, music, SR

— [Thomas Tuke], *Heavenly Directions to the Holy Land*, religious tract, SR

Oct 16 — Stoughton, *Dignitie of Gods Children and Baseness of Others*, religious tract, SR

— Cyril Tourneur, *Poem on the Death of Sir Francis Vere*, SR

Oct 19 — Jacobus Arminius d. (b. 1560)

Winter — The Plague strikes London in the worst outbreak since 1603; theaters remain closed for 1½ months

Nov 10 — Arthur Hopton, *Bacculum Geodeticum*, scientific treatise, SR

— Thomas Tuke, *Picture of a True Protestant*, religious tract, SR

Nov 13 — W. M., *Fortune Teller: The Man in the Moon Telling Fortunes*, SR

Nov 14 — Rowland Vaughan, *Water Workes: Making of Bad Grounds Fruitful*, agricultural treatise, SR

Nov 15 — Henrietta Maria, youngest daughter of Henry IV, King of France and Marie de Médici, and future Queen of England, b.

Nov 16 — R. M., *True Touchstone for a Counterfeit Catholic*,

SR
Dec — Barnabe Barnes buried (b. 1571)
Dec 2 — John Donne, *Pseudomartyr*, religious treatise, SR
Dec 14 — *Purpose and Ends of the Plantation in Virginia*, tract, SR
— Edmond Gardiner, *Gardiners Garden: Triall of Tabacco*, medical tract, SR
Dec 18 — *Morus Foeneratoris: The Usurer's Bite*, tract, SR
— George Herbert matriculates at Trinity College, Cambridge
Dec 22 — [John Selden], *Duello*, SR

Decade Two: 1610-1619
Rumours of War

1610

Bishop Lancelot Andrewes, *Responsio ad Apologiam Cardinalis Bellarmini...*, published

Sir Francis Bacon, *The Beginning of the history of Great Britain* (published 1657

Francis Beaumont and John Fletcher, *The Maid's Tragedy*

Thomas Campion, *Two Books of Airs*

Robert Dowland, *A Musicall Banquet*, published, lute-music; with lyrics by Edward DeVere, 17th Earl of Oxford; Robert Devereux, 2nd Earl of Essex; and others

Giles Fletcher, *Christ's Victorie, and Triumph in heaven, and earth, over and after death*[101], published at Cambridge, establishing Fletcher's position as pre-eminent religious poet at Cambridge

Orlando Gibbons, *Fantasies of Three Parts*[102]

Sir Arthur Gorges, English translation of Sir Francis Bacon, *The wisedome of the ancients, written in Latine by the Right Honourable Sir Francis Bacon Knight, Baron of Verulam and Lord Chancelour of England. Done into English...*, published

Joseph Hall, *An Apology against the Brownists*, Hall's first directly political polemic

Francis Herring, *Popish Pietie*, treatise dealing with the Powder

---

101. The only edition to appear during Fletcher's lifetime, and, apart from commemorative poems for Prince Henry and Princess Elizabeth, Fletcher's only English poetry

102. A collection of chamber music.

Treason, "that monstrous birth of the Roman harlot

David Owen, *Herod and Pilate Reconciled: Or, The Concord of Papist and Puritan ... for the Coercion, Deposition, and Killing of Kings*, scholarly tract declaring that Kings are answerable to God alone

William Shakespeare, *The Tempest* (?), *Cymbeline*, *The Winter's Tale*

'William Sh.,' *Mucedorus*, published (1st appearance, 1598; 17 editions by 1700)

Cyril Tourneur, *The Atheist's Tragedy: or, The Honest Man's Revenge*, performed

Lucius Cary, 2nd Viscount Falkland, b.

Charles Hoole b

Matthew Newcomen b.

Bathsua, or Basua, Pell b. (afterward Bathsua Makin

David Teniers II b.(painter)

Sir Thomas Roe commands James's third attempt to colonize Guiana

Jan — John Donne, *Pseudo-Martyr*, anti-Catholic tract

— Sidney Godolphin b.

Jan 1 — George Herbert sends two sonnets to Lady Danvers

Jan 5 — Torquato Tasso, *Heroic Combat between Raymunde and Argantes*, SR, translation from *Gerusalemme Liberata*

Jan 10 — George Carleton, *Jurisdiction Regal, Episcopal, Papal*, SR

Jan 14 — *The Five Articles of Remonstrance*, a systematized statement of the teachings of Jacobus Arminius, drawn up by his followers in The Hague; subsequently published in July

Jan 24 — James I receives a copy of *Pseudo-Martyr*[103]

---

103. This volume helped convince James I—who was by his own estimation no mean hand at theological disputation (it has been said of James that, as a King, he was a tolerable theologian)—of Donne's polemical abilities, sufficiently for James to make it clear that any hopes Donne might have for preferment would have to include his entering the ministry.

Feb 3 — John Webster, Puritan preacher, b.

Mar — Galileo Galilei, *Nuncius Siderius* (*Message from the Stars*), pamphlet, announces the discovery and refinement of the telescope

Mar 4 — William Dobson, b. (portraitist)

Apr 2 — E. B. [Edmond Bolton], *Element of Armoryes*, SR

Apr 4 — Arthur Dent, *Opening of Heaven Gates*, SR

Apr 19 — Thomas Dekker, *Shoemaker's Holiday*, play, SR

May 8 — William Crashaw, *The Jesuittes Gospel*, SR

— Pierre du Moulin, *Oppositions of the Word of God with Roman Doctrine*, SR

— William Folkingham, *Feudigraphia: surveying Methodized*, SR

May 14 — Assassination of Henry IV of France by François Ravaillac, a Catholic extremist (Ravaillac executed, May 27)[104]

May 15 — William Barley, *The Lamentable complaint of Fraunce, for the death of the late King Henry 4...*, published, broadside ballad

Jun 3 — William Cavendish made Knight of the Bath

Jun 4 — William Camden, *Britannia; or, A Chorographical Description of England, Scotland, and Ireland*, English translation by Philemon Holland[105]

— Prince Henry created Prince of Wales

Jun 5 — Samuel Daniel, *Thetys Festival*, performed as part of the installation festivities for the Prince of Wales; Daniel's second and final masque written at Queen Anne's request; thereafter published in quarto

Jun 10 — George Marcelline, *Triumphs of King James I*, SR

— Lady Arabella Stuart m. William Seymour, grandson of the

---

104. Hyder Rollins notes the English interest in the assassination, with books on the subject registered for publication on May 10 (which would have been a week after the assassination, using English dating), May 14, May 30 (three items), 1610; January 12, 1611, and October 10, 1611 (*Pepysian Garland*, p. 24).

105. The original Latin edition had appeared in 1586.

Earl of Hertford, without James' permission, thus placing the Stuart monarchy and succession potentially at risk

Jun 12 — *Chester's Triumph in Honor of the Prince*, SR Jun 27

Jun 27 — Lady Arabella and William Seymour imprisoned in the Tower of London

Jul 11 — Robert Linacre, *Short Catechism for Little Children against Popery*, SR

Jul 14 — Daniel Price, *Creation of the Prince*, SR

— Plague in London closes the theaters

Jul 20 — Henry, Prince of Wales, *Princes Prayers*, SR

Aug — Ben Jonson, *The Alchemist*, performed at Oxford, London's theaters still being closed

Sep 20 — Ben Jonson, *Epicoene, or the Silent Woman*, SR

Oct 2 — Mrs. Aemili Lanyer, *Salve Deus Rex Judæorum*, SR, 2 editions

Oct 3 — Ben Jonson, *The Alchemist*, SR; *Sejanus, His Fall*, SR; *Volpone*, SR[106]

Oct 4 — Joseph Hall, *The Sixth Decade of Epistles* (Volume 3), SR

Oct 8 — John Davies of Hereford,[107] *The Scourge of Folly*, SR

Oct 16 — Isaac Casaubon[108] arrives in England, largely through the influence of Bishop Lancelot Andrewes

Oct 31 — [John Marston?], *Histriomastix, or the Player Whipte*, SR by Thomas Thorpe

Nov 2 — Francis Herring, *Popishe Pyetye*, SR

—Richard Bancroft, Archbishop of Canterbury, d.

Nov 26 — Thomas Coryate, *Coryates Crudities Hastily gobled up in five Moneths travels in France, Italy, &c*; includes

---

106. This edition of Jonson's play also included the first appearance of John Donne's tribute to the playwright, "Amicissimo et Meritissimo Ben Jonson."

107. So named to differentiate him from Sir John Davies.

108. An eminent continental scholar whose studies demonstrated the ahistorical approach Renaissance philosophers and theologians had taken toward the purported writings of Hermes Trismegisthus.

commendatory poems by John Donne; and *Coryats Crambe, or his Coleworte twice Sodden*
— John Selden, *Jani Anglorum*, SR, legal treatise
Dec — Elizabeth Drury d. (b. 1596); subject of John Donne's *Anniversaries*

1611

Lancelot Andrewes, *Scala Coeli: Nineteene sermons concerning prayer. The first six guiding to the true doore: the residue teaching how so to knocke thereat that wee may enter...*, published

Authorized Version, King James Bible

Francis Beaumont and John Fletcher, *A King and No King*, performed

George Chapman, *The Iliads of Homer; prince of poets. Never before in any language truly translated. With a comment uppon some of his chiefe places; donne according to the Greek by Geo: Chapman*, translation of Homer, (published as early as 1609?); *The Revenge of Bussy d'Ambois*, published

John Florio, *Queen Anna's New World of Words, or Dictionarie of the Italian and English tongues....*

Ben Jonson, *Catiline His Conspiracy*

Amelia Lanier, *Salve Deus*, with "A Description of Cooke-ham"

Thomas Middleton, *Roaring Girl*, SR, play

Parthenia or the Maydenhead of the first musicke that ever was printed for the Virginalls, published (?), with music by William Byrd, John Bull, and Orlando Gibbons

Thomas Ravenscroft, *Melismata. Musicall phansies*, published

John Speed, *Historie of Great Britaine*

Edmund Spenser, *The Faerie Queen: The Shepheards Calendar: Together with the other Works of England's Arch-Poët, Edm. Spenser: Collected into one Volume*, published

John Webster, *The White Devil*, written and performed (?)

Giles Fletcher, the Elder, d. (b. 1548)[109]
William Cartwright b.
John Pell b. (brother of Bathsua Pell)
James I begins selling a new rank of nobility, the *Baronet*, or hereditary knighthood, for between £750 and £1,095; gradually the sale expands to include earldoms and other peerages for up to £10,000[110], causing dissension, envy, and anger
George Abbot, appointed Archbishop of Canterbury[111]
Thomas Carew, B.A., Merton College, Oxford
Phineas Fletcher, Fellow of Cambridge University
Henry King, B.A., Christ Church, Oxford University

Jan 1 — Ben Jonson, *Oberon, The Faery Prince. A Masque of Prince Henry's*, produced
Jan 7 — James Harrington b.
Jan 24 — John Donne, *Conclave Ignatii...apologia pro Iesuites*, SR
Jan 25 — J. Sanford, *Propulaion, Entrance to the Spanish Tongue*, SR[112]
Jan 31 — Thomas Carew, B.A., Oxford University
Feb 13 — Ben Jonson, *Love Freed from Ignorance and Folly*,

---

109. A minor poet in his own right, Giles Fletcher, the Elder, was the father of Giles and Phineas Fletcher (both much more substantial poets than their father) and uncle to John Fletcher, the dramatist. Frank S. Kastor states that, "in addition to influencing John Milton's work, Giles Fletcher, his sons Phineas and Giles, and their first cousin, John, the dramatist, comprise one of England's largest, most significant family of writers. Their works form part of the same great renascence in English literature as Milton's. Their lives span that most important hundred years in English cultural history, 1550-1650, which includes Renaissance, Reformation, and the revolutionary Civil Wars..." (*Milton Encyclopedia*, III, p. 105).

110. In modern equivalents, roughly £200,000, which must have provided a healthy infusion of funds into James' strained coffers.

111. Much of the religious and political history of England over the next several decades stems from a deep antagonism between Archbishop Abbot and his ultimate successor, William Laud.

112. Sanford also published introductions to Italian, French, and Latin.

the last masque written by Jonson for Queen Anne

Mar 16 — [William?] Barcley, *Authority of the Pope over Temporal Kings*, SR

Mar 19 — Thomas Ravenscroft, *Melismatal Musicall crochettes, Part I*, SR, music

Mar 25 — Sir Robert Carr elevated to the peerage as Viscount Rochester, the first of James's Scots followers elevated to the House of Lords

Apr — John Chalkhill admitted to Trinity College, Cambridge

Apr 8 — The Council of Virginia advertises for 300 men to remove to the Colony

Apr 11 — Simon Forman records seeing a performance of William Shakespeare, *Macbeth*[113]

Apr 12 — [Sir Walter Raleigh], *History of the World*, SR, although the book did not appear (anonymously) until 1614[114]

Apr 20-29 — Simon Forman records seeing a performance of William Shakespeare, *Cymbeline*

Apr 22 — William Byrd, *Psalmes, Songes, & Sonnetts*, SR, music for viols and other instruments

Apr 23 — William Crashaw, *Manuale Catholicorum*, SR

Apr 30 — Simon Forman records seeing a performance of William Shakespeare, *Richard II*; his account includes lines that do not appear in printed versions[115]

May — Sir Robert Carr, Viscount Rochester, created a Knight

---

113. Curiously, this frequently maligned astrologer-*cum*-healer, often referred to by critics and scholars as a mountebank, a conman, and a lecher (his primary claim to fame would seem to be that he contributed yet another word to the English language to describe the sex act, halek), provides several of the surviving eye-witness accounts to performances of Shakespeare's plays (see A. L. Rowse, *Sex and Society*; for a less sympathetic but still authentic-seeming view, see Stanley Stewart's novel, *The King James Version*.)

114. The book was entered again, in Raleigh's name, three days later, on April 15, 1611.

115. A. L. Rowse, *Sex and Society*, p. 13. The political overtones of the play apparently still reverberated, a decade or so after the Essex affair.

of the Garter

May 13 — Prince Charles created a Knight of the Garter

May 15 — Simon Forman records seeing a performance of William Shakespeare, *The Winter's Tale*

May 17 — William Vaughan, *Spirit of Detraction coniured in Three Circles*, SR, religious tract

May 18 — John Donne, *Ignatius, His Conclave, or His Inthronisation in a Late Election in Hell...*, SR

May 20 — John Brinsley, *Ludus Literarius: Or, The Grammar Schoole*, handwriting manual, dedicated to Prince Henry and Prince Charles

Apr — Robert Carr, Viscount Rochester, made a Privy Councillor at age 25

Jun 2 — Lady Arabella Stuart escapes confinement in the Tower; attempts to flee to France; is retaken and re-confined in the Tower

Jun 26 — Arthur Hopton, *Speculum Topographicum: Topographical Glass*, SR, scientific treatise

Jun 28 — William Cecil, *Councell of a Father to his Son: 10 Precepts*, SR

Aug 6 — *Latest News from Virginia*, SR, ballad

Aug 9 — Henry Peacham, *Minerva Britanna, Emblems and Impresas*, SR

Aug 29 — James I confirms William Laud as President of St. John's College, Oxford, following a contested and acrimonious election[116]

Sep 12 — Simon Forman buried, after accurately predicting the date of his own death

Sep 14 — Cyril Tourneur, *The Atheist's Tragedy; or, The Honest Man's Revenge*, published

Oct 4 — J. Taylor, *Sculler Antipapa rowing from Tyber to Thames*, SR

---

116. Foremost among Laud's antagonists was George Abbot, Archbishop of Canterbury, who continued to block Laud's attempts to gain preferment; in spite of the irregularities associated with his election, Laud remained as President of the College for a decade.

Oct 14 — Thomas Heywood, *The Golden Age, with the Lives of Jupiter and Saturn*, SR

Nov — John Donne, *The First Anniversary* and "A Funeral Elegy," published[117]

Nov 1 — William Shakespeare, *The Tempest*, performed at Court

Nov 4 — Arthur Dent, *Exposition upon the Lord's Prayer*, SR

Nov 5 — William Shakespeare, *The Winter's Tale*, performed at Court

Nov 18 — Ben Jonson's last surviving child, Ben, buried, St. Anne's Church, Blackfriars[118]

Nov 23 — Nathan Field, *Woman is a Weathercock*, SR

Nov 27 — Pierre du Moulin, *Defense de la foy Catholique...*, SR

Dec — Leonora Baroni b.

Dec 13 — Gates Dale, *Articles, Lawes & Order for Virginia*, SR

Dec 16 — Christopher Marlowe, *Edward II*, SR, drama

Dec 24 — S. Ruytinck, *Golden Legend of the Romish Church*, SR

---

117. *The First Anniversary* was the among the first of Donne's poems to see publication; during his lifetime only a handful of his poems were published, the majority circulating in manuscript among a coterie of fellow poets and writers. Only after his death would his poetry be available to the general reading public—a frequent situation during the period. In later decades, his songs became some of the most frequently reprinted (and pirated) verse of the century.

118. Jonson survived all of his children; biographical data suggests that following the death of his last child, Jonson may have essentially separated from his wife. Given the high mortality rate among children at the time, Jonson's case is not entirely atypical; a century later, Queen Anne would outlive her husband and all five of her children to survive childbirth, leaving no immediate heirs and thus precipitating the Hanoverian succession.

1612

Lewis Bayly of Evesham (thereafter Bishop of Bangor), *The Practice of Piety*, published, Puritan treatise (50 editions by 1673 in multiple Continental languages)

George Chapman, *Caesar and Pompey*

William Corkine, *Seconde Book of Ayres*, published, lute-music

Thomas Deloney, *Thomas of Reading*, prose (novel?), 4th edition[119]

John Donne, *The Second Anniversary*, published as "Of the Progress of the Soul"

John Dowland, *A Pilgrim's Solace*, published, lute-music

Orlando Gibbons, *First Set of Madrigals and Motets of Five Parts*, published

Thomas Heywood, *Apology for Actors*

Ben Jonson, *To Penshurst*[120]

Francis Beaumont, *The Knight of the Burning Pestle*

John Fletcher and William Shakespeare (?), *Cardenio* (lost play, perhaps written 1612-13)

John Smith of Jamestown, *The Proceedings of the English Colony in Virginia* published

---

119. This is the earliest surviving issue of the novel, identified on the title page as the 4th edition; the book was probably first published in 1598-1599.

120. Jonson's poem is generally regarded as initiating the seventeenth-century vogue for topographical poems, although recent scholarship suggests that he may have been anticipated by Amelia Lanier by a year or so. The poem is also a central document in the century's near sanctification of Sir Philip Sidney as the quintessential patron of English Protestant poetry.

W. Turner, *Turners dish of lentten stuffe, or a galymaufery*, broadside ballad
John Webster, *The White Devil*, printed
Battista Guarini d. (b. 1538)
Elizabeth Jane Weston d. (b. 1582)
Richard Crashaw b.(?)
Edward King b.
Thomas Young arrives in England from Scotland
George Chapman arrested for debt

Jan 12 — Ben Jonson, *Love Restored (The Prince's Masque)*, performed[121]
Jan 17 — William Easte, *Vive Memor Mortis: Mirrour of Man's Mortality*, SR
— Sir Thomas Fairfax b.
Jan 21 — *Men Bayted in a Beares Skin*, ballad, SR
Feb 1 — Robert Daborn, *A Christian Turned Turk: Ward & Danseker*, SR
Feb 7 — Michael Drayton, *Poly-Olbion, Part I*
— Jacques Guillemeau, *Child Birth: Happy Delivery of Woman*, SR, medical treatise
— Thomas Killigrew b.
Feb 8 — Samuel Butler baptized
Feb 15 — Richard Niccols, *Twynnes Tragedye*, SR
— Cyril Tourneur, *The Noble Man*, SR
Feb 24 — The Virginia Company publishes a lottery for Virginia
Mar — Leggatt and Wrightman, two Arian adherents, burned for heresy; last burnings for heresy in England
Mar 17 — George Thompson, *Hunting of the Romayne Beast*, SR
Spring — Ben Jonson acts as tutor abroad to Walter, son of Sir

---

121. Given the title, it is possible that Prince Henry performed in the masque, although the surviving thext does not so indicate. Unlike most court masques, this one was performed with restraint and economy, costing as little as £280.

Walter Raleigh, stopping in Paris, Brussels, Antwerp, and Leiden[122]

Apr — John Donne in Paris; letter to George Gerrard concerning the *Anniversary* poems

Apr 16 — William Cowper, *Christ's Descent, Consecration, and Combat with Sathan*, SR

Apr 17 — George Chapman, *Revenge of Bussy D'Ambois*, SR, play; *The Widowes Teares*, SR, play

Apr 20 — Francis Herring, *Poemata miscellanea*, dedicated to Henry, Prince of Wales, SR

— Samuel Rowlands, *Knaves of Hartes: hayle fellowe well mett*, SR

May — Contract signed for the marriage of Princess Elizabeth to Frederick, Elector Palatine

May 9 — Henry Parrot, *Stultorum Laquei: Spryngese for Woodcockes*, SR

— John Taylor, the Water Poet[123], *Laugh and Be Fat*, parody of Thomas Coryate

May 12 — William Shakespeare signs affidavit in the case of Belott v. Mountjoy in London

May 15 — Ben Jonson, *Epigrams*, SR

May 24 — Robert Cecil, Earl of Salisbury, chief minister to Elizabeth I and James I, and architect of the peaceful succession of James I, d. (b. 1563?); his death opens prospects for

---

122. Jonson's tenure as tutor was notorious for his inability to control either himself or his student. One account has Jonson, drunk, being paraded through the streets of Catholic Paris in a cart, stretched out in parody of the Crucifixion. His treatment of Comus in a court masque as fat, drunken, and naked may have had some connections to his own experiences.

123. Taylor was a well-known character and personality during the period. A boatman on the Thames, he earned his sobriquet "The Water Poet" by entertaining his passengers with his doggerel verse. During the summers, he undertook tours which resulted in travelogues and pamphlets that were, in their own turn, widely popular. More serious readers, critics, and students of literature were at times affronted by his popularity, especially in light of the small talent he seems to have possessed. This particular title was reported by the *Dictionary of National Biography* as ordered burned.

advancement for his cousin, Sir Francis Bacon

May 27 — *England's General Tears for Salisbury*, SR, ballad

— *Hurte in a Pot of Good Ale*, SR, ballad

— *Shakeragges highe waye to hell*, SR, ballad

Jun 25 — Gervase Markham[124], *New Book of English Husbandrye*, SR

Jun 26 — Roger Manners, 5th Earl of Rutland, d. (b. 6 Oct 1576)[125] Jun 27

— *Circumference of the Earth: Northwest Passage* SR, travel tract

— Samuel Daniel, *History of England*, SR

Jul 6 — *Bloodshed Revenged*, SR, ballad

— Christopher Lawne, *Prophane Schisme of the Brownistes*, SR, religious tract

Jul 15 — **John and Sara Milton's daughter Sara b, London**

Jul 17 — The Virginia Company publishes the articles for its second lottery

Jul 21 — Nine witches tried and convicted in Northamptonshire

— Thereafter: *The Witches of Northamptonshire*, pamphlet

— *A Briefe Abstract of the Arraignment of Nine Witches at Northampton, July 21, 1612*, manuscript account written

Jul 23 — Richard Johnson, *Remembrance of the Honors Due to the life and Death of Robert Earle of Salisbury...*, SR, memorial to William Cecil, 1st Earl of Salisbury

Aug 2 — Thomas Carew, admitted to Middle Temple to study law

Aug 6 — **John and Sara Milton's daughter Sara buried, London**

Aug 7 — Samuel Purchas, *Purchas His Pilgrimage; or, Relations of the World and the Religions observed in all Ages*

Aug 12 — *The Burning of Tyverton*, SR, ballad

Aug 19 — *I Cannot be Enamored on Her Face*, SR, ballad

---

124. Also Jarvis or Jarvase, yet another example of the free-wheeling attitude of the time toward spelling names.

125. Rutland is occasionally considered as one of several candidates for the 'true' author of Shakespeare's plays.

Sep 9 — Anne Marbury m. William Hutchinson
Sep 11 — John Owen, *Epigrammatum*, SR
Sep 28 — Ben Jonson, *Epicoene, or the Silent Woman*, SR re-assigned
Oct 1 — General Sessions of the Peace, "An Order for suppressing of Jigges at the ende of Playes," passed; all jigs, rhymes, and dances—which encourage cut-purses and tumults—abolished
Oct 3 — Thomas Adams, *Heaven and Earth Reconciled*, visitation sermon preached at St. Paul's, Bedford[126]
Oct 12 — Sir Francis Bacon, *Essays*, 2nd edition, SR
Oct 16 — Frederick V, Elector Palatine, arrives in England to marry the Princess Elizabeth
— *Entertainment of the Palsgrave* (Frederick V, Elector Palatine), SR
Oct 23 — *England's Welcome to County Palatine* (Frederick V, Elector Palatine), SR, ballad
Nov 5 — *The Papists' Powder Treason*, allegorical engraving printed to commemorate the Gunpowder Plot[127]
Nov 6 — Henry Frederick, Prince of Wales d. of typhoid fever at age eighteen, leaving a relatively unprepared Charles heir to the throne
— Prince Charles created Duke of Cornwall shortly thereafter
— After Henry's death, Sir Walter Raleigh ceases work on *The History of the World*
— Alexander Gill, *Threnody* for Prince Henry, published when Gill is fourteen
— George Herbert, *In Obitum Henrici Principis Walliae*, in *Epidecium Cantabrigiense*
— William Laud, Latin elegy to Prince Henry in *Justa Oxoniensium*, a collection issued by Oxford University

---

126. Adams was referred to by his contemporaries as the "Shakespeare of the Puritans" (John Brown, *Bunyan*, 8)

127. Following the death of Prince Henry Frederick the next day, the engraving was withdrawn, to be reissued during the anti-Catholic fervor accompanying the Popish Plot later in the century

— In all some fifty printed tributes to Prince Henry will appear (a number of them are listed below)

Nov 7 — Thomas Potts, *Discovery of Witches in Lancaster*, SR

— John Taylour, *Great Brittaynes greatest Woe: Elegy on Prince Henry*, SR

Nov 16 — Clement Cotton, *Myrrour of the Martyrs*, SR

Nov 19 — W. Turner, three ballads, SR

Nov 20 — Sir John Harington d. (b. 1561?)

Nov 27 — Joshua Sylvester, *Lachrymae Domesticae: for Prince Henry*, SR

Nov 28 — J. Maxwell, *Life and Death of the Peerless Prince, with Poems*, SR

Nov 30 — John May, *State of Clothinge now used in England*, SR

Dec — The King's Men, William Shakespeare's Company, perform some twenty plays in honor of Frederick V and Princess Elizabeth, including *Much Ado About Nothing, Othello, Julius Caesar*, and *The Tempest*

Dec 5 — *Farewell Prince Henry*, SR, ballad

— *Obsequies and Funeralls of Prince Henry 6 Dec. 1612*, SR

— Daniel Price, *Lamentations for Prince Henry: Two Sermons before His Majesty 10 & 15 Nov. 1612*, SR

Dec 7 — Prince Henry buried in Westminster Abbey

— Frederick V and his uncle, Maurice of Nassau, elected to the Order of the Garter

— *Complaint against Death*, SR, ballad

— *Englands Sorrow*, SR, ballad

Dec 11 — George Chapman, *Epicede*, SR, poem in honor of his patron, Prince Henry

Dec 17 — Elizabeth Cary, Lady Cary, *The Tragedy of Mariam, The Faire Queen of Jewry*, SR, first tragedy written by an English woman; published 1613

— Sir John Davies, *Muses Teares for the Loss of Their Hope*, SR, elegy for Prince Henry

— Richard Niccols, *Epicedium: Three Sisters Tears for Henry*,

SR, elegy for Prince Henry

— Leonella Sharpe, *Oratio Funebris Henrii Walliæ*, SR

Dec 18 — A. B. [George Wither], *Prince Henrys Obsequies, or mournfull elegies*, SR

Dec 19 — Sir John Davies, *Description of the Estate of Ireland under James I*, SR

Dec 20 — William Welwod, *Sea Lawes*, SR, maritime treatise

Dec 22 — J. Bertant, *Microcosmographia*, SR

Dec 25 — Cyril Tourneur and John Webster, *Funeral elegies on the Death of Prince Henry*, SR

Dec 27 — Betrothal night for Frederick V and Princess Elizabeth

1613

Giovanni Andreini, *L'Adamo*, comedy on the Fall of Man[128]
Robert Anton, *Moriomachia*, prose, satirical anti-romance
Lewis Bayly, *The practice of Piety*, 3rd edition
Francis Beaumont and John Fletcher, *The Knight of the Burning Pestle*
William Byrd, *Fantasia for Viol*
I. C. [J. C.?], editor, *Alicilia*, including reprint of John Marston, *The Metamorphosis of Pigmalions Image* (full text rpt. 1619, 1628)
John Coprario, *Songs of Mourning*, published, lute-music
John Florio, *Essayes on Morall, Politike, and Millitarie Discourses of Lo. Michaell de Montaigne*, translation of Michel de Montaigne, dedicated to Anne of Denmark
Lachrymæ Lachrymarum, elegies by George Herbert, John Donne, and others in tribute to Prince Henry[129]
James Speght, *A Briefe Demonstration, who have, and are of*

---

128. Voltaire suggested in his 1732 *Essai sur la poésie épique* that Milton had attended a performance of the play in Florence in 1638 and that Andreini (and through Andreini, Hugo Grotius) had thus influenced Milton's decision to write a tragedy—later revised to epic—on the same subject. (*Milton Encyclopedia*, I, p. 46)

129. This was only one of many volumes published in memory of the Prince. Henry's death elicited a massive outpouring of such elegiac tributes, outstripping in number even those composed to commemorate the death of Sir Philip Sidney a quarter of a century earlier. Since by the opening decades of the Seventeenth Century, Sidney had become generally regarded as the archetype of the Courtier, the poetic responses to Henry's death suggest the extraordinary regard in which the young prince was held.

the certainty of their salvation, that have the Spirit of Christ, published, Calvinist tract
Edmund Spenser, *Prosopopoia, or Mother Hubberd's Tale*
John Webster, *Duchess of Malfi*, performed by the King's Men at Blackfriars
Alphonso Lanier, Amelia Lanier's husband, d. (b. ?)
Anne Dudley b.(?) (afterward Anne Bradstreet)
Richard Crashaw b.(?)
Thomas Carew, secretary to Sir Dudley Carleton, Ambassador to Italy (to 1615
Thomas Dekker imprisoned for debt (until 1619)
Hope Theater, contract signed for construction

Jan 12 — *Britain's Greatest Comfort: Prince Charles*, SR, ballad
— Barnaby Riche, *Excellencie of Good Women*, SR
Jan 14 — *Song of Lady Elizabeth and Palatine*, SR, ballad
Jan 16 — *Inhumane Murder by William Hollis*, SR, pamphlet
— *Inhumane Murder by William Hollis*, SR, ballad
— George Wither, *Abuses Stript and Whipt. Or Satirical Essays*, verse essays, dedicated to himself
Jan 21 — Thomas Dekker, *Strange Horse Race Ending in Catchpolles Masque*, SR
Jan 23 — *Witches Lately Condemned at Bedford*, SR, pamphlet, "With a strange triall how to know a witch"
Jan 27 — *Powerful Earthquake in Munster*, SR, pamphlet
Jan 28 — Sir Thomas Bodley d. (b. 1545), founder of the Bodleian Library, Oxford
Jan 30 — *Celebration of Elizabeth and Palatines Nuptialles with a Sea Fight*, SR, ballad
— John Taylor, *Celebration of Elizabeth and Palatines Nuptialles with a Sea fight*, SR, pamphlet
Feb 7 — Frederick, Elector Palatine, invested Knight of the Order of the Garter at Windsor
Feb 8 — Henry Peacham, *The Period of Mourninge*, SR
Feb 10 — George Wither, *Epithalamion on the Marriage of* ...

Lady Elizabeth, SR

Sunday, Feb 14—St. Valentine's Day — Princess Elizabeth m. Frederick V at the Royal Chapel, Whitehall; marriage performed by George Abbot, Archbishop of Canterbury[130]

— Thomas Campion and Inigo Jones, *The Lords' Masque*

— John Donne, *Epithalamion, or Marriage Song*

— Anthony Nixon, *Great Britains General Joyes*, SR, ballad

— Samuel Butler baptized

Feb 15—Shrove Monday — George Chapman and Inigo Jones, *The Memorable Masque of the Two Households of Inns of Court, The Middle Temple, and Lincoln's Inn*, in honor of Frederick V and Princess Elizabeth, performed; published shortly thereafter in quarto[131]

— Thomas Heywood, *Marriage Triumphe in an Epithalamion*, SR

Feb 16 — Francis Beaumont, *Gray's Inn and Inner Temple masque*, with Sir Francis Bacon as principle 'contriver' scheduled for production[132]

Feb 17 — George Herbert, B.A., Cambridge University

Feb 18 — *Marriage...Shewes...Masques, Revels*, SR

---

130. Much of the grief felt in England following Prince Henry's death was transmuted into more positive emotions at the wedding of Princess Elizabeth. A poet herself, she remained a vivid presence in English imagination as the Winter Queen, long after the death of her husband.

Of the wedding itself, Frances Yates writes: "...all the treasures of the English Renaissance were outpoured, and London went wild with joy at what seemed a continuation of the Elizabethan age in this alliance of a new, young Elizabeth with the leader of the German Protestants and a grandson of William the Silent." Yates further stresses the fact that while Frederick was a Calvinist, the ceremony was strictly Anglican, with Frederick making his responses in English. (*Rosicrucian Enlightenment*, p. 1, 4).

131. Producing this masque cost the two Inns of Court £2,255.

132. The masque, part of the festivities celebrating the wedding of the Princess Elizabeth and the Elector Palatine, was attempted but not produced, due to the press of spectators, so packed that the masquers could not make their way from the Thames (part of the masque's landscape) to their royal audience (Jardine and Stewart, 336).

Feb 20 — Francis Beaumont, *Masque of the Inner Temple and Gray's Inn* in honor of Frederick V and Princess Elizabeth, performed on the second attempt (SR: Feb 27)

Feb-Apr — Frederick visits Oxford and Cambridge; he is welcomed to the latter with appropriate Latin verses by George Herbert

Mar 10-11 — William Shakespeare, deeds for Blackfriars gatehouse, London, signed

Apr 8 — *Relation and Picture of a Strange Monster*, SR

Apr 13 — Louis XIII of France, *The French King's Declaration confirming Nantes*, SR, translation

Apr 16 — *Farewell to Palatine and Elizabeth*, SR, ballad

Apr 21 — Sir Thomas Overbury imprisoned in the Tower

Apr 25 — Frederick V and Elizabeth depart for The Hague

April 27/28 — Thomas Campion, *The Caversham Entertainment*, masque by Lord Knollys to Queen Anne on her progress to Bath

May — James I instructs George Abbott, Archbishop of Canterbury, to begin proceedings to nullify Lady Frances Howard's seven-year marriage to Robert Devereux, 3rd Earl of Essex[133]

May 4 — Joseph Hall, *An Holy Panegyricke*, SR, sermon

May 15 — Mark Rydley, *Magneticall Bodies and Motions*, SR, scientific treatise

May 26 — Sir Henry Vane baptized

Jun 10 — William Crashaw, *Dialogue between Soul and Body*, SR

Jun 16 — *Shepherd's Song before Queen Anne in 4 Parts*, SR

Jun 20 — John Cleveland christened

Jun 29 — The Globe Theater burns as a result of sparks ignited by cannon-fire during the premier (?) performance of William Shakespeare's *Henry VIII*[134]

---

133. At the time of the ceremony, Essex had been fourteen and Lady Francis thirteen; almost immediately thereafter, Essex left England for the continent.

134. The performance and the fire are described in a letter from Sir Henry

Jun 30 — *Overthrow of the Famous Theater: 'Globe'*, SE entry, ballad

— *Sudden Burning of the 'Globe ' 29 June 1613*, SR, Ballad

Aug 2 — John Taylor, the Water Poet, [*Coryate's*] *Escape from Drowninge*, SR

Aug 15 — Jeremy Taylor baptized

Aug 17 — *Damage done by Fire and Storm in Germany*, SR, news tract

Aug 25 — *Wycked Wylles Sauce*, SR, ballad

Sep 15 — Sir Thomas Overbury d., imprisoned in the Tower (b. 1581)[135]

Sep 25 — Frances Howard, Countess of Essex, secures her annulment (nullity) from Robert Devereux, 3rd Earl of Essex

Sep 23 — Robert Harcourt, *Voyage to Guiana*, SR, traveler's account

Oct 8 — Arthur Saul, *Famous Game of Chesse Play*, SR

Oct 27 — Sir Francis Bacon appointed Attorney-General; Sir Edward Coke named Chief Justice of the King's Bench, clearing the way for Bacon's advancement

Oct 27 — Samuel Rowlands, *Knaves of Diamonds & Spades*, SR

Nov 3 — Thomas Middleton, *Triumph of Truth*, SR, pageant

Nov 13 — Robert Carr, James's Scots favorite, created 1st Earl of Somerset

Nov 15 — William Browne of Tavistock, *Britannia's Pastorals, Part I*

Dec 1 — Galileo Galilei, *Letters on the Solar Spots*, written,

---

Wotton to Sir Edmund Bacon, July 2, 1613. Evans, *Riverside Shakespeare*, p. 56

135. Overbury's death in the Tower, at the time bruited to be by poison, ultimately led to the downfall of King James' favorite at court, Robert Carr, Earl of Somerset, and his new wife, Lady Frances Howard. Overbury's death cleared the way for the marriage, but subsequent discoveries of Lady Francis' possible complicity in that death (and others) overcame even James' affection for his favorite. For an accurate and highly readable fictional account of the affair, see Stanley Stewart, *The King James Version*; and Beatrice White, *Case of Ravens*.

announces Galileo's acceptance of the Copernican universe

Dec 13 — G. M. [Gervase Markham], *Cheap & Good Husbandrye*, SR

— Sir Thomas Overbury, *A Wife (now a Widow)*, SR

Dec 25 — Thomas Campion, *The Somerset Masque*, wedding masque for Robert Carr, 1st Earl of Somerset, and Lady Frances Howard; the masque produced by Inigo Jones

Dec 26 — Ben Jonson, *Challenge at Tilt*, produced by Inigo Jones; wedding masque for Robert Carr, 1st Earl of Somerset, and Lady Frances Howard

— Robert Carr, Earl of Somerset, m. Lady Frances Howard, with court celebrations lasting until Twelfth Night

Dec 29 — Ben Jonson, *The Irish Masque at Court*, produced by Inigo Jones; wedding masque for Robert Carr, Earl of Somerset, and Lady Frances Howard

1614

Music by John Milton, Sr., and Henry Lawes included in Sir William Leighton's *The Tears or Lamentations of a Sorrowful Soul*

John Bodenham, ed., *England's Helicon*, augmented edition

William Browne of Tavistock, *Inner Temple Masque; Shepheards Pipes*, influenced by Edmund Spenser, *Shepheards Calendar*

Richard Carew of Anthony, *The Excellency of the English Tongue*, published with William Camden, *Remains*

Isaac Casaubon, *De rebus sacris et ecclesiasticis exercitationes XVI. Ad Cardinalis Baronii Prolegomena in Annales*, published in London[136]

Anthony Copley, *Wits, Fits, and Fancies*[137], jest-book, 2nd edition

John Coprario, *The Masque of Squires*, published

John Day, *Day's Dyall*,[138] theological treatise

---

136. Casaubon treats the origins and dating of the sybillina and the *Hermetica*, concluding that the *Hermetica* postdated the beginning of the Christian Era. While not denying the possible existence of Hermes Trismegistus, or that such an individual might have lived before Moses' time, Casaubon denies the authenticity of written materials ascribed to such a person. (Walter Scott, *Hermetica*, p. 41).

137. First published in 1595, Copley's collection consisted largely of translations from a Spanish jest book of the sixteenth century, compiled by Melchio dr Santa Cruz. The 1614 edition included 1,100 jests.

138. C. A. Patrides suggests that Day's discussions of metaphors used to define the Trinity is of particular importance in understanding Milton's lan-

Phineas Fletcher, *Piscatorial Eclogues*, completed; *Sicelides*, drama

Edward Grimestone, *History of Louis XI*, translation from the French original by Pierre Matthieu[139]

Thomas Middleton, *Women Beware Women*; *The Witch*, performed

Sir Thomas Overbury, *A Wife: Now the Widow of Sir Tho: Overburie Being a most exquisite and singular poem of the choyse of a Wife. Whereunto are added many witty Characters, and conceited Newes...* (5th impression)

William Covell d. (b. ca. 1560)

Robert Smythson d. (b. 1534?), first English "Architector"; buried at Wollaton Hall

Sir Robert Wroth, husband to Lady Mary Sidney Wroth, d. (b. 1576

Katherine Boyle b. (afterward Lady Ranelagh)

John Lilburne b.

Fulke Greville made Chancellor of the Exchequer (to 1622)

Robert Burton, B.D., Christ Church, Oxford[140]

Henry King receives M.A., Christ Church, Oxford University

Jan 1 — John Wilkins b. (Afterwards Bishop of Chester)

Jan 6—TWELFTH NIGHT — Anon. [J.G., W.D., T.B.], *Masque of Flowers* presented at Whitehall by the gentlemen of Gray's Inn, at the end of celebrations for the Somerset's marriage[141]

Jan 7 — Pitiscus, *Trygonometry or the Doctrine of Triangles*, SR, mathematical treatise

Jan 10 — Ben Jonson, *Irish Masque*, repeat performance at the

---

guage in Paradise Lost. *Bright Essence*, p. 10.

139. Louis XI was, for the period, an icon for the tyrannical, autocratic ruler. See David Underdown, *A Freeborn People*, p. 32.

140. Burton was elected to Christ Church in 1599; for the next forty years, he lived at the University.

141. John Chamberlain notes that the cost of the masque—some £2,000—was being covered by Sir Francis Bacon.

wish of James I

Jan 21 — J. G., W.D., T.B, *Maske of Flowers by Grays Inn*, SR to Robert Wilson, with dedication to Sir Francis Bacon

— Anthony Painter, *Judgment of God upon a Carryer that blasphemed*, SR

Jan 26 — Sir Francis Bacon, *The charge of Sir Francis Bacon, knight, his Majesties Attourney general, touching Duells, upon an information in the Star-chamber against Priest and Wright*, SR by Robert Wilson

Jan 29 — J. Barbier, *Janua Linguarum: Gate of Language*, SR, educational treatise

Feb 13 — [William] Lithgow, *Payneful peregrination to Europe, Asia & Africa*, SR, traveler's account

Mar 9 — Alexander Whitaker, *True Discourse of the Present Estate of the English in Virginia*, SR

Mar 16 — George Chapman, *Perseus and Andromede* (*Andromeda Liberata*), SR, dedicated to Robert Carr, 1st Earl of Somerset[142]

Mar 29 — Sir Walter Raleigh, *History of the World*, published anonymously; at the sign of the Crane, St. Paul's Churchyard; unfinished; concludes at 130 BC; Volume I subsequently recalled by King James for censuring princes

Spring

George Wither imprisoned for satirical comments contained in *Abuses Stript and Whipt*

Apr 5 — James I summons his second Parliament

— John Donne sits as M.P. for Taunton

Apr 7 — El Greco (Domenikos Theotocopoulos) d. (b. 1541); Spanish painter, born in Crete

— Gervase Markham, *2nd Part of English Husbandry*, SR

Apr 8 — Lentulus, *Italian Grammar*, SR, educational

May 4 — Samuel Rowlands, *A Fooles Bolt is soone Shott*, satirical pamphlet

---

142. The poem is an allegorical treatment of the rescue of Andromeda (Lady Frances) by Perseus (Somerset) after she has been chained to a barren rock (Essex) to suffer the depredations of a sea-beast (public opinion).

May 14 — [Christopher Brooke?], *Ghost of Richard III*, SR, poem/political pamphlet
May 15 — Thomas Evans, *Oedipus in Three Cantoes*, SR, poem
May 27 — Sir Arthur Gorges, *Lucans Pharsalia translated into English verse..., with the Warre of Caesar and Pompey*, SR, epic
May 29 — Sir Ralph Winwood receives the oath as Secretary of State
Apr 7 — James I opens Parliament
Jun 10 — James I dismisses the Addled Parliament after only two months, with no legislation passed
Jun 22 — Robert Bruce, *Misterye of the Lordes Supper*, SR
Jun 28 — Nicholas Breton, *I would and I Would Not*, SR
— *Publication for the Plantation in Guiana*, SR, pamphlet
Jun 30 — Thomas Tuke, *Christians Lookinge Glasse*, SR
Jul 1 — Sir William Cornwallis d. (b. 1579?)
Jul—CALENDS OF JULY — Isaac Casaubon d. (b. 1560)
Jul 10 — Arthur Annesley b. (afterward 1st Earl of Angelsey)
Mid-Jul — Christian IV of Denmark arrives unexpectedly for a visit, interrupting James' summer progress
Aug 1 — King Christian of Denmark departs England from Gravesend
Aug 3 — James I, resumes his interrupted progress; first meets his new favorite, George Villiers, at Apethorpe
Aug 8 — George Wither, *Satire dedicated to His Majesty*, SR
Aug 20 — William Martyn, *History of the Normans and Kings of England*, SR
Sep 5 — *Killing of the Serpent in Sussex*, SR, ballad
Oct 3 — George Herbert sworn a minor fellow at Trinity College, Cambridge
Oct 8 — George Wither, *Thirsis Hunting Day* (*Shepherd's Hunting*), SR, written while Wither is imprisoned
Oct 12 — Henry More b., philosopher
Oct 20 — Ralph Hammer, *Narration of the Present State of Virginia*, SR

Oct 22 — *Warres of the Low Countryes*, SR, ballad

Nov 1 — Ben Jonson, *Bartholomew Fair*, performed at Court

Nov 2 — George Chapman, translation of Homer's *The Odyssey*

Nov 4 — George Villiers acknowledged as the new favorite in James' Court

Before Dec 16 — John Webster, *Duchess of Malfi*, first performed (?)

Dec 16 — William Ostler, who first acted the part of Antonio in John Webster, *Duchess of Malfi*, d.

Dec 22 — The Archbishop of Canterbury directs the Stationers Company to suppress Sir Walter Raleigh's *The History of the World*[143]

Dec 29 — Joshua Sylvester, *Second Session of the Parliament of Virtues*, SR

---

143. In spite of such attempts, Raleigh's book would see ten editions during the century and would be read and appreciated by John Hampden, John Milton, Oliver Cromwell, and others.

1615

William Browne of Tavistock, *Ulysses and Circe* (*The Inner Temple Masque*)[144]

William Gouge, *Exposition of the Song of Solomon*, published

Joseph Hall, *A Recollection of such Treatises as have bene heretofore severally published, and are nowe revised, corrected, augmented. By Jos: Hall Dr of Divinity*[145]

Thomas Kyd[146], *The Spanish Tragedy*, published

Thomas Stanley, *A Platonick Discourse upon Love*, translation of Giovanni Pico della Mirandola

John Stephens, *Satyrical Essayes Characters and Others. Or Accurate and quick Descriptions, fitted to the life of their Subjects*, published

John Webster, editor, Sir Thomas Overbury, *Characters*, 3rd edition

George Wither, *Shepheards Hunting*, published, written in Marshalsea Prison; influenced by Edmund Spenser,

---

144. An influential work for Milton.

145. Bishop Hall's *Recollection* was reprinted in 1617, 1621, 1625, 1633, 1634, 1639, 1647, 1662. His works were among the first English books translated into French; in addition, during the century his *Characters* were translated into French and Dutch.

146. Thomas Kyd (1558-1594), an important figure in the development of the Elizabethan revenge tragedy, is also interesting in his connections with the death of Christopher Marlowe; see Leslie Hotson, *The Death of Christopher Marlowe*; William Urry, *Christopher Marlowe and Canterbury*; Charles Nicholl, *The Reckoning*; and other studies—historical and fictional—of Marlowe's life and death.

Shepheards Calendar; *Fidelia*, pastoral
Mary Barret b
Laurence Clarkson b.
Sir John Denham b., in Dublin
John Lilburne b. (?)[147]
Henry Oldenburg b. (?), in Bremen
Dr. Nathan Paget b.
Phineas Fletcher resigns his fellowship, Cambridge University
George Herbert, M.A. and Major Fellow, Trinity College, Cambridge
Inigo Jones appointed Royal Surveyor (through the outbreak of the Civil War)

Jan 6—TWELFTH NIGHT — Ben Jonson, *The Golden Age Restor'd*
Jan 9 — Samuel Hieron, *Certayne Usefull Meditations on Death*, SR
Jan 20 — Ben Jonson, *Certayne Masques at the Court*, SR
Jan 23 — John Donne ordained priest at King James' request by Dr. John King, Bishop of London
Jan 30 — **John and Sara Milton's daughter Tabitha baptized**
Feb — John Donne appointed Royal Chaplain
Feb 8 — Joseph Swetnam, *Arraignment of Lewd, Idle, froward and unconstant women: Or the vanitie of them, choose you whether*, epistolary preface by 'Thomas Tel-troth', SR, published to much contemporary critical controversy; ten editions before 1637, anti-feminist tract
Mar 7-11 — James I visits Cambridge University
— John Donne, D.D., Cambridge University, by royal decree[148]

---

147. Lilburne's father had the intriguing distinction of being the last man in English history to demand settlement of a civil suit through trial by battle (Joseph Frank, *The Levellers*, p. 12)

148. James's presence at Cambridge, as well as the rapidity of Donne's preferment in the Church, suggest how strongly the king felt concerning what he perceived as Donne's qualifications for the ministry; subsequent events, including Donne's increasing reputation as the most capable ser-

Mar 7 — Mr. Cecill, *Emilia*, Latin play presented for James I by St. John's College

Mar 8 — George Ruggles, *Ignoramus*, 5-hour play performed for James I, satirizing Sir Edward Coke; presented by Clare College

Mar 9 — Mr. Tomkis, *Albamazar*, presented for James I by Trinity College

Mar 10 — Mr. Brookes, *Melanthe*, pastoral presented for James I

Mar 11 — Phineas Fletcher, *Sicelides*, presented for the King by King's College, even though James I had left Cambridge

Mar 12 — *Murder in Lancashire*, SR, ballad

Mar 21 — William Camden, *Historia* (History of England from 1558-1588), in Latin, SR

Apr 3 — William Bradshaw, *Of Justification*, SR, religious treatise

Apr 14 — **John Milton, Sr., acting as an assistant in the Company of Scriveners**

Apr 18 — Sir John Harington, *Epigrams never yet printed*, SR

Apr 23—St. George's Day — George Villiers knighted, appointed Gentleman of the King's Bedchamber, both at Queen Anne's request

Apr 24 — John Fletcher, *Cupid's Revenge*, SR

Apr 26 — Francis of Sales (St. Francis de Sales), *Introduction to a Devout Life*, SR, translation of meditation handbook

Apr 30 — John Donne's earliest extant sermon, presented at Greenwich

May 3 — William Cecil, *Precepts for the Ordering of a Man's House*, SR

May 4 — Nicholas Breton, *Characters upon Essaies Morall and Divine*

Jul — Sir Ralph Winwood receives reports that Sir Thomas Overbury had been murdered with the complicity of Lady Frances Howard

---

monizer of his day, proved James correct on this point, at least.

Jul 19 — Charles Emanuel I, *The Emperor's Decree on Wars of Savoy and Mantua*, SR

— Samuel Hieron, *Dignity of Preaching*, SR

Aug 3 — **John and Sara Milton's daughter Tabitha buried**

Sep 5 — Lady Arabella Stuart d., still imprisoned in the Tower; last familial threat to James Stuart's monarchy removed

Sep 8 — Joseph Hall, *Contemplations upon Holy Scripture, Volume 3*, SR

Sep 26 — John Trundle, *The Arraignement of John Flodder and his wife...for burning the Towne of Windham...*, SR, broadside ballad, stridently anti-Papist

Oct 13 — James I orders a full inquiry into the complicity of the Earl and Countess of Somerset in the death of Sir Thomas Overbury; the commission headed by Sir Edward Coke

Oct 19 — Richard Weston tried for the murder of Sir Thomas Overbury

Oct 25 — Richard Weston executed

Oct 27 — Frances Howard Carr, Countess of Somerset, placed in close custody at Blackfriars for complicity in the death of Sir Thomas Overbury

Oct 29 — Nicholas Breton, *Worthies and Unworthies of this Age*, SR

— James I, *Father's Blessing, or 2nd Counsell to his Son*, SR

Nov — Robert Armin d. (b. c.1565), comic actor in the acting company associated with William Shakespeare

Nov 2 — William Gough, *Whole Armour of God*, SR

— Robert Carr, Earl of Somerset, committed to the Tower for complicity in the death of Sir Thomas Overbury

Nov 7 — Anne Turner arraigned for the murder of Sir Thomas Overbury

Nov 12 — Richard Baxter b.

Nov 14 — Anne Turner executed at Tyburn

Nov 16 — Sir Gervase Elwes arraigned for complicity in the death of Sir Thomas Overbury

Nov 20 — Sir Gervase Elwes executed on Tower Hill

Nov 23 — T. Brewer, *Mrs Anne Turners Repentance for*

Overbury's Murder, SR, pamphlet

Nov 24 (?)— **John and Sara Milton's son Christopher b., London**

Nov 25 — *Sir Thomas Overbury's Ghost*, SR, pamphlet

Nov 26 — John Davies of Hereford, *A Select Second Husband for Sir Thomas Overbury's Wife*, SR

— Godfrey Goodman, Bishop of Gloucester *Fall of Man*, SR

Nov 27 — James Franklin tried for complicity in the murder of Sir Thomas Overbury

Nov 29 — Thomas Dekker, *Artillery Garden*, SR

Dec 3 — **Christopher Milton baptized, All Hallows Church**

Dec 5 — Miguel de Cervantes, *Don Quixote, Part 2*, SR, translation

Dec 19 — Sir Gervase Elwes, *Jervis Elowaies death speech at the Tower*, SR, pamphlet

Dec 23 — Joshua Sylvester, *Jobe Triumphant in his Tryall*, SR

1616

Music by John Milton, Sr. included in Thomas Myriell's *Tristitiæ Remedium* (unpublished)
Johann Valentin Andreæ, Chemical Wedding of Christian Rosencreuz, published, Strasbourg, Germany; key Rosicrucian document
Dr. Francis Anthony, *The Apologie: a defense of a verity concerning Aurum Potabile*, medical treatise with case histories concerning the efficacy of potable gold
Thomas Beard, *A retractive from the Romish religion*, treatise by Oliver Cromwell's schoolmaster
Nicholas Breton, *The Good and the Badde, or Descriptions of the worthies, and Unworthies of this Age*, characters, published
William Browne of Tavistock, *Britannia's Pastorals, Part II*
George Chapman, translation of *The Whole Works of Homer*
Sir William Cornwallis, *Essayes; or Rather Encomions, Prayses of Sadnesse; and Essayes of Certain Paradoxes*
Thomas Coryat, *Greetings from the Court of the Great Mogul*, published
John Cotta, *The Triall of Witchcraft*, published
T. F., *Miraculous Newes, From the Cittie of Holdt, in the Lordship of Munster (in Germany) the twentieth of September last past. 1616. Where There Were Plainly beheld three dead bodys rise out of their Graves, admonishing the people of Judgements to Come*, published, translation of contemporary new-pamphlet

John Fletcher, *Mad Lover* and *Loyal Subject*, published

Robert Fludd, *Compendious Apology for the Fraternity of the Rosy Cross...*, published, Leiden, Netherlands

(Thomas Gainsford), *The Rich Cabinet furnished with varietie of Excellent discriptions, exquisite Charracters, witty discourses, and delightful Histories*, translated in part from Giovanni della Casa[149]

Bishop Francis Godwin, *Annales*, Latin history of the reigns of Henry VIII, Edward VI, and Mary I

Godfrey Goodman, Bishop of Gloucester, *The Fall of Man, or the Corruption of Nature, prooved by the Light of our naturall Reason*, published

James I, *Works*, edited by Prince Charles; includes *The TrewLaw of Free Monarchies*, James' first political treatise (1598)

Ben Jonson, *The Devil is an Ass*

Christopher Marlowe, *Dr Faustus*, B-text, published

Thomas Middleton, *Civitatis*

John Rolfe, *True Relation of the State of Virginia*

Thomas Tuke, *Discourse Against Painting and Tincturing of Women*

William Whateley, *A Bride-Bush: Or, a Direction for Married Persons*, manual, published

Joseph Beaumont b.

William Faithorne, the Elder, b.; artist

Alexander More (Morus) b.

John Owen b.

Isaac Penington b.

John Thurloe b.

Bishop Lancelot Andrewes appointed to the Privy Council

Sir Thomas Browne admitted to a scholarship at the Westminster School

Sir Edward Coke removed as Chief Justice of the King's Bench for his support of law over monarchical or ecclesiastical prerogative

---

149. Della Casa's poetry provided a major source for Milton's concept of the heroic sonnet.

Inigo Jones begins construction on the Queen's House at Greenwich (completed 1635)[150]
Ben Jonson appointed Poet Laureate

Jan 4 — Sir George Villiers appointed Master of the Horse, a post frequently held by the monarch's current favorite; official salary is 100 marks (£66 13s. 4d.) plus gratuities and privileges

Jan 6—TWELFTH NIGHT — Ben Jonson, *Mercury Vindicated from the Alchemists at Court. By Gentlemen the King's Servant*[151]

Jan 20 — *Portraiture of Sir Thomas Overbury*, SR

Jan 25 — William Shakespeare receives the first draft of his will

Jan 28 — Sir Thomas Overbury, *Observations of his Travelles*, SR

Feb 6 — Ben Jonson granted a Royal Pension, £10 a year[152]

Feb 26 — Dorothy Leighe, *A Mother's Blessing*, SR (15 editions by 1630, 4 additional editions between 1630 and 1640)

Mar — Sir Dudley Carleton departs for a mission to the Netherlands; Thomas Carew part of the retinue

---

150. Among the first Palladian, neo-classical structures in England and, along with the Banqueting House in Whitehall, one of Jones' few architectural works to survive into this century.

151. David Lindley argues that *The Golden Age Restored* was the masque chosen for 1616.

152. This in addition to his salary of £60 a year, at a time when the cost of producing one Royal Masque might well exceed £3,000, not including richly jeweled costumes for individual noble or Royal participants. At least once during James' reign, jewelers complained that because of the requirements of a royal masque, there was not a pearl to be found in the city of London.

As a matter of interest, Charles Nicholl suggests that late sixteenth-century and early-seventeenth-century monetary amounts can be roughly translated into modern purchasing power by multiplying the original sum by 500. Thus Jonson's £10 pension would be approximately £5,000 today (*Reckoning*, "Acknowledgments" [n. p.]. Other estimates vary from five to twenty times modern sums.

Mar 6 — Francis Beaumont d. (b. 1584?); buried in Westminster Abbey near Geoffrey Chaucer and Edmund Spenser

Mar 12 — Cicero, *Tullies Offices: Translated Grammatically*, SR

Mar 15 — Bernard Salignaus, *Principles of Arithmatick*, SR

— George Herbert, M.A. from Trinity College, Cambridge; sworn a major fellow

Mar 17 — Sir Walter Raleigh released from the Tower, through the influence of the Villiers family

Mar 19 — Francis Beaumont and John Fletcher, *The Scornful Lady*, SR

Mar 24 — John Berkenhead (or Birkenhead) b.

Mar 25 — William Shakespeare signs the final copy of his will in three places[153]

Apr — Sir George Villiers and the Earl of Rutland appointed to the Order of the Garter

Apr 4 — Catherine Smith buried, shortly after her son, John Smith, b. (?)[154]

Apr 21 — John Donne's second dated sermon, preached at Whitehall

Apr 23 — Miguel de Cervantes d (b. 1547

— William Shakespeare d. (b. 1564)

— Oliver Cromwell admitted a fellow commoner, Sidney Sussex College, Cambridge[155]

Apr 25 — William Shakespeare buried, Church of the Holy Trinity, Stratford-on-Avon

— At a time when memorial elegies are increasingly common, Shakespeare's death passes entirely unremarked by either

---

153. Scholars continue to debate the authenticity of the signatures. Several experts in Elizabethan handwriting have argued persuasively that each of the three signatures was written by a different hand, thus putting three of the six extant examples of Shakespeare's signature into doubt

154. The Cambridge Platonist, not the explorer and adventurer.

155. Sidney Sussex, founded in 1598, was already notorious by the time of William Laud as a hotbed of Puritanism; Cromwell's attendance there should not be considered a coincidence.

MILTON'S CENTURY | 115

the dramatists or the poets of London[156]

May — Margaret Clifford, Countess of Cumberland, d. (b. 1560?); patron of Amelia Lanier

May 24 — Lady Frances Howard, Countess of Somerset, arraigned before the House of Lords for the death of Sir Thomas Overbury; judged guilty and imprisoned for six years

May 25 — Robert Carr, Earl of Somerset, arraigned before the House of Lords for the death of Sir Thomas Overbury; judged guilty and imprisoned for six years

May 12 — John Downame, *Plea of ye Poore*, SR

Summer — Ben Jonson, *Works*[157]

Jun 3 — John Smith of Jamestown, *Description of New England*

Jun 5 — *Tobacco and the Fidlers Catch*, SR, ballad

Jun 6 — Barnabe Rich, *Lookynge Glasse for Ladies*, SR

Jun 7 — *Picture of Sir George Villiers*

Jun 9 — Sir Francis Bacon appointed to the Privy Council[158]

Jun 10 — Sir William Cornwallis, *Essayes, or Rather Encomiums; and Essayes or Certain Paradoxes*

Jun 17 — Thomas Cooper, *Misterye of Witchcraft*, SR

— John Deacon, *Tobacco Tortured, or the Filthie Fume of Tobacco Refined*, SR

Jul — John Smith, a thirteen-year-old boy, charges fifteen elderly Leicestershire women with witchcraft; nine of the

---

156. In addition—and perhaps more curiously—the few contemporary references to Shakespeare almost all refer to him as either a poet or a writer of comedies, making no reference to him as author of the great tragedies.

157. Jonson's temerity in publishing his plays in a volume entitled *Works*, and in publishing it during his lifetime, marks a radical shift toward the more openly public role poets and dramatists would take during the remainder of the century.

158. Bacon's promotion was, in part at least, due to his handling of the King's case against the Earl of Somerset, who had been Bacon's patron. This action, together with his legal involvement in the case of an earlier former patron, the Earl of Essex, gives a distinctly negative sense to his reputation, both contemporary and modern.

women are hanged
Jul 3 — Frances Howard Carr, Countess of Somerset, officially pardoned by James I
Jul 18 — Frances Bunney, *Justification by Faith Only*, SR, pamphlet
— Thomas Granger, *Tree of Good and Evil*, SR
Jul 27 — George Chapman, translation of *Hero and Leander*, SR
Aug — James I examines John Smith, determines that the charges against the women are false[159]
— Sir Walter Raleigh, under death-sentence in the Tower, receives permission to head an expedition to Orinoco
Aug 27 — Sir George Villiers created Baron Whaddon and Viscount Villiers simultaneously by James I, making Villiers a peer with grants of lands worth nearly £30,000
Aug 31 — William Alexander, *Additions to the Arcadia*, SR
Sep — George, Viscount Villiers, appointed Lord Lieutenant of Buckinghamshire
Oct 20 — *Miraculous Signs in Holdt*, SR, pamphlet
— *Miraculous Signs in Holdt*, SR, ballad
Oct 24 — John Donne appointed Reader in Divinity to the Benchers of Lincoln's Inn
Oct 29 — Anthony Munday, *Golden Fishings: The Lord Mayor's Show*, SR
Oct 31 — Prince Charles arrives by river from Richmond
— Thomas Middleton, water masque on the Thames to celebrate Charles' arrival
Nov 4 — Prince Charles created Prince of Wales
Nov 14 — Barten Holyday, translation of Persius Flaccus, *Satires*, SR
— Rachel Speght, *A Mouzell for Melastomus* ('A Muzzle for Black-Mouth'), *The Cynicall Bayter of, and foule mouthe Barker against Evahs sex. Or an Apologeticall Answere to*

---

159. James considered himself an expert on witchcraft and other issues of a spiritual and metaphysical nature, publishing several volumes on related subjects.

that Irreligious and Illiterate Pamphlet made by Io. Sw. And by him Intituled, The Arraignment of Women, with *Certaine Quares to the bayter of Women with Confutatio of some part of his Diabolicall Discipline*, SR; title page dated 1617, response to Swetnam' satire on women

Nov 15 — William Camden, *History of England in English 1558-1588*, SR

Nov 21 — William Laud appointed Dean of Gloucester

Nov 23 — Richard Hakluyt, d. (b. 1552/1553)

Dec 13 — Joshua Sylvester, *Tobacco Battered or the Pipes Scattered*, SR

Dec 17 — Roger L'Estrange b. (d. 1704)

Dec 25 — Ben Jonson, *Christmas His Masque (Christmas His Showe)*, performed

1617

Thomas Campion, *Third and Fourth Books of Ayres*

Thomas Campion (?), George Mason, and John Earle, *The Entertainment at Brougham Castle*, masque performed

Robert Fludd, *The Apologetic Tractatus for the Society of the Rosy Cross*, published at Leiden, Netherlands; *Ultriusque Cosmi Maioris et Minoris Metaphysica, Physica atque Technica Historia, in duo Volumina...divisa* (*History of the Two Worlds*), two volumes published as a single folio at Oppenheim, Germany[160]

Hugo Grotius, *Christus Patiens*, published in Leiden

'Constantia Munda', *The Worming of a mad Dogge: Or, a Soppe for Cerberus the Jaylor of Hell. No Confutation byt a sharpe Redargation of the bayter of Women*, tract, pseudonymous response to Joseph Swetnam

Sir Walter Raleigh, *The History of the World* 2nd edition, with name and portrait

Julius Caesar Scaliger, *Poetices libri septem*, 5th edition, published in Heidelberg

'Ester Sowernam', *Ester hath hang'd Haman; or, An answere to a lewd Pamphlet, entituled The Arraignment of Women, with the arraignment of lewd idle, froward, and unconstant men, and Husbands...*, tract, pseudonymous response to Joseph Swetnam

Edmund Spenser, *Works*, 2nd folio

---

160. An extensive treatment of microcosm and macrocosm as they relate to philosophy, alchemy, etc.

Joseph Swetnam, *The Schoole of the Noble and Worthy Science of Defence*, manual on fencing; with some responses to Rachel Speght, *Mouzell for Melastomus*

Edward Vaughan, *A Plaine and Perfect Method for the Easie Understanding of the Whole Bible*, published

John Webster, *The Devil's Law Case*, written (?); *The Duchess of Malfi*, performed in a revised revival

Thomas Young, *Englands Bane: or, The Description of Drunkennesse*, published

Thomas Coryate d. (b. 1577; of dysentery while traveling in Surat)

Ralph Cudworth b.

Vavasour Powell b.

Henry King m. Anne Berkeley

Matthias I, the Hapsburg Holy Roman Emperor, resigns the Crown of Bohemia in favor of his cousin, Ferdinand of Styria, a Jesuit-trained Catholic

Lucy, Countess of Bedford, travels to Germany as chief attendant to Elizabeth of Bohemia

Bishop Lancelot Andrewes appointed to the Privy Council in Scotland

James Shirley receives B.A. from Cambridge

Sir John Denham moves to Surrey, in the area of Coopers Hill

Ladies Hall, Deptford, Kent, founded; first public school for "young gentlewomen," emphasizing needlework

Jan 5 — George, Viscount Villiers, created Earl of Buckingham

Jan 6—TWELFTH NIGHT — Ben Jonson, *The Vision of Delight*

— Pocahontas presented at Court to Queen Anne

Jan 7 — *Machiavellis Dogge*, SR

Jan 15 — Joseph Hall, *Quo Vadis? a just Censure of Travell, as it is commonly undertaken by the gentlemen of our nation*, SR

Jan 30 — William Sancroft b. (later Archbishop of Canterbury)

Feb 4 — George Villiers, Earl of Buckingham, appointed to the Privy Council

Feb 12 — John Davies of Hereford, *Wittes Bedlam*, SR

Feb 15 — *Whale cast up neare Harwich, Feb. 1617*, SR, news pamphlet

Feb 18 — John Woodall, *The Chirurgions Mate*, SR, medical treatise

Feb 21 — Nicholas Byfeilde, *Direction for Private Reading of the Scripture*, SR

— Francis Herring, *Mischiefes Misery or Romes Master Peece*, SR, expanded version of *Popishe Pyetye*

Feb 22 — Ben Jonson, *Lovers Made Men*, masque, produced for Lord Hay by Lucy Harington Russell, Countess of Bedford

Mar 5 — Sir Thomas Egerton, Lord Chancellor Ellesmere (b. 1540?), on his death-bed, surrenders the Great Seal

Mar 7 — Sir Francis Bacon, appointed Lord Keeper of the Seal (the office held during Elizabeth's reign by his father), in part through the intercession of the Earl of Buckingham

Mar 8 — J. Salkeld, *Treatise of Paradice*, SR

— J. Harper, *Jewel of Arithmiticke*, SR

Mar 24 — Sir John Berkenhead b.

— John Donne receives the honor of preaching at St. Paul's Cross

Mar 29 — Abraham Man, *Amulett or Preservative against Sickness and Death*, SR

— Sir Walter Raleigh sets sail from Dover for his Guiana expedition

Apr 14 — *Petition of Poore Prisioners Gail of Fleet*, SR

Apr 17 — Christopher Marlowe, *Edward II*, SR, tragedy[161]

Apr 26 — John Hayward, *Holie poem betwixt Justice & Mercy*, SR

May — George Villiers, Earl of Buckingham, appointed to the Scottish Privy Council, a rare honor for an English peer

May 22 — Samuel Rowlands, *The Bride*, SR

May 23 — Elias Ashmole b.

---

161. It seems instructive to note the timeliness of republishing Marlowe's play, given the simultaneous and meteoric rise of the current Court favorite, George Villiers.

Jun — Sir Francis Bacon appointed to the Privy Council

Jun 21 — William Pratt, *Arithmeticall Jewell with the use of small tables*, SR, mathematical treatise

Jun 24 — Robert Cromwell, Oliver Cromwell's father d., probably marking the end of Cromwell's education at Cambridge

Summer — Amelia Lanier begins keeping school in St. Giles in the Fields

Jul — James I opens the Scottish Parliament, with the Earl of Buckingham as the only English peer present in the Procession of State

— Oliver Cromwell leaves Sidney Sussex College

Jul 13 — **John Milton, Sr., publishes commendatory sonnet in John Lane,** *Guy, Earl of Warwick*

Jul 17 — *Palatinate Wars 20 & 23 July 1622*, SR

— Ferdinand of Styria confirmed as King by Bohemian Council of State

Jul 18 — *Slaughter of English in Bergen-Op-Zone*, SR

Jul 20 — Richard Ferrers, *Worth of Woemen*

Jul 26 — John Johnson, *Astronomicall Arithmeticke*, SR

Aug 8 — Anne More Donne gives birth to a stillborn child

Aug 15 — Anne More Donne d., at age 33 (b. 1584), after giving birth to twelve children in fifteen years[162]

Aug 25 — Frances Aylesbury baptized

Sep 7 — Aesop, *Pueriles Confabulutumculae* (*Fables*), translated by John Brinsley, SR

Oct 2 — George Herbert appointed *sublector quartae classis*, Trinity College, Cambridge

Oct 5 — Dorothy Sidney baptized; daughter of Robert Sidney,

---

162. While the facts might suggest an overbearing attitude on Donne's part as husband, most of the women of the period endured equally compressed periods of pregnancy. Reports of seventeen to nineteen births within twenty years are common, although many of those might have been stillbirths, and of the live births only three or four children might survive until their teens. What evidence survives in this instance suggests a close affection between John and Anne Donne.

2nd Earl of Leicester[163] (afterward Countess of Sunderland)
Oct 9 — Henry Fitzgeffrey, *Satirical Epigrams*, SR
Oct 16 — John Willis, *Nemonica, with an Art of Memory*, SR, English version of an earlier Latin treatise by Willis
Oct 22 — James Maxwell, *Primitive Pattern for the Church of Scotland*, SR, religious treatise
Nov 6 — James Hay m. Lucy Percy[164]; King James presides at the wedding
Nov 10 — B. Pirckheimer, *Praise of the Gout: Goutes Apologie*, SR, medical treatise
— Thomas Young, *Englands Bane*, SR
Nov 20 — Sir Dudley Carlton, *Speech in the Low Countries*, SR, translation
Dec 1 — William Crashaw, *Milke for Babies: Catechism*, SR
— Roger Williams, *Accions of the Low Countries*, SR
Dec 13 — Harum White, *Repentance of Mary Magdalyne*, SR
Dec 15 — John Willis, *Stenographia, Sive Ars Compendiose Scribendi*, SR, treatise on writing

---

163. Her grandfather was Henry Percy, 9th Earl of Northumberland, friend of Raleigh and at this time still a prisoner of James I in the Tower.

164. James Hay was a fellow-Scot and an early Court favorite of James I; his new wife was the daughter of the imprisoned "Wizard Earl," Henry Percy, Earl of Northumberland. Following the marriage, Percy's imprisonment was gradually lightened, leading to his eventual release from the Tower.

1618

John Milton begins tutorials with a young Scots Puritan minister, Thomas Young
Cornelius Janssen paints portrait of the young Milton[165]
Martin Billingsley,[166] *The Pens Excellencie or The Secretaries Delight*, handwriting manual
Thomas Deloney, *Canans Calamitie Jerusalems Misery, or The dolefull destruction of faire Jerusalem by Titus...*, verse history (SR Jan 1598)
[Thomas Heywood?], *Swetnam the Woman-hater Arraigned by Women...*, drama, performed at the Red Bull
Philip Massinger, Thomas Middleton, William Rowley, *The Old Law*, written
Edmund Rudierd, *The Thunderbolt of Gods Wrath*, abridgement of Thomas Beard[167], *The Theatre of Gods Judgments*

---

165. That the Janssen portrait shows the young Milton in the short hair style adopted by Puritans more likely reflects the preferences of his Puritan tutor than of his family. In terms of the confidence placed by John Milton, Sr., in his son's potential, it is interesting that, while there are several portraits of the poet as a child or youth, none exist for the father, mother, brother, or sister. Janssen was a well-received painter in the English court.

166. Part of Billingsley's authority on the subject of penmanship as an adjunct to political power stemmed from his position as tutor to Prince Charles, the future Charles I.

167. Thomas Beard was Oliver Cromwell's schoolmaster and one of the most influential late-Elizabethan writers on the workings of God's Providence in human history. Beard's works were reprinted a number of times during the 17th Century.

(1597)

Thomas Taylor, *Christs Combate and Conquest: or, the Lyon of the Tribe of Judah*, published

Mary Ward, account of her missionary endeavors in England as a Catholic (1608-1618), written

William Bradshaw d. (b. 1571); Puritan leader

Henry Bennet b. (afterward 1st Earl of Arlington)

Abraham Cowley b.

John Smith b. (Cambridge Platonist)

Richard Lovelace b.

James Nayler b.

Sir Edward Sherbourne b. (d. 1702)

Isaac Vossius b

Sir Kenelm Digby attends Oxford University

George Herbert, appointed Praelector, or Reader in Rhetoric, Trinity College

Jan 1 — George Villiers created Marquis of Buckingham, at age twenty-five[168]; as Marquis, he outranks all peers of the rank of Earl or below

— Thereafter: George Herbert, official congratulatory letter to Buckingham

Jan 4 — John Murrell, *New Booke of Cookery*, SE entry

— James Shirley, *Echo and Narcissus*, SR, first poems

---

168. The dates and occasions of George Villiers' rapid rise from country gentleman to holding positions of influence and power (or Robert Carr's, or Francis Bacon's, for that matter) are perhaps not in themselves significant, but they do indicate much about the arbitrary and eccentric manner of Stuart politics during the period—a form of politics that invariably created envy and ill-will that could always conceivably turn against the favorite... and possibly against the monarch.

Concerning the last rank, Roger Lockyer writes: "There was some surprise that the marquisate, like the earldom, was of Buckingham, but Carleton was told by another informant that 'the King would have it so, because he so much affects the name of Buck'. The reference, of course, is to the hunting field, where Buckingham and his master spent much of their time together, but the sexual implications should not, perhaps, be overlooked" (*Buckingham*, p. 33).

published
— Sir Francis Bacon, appointed Lord Chancellor

Jan 6—TWELFTH NIGHT — Ben Jonson, *Pleasure Reconciled to Virtue*, masque commemorating Prince Charles's investiture as Prince of Wales; James I impatiently demands dancing, and the new Marquis of Buckingham leaps up to accommodate him; masque subsequently revised and performed as *For the Honour of Wales*

Jan 13 — Nathanael Culverwel baptized

Jan 22 — Thomas Middleton, *Dick Divers-Deep, or Owles Almanacke*, SR

Feb 2—CANDLEMAS NIGHT — [Thomas Pestell?], *The Coleorton Masque*, presented by Sir Thomas Beaumont to Sir William Seymour and Frances Devereux Seymour

Feb 10 — William Crashaw, *Parable of Poyson*, SR

Feb 11 — Geffray Mynshul, *Certain Characters and Essayes of Prison and Prisoners*

Feb 15 — John Smith baptized; later an influential member of the Cambridge Platonists

Feb 18 — John Brinsley *Ouids Metamorphosis translated grammatically, and also according to the propriety of our English tongue, so farre as grammar and the verse will well beare*, SR

Mar 4 — John Sprint, *Necessity of Conformity*, SR

Mar 17 — R. M., *Relation of the Government of Rawleigh's Fleet*, SR

Spring — *The Peacemaker*, published, anonymous treatise; the style generally resembles Lancelot Andrewes', with passages by other hands, including King James; published bearing the royal arms, indicating James's approval of its primary tenet: "*Beati pacifici*"

Apr — John Selden, *History of Tithes*, published, opposing all ecclesiastical claims to authority and ignoring the claim to Divine Right

Apr 8 — Paul Baines, *Main Points of Christian Religion...*, SR

Apr 20 — Bartholomew Holyday, *Marriages of the Artes*, SR

Apr 21 — William Barlow, *Magneticall Advertisements*....

Apr 22 — Joseph Hall, *Contemplations on Holy Story, Vol. 4*, SR; *Sermon at Spittle: Righteous Mammon*, SR

May — Protestants on the Bohemian Council of State reject the election of Ferdinand of Styria as King of Bohemia

— Sir John Elyot knighted

May 14 — Hesiod, *Georgics*, translated by George Chapman, SR

May 26 — Sir John Harington, *The Most Elegant and Witty Epigrams of Sir John Harington, Book IV*, SR

May 30 — Richard Brathwayte, *Exquisite Discourse of Epitaphs*, SR; *Good Wife: A Rare One Amongst Women*, SR

Jun 2 — William Hornby, *Scourge of Drunkenness*, SR

Jun 14 — George Wither, *Discourse of Love, or Songes, Sonnettes, and Elegies*, SR

Jun 21 — Sir Walter Raleigh returns from a disastrous expedition to Guiana, to find an order for his arrest waiting him

Jun 28 — Lucan, *Bello Civili Caesaris et Pompei* (*Civil War*), SR

— Edmund Willis, *An Abbreviation of Writing by Character*, manual of shorthand

Jul 2 — Paul Baine, *Christian Garment*, SR

Jul 12 — Sir Francis Bacon created Baron Verulam of Verulam; at the same time, Buckingham's mother created Countess of Buckingham

Jul 15 — Michael Barrett, *Vineyard of Horsemanship*, SR

Jul 20 — Stephan Jerome, *Origen's Repentance*, SR

Jul 24 — John Taylour, *Verses upon the Kings of England from Brute to James I*

Aug 2 — Sir Robert Sidney, Sir Philip Sidney's brother, created 2nd Earl of Leicester

— Two additional earldoms awarded, Devonshire and Warwick, at a cost of £10,000 each[169]

---

169. Samuel Gardiner writes: "So little shame did James feel about the matter that he actually allowed the greater part of the price to be entered in the receipt-book of the Exchequer," adding that one of the candidates, Lord

Aug 7 — Francis Beaumont and John Fletcher, *A King and No King*, SR

Aug 10 — Sir Walter Raleigh again committed to the Tower

Aug 17 — Sir Francis Bacon begins active investigation into Sir Walter Raleigh's case

Sep 17 — John Owen, *Epigrams*, SR

Sep 28 — Joshua Sylvester d. (b. 1563)

Oct — Sir Walter Raleigh composing *The Art of War by Sea*

Oct 14 — Peter Lely b., as Peter van der Faes, in Westphalia[170]

Oct 19 — John Harmar, *The Mirrour of Humility*, translation of Daniel Heinsius, *In Theophania...homilia* (published, Leiden, 1612), theological treatise

Oct 22 — Joannes Scapula, *Lexicon Graecolatinum*, SR

— Sir Walter Raleigh appears for the last time before the commissioners appointed to examine his case, including Sir Francis Bacon; Bacon pronounces the death sentence

Oct 29 — Sir Walter Raleigh executed (b. 1552?)[171]

Nov 2 — John Taylor, the Water-Poet, *The Pennyles Pilgrimage or the Money-lesse Perambulation of John Taylor, Alias The King's Majesties Water-Poet; How He TRAVAILED on Foot from London to Edenborough in Scotland, Not Carrying any Money To or Fro, Neither Begging, Borrowing, or Asking Meate, Drinke, or Lodging*, Published, verse account of a journey through England

Nov 14 — Thomas Middleton, *Parliament of Threadbare Poets*, SR (original entry, 1608)

Nov 21 — John Chamberlain: "We are so full still of Sir Walter

---

Rich (elevated to the earldom of Warwick), had been involved in piracy to a far greater extent than had cost Sir Walter Raleigh his head, concluding that "With him piracy had degenerated into a mere commercial speculation" (*History*, III, 215.)

170. Acknowledged as the best painter of his time in England, Lely took his name from the house in which his father had lived in the Netherlands, identified by a sign with a Lily.

171. Raleigh's son, formerly Ben Jonson's pupil, had been killed during the ill-fated Orinoco expedition that sealed Raleigh's death sentence.

Raleigh that almost every day brings forth somewhat in this kind, besides divers ballets (i.e., ballads), wherof some are called in, and the rest such poore stuffe as are not worth the overlooking"[172]

— No ballads on Raleigh are officially entered in the *Stationers' Register*, but a many appear, including: *Sir Walter Rauleigh his lamentation: Who was beheaded in the old Pallace at Westminster the 29. Of October. 1618*, broadside ballad, written to the tune of *Weiladay*

Nov 26 — Sir Lewis Stucley, *Petition*, published by the King's printer, an attack on Sir Walter Raleigh's death speech as libellous to him[173]

Nov 27 — Sir Lewis Stucley, *Declaration*, published, a further attack on Raleigh's reputation

Winter — Ben Jonson 's walking trip through Scotland begins

Dec — John Selden called before James I; they amicably discuss the number of the Beast in Revelations, avoiding the issue of Tithes or Divine Right

Dec 11 — E. Brett, *Of Hawks and Hawking*, SR

Dec 16 — Thomas Gataker, *The Nature and Uses of Lottes*, SR

---

172. Hyder Rollins, *A Pepysian Garland*, p. 89.

173. Stucley was in fact Raleigh's cousin, and had inhibited Raleigh's escape when arrest became imminent. The tract was popularly thought to be by a Court official—most probably Sir Francis Bacon himself; again, what was perceived as Bacon's ill-usage of a former patron further diminished his reputation.

1619

Sir Francis Bacon *The Wisdom of the Ancients*, translation into English as *De Sapientia Veterum*
Richard Bernard, *A Key of Knowledge for the Opening of... Revelation*
Thomas Blundeville, *The Arte of Logicke. Plainly taught in the English Tongue...*, published
Lady Anne Clifford, *Diary*, completed (1603-1619
Thomas Deloney, *The pleasant history of John Winchcomb, in his younger years called Jack of Newbery, the famous and worthy Clothier of England...*, novel (?) 8th edition (1st edition, 1597
Michael Drayton, *Poems*, revised; includes the final version of his sonnet sequence, *Idea's Mirror* (1594)
Richard Gethinge, *Calligraphotechnia*, handwriting manual
William Shakespeare, *King Lear*, printed (2nd quarto)
John Webster, *The Devil's Law-Case*, performed
The Wonderful Discoverie of the Witchcrafts of Margaret and Phillippa Flower, 1619, published
William Chamberlayne b.
Carlo Dati b.
Francis Higginson b.
John Lambert b.
The Thirty Years War begins with the overthrow of the Elector Frederick as King of Bohemia by Catholic forces; Frederick and Elizabeth, holding their court-in-exile at The Hague, thereafter frequently referred to as the "Winter King and

Queen of Bohemia"; Elizabeth also referred to as the "Queen of Hearts"[174]

Lancelot Andrewes consecrated Bishop of Winchester

Thomas Carew, accompanies Edward, Lord Herbert of Cherbury to France

Alexander Gill, the Younger, begins teaching at St. Paul's School at age 22

John Selden arraigned before a High Commission, forced to sign a submission admitting to Divine Right, not allowed to sell his book, and forbade to write any rejoinders or replies

Early 1619 — King James seriously ill, with concerns at Court that he might not survive

Jan — Ben Jonson concludes his extended visit with William Drummond of Hawthornden

Jan 1 — J. Bambridge, *Astronomicall Discussion of the Late Blazing Starre*, SR

Jan 9 — Thomas Mason, *A Revelation of the Revelation*, SR, religious treatise

Jan 12 — John Denison, *The Heavenly Banquet*, SR

— Thomas Morrice, *An Apology for Schoolmasters...*, SR

Jan 20 — Patrick Hannay, *The Happy Husband: or, Directions for a Maid to choose her Mate*, published

Jan 22 — Fontanus Saxum, *Interpretation of the New Blasing Star last Nov.*, SR

Jan 25 — J. Borreel, *Demonstration of the Late Comet*, SR

---

174. James I was severely censured for not sending military aid to Frederick, who was after all, not only a fellow Protestant and a reigning King, but James' son-in-law and princely husband of James' enormously popular daughter, Elizabeth. James was, however, more concerned with the wider implications of English intervention on the Continent and seems—particularly in his efforts to marry his son Charles to a Catholic princess, either of Spain or of France—more intent on creating a balance of power and forestalling war than throwing himself, and England, into a religious struggle. James has been frequently disparaged as a monarch by historians, but at the least he did keep England relatively free from the disastrous entanglements of the Thirty years' War

Jan 28 — George Villiers, Marquis of Buckingham, appointed Lord Admiral of the Navy (position held through James' death in 1625)

Feb — James I, *Meditation upon the Lord's Prayer*, dedicated to George Villiers, Marquis of Buckingham

— John Hay, Lord Doncaster, appointed to the Bohemian embassy on the Eve of the Bohemian crisis[175]

Feb 11 — William Innis, *The Domesticke Church*, SR

Feb 22 — Queen Anne, desperately ill and bedridden

Mar — Three women tried for witchcraft in Leicestershire

Mar 2 — Anne of Denmark, Queen-Consort of England, d., of dropsy at the age of 44 (b. 1574)[176]

— Thereafter: Patrick Hannay, *Elegies on the Death of Queene Anne*, published

Mar 6 — Cyrano de Bergerac b., in Paris, France

Mar 8 — *Discovery of the Jesuits in Secret Consultation*, SR

Mar 20 — Matthias I, Holy Roman Emperor, d., exacerbating the issue of succession to the Crown of Bohemia

Mar 22 — Edward Popham, *Looking-glasse for the Soule, and a definition thereof*, SR

Apr 6 — [William Fennor], *Pasquilles Palynodie: A Pint of Poetry*, SR

Apr 12 — William Heale, *An Apologie for Weemen*, SR

Apr 13 — William Schouten, *Voyage and Discovery of a New Passage into the South Sea*, SR

Apr 14 — James I, letter to John Hay, Lord Doncaster, directing him to work for a peaceful resolution in Bohemia[177]

---

175. Doncaster's involvement may have helped precipitate the crisis, since, rather than acting as an objective mediator between the two parties, Doncaster arrived in Bohemia a staunch defender of the claims of Frederick V

176. Anne Oldenburg was the daughter of Frederick II, King of Denmark and Norway, and Sophia of Mecklenburg-Güstrow. She had married James VI, King of Scotland, on 24 Nov 1589, at the age of fifteen, and bore him seven children.

177. James saw the situation as an opportunity to put into effect his ideals

Apr 15 — Mary de Medici, *Remonstrance & Reasons for her Escape*, SR, political pamphlet
Apr 18 — John Donne, "Sermon of Valediction at my going into Germany, at Lincoln's Inn"
Apr 28 — Francis Beaumont, *The Maides Tragedy*, SR
May 7 — John King, *Thanksgiving for His Majesty's Recovery*, SR, sermon
May 12 — John Hay, Lord Doncaster, departs for Bohemia
— John Donne accompanies him on the diplomatic mission to Germany
May 13 — Queen Anne buried at Westminster Abbey, thirteen weeks after her death
— Edward, Lord Herbert of Cherbury, leaves London as Ambassador to France; Thomas Carew part of the retinue
May 15 — Patrick Hannay, *Two Elegies on the Death of the Queen*, SR
May 17 — Ben Jonson receives honorary M.A. degree from Oxford
May 26 — *Postures of Musketterian and Pikeman with Arms*, SR, broadsheet
Jun 1 — *Matters in Bohemia, Austria, Poland, Silesia, & France from 2 Mar 1618*, SR, news pamphlet
Jun 2 — Patrick Adamson, *Latin Poems upon Job*, SR
Jun 8 — Samuel Crooke, *Duell with Death (Death Subdued)*, SR, sermon
Jun 12 — Samuel Purchas, *Microcosmos, or the History of Man, Relating the wonders of his Generation, vanities in his Degeneration, Necessity of his Regeneration*, SR
Jun 17 — *Indentures to Bind Children Apprentices*, SR by

---

as outlined in *The Peacemaker*. His instructions to Doncaster read: "Let the King keep the oath which he took at his coronation. Let the Jesuits cease to meddle with political affairs. Let prisoners on both sides be released, and let the Protestants enjoy the rights and liberties to which they are entitled" (cited in Samuel Gardiner, *History*, III, p.300). Gardiner's assessment of the King's good intentions seems apt: "The advice was excellent, but the man could have but little knowledge of human nature who fancied that a deep and envenomed quarrel could be appeased by such vague generalities."

direction of the Churchwardens and overseers of the poor

Jul — James refuses to send troops to support an offensive in Bohemia on the part of Frederick V, agreeing only to defensive measures should they be needed

— Doncaster continues to seek for a peaceful resolution of the conflict, meeting with Ferdinand in Salzburg and Spanish representatives in Frankfurt; James' hopes for peace in Europe dwindle

Jul 10 — Thomas Middleton, *The Masque of Heroes* (*Inner Temple Masque*)

Aug 13 — George Withers, *Preparation to the Psalter*, SR

Aug 16 — Rebellious Bohemians depose Ferdinand of Styria and offer the crown of Bohemia to Frederick V, Elector Palatine

Aug 18 — Ferdinand of Styria unanimously elected Holy Roman Emperor at Frankfurt[178]

— Doncaster retires to Spa, to avoid appearances of responsibility for the coming conflict

Aug 20 — John Mayer, *A Patterne for Woemen with St. Jerome's Discourse*, SR

Aug 21 — Henry Lyte, *Art of Tennes*, SR, educational pamphlet

Sep 3 — Virgil, *Eclogues & De Apibus*, translation by Brinsley, SR

— Robert Whitell, *Way to Celestial Paradise*, SR

Sep 12 — James refuses to make any decision relating to the Bohemian Crown

Sep 13 — John Calvin, *Lectures upon Jeremiah*, SR, translation into English

Sep 17 — Ferdinand II, Holy Roman Emperor, *Reasons for Electing a New King*, SR, translation from Latin

Sep 18 — Samuel Rowlands, *The Night Raven*, SR

Sep 28 — Frederick V unilaterally accepts the Crown of

---

178. Not even the representative of Frederick V, the Elector Palatine, spoke against Ferdinand's election.

Bohemia[179]

Oct 11 — Thomas Dekker, *Dekker's Dream*, SR

Oct 14 — Samuel Daniel d. (b. 1562)

Oct 17 — *Swetnam the Woemen Hater Arraign'd by Woemen*, SR

Oct 21 — George Herbert appointed temporary University Orator, Cambridge[180], during the absence of Sir Francis Nethersole

Oct 31 — Frederick V and Elizabeth enter Prague

Nov — Frederick V and Elizabeth crowned as King and Queen of Bohemia

Nov 8 — *A Help to Memory and Discourse*, SR, educational treatise

Nov 10 — René Descartes experiences a series of three dreams that result in a "vision of science expressed in mathematics"[181]

Nov 19 — William Gouge, *Brief of the Old and New Testament Prophecies*, SR

Dec 17 — Prince Rupert of the Rhine[182] b., to Frederick V and

---

179. Frederick wrote in a letter to his uncle, the Duke of Bouillon, dated September 24/October 4, that his sole purpose in accepting the Crown, already claimed by a fanatically militant Catholic in Ferdinand of Styria, was that it was "a divine calling which I must not disobey...my only end is to serve God and His Church" (cited in Frances Yates, *Rosicrucian Enlightenment*, p. 19; Samuel Gardiner, *History*, III, p. 311). With two such strident opposites asserting their right to the same Crown, war was inevitable; over the next thirty years, the consequences of Frederick's decision altered the social and political face of Europe.

180. Herbert's election to this position constituted more than an academic honor. Previous University Orators had progressed to seats on the Privy Council, and for the young Herbert, his appointment signaled a beginning step to a promising political career.

181. Naomi Zack continues: "...and the three famous dreams..., which he interpreted as a divinely sanctioned revelation of his destiny to unify all of the quantifiable sciences under mathematics" (*Bachelors of Science*, p. 37).

182. Prince Rupert was the grandson of James I through Elizabeth, 'The Winter Queen,' and her husband Frederick; thus Rupert was first cousin

Elizabeth of Bohemia (afterward Duke of Bavaria)
Dec 6 — Samuel Rowlands, *A Payre of Spy Knaves*, SR
Dec 18 — Thomas Gataker, *Marriage Duties*, SR
Dec 27 — Christopher Newstead, *Apologie for Woemen, Womens Defence*, SR

---

to King Charles I Some historians have attributed the Royalists' defeat in the Civil War in part to Rupert's misplaced sense of the chivalric and the romantic, and his disdain for the commoners that composed and at times commanded the Parliamentarian forces. Not entirely inaccurately, he was referred to as "the Mad Cavalier" because of his impetuosity, especially in battle.

Decade Three: 1620-1629
Jacobean to Caroline

1620

End of Milton's tutorial with Thomas Young
Milton begins attending St. Paul's School, London, under high master Alexander Gill, the Elder. While at the school, Milton becomes acquainted with Alexander Gill, the Younger, and with Charles Diodati, son of an influential Italian physician
Owen Feltham, *Resolves, Divine, Morall, Politicall*, 1st printing with frequent reprints
James I, *Meditation upon St. Matthew's Gospel* published, including a meditation on the Crown of Thorns[183]
James Granger, *Syntagma Logicum, or The Divine Logicke*, published
[Thomas Heywood?], *Swetnam the Woman-hater Arraigned by Women...*, drama, published
Thomas May, *The Heir*, produced
Lady Grace Mildmay d. (b. 1552)[184]
Alexander Brome b.
Richard Flecknoe b. (?)
Nicolaas Heinsius b.
Thomas Young departs for Hamburg, Germany, to serve as a chaplain to an English congregation there
Edmund Waller admitted to King's College, Cambridge

---

183. Possibly a reflection of James' irresolute and ultimately disastrous delaying during the Bohemian crisis, which involved a crown of another sort. James speaks of the mock coronation of Christ as a "pattern of a king's inauguration" (Samuel Gardiner, *History*, III, p. 327).

184. Author of an unpublished journal cited by Bush, *English Literature*.

Jan — John Donne returns from diplomatic mission to Germany

Jan 3 — Frederick V referred to in a Jesuit communiqué: "He will only be a winter-king," a source for his subsequent familiar title[185]

Jan 6—TWELFTH NIGHT — Ben Jonson, *News from the New World Discovered in the Moon*, masque

Jan 10 — Francis Beaumont and John Fletcher, *Philaster*, SR

Jan 15 — Thomas Dekker and John Day, *The Life & Death of Guy of Warwick*, SR

Jan 20 — William Gamage, *Lindsey Woolsey*, SR (reprint of 1613 Oxford issue)

Jan 21 — George Herbert appointed Public Orator, Cambridge University

Jan 29 — Joshua Sylvester, *Perspective Spectacles and Divers Meditations*, SR, combined issue of Sylvester's translations from Du Bartas and his own works

— Lucy Apsley b. (afterward Lucy Hutchinson)

Feb 1 — *Portraiture of the King in Parliament Robes* SR

— Edmond Rue, *Twelve Rules introducing the Art of Latin*, SR

Feb 9 — *Hic Mulier, or the Man-Woman*, SR

Feb 16 — *Haec Vir, or the Woeman-Man, Reply to Hic Mulier*, SR

Mar 1 — Thomas Campion d., probably of the plague (b. 1567)

Mar 22 — Florio, John, *The Decameron, containing an hundred pleasant nouels...*, translation of Giovanni Boccaccio, *Decameron*, (?), SR with addition: "recalled by my Lord of Canterburyes command"

Mar 28 — Thomas Gibson, *Shematismus, seu de figuris gramatices*, SR, educational treatise

Apr 3 — Edmund Gunter, *Canon Triangulorum*, SR, mathematical treatise

Apr 4 — Virgil, *Aeneid II*, translation by Wroth, SR

Apr 8 — John Melton, *Astrologaster, or the Figure Caster*, SR,

---

185. Samuel Gardiner, *History*, III, p. 317.

scientific treatise

Apr 11 — Francis Quarles, *A Feast for Worms. Set forth in a poeme of the history of Jonah*, published (reprint 1626

Apr 29 — *Muld Sacke, Apologie of Hic Mulier...*, SR, pamphlet demanding political, religious, social, agricultural, and financial reform

May 5 — John Selden, Letter to Buckingham, his ironical last word on the issue of Divine Right raised by *History of Tithes*

— Tobias Venner, *Via Recta: Nourishment and the Preservation of Health*, SR

May 9 — John Rous elected Chief Librarian of the Bodleian Library

May 15 — Gervase Markham, *Hungers Prevention: The Art of Fowling*, SR

May 16 — George Villiers, Marquis of Buckingham, m. Lady Katherine Manners, daughter of the Catholic (but immensely wealthy) Francis Manners, 6th Earl of Rutland

May 19 — Thomas Wilson, *Saints by Calling, Called to be Saints*, SR

May 22 — Thomas Gataker, *The Popes Pride and the Papistes Poll*, SR

— John Taylor, the Water Poet, *Praise of Hempseed*, SR

Jun 9 — John Davies of Hereford, *The Writing Scholemaster*, SR, educational treatise

Jun 12 — Richard Crakanthorpe, *Sermon on Predestination*, SR

Summer — James' vacillating stances toward his son-in-law give Spain and Germany tacit permission to invade Bohemia

Jul 4 — Thomas Middleton, *World Tossed at Tennis*, SR, masque

Jul 10 — William Folkingham, *Art of Brachigraphy*, SR, educational treatise

Mid-Aug — Marchamont Needham (Nedham) b.

Aug 21 — Marchamont Needham baptized, at Burford, near

Oxford

Aug 22 — Oliver Cromwell m. Elizabeth Bourchier, St. Giles Church, Cripplegate

Aug 26 — Richard Whitbourne, *Discovery of Newfoundland*, SR, traveler's account

Sep 4 — Spanish forces under the Catholic League invade Palatinate territory

Sep 6 — *Mayflower* sails for New England

Sep 23 — [Thomas Venner], *The Taking of the Fume of Tobacco*, SR, medical tract

Oct 10 — John Ford, *The Line of Life*, SR

Oct 12 — Francis Bacon, *Novum Organum* appears (incomplete version)

Oct 29/Nov 8 — Battle of White Mountain; Frederick V defeated by Catholic forces, which force him into exile at The Hague[186]

Oct 31 — John Evelyn b. (d. 1706)[187]

---

186. "Historians have noted the effect on the internal history of England of the extraordinary Bohemian enterprise and its failure. They have seen that James I, conducting his foreign policy by 'divine right' and without consulting Parliament, which was unanimously in favour of supporting the King of Bohemia, was beginning a train of events which would eventually destroy the Stuart Monarchy. It was not only the internal government of the country without consulting Parliament which aroused anger; it was the pursuit of a foreign policy against the wishes of Parliament, or without consulting Parliament, which also aroused deep anger, and that not only among members of Parliament but among the people generally, of all classes" (Frances A. Yates, *Rosicrucian Enlightenment*, p. 24). Given the consequences for himself, his son, and England, of James' treatment of his daughter and son-in-law, exacerbated by Elizabeth Stuart's enduring popularity in England up to and beyond the Restoration of Charles II, this episode provides one key to understanding much that would happen during the next four decades.

187. Evelyn notes in his Diary that his father. Richard Evelyn, "was married at St. Thomas's, Southwark, 27th January, 1613. My sister Eliza was born at nine at night, 28th November, 1614; Jane at four in the morning, 16th February, 1616; my brother George at nine at night, Wednesday, 18th June 1617; and my brother Richard, 9th November 1622" (p. 1). Five children in less than ten years was well within the norm for the time, as were the senior Evelyns' ages at the time of John's birth—Richard was 33, Eleanor

Nov 2 — James Warre, *Truths Touchstone*, SR, anti-Catholic religious tract

Nov 8 — Guillaume de Saluste du Bartas, *A Commentary on du Bartas*, translation by Lodge, SR

— *Picture of the King of Bohemias Eldest Son*, SR

Nov 9 — Robert Newton, *Countess of Montgomery's Eusebeia*, SR

Nov 17 — Webbe, Joseph, *The Familiar Epistles of M. T. Cicero Englished amd conferred with the: French, Italian and other translations*, SR

Nov 20 — Thomas Vicars, *Manuductio ad artem Rhetoricam* (Manual on the Art of Rhetoric), SR

Nov 24 — Martin Fotherby, *Atheomastix: Clearing Four Truths against Atheists*, SR

— Richard Montagu, *Diatribe upon the first part of the late History of Tythes*, SR

Dec 4 — George Buchanan, *Ecphrasis paraphraseos in psalmos Davidis* (Psalm paraphrases in Latin), SR[188]

Dec 8 — George Wither, *Songs and Prayers in the Old Testament*, SR, collection

Dec 11 — John Smith, of Jamestown *New Englands Tryall*, SR

---

23. The only unusual element in the narrative is the fact that five children survived to adulthood. Eliza (Darcy) died first, in childbirth, at just over twenty years of age, in 1634; Elleanor a year later at age 38, and Richard five years following, in December of 1640, at about 56. In contrast, none of Ben Jonson's children survived to their teens. Evelyn himself lived to his eighty-sixth year.

188. This might likely be the edition Milton consulted in constructing his own psalm paraphrases in his youth, which show the influence of Buchanan's work.

1621

John Milton, Sr., music for six psalms in Thomas Ravenscroft's *Whole Book of Psalms*
John Barclay, *Argenis*, Latin romance
Robert Burton, *Anatomy of Melancholy*, 1st edition; reprints in 1624, 1628, 1632, 1638
John Ford, Thomas Dekker and William Rowley, *The Witch of Edmonton*, written
Mrs. Dorothy Leigh, *The Mothers Blessing*, 7th edition
Philip Massinger, *The Maid of Honor*, and *A New Way to Pay Old Debts*, written (?)
Thomas Middleton, *Women Beware Women*, performed (?)
Sir Walter Raleigh, *History of the World*, 1st complete edition
Joshua Sylvester, *Du Bartas His Divine Weekes and Works, Second Week*, published
Tobacco consumption since 1614 averages 140,000 pounds annually, or less than an ounce per capita
Lucy, Countess of Bedford, attends Elizabeth of Bohemia at The Hague

Jan 6 — Richard Preston, *The Lords Supper: Doctrine of the Sacrament*, SR
Jan 7 — John Donne, sermon before Lucy Harington Russell, at Harington House
Jan 10 — Francis Quarles, *Hadassa or the History of Queen Hester*
Jan 13 — R. W., *Looking Glass for Papists to see Deformities*,

SR
Jan 16 — Thomas Clark, *The Pope's Deadly Wound*, SR
Jan 18 — Rachel Speght, *Moralities Memorandum: with a Dream prefixed, imaginarie in manner; reall in matter*, SR
Jan 22 — William Laud appointed Prebend of Westminster
Jan 27 — Sir Francis Bacon, elevated to Viscount St. Albans
Jan 30 — James I opens Parliament with Sir Francis Bacon at his side as Lord Chancellor
— Edmund Waller M.P. for Amersham at age sixteen
Feb 3 — *Portraiture of Francis Manner, Earl of Rutland*, SR
Feb 8 — Stephen Denison, *Doctrine of Both the Sacraments*, SR
Feb 12 — Tilsley, *Animaversions upon Mr Seldons History of Tithes*, SR
Feb 16 — Alexander Gill, the Elder, *Logonomia Anglica*, SR
— Lewes Hughes, *Goodness of God toward the Summer Islands*, SR
— John Taylor, *Praise, Antiquity, and Commodity of Beggery*, SR
Feb 26 — N. S., *Merry Jests concerning Popes, Monkes & Fryers*, SR
— *An Astronomical Glass or Table Almanacke*, SR
Feb 28 — Stephen Denison, *Lawfulness of Kneeling in Receiving the Sacrament*, SR
Mar 14 — The Committee for Inquiring into Abuses in the Courts of Justice presents its report to the House, followed by two claims against Sir Francis Bacon, Buckingham's protégé
Mar 15 — William Laborer, *The Art of Short English Writing*, SR
Mar 17 — Sir Francis Bacon formally accused of accepting bribes
Mar 22 — Three new charges brought against Sir Francis Bacon
Mar 23 — Richard Brathwaite, *Times Curtain Drawne: Anatomie of Vanitie*, SR, moral treatise

Mar 26 — Ashmore, John, *Certain Selected Odes of Horace, Englished and their arguments Annexed. With poems (antient and modern) of divers subiects translated*, SR

Mar 30 — John King, Bishop of London, d.; funeral sermon by John Donne

Mar 31 — Andrew Marvell b., Yorkshire

Apr 7 — Alexander Cooke, *More Work for a Masse Priest*, SR

Apr 12 — Charles Goldwell, *Reason's Metamorphosis & Restauration*, SR, philosophy

May 3 — Sir Francis Bacon impeached and the Great Seal of England removed from his custody[189]

May 10 — Thomas Culpepper, *Tract against Usury Presented to Parliament*, SR

May 18 — *Seamonster, a Sea-Man, taken between Denmark and...*, SR, news pamphlet

May 31 — William Mason, *Handful of Essaies or Imperfect Offers*, SR

— John Taylor, the Water poet *Superbiae Flagellum: Whip of Pride*, SR

— Sir Francis Bacon taken from York House to the Tower

Jun — Sir Francis Bacon freed but never again to be allowed to hold public office or approach within twelve miles of London[190]

---

189. While Bacon was the immediate target of the impeachment, evidence suggests that Parliament used him as a 'whipping-boy' to express dissatisfaction with the Duke of Buckingham and James I, both of them untouchable. Bacon proved more vulnerable than his masters. Bacon's principle offense was taking bribes while a judge; his defense was that, while he had taken the bribes (it was impossible to survive otherwise, given the economics of the Jacobean court system), he had never allowed the bribes to interfere with his dispensing of justice.

190. The latter term was a standard punishment for those in disfavor, since the prohibition made it impossible to cultivate the necessary contacts at Court for preferment, which often led to bankruptcy or ruin; or, in more extreme cases, it presumably kept would-be assassins, rebels, and traitors a reasonably safe distance from the Monarch's person and the Royal Treasure immured in the Tower. Throughout the century and well into the next, the

Jun 4 — Parliament adjourns

Jun 16 — George Wither, *Withers His Motto*, satire resulting in a second term of imprisonment

Jun 21 — Thomas Taylor, *Brief View of Gods Speciall Mercyes*, SR

Summer — Ben Jonson, *The Gypsies Metamorphosed*, performed; a private masque commissioned for George Villiers

Jul 8 — Jean de La Fontaine b, Fabulist and perhaps the most widely read French poet of the centiry

Jul 11 — *Portraiture of the Cittie of Rochelle*, SR

Jul 13 — Lady Mary Sidney Wroth,[191] *The Countess of Montgomery's Urania*, SR first published fiction written by an English woman; *Pamphilia to Amphilanthus*

Jul 18 — Henry Percy, 9th Earl of Northumberland, and other political prisoners released from the Tower to honor King James' birthday; Percy persuaded to leave after sixteen years imprisonment[192]

---

prohibition stood for all Catholics, even though it was rarely enforced except in times of recurrent anti-Papist fervor; for that reason, for example, Alexander Pope and his family resided in nearby Twickenham, rather than London proper.

191. Niece to Sir Philip Sidney and Mary Sidney Herbert, Countess of Pembroke (and Lady Mary's goddaughter); and daughter of Sir Robert Sidney, Philip's younger brother and later 2nd Earl of Leicester.

192. Not that Percy particularly enjoyed his life in the Tower, although his gathering of scholars and his substantial library, coupled with his relative freedom from incurring additional charges of treason and conspiracy while in prison, might have made life there less than onerous. His cell was large, commodious, and comfortable; he was allowed frequent visitors; his food was prepared in his own kitchen in a house he had rented close by; he was even allowed to build a small outbuilding within the Tower courtyards in which to conduct chemical—and alchemical—experiments. He might even have suffered from the prisoner's occasional fear of living in the outside world. However, in this instance, Percy seemed primarily reluctant to accept what he saw as a favor emanating from his son-in-law, John Hay, whom he disliked as a Scot and as a Court favorite of James I.

After his release from the Tower, the old Earl (he was fifty-seven at the

Jul 20 — Thomas Gataker, *Small Spark to Kindling Sorrow for Syon*, SR

Jul 28 — [George Shaw], *Doctrine of Dying Well*, SR

Aug 5 — Ben Jonson, *The Gypsies Metamorphosed*, repeat performance for the Earl of Rutland; third performance later at Windsor

Aug 6 — Rachel Speght m. William Procter[193]

Sep 2 — Thomas Middleton, *The Faire Quarrell*, SR

Sep 7 — *What's the News Now?*, SR, ballad

Sep 10 — Isaac Casaubon, *Pietas*, SR

Sep 20 — *Portraiture of the King and Queen of Bohemia &c.*, SR

Sep 25 — Mary Sidney Herbert, Countess of Pembroke, d. (b. 1561)[194]

Oct 6 — William Shakespeare, *Othello, the Moor of Venice*, SR

Oct 23 — William Paseus, *Portraiture of the King Sitting in a Chair, the Prince Standing*, SR

Oct 30 — John Brinsley, *Consolation for our Gramer Schoole*, SR

Nov (?)— Sir Francis Bacon receives a limited Royal pardon

Nov 1 — John Willis, *Scholemaster to the Art of Stenography*, SR

Nov 6 — *Germany: News to 29 Oct. 1621*, SR, news pamphlet

Nov 16 — *Silver Age* and *Brazen Age*, SR, ballads

---

time, considered well advanced in years for the period) traveled to Bath in a carriage drawn by eight horses; the story circulated that he had done so to reinforce the superiority of his rank and title to that of Buckingham, who had recently toured parts of England in a carriage drawn by six horses.

193. Nothing further is known about Speght's life, including her death or burial dates. She was born about 1597.

194. Sir Philip Sidney's sister and one of the most influential Protestant female patrons of literature during the first two decades of the century, second only in influence to Elizabeth I herself. Much of her effort was devoted to preserving and enhancing her brother's literary reputation. See Margaret Hannay, *Philip's Phoenix*.

Nov 17 — Queen Elizabeth's Accession Day celebrated (annually)
— William Laud resigns as President of St. John's College, Oxford
Nov 18 — William Laud consecrated Bishop of St. David's, Wales
Nov 19 — William Laud sits as a member of the House of Lords
— John Donne elected Dean of St. Paul's Cathedral, London
— John Donne preaches his first sermon as Dean of St. Paul's
Nov 21 — Francis Rouse, *Diseases of the Times, Attended by their Remedies*, SR
Nov 24 — Henry Petre, *Brachygraphie*, SR
Nov 25 — Henry King preaches publicly at St. Paul's Cross
— Thereafter: Henry King, *A Sermon Preached at Pauls Crosse, the 25. Of November, 1621*, published
Dec 7 — Philip Massinger and Thomas Dekker, *Virgin Martyr*, SR
Dec 9 — Fortune Theater destroyed by fire
Dec 11 — Samuel Purchas, *Hakluytus his Posthumus or Purchas his Pilgrim...*, SR, traveler's account
— Virgil, *Deus Nobis: Dido's Death*, SR, English translation to be published with the Latin original
Dec 23 — Heneage Finch b., brother of Anne Finch (and later 1st Earl of Nottingham)

1622

David Browne, *The New Invention, Intituled Calligraphia: or, The Art of Faire Writing*, handwriting manual

Thomas Carew, commendatory verses to Thomas May's comedy, *The Heir* (produced 1620); Carew's first published verse

William Gouge, *Of Domesticall Duties: Eight Treatises*, published

Hugo Grotius, *De Veritate Religione Christianæ*[195]

Patrick Hannay, *The Nightingale Sheretine and Mariana. A happy Husband. Elegies on the death of Queene Anne. Songs and Sonnets*, published

The Interpreter, Wherein three principal Terms of State, much mistaken by the Vulgar, are clearly unfolded, published, poem,[196] defining 'Puritan,' 'Protestant,' and 'Papist'

Elizabeth Josceline, *The Mothers Legacy to her Unborn Child*, published; three editions by 1625[197]

---

195. Milton later read the work and explored many of its ideas.

196. A Puritan, the poem asserts, "says, with all his heart, 'God save the King / And all his issue!'"; a Protestant, on the other hand, "makes, within his heart, God of his King"; while the "Romanist is such an other things / As would, with all his heart, murder the King." The anonymous author makes little secret of which party merits proper attention. Charles Harding Firth, *Stuart Tracts*, pp. 235ff.

197. Elizabeth Brooke (b. c 1596; m. 1616) died just over a week after the birth of the child for whom she wrote her book; that her need to communicate with the child she knew she might not live to watch grow up touched a sympathetic chord among her contemporaries is abundantly witnessed by

Elizabeth Knyvet, Countess of Lincoln, *The Countess of Lincoln's Nursery,* including a plea for breast-feeding rather than the far more common practice of wet-nursing; foreword by Thomas Lodge

Gervase Markham and William Sampson, *Herod and Antipater, a Tragedy*

Thomas May, *The Heir an Excellent Gentleman*, play, published

Thomas Middleton, with William Rowley, *The Changeling*, performe*d*

John Owen, *Epigrammatum Ioannis Owen Oxoniensis Cambro-Britanni libri tres*

George Wither, *Juvenilia*, incomplete collection of his works; marks the end of Wither's effective poetic career, although he continued to write

Inigo Jones completes the Whitehall Banqueting House, one of the first structures in England to reflect the influence of the new Classical Palladian style

John Owen d. (b. 1564), the "English Martial"

Anne Murray b. (?), diarist (afterward Lady Anne Halkett)

Jane Savage m. Lord John St John Paulet, 5th Marquis of Winchester

Jan — Robert Carr, Earl of Somerset, and Frances Howard Carr, Countess of Somerset, released from confinement in the Tower

Jan 6—Twelfth Night — Ben Jonson, *The Masque of Augurs*

Jan 15 — Molière (Jean Baptiste de Poquelin) b

Jan 17 — John Hayward, *Davids Teares*, SR

Feb 9 — Sir Francis Bacon, *History of Henry VII*, SR (published 1629)

Feb 21 — John Johnson, *Arithmaticke*, SR

Mar 6 — Michael Drayton, *Poly-Olbion, Part I*

Mar 22 — Robert Cushman, *Sermon at Plimouth in New England 9 Dec 1621,* "together with a preface shewing the

---

the popularity of her book. Antonia Fraser, *The Weaker Vessel*, p. 69.

state of the countrie and the condition of its inhabitants," SR

— Massacre in the Virginia Colony

Mar 27 — *Pens Paradice or the Pens Alphabet*, SR

Mar 30 — Robert Vaughan, *Portraict of Nine Modern Worthies of the World*, SR[198]

Apr 13 — Nicholas Breton, *Strange News Discovered by a Strange Pilgrim*, SR

Apr 17 — Henry Vaughan and Thomas Vaughan b.; twins

Apr 22 — John Knight of Broadgates Hall, Oxford University, preaches a sermon advocating tyrannicide; Knight's action reported to James I by William Laud, who subsequently writes *Directions for controlling sermons in England*[199]

May 3 — Thomas Adams, *Cittie of Peace*, SR

May 16 — Dennis Webster, *The Blacksmiths Dream*, SR

— *Triumph for Brunswick and Lauenburgh in Westphalia*, SR, news pamphlet

May 18 — *Currant of News 14 May 1622*, SR

May 25 — William Crashaw, *Meat for Men*, SR, religious tract

May 27 — *Battailes in the Palatinate since the King's Arrival*, SR, news pamphlet

May 29 — Patrick Scott, *Atheisme Dismantled*, SR

— *Currant of News: Defeat of Leopolus by Brunswick*, SR, news pamphlet

Jun 10 — *More News from the Palatinate*, SR

Jun 19 — *A Relation of the Most Lamentable Burning of the Cittie of Corke, in the west of Ireland, in the Province of Monster, by Thunder and Lightning. With other most dolefull and miserable accidents, which fell out the last of May 1622 after the prodigious battell of the birds called Stares, which fought strangely over and neare that Citie the 12. & 14. Of*

---

198. The worthies include Mahomet, Soliman, Tamberlaine, Charles V, Scanderbeg, Edward III, Henry IV of France, and Sir Philip Sidney

199. It is a mark of Laud's increasing ascendancy that the prelate of a poor, undistinguished bishopric in Wales was selected to write the response, a copy of which was sent to the Archbishop of Canterbury.

May 1621. As it hath been Reported to divers Right honourable Persons, SR, pamphlet, printed in London for Nicholas Bourne and Thomas Archer. Refers to earlier broadside ballads, including:

— *A Battell of Birds, Most strangly fought in Ireland, upon the eight day of September last, 1621. Where neere unto the Citty of Corke, by the river Lee, weare gathered together such a multytude of Stares, or Starlings, as the like for number, was never seene in any age*, written to the tune of *Shores Wife or Bonny Nell*

— *The Lamentable Burning of the City of Corke...*, to the tune of *Fortune my Foe*

Jun 21 — Alexander Cooke, *Yet More Work for a Masse-Priest*, SR

Jun 29 — John Barclay, *Argenis*, SR, Latin romance

— William Murrell, *News from Newe England*, SR

Jul 1 — David Pareus, *Commentaries* on the Bible, condemned, declared seditious, and publicly burned

Jul 3 — Henry Peacham, *The Complete Gentleman*, educational treatise

— John Donne becomes a member of the Virginia Company

Jul 10 — Cutter, *A Pleasant New song, Of the Backes complaint, for bellies wrong: or a farwell to good fellowship*, to the tune of *A, B, C*, SR, broadside ballad

Aug 1 — *Weekly News throughout Christendome*, SR

Aug 9 — Nicholas Breton, *Oddes: or, All the World to Nothing*, SR

Aug 19 — *Courant from the 16. July to 6 Aug. 1622*, SR

Aug 27 — *Husband who Murdered 18 wives by Witchcraft in Prague*, SR

Aug 31 — *Map of the World*, SR

Sep 1 — William Laud debates the Jesuit Father Fisher at Windsor, with James I, Prince Charles, the Duke of Buckingham, and Buckingham's mother in attendance[200]

---

200. Mary Villiers, Buckingham's mother, was contemplating conversion to Rome. Laud therefore would have seen his debate as a public service to

Sep 2 — *Currant of News: Storm at Plimouth 3 Sept. 1622*, SR
Sep 11 — [Christopher Brooke], *Late Massacre in Virginia*, SR
— John Taylor, the Water Poet, *York for My Money: A Wherry Ferry Merry*, SR
Sep 20 — Sir Francis Bacon, *Historial Naturalis et Experimentalis*, SR
Sep 24 — J. P., *Anabaptismes Mistery of Iniquity Unmasked*, SR
Oct 31 — John Donne, *Sermon: They Fought from Heaven*, SR
Nov — Sir Francis Bacon, *Historia Ventum*
Nov 4 — Patrick Scott, *Calderwoods Recantation for Ministers in Scotland*, SR
Nov 8 — George Chapman, *Pro Vere Autumni Lachrymæ*, SR
Nov 28 — John Donne, *Sermon: Acts 1: 8, to the Virginia Company*, SR
Dec 15 — Edward Herbert, Lord Herbert of Cherbury, *De Veritate*, dedication to George Herbert, dated
Dec 27 — George Wither, *Cantica Sacra: Ten Hymns*, SR
Dec 28 — St. Francis de Sales, Bishop of Geneva, d. (b. 1567)[201]
Dec 31 — *Legend of the Jesuits*, SR

---

the Crown, the State, and the Church, particularly since he was able to sway her from her course (at least temporarily).

201. The Salesian mode of meditation, based on the writings of St. Francis, provided an alternative to the more rigidly constructed Ignatian meditation, modelled on the writings of Ignatius of Loyola. Many of Crashaw's poems, especially "The Weeper," repay close readings as Salesian meditations. See also Louis Martz, *The Poetry of Meditation*.

1623

Robert Aylett, *Joseph*, brief Biblical epic structured on the Book of Job

Francis Bacon, *History of the Reign of Henry VIII*, written (?; published 1629)

William Camden, *Remaines, concerning Britaine: the third impression reviewed, corrected, and encreased*, published

Tommaso Campanella, *Civitas Solis*, utopian treatise, published

Thomas Deloney, *Thomas of Reading. Or, The Sixe worthie Yeomen of the West*, 5th edition, corrected and enlarged, prose fiction

William Drummond of Hawthornden, *Flowres of Sion*, with *A Cypresse Grove*, published (reprint 1656, 1659)

John Ford, Thomas Dekker and William Rowley, *The Witch of Edmonton*

John Donne, *Three Sermons upon Special Occasions*

Philip Massinger, *The Bondsman*, written

Thomas Scott, *Vox Dei*, published, with an engraving of "Christ Triumphing over Sin, Death, and Hell," by Crispin van de Passe

John Webster, *Duchess of Malfi*, printed

George Wither, *Hymns and Songs of the Church*

Giles Fletcher d. (b. 1585)

Margaret Lucas, afterward Margaret Cavendish, Duchess of Newcastle, b.[202]

---

202. "Margaret Cavendish tried her hand at virtually every genre available: poetry, short-story, letter, biography, autobiography, essay, drama, natural

Ben Jonson m., St. Giles Cripplegate
Christopher Villiers created 1st Earl of Angelsey

Early 1623 — Sir Thomas Browne, enrolls at Broadgates Hall (after 1624, Pembroke College), Oxford
Jan 6—TWELFTH NIGHT — Ben Jonson *Time Vindicated to Himself and to His Honours*, masque
Jan 7 — James Forestus Hart, *Arraignment of Urines*, SR, medical treatise
Jan 16 — John Lambe [Giovanni Lambi], *A Revelation...of Alchemy*, SR, scientific treatise
Jan 20 — Philip Massinger, *The Duke of Milan*, SR
Jan 27 — *Currant of News: Vision in Freezland*, SR
Feb — Massacre at Amboyna; destruction of the English colony by Dutch forces
— Thereafter, a number of pamphlets and broadside ballads, both in English and in Dutch
Feb 7 — **Charles Diodati, Milton's closest childhood friend, removed from St. Paul's School to be matriculated at Trinity College, Oxford**
— Demosthenes, *Oration*, SR, translation
Feb 15 — Henry Cockeram, *English Dictionary...*, SR
Feb 17 — Joseph Hall, *Contemplations, Volume 6*, SR; *The Great Imposter*, SR, sermon; *Deceit of Appearances*, SR, sermon delivered before the Court at Theobalds
Feb 18 — Prince Charles and George Villiers set out on an incognito journey to Spain, as John and Thomas Smith, intending to negotiate for Charles to marry the Infanta
Mar 12 — George Herbert presents King James with an Oration and an Epigram upon the King's departure from Cambridge University
Spring — Nathaniel Butler, *The Unmasked Face of Our Colony in Virginia*, pamphlet, attacking government administration of the colony

---

history, and imaginary voyager" (Paul Salzman, *English Prose Fiction*, p. 293).

Easter term — Sir John Suckling matriculates at Trinity College, Cambridge

Apr 2 — *Arrival and Entertainment of Prince Charles in Spain*, SR, news pamphlet

Apr 3 — Vice-Chancellor of Cambridge, *Orations to His Majesty and the Ambassadors of Spain and Flaunders*, SR

Apr 10 — Privy Council considers allegations in Nathaniel Butler's attack on administration of the Virginia Colony

Apr 24-25 — Robert Herrick (b. 1591) ordained deacon and priest

Apr 28 — Thomas Gataker, *Discussion of the Popish Doctrine of Transsubstantiation*, SR

May — George Villiers created Duke of Buckingham while in Spain, the only non-Royal Duke in England and the first commoner raised to the rank in nearly a century[203]

May 14 — William Painter, *Chaucer New Painted*, SR

May 22 — Privy council confiscates all records of the Virginia Company

May 26 — Owen Feltham, *Resolves, Divine, Morall, Philosophicall*, SR

— William Petty b.

Jun 6 — Edmond Jessop, *Errors of English Anabaptists*, SR

Jun 13 — John Donne, *Sermon on Ascension Day*, SR

Jun 19 — Blaise Pascal b.

— Edward Sutton, *Anthropophagus: Caution for the Credulous*, SR

Jun 20 — Joseph Hall, Bishop of Exeter, *Contemplations on the Old Testament, Volume 7*, SR

Jul 2 — J. Walker, *Glass for Papists and Puritans*, SR, religious

---

203. Prince Henry had been Duke of Cornwall, and Prince Charles, Duke of York. In 1551, Sir John Dudley had been raised to Duke of Northumberland by Edward VI; the Dukedom of Norfolk had been occupied from 1553 to 1572, when the fourth duke had been found guilty of treason. Through his elevation to stature of Duke, Buckingham thus became the ranking peer, excluding only Prince Charles, in England. According to some contemporaries, Buckingham's greatest claim to the honor of a Dukedom lay in the shapeliness of his legs when he danced.

tract

Jul 4 — William Byrd, composer, d. (b. 1543)

Jul 5 — Andres de Almansa and Andres de Mendoza, *Two Royal Entertainments for Prince Charles by His Majesty... Spain*, SR

Jul 18 — *An Unpleasant Old Woman*, SR, ballad

— G. C. [George Carleton], *Madness of Astrologers...*, SR

— C. Colton, *Martirs Flowers*, SR, religious tract

Aug — Sir Henry Herbert, brother of George Herbert, knighted and subsequently appointed Master of the Revels at Court[204]

Aug 19 — *Dictionary in English and Latin*, SR

Aug 25 — J. M.. [John Mico], *Spirituall Food*, SR, 2nd edition of *a Pill to Purge Popery*

Aug 29 — Ælfric, *Saxon Treatise on the Old & New Testament*, SR

— [John Leech], *Epigrammatica*, SR

Sep — Sir Kenelm Digby knighted by James I

Sep 3 — *Book of Jigges in Three Parts*, SR, music

Sep 27 — Daniel Donne, *Subpoena from the Star-Chamber of Heaven*, SR

Sep 28 — *Abuses of the Romish Church Anatomized*, SR

Oct 2 — Ben Jonson, English translation of John Barclay's *Argenis*, SR[205]

Oct 5 — Prince Charles and George Villiers return from their incognito journey to Spain, their negotiations having failed

— Thomas Herbert, brother to Edward, Lord Herbert of Cherbury, and George Herbert, commands one of the ships carrying Charles to England

— Charles' return—and the failure of negotiations for a Spanish marriage—inspires spontaneous public celebrations eclipsed

---

204. As Master of Revels, Herbert exercised considerable influence over all dramatic presentations, at Court and otherwise.

205. The popularity of Barclay's Latin prose romance stimulated King James to request that Jonson translate the work into English; the manuscript was apparently among those lost in the fire that destroyed Jonson's home.

only by those commemorating the Gunpowder Plot[206]
— Thereafter: Edmund Waller composes his first public work, a poem based on Charles' journey, which establishes his reputation at Court
Oct 7 — John Taylor, *Britain's Joy: Prince Charles' Welcome in Spain*, SR
Oct 8 — George Herbert, *Oratio Caroli Reditum ex Hispanjis celebrans*, University Oration presented before Charles, apparently Herbert's last immediate contact with the Royal Family[207]
Oct 9 — *Wandering Jew*, SR, ballad
Oct 13 — Francis Bacon, *De Augmentis Scientiarum*, an expansion of *The Advancement of Learning*, SR (published 1629)
— *Joyful Return of Prince Charles*, SR
— Francis Quarles, *Job Militant*, SR
Oct 18 — George Close, *Rock of Religion Christ not Peter*, SR
Nov — King James again seriously ill
— George Herbert, M.P. for Montgomery
Nov 1 — Francis Beaumont and John Fletcher, *The Mayd of the Mill*, performed at court
Nov 7 — **John Milton signs as witness to the marriage contract between Anne Milton and Edward Phillips**
Nov 8 — William Shakespeare, *Mr. William Shakespeare's Comedies, Histories, and Tragedies* (First Folio), SR
Nov 9 — William Camden d. (b. 1549/1551)
Nov 14 — Edward Winslow, *Plymouth Plantation and the*

---

206. David Underdown argues that the two most memorable public events of the early seventeenth century were the Gunpowder Plot and the failure of the Spanish marriage: "A local scribe at Symondsbury in Dorset usually recorded in his chronology only variations in the weather and their impact on the harvest; the Prince's return from Spain the only political event he listed" (*A Freeborn People*, p. 50).

207. This oration may have marked the end of Herbert's hopes for advancement at Court, since Charles' political ambitions and directions were clearly opposed to Herbert's.

Providence of God, SR, religious pamphlet

Nov 22— **John Milton's sister Anne m. Edward Phillips**

Late Nov — John Donne striken with a serious illness, shortly before Dec 1

Dec 3 — Constance Donne, John Donne's eldest daughter, m. Edward Alleyn[208]

Dec 6 — Donne passes the crisis in his illness

Dec 7 — Samuel Ward, *Sermon: Peace Offering for the Prince's Return*, SR

Dec 13 — Thomas Taylor, *Glass for Gentle Woemen to Dress By*, SR, religious tract

Dec 14 — *128 Ballads Old, Often Printed...*, SR, ballads

Dec 17 — Thomas Reeve, *Mephibosheths Hearts Joy on the Sovereigns Safety*, SR

Dec 28 — James I issues writs for Parliament to assemble

---

208. Alleyn, aged fifty-seven, was a retired actor who had once garnered acclaim with his performances in Christopher Marlowe's *Tamburlaine*.

1624

John Milton, Paraphrases on Psalms 114 and 136

Sir Francis Bacon, *Considerations touching a War with Spain*, written (published 1629); *New Atlantis*, written (published 1627); *Magnalia Naturæ*, written (published 1627)

Camdeni Insigni, tributes to William Camden published at Oxford, including Charles Diodati's sole published poem and Sir Thomas Browne's first published work

Pierre du Moulin, *The Elements of Logick..., Translated...by Nathanael De-Lawne*

John Gee, *The Foot out of the Snare, or Detection of Practices and Impostures of Priests and Jesuits in England*, published

Edward Herbert, Lord Herbert of Cherbury, *De Veritate (Of Truth)*[209]

Herman Hugo, *Pia Desideria*, a continental emblem collection; subsequently a source for Francis Quarles

Henry King, "An Exequy," written on the death of his wife

W. B. [William Laud], *A Relation of the Conference between W. Laud and Mr Fisher, the Jesuite*, published at James's command, appended to Francis White, *A Replie to the Jesuit Fisher's answere*

Thomas Middleton, *A Game at Chess*, performed; Middleton's final play

Richard Montague, *A Gagg for the New Gospell? No: a New*

---

209. Cherbury's treatise is often considered one of the founding documents of English Deism; he was also a poet of some strength and note whose work, though modeled on that of John Donne, is considerably more philosophical, especially Neo-Platonic philosophy.

Gagg for an Old Goose, an extreme attack on Calvinist puritans

Francis Quarles, *Sion's Elegies*

John Smith of Jamestown, *The generall historie of Virginia, New England & the Summer Isles : together with The true travels, adventures and observations, and A sea grammar*

Edward Winslow, *Good Newes from New-England*, published

Esther Inglis d. (b. before 1574)

Samuel Crossman b.

War with Spain

Duke of Buckingham functions as the chief minister of England in all but name

James I pardons Robert Carr, 1st Earl of Somerset

Sidney Godolphin admitted to Exeter College, Oxford

Jan 6—TWELFTH NIGHT — Ben Jonson, *Neptune's Triumph for the Return of Albion*, scheduled, postponed, and finally abandoned[210]

Jan 9 — John Donne, *Devotions upon Emergent Occasions*, SR

Jan 12 — Elizabeth Josceline, *Mother's Legacy to her Child*, SR

Jan 18 — Henry Mason, *The Art of Lying Covered by Jesuits: Equivocation*, SR

Jan 24 — *A Gag for the Pope*, SR

— Henry Wotton, *Elements of Architecture*, SR

Jan 29 — William Udall, *Life, Death & Fortunes of the Blessed Mary Steward*, SR

Feb 16 — Lodovic Stuart, 2nd Duke of Richmond and Lennox, Lord High Steward, d.

Feb 19 — Parliament summoned by James, its opening delayed by the death of the Duke of Richmond and Lennox; George

---

210. According to rumors, the French and Spanish ambassadors refused to attend the same performance and it became impossible to determine which of the two should receive precedence by being invited to the premier performance of the masque; it was easier simply to cancel the masque.

Villers, 1st Duke of Duke of Buckingham, tries to manipulate Lords against Commons over the issue of negotiations with Spain

— Nicholas Ferrar serves as M.P., possibly renewing his friendship with George Herbert

— George Herbert, M.P. for Montgomery (through May 29, 1624)

— Edmund Waller, M.P. for Ilchester, Somerset, the first of five or six Parliaments in a career in the House of Commons that spanned over 50 years

Mar — John Donne appointed to the vicarage of St. Dunstan's in the West, Fleet Street; Izaak Walton, his later biographer, is among his parishioners

Mar 12 — Philip Massinger, *Bondsman*, SR

Mar 17 — Martin Fist, *Meat for Men: A Brief Catechism*, SR

— Thomas Reeve, *Seamans Sacred Safety*, SR, religious tract

Mar 20 — William Camden, *True History of Queen Elizabeth*, English translation from the French translation by Darcye, SR

Apr — Edward Herbert, Lord Herbert of Cherbury, recalled as Ambassador to France

May 3 — Anthony Magino, *Strange Prediction for the Present Year*, SR

May 6 — James I, last proclamation against Jesuits and seminary priests

— Thereafter: *A New-yeeres-gift for the Pope. Come see the difference plainly decided, betweene Truth and Falshood..., broadside ballad, printed, to the tunne of thomas, you cannot....*

Jun 1 — Henry Ainsworth, *Song of Songs in English Meter*, SR

Jun 2 — Anthony Wotton, *Run from Rome*, SR

Jun 11 — Thomas Beard, *Antechrist the Pope of Rome*, SR

— John Penkethman, *Table of Interest at a Rate of 10 or 8£/100*, SR, business tract

— George Herbert granted six-month leave of absence as

University Orator
Jun 24 — [Thomas Wray], *Sundry Laws against Swearing*, SR
— George Fox[211] b.
Jul 2 — Edward Gurney, *Romish Chaine*, SR
Jul 12 — John Smith of Jamestown, *History of Virginia, Summer Islands, New England...*, SR
Jul 27 — James Ussher, *Universality & Unity of the Church & Catholicke Faith*, SR
Jul 9 — Ben Jonson, *The Masque of Owls*, presented before Prince Charles at Kenilworth
Jul 28 — John Jeffries, *News from Virginia*, SR
Sep 7 — William Alexander, *Incouragement to the Colonies*, SR
Sep 10 — Thomas Sydenham b.
Sep 12 — *Graces & Prayers for Children*, SR
Sep 16 — Thomas Farnaby, *Figurae, Tropi et Schemata*, SR
— J. Morgan, *Most Bloody Murther by Tindall of his Mother*, SR
Sep 19 — Joseph Hall, preaches "The True Peace Maker" before James I at Theobalds[212]
Sep 22 — Joseph Hall, *The True Peace Maker*, SR
— Thomas Wise, *Animadversion upon Lilyes Grammer*, SR
Oct 7 — James Hart, *Anatomy of Urines*, SR, medical treatise
Oct 14 — Pierre du Moulin, *Logicke*, SR
— *Dutch tortures of the English at Ambona in the East Indies*, SR
Oct 18 — John Mayer, *Antidote against Popery*, SR
Oct 27 — Infant son baptized, born to William Davenant (18 years of age) and his wife Mary (surname unknown)
Nov 2 — William Andrews, *Divers Epigram...*, SR
— Daniell Cawdry, *Humilities the Saintes L:ivery*, SR

---

211. Fox published well over 250 tracts and pamphlets, establishing many of the basic tenets of the Quakers.

212. As with many sermons of the time, Hall's is consciously aware of explicit and implicit comparisons of James I—'England's Solomon'—with the biblical Solomon.

Nov 3 — George Herbert given permission to be ordained a deacon by lord Keeper John Williams, Bishop of Lincoln, under dispensation by the Archbishop of Canterbury

Nov 6 — William Crashaw, *Preparative to the Jubilee at Rome*, SR

Nov 15 — Sir Francis Bacon, *Apopthegemes owld and new*, SR

Nov 25 — William Gill, *Ignis fatuus, or the Elf Fyer of Purgatory*, SR

Dec 4 — Sir Francis Bacon; *Translations of Certain Psalms into English*, SR, dedicated to George Herbert

Dec 14 — *A Comfortable new Ballad of a Dreame of a Sinner, being very sore troubled with the assaults of Sathan*, broadside ballad, registered, to the tune of *Roger*

Dec 16 — George Herbert ceases to act as University Orator, his functions being taken by his deputy

1625

Milton[213] constantly in residence at Christ's College, Cambridge, until 1632, with occasional exceptions of vacations and short trips to family homes
John Milton, "*Ignavus satrapam*" (Slothful sleep…) (?)[214]
William Browne of Tavistock, *Britannia's Pastorals*, Parts I and II, reprinted
John Donne, *Five Sermons*
Ben Jonson, *The Staple of News*
Philip Massinger, *A New Way to Pay Old Debts*
William Morrell, *Nova Anglia*, poem based on New England experiences, published in Latin and English in London
Jan Bruegel, the Elder, d. (b. 1568); continental painter
Thomas Lodge d. (b. 1557/8)
Thomas Stanley b.
Edward Herbert, Lord Herbert of Cherbury, recalled from French embassy in disgrace
Henry King, D.D., Christ Church, Oxford University
James Ussher, appointed Archbishop of Armagh

Jan 1 — John Barclay, *Argenis,* SR
Jan 3 — Gervase Markham, *Souldiers Accidence*, SR

---

213. Hereafter, references to 'Milton' will refer exclusively to John Milton, Jr., the poet.

214. The eight Latin lines beginning "*Ignavus satrapam*" appear undated in *Milton's Commonplace Book*. I follow Merritt Y. Hughes (*Complete Poems*) in placing them after the Psalm paraphrases.

— Robert Sherwood, *The French Tutor*, SR, educational book
Jan 12 — **Anne Phillips b.** (Milton's niece)
— Theodor Heringe, *Triumph of the church over Water & Fire*, SR
— Humphrey Lind, *Ancient Characters of the Visible Church*, SR
Jan 22 — Thomas Jackson, *Errors concerning the Verity Unity and Attributes of Deity*, SR
Jan 24 — **Mary Powell, Milton's future wife, baptized**
Feb — James Shirley, *Loves Tricks*, licensed
Feb 12 — **Milton admitted to Christ's College, Cambridge, with William Chappell as his tutor**
Feb 18 — Richard Montagu, *Appello Caesarem. A Ivst Appeale from Two Vniust Informers*, attack on Calvinist puritans, SR
Feb 20 — John Penkethman, *Preparative to Purchase: Interest Table at 8£/100*, SR
Feb 26 — Alexander Spicer, *Elegies on the Death of Lord Chichester*, SR
Mar 2 — James Hamilton, 2nd Marquis of Hamilton d.
Mar 13 — Francis Bacon, *Essays*, 3rd edition (final format)
— J. Stradling, *Divine Poems to the Kings Most Excellent Majesty*, SR
Mar 25 — Giambattista Marino d. (b. 1569)[215]
Mar 26 (?)—**John Milton, Letter to Thomas Young, dated from London before Milton begins residence at Cambridge**
Mar 26 — James VI and I, King of Scotland and England, the "wisest fool in Christendom,"[216] d. (b. 1566)

215/ After whom "Marinism" is named, a continental poetic style analogous to Baroque in sculpture and architecture. Marino is often seen as an influence on the English Metaphysical poets, particularly Richard Crashaw.

216. Not the most capable of England's monarchs, James nonetheless proved more resilient (some might argue less overtly stupid) than his son Charles I. Quips made at the time referred to "King Elizabeth and Queen James," in recognition of the vast differences between his mode of ruling and his predecessor's.

Mar 27 — Accession of King Charles I, at age 25

Apr — First signs of Plague appear in London

Apr 3 — John Donne, *First Sermon Preached to King Charles,* presented; included shortly thereafter in *Four Sermons upon Special Occasions*, Donne's first published collection

Apr 4 — Sir Francis Bacon, *Operum*, SR

Apr 9 — **Milton matriculates at Christ's College, Cambridge University**

Apr (?) — **John Milton, *Prolusion V: In Scholis Publis***

— **John Milton, "*Apologus de Rustica et Hero*" (Fable of the Peasant and the Landlord)**

— **John Milton, "*Carmina Elegiaca*" (Elegiac Verse**

— **John Milton, "*Mane citus lectum fuge*"**

May 1 — MAY DAY — Proxy marriage between King Charles I and Henrietta Maria of France (sister of Louis XIII), in Paris

May 7 — James I buried in Westminster Abbey

— John Williams, Bishop of Lincoln, preaches *Great Britain's Solomon*, funeral sermon for James I, at Westminster Abbey

— Herbert Thorndike speaks the Cambridge University commemorative oration for James I, rather than George Herbert, who is still officially the University Orator

— Reported Plague deaths double over those of the previous week

May 18 — Charles I calls his first Parliament in Oxford

— George Herbert, M.P. for Montgomery

Jun — Plague deaths rise to 500 per week

Jun 5 — Orlando Gibbons, organist of the Chapel Royal for James I, d. (b. 1583)

Jun 12 — Arrival of Henrietta Maria in England

Jun 13 — Marriage of King Charles I to Henrietta Maria solemnized at St. Augustine's, Canterbury

Jun 18 — Charles I's first Parliament meets

Summer — Nicholas Ferrar leaves London due to Plague, founds Little Gidding, a non-monastic religious community in the vicinity of Bemerton, near Salisbury

Jul 10 — Henry King, *David's Enlargement: Two Sermons. Upon the Act Sunday, Being the 10th of Jul. 1625*

Jul 11 — Parliament adjourns because of the Plague

Jul 28 — Lady Eleanor Touchet Davies receives a vision that leads to a twenty-seven year career as a prophet[217]

— Thereafter: Lady Eleanor Davies, *Warning to the Dragon and All His Angels* the first printed of over sixty prophetic tracts; the introduction concludes with the anagram "A snare o devil" and the tract with "O a Sure Daniel

Jul 31 — 5,000 dead from Plague

Aug or Sep — John Florio, d., of the plague (b. 1553?)

Aug 12 — Parliament dissolved

Aug 29 — John Fletcher d. (b. 1579), of the plague

Aug 31 — 19,000 dead from Plague

Sep — 40,000 dead from Plague; death count still reaching 5,000 per week[218]

Oct 10 — Sir Arthur Gorges buried (b. 1557)

Nov — Only 100 reported dead from Plague during the first week

Dec — John Fletcher, buried at St. Saviour's, Southwark

Dec 10 — **Charles Diodati, B.A., Trinity College, Oxford**

Dec 21 — George Herbert, in residence at the house of Sir John Danvers, his step-father; John Donne also in residence, due to the Plague

---

217. She was "Awakened by a voyce from HEAVEN," which she identified as the prophet Daniel, who told her that "There is Ninteene yeares and a halfe to the day of Judgement and you as the meek Virgin" Throughout her career, she associated herself, through anagrams on her various names (Eleanor Davies, Eleanor Audley, Eleanor Touchet) with the prophet Daniel. ("Eleanor Davies, Her Appeal to the High Court"; Esther S. Cope, *Prophetic Writings*, p. xi.)

218. Until 1665, this was considered the "Great Plague." Coincidentally—and for those involved, at times frighteningly—the accession of a Stuart monarch seemed to coincide with outbreaks of the Plague, possibly one reason for the sense of foreboding and doom that early settled on London thirty years later when a new outbreak followed by only a few years the accession of the third Stuart king.

1626

Sir Francis Bacon, *The New Atlantis*

Nicholas Breton, *Fantastickess: Serving for a Perpetual Prognostication*

William Davenant, *The Tragedy of Albovine, King of the Lombards*, written but not produced, Davenant's first play

Thomas Deloney, *The Pleasant Historie of John Winchcomb, In his yonguer yeares called Jack of Newbery, the famous and worthy Clothier of England...*, 10th issue, prose fiction, published

Ben Jonson, *The Staple of News* (or 1625?)

Philip Massinger, *The Roman Actor*, written

Sir Thomas Overbury, *His Observations in his Travels upon the State of the Seventeen Provinces, as They Stood Anno Domini 1609...*, published

Henry Parrot, *Cures for the Itch. Characters. Epigrams. Epitaphs. By H. P*

William Prynne, *The Perpetuitie of a Regenerate Mans Estate*, Prynne's first published political tract[219]

Peter Ramus, *The Art of Logick. Gathered out of Aristotle and set in due forme...by Peter Ramus*, translated by Anthony

---

219. "The most famous Star Chamber case in which both Laud and the elder Vane participated was that of William Prynne, a Presbyterian lawyer who believed that he had been called into the world to seek out sin and write books against it. From the standpoint of sheer production, he was triumphantly successful in this calling. As Anthony Wood said, 'I verily believe, that if rightly computed, he wrote a sheet for every day of his life'" (J. H. Adamson and H. F. Holland, *Sir Harry Vane*, p. 127).

Wotton

George Sandys, translation of Ovid, *Metamorphosis* (enlarged, 1632)

Thomas Scot, *Sir Walter Raleigh's Ghost is England's Forewarner*, tract

James Shirley, *The Wedding*

Sir William Vaughan, *The Golden Fleece*, description of Newfoundland, published in London

John Wilson, *A song of Deliverance for the Lasting Remembrance of Gods wonderful Works*, didactic poem by a New England colonist

Nicholas Breton d. (b. 1555?), shortly after the publication of *Fantastickes*

Salomon de Caus[220] d. (b. 1576), landscape architect and horticultural engineer; designed gardens at Somerset House and elsewhere

Oliver Ormerod d. (b. ca. 1580)

William Rowley d. (b. 1585)

Emeric Bigot b., in Rouen, France

Mary Boyle b.[221]

Henry Oldenburg b. (?), in Bremen, Germany

Christoph Peter b.

Aubrey de Vere, 20th Earl of Oxford, b. (d. 1703)

War with France

Sir Thomas Fairfax enters St. John's College, Cambridge

Edward King admitted to Christ's College, Cambridge

Jan — Sir Robert Howard b.

Jan 1 — Henry Lawes appointed Epistoller in the Chapel Royal

Jan 15 — John Donne, *The First Sermon after our Dispersion by the Sickness*, delivered at St. Dunstan's

Feb 2 — King Charles I, crowned at Westminster; Queen

---

220. Credited with inventing the steam engine.

221. Mary Boyle Rich, later Countess of Warwick, left an autobiography that remained unpublished until 1848

Henrietta Maria refuses to participate in—or even to watch—the Protestant ceremony

Feb 9 — Charles I opens his second Parliament; debate in Commons gradually turns to accusations against Buckingham as Lord Admiral for failure to execute properly the War against Spain

— Sir John Elyot emerges as a leading orator and opponent of Charles and Buckingham; imprisoned for his outspokenness

Feb 18 — Cyril Tourneur d. (b. 1580?), in Kinsdale, Ireland

Feb 20 — John Dowland, song writer and lute player, buried (b. 1563)

Feb 24 — John Donne, *A Sermon Preached to the King's Majesty*, presented

Mar — **Milton's quarrel with his tutor, William Chappell, which results in his being rusticated from college; Lent term**

— **Milton returns to college; he is assigned a new tutor, Nathaniel Tovey**

Mar 12 — **John Aubrey, Milton's first biographer, b.**

Mar 15 — Charles I thanks Commons for their expressed loyalty to him and to the Crown, but notes that certain members seem intent on destroying those he has favored, particularly the Duke of Buckingham[222]

— Commons determines that to ease England's current crises, the Duke of Buckingham must be removed from power[223]

Mar 25 — Commons' Committee for Evils, Causes and Remedies

---

222. Roger Lockyer, *Buckingham*, p. 313.

223. Having demonstrated to their own satisfaction their ability to maneuver and defeat one king's third-in-command, Sir Francis Bacon, Commons essentially decided to go after another king's second-in-command, Buckingham. Throughout much of the debate over both Bacon and Buckingham, Commons insisted on their loyalty to the King, who had, after all, only been persuaded from his true course by evil and corrupt councilors. Not for another two decades would Charles himself—and the monarchy—become the focus of direct attack.

presents accusations against the Duke of Buckingham

May 27 — William II, Stadtholder of Orange, b.

Apr 9—EASTER SUNDAY — Sir Francis Bacon, First Baron Verulam, Viscount St. Albans, d. (b. 1561)

Apr 20 — Commons determines to proceed formally against Buckingham

— Alice Barnham Bacon, widow of Sir Francis Bacon, m. John Underhill, her gentleman-usher

Apr/May — **John Milton, *Elegy I: Ad Carolum Diodatum* (To Charles Diodati)**

May 10 — *The Commons' Declaration and Impeachment against the Duke of Buckingham, presented to the House of Lords*[224]

Jun — Charles creates six new peers to vote for Buckingham in the House of Lords but the outcome still remains equivocal

Jun 1 — Charles forces Cambridge University to elect Buckingham its Chancellor; in spite of the King's pressure,

---

224. The first paragraph of the indictment lists Buckingham's official titles and honors: "George, Duke, Marquis and Earl of Buckingham, Earl of Coventry, Viscount Villiers, Baron of Whaddon, Great Admiral of the kingdoms of England and Ireland, and of the principality of Wales and of the dominions and islands of the same, of the town of Calais and the marches of the same, and of Normandy, Gascony, and Guienne, General Governor of the seas and ships of the said Kingdoms, Lieutenant General, Admiral, Captain General and Governor of His Majesty's Royal Fleet and Army, lately set forth, Master of the Horse of our Sovereign Lord the King, Lord Warden, Chancellor, and Admiral of the Cinque Ports and of the members thereof, Constable of Dover Castle, Justice in Eyre of all the forests and chases on this side of the river of Trent, Constable of the Castle of Windsor, Gentleman of His Majesty's Bedchamber, one of His Majesty's most Honourable Privy Council in his realms both in England, Scotland, and Ireland, and Knight of the most honourable Order of the Garter...." The articles of impeachment then specify that among his "misdemeanours, misprisions, offences, crimes, and other matters," Buckingham is not only too young and too inexperienced to meet his multiplicity of responsibilities, "which said offices were both carefully and sufficiently executed by several persons of such wisdom, trust, and ability"; but that he gained several of the most important through bribery and the exchange of money. (Samuel Gardiner, *Constitutional Documents*, p. 7-8)

the election is close and hotly contested

Jun 4 — Nicholas Ferrar ordained a deacon by William Laud

Jun 8 — *The Humble Answer and Plea of George Duke of Buckingham to the Declaration and Impeachment made against him before your Lordships, by the Commons House of Parliament*, presented to the House of Lords

Jun 12 — "Terrible Monday," accompanied by thunderstorms believed to have been conjured by Dr. John Lambe, the Duke's magician[225]

Jun 15 — Charles I dissolves Parliament, begins the thirteen-year Personal Rule without Lords or Commons

Jun 20 — William Laud, nominated as Bishop of Bath and Wells

Jun 30 — Sir Thomas Browne, B.A., Pembroke College, Oxford University

Jul 5 — George Herbert, already ordained a deacon, installed by proxy into the canonry and prebend of Leighton Ecclesia and canon of Lincoln Cathedral

Jul 7 — Charles I, *The King's Letter and Instructions for the Collection of a Free Gift*, presented to the people of England, with instructions to County Justices of the Peace, as a means of financing government without recourse to Parliament; the request fails

Jul 13 — Robert Sidney, 2nd Earl of Leicester, d.(b. 1563)

— George Villiers, 1st Duke of Buckingham, installed as

---

225. "On 12 June 1626, the day that the King and Buckingham were believed to have decided to abort the impeachment proceeding by dissolving Parliament, there was a great thunderstorm in London, apparently accompanied by a tornado—a 'tempest whirling and ghoulish'—which opened the graves of some of the victims of the previous year's plague epidemic. The day was long remembered as the 'terrible Monday': some thought Dr. Lambe had caused it, and a gentleman was reported to have said that 'one of the Duke's devils did arise' in it" (David Underdown, *A Freeborn People*, p. 35). Underdown continues by nothing that while modern minds might scoff at the idea of magically conjured storms and devils, many during the century would have believed such stories and based their actions, their beliefs, and their lives upon them.

Chancellor of Cambridge University; George Herbert acts as University Orator for the last time

Aug 18 — Jeremy Taylor admitted to Gonville and Caius College, Cambridge

Sep/Oct — Samuel Purchas d. (b. 1577), travel wriiter

Sep 16 — Richard Ridding resigns his position as Beadle of Cambridge University, after some thirty years of service

Sep 19 — Richard Ridding makes his will

— **Thereafter: John Milton,** ***Elegy II: In Obitum Praeconis Academici Cantabrigiensis*** **(On the Death of the Beadle of Cambridge University), written in memory of Richard Ridding**

Sep 23 — Charles I, *The Commission and Instructions for Raising the Forced Loan in Middlesex*, presented to George Abbot, Archbishop of Canterbury and forty others, as a means of raising revenues without Parliament

Sep 25 — Lancelot Andrewes, Bishop of Winchester, d. (b.1555), leaving John Donne acknowledged as pre-eminent preacher of the day

— **Thereafter: John Milton,** ***Elegy III: In Obitum Praesulis Wintoniensis*** **(On the Death of the Bishop of Winchester), in memory of Lancelot Andrewes**

Oct 4 — Richard Cromwell b. (d. 1712)[226], third son of Oliver Cromwell

Oct 6 — Nicholas Felton, Bishop of Ely, d. (b. 1556)[227]

— **Thereafter: John Milton,** ***In Obitum Praesulis Eliensis*** **(On the Death of the Bishop of Ely)**

21 Oct — John Gostlin, Vice-Chancellor of Cambridge University, d.(b. 1566)

— **Thereafter: John Milton,** ***In Obitum Procancellarii Medici***

---

226. Following the Restoration, Richard Cromwell remained on the Continent until about 1680, living under the name of John Clarke. He returned to England and, still using the name of Clarke, passed thirty-two uneventful years, until his death in his seventies (12 July 1712).

227. Friend of Lancelot Andrewes, fellow and Master at Pembroke College, Cambright, and a translator of the King James Version of the Bible.

(On the Death of the Vice-Chancellor, a Physician)

Oct 26 — Henry Lawes appointed a Gentleman of the Chapel Royal

Nov (?)— **John Milton, *In Quintum Novembris* (On the Fifth of November), Latin mock-heroic poem on the Gunpowder Plot**

— **John Milton, Latin epigrams on the Gunpowder Plot: "*In Proditionem Bombardicam*" (On the Gunpowder Plot); "*In Eandem*" (On the Same), "*In Eandem*," "*In Eandem*,"; "*In Invetorem Bombardæ*" (On the Inventor of Gunpowder)**

— **John Milton, "The Fifth Ode of Horace, Lib. I"**

Nov 8 — Richard Ridding's will proved

Nov 11 — Lancelot Andrewes, Bishop of Winchester, buried

Dec 8 — Christina, afterward Queen of Sweden, b

— Sir John Davies d. (b. 1569)[228]

---

228. Author of *Orchestra, or a Poem of Dancing*, an archetypal Elizabethan illustration of the pervasive belief in Cosmic Order and Harmony; the breakdown of this belief is one of the hallmarks of the seventeenth-century and of the transition from a Renaissance to a Modern conception of the universe.

1627

John Bastwick, *Elenchus religionis papisticæ*, published, anti-Episcopacy tract

Drayton, Michael, *The Battaile of Agincourt*, poem

Phineas Fletcher, *Locustæ; or, The Apollyonists*[229]; *Britain's Ida*

George Hakewell, *Apology or Declaration of the Power and Providence of God in the Government of the World*[230]

Thomas James, *Index Generalis*, published[231]

Mallery, Phillippe de, *Typus Mundi*, Continental emblem collection; later source for Francis Quarles

Thomas May, complete translation of Lucan, *Pharsalia*

Joseph Mede, *Clavis Apocalyptica* (Key of the Revelations), Latin treatise, combines mathematics, history, and theology to determine the date for the End of the World—between

---

229. Similarities between this brief epic and Milton's Latin poems on the Gunpowder Plot, particularly *In Quintum Novembris*, have suggested to some scholars that the younger poet may have read Fletcher's work while it was still in manuscript. Albert C. Baugh indicates that the poem had been circulating in manuscript for some fifteen years before its publication (*Literary History of England* 682).

230. Within a year, Milton would be defending Hakewell's conclusions.

231. Based on an historical series of Catholic lists of proscribed books, generally titled an *Index*, James' list, prepared during his tenure as librarian at the Bodleian Library, became in effect a list of books to be acquired. According to Jonathan Green (*Encyclopedia*, p. 133), the Bodleian continued to use James' *Index* as a guide to buying books well into the twentieth century.

1625 and 1716, with either 1654 or 1670 most likely as possibilities[232]

Lady Katherine Paston, Correspondence 1603-1627 completed (published, 1941)

William Prynne, *The Perpetuities of a Regenerate Mans Estate*, 2nd edition[233]

John Hall b. (d. 1701)

Susanna Harvey b. (d. 1709; afterward Susanna Hopton

Dorothy Osborne b

Cyriack Skinner b., grandson of Sir Edward Coke

Alice Wandesford b. (d.1706)[234]

Christopher Wase b

Edmund Waller m. Anne Banks, considered one of the greatest "matrimonial prizes of the day"[235]

Sir John Suckling admitted to the Inns of Court

Robert Herrick appointed Chaplain to George Villiers, 1st Duke of Buckingham

John Cleveland admitted to Christs College, Cambridge

Humphrey Moseley admitted freeman to the Stationers Company

Jan 12 — William Davenant, *The Cruell Brother. A Tragedy*, licensed by Sir Henry Herbert, Master of the Revels; thereafter produced at Blackfriars Theater by "His Majesty's Servants"; Davenant's first stage production

Jan 25 — Robert Boyle b., fourteenth of fifteen children of Lady

---

232. Christopher Hill, *Milton and the English Revolution*, p. 33.

233. A suggestion of Prynne's lifelong devotion to religious reform is found in the fact that this 'pamphlet' runs some 656 pages.

234. Alice Wandesford Thornton wrote an extensive *Autobiography*, published in 1873.

235. Julia Cartwright, *Sacharissa*, p. 17. Cartwright continues to note that Waller's arranging the match was "a feat which, according to Clarendon, made him more famous than all his wit, fine arts and poetry."

Catherine Fenton and Richard Boyle, 1st Earl of Cork[236]

Feb 8 — Robert Sibthorp preaches a sermon in Northampton in which he argues the King's absolute power to do "whatsoever pleaseth him. Where the word of the King is there is power"—a challenge to Puritans and other Dissenters[237]

— Thereafter: Robert Sibthorp, *Apostolic Obedience*, licensed by Bishop Laud over the objections of Archbishop Abbott; Laud rewarded by a seat on the Privy Council

Mar/Apr (?)— **John Milton, *Elegy IV: Ad Thomam Junium, Præceptorem suum, apud mercatores Anglicos Hamburgæ agentes Pastoris munere Fungentem* (To Thomas Young, His Tutor, performing the duties of a pastor among the English merchants resident in Hamburg)**

— **John Milton, *Prolusion IV: In Rei Cujuslibet interitu...***

Mar 25 — Ann Harrison b. (afterward Ann Fanshawe), memoirist

Apr 1 — John Donne accused by William Laud, Bishop of Bath and Wells, of preaching Low Church doctrine before the King

Apr 4 — Charles I forgives Donne, due to the influence of court favorites

Apr 19 — Sir John Beaumont d. (b. 1583)

May 3 — Edward Russell, 3rd Earl of Bedford, d. (b. 1573)

May 27/31 — Lucy Harington Russell, Countess of Bedford and one of the period's great patrons of literature and art,[238] d. (b. 1581), leaving no living children

---

236. Richard Boyle was generally accounted the wealthiest man in England.

237. Charles Carlton, *Archbishop William Laud*, p. 63.

238. Lucy Harrington Russell, "wife of Edward, third Earl of Bedford, was easily the most important patroness of the Jacobean court, except for Queen Anne herself" (Barbara K. Lewalski, "Lucy, Countess of Bedford," p. 52). Among the poets and musicians indebted to her for patronage were John Donne, Michael Drayton, Ben Jonson, Samuel Daniel, John Dowland, John Davies of Hereford, and George Chapman. Her circle of relatives included Sir Philip Sidney and Sir John Harington, translator of Ariosto.

Jun — Charles dispatches a fleet under the Duke of Buckingham to raise the siege of La Rochelle on the Isle of Rhé
Jun 8 — Magdalene Newport Herbert Danvers buried
Jul 1 — John Donne, memorial sermon for Magdalene Newport Herbert Danvers, preached at Chelsea
Jun 11 — **Milton lends Richard Powell (Mary Powell's father and his future father-in-law) £500, a debt that will have repercussions for the remainder of Milton's life**
Jul 4 — Thomas Middleton buried (b. 1580), at Newington
Jul 7 — John Donne, *A Sermon of Commemoration of the Lady Danvers*, published
— George Herbert, *Memoriæ Matris Sacrum*, nineteen Greek and Latin memorial elegies for his mother, SR[239]
Oct-Nov — Efforts to relieve the Island of Rhé and raise the siege of La Rochelle fail; Buckingham returns to England
Dec 29 — Henry Condell, associate of William Shakespeare, and 'projector' of the First Folio, buried, St. Mary Aldermanbury

---

[239]. These memorial poems were the only of Herbert's poetic achievements to see print during his lifetime.

1628

John Milton, "On the Death of a Fair Infant Dying of a Cough" (1626?)

John Milton, *De Idea Platonica quemadmodum Aristoteles Intellexit* (On the Platonic Idea as Understood by Aristotle), possibly written as late as 1630 (?)

John Milton, *Prolusion I: Utrum Dies an Nox præstantior sit?* (?)

John Milton, *Prolusion III: Contra Philosophiam Scholasticam* (?)

Henry Burton, *The Seven Vials*

Sir Edward Coke, *First Part of the Institutes of the Lawes of England*, in four parts through 1644

John Earle, *Micro-cosmographie. Or, a Peece of the World Discovered; in Essays and Characters,* (1st edition; enlargements in 1629, 1633)

Joseph Fletcher, *The Historie of the Perfect-Cursed-Blessed Man*

Phineas Fletcher, *Venus and Anchises: Brittain's Ida*, published, attributed to Edmund Spenser by Thomas Walkley, the publisher

John Ford, *The Lover's Melancholy*, produced

Joseph Hall, Bishop of Exeter, *Contemplations upon the Principal Passages in the Holy Story*, 8 volumes, completed (1612-1628)

Joseph Hall, Bishop of Exeter, *The Old Religion: A treatise of... the differences betwixt the Reformed and Roman Church...*,

published

William Harvey, *Exercitatio anatomica de motu cordis et sanguinis in animalibus* (Anatomical Essay on the Motion of the Heart and Blood in Animals), published

Thomas Hobbes, translation of Thucydides, *History of the Peloponnesian Wars*

P. M. [Pierre Matthieu], *The powerfull favorite, or, The Life of Ælius Sejanus*, translated twice; implied direct parallels with the Duke of Buckingham

Thomas May, translation of Virgil, *Georgicks*

William Prynne, *Healthes Sickness*, attack on current manners; *The Unloveliness of Lovelocks*, published, attack on the 'womanish' fashion for long hair[240]

Sir Walter Raleigh, *The Prerogative of Parliaments in England*, published (written 1615?)

Henry Reynolds, *Tasso's Aminta Englisht*, published

Thomas Spenser, *The Art of Logicke, delivered in the precepts of Aristotle and Ramus*, published

George Wither, *Britain's remembrancer, containing a narration of the plague lately past; a declaration of the mischiefs present; and a prediction of judgments to come*, published (extracts rpt 1642, 1643)

Samuel Rowlands d. (?, as late as 1630; b. 1570?)

Alexander Leighton, *Syon's Plea against the Prelacy*, published, subsequently ordered burned (1630?)

Roger Manwaring, *Religion and Allegiance*, collected sermons, burned by order of Charles I; *By the King, a proclamation for the calling in, and suppressing of two sermons, preached and printed by Roger Manwaring, Doctor in Diuinity, intituled Religion and Allegiance*

Richard Montagu appointed Bishop of Chichester, recognizing

---

240. David Underdown sees in such texts, with their strict compartmentalizing of "masculine" and "feminine" characteristics equated with virtues and vices respectively, a literary manifestation of the people's fear of political inversions during the period. See *A Freeborn People*, "Custom and Inversions,'"pp.43-67)

his support for Charles I and William Laud
George Villiers, 1st Duke of Buckingham, publicly if anonymously identified with the tyrant, Louis XI of France

Jan — Richard Montagu, *Appello Caesarem*, burned
Jan 22 — Anne Phillips buried, St. Martin-in-the-Fields (Milton's niece)
Jan 28 — George Herbert officially resigns his position as University Orator, Cambridge[241]; Robert Creighton appointed his replacement
Jan 30 — George Villiers, 2nd Duke of Buckingham, b
Mar 15 — John Bull, composer, d.(b. 1562?), in exile in Antwerp, Netherlands
Mar 17 — Charles I's Third Parliament convenes
— Oliver Cromwell enters Commons as the elected M.P. for Huntington
Mar 28 — Thomas Young returned to England, inducted into vicarages in Stowmarket, Suffolk
Apr 25 — Sir William Temple b
May 1 — **John Milton, Elegy VII, written**
May 20 — **John Milton, Letter to Alexander Gill, written**
May 27 — *Petition of Right* passed by Commons and Lords
— Sir John Elyot again a leader of the opposition
Jun — **John Milton, "Naturam non Pati Senium" (That Nature is not Subject to Old Age), verse exercises**
Jun 2 — Charles I gives Parliament an unsatisfactory, hedging response to the *Petition of Right*, leading to further anger against the Duke of Buckingham, the "common enemy of the kingdom"[242]
Jun 5 — Sir Edward Coke refers in Parliament to Buckingham as "the cause of all our miseries," in spite of James' explicit

---

241. Just as his accepting the position indicated his intention to pursue a political career, so his resignation indicates his new decision to dedicate himself to the Church and withdraw from social and political spheres.

242. Roger Lockyer, *Buckingham*, p. 439.

prohibition against such claims[243]
— Edward Kirton, in a speech before Commons: "The Duke is an enemy to the kingdom, and so to the King; and I hope every good subject will before long draw his sword against the enemies of the King and kingdom"[244]
— Hugh Pyne: "I think we can hardly tax the man in question without blaming a greater power"[245]

Jun 7 — The petition exhibited to His Majesty by the Lords Spiritual and Temporal, and Commons in this present Parliament assembled, concerning divers Rights and liberties of the Subjects, with the King's Majesty's Royal Answer thereunto in full Parliament (The Petition of Right), presented to Charles
— Charles I appeases Commons by accepting the Petition of Right according to traditional formula

Jun 13-14 — John Lambe, an astrologer associated with the Duke of Buckingham, hence called the "Duke's Wizard," killed by a London mob
— Thereafter: Martin Parker, "The Tragedy of Doctor *Lambe*, The great suposed Coniurer, who was wounded to death by Saylers and other Lads, on Fryday the 14. of June 1628. And dyed in the Poultry Counter, neere Cheap-side, on the Saturday following,"[246] broadside Ballad, to the tune of

---

243. David Underdown, *A Freeborn People*, p. 36.

244. David Underdown, *A Freeborn People*, p. 38-39.

245. David Underdown, *A Freeborn People*, p. 40. Underdown identifies this statement as the sole recorded suggestion of the Monarch's complicity in Buckingham's guilt, adding, "it is astonishing that no action was taken against him, It may be that hardly anyone heard him—during his speech the members' attention would have been fixed on the Speaker, who just entering the House with the message adjourning them until the next day" (pp. 40-41).

246. The date Parker gives in his ballad is incorrect; Lambe was assaulted on the 13th and died on the 14th. The broadside also includes a woodcut of a magician conjuring, taken from the first edition of Christopher Marlowe's Dr. Faustus.

Gallants come away

— *A Briefe Description of the Notorious Life of John Lambe, otherwise called Doctor Lambe. Together with his Ignominious Death*, printed in Amsterdam

— John Rous, Bulstrode Whitelock, Joseph Mead and others, journal entries and other references to Lambe's death[247]

Jun 18 — Coronation of Charles I at Edinburgh, Scotland

Jun 20 — William Cavendish, 2nd Earl of Devonshire and patron to Thomas Hobbes, d. (b. 1590

Jun 23 — Roger Manwaring makes his submission to Commons for his earlier publication of *Religion and Allegiance*

Jul — **John Milton, "At a Vacation Exercise in the College, Part Latin, Part English**

— **John Milton, *Prolusion VI: Exercitationes nonnunquam...***

Jul 2 — **John Milton, Letter to Alexander Gill, the Younger, written, perhaps describing the previous set of verses**

— William Laud consecrated Bishop of London

Jul 8 — **Charles Diodati, M.A., Trinity College, Oxford**

Jul 9 — Alice Davis found guilty of murdering her husband

— Thereafter: "The Unnaturall Wife: Or, the lamentable Murther, of one goodman *Davis*, Locke-Smith in Tuytle-streete, who was stabbed to death by his Wife, on the 29. of June 1628. For which fact, She was Araigned, Condemned, and Adiudged to be Burnt to Death in *Smithfield*, the 12. Of July 1628," broadside ballad, printed by Margaret Trundle, widow of John Trundle; to the tune of *Bragandary*

Jul 10 — Sir John Danvers (George Herbert's step-father) m. Elizabeth Dauntesey

Jul 21 — **John Milton, Letter to Thomas Young**

Jul 22 — Sir Thomas Wentworth raised to the peerage

---

247. While Lambe's death is not in itself significant historically or politically, it did supply an opportunity for England to express its almost irrational hatred of the Duke of Buckingham. Lambe's association with Buckingham figures prominently in the many contemporary references to his death.

Jul 27 — Peter Smart, sermon, refers to the Cathedral altar as a "damnable idol"[248]

Aug — George Villiers, 1st Duke of Buckingham, prepares a second fleet to sail against the Isle of Rhé

Aug 23 — George Villiers, 1st Duke of Buckingham, assassinated (b. 1592), by John Felton

Sep — Fulke Greville, 1st Lord Brooke, d. (b. 1554)

Sep 1 — Alexander Gill, the Younger, publicly remarks on the King's stupidity and the Duke of Buckingham's failings, while admiring Felton's courage

Sep 4 — Alexander Gill, the Younger, arrested in his classroom at St. Paul's School for drinking to Felton's heath[249]

Sep 7 — The Duke of Buckingham's fleet sets sail for the Isle of Rhé under the command of Robert Bertie, 1st Earl of Lindsey; returns in October in defeat

Sep 18 — George Villiers, 1st Duke of Buckingham, buried, in Westminster Abbey

Oct 2 — Charles I indicates his intention to elevate William Laud to the See of Canterbury when it becomes vacant

Oct 19 — Ben Jonson ill with stroke; partially paralytic; stroke probably occurred between October 19, 1628, and January 19, 1629

Oct 28 — Protestant La Rochelle falls to French Catholic forces

— Thereafter: Martin Parker, "Rochell her yeelding to the obedience of the French King, on the 8. of October 1628. After a long siege by Land and Sea, in great penury and want," broadside ballad, to the tune of *In the dayes of old*

---

248. In addition, Smart "added that bishops were 'Rome's dastardly brood, still doting on their mother, the painted harlot of Rome', and defined an Arminian as an 'arch-heretic and enemy of God,'" giving High-Church Anglicans such as William Laud a foretaste of Puritan reactions to reforms advocated by Charles I and his Bishops (Charles Carlton, *Archbishop William Laud*, p. 62).

249. For particulars on the affair, especially the extent of Gill's comments about Buckingham, James I, and Charles I, see Christopher Hill, *Milton and the English Revolution*, p. 28. Gill's sentence is detailed in *Milton Encyclopedia*, Vol. 3, p. 129.

Nov 6 — Star Chamber sentences Alexander Gill, the Younger., to severe penalties; by November 22, however, he has been imprisoned, with none of the other stipulations followed

Nov 27 — John Felton brought to trial, pleads guilty, and is forthwith sentenced to death

Nov 29 — John Bunyan baptized

— John Felton hanged at Tyburn

Dec — Thomas Wentworth, 1st Earl of Strafford, appointed President of the Council of the North

1629

John Milton, *Prolusion II: De Sphærarum Concentu*
John Milton, "Song: On May Morning"
Lancelot Andrewes, *XCVI Sermons*, edited by William Laud, Archbishop of Canterbury, and John Buckeridge, Bishop of Ely, first of four volumes of collected sermons; *Two Answers to Cardinall Perron, and two Speeches in the Starr-Chamber,* published
Sir John Beaumont, *Bosworth-field*, collection of poems
Sir William Davenant, *The Siege* and *The Just Italian*, plays, licensed and produced; *The Tragedy of Albovine, King of the Lombards*, published, Davenant's first published play, including commendatory verses by Edward Hyde, future Earl of Clarendon, dedication to Robert Carr, Earl of Somerset
Thomas Morton, *A Treatise of the Threefold State of Man*, published
James Shirley, *Wedding*, published
John Taylor, the Water Poet, *Wit and Mirth*, jest-book
Lady Katherine Paston d. (b. 1578)
Thomas Shelton d. (?)
John Speed d. (b. 1552).[250]
Ezekiel Spanheim b. (d. 1710), in Geneva
Katherine Boyle m. Arthur Jones, 2nd Viscount Ranelagh
Sir Thomas Browne begins European medical studies at

---

250. Speed, the author of a *History of Great Britaine under the Conquests of ye Romans, Danes and Normans*, was married for 57 years to his wife, who bore him 22 children (according to his monument in the Church of St. Giles, Cripplegate)

Montpelier, Padua, and Leiden (to 1633)
William Laud made Chancellor of Oxford
Robert Herrick appointed Vicar of Dean Prior, Devonshire
Benjamin Whichcote, B.A., Emmanuel College, Cambridge

Jan — Charles I convenes the Second Session of his Third Parliament

Jan 30 — Commons attacks Papists and Arminians, declaring both enemies of God and of England; Bishop Laud one target of Commons' diatribe

Feb 10 (?)— **Milton signs the *University Subscription Book*, Christ's College, Cambridge, as supplicant for the B.A degree**

Mar 2 — Charles I dissolves Parliament, which will not meet again until 1640; beginning of the Personal Rule[251]

— Sir John Elyot and seven other leaders of Commons imprisoned

— Thereafter, Sir John Elyot, *The Monarchy of Man*, written during his imprisonment,

Mar 5 — George Herbert m. Jane Danvers, cousin to Sir John Danvers (his step-father), reportedly (by Walton) only three days after first meeting her[252]

Mar 26 — **Milton receives A.B. degree; signs the *University Subscription Book***

Mar 27 — Ben Jonson, "An Epigram to Our great and Good King Charles on His Anniversary Day, 1629"

Mar 28 — Thomas Hobbes, *Eight Books of the Peloponnesian Warre, Written by Thucydides, the Sonne of Olorus:*

---

251. "...for England, the most gloomy, sad and dismal day that had happened in five hundred years," according to a contemporary (Hugh Ross Williamson, *Four Stuart Portraits*, p. 98).

252. Herbert's rapid marriage to a young lady whom he had never met but whose family was known to him suggests that John Milton's later marriage to a woman much younger than himself, after a similarly brief acquaintance, might not be as unusual as twentieth-century readers imagine. By all accounts, Herbert's marriage, though short, was thoroughly happy.

Interpreted with Faith and Diligence Immediately out of the Greeke by Thomas Hobbes, Secretary to the Late Earle of Devonshire, SR (re-issued, 1634, 1648); publication delayed by the death of William Cavendish, 2nd Earl of Devonshire

Apr — Peace declared in the war between England and France

— **John Milton:** *Elegy V: In Adventum Veris* **(On the Coming of Spring)**

Apr 2 — Edward Herbert created Lord Herbert of Cherbury by Charles I

Apr 17 — John Donne, Honorary M.A. from Cambridge University, for writing *Pseudo-Martyr*

May 19 — Henrietta Maria gives birth to her first son, named Charles

May 20 — Prince Charles d., less than a day after his birth

Jun 1 — *The Western Knight, and the young Maid of Bristol, Their loves and fortunes related*, broadside ballad, "to a pretty amorous tune"

Jun 11 — Sir Thomas Browne, M.A., Oxford University

Jun 20 — T. F., *A Fooles Bolt is soone shot...*, SR, broadside ballad, to the tune of *Oh no no no not yet*

— Martin Parker, *The Father hath beguil'd the Sonne...*, SR, broadside ballad, to the tune of *Drive the cold Winter away*

Jun 22 — Martin Parker, *Fourpence halfepenney Farthing: Or, A Woman will haue the Oddes*,[253] SR, broadside ballad, to the tune of *Bessy Bell,* or *a Health to Betty*

Jul 23 — Martin Parker (?), *The Son Beguiles the Father*, SR, broadside ballad (now lost)

Summer — Sir Lucius Cary d. of smallpox (b. 1610); his death occasions Ben Jonson's *To the Immortal Memory and Friendship of the Noble Pair, Sir Lucius Cary and Sir Henry*

---

253. "This ditty shows Martin Parker in a naughty mood, but seems desirable in print merely because it is his work. No other ballad-writer was half so clever in dealing inoffensively, as far as concerns language, with an offensive situation. In his class he was a master of innuendo. This 'Jest' maintained its popularity for years," well into the 1680s (Hyder Rollins, *Pepysian Garland*, p. 323)

Morison, the "first sustained Pindaric ode in English"[254]
Oct 21 — Peter Sterry enters Emmanuel College, Cambridge
Dec 9 (?)— **"Onslow" portrait painted, depicting Milton as the "Lady" of Christ's College**
Dec 25 — **John Milton, "On the Morning of Christ's Nativity"**
— **John Milton, *Elegy VI: Ad Carolum Diodatum, Ruri Commorantem* (To Charles Diodati, When He was Visiting in the Country)**

---

254. David Riggs, *Ben Jonson: A Life* (Cambridge MA: Harvard UP, 1989), p 312.

Decade Four: 1630-1639
Retirement and Preparations

1630

John Milton, Sr., retires to Horton, Buckinghamshire
John Milton, begins keeping his Commonplace Book (?)
John Milton, begins writing the "Trinity ms," which ultimately lists a number of dramatic and poetic plans
John Milton, "Canzone"
John Milton, Sonnet I "O Nightingale!"
John Milton, Sonnet II *"Donna Leggiadra!"* (Beautiful Lady!)
John Milton, Sonnet III: *"Qual in Colle Aspro"* (As on a Rugged Mountain)
John Milton, Sonnet IV: *"Diodati, e te'l Dirò"* (Diodati, and I Will Say It to You)
John Milton, Sonnet V: *"Per certo i bel vostr' occhi"* (In Truth, Your Fair Eyes)
John Milton, Sonnet VI: *"Giovane piano, e semplicetto amante"* (Young, Gentle, and Candid Lover)
John Milton, *Elegy VII* (as early as 1628?)
John Milton, "On Shakespeare, 1630" composed (?); published in the *Second Folio* (1632) as "An Epitaph on the Admirable Dramatic Poet W. Shakespeare" [255]
Thomas Dekker, *The Honest Whore, Part II,* printed

---

255. It is possible that the young Milton was quite familiar with Shakespeare's work, since his Bread Street home was only a few blocks from the Blackfriars Theater where Shakespeare's company often performed. For a discussion of a key image in this poem—the "star-ypointing pyramid"—see Leslie Hotson, *Mr. W. H.*, and his discussion of the Elizabethan usage of the word pyramid as meaning primarily an obelisk (pp. 85-86).

Michael Drayton, *The Muses Elizium, lately discovered, by a new way over Parnassus*, poetry

William Drummond of Hawthornden, *Flowres of Sion*, poems, published at Edinburgh

Joseph Hall, Bishop of Exeter, *Certain Irrefragable Propositions*, published

Diana Primrose, *Chaine of Pearle*[256]

William Prynne, *Anti-Arminianism*, published

Francis Quarles, *Divine Poems*

Thomas Randolph, *Aristippus, Or, The Joviall Philosopher*, printed; Randolph's first published work

John Smith of Jamestown, *Continuation of the Generall Historie of Virginia, the Summer Islands, and New England, 1624-1629*; *The True Travels...of Captaine John Smith*

John Taylor, the Water Poet, *All the workes of John Taylor the water-poet. Beeing sixty and three in number. Collected into one volume by the author*, in folio[257], collection of tour pamphlets and other publications (1st of ten editions in five years); *The Great Eater, Of Kent, Or Part of the Admirable Teeth and Stomacks Exploits of Nicholas Wood, of Harrisom in the County of Kent. His Excessive Manner of Eating without manners, in a strange and true manner described*, 20-page pamphlet

Giles Widdowes, *The Schysmatical Puritan*, sermon, with anti-Puritan preface (2nd edition, 1631)

Tomasso Campanella d. (b. 1568)

Johannes Kepler d. (b. 1571)

Christopher Villier, 1st Earl of Angelsey, d. (b. before 1600)

Sophia Simmern of Brunswick, Electress of Hanover, b., at The Hague[258]; twelfth child of Frederick V, Elector Palatine, and

---

256. A versified allegory celebrating the virtues of Queen Elizabeth I.

257. Zall emends the description to "sumptuous folio" (*Nest*, p. 121)

258. Before her death without surviving issue, Queen Anne indicated that Sophia, Electress of Hanover, should be her successor. Since the latter died shortly before Anne's death, Sophia's son, George, accordingly ascended the English throne as King George I

Princess Elizabeth

Anna Weamys b.(?)[259]

Gustavus Adolphus, King of Sweden, emerges as Protestant hero in the European wars

William Laud, Bishop of Bath and Wells, appointed Chancellor of Oxford University

Edward King appointed fellow of Christ's College, Cambridge; by royal mandate

Inigo Jones directed to oversee repairs on St. Paul's Cathedral[260]

John Lilburne apprenticed to a clothier in London

Peter Paul Rubens, though Flemish, arrives in England as a Spanish diplomatic representative

Roger Williams leaves for Massachusetts Bay Colony, New England

Jan 16 — Henry, Lord Hastings, b

Mar 12 — Martin Parker, *The He-Divell: or, If This womans husband use her well, Ile say some kindnesse may be found in Hell*, broadside ballad, registered by Francis Grove, to the tune of *The Shee-divell*

Mar 28 (?) — **John Milton, "The Passion" written, apparently as a sequel of sorts to the Nativity Ode. Milton comments: "This subject the Author finding to be above the years he had, when he wrote it, and nothing satisfied with what was begun, left it unfinisht," yet he preserved**

---

259. No dates are known for Weamys, but a birth around 1630 seems probable, since she is not yet twenty in 1650.

260. Old St. Paul's had lost its spire in a fire during the middle of the preceeding century, and by the end of James' reign had fallen into a state of disrepair. Booksellers' stalls crowded its outer walls; book-dealers and others (including prostitutes) used its central nave as a meeting place. Contemporary visitors include reports of well-dressed gentlemen urinating on the inner columns, and in general the building had become more of a convenient landmark than a house of worship. The decline became more prominent during the Commonwealth, when for a time part of the Cathedral became an impromptu alley for ninepins. Jones' repairs included a neo-Classical portico, subsequently destroyed in the Great Fire.

it to include in the *Poems of 1645*
Spring — John Donne's last sermons delivered at St. Paul's
Apr — Plague breaks out in Cambridge
Apr 8 — Thomas Middleton, *Chast Mayd in Cheape-side*, SR
Apr 10 — William Herbert, 3rd Earl of Pembroke and Chancellor of Oxford, d.
Apr 16 — Charles Diodati attends the University of Geneva in Switzerland, studying theology
— George Herbert presented with the living of Fugglestone-with-Bemerton
Apr 17 — Cambridge University closed because of the Plague until January 1631
Apr 26 — George Herbert installed in his rectorship at Bemerton by John Davenant, Bishop of Salisbury
Apr 28 — William Laud, elected Chancellor of Oxford University
— Charles Cotton b.
May 29 — Prince Charles b., second son of Charles I[261]; subsequently created Prince of Wales (afterward Charles II)
Jun 1 — Lady Anne Clifford, Countess of Dorset, m. Philip Herbert, 4th Earl of Pembroke and Earl of Montgomery
Jun 10 — Edward King receives a fellowship from Christ's College; Milton may have anticipated receiving it himself
Jun 17 — **Milton's first reading of Pindar's poems**
Aug — **Edward Phillips b. to Anne Phillips, Milton's sister**
— Charles I contemplates appointing John Donne to a bishopric
Sep 19 — George Herbert ordained a priest by John Davenant, Bishop of Salisbury
— Sir John Suckling knighted by Charles I (purchased honor)
October (?) — Sir Thomas Browne begins courses at Montpelier, in France
Oct 12 — John Heming, associate of William Shakespeare and 'projector' of the First Folio, buried

---

261. The first son born to Charles I, also named Charles, died in infancy.

Oct 29 — Robert Herrick installed as vicar of Dean Prior

Nov 4 — Richard Barry b. (afterward 2nd Earl of Barrymore)

Nov 30 — Alexander Gill, the Younger, pardoned—avoiding having his ears lopped off—and released from prison[262]

Dec 13 — John Donne draws up his final will

Dec 20 — *John Jarrett*, broadside ballad, SR by Francis Grove, to the tune of *The Wiving Age*

---

262. To make the punishment even more gruesome, Gill was to have lost one ear at Oxford and the other at London. (Don M. Wolfe, *Milton and His England*, 9)

1631

John Milton, "L'Allegro" (?)
John Milton, "Il Penseroso (?)
Jacobus Arminius, *Opera Theologica*
Richard Braithwaite, *The English Gentlewoman*, published; *Whimzies, Or, A New Cast of Characters*
Thomas Deloney, *The Garland of Good Will. Divided into three parts: Containing many pleasant Songs, and pretty poems, to sundry new Notes*, reprint (1st edition 1604?; SR Aug 27, 1596)
Phineas Fletcher, *Piscatorial Eclogues,* published
John Ford, *'Tis Pity She's a Whore* (?), *The Broken Heart*
Thomas Fuller, *Davids Hainous Sinne*, prose
Thomas Heywood, *The Fair Maid of the West* published; *Englands Elizabeth*
Ben Jonson, *The New Inn, Bartholomew Fair, The Devil is an Ass, The Staple of News*, published in folio
William Prynne, *Lame Giles his Haultings*, published, attack on Arminian/High-Church reforms led by William Laud
Francis Quarles, *The History of Samson*
Wye Saltonshall, *Picturæ Loquentes. Or Pictures Drawne forth in Characters*
Aurelian Townshend, *Albions Triumph and Tempe Restord*, printed, masques
Robert Bolton d. (b. 1572)
Sir Robert Cotton d. (b. 1571)[263]

---

263. Important less than a writer than as a collector, Cotton was responsi-

Michael Drayton d. (b. 1563); buried in Westminster Abbey, with an inscription ascribed to Ben Jonson
Captain John Smith of Jamestown[264] d. (b. 1579/80)
Michael Wigglesworth b. (d. 1705)
John Cleveland, B.A., Cambridge University

Jan 1 — Thomas Hobson, university carrier, d.[265]
— By this time, nearly 350 people have died in Cambridge of the plague
Jan 6—TWELFTH NIGHT — Ben Jonson, *Love's Triumph through Callipolis*, masque[266]
Jan 8 — Henry Lawes appointed to the King's Musick as a musician for voices
Jan —Plague subsides in Cambridge; 3,487 dead
— John Milton, "On the University Carrier: Who Sicken'd

---

ble for amassing the library that served as a central repository for irreplaceable documents, including the unique copies of *Beowulf, Sir Gawain* and the *Green Knight*, and many others.

264. Of John Smith's chief claim to fame—his relationship with Pocahontas—Samuel Gardiner asserts: "In England, but for the mendacity of Smith, her name would probably soon have been forgotten, along with those of so many of her race who have from time to time visited our shores. He was at this time looking about for fresh employment, and saw that the best chance of acquiring notoriety lay in connecting his name with hers. He accordingly invented that touching story which has, for two centuries and a half, charmed readers of all ages. Of the many poetical fictions which historical inquiry in our day (i.e., 1883) is clearing away, there is none which will be surrendered with such regret as that which tells how the captive Englishman condemned to death was saved by the intervention of the daughter of his captor" (*History*, III, 158).

265. Thomas Hobson (1544-1631), the University Carrier, had driven a carriage each week between London and Cambridge for over seventy years—from 1564 to 1631. His habit of assigning students the horse nearest the door, and hence the most rested horse, gave rise to the phrase "Hobson's choice," still current in English.

266. The debate between Ben Jonson and Inigo Jones over the primacy of words or spectacle in masques draws to a climax at roughly this time, with Jones' perspective edging out Jonson's.

in the Time of His Vacancy, Being Forbid to Go to London, by Reason of the Plague
— John Milton, "Another on the Same"
— John Milton, "Upon old Hobson…" (?)[267]

Feb 15 — **Milton's brother Christopher matriculates at Christ's College; Nathaniel Tovey serves as his tutor as well. Milton has returned to Cambridge from London**

Feb 20 — Thomas Osborne, b. (d. 1712), later Earl of Danby and 1st Duke of Leeds

Feb 22 — SHROVE-TIDE — Ben Jonson and Inigo Jones, the "inventors," *Chloridia* (*Rites to Chloris and Her Nymphs*), masque, performed by Queen Henrietta Maria and her Ladies

Feb 25 — John Donne preaches *Death's Duel*, his last sermon at court

Mar 31 — John Donne, Dean of St. Paul's, d. (b. 1572)

Apr 15 — Jane Paulet, Marchioness of Winchester, d., at age twenty-three

— **Thereafter, John Milton, "An Epitaph on the Marchioness of Winchester"**[268]

Sir Henry Vane, the Younger, arrives in Vienna on his first diplomatic mission

Apr 26 — Sir John Denham registers at Lincoln's Inn

May — Oliver Cromwell, having sold his property, leaves Huntingdon, possibly intending to emigrate to New England[269]

May 5 — Richard Lovelace appointed Gentleman Waiter Extraordinary to Charles I, an honorary position

May 14 — Mervyn Touchet, 2nd Earl of Castlehaven, brother of

---

267. Milton's authorship of a third Hobson poem has been argued, and the arguments noted, by W. R. Parker, Merritt Y. Hughes, and others.

268. It is interesting to compare Milton's poem to Paulet with Ben Jonson's on the same subject; William Camden and William Davenant also contributed memorial elegies.

269. Cromwell's kinsman, John Hampden, was an associated of Lord Say, who then held the patent for the Connecticut Colony. Tradition persists that Cromwell intended to relocate to the Colony.

Lady Eleanor Davies and brother-in-law to John Egerton, 1st Earl of Bridgewater, executed for sexual offenses following a scandalous trial[270]

Summer — **Milton vacations in the country** (?)

Jun 26 — John Egerton, Earl of Bridgewater, made President of the Council of Wales

Jul 8 — John Egerton, Earl of Bridgewater, made Lord Lieutenant of Wales

Aug 9 — John Dryden b., Canons Ashby, Northamptonshire

Aug 14 — John Dryden christened

Sep — Charles Diodati withdraws from theological studies to study medicine

Sep 19-26 — **John Milton, Sr., living at Bread Street; some time thereafter, he removes from Bread Street to Hammersmith, a suburb west of Westminster**

Fall (?) — Sir Thomas Browne begins study at the university in Padua, Italy (through Autumn 1632?)

Oct — **John Phillips b. to Anne Phillips, Milton's sister** (?)

— Plague diminishes in Cambridge

— Sir Henry Vane, the Elder Ambassador to Gustavus Adolphus, King of Sweden, in Germany; Sir John Suckling accompanies the embassy

Nov 4 — Princess Mary Henrietta, daughter of Charles I and Henrietta Maria, b.[271]

Nov 18 — Sir John Denham, at Trinity College, Oxford; no evidence of completing his degree

Dec — Henry More, at Christ's College, Cambridge

Dec 17 — William Hatcliffe makes his Will[272]

---

270. A number of critical and scholarly studies have investigated the possible relationship between the Castelhaven scandal and Milton's decision to write Comus as a moral—and perhaps as a healing—masque.

271. Mary later married Prince Willem II of Orange and became the mother of Willem III, Prince of Orange (subsequently King William III of England).

272. Leslie Hotson's candidate for the 'Young Man" of Shakespeare's Sonnets (*Mr. W. H.*, p. 299)

1632

Milton retires to his father's homes in Hammersmith and later Horton, until 1638
Richard Brome, *Play of the Novella*, written[273]
Sir William Cornwallis, *Essayes*, reprinted posthumously
John Donne, *Death's Duel*, published
Sir Robert Filmer, *Patriarcha, The Natural Power of Kings Defended against the Unnatural Liberty of the People*, pro-monarchical treatise responding to the general fear of a populist government
Giles Fletcher, *Christ's Victorie, and Triumph*, edited by Phineas Fletcher (?); reprinted, 1640
Galileo, *Dialogo sopra I due massimi sistemi del mondo Tolemaicho e Copernicano* (Dialogues concerning the Two Chief World Systems of Ptolemy and Copernicus), results in imprisonment by the Inquisition
George Herbert, *A Priest to the Temple; or, The Country Parson His Character and Rule of Holy Life*, completed (published 1652)
Ben Jonson, *The Magnetic Lady; or, The Humours Reconciled*
The Lawes Resolutions of Womens Rights, or the Lawes Provision for Women, severely limiting legal rights of women
Philip Massinger, *A New Way to Pay Old Debts*
Francis Quarles, *Divine Fancies: digested into epigrammes, meditations, and observations* (reprinted 1633, 1636, 1638,

---

273. Aphra Behn would subsequently borrow elements from this play in writing *The Rover*.

1641

Sir Walter Raleigh, *Instructions to his Son*

Thomas Randolph, *The Jealous Lovers*, presented by students before the King and Queen at Cambridge

Rembrandt van Rijn, *Anatomy Lesson of Dr. Nicolaes Tulp*, painted

James Shirley, *The Ball*, satirical comedy

Thomas Dekker d. (b. 1570/72?)

Luca Giordano b. (d. 1705); religious painter

Lucy Apsley m. John Hutchinson

William Harvey, appointed Physician to Charles I (to 1646)

Sir John Berkenhead attends Oriel College, Oxford

Thomas Randolph, M.A., Trinity College, Cambridge

Jan 1 — Katherine Fowler b. (afterwards Mrs. Katherine Philips, "The Matchless Orinda")[274]

Jan 6 — Aurelian Townshend and Inigo Jones, *Albion's Triumph*, masque

Jan 11 — Katherine Fowler baptized

Jan 12 — Sir Thomas Wentworth, afterward 1st Earl of Strafford, appointed Lord Deputy of Ireland, strengthening Charles I's hold over that nation

Feb 13 — William Hatcliffe's will proved and executed, (Hatcliffe b. 1568)

Feb 14—S<small>HROVE</small> T<small>UESDAY</small> — Aurelian Townshend, *Tempe Restored, a Masque, presented by the Queen and fourteen ladies*, performed; thereafter printed

Apr — **John Milton, *Prolusion VII: Beatiores reddit***

---

274. Katherine Fowler's life was connected with other key writers of the period. A childhood friend who remained close to her for the rest of her life was Mary Aubrey ("Rosania'), a cousin of John Aubrey. And her mother, Katherine Oxenbridge Fowler, remarried following the death of John Fowler; her new husband, Sir Richard Phillips, was the widower of Elizabeth Dryden, John Dryden's aunt. Whether aware of the tenuous family connection or not, Dryden was one of Philips' strongest supporters as a poet. Coincidentally, Mary Aubrey married into the Montagu family and was thus known to and admired by Samuel Pepys.

Homines…
— Sir John Suckling returns to London, bearing confidential dispatches from Sir Henry Vane, the Elder
May 9 — Ralph Cudworth enters Emmanuel College, Cambridge
Jul 3 — **Milton signs the graduation book,** *University Subscription Book*, **for Christ's College, Cambridge, and receives M.A. degree, cum laude**
July — **Milton retires to Hammersmith, near London, and later Horton, in Buckinghamshire, to begin intensive individual study and preparation for his poetic calling**
— **Milton begins his Commonplace Book (?)**
(?)— **John Milton, "On Shakespeare" published anonymously (written as early as 1630?)**
— William Shakespeare, *Second Folio*
Aug 9 — Henry Lawes serves in the King's Musick as musician for lute and voice
Aug 10 — Henry Reynolds, *Mythomystes, wherein A short Survay is taken of the Nature and Value of true poesy and depth of the ancients above our moderne poets*, published
Aug 23 — John Bancroft appointed Bishop of Oxford
Aug 29 — John Locke b. (d. 1704)
Sep — Ben Jonson referred to by John Pory as "Ben Jonson, who I thought had been dead."[275]
Sep 14 — **Legal documents indicate John Milton, Sr., now in residence at Hammersmith**
Sep 22 — **Christopher Milton leaves Cambridge, enters the Inner Temple**
Oct 20 — Sir Christopher Wren b.
Oct 31 — Jan Vermeer b, Delft, Netherlands
Nov — **Milton's brother, Christopher, admitted to the Inner Temple, London, as a law student**
— Gustavus Adolphus, King of Sweden, and continental champion of the Protestant cause, d., at the Battle of Lutzen,

---

275. David Riggs, *Ben Jonson*, p. 331.

Germany[276]; succeeded by six-year-old Queen Christina
— William Prynne, *Histrio-mastix: The Player's Scourges* (dated 1633, published 1632)[277]
Nov 5 — Henry Percy, 9th Earl of Northumberland, the "Wizard Earl," d. (b. 1564), in retirement at Petworth
Nov 24 — Baruch (Benedict) Spinoza b.
Nov 27 — Sir John Elyot d. (b. 1592), of tuberculosis while imprisoned in the Tower for his conduct in Parliament, considered a Martyr to the Puritan cause
Nov 29 — Frederick V, Elector Palatine and "Winter King" of Bohemia, d. (b. 1596), of the plague, in Germany; Elizabeth, the "Winter Queen," holds court-in-exile at The Hague[278]
Dec 9 (?)— **John Milton, Sonnet VII: "How Soon Hath Time"**
— **John Milton, *Arcades* performed before Alice Spenser**[279],

---

276. At the time Gustavus Adolphus died, England had participated in secret negotiations with Catholic Spain against Sweden and the Netherlands, a fact known to only a few in England. Later that year, England agreed to help subsidize the cost of Spain's warfare in the Netherlands.

277. Prynne is credited with over 200 pamphlets and books; this specimen is "a thousand-page diatribe against stage plays without a mention of Shakespeare, Marlowe, or Jonson, abounding in long citations from the church fathers" (Don M. Wolfe, *Complete Prose*, I. 40). A passage cited by J. H. Adamson and F. H. Holland suggests the principle elements of Prynne's style: "What else are the residue of our assiduous play-haunters, but adulterers, adulteresses, whoremasters, whores, bawds, panders, ruffians, roarers, drunkards, prodigals, cheaters, idle, infamous, base, profane and godless persons, who hate all grace, all goodness, and make a mock of piety" (*Sir Harry Vane*, p. 127).

278. Increasingly during this time, the distant (and therefore easily romanticized) Protestant Queen of Bohemia became the pivot of imagination for many English Puritans; eventually, some pamphlets went so far as to suggest that her brother, Charles, should be deposed in her favor. She retained her romantic image to the end of her life.

279. A distant relation of Edmund Spenser (and widow of Ferdinando Stanley, Earl of Derby, a cousin to Queen Elizabeth I and occasionally touted candidate for succession as King of England upon Elizabeth's death), Alice Spenser establishes a dynamic link between Elizabethan and

Dowager Countess of Derby, at Harefield, some ten miles from Horton; accompanying music written by Henry Lawes

Dec 17 — Anthony Wood (Anthony à Wood) b.

Seventeenth-Century poetry; she had long before received the dedication of Spenser's *The Teares of the Muses*, and now receives the praise of Spenser' most acclaimed successor

1633

John Milton, Letter to a Friend (published 1674
John Milton, "On Time"; "to be inscribed on a clock case"
John Milton, "Upon the Circumcision"
John Milton, "At a Solemn Music"
A Banquet of Jests, 1st edition (of nine) published, the most popular jest-book of the mid-century[280]
Robert Bolton, *M. Boltons Last and Learned Worke of the Foure Last Things, Death, Judgment, Hell, and Heaven*, Puritan devotional treatise, with biographical preface by Edward Bagshawe
Abraham Cowley, *Poetical Blossoms*[281]
Lady Eleanor Davies, *Woe to the House*, broadsheet, published in Amsterdam, prophesying doom to the house of Derby, with anagrams on Mervin Audeley, Elizabeth Stanley and Anna Stanley[282]; *Given to the Elector*, published in Amsterdam,

---

280. The book was frequently associated with the name of Archee Armstrong, official court jester to Charles I; subsequent editions of a *Banquet of Jests* in fact attributed authorship to Armstrong who, although litigous by nature, seems never to have brought suit for the misuse of his name.

281. Published when the author was a precocious fifteen, with the earliest poems dating from five years earlier. It is significant to compare Cowley's rapid assertion of poetic powers with Milton's much slower (to some minds almost retarded) development as a poet.

282. Mervin Audeley="M'evel vineyard"; Elizabeth Stanley="That Jezebel Slain"; Anna Stanley="A lye Satann." Anna Stanley was married to Davies' brother, Mervin Touchet, 2nd Earl of Castlehaven, who was tried

verse pamphlet

John Donne, *Songs and Sonets; Paradoxes*, published; the first edition (only) contains prefatory poem signed "Thos: Browne"[283]

Giles Fletcher, the Elder, *De Literis Antiquæ Brittaniæ*, Latin poem edited and published by Phineas Fletcher; contains the myth of Sabrina Milton incorporates into *Comus* (1634)

Phineas Fletcher, *The Purple Island*, published, begun before 1610

John Ford, *'Tis Pity She's a Whore*, published; *Love's Sacrifice*, published; *The Broken Heart*, published

Fulke Greville, 1st Lord Brooke, *Certaine learned and elegant workes of the Right Honourable Fulke Lord Brooke, written in his youth, and familiar exercise with Sir Philip Sidney*

Henry Hawkins, *Parthenia Sacra*, devotional emblems of the Virgin Mary

George Herbert, *The Temple*[284]

Robert Herrick, first published poems

Christopher Marlowe, *The Jew of Malta*, performed and published

Philip Massinger, *The Guardian*, written

Edmund Spenser, *A View of the State of Ireland, Written Dialogue-wise between Eudoxus and Irenaeus, By Edmund Spenser Esq. in the yeare 1596*, published

---

and executed in 1631 for sodomy and accessory to rape. This relationship creates a complex genealogical relationship between Lady Eleanor Davies and the Touchet family, including the Earls of Castlehavens; Alice Spenser, Dowager Countess of Derby and widow of Ferdinando Stanley, 5th Earl of Derby, and the Egertons, including the Earl of Bridgewater for whom Milton wrote *Comus*.

283. Edmund Gosse suggests that the poem was contributed by Sir Thomas Browne.

284. "The number of editions of *The Temple* indicates that Herbert was the most popular religious writer within his own century aside from the voluminous Frances Quarles; and except for John Cleveland, he was the most popular of the so-called 'metaphysical poets,' sacred or profane" (Joseph Summers, *George Herbert*, p. 11)

Thomas Taylor, *Christ's Victorie over the Dragon: or Satans Downfall*, published
Arthur Wilson, *The Swisser*, performed at Blackfriars
Robert Browne d. (b. 1550), founder of the first Brownists or Congregationalists
Francis Godwin, Bishop of Llandaff and of Hereford d. (b. 1562)
Lady Margaret Hoby d (b. 1552)
Wentworth Dillon, b. (later 4th Earl of Roscommon)
Edward Lawrence b.
George Saville, b. (later 1st Marquis of Halifax)
Mary Barret m. John Dyer
John Cotton[285] flees to New England aboard the *Griffin*

Jan 9 — Walter Montagu, *The Shepherd's Paradise*, pastoral drama, acted, with Queen Henrietta Maria and other court ladies among the performers
Feb (?)— George Herbert delivers his poems in manuscript to Nicholas Ferrar at nearby Little Gidding[286]
Feb 1 — William Prynne sentenced to life-imprisonment for his satirical attack on women on stage in *Histrio-Mastix*
— William Prynne, *Histrio-Mastix*, burned
Feb 23 — Samuel Pepys b. (d. 26 May 1703)
Feb 25 — George Herbert dictates his will
Mar 1 — George Herbert d. (b. 3 Apr 1593)
Mar 2 — Samuel Pepys baptized, St. Bride's Church
Mar 3—QUINQUAGESIMA SUNDAY[287] — George Herbert buried at St. Andrew's Church, Bemerton
Apr — Inigo Jones begins extensive renovations to old St. Paul's

---

285. It is a mark of Cotton's influence in New England that the most important town in Massachusetts was renamed after the location of Cotton's living in Boston, Lancastershire.

286. According to Izaak Walton's account. Herbert is said to have asked Ferrar to publish the works if Ferrar felt that they would be of benefit to any needing soul; otherwise, Ferrar was to destroy them.

287. Last Sunday before the beginning of Lent.

Cathedral[288] (through 1642; destroyed by fire in 1666)

Apr 5 — Nathaniel Culverwel enters Emmanuel College, Cambridge

May 7 — Ben Jonson, *The Tale of a Tub*, licensed by the Revels Office

May 29 — Martin Parker, *The Faire Maides Apology: or, Cupids Wrongs Vindicated*, SR, broadside ballad

End of May — Ben Jonson, *Entertainment at Welbeck* presented for Charles I at Welbeck

Jun 30 — Galileo removed from close confinement; spends the remainder of his life under house arrest on his farm at Arcetri in Tuscany—**thus, Milton's subsequent reference to the "Tuscan artist," *Paradise Lost* I.288**

Aug 4 — George Abbott, Archbishop of Canterbury, d. (b. 1562)

Aug 10 — Anthony Munday d. (b. 1553?/1560?)

Aug 29 — William Laud formally elected Archbishop of Canterbury

Sep 19 — Bishop William Laud consecrated as Archbishop of Canterbury

Oct 3 — William Juxon appointed Bishop of London by Archbishop William Laud

Oct 14 — Lady Eleanor Davies summoned to the Court of High Commission to account for "compiling and publishing certain fanatic and scandalous pamphlets"—including *Given to the Elector*—containing her prophecies as "Reveale o Daniel" (anagram on her name); her books subsequently ordered burned[289]

Oct 16 — James, Duke of York (later King James II), b. to Charles I and Henrietta Maria

Oct 18 — Charles I, *The King's Majesty's Declaration to his subjects concerning lawful sports to be used*, published

---

288. Although destroyed in the Great Fire, Jones' addition of a classically inspired portico to the west front of the building in turn influenced Sir Christopher Wren's designs for the new cathedral.

289. Antonia Fraser, *The Weaker Vessel*, p. 158

Oct 24 — James, Duke of York, christened by the Archbishop of Canterbury

Nov 3 — Act of the Privy Council on the Position of the Communion Table at St. Gregory's, recorded[290]

Dec — Sir William Davenant, *The Wits*, completed

— Sir Thomas Browne, M.D. from the University at Leiden, Netherlands; shortly thereafter, returns to England

Dec 11 — Richard Harper registers *A Warning for all desperate Women. By the example of Alice Davis who for killing of her husband was burned in Smithfield the 12 of July 1628. To the terror of all the beholders*, broadside ballad, to the tune of *The Ladies Fall*

Dec 14 — Andrew Marvell, at Trinity College, Cambridge

---

290. Chief among the burning issues of the day, largely stimulated by William Laud's obsession in the matter, was the positioning of altar and communion table in churches. One's stance on this matter was, in good measure, an indication of one's position toward Anglicanism, Catholicism, Puritanism, Presbyterianism, Calvinism, and a host of lesser –isms. In this instance, Charles approved removing the table from the middle of the chapel and resituating it at the west end, "altar-wise," thus indicating his agreement with the Laudian Arminians in this matter.

1634

John Milton, Sr., offered mastership, Scrivener's Company
John Milton purchases a copy of Euripides' plays, suggesting an increasing interest in Greek drama[291]
John Milton, "*Philosophus ad Regem*" (Latin epigram) (?)
Richard Crashaw, *Epigrammatum sacrorum liber*
John Ford, *Perkin Warbeck,* published
William Habington, *Castara*, lyric sequence
Gervase Markham, *The Art of Archerie, Shewing how it is most necessary in these times for this Kingdom, both in Peace and War, and how it may be done without Charge to the Country, Trouble to the People, or any Hindrance to Necessary Occasions. Also, of the Discipline, the Postures, and whatsoever else is necessary for the attaining to the Art*
Joseph Swetnam, *The Arraignment of Lewd, Idle, Froward, and Unconstant Women: Or, the vanitie of them; chuse you whether,* published, later edition[292]
John Taylor, *The Needles Excellency: A New Booke wherein are diuers Admirable Workes wrought with the Needle. Newly inuented and cut in Copper for the pleasure and profit of the Industrious*, 10th edition
Edmund Waller, begins writing Sacharissa poems to Dorothy Sidney (until c. 1638)

---

291. Preserved in the Bodleian Library (William Riley Parker, "The Date of Samson Agonistes Again," p. 167).

292. Swetnam's was a "sensationally popular' book for the period (David Underdown, *A Freeborn People*, p. 64-65).

George Wither, *Emblems*
Lettice Knollys, Countess of Essex, d. (b. 1541)
Cornelius Van Drebbell d., in London; inventor of the thermometer and other devices (b. 1572, Alkmar Holland)
John Webster d. (dead by 1634?)[293]
Nathaniel Wanley b.
John Cleveland, Fellow of St. John's, Cambridge
Marchamont Needham, enrolled at All Soul's College, Oxford

Jan 9 — Sir William Davenant, *The Wits*, comedy, approved by Sir Henry Herbert, Master of the Revels, with corrections by, and at the insistence of, Charles I
Jan 19 — Sir William Davenant, *The Wits*, licensed for performance; thereafter acted at Blackfriars
Jan 28 — Sir William Davenant, *The Wits*, performed at Blackfriars Theater
Feb 4(?)— James Shirley, *The Triumph of Peace*, masque, performed in the Banquet Hall, Whitehall; sets by Inigo Jones; re-staged within a fortnight
Feb 18—SHROVE TUESDAY — Thomas Carew, *Coelum Britannicum*, produced at the Banqueting Hall before Charles I; John, Lord Brackley, and Thomas Egerton are among the actors; stage-sets by Inigo Jones and music by Henry Lawes[294]
Mar 26 — Sir John Berkenhead, at Oxford University, age 17
Apr 8 — William Shakespeare, *The Two Noble Kinsmen*, SR
Apr 29 — William Prynne stripped of his university degrees, after being pilloried twice, having his books publicly burned, and being sentenced to lose both of his ears (which would disqualify him to be a minister)

---

293. John Webster represents a rather extreme example of the lack of biographical information about many pre-Miltonic writers. All that scholars can say definitely about Webster's life is that he was probably born in the decade of the 1570s and was referred to as dead by 1634.

294. Carew's only masque was commissioned by Charles I as a return offering for to Henrietta Maria for her masque, presented on Twelfth Night.

May 4 — **Alice Spenser, Dowager Countess of Derby, celebrates her seventy-fifth birthday; possible occasion for Milton's** *Arcades* **(?)**

— George Chapman d. (b. 1559?)

Jun 25 — John Marston d. (b. 1575)

— Sir John Denham m. Ann Cotton

Jun 27 — Richard Lovelace matriculates as Gentleman Commoner, Gloucester Hall, Oxford

Jul 16 — *No Naturall Mother, but a Monster. Or, the exact relation of one, who for making away her owne new borne childe, about Brainford neere London, was hang'd at Teybourne, on Wednesday the 11. Of December, 1633*, SR, broadside ballad, to the tune of *Welladay*

Jul 30 — Ben Jonson, *Love's Welcome. The King and Queen's Entertainment at Bolsover, at the Earl of Newcastle's*, performed; Jonson's last entertainment, written for William Cavendish, then Earl of Newcastle[295]

Sep 3 — Sir Edward Coke d. (b. 1552)

Sep 18 — Ben Jonson granted a pension from the city of London, at the request of Charles I

Sep 29 — **John Milton,** *A Mask at Ludlow* **(afterward called** *Comus***) performed as part of the ceremonies associated with the installation at Ludlow Castle of John Egerton, 1ˢᵗ Earl of Bridgewater, as President of the Council of Wales**[296]

Fall — Anne Marbury Hutchinson and William Hutchinson arrive at Boston, in New England

Oct 20 — First writs issued from Charles' council requiring Ship-Money[297]

---

295. Estimates place the cost of the masque at between £14,000-£15,000.

296. The "Chronology" in Flannagan's 1998 Riverside Milton gives Egerton's Christian name as 'Thomas.' Thomas Egerton, Sir John Egerton's father, had married Alice Spenser, Dowager Countess of Derby, in 1600, following the death of her first husband, Ferdinando Stanley, 5th Earl of Derby (d. 1594).

297. At a time when Charles was in need of money, his advisors, taking

Nov — **John Milton, Translation of Psalm 114 into Greek**
— Sir John Digby (brother to Sir Kenelm Digby) cudgels Sir John Suckling, a competitor for the hand of Anne Willoughby
— Later in November: Suckling retaliates by attacking Suckling near Blackfriars Theater with a group of sixteen others
Nov 20 — Sir William Davenant, *Love and Honor*, licensed by Sir Henry Herbert
Dec 4 — **John Milton, Letter to Alexander Gill, the Younger, commending Gill's Greek poetry**
Dec 12 — Sir William Davenant, *Love and Honor*, performed at Blackfriars

---

advantage of an ancient statute by which port-cities, and occasionally inland cities, were required to provide ships to insure the public welfare. By levying ship-money with increasing severity, Charles' government transformed it into a general tax that would allow him to finance his needs without resorting to calling Parliament. The ship-money was also among the key issues over which Commons chose to debate Charles' authority. Henry Hallam reports that the ship-money impositions cost the city of London alone some £35,000 (Henry Hallam, *Constitutional History*, II, p. 10)

Christopher Hill summarizes the effect of the ship-money on England as follows: "The judgment in 1637, that (John) Hampden must pay shocked the propertied class. For if Ship Money was legal, non-parliamentary government had come to stay" (*God's Englishman*, p. 33)

1635

Milton moves from Horton to Hammersmith, seventeen miles west of London (roughly mid-year)
John Bastwick, *Flagellum Pontificis*, published
Daniel Dyke, *Michael and the Dragon, or Christ Tempted and Satan Foyled*, published in *Two Treatises: The One of Repentance, the Other of Christs Temptations*
Alexander Gill, the Elder, *Sacred Philosophy of the Holy Scriptures*, includes a denunciation of mortalism as heresy
Hugo Grotius, *Christus Patiens*, Latin drama
William Habington, *Castara*, 2nd edition
Haywood, Thomas. *The Hierarchie of the blessed Angells. Their Names, orders and Offices. The Fall of Lucifer with His Angells*, published in London; engravings by John Droeshout
Francis Quarles, *Emblemes*
John Reynolds, *The Triumph of Gods Revenge against The Crying and Execrable Sinne of (Willfull and Premeditated) Murther*, short-fiction collection illustrating God's providence against sinners; first five stories published in 1621[298]
James Shirley, *The Traitor*
Anthony Stafford, *The Femall Glory*, an exercise in Laudian elevation of Mary
John Swan, *Speculum Mundi*

---

298. *The Triumphs of Gods Revenge* is a collected edition of some thirty narratives Reynold published in smaller collections of five stories each, beginning in 1621. The collections saw multiple reprints during the period.

John Taylor, the Water Poet, *Bull, Beare, and horse*, jest-book

Thomas Taylor, *Christ Revealed: or the Old Testament Explained*, published

George Wither, *A Collection of Emblems, Ancient and Modern*

Jacques Callot d. (b. 1592/3); Continental religious painter[299]

Edward Fairfax d. (b. 1580?); translator

Thomas Randolph d.; dramatist

Thomas Betterton b. (?; d. 1710); actor

Sir George Etherege b.(?)

Robert Hooke b. (d. 1703)

Thomas Sprat b. (afterward Bishop of Rochester; d. 1713)

Founding of the Académie Française

John Bastwick tried by a Court of High Commission, with his books seized and ordered burned

John Cleveland, M.A., Cambridge University

Sir Richard Fanshawe, secretary to Lord Aston, Ambassador to Spain

Hugo Grotius represents Sweden at the French Court

Sir Francis Kynaston founds Museum Minervæ, an academy based on theories of educational reform

Amelia Lanier petitions Charles I for back-revenues on her husband's patent (surcharge on loads of hay and straw sold in London and Westminster)

Andrew Marvell enters Trinity College, Cambridge (?)

Sir Henry Vane, the Younger sails for New England with Hugh Peters and John Winthrop; elected governor of the Boston colony at age twenty-three

Jan 1 — Ben Jonson, *Pan's Anniversary*, New Year's masque for Charles I (written in 1620 for James I)

Feb 10 — Sir William Davenant, *The Temple of Love*, masque, performed at Court on commission by Henrietta Maria; Davenant's first masque; production by Inigo Jones[300]

---

299. Roland M. Frye discusses Callot's *The Temptation of Saint Anthony* as part of the iconographic heritage Milton employed in *Paradise Lost* and *Paradise Regained*.

300. Henrietta Maria was so entranced by the masque—which Inigo Jones

Feb 21 — Thomas Flatman b.

Mar 17 — Thomas Randolph buried (poet and dramatist)

Before Mar 25 — Sir William Davenant, *The Temple of Love*, masque, printed Jul 7

— Sir Henry Vane, the Younger, letter to his father asking his father's approval to travel to Massachusetts

Jul 28 — Richard Corbett, Bishop of Oxford and Norwich, d. (b. 1582)

Aug 1 — Sir William Davenant, *News from Plymouth*, comedy, licensed by Sir Henry Herbert, for production at the GlobeSep

— The *Abigail* sets sail for New England; passengers include sir Henry Vane, the Younger

Oct 14 — Jeremy Taylor leaves Cambridge University for Oxford; admitted M.A. at University College, Oxford, within the week

Oct 19 — Sir Thomas Browne, *Religion Medici*, composed at approximately this date[301]

Nov 1 — Sir Henry Vane, the Younger, accepted in full membership by the Boston church

Nov 16 — Sir William Davenant, *The Platonic Lovers A Tragaecomedy*, licensed by Sir Henry Herbert

Nov 17 — Alexander Gill, the Elder, d. (b. 1565)

Nov 18 — Alexander Gill, the Younger, succeeds in orienting himself sufficiently to Laudian and Royalist perspectives to be appointed Head Master of St. Paul's School following his father's death

Dec 28 — Princess Elizabeth, daughter of Charles I and Henrietta Maria, b.

---

referred to as the "Queenes Masque of Indianes"—that she insisted on three performances rather than one. Production costs for the masque reached £1,400 (Arthur H. Nethercot, *Sir William Davenant*, p. 122-123).

301. For a discussion of internal evidences for this dating, see Edmund Gosse, *Sir Thomas Browne*, p. 20

1636

Henry Burton, *A Divine Tragedy lately acted*, tract illustrating God's judgments on Sabbath-breakers
Pierre Corneille, *Le Cid*
Abraham Cowley, *Poetical Blossoms*, 2nd edition, with *Sylvia* added
John Davies of Hereford, *The Writing Schoolmaster or the Anatomie of Faire Writing*[302]
Sir John Denham, translation of Virgil, *Aeneid, Book II*
Daniel Featley, *Clavis Mystica: A Key to Opening Divers Difficult and Mysterious Texts of Holy Scripture*, published
Jasper Fisher, *The Priest's Duty and Dignity*, sermon
Samuel Hoarde, *The Soules Miserie*
William Prynne, *A Looking-Glasse for All Lordly Prelates*; *News from Ipswich*, attacking William Laud as an "Arch-Agent for the Devil
George Sandys, *Paraphrase upon the Psalms*, published
George Wither, *The Nature of Man*

---

302. Thomas Fuller, *Worthies of England*: "John Davies of Hereford… was the greatest Master of the Pen that england in her age beheld, for 1. Fast-Writing, so incredible his expedition. 2. Fair-Writing, some minutes' Consultation being required to decide whether his lines were written or printed. 3. Close-writing, A Mysterie indeed, and too Dark for my Dimme Eyes to discover. 4. Various-writing, Secretary, Roman, Court, and Text. The Poeticall fiction of Bryareus the Gyant, who had an hundred hands, found a Moral in him, who could so cunningly and copiously disguise his aforesaid Elemental hands, that by mixing he could make them appear an hundred, and if not so many sorts, so many Degrees of Writing" (cited in Jonathan Goldberg, *Writing Matters*, p. 129).

Nicholas Boileau (Nicholas Boileau-Despreaux) b. (d. 1711)
Joseph Glanvil b.
Thomas Tenison b. (afterward Archbishop of Canterbury; d. 1715)
Ship Money collections bring in 96½% of assessments[303] (compare with 1638 responses)
Outbreak of the Plague kills 10,400, out of a total of 23,000 deaths from all causes
William Laud, Archbishop of Canterbury, and William Juxon, Bishop of London, appointed to Privy Council[304]; bishops now hold State Offices as well as ecclesiastical ones
Peter Sterry elected Fellow at Emmanuel College, Cambridge
Richard Farnham and John Bull, London weavers, assert that they are the Two Witnesses prophesied in Revelations 11:3

Jan — Roger Williams exiled from Massachusetts Bay Colony to Narragansett Bay (Rhode Island) for his views on religious toleration
Jan 14 — Jeremy Taylor, Fellow of All Saints College, Oxford, through the influence of William Laud
Jan 19 — Sir William Davenant, *The Witts, as it was Acted without offense...*, licensed for printing; *The Platonic Lovers A Tragaecomedy*, licensed for printing (SR, Feb 4)
Feb 18 — Sir William Davenant, *The Triumphs of the Prince D'Amour*, SR
Feb 24 — Sir William Davenant, *The Triumphs of the Prince D'Amour*, masque, performed at the Middle Temple before Henrietta Maria, Prince Rupert, and others
Mar 3 — Sir Henry Vane, the Younger, made freeman of the Massachusetts colony
Mar 6 — William Juxon, Bishop of London, appointed Lord

---

303. Christopher Hill, *God's Englishman*, p. 34.

304. The consequence of the appointments is that now the ecclesiastical Lords hold secular offices as well, including State Offices; increasingly during the next several years, William Laud will accumulate power at multiple levels in the religious and the political hierarchies.

Treasurer[305]

Apr 6 — John Smith enters Emmanuel College, Cambridge

May 25 — Sir Henry Vane, the Younger, elected Governor of the Massachusetts Colony

Jun — Outbreak of Plague increases in London

— Theaters closed for some months

Aug — Governor Henry Vane donates £10 toward establishing a free school at Newtown, Massachusetts Colony[306]

Aug 29 — Charles I and Henrietta Maria officiate at the opening of the new quadrangle at St. John's College, Oxford, constructed by William Laud at a cost of £5,000

— William Strode, *The Floating Island*, performed before Charles I and Henrietta Maria at Oxford[307]

Aug 30 — William Cartwright, *The Royal Slave*, performed before Charles and Henrietta Maria at Oxford; thereafter performed at Court[308]

---

305. Archbishop William Laud's diary entry for the day reads: "Sunday, William Joxon, lord bishop of London, made lord high-treasurer of England: no churchman had it since Henry VII.'s time. I pray God bless him to carry it so that the church may have honour, and the king and the state service and contentment by it. And now, if the church will not holde themselves up under God, I can do no more" (cited in Henry Hallam, *Constitutional History*, II, p. 30n). Hallam himself refers to Juxon as a "creature" of Laud's but further notes that "It must be added that Juxon redeemed the scandal of his appointment by an unblemished probity, and gave so little offence in this invidious greatness, that the long parliament never attacked him, and he remained in his palace...without molestation until 1647" (p. 31n). As Bishop of London, Juxon officiated at the execution of Charles I.

306. Two years later, in 1638, after Vane had returned to England, a minister in Charlestown, Massachusetts Colony, named John Harvard, donated an additional £800 toward this same school, which was subsequently named for him: Harvard College, later Harvard University.

307. Strode was the University Orator; one viewer responded to Strode's theatrical endeavor by commenting that 'it was the worst that he ever saw but one he saw at Cambridge" (Charles Carlton, *Archbishop William Laud*, p. 142)

308. The date for the performance is given as 30 April by Autrey Wiley, *Rare Prologues*, p. 20.

Aug 31 — Prince Rupert of the Rhine, M.A. from Oxford

— Richard Lovelace receives M.A. from Oxford, as part of the celebrations accompanying the Royal visit

Nov 5 — Dr. Henry Burton preaches two anti-prelatical sermons, printed within the next month as *For God and King*

Dec — Lady Eleanor Davies vandalizes the altar hangings at Lichfield Cathedral, sits on the bishop's throne, and declares herself primate; she is subsequently confined to Bethlehem Hospital (Bedlam)

Dec 7 — Governor Henry Vane request release from his position to return to England; his request denied by the Colony council

1637

John Milton, *A Maske presented at Ludlow Castle, 1634: on Michaelmasse night, before the right honorable John, Earle of Bridgewater, Viscount Brackly, Lord President of Wales* (*Comus*), edited by Henry Lawes, published anonymously

William Austen, *Haec Homo. Wherein the Excellency of the Creation of Woman is described. By way of an essay*

John Bastwick, *The Letany of John Bastwick*, published in four parts

William Chillingworth, *The Religion of Protestants A Safe Way to Salvation*[309]

Abraham Cowley, *Poetical Blossoms*, 3rd edition

René Descartes, *Discourse on Method*

Ralph Knevet, *Funerall Elegies: Consecrated to the Immortall memory of the Right Honourable the Lady Katherine Paston late wife to the truly noble and heroicke, William Paston of Oxford Esquire*

Shakerly Marmion, *Cupid and Psiche, or an Epic Poem of Cupid and His Mistress. As it was lately presented to the Prince Elector*, in Two Books, published; dedicated to Charles Louis, Elector Palatine

Musa Cantabrigiensis, collection in memory of Princess Anne; with Latin and Greek poems by Andrew Marvell

---

309. As late as the mid-nineteenth-century, on historian will note that Chillingworth's treatise "is generally admitted to be the best defence which the Reformers have been able to make against the Church of Rome" (Henry Thomas Buckle, *History*, Vol. I, p. 347).

William Prynne, *A Breviate of the Prelates Intolerable Usurpations*
John Trapp, *Gods Love-Tokens, and the Afflicted Mans Lessons*, published[310]
Robert Fludd d. (b. 1574)
Philemon Holland d. (b. 1552)
Alice Spenser, Countess of Derby, d. (b. 1559)
Susanna Perwick b.
Thomas Traherne b.(?, possibly as late as February 1639)
Papal delegate formally received in England for the first time since the reign of Mary I
Sir Thomas Browne incorporated M.D., Oxford; begins his life-long practice in Norwich
Abraham Cowley enters Trinity College, Cambridge
Archee Armstrong, official jester to James I and Charles I, dismissed from office for insulting Archbishop William Laud
Peter Sterry, M.A., Cambridge University
St. Francis de Sales, *Praxis Spiritualis; or, the Introduction to a Devout Life*, burned at Smithfield[311]
First operas performed in the Teatro di San Cassiano, Italy

Jan 1 — Sir William Davenant, *Love and Honor*, revived as a New Year's Play at the request of Queen Henrietta Maria, Hampton Court
Feb 1 — Henry Burton imprisoned by Archbishop William Laud
Mar 5 — Benjamin Whichcote ordained deacon and priest on the same day

---

310. Trapp's text treats Samson as one with the Beast of Revelations, and hence an enemy of God—the alternative reading of Samson as emblem available to Milton while writing *Samson Agonistes*. (Joseph Anthony Wittreich, *Interpreting Samson Agonistes*, p. 361.)

311 The books had been licensed for publication by Archbishop Laud, but changes in the text during printing led to its being recalled and burned (Jonathan Green, *Encyclopedia*, p. 26).

Mar 11 — William Prynne, Henry Burton, and John Bastwick arraigned before Star Chamber by William Laud for publishing (unlicensed) attacks on bishops

Mar 17 — Princess Anne, b. (daughter of Charles I)

Spring — William Laud's *Prayer Book* imposed upon the Scottish Church without discussion or approval by Kirk or Parliament

Apr 3 — **Sara Jefferay Milton d. at about 65 years of age**

Apr 6 — **Sara Jefferay Milton buried, Horton parish church**

Apr 18 — John Lilburne whipped through the streets of London, receiving two hundred strokes as punishment

— Massachusetts Governor Henry Vane sets in motion war against the Pequot Indians[312]

May — Amelia Lanier petitions the Privy Council for redress against her brother-in-law

May 17 — Sir Henry Vane defeated by John Winthrop in the election for the Governorship of Massachusetts

— Thereafter: Sir Henry Vane, the Younger, *A Brief Answer to a Certain Declaration*, published in Boston, Massachusetts, argument against religious exclusion

Summer — Sir John Suckling, *The Wits, or A Session of the Poets*, written

Jun 14 — William Prynne sentenced by the Star Chamber to further punishment; Henry Burton and John Bastwick convicted

Jun 30 — Henry Burton, William Prynne, and John Bastwick hideously punished for their writings[313]

---

312. J. H. Adamson and H. F. Holland note of this action: "And thus irony was heaped upon irony. Vane had opposed formalisms in Vienna and London only to find them flourishing, under different forms, in Boston. And refusing to take up arms himself, he was forced by circumstances to set in motion the forces that would soon culminate in America's first national crime against conscience. It was a pacifist in principle who gave the orders that would result in the obliteration of the Pequot nation" (*Sir Harry Vane*, p. 98)

313. Burton was condemned by the Star Chamber to be fined £5,000, to be disqualified to serve as a minister, to lose his university degrees, to be pillo-

— Thereafter: *A Briefe Relation of certail speciall and most materiall passages, and speeches in the Starre Chamber occasioned and delivered ... at the censure of those three worthy Gentlemen, Dr. Bastwicke, Mr. Burton and Mr. Prynne, as it hath been truly and faithfully gathered from their owne mouthes by one present at the said Censure*, illicitly published, unlicensed

— Henry Burton, *For God and King*, subsequently burned

Jul 11 — Charles I, *A Decree of Starre-Chamber, Concerning Printing*, establishes strict control and censorship over publishing; reduces the number of licensed printers from the original 97 (1557) to twenty[314]

Jul 28 — Dr. Henry Burton, while being transported from prison to Lancaster Castle, cheered by a London crowd estimated at 100,000[315]

Aug-Sep — Sir John Suckling, *An Account of Religion by Reason*, religious treatise, composed during Suckling's stay at Bath with William Davenant

Aug 3 — Sir Henry Vane sets sail from Boston to return to England

Aug 6 — Ben Jonson d. (b. Jun 11, 1572)

---

ried, imprisoned for life, and lose both of his ears. Prynne received essentially the same sentence, received brands on his cheeks identifying him as a "seditious libeler," and lost the remaining fragments of his ears. "When the sentences were carried out on June 30, Prynne's stumps were sawed instead of cut off, and Burton's ears were sheared so close to his head that his temporal artery was opened, and the blood gushed out upon the scaffold" (Don M. Wolfe, *Complete Prose*, I, 43-44). Prynne accepted his mutilation with more than heroic martyrdom, claiming that the branded 'SL' identified his 'scars of Laud' ('Stigmana Laudis') as marks of honor in God's service (J. H. Adamson and F. H. Holland, *Sir Henry Vane*, p. 128).

314. Sirluck refers to the act as "the fruit of a century of experience in the control of the press" and "the most elaborate instrument in English history for the suppression of undesired publication; nothing was unforeseen except the determination with which it was defied." *Complete Prose*, Vol. II, 159. See also William Haller, *Tracts*, Vol. I, p. 9n.

315. Don M. Wolfe, *Complete Prose*, I, 44.

— Ben Jonson, *The Sad Shepherd; or, A Tale of Robin Hood*, unfinished pastoral comedy

Aug 10 — **Edward King d.; Milton's fellow student at Christ's College, his death provides the occasion for *Lycidas***

Aug 17 — Ben Jonson buried

Aug 30 — Synod convenes in Massachusetts in a futile attempt to reconcile religious differences in the Colony

Fall — Sir John Suckling, *A Sessions of the Poets*, sung before Charles I at the King's request

Oct 4 — Richard Lovelace enrolled at Cambridge University

Oct 24 — Marchamont Needham, B.A., Oxford University

Nov — **John Milton, *Lycidas* written**

— Ship-money case opens against John Hampden

Nov 2 — **John Milton, Letter to Charles Diodati, outlining the poet's departure from London**

Nov 23 — **John Milton, Letter to Charles Diodati; describes study at Horton**

Dec — John Lilburne arrested on his return from Holland, for publishing seditious materials in Rotterdam and smuggling them into England

— Sir John Suckling, *Aglaura*, magnificently produced at Court during the Christmas festivities, at a cost of £300-£400 from Suckling's own pocket

Dec 4 — Nicholas Ferrar d.

(?)— **John Milton, *Ad Patrem* (To His Father); possibly written as early as 1632 (?)**[316]

---

316. Of this stage in Milton's life, Elbert Hubbard writes that he was "thirty-two years of age, and had never earned a sixpence" (*John Milton*, p. 16), an assessment that Milton would have to had acceded to but, as the Latin poem to his father illustrates, would have attempted to ameliorate. During the time of his retirement, he explains, he was not merely lounging about but rather preparing to become England's premier poet.

1638

Milton assiduously studying the writings of John Selden, a leading Erastian scholar[317]

John Milton, *Lycidas* appears as the final selection in a collection of Latin and English verse, *Justa Eduardo King Naufrago* (In Memory of Mr. Edward King, Shipwrecked) at Cambridge[318]

The Anatomy of a Woman's Tongue, published

Robert Chamberlain, *Nocturnall Lucubrations*, poems (re-issue, 1652)

Abraham Cowley, *Love's Riddle*, pastoral drama

[Bishop Francis Godwin], *Voyage to the Moon*, satirical fiction, imaginary-voyage narrative, anonymous translation from Godwin's original Latin by E. M. [Edward Mahon]

Martin Mersenne (Mersennus), *Harmonie Universelle, On the Nature of Sound, On Stringed Instruments, On Percussion Instruments, On Organs, On Compositions,* and *On Various Kinds of Music* (Latin reprint, 1650)

John Pell, *An Idea of Mathematics written by Mr John Pell to*

---

317. Erastianism, named after a Swiss theologian, Thomas Erastus (1524-1583), allowed the State primacy over the Church, a position subsequently carried to extremes by Archbishop William Laud. William B. Hunter suggests that Milton began as an Erastian, then gradually moved toward full anti-Erastian rhetoric in *A Treatise of Civil Power* (*Milton Encyclopedia*, III, p. 68).

318. Twenty-three poems in Latin and Greek, followed by thirteen in English. The section of English poems has a separate title-page reading *Obloquies to the Memorie of Mr Edward King* Anno Dom. 1638.

Samuel Hartlib
Ericius Puteanus, *Comus*, dream-vision; published
Francis Quarles, *Hieroglyphics of the Life of Man*, emblems
Thomas Randolph, *Poems; with the Muses Looking-glass*, published; *Amyntas, or The Impossible Dowry*, pastoral
George Sandys, *Paraphrase upon the Divine Poems*, with music by Henry Lawes
Sir John Suckling, *Aglaura*, published[319]
N. W. [Nathaniel Whiting], *Le hore di recreatione: or, The Pleasant Historie of Albino and Bellama... (with) Il Insonio Insonadado, or a sleeping-waking Dreame...*, published
John Wilkins, *The Discovery of a World in the Moon*, published (enlarged, 1640)
Joseph Mead d. (b. 1586)
Philip Ayres b. (d. 1712)
Lady Elizabeth Howard b. (?)
Thomas Shadwell b. (as late as 1642?)
Lucy Apsley m. John Hutchinson
Ship Money collections bring in only 39% of assessed monies[320]
Richard Busby appointed Headmaster, Westminster School[321]
Amelia Lanier petitions the Privy Council in the matter of her brother-in-law; the Council gives the petition to the Lord Mayor so that "His majesty shall not be further troubled to interpose"[322]
Richard Montagu appointed Bishop of Norwich, recognizing his support for Charles I and William Laud
Galileo's blindness complete

---

319. The copy of *Aglaura* preserved in the Huntington Library, San Marino CA, bears the signature of J. Brackeley, the Lord Brackeley who had earlier acted in Milton's *Comus*

320. Christopher Hill, *God's Englishman*, p. 34.

321. Among others, Busby's students would include Sir Christopher Wren, John Locke, Robert Hooke, and Matthew Prior.

322. Cited in A. L. Rowse, *Sex and Society*, p. 117.

Early 1638 — *Jonsonus Viribus*, published, commemorative poems to Ben Jonson

Jan 7 — Sir William Davenant, *Britannia Triumphans: A Masque...*, the King's Twelfth-Night masque, performed on the Sunday after Twelfth Night[323]

Jan 8 — Sir William Davenant, *Britannia Triumphans*, licensed for printing

Jan 24 — Charles Sackville b. (d. 1706; afterward, 6th Earl of Dorset)

Late Jan-early Feb — Sir John Suckling, *Aglaura*, tragedy, produced by the King's Company at Blackfriars Theater and later at Court (at Suckling's expense)

Feb 2 — Abraham Cowley, *Naufragium Joculare*, Latin comedy, acted at Trinity College, Cambridge; published thereafter

Feb 6 — SHROVETIDE — Sir William Davenant, *Luminalia, or the Festivall of Light*, masque, with sets by Inigo Jones

Feb 13 — John Lilburne convicted of publishing seditious books (punished Apr 18)

Feb 26 — Sir William Davenant, *Madagascar, with Other Poems*, poems, receive imprimatur for publication (SR, Mar 13)

Feb 27 — The Scottish National Covenant published

Spring — **Milton calls on Sir Henry Wotton for advice concerning Milton's continental tour**

Mar — Anne Marbury Hutchinson tried by her congregation in Boston; she is subsequently excommunicated and cast out of the Colony

Mar 12 — John Lilburne, *A Christian Mans Triall*, written while Lilburne is in prison awaiting punishment (Feb 13, Apr 18)

Mar 22 — Anne Hyde b., at Cranborne Lodge, Windsor (afterward Duchess of York)

Mar 23 — Jeremy Taylor receives the benefice of Uppingham, Rutland

---

323. Charles II and Henrietta Marie ordered a special building constructed for the presentation of this masque—to be disassembled after the production—at a cost of nearly £2,500. Charles' own costume cost £150.

Apr 3 — Sir John Suckling, *Aglaura*, tragi-comedy (with a new fifth act), produced at the Cockpit Theater before the King and Queen; later published in folio

Apr 13 — **Milton receives a letter from Wotton, advising Milton on the itinerary for his Italian journey**

Apr 18 — John Lilburne whipped through the streets of London
— Thereafter: John Lilburne, *A Worke of the Beast, or A Relation of a most unchristian Censure, Executed upon John Lilburne, (now prisoner in the fleet), the 18th of April 1638. With the heavenly speech uttered by him at the time of his suffering. Very usefull for these times both for the encouragement of the Godly to suffer, And for the terrour and shame of the Lords adversaries. Printed in the yeare the Beast was Wounded 1638*, unlicensed, anonymous publication

Apr 23 — Sir William Davenant, *The Unfortunate Lovers*, tragedy, acted at Blackfriars

May — **Milton leaves Horton; his Italian journey commences**

May 4 — Henry Vaughan admitted to Oxford

May/Jun — **Milton visits Hugo Grotius, a leading continental scholar and poet, in Paris, with an introduction by John Scudamore; Leaves France**

Jun 4 — William Cavendish, Earl of Newcastle, appointed governor for Prince Charles

Jun/Jul — **Milton passes through Nice and Genoa**

Jul — **Milton arrives in Pisa**

— Sir John Suckling, *A Ballade. Upon a Wedding*, composed for the marriage of John, Lord Lovelace and Lady Anne Wentworth

Aug 27 — **Charles Diodati buried, St. Anne's Churchyard, Blackfriars, London; Milton will not know of his friend's death for several months**

Aug/Sep 10 — **Milton visits in Florence**

Sep — **Milton reports meeting Galileo**[324]

---

324. One indication of Galileo's importance to Milton is found in the fact that the astronomer is the only one of Milton's contemporaries to appear in

— John Lilburne, *Come out of her my people*, 3rd political pamphlet, published
— Sir William Davenant appointed Poet Laureate, more than a year after Ben Jonson's death
Sep (?)— **John Milton, "*Ad Salsillum poetam romanum ægreotantum*" (To Salsili, a Roman Poet, Being Ill)**
Sep 10 — **John Milton, Letter to Benedetto Buonmatthei**
Sep 16 — **Milton reads his Latin poem at a meeting of the Academia degli Svogliati (Academy of the Disgusted)**
Oct — **Milton leaves Florence and travels to Siena and Rome**
Oct 30 — **Milton dines at English Jesuit College in Rome**
Nov 5 — Jeremy Taylor, Guy Fawkes Day Sermon, Oxford[325]
Nov 20 — Sir William Davenant, *The Fair Favorite*, performed at the Cockpit before the King and Queen
— Sir John Suckling, appointed Gentleman of the Privy Chamber Extraordinary (purchased honor)
— Thomas Carew appointed Gentleman of the Privy Chamber Extraordinary
Nov 28 — Alexander Lindsay resigns as Bishop of Dunkeld
Nov/Dec — **Milton departs from Rome for Naples, where he meets with Giovanni Baptista Mansus, Marquis of Villa[326]**
Dec 11 — Sir William Davenant, *The Fair Favorite*, performed again for the King and Queen

---

Paradise Lost.

325. This sermon, by the 25-year-old Taylor, is the earliest work for which we have a printed record.

326. Mansus provided yet another connection for Milton with the illustrious past (as had Alice Spenser). Mansus had been the patron of Torquato Tasso, a central epic poet and theorist of the sixteenth century. Imprisoned as mad in 1579, Tasso remained incarcerated for seven years; following his release he stayed several times with Mansus. Tasso claims a central position in Milton's preparation to write *Paradise Lost*—the older poet was the author of several epics, including *Gerusalemme Liberata* and of a ten-book *Discourses on the Heroic Poem*.

Dec 13 — Sir William Davenant receives an annuity of £100 as Court Poet from Charles I[327]

Dec 20 — John Lilburne, *The Poore Mans Cry*, dated, published 1639

Dec 30 — Elizabeth Minshull baptized, Wistaton, Chester

Winter — **John Milton, *Mansus***

---

327. Davenant did not receive the official appellation of 'Poet Laureate,' although his contemporaries referred to him as such. His successor, John Dryden, was the first English poet to be so recognized by Letters Patent from the Monarch. (Alfred Harbage, *Davenant*, p. 65)

1639

Milton reads John Speed's *Historie of Great Britaine* (between 1639 and 1641?)[328]
John Milton, outlines for Tragedies (?; as late as 1642?)
John Milton, outlines for a drama on the Fall of Man, drafted
Johannes Beverovicious, *The Excellency of the Female Sex*, published
William Cartwright, *The Royall Slave*
Robert Chamberlain, *Conceits, Clinches, Flashes, and Whimzies*, jestbook, the first to emphasize punning
John Amos Comenius, *Janua Linguarum Reserata* (1631), translated by John Robotham as *The Gate of Languages Unlocked*; *Conatuum Pansophicorum Dilucidatio*, published
John Ford, dedication to *The Lady's Trial*; last certain historical record of Ford
Thomas Fuller, *The History of the Holy Warre*
John Lilburne, *Come out of her my People*, published
Francis Quarles, *Emblemes*, published with *Hieroglyphikes of the Life of Man*, together one of the most popular books of verse in the century (reprinted, 1643, 1658, 1660, 1663, 1669, 1676 1683, 1684, 1696, and others)
Nicolo Sabbatini, *Practica di fabricar scene e machine ne' teatri*, published in Italy, with directions for constructing

---

328. Speed's volume provided a number of historical entries for Milton's *Commonplace Book*, as well as background and information for his own *History of Britain*

stage effects

Richard Sibbs, *Bowels Opened, or, A Discovery of the Neere and deere Love, Vnion and Communion betwixt Christ and the Church, and consequently betwixt Him and every beleeving soule*, published

Thomas Young, *Dies Dominica* (The Lord's Day), sabbatarian tract, published anonymously

Elizabeth Cary, Viscountess Falkland, d. (b. 1585)

Shakerley Marmion d.

Josias Nichols d. (b. ca. 1555)

Thomas Ellwood b. (d. 1713)

Jean Baptiste Racine b.

Sir Charles Sedley b. (?; d. 1701)

Abraham Cowley receives B.A., Trinity College, Cambridge

Henry More, M.A., Christ's College, Cambridge; shortly thereafter, elected Fellow and Tutor

Andrew Marvell, B.A., Cambridge University

Jan/Feb — **Milton in residence in Rome**

Jan 21 — Thomas Carew and Sir John Suckling mentioned as the best wits of the time

Jan 29 — Sir John Denham called to the Bar

Feb — **Milton attends an entertainment at Casa Barberini, home of Cardinal Francesco Barberini[329]; the next day, Milton meets with Barberini in a private audience**

---

329. Barberini served as prime minister of Rome and chief counselor to his uncle, Pope Urban VIII. He was known as a patron of the arts and, among other things, the founder of the Barberini Library, which must have appealed to Milton. Still, there is something intriguing in the image of a firebrand young English Protestant—brought up in a milieu that included Gentillet's *Contra-Machiavel*; images of 'politic Italians' on the stage going back at least as far as Marlowe's plays; and the schemes and scandals of the previous generation centering on Papal interference (or what was popularly believed to be such interference) in English life—being greeted courteously and apparently with some honor by one of the Princes of the Church. Clearly there was in Milton something, beyond the stereotypic portrait of Puritan dourness, that proved enormously charismatic.

Feb (?) — **John Milton, *"Ad Leonoram Romæ Canentem"*[330] (To Leonore Singing in Rome)," to Leonora Baroni**
— **John Milton, *"Ad Eandem"* (To the same)**
— **John Milton, *"Ad Eandem"* (To the same)**
Feb 11 — George Grahame resigns as Bishop of Orkney
Mar 17 — **While in residence in Florence. Milton again attends the Academia degli Svogliati and reads Latin poetry**
Mar 24 — **Milton again attends the Academia degli Svogliati**
— **Milton receives Latin encomia[331] from Carlo Dati and Antonio Francini**
Mar 26 — Sir William Davenant receives the King's Patent to build a playhouse; the theater is never constructed
Mar 27 — Henry Valentine, Royal Chaplain, *God Save the King*, sermon at St. Paul's Cathedral, printed immediately thereafter
— Charles I leaves London to lead the Northern Army against rebellious Scots in the First Bishops' War
Mar 30 — **John Milton, Letter to Lukas Holsten, Vatican librarian**
Mar 31 — **Milton attends the Academia degli Svogliati**
Apr — **Milton arrives at Venice**
— **Henry Lawes, Letter to Milton, assuring Milton "sufficient warrant, to Justify yor goinge out of the Kings Dominions"**
— Sir John Denham is one of twenty-five Middlesex gentlemen who refuse contributions to support Charles I's war with Scotland
Apr 13 — Sir Henry Wotton, Letter to Milton concerning the latter's travels

---

330. While some readers and critics have seen Milton's poems to the premier singer of her day as evidence of a youthful infatuation, if not love, John Shawcross argues that "Milton's praise of Leonora seems hyperbolic, but it is standard and not excessive when compared with others'. There is nothing suggestive of love poetry..." (*Milton Encyclopedia*, I, p. 127)

331. *Encomium*: A formal poem of praise

May 5 — John Lilburne, *Letter to the Apprentices of London*, pamphlet urging apprentices to march on Lilburne's behalf

Jun — Thomas Stanley admitted to Pembroke Hall, Cambridge

Jun 10 — **Milton visits Cerdogni family home in Geneva and signs their family album; visits John Diodati, Professor of Theology and uncle to Charles Diodati. Milton may have learned of Charles Diodati's death at this time**[332]

Jun 16 — Anne Reeves[333] christened, St. Giles, Cripplegate

Jun 18 — Pacification of Berwick (Articles of Pacification) concludes the First Bishops' War disastrously for Charles I

Jun 24 — Treaty of Berwick signed

Jul (?) — **Milton returns through France to England**

Jul 8 — Henry, Duke of Gloucester b.

Jul 20 — Dorothy Sidney ("Sacharissa") m. Henry Spencer, Baron Spencer of Althorp, at Penshurst, the Sidney home,

Aug 1 — **Milton takes up residence in London. He establishes a school in St. Bride's Churchyard, London, where he begins teaching his Philips nephews, John and Edward; later he includes sons of several aristocratic families among his students**

Oct 25 — An audit of the books indicates that Inigo Jones has completed his Corinthian portico for St. Paul's Cathedral

Dec — Sir Henry Wotton d. (b. 1568)

— Thomas Stanley matriculated, Cambridge University

— Sir Aston Cockayne, *A Masque at Bretbie*, performed on Twelfth Night

Dec 4-11 — A number of ballads appear, both registered and unregistered, relating to the "hog-faced woman," then in London, including:

— *The Woman Monster*

— *A Maiden Monster*

— *A Strange Relation of a Female Monster*

---

332. Diodati's villa on Lake Geneva later became famous through the residence of Lord Byron and company there in 1816.

333. Later providing the opportunity for satire as John Dryden's mistress.

- *A New Ballad of the Swines-faced Gentlewoman*
- *A Wonder of these Times*
- Laurence Price, *A Monstrous shape. Or, a Shapeless Monster. A Description of a female creature borne in holland, compleat in every part, save only a head like a swine, who hath travailed into many parts, and is now to be seene in LONDON*, broadside ballad, not registered, to the tune of *The Spanish Pavin*

Dec 5 — *A Certaine Relation of the hog-faced Gentlewoman called Mistris Tannakin Skinker, who was borne at Wirkham a Neuter Towne between the Emperour and the Hollander, scituate on the river Rhyne. Who was bewitched in her mothers wombe in the year 1618, and hath lived ever since unknowne in this kind to any, but her Parents and a few other neighbours. And can never recover her true shape tell she be married &c. Also relating the cause, as it is since conceived, how her mother became so bewitched*, published

(?)— **John Milton, *Epitaphium Damonis* (*Damon's Epitaph*), Milton's tribute to Charles Diodati and his last extended exercise in Latin verse-pastoral**

Decade Five: 1640-1649
Civil War and the Execution of a King

1640

John Milton, "On Shakespeare" reprinted, attributed to I. M.

John Milton, Hobson poem appears—unauthorized—in *A Banquet of Jests* (see below) and in *Wit's Recreation*

Sir Francis Bacon, *Certaine Considerations Touching the Better Pacification and Edification of the Church of England*, two reprints

A Banquet of Jests, published anonymously but subtitled "The King's Jester to the Reader," connecting the book with Archee Armstrong

Francis Beaumont, *Poems...The Hermaphrodite. The Remedie of Love. Elegies. Sonnets, with other Poems* (reprinted 1653)

Richard Braithwaite, *Ar't Asleepe Husband? A Boulster Lecture*, popular tract, with engraving by William Marshall

Thomas Carew, *Poems*, edited by Aurelian Townshend (reprinted 1642, 1651, 1653, 1671)

Robert Chamberlain, *The Swaggering Damsel*

John Cotton, John Wilson, and Richard Mather, *The Whole Booke of Psalmes Faithfully Translated into English Metre* (Bay Psalm Book), published in Massachusetts, the first book printed in New England

Edward Dacres, *Nicholas Machiavel's Prince*

John Donne, *LXXX Sermons*

Mildmay Fane, 2nd Earl of Westmorland, *Raguaillo D'Oceano*, produced

John Goodwin, *The Saints Interest*, published

Robert Greville, 2nd Lord Brooke, *The Nature of Truth*, published, defense of independency in belief

William Habington, *The Queen of Aragon*, drama; *The History of Edward IV*; *Castara*, 3rd edition

George Herbert, *Outlandish Proverbs*, collection of 1032 proverbs of non-English origin

Christopher Harvey, *The Synagogue: Or, The Shadow of the Temple ... In Imitation of Mr George Herbert*, published[334]

Thomas Hobbes, dedication to *The Elements of Law, Natural and Politique*, dated

Ben Jonson, *The Workes of Ben Jonson. The Second Volume*; edited by Sir Kenelm Digby; *English Grammar*

Henry Parker, *The Case of Shipmony*, published, arguing that the highest good is the health of the commonwealth

Martin Parker, *Well met neighbour: or, A dainty discourse betwixt Nell and Sisse*, broadside ballad

Thomas Randolph, *Poems*, 2nd edition

Edward Reynolds, *A Treatise of the Passions and Faculties of the Soule of Man*, published

George Sandys, *Christs Passion*, English translation of Hugo Grotius, *Christus Patiens* (Latin)

George Sandys, *Ovids Metamorphosis Englished Mythologizd and Represented in Figures*

John Selden, *A Briefe Discourse Concerning The Power of The Peeres and Comons of Parliament, in point of Judicature, Written by a Learned Antiquerie, at the request of a Peere of this Realme...*, published

John Tatham, *The Fancies' Theater*, poetry

"'Mary Tattle-well' and 'Jane Hit-him-home,' spinsters," *The*

---

334. "Harvey may have understood that art and wit and grace were inextricable in *The Temple*, but the understanding did him little good. Despite his close imitation of Herbert in subjects, language, stanza forms, and rhythms, most of his poems are very bad"; in spite of this, copies of Harvey's poems were often bound with Herbert's *The Temple* for the two next centuries (Joseph Summers, *George Herbert*, p. 12). More successful in integrating Herbert's vision with their own were Richard Crashaw and Henry Vaughan

Women's Sharpe Revenge, tract discussing grievances about education and employment

John Taylor, the Water Poet, *Differing Worships, or, the oddes, betweene some knights service and God's. Or Tom Nashe his ghost*, published, poetry

William Whateley, *Prototypes, or the Primarie Precedent Presidents Out of the Booke of Genesis...*

Wit's Recreation. Selected from the finest fancies of moderne muses, published, anthology

John Ford d. (?; b. 1586)

Peter Paul Rubens d. (b. 1577)

Lady Mary Sidney Wroth d.[335] (b. 1586?)

Sir James Chamberlayne b.

John Crowne b. (d. 1712)

William Wycherley b. (?; d. 1715/16)

Press censorship allows only 22 pamphlets to be printed (cf. 1642)

Sir Thomas Fairfax knighted

George Thomason begins collecting books and pamphlets, eventually amassing some 22,000 items, including all but nine of Milton's titles; Thomason frequently dated materials and identified anonymous authors

Bathsua Makin governess to Princess Elizabeth (to 1644)

Jan 7 — Alexander Gill, the Younger, removed as Head of St. Paul's School

Jan 12 — Thomas Wentworth created 1st Earl of Strafford[336]

Jan 21 — Sir William Davenant, *Salmacida Spolia. A Masque*

---

335. Lady Mary Wroth may have died as late as 1653. She was Sir Philip Sidney's niece, daughter of Robert Sidney, 2nd Earl of Leicester (1563-1626, nephew of Robert Dudley, 1st Earl of Leicester).

336. Wentworth's son was created Baron Raby at the same time. Since Sir Henry Vane, the Elder, owned Raby Castle and had ambitions to the title himself, Wentworth's actions brought upon him the ire of both Vanes, elder and younger; the latter's testimony would be a crucial part of Wentworth's subsequent attainder and execution.

Presented by the Kings and Queenes Majesties at Whitehall..., performed, Davenant's last masque and the last Caroline masque[337]; with Inigo Jones; re-staged 1640

Jan 25 — Robert Burton d. (b. Feb 8, 1577), with the suggestion of suicide by hanging

Jan 26 — **Christopher Milton called to the bar**

Feb — Sir John Suckling commissioned Captain, to raise a troop of 100 to support Charles I in Scotland

— Sir Henry Vane, the Elder, appointed Secretary in place of Sir Edward Coke, a political affront to Thomas Wentworth, 1st Earl of Strafford

Feb 10 — Bishop Joseph Hall, *Episcopacie by Divine Right Asserted*

Feb 15 — Izaak Walton, *Life of Dr. John Donne*

Mar 18 — Philip Massinger d. (b. 1583)

Mar 21 — Thomas Carew d. (b. 1594/95)

Mar 23 — Thomas Carew buried

— Thomas Carew, *Works*, SR, licensed to Thomas Walkley (approved on 29 April)

Apr 13 — Charles I forced to summon Parliament—the Short Parliament

Apr 17 — John Pym addresses Parliament, outlining Charles' constitutional, financial, and religious problems, alluding to Henrietta Maria's Papist influence

Apr 23 — Commons refuses to vote Charles I subsidies without imposing their conditions

Apr 26 — Robert Herrick, *The severall Poems written by master Robert Herrick*, registered

---

337. "Even more than *Britannia Triumphans*, *Salmacida Spolia* was a *Tendenzschrift*, in which the collaborators recognized the crisis and tumult of the times and endeavored to allay the anxieties of themselves, their audience, and their readers by reassuring the world that a 'secret Wisdom,' in the person of Charles I,...would appear with his consort and reduce the threatening storm to a beneficent and lasting calm" Arthur H. Nethercot, *Sir William Davenant*, 176-177). The masque cost £1,400 to produce. Unusual even by Caroline standards, both Charles I and his Queen performed in the masque, giving its political message additional import.

Apr 30 — Sir John Suckling, M.P. for Bramber, Sussex, until May 5

May 4 — Charles I offers to surrender claims to Ship Money in exchange for twelve subsidies (£840,000)

May 5 — Charles dismisses Parliament at the suggestion that Commons intended to invite Lords to meet and discuss the threatening war with Scotland

— Thereafter: broadsheets attacking Archbishop William Laud, one including the anagram on his name, "WELL AM A DIVIL" and another urging London apprentices to march on Lambeth Palace on May 11

May 11 — A mob of five hundred storm Lambeth Palace demanding custody of Archbishop William Laud

Jun 4 — Northumberland writes, concerning the dissolution of Parliament and the discontent that it generates: "It is impossible that things can long continue in the condition they are now in; so general a defection in this kingdom hath not been known in the memory of any!"[338]

Jun 23 — Sir Henry Vane, the Younger, knighted

Jun 26 — Thomas Carew, *Poems. By Thomas Carew Esquire...*, published

Jun 27 — Sir William Davenant assumes management of the King and Queen's Boys at the Phoenix (or Cockpit) in Drury Lane

Jun 30 —**Milton repossesses Richard Powell's land in Wheatley, Oxfordshire, for non-payment of the £500 debt**

Summer — **John Milton, *Epitaphium Damonis*, printed**

— **John Milton, plans for tragedy called *Paradise Lost* entered in the Trinity Ms. (?)**

— Second Bishops' War

Jul — The government seizes £150,000 in privately owned bullion stored for safe-keeping in the Tower of London; the act precipitates a rash of bankruptcies

---

338. Henry Hallam, *Constitutional History*, II, p. 68.

Jul 1 — Sir Henry Vane, the Younger, m. Frances Wray

Jul 10 — Aphra Johnson b. (afterward Aphra Behn, "the Incomparable Astraea")

Late Jul — Charles I offers not to debase the coinage in exchange for a loan of £200,000; London refuses

Aug 28 — Petition of Twelve Peers for the Summoning of a New Parliament, presented to Charles I

— Conclusion of the Second Bishops' War; English forces defeated by the Scots at Newburn Ford, near Newcastle

Sep 4 — Scots Army invades, occupies Durham and controls Northumberland

Oct 4 — John Lilburne, *A Copy of a Letter ... to the Wardens of the Fleet*, dated

Oct 21 — Scots Army agrees to cease hostilities, in exchange for £25,000 a month support; move forces Charles I to attempt again to wrench subsidies from Parliament

— Thereafter: Thomas Wentworth, 1st Earl of Strafford returns to London from Yorkshire

Oct 26 — Treaty of Ripon concludes the Second Bishops' War disastrously for Charles I

Nov 3 — The Long Parliament, which will sit until 1653, convenes at Westminster; actions of the Long Parliament include

— Impeachment of Thomas Wentworth, 1st Earl of Strafford

— Impeachment of William Laud, Archbishop of Canterbury

— Thereafter: Sir John Suckling, *To Mr. Henry German. In the Beginning of Parliament, 1640*, political tract defining Suckling's Royalist sympathies

Nov 7 — Parliament orders the release of three anti-prelatical activists, William Prynne, John Bastwick, and Henry Burton; the three are to appear before Commons

— Sarah Burton petitions Commons directly on behalf of her husband

Nov 9 — Oliver Cromwell addresses Parliament, delivering a petition from John Lilburne, then a prisoner in the Fleet

Nov 10 — Henry Burton released by Commons

Nov 11 — The Root and Branch Petition, presented to Parliament arguing against episcopal government, signed by 15,000[339]

Nov 13 — The Earl of Northumberland, in a letter to Leicester, addresses the current hatred of Thomas Wentworth, 1st Earl of Strafford[340]

Nov 28 — William Prynne and Henry Burton arrive in London and are welcomed with crowds and cheers[341]

Late Nov — Thomas Wentworth, 1st Earl of Strafford, arrested and committed to the Tower

Dec — William Prynne, *Lord Bishops, None of the Lords Bishops*

Dec 4 — John Bastwick arrives in London to an enthusiastic reception

Dec 8 — Princess Anne, d. (daughter of Charles I)

Dec 18 — Harbottle Grimstone urges Parliament to indict Archbishop William Laud for high treason

Dec 30 — Parliament entertains a Bill to mandate annual parliamentary sessions, later adjusted to Triennial sessions

---

339. The petition was submitted to Commons on behalf of "many of His Majesty's subjects in and about the City of London, and several Counties of the Kingdom" (Samuel Gardiner, *Constitutional Documents*, p. 137).

340. "A greater and more universal hatred was never contracted by any person than he has drawn upon himself. He is not at all dejected, but believes confidently to clear himself in the opinion of all equal and indifferent-minded hearers, when he shall come to make his defence. The king is in such a straight that I do not know how he will possibly avoid, without endangering the loss of the whole kingdom, the giving way to the remove of divers persons, as well as other things that will be demanded by the parliament. After they have done questioning some of the great ones, they intend to endeavour the displacing of Jermyn, Newcastle, and Walter Montage" (Henry Hallam, *Constitutional History*, II, p. 78n)

341. Wolfe adds that a crowd of 10,000 followed Burton from Charing Cross to London

1641

Milton acquainted with George Thomason, although the latter never publishes Milton's works

John Archer [Henry Archer?], *The Personall Reigne of Christ upon Earth*, pamphlet; multiple editions thereafter

[Robert Baillie], *An Antidote against Arminianisme; or, A Plain and Brief Discourse Wherein the State of the Question in All the Five Infamous Articles of Arminius Is Set Downe, and the Orthodox Tenets Confirmed by Cleere Scriptural Grounds. Framed of Purpose for the Capacity of the More Simple Sort of People*, published (reprint 1652)

John Ball, *A Treatise of the Covenant of Grace; Wherein ... Divers errours of Arminians and Others are Confuted*

A. B. [Alexander Brome?], *A Canterbury Tale. Translated out of Chaucer's old English Into our Now Usual Language*

The Arminian Nunnery; or, A Brief Description & Relation of the late erected Monasticall Place, called the Arminian Nunnery at Little Gidding in Huntingdon-shire, pamphlet, attack on Nicholas Ferrar, addressed to Parliament

John Barnard, compiler, *First Book of Selected Church Music, consisting of Services and Anthems, such as are now used in Cathedrals and Collegiate Churches of this Kingdom, never before printed...*, with music by William Byrd, Orlando Gibbons, William Munday, and others

John Bastwick, *The Confession of the faithfull Witnesse of Christ, Mr. John Bastwick Doctor of Physick*, published, Puritan defense and account of his punishment by Star

Chamber

Henry Burton, *The Sounding of the Two Last Trumpets*, tract

T. B., *Newes from Rome, Or, a Relation of the Pope and his Patentees Pilgrimage into Hell, with their entertainment, and the Popes return back again to Rome*

William Cartwright, *To the Right Honourable Philip Earle of Pembroke*

Certain Briefe Treatises, Written by Diverse Learned Men, Concerning the Ancient and Moderne Government of the Church, compiled by Archbishop James Ussher (?); includes works by Richard Hooker, Lancelot Andrewes, Martin Bucer, John Rainolds, James Ussher, and others

Lady Eleanor Davies, *The Lady Eleanor, Her Appeale to the High Court of Parliament*, published, recounts her calling as a prophet; concludes with anagram on *Daniel*, "I end all"

Sir John Denham, *The Sophy*, tragic melodrama in blank verse, performed

René Descartes, *Meditationes de Prima Philosophia*, published in Paris

John Dury, *A Summary Discourse concerning the work of Peace Ecclesiastical*, treatise devoted to creating unity among the Protestant churches of Europe

John Foxe, *Acts and Monuments of these latter perillous dayes, touching matters of the Church*, or *Foxe's Book of Martyrs*, new issue, edited by Foxe's son

William Habington, *Observations upon History*

Samuel Hartlib, *A Briefe Relation of that which hath been lately attempted to procure Ecclesiasticall Peace*, companion tract to John Dury's *summary Discourse*

Ben Jonson, *Timber: Or Discoveries Made Upon Men and Matter*

Hanserd Knollys (?), *A Glimpse of Sions Glory*, Baptist tract

John Lilburne, *A Christian Mans Triall*, published; written while Lilburne is in prison awaiting punishment (Feb 13, Apr 18)

Joseph Mede, *The Apostacy of the Latter Times*

William Prynne, *A New Discovery of the Prelates Tyranny,*

published, account of his punishment by Star Chamber; The Antipathie of the English Lordly Prelacie, Both to Regall Monarchy, and Civill Unity, published

The Recantation and Humble submission of Two Ancient Prelates of the kingdome of Scotland..., contains statements by Alexander Lindsay and George Grahame

Sir John Suckling, *The Goblins*, drama completed (begun after 1637?)

George Walker, *Socinianisme in the Fundamentall point of Justificatio*

Edmund Waller, *Speech Against Prelates Innovations*; *Mr Waller's Speech in the Painted Chamber*

[Robert Wild], *Alas Poore Scholler, whither wilt thou goe: or strange alterations which at this time be, there's many did thinke they never should see*, broadside ballad

John Bancroft, Bishop of Oxford, d. (b. 1574)

Thomas Heywood d. (b. 1574?)[342]

Sir William Vaughan d. (b. 1577)

Richard Jones b. (d. 1711; afterward 1st Earl of Ranelagh)

Thomas Rymer b. (d. 1713)

Mary Boyle m. Charles Rich (afterward 4th Earl of Warwick)

Outbreak of Plague in London

John Pocklington, *Sunday no Sabbath* (sermons) and *Altare Christianum*, both ordered burned

Early 1641 — Sir John Suckling, *Brennoralt, or The Discontented Colonel*, political play, composed

Jan — Bishop Joseph Hall, *An Humble Remonstrance to the High Court of Parliament*, arguing for episcopal government of the church

— Alexander Henderson, *The Unlawfulness and Danger of Limited Prelacie*, published, rejoinder to Hall's arguments

— Henry Parker, *A Discourse concerning Puritans*, published, defense of Parliament and the people against prelates

---

342. Heywood is credited with having written, revised, altered, collaborated on, or otherwise had a hand in some 220 plays.

— Roger Boyle, then Lord Broghill, m. Lady Margaret Howard
— Thereafter: Sir John Suckling, *A Ballad upon a Wedding* to commemorate the marriage

Jan 8 — Sir John Suckling, letter to the Earl of Newcastle, inviting his participation in the Army Plot[343]; Henry Percy, Captain Billingsley, William Davenant, and Henry Jermyn are among the plotters

Jan 19 — Parliamentary committee reports discuss a Triennial Bill

Feb 2 — Abraham Cowley, *The Guardian*, performed at Trinity College, Cambridge, in honor of Prince Charles

Feb 12 — Mildmay Fane, 2nd Earl of Westmorland, *Candy Restored*, produced at Althorpe

Feb 15 — The Triennial Act: An Act for the preventing of inconveniences happening by the long intermission of Parliaments, passed

Feb 21 — John Goodman, a Catholic priest, condemned to death by Parliament but reprieved by Charles I after the intervention of a Papal agent

Feb 24 — John Pym charges Archbishop William Laud in the House of Commons with treason

— Thomas Wentworth, Earl of Strafford, defends himself before the House of Lords

Feb 26 — Impeachment charges against Archbishop William Laud carried to the House of Lords and read by John Pym

Mar — James Shirley, *The Cardinal*, licensed

Mar 1 — Archbishop William Laud imprisoned in the Tower; on the way, vocal crowds threaten him

Mar 5 — Charles Howard, Lord Andover moves in the House of Lords that the Star Chamber be abolished; earlier proposals had merely addressed regulating the Court

Mar 11 — Bishops barred by Commons from any legislative or judicial functions, including sitting in the Court of the Star Chamber

---

343. An attempt at strengthening the government of Charles I through military intervention

Mar 12 — Abraham Cowley, *The Guardian*, performed at Trinity College in honor of Prince Charles (published 1650)[344]

Mar 20 — Smectymnuus[345], *An Answer to a Book Entitled An Humble Remonstrance by Joseph Hall*

— **John Milton, "A Postscript" to** *An Answer*[346]

Mar 23 — John Pym opens the case against Thomas Wentworth, 1st Earl of Strafford, in Commons

Apr 10 — Sir Henry Vane, the Younger, testifies against Thomas Wentworth, 1st Earl of Strafford

Apr 12 — Bishop Joseph Hall, *A Defence of the Humble Remonstrance*

— Parliament passes a Bill of Attainder against Thomas Wentworth, Earl of Strafford, allowing for his execution without trial, since it is impossible to substantiate charges of treason

Apr 13 —Richard Montagu, Bishop of Chichester and of Norwich, d. (b. 1577)

Apr 20 — Earlier Star Chamber sentences against William Prynne revoked; he is restored to his degrees and membership at Lincoln's Inn

Late Apr — Sir John Suckling raising troops, ostensibly for service in Portugal

May — **John Milton,** ***Of Reformation Touching Church-Discipline in England: And the Causes that hitherto have hindered it. Two Bookes, Written to a Friend***, **Milton's first anti-prelatical tract, published (the only edition during Milton's lifetime)**

May 3 — Commons interrogates Sir John Suckling concerning

---

344. *The Guardian* was later revised, performed, and published as *Cutter of Coleman Street*

345. The acronym 'Smectymnuus' identifies the clergymen principally involved in writing the pamphlet: Stephen Marshall, Edmund Calamy, Thomas Young, Matthew Newcomen, and William Spurstowe (the 'w' in his Christian name being represented as a doubled 'u').

346. Attributed to Milton by Mason, Will T. Hale, and Don M. Wolfe. See Don M. Wolfe' preface to the "Postscript," *Complete Works*, I, 961-962.

his troops
May 4 — Parliament adopts a Protestation of Loyalty to the Protestant Religion (i.e., Church of England)
May 5 — Thomas Wentworth's death decreed by Commons; Strafford himself urges Charles I to sign the Bill of Attainder for fear of the consequences should Charles try to act in his behalf
May 6 — Sir John Suckling flees to France following the Army Plot and an abortive attempt to free the Earl of Strafford
May 8 — Charles I issues a formal warrant requiring the five members of the Army Plot to appear to answer charges against them
May 9 — A mob, opposed to the Earl of Strafford, storms Whitehall, threatening the Queen and her children unless the Earl is condemned
May 10 — The Act for the Attainder of the Earl of Strafford, passed by Parliament
— *An Act to prevent inconveniences which may happen by the untimely adjourning, proroguing, or dissolving of this present Parliament*, passed by Lords and Commons
— Charles I signs the Earl of Strafford's death warrant, acquiescing to Parliament's demands and betraying a long-time supporter
May 11 — Charles I pleads that Strafford be sentenced to life imprisonment rather than execution
— Charles I signs the bill prohibiting dissolution of Parliament without Parliament's consent
May 12 — Sir William Davenant apprehended while trying to escape England
— Thomas Wentworth, 1st Earl of Strafford, beheaded without benefit of trial; a crowd of some 200,000 celebrate
— Sir John Denham, "On the Earl of Strafford's Tryal and Death," supporting Strafford
— Princess Mary m. William II, Stadtholder of Orange[347]

---

347. Their son, William III, would marry Mary, daughter of Charles II; the couple would ultimately become co-monarchs of England as William

May 14 — Sir John Suckling arrives in Paris, after which nothing specific is known about his activities leading to his death before the end of 1641

May 15 — Sir William Davenant called as a prisoner before the House for complicity in the Army Plot

— *Diurnall Occurrences*, a pro-Parliament news-book, publicly chronicles the Army Plot

May 20 — Robert Moray admitted into Masonic lodge, Edinburgh[348]

May 21 — James Ussher, Archbishop of Armagh, *Judgment of Dr. Rainoldes touching the Originall of Episcopacy*, registered

May 27 — Oliver Cromwell, Oliver St. John, Arthur Haselrig, and Sir Henry Vane the Younger propose a 'root and branch' bill to Commons, abolishing episcopacy

May 31 — Peloni Almoni, Cosmopolites [pseudonym], *A Compendious Discourse, proving Episcopacy to be of Apostolicall and Consequently of Divine Institution*, dated

Jun — John Taylor, *A Swarme of Sectaries and Schismatiques, wherein is discovered the strange preaching (or prating) of such as are by their trades Coblers, Tinkers, Pedlers, Weavers, Sow-gelders, and Chymney Sweepers*, verse essays attacking Puritans and mechanic preachers

Jun 11 — Sir Henry Vane, the Younger, *Henry Vane His Speech in the House of Commons, at a Committee for the Bill against Episcopall-Government*, Vane's first major address, delivered and printed; urges abolition of the Anglican establishment, "root and branch"

Jun 20 — Henry Burton, *Englands Bondage and Hope of Deliverance*, sermon defending free conscience and independent government of congregations

Jun 25 — 'Smectymnuus,' *A Vindication of the Answer to the*

III and Mary II.

348. Frances A. Yates (*Rosicrucian Enlightenment*, p. 210) argues for this as the first authenticated reference to a Masonic initiation in England.

Humble Remonstrance

Jun-Jul — **John Milton,** *Of Prelatical Episcopacy and Whether it may be deduc'd from the Apostolical times by vertue of those Testimonies which are alledg'd to that purpose in some late Treatises: One whereof goes under the name of James Arch-Bishop of Armagh,* **anonymous, although Milton's authorship is known by July**

Jul — Henry Burton, *The Protestation Protested*, published, response to Parliament's Protestation of Loyalty

— *The Brownist Conventicle: or an Assemble of Brownists, Separatists, and Non-Conformists, as they met together at a private house to heere a Sermon of a brother of theirs neere Aldgate, being a learned Felt-maker*, with an indecent woodcut illustrating the actions of the separatists

— John Evelyn records in his diary his reception by Elizabeth of Bohemia at The Hague

Jul 5 — *An Act for the Regulating the Privy Council and for taking away the Court commonly called the Star Chamber*, passed

— *An Act for the repeal of a branch of a Statute primo Elizabethae, concerning Commissioners for causes ecclesiastical*, passed, abolishing the Court of High Commission

— Abolition of the Court of the Star Chamber eliminates official censorship in England

— Thereafter: subsequent abolishing of arbitrary legal jurisdiction embodied in the High Commission, the Court of the President and Council of the North at York, the Court of the President and Council of Wales, and others[349]

Jul 6 — Edmund Waller, *M.r Wallers Speech in Parliament*, attacks ship-money; sells 20,000 copies in one day[350]

Jul 8 — Sir William Davenant released on £4000 bail by the House, following his *Petition* to the House

---

349 Henry Hallam argues that the effect of such courts had been to "deprive one third of England of the privileges of the common law" (*Constitutional History*, II, p. 74-75).

350. Don Wolfe, *Complete Prose*, I, 130.

Jul-Sep (?)— **John Milton,** *Animadversions upon the Remonstrant's Defense against Smectymnuus*, **published anonymously**[351]

Jul 28 — Bishop Joseph Hall, *A Short Answer to the Tedious Vindication of Smectymnuus*

Aug — *A Discovery of Six Women Preachers ... with a Relation of their names, manners, life and doctrine,* critique of sectaries

— Thomas Edwards, *Reasons against the Independent Government of Particular congregations,* published

Aug 7 — *An Act for the declaring unlawful and void the late proceedings touching Ship-money, and for the vacating of all recordsand process concerning the same,* passed

Sep — *A Discovery of 29 Sects here in London,* critique of sectaries

— *New Petition of the Papists,* published

Sep 1 — Commons proposes that communion tables be places in accordance with Puritan beliefs[352]

Sep 9 — Long Parliament recesses

Sep 21 — John Amos Comenius, eminent Moravian scholar and educator, arrives to visit his correspondent and fellow educational reformer, Samuel Hartlib of Prussia

Oct — Robert Baillie, *The Unlawfulness and Danger of Limited Episcopacie,* published

— Katherine Chidley, *The Justification of the Independent Churches of Christ, Being an Answer to Mr Edwards his Booke etc.,* response to Thomas Edwards, *Gangræna*; Chidley is the first woman to emerge as a major voice in the pamphlet wars

---

351. Rudolf Kirk's preface in the *Complete Works,* I, 653, suggests that Milton's book probably preceded Hall's *Short Answer.*

352. In a controversy that presaged Jonathan Swift's 'Big-Endians' and 'Little-Endians', discussion raged as to whether the communion should be placed at the east end of the church, surrounded by a rail and raised by steps (the Laudian Anglican position); or at the center of the church, with neither steps nor rail (Puritan position).

— *Description of the Sect called the Family of Love, with their place of Residence. Discovered by Susannah Snow*, tract critiquing sectaries

Oct 21 — Irish Catholics rebel against the English garrisons in Ireland

Oct 25 — Samuel Hartlib, *A Description of the Famous Kingdom of Macaria*, utopian tract

Nov — *A Curb for Sectaries and bold Propheciers, By which Richard Farnham the Weaver, James Hunt the Farmer, M. Greene the Felt-Maker, and all other the like bold Propheciers and Sect Leaders may be Bridled*, pamphlet

— Robert Greville, 2nd Lord Brooke, *A Discourse Opening the Nature of that Episcopacie which is Exercised in England*, reasoned attack on prelacy (2nd edition, 1642)

— *Humble Petition of the Brownists*, published

— Henry Parker, *The True Grounds of Ecclesiasticall Regiment*, published, defense of Parliament and the people against prelacy

— *Religions Enemies. With a brief and ingenious Relation, as by Anabaptists, Brownists, Papists, Familiarists, Atheists, and Foolists, sawcily presuming to tosse Religion in a Blanquet*, pamphlet

— Grand Remonstrance against Charles I submitted to Commons; Charles still retains substantial support in the House

Nov 1 — News of the Irish Rebellion reaches England

Late Nov — First weekly pamphlet summarizing Parliamentary events published; forerunner of the spate of *Diurnals*, *Intelligencers*, and *Mercuries* that characterize the Civil War period

Dec — Sir Anthony Van Dyck buried, old St. Paul's Cathedral (b. 1599)[353]

Dec 1 — The Grand Remonstrance, with a Petition of the House

---

353. Though Flemish by birth, Van Dyck served as Court Painter to Charles I.

of Commons, presented to Charles I at Hampton Court[354]

Dec 4 — The Long Parliament formally rejects tolerance for the Papist religion in Ireland or elsewhere

Dec 19 — *The Discovery of a Swarme of Separatists, or a new Leathersellers Sermon*, pamphlet

— *New Preachers, new. Greene the felt-maker, Spencer the horse-rubber, Quartermine the brewers clarke*, anti-sectarian pamphlet

Dec 21 — *A Tale in a Tub; or a Tub Lecture, as it was delivered by My-heele Mendsoale, an Inspired Brownist, in a meeting-house near Bedlam*, anti-sectarian pamphlet

Dec 23 — Charles I, The King's Answer to the Petition Accompanying the Grand Remonstrance[355]

Dec 30 — Bishop Joseph Hall committed to the Tower

---

354. The Grand Remonstrance asserted Commons' loyalty and its conviction that the troubles of the times were due explicitly to the King's evil advisors rather than to the King himself, and "humbly" requested that Charles respond to their petition to have Bishops deprived of all legislative functions and their power over the clergy curtailed, thus diminishing the threat of a return to Rome; that Charles remove from his Privy Council all such advisors as acted in contravention to Parliament's will; and that the recent Irish rebels not be made to suffer for their actions. In effect, the Remonstrance—taking into account its 204 individual points—contained the sum of Commons' indictments against the monarchy at the time, but fell short of laying the blame for those failings at Charles' feet.

355. Charles first noted the Commons' disrespect in having published the Grand Remonstrance before he had a chance to read it or respond to it; then rejected each of the accompanying petition's three points—limits on Bishops, revisions to his Privy Council, and amnesty for the Irish Rebels as far as alienation of their property was concerned.

1642

John Milton, publishes Sir Walter Raleigh, *Maxims of State*[356]
John Milton, verses for a dramatic version of *Paradise Lost* (or as late as 1652)[357]
John Berkenhead, editor of the Royalist *Mercurius Aulicus* (through 1645)
Sir Thomas Browne, *Religio Medici*, pirated edition
Thomas Carew, *Poems. By Thomas Carew Esquire...*, 2nd edition
Sir Edward Coke, *Second Part of the Institutes of the Lawes of England*
John Cotton, *The Powring out of the Seven Vials*, Puritan tract, associating Anglicanism with the Beast of Revelations
John Eaton, *Honey-Combe of Free Justification*, Familist or Antinominian pamphlet
An Exact Description of a Roundhead, and a Long-Head Shag-Poll, defense of Puritans and attack on Cavaliers, published
Fearfull News from Coventry: or A true Relation and Lamentable Story of one Thomas Holt of Coventry a Musitian who

---

356. Christopher Hill, *Milton and the English Revolution*, p. 60. Hill's discussion emphasizes Milton's admiration for Raleigh, a link with Elizabethan and Spenserian culture.

357. Any discussion of Milton's intention to write for the stage, or of his writing dramatic works in general (including *Samson Agonistes*, which he notes was never intended to be acted), needs to keep in mind that from 1642 to 1660, public theaters were closed. See William Riley Parker, "The Date of *Samson Agonistes* Again," 164.

through Covetousnesse and immoderate love of money, sold himselfe to the Devill, with whom he had made a contract for certaine yeares—And also of his Lamentable end and death, on the 16 day of February 1641, pamphlet

Nathaniel Fiennes, *True and Exact Relation of both the Battles fought by ... Earl of Essex against the Bloudy Cavaliers*, published; *A Narrative of the Late Battle before Worcester taken by a Gentleman of the Inns of Court from the mouth of Master Fiennes*

Henry Ferne, *The Resolving of Conscience, Upon this Question, Whether upon such a Supposition or Case, as is now usually made (The King will not discharge his trust, but is bent or seduced to subvert Religion, Laws, and Liberties) Subjects may take Arms and Resist?*, published at Cambridge (reprinted at London, 1642)

Thomas Fuller, *The Holy State and the Profane State*, characters and essays; *The Good Wife*

Thomas Hobbes, *De Cive*

Sir Francis Kynaston, *Leoline and Sydanis. A Romance of the Amorous Adventures of Princes...*, with *Cynthiades. Or Amorous Son(n)ets*, published

Henry More, *Psychodia Platonica*, poems

Jeremy Taylor, *Episcopacy Asserted*, in defense of Charles I and Royal prerogative

John Taylor, *Mad Fashions, od fashions, all out of fashions, or, the Emblems of these distracted times*, satirical pamphlet, published

Sir Henry Wotton, *A Short View of the Life and Death of George Villiers, Duke of Buckingham*

John Chalkhill d. (b. 1595)

Sir Francis Kynaston d. (b. 1587)

David Owen d. (?) (b. ca. 1580?)

Guido Reni d. (b. 1575); continental painter[358]

---

358. Roland M. Frye discusses the influence of such works as Reni's Michael and Satan (Santa Maria della Concezione, Rome) on Milton's visual imagination.

Edward Taylor b., Leicestershire (d. 1729, Westfield, Massachusetts)

Benjamin Thompson b. (d. 1714)

Abraham Cowley, M.A., Trinity College, Cambridge University

Henry King appointed Bishop of Chichester

Relaxation of press censorship allows 1,966 pamphlets to be printed[359] (cf. 1640)

Rembrandt van Rijn, *Night Watch*, painted

Jan — Some 400 women petition the House of Lords for redress in matters of trade and living conditions

— Joseph Hall, *Confutation of Smectymnuus*

Jan 3 — Attorney General Edward Herbert[360] confronts the House of Lords with impeachment articles against five members of Commons and one member of Lords. The House refuses to act; Commons refuses to allow the King's Sergeant at Arms to arrest the five members

Jan 4 — Charles I personally—and unsuccessfully—attempts to arrest the five members of Commons at Westminster after discussions begin concerning possible impeachment of Queen Henrietta Maria[361]

— Commons adjourns to the City of London

— Thereafter: Sir John Denham, "To the Five Members of the Honourable House of Parliament: the humble Petition of the Poets," written, verse satire on the Five Members

Jan 8 — Galileo Galilei d. (b. 1564)

Jan 11 — Commons returns to Westminster, having defeated

---

359. Christopher Hill, *Milton and the English Revolution*, p. 65.

360. Cousin to Edward Herbert, Lord Herbert of Cherbury, and the poet George Herbert.

361. The five members of Commons were John Pym, John Hampden, Sir Arthur Haselrig, Denzil Hollis, and William Strode; one member of the House of Lords, Edward Montagu, Baron Montagu of Kimbolton, later created Earl of Manchester, was also included in the impeachment. Hampden was related to Oliver Cromwell and, interestingly enough, to Edmund Waller.

Charles' attemts to arrest its members

Jan 12 — King Charles I flees London; the First Civil War begins

— John Amos Comenius, *A Reformation of Schooles*, appears, translated by Samuel Hartlib

Jan 24 — John Goodwin, *Imputatio Fidei, or, A treatise of justification...*, published, argument for individualism in belief

— Cheapside Cross destroyed by a sectarian mob

After Jan 24 — Richard Overton, *Articles of High Treason Exhibited against Cheap-Side Cross*, published; Overton's first signed pamphlet, anti-prelatical tract

— *The Doleful Lamentation of the Cheap-side Cross: Or, Old England Sick of the Staggers*, pamphlet, one of a number responding to the mob's actions

Jan 29 — Commons passes the Licensing Ordinance for the Company of Stationers, the act that will elicit Milton's *Areopagitica*

Jan-Feb — **John Milton, *The Reason of Church Government Urg'd against Prelaty by Mr. John Milton. In two Books*, published in response to Certain Briefe Treatises..., focusing on essays by Lancelot Andrewes and James Ussher**

Feb 13 — *An Act for disenabling all persons in Holy Orders to exercise any temporal jurisdiction or authority* (Clerical Disabilities Act), passed; the statute to become effective as of February 15; prelates barred from sitting in the House of Lords

Feb 23 — Queen Henrietta Maria sets sail for Holland, escaping with the Crown Jewels; Sir William Davenant is among her supporters (?)

— William II, Stadtholder of Orange, and his bride, Princess Mary, depart England for Holland[362]

Mar — After a year and a half with no licensing ordinances, Parliament orders that action be taken to stop the flood of

---

362. At the time, William II was fifteen, and Mary, eldest daughter of Charles I, was nine.

unsanctioned publications
— Richard Overton, *New Lambeth Fayre*, anti-prelatical tract
Mar 5 — *An Ordinance of the Lords and Commons in Parliament, for the safety and defence of the kingdom of England and dominion of Wales* (Militia Ordinance), proposed by Commons,[363]
Mar 19 — Charles I situated at York, 200 miles north of London
Late Mar (?) — ***A Modest Confutation of a Slanderous and Scurrilous Libel, Entitled, Animadversions upon the Remonstrants Defence against Smectymnuus*, published, possibly by Joseph Hall, Bishop of Norwich, and/or his son, Robert Hall; response to *Animadversions* with direct vilification of Milton**
Apr 5 — Sir John Suckling, *The Discontented Colonel* (*Brennoralt*), SR by Francis Egglesfield
After Apr 8 (?) — **John Milton, *An Apology Against a Pamphlet call'd A Modest Confutation of the Animadversions upon the Remonstrant against Smectymnuus, etc.*, published, Milton's fifth and final anti-prelatical tract**
Apr 17 — The Kentish Petition, orchestrated by Sir Edward Dering, presented to Parliament by the clergy, gentry, and common people of Kent, in favor of episcopal government; ordered burned by the common hangman
Apr 30 — Richard Lovelace presents Sir Edward Derings' Kentish Petition to Commons; he is thereafter imprisoned at the Gatehouse
May — Sir Edward Dering, *Four Speeches made by Sir Edward Dering*, speeches on religion, burned by the common Executioner when the author refused to ally completely with the Puritan parliament; Dering committed to the Tower for a week
— John Aubrey enters Trinity College, Oxford
May (or June) (?) — Sir John Suckling, d., possibly a suicide

---

363. The bill proposed that Parliament appoint Lords lieutenants for each country, effectively placing all military bodies directly under Parliamentary control; Charles I strongly opposed the proposal.

by poison, in Paris, following a failed conspiracy to rescue Thomas Wentworth, 1st Earl of Strafford

May 5 — Bishop Joseph Hall released from the Tower, fined £5,000

May 21 — Henry Parker, *Some few Observations upon his Majesties Late Answers*, defense of Parliament

— Great Seal removed from London by Sir Edward Lyttleton, Lord Keeper of the Seal

— **Milton leaves his London home for a visit to Oxford, at the time the King's headquarters, and Forest Hill, home of Richard Powell**

May 27 — Charles I, *A Proclamation, forbidding all His Majesty's subjects belonging to the trained bands or militia of this kingdom to rise, march, muster or exercise, by virtue of any Order or Ordinance of one or both Houses of Parliament, without consent or warrant from His Majesty, upon pain of punishment according to the laws* (Proclamation Condemning the Militia Ordinance), "By the King"

May 29 (or early June?) — **Milton m. Mary Powell near Forest Hill, in the vicinity of Oxford, the King's new headquarters; Milton had been visiting at her father's home for only a few weeks when they were married**

Jun 1 — The Nineteen Propositions sent by the two Houses of Parliament to the King at York, accepted by the House of Lords[364]

Jun 6 — *A Declaration of the Lords and Commons in Parliament concerning His Majesty's proclamation, the 27th of May, 1642*, approved

Jun 8 — A True Relation of the Proceedings of the Scots and

---

364. The propositions imposed additional limits on the Crown's power, making virtually all of Charles' legislative actions subject to review and approval by Parliament, further restricting Papists' participation in Commons and Lords, controlling the education of the King's children, demanding that Charles disband his personal guard and other military forces, and other encroachments on Crown powers—all couched in appropriately courteous and diplomatic language. The sense of an ultimatum is, however, difficult to miss.

English Forces in the North of Ireland, burned

Jun 20 — John Amos Comenius leaves England for Sweden

Jun 21 — Richard Lovelace released from prison on bail, by order of Commons; he is forbidden to aid Royalist forces or leave the city of London

Jul 27 — *The Round-Head Uncovered*, depicting Roundheads as anti-Puritans

Jun 29 — William Sedgwick, *Zions Deliverance and her Friends Duty*, sermon delivered before Commons

Jul — **Milton returns to London with his wife**

Jul 2 — [Henry Parker], *Observations upon some of his Majesties late Answers and Expresses*, published (2nd edition, 1642)

Jul 6 — Parliament resolves to raise 10,000 men to confront Charles I

Jul 9 — *Animadversions upon those Notes which the late Observer hath published*, response to Henry Parker written from Oxford, the King's camp

— Parliament appoints Robert Devereux, 3rd Earl of Essex, its general

Jul 12 — Parliament resolves to raise an army, under the command of the Robert Devereux, 3rd Earl of Essex, "for the safety of the King's person, defense of both Houses of Parliament, and of those who have obeyed their orders and commands, and preserving of the true religion, the laws, liberty and peace of the kingdom"[365]

Jul 17 — Henry Parker, *A Petition humbly desired to be presented to his Majestie*, published, defense of the people against claims of royalty

Jul 20 — *Religions Lotterie, or, the Churches Amazement...*,

---

365. Devereux, as the young husband of Frances Howard, had been forced by an earlier Stuart monarch into accepting both a divorce and a public statement attesting to his impotence (at least with Frances Howard); some have argued this background as a reason why the son of Elizabeth's last favorite should find himself commanding the armies against the King. Certainly Essex was the highest ranking peer to declare for Parliament in the Civil War.

pamphlet, listing nonconformist sects with brief descriptions

Jul 28 — Henry Parker, *The Danger to England observed upon its deserting Parliament*, published, discussion of social contract as basis for law

Aug — **Mary Powell visits her home in Forest Hill, near Oxford**

— Sir John Denham, *Cooper's Hill*, published in London, first of four pirated editions (1642, 1650, 1653); *The Sophy*, drama, published

Aug 3 — *An Answer or necessary Animadversions upon some late Impostumate Observations*, response to Henry Parker

Aug 6 — Sir John Denham, *Coopers Hill* (3rd draft) SR by Thomas Walkeley; *The Sophy*, tragedy, SR by Thomas Walkeley

— Henry Parker, *Animadversions Animadverted*, reply to his Oxford attacker

Aug 18 — William Prynne, *A Soveraign Antidote*

Aug 22 — Charles I raises his standard at Nottingham

— The Civil War officially begins

Aug 23 — *A Puritane Set Forth in His Lively Colours: Or, K. James his description of a Puritan. Whereunto is added, The Round-heads Character, with the Character of an Holy Sister*, denunciation of Puritans and Round-Heads

Aug 26 — Commons passes a further order to enforce licensing laws

Sep 12 — *King James: his Judgement of a King and a Tyrant*, burned

Sep 19 — William Ball, *A Caveat for Subjects*, attack on Henry Parker

Sep 21 — **A note in Milton's copy of Sir John Harington's 1591 translation of Ludovico Ariosto, *Orlando Furioso*, indicates that Milton has read the poem twice**

Sep 29 — **Mary Powell scheduled to return to London, but she does not**

— William Stanley, 6ᵗʰ Earl of Derby, d. (b. 1561)³⁶⁶

Oct — **Milton requests that his wife return to him; she refuses.**

— **Milton's brother Christopher announces himself a Royalist and begins service in the King's cause**

Oct 5 — *A Speedy Post from Heaven to the King of England*, burned

Oct 8 — Lucius Cary, 2ⁿᵈ Viscount Falkland, letter to the Earl of Cumberland concerning the Battle of Worcester, publicly burned

Oct 21 — John Goodwin, *Anti-Cavalierisme, or, Truth Pleading As well the Necessity, as the Lawfulness of this present War, for the suppressing of that Butcherly brood of Cavaliering Incendiaries, who are now hammering England, to make an Ireland of it...*, sermon-tract published as a call to public action (2ⁿᵈ edition 1643)³⁶⁷

Oct 23 — Battle of Edgehill, first major conflict in the Civil War; Oxford (and Forest Hill) now at the center of the Royalist camp

Nov 4 — John Goodwin, *The Butchers Blessing*, sermon-tract designed as a call to public action

Nov 10 — William Walwyn, *Some Considerations Tending to the Undeceiving Those, Whose Judgements are Misinformed by Politique Protestations, Declarations, &c. Being a necessary discourse for the present times, concerning the unseasonable difference between the Protestant and the Puritan*, pro-toleration tract

Nov 11 — Sir William Davenant leaves Holland to become Lieutenant General of Ordnance under William Cavendish, Earl of Newcastle, in the Royalists' northern army

---

366. Derby is among several candidates considered as the 'true' author of Shakespeare's plays.

367. Goodwin argued that the King had been seduced from seeking the good of the people by the influence of the Cavaliers, courtly favorites without the people's good at heart; he repeated the argument in *The Butchers Blessing*.

Nov 13 (?)— **John Milton, Sonnet VIII: "Captain or Colonel, or Knight in Arms:**

Nov 20 — Sir Dudley Digges, *Answer to a Printed Book*, response to Henry Parker

Nov 27 — Barbara Villiers (later Countess of Castlemaine, Duchess of Cleveland) b. (d. 1708)

Nov 29 — Charles Herle, *An Answer to Misled Doctor Fearne*, published

Dec 19 — Edward Sackville, 2nd Earl of Dorset, writes to Sir Kenelm Digby, strongly recommending that Digby read the (pirated and anonymous) edition of Sir Thomas Browne's *Religio Medici*

Dec 23 — Sir Kenelm Digby writes to Sackville, praising *Religio Medici* enthusiastically; shortly thereafter begins writing a critical essay on the book[368]

Dec 25 — Sir Isaac Newton b.

Dec 29 — Charles Herle, *A Fuller Answer*, expanded version of *An Answer to Misled Doctor Ferne*, published

---

368. For the importance—and relative lack—of critical authority in seventeenth-century England, see Edmund Gosse, *Sir Thomas Browne*, p. 54. Gosse argues that Digby's published response to the *Religio Medici* in part rescued it from the oblivion into which other books—notably Milton's 1645 *Poems*—sank during the period.

1643

John Milton, Sr., music published in William Slatyer, *The Psalmes of David*

Johannes Alsted, *The Beloved City; or, the Saints Reign on Earth a Thousand Yeares asserted*, Fifth-Monarchist pamphlet, translated by W. Burton

Henry Burton, *A Narration of the Life of Mr. Henry Burton*, published, account of his punishment by Star Chamber

Giles Fletcher, *The History of Russia*, reprinted[369]

Joseph Mede, *The Key of the Revelation, Translated into English by Richard More...*, published

David Owen, *Puritano-Jesuitismus, the Puritan Turned Jesuit*, reprint of *Herod and Pilate Reconciled* (1610)

Roger Williams, *A Key to the Language of America*, treatise on Indian languages, with moralizing poems

William Browne, of Tavistock, d. (?; possibly as late as 1645; b. 1590/91?)

William Cartwright d.

Robert Greville, 2nd Lord Brooke, Parliamentary General, d.

Aurelian Townshend d. (b. 1583)

Louis XIV, King of France, b. (d. 1715)

Richard Crashaw flees Cambridge shortly before Cromwell and his forces eject Laudians

Edward Hyde admitted to the Privy Council by Charles I as

---

369. The original edition, *Of the Russe Common Wealth*, had first appeared in 1591. As George B. Parks notes in his introduction to Milton's *Brief History*, the poet was well acquainted with the works of the Fletchers at an early date (Maurice Kelley, ed. *Complete Prose*, VIII, p. 455-456).

Chancellor of the Exchequer

Inigo Jones deprived of all offices as a Royalist

Jeremy Taylor, D.D. from Oxford, at the King's bequest as a reward for *Episcopacy Asserted*

George Wither captured by Royalists; rescued by Sir John Denham, who argued that as long as Wither was alive, Denham would "not be the worst poet in England."[370]

Jan — *Mercurius Aulicus, a Diurnal communicating the intelligence and affaires of the Court to the rest of the Kingdome*, begins publication at Oxford, edited by Dr. Peter Heylyn, written predominantly by John Berkenhead; Royalist newspaper

Jan 3 — Lady Eleanor Davies, *To the Most Honorable the High Court of Parliament Assembled*, dated and identified as "The Holy Ghosts New-yeares-gift"

Jan 6 — William Prynne, *A Revindication of the Anoynting and Priviledgs of faithfull subjects*

Jan 25 — *The Midwife's Just Petition: or, a Complaint of diverse good Gentlewomen of that faculty; Shewing to the whole Christian world their just cause of their sufferings in these distracted Times, for their want of Trading*

Jan 26 — Sir John Spelman, *View of a Printed Book*, attack on Henry Parker

Jan 31 — 'Martin Marprelate,' *The Character of a Puritan*, re-issue by Richard Overton

Feb — Henrietta Maria disembarks in Yorkshire with weapons purchased by pawning her personal jewels[371]

Feb 1 — Griffith Williams, Bishop of Ossory, *Vindiciae Regum*, response to John Goodwin, *Anti-Cavalierisme*

Feb 10 — Sidney Godolphin buried at Okehampton; d. in a skir-

---

370. Bruce King, *Seventeenth-Century English Literature*, p. 72.

371. Continental financiers demurred about loaning the Stuarts money against the Crown Jewels, since ownership of those jewels was at the moment seriously in question.

mish at Chagford[372]

Feb 11 — William Bridge, *The Wounded Conscience cured*, published by order of the House of Commons, response to Henry Ferne

Mar — Parliament passes an additional ordinance to strengthen licensing laws

Mar 2 — General Robert Greville, 2nd Lord Brooke, d., while besieging Lichfield Cathedral

Mar 3 — Sir Thomas Browne, letter to Sir Kenelm Digby, requesting that the latter not publish a critical discussion based on the anonymous, pirated, and corrupt text of *Religio Medici*

Mar 7 — *Christus Dei*, attack on Henry Parker

Mar 14 — Parliamentary commission including Sir Henry Vane, John Pym, Oliver Cromwell, and others grants Roger Williams a patent for his settlement in Rhode Island

Mar 16 — William Prynne, *The Treachery and Disloyalty of Papists to their Soveraignes*

Mar 23 — Sir John Denham, *Mr. Hampdens speech occasioned upon the Londoners Petition for Peace*, to the tune of *I went from England*, broadsheet satire against Hampden

Mar 25 — Lady Eleanor Davies, *Samson's Legacie*, dated

Mar 27 — Parliament passes a Sequestration Ordinance, ruling that Royalists would have their property confiscated, the proceeds to fund Parliament's war against the King

Late Mar — Sir Kenelm Digby, *Observations upon Religio Medici*

— Shortly thereafter: Sir Thomas Browne, *Religio Medici*, authorized edition[373], printed by the same publisher responsible for two pirated editions, Andrew Crooke

---

372. Godolphin's poems were first published as a whole in 1906 by George Saintsbury.

373. "The almost immediate translation into Latin made Browne's 'private exercise' a European book—perhaps the first literary (as distinct from learned) English book to reach a wide continental audience since More's *Utopia*" (Norman Endicott, *The Prose of Sir Thomas Browne*, p. x).

Apr — Stationer's Company publishes a *Remonstrance* demanding the right to appoint licensers and strictly regulate all printing

Apr 11 — John Goodwin, *Os Ossorianum or a Bone for a Bishop to Pick*, response to Griffith Williams, *Vindiciae Regum*

Apr 14 — Herbert Palmer and others, *Scripture and Reason Pleaded for Defensive Armes...Published by Diverse... Divines*, response to Henry Ferne, printed by order of the House of Commons

Apr 15 — *A Review of the Observations*, attack on Henry Parker

— William Prynne, *The Soveraigne Power of Parliaments*, Part I

Apr 18 — Henry Ferne, *Conscience Satisfied*, response to his attackers

Apr 27 — **John Milton, Sr., comes to live with Milton; more pupils attend Milton's in-home school**

Apr 29 — *A Most Miraculous and Happy Victory obtained by James Chidleigh...against Sir Ralph Hopton and His Forces*, Parliamentarian pamphlet, published; subsequently parodied by Sir John Denham, *A Western Wonder*

May — Commons in Westminster impeaches Henrietta Maria, nicknamed "the Generalissima," for her successes in furnishing Charles I with arms, soldiers, and money

Mid-May — Sir John Denham, *A Western Wonder*, written, verse satire against the Roundheads

May 17 — Charles Herle, *Answer*, response to Henry Ferne, *Conscience Satisfied*

May 24 — Philip Hunton, *Treatise of Monarchie*, published (reprinted 1680, 1689)

May 31 — Edmund Waller arrested in conjunction with "Waller's Plot" to deliver London to King Charles I[374]

Summer — Bristol and Exeter surrender to Royalist forces

---

374. Waller, a moderate Royalist, was related by marriage to two of the leading Parliamentarians of the Civil War, John Hampden and Oliver Cromwell.

under Prince Rupert and Prince Maurice[375]
— In view of losses by Parliamentary forces under Fairfax at Adwalton Moor and William Waller at Roundway Down, Parliament expresses dissatisfaction with Robert Devereux, 3rd Earl of Essex, as Parliamentary commander
— Roger Williams arrives in London to work for recognition of the Rhode Island Colony

Jun — Parliament abolishes the episcopal system of church government as evil and offensive; Westminster Assembly of Divines appointed to minister ecclesiastical affairs
— Henry Spencer, Baron Spencer, created 1st Earl of Sunderland; Dorothy Sidney Spenser, now Countess of Sunderland

Jun 3 — Vestry records for Chatham, in Kent, record that parishioners obliterate writing and paintings on church walls

Jun 4-5 — Parishioners at Chatham move the communion table into the center of the church, as ordered by Parliament

Jun 12 — Parishioners in Chatham, Kent, destroy medieval choir stalls as promoting superstition and build new pews in the chancel

Jun 14 — Parliament passes final version of the Licensing Order (Ordinance for Printing), forbidding the printing of materials unlicensed by Parliamentary appointees or unregistered with the Stationers' Company[376]
— Twelve clergymen appointed to license books treating with divinity
— **Thereafter, Milton begins work on a treatise on freedom of the press, subsequently addressed to Parliament and**

---

375. Rupert was the third son and Maurice the fourth son of Frederick V, Elector Palatine and Elizabeth of Bohemia, hence cousins to Charles I.

376. "The ordinance threatened, among others, an anonymous radical who had written a tract in favor of divorce, which opened the door, it was said, to all immortality and the destruction of religion. The young poet whose unhappy married life had motivated that tract, now doubly alarmed, began to pen a defense of freedom of the press. When it was finished he would address it to the Parliament and call it *Areopagitica*" (J. H. Adamson and H. F. Holland, *Sir Harry Vane*, p. 187).

published as *Areopagitica*

Jun 15 — Special day of Thanksgiving declared by Parliament for the discovery of Waller's Plot; Edmund Calamy and Stephen Marshall preach before Lords and Commons respectively

Jun 23 — William Prynne, *The Soveraigne Power of Parliaments, Part II*

Jun 24 — John Hampden d., of wounds in battle against Prince Rupert

Jul — Sir John Denham, *A Second Western Wonder*, verse satire ridiculing the Roundheads

Jul 4 — Edmund Waller, *Speech 4 July 1643*, published

Jul 6 — Matthew Newcomen preaches, *The Craft and Cruelty of the Churches Adversaries*, the opening sermon for the Westminster Assembly

Jul 14 — Henrietta Maria joins Charles I at his court at Oxford, replenishing the treasury and urging him not to compromise with his opponents

Jul 21 — William Spurstowe preaches before both houses of Parliament

Jul 24 — William Bridge, *The Truth of the Times Vindicated*, response to Henry Ferne, *Conscience Satisfied*

Fall — Edmund Waller remanded into custody in the Tower of London

Aug — Women's Peace Petition forcibly presented at Westminster by a group varyingly estimated at from 200 to 6,000 women

— Anne Marbury Hutchinson killed by Indians, Pelham Bay, Long Island, New York (b. 1591

Aug 1 — **John Milton, *The Doctrine and Discipline of Divorce restor'd to the good of both sexes from the Bondage of Canon Law and other mistakes to Christian freedom, guided by the rule of charity, etc.*, 1st edition, published unlicensed, anonymous, under the imprint of Thomas Paine and Matthew Simmons**

Aug 5 — *Time's Distractions*, one of the final masque-like plays of Charles' reign, probably completed, performed shortly thereafter[377]

Aug 14 — *An Examination of the Observations*, attack on Henry Parker

Aug 16 — Marchamont Needham, first issues of *Mercurius Britanicus*, newspaper in opposition to the Royalists' *Mercurius Aulicus*[378]

Aug 21 (?)— Sir William Davenant arrives in Oxford with dispatches from the Earl of Newcastle; remains there to fight in the King's forces

Aug 26 — The Solemn League and Covenant, negotiated in Scotland by Sir Henry Vane, the Younger, arrives in Westminster

Aug 28 — William Prynne, *The Soveraigne Power of Parliaments, Part III*

Sep 7 — Roger Williams, *Key into the Language of America*, published in London

Sep 18 — Gilbert Burnet b. (d. 1715; afterward Bishop of Salisbury)

Sep 19 — William Walwyn, *The Power of Love*, tract urging tolerance of sects, particularly the Family of Love

Sep 20 — Forces under Robert Devereux, 3rd Earl of Essex, confront Royalist forces under Prince Rupert at the Battle of Newbury (Siege of Gloucester)

---

377. The play is anonymous and unnamed, existing in a single copy in the British Museum MS Egerton 1994, the tenth of fifteen plays in the collection. The plays' modern editor assigned the title *Time's Distractions*, which I use here. Suggested possible authors include Mildmay Fane, Earl of Westmorland, and George Chapman, although there is no substantial evidence for either. For a full discussion of the play, its backgrounds, its position in Caroline drama, and its intrinsic and extrinsic values, see Diane Weltner Strommer, *Time's Distractions*.

378. The primary writer/editor for the Royalist counterpart, John Berkenhead, lost no time in pointing out that the masthead for the newsletter had misspelled the word *Britannicus*; such was the rivalry between the two papers that *Mercurius Britanicus* never corrected the initial error (Joseph Frank, *Cromwell's Press Agent*, p. 15).

— Lucius Cary[379], 2nd Viscount Falkland and Secretary of State to Charles I, d. in the battle

— Sir William Davenant knighted during the Siege of Gloucester

Sep 21 — John Bradshaw appointed Judge of the Sheriff's Court

Sep 25 — *A Solemn League and covenant for Reformation and Defence of Religion, the honour and happiness of the King, and the peace and safety of the three kingdoms of England, Scotland and Ireland*, adopted, pledging England and Parliament to substantial religious reforms

Sep 27 — Anthony Burgess, *The Difficulty of, and the Encouragements to a Reformation*, sermon preached before Commons

Fall (?)— *A Letter of Mr. Cotton Teacher of the Church in Boston, in New England to Mr. Williams a Preacher There*, defense of the actions of the Colony in exiling Roger Williams, apparently published by Williams himself preparatory to his publishing his remonstrance (see 5 Feb 1644)

Oct 25 — Sir Henry Vane returns to London following negotiations in Scotland

Nov 1 — Henry Ferne, *A Reply unto severall Treatises pleading for the Armes now taken up by Subjects*, response to his detractors, including William Bridge, Charles Herle, Philip Hunton, and the authors of *Scripture and Reason*

Nov 25 — Lady Eleanor Davies, *The Star to the Wise. To the High Court of Parliament, the Honorable House of Commons: The Lady Eleanor her Petition; Shewing cause to have her Book Licensed, BEING the Revelations Interpretation*,[380] dated

---

379. Cary was in essence the Sir Philip Sidney of the Civil War—the epitome of chivalric and gentlemanly behavior, admired by Royalists and Parliamentarians alike, whose death was mourned by many

380. Only one of Lady Eleanor Davies' many pamphlets was officially published as bearing the requisite registry with the Stationers' Company and authorization by the Archbishop of Canterbury, the Bishop of London, or an appropriate designatee.

Dec 8 — John Pym d., of cancer (b. 1583)

Dec 15 — John Pym buried; Sir Henry Vane, the Younger, acting as pallbearer[381]

Dec 28 — *Certaine Considerations to Dis-swade Men from further Gathering of Churches*, tract attempting to stop the proliferation of Independent congregations

---

381. None of the Scots delegation in London attended the funeral, indignantly claiming that all such rites smacked of Popery

1644

William Barton, *The Book of Psalms in Metre. Close and Proper to the Hebrew*, published

Thomas Brightman, *The Workes of that Famous, Reverend, and Learned Divine, Mr. Tho. Brightman*, published

Sir Thomas Browne, additional issues of *Religio Medici*, including Latin translations by John Merryweather, published in Leyden and Paris

John Bulwer, *Chirologia: or the Naturall Language of the Hand. Composed of the Speaking Motions, and Discoursing Gestures thereof. Whereunto is added Chironomia: Or, the Art of Manuall Rhetoricke. Consisting of the Naturall Expressions, digested by Art in the Hand, as the chiefest Instrument of Eloquence....*[382]

Sir Edward Coke, *Third Part and Fourth Part of the Institutes of the Lawes of England*

Sir Kenelm Digby, *Of Bodies; Of the Immortality of the Soul*, published in Paris

William Lilly, *A Prophecy of the White King*[383]; *England's Prophetical Merlin*, almanac, as *Merlini Anglici Ephemeris* through 1682

---

382. Bulwer's work is the first treatise on oratorical gesturing in English, accompanied by references to classical authorities and illustrations of the various hand positions discussed.

383. One of a series of annual astrological treatises by Lilly, a number of them annual almanacs, *A Prophecy of the White King*, supposedly already a thousand years old, sold 1,800 copies in one day (B. S. Capp, *Fifth Monarchy Men*, p. 18).

William Prynne, *Breviate of the life of William Laud, Archbishop of Canterbury, extracted for the most part verbatim out of his Diary, and other items out of his own hand*, edited to reflect to Laud's discredit

Robert Stapleton, English translation of Juvenal, *Satires*, first six satires

To day a man, To morrow none: Or, Sir Walter Rawleighs Farewell to his Lady, The night before hee was beheaded: Together with his advice concerning HER and her SONNE, published, prose and verse pamphlet

Thomas Weld, *Antinomians and Familists Condemned by the Synod of Elders in New England*

William Chillingworth d.

Alexander Gill, the Younger, d (?; b. 1597)

Francis Quarles d. (b. 1592)

George Sandys d. (b. 1578)

Edward Ravenscroft b. (?, or 1654; fl. 1671-1697; d. 1704)

Princess Elizabeth concludes her schooling under Bathsua Makin

Abraham Cowley ejected from Cambridge, moves to St. John's College, Oxford

Globe Theater dismantled by Sir Matthew Brand

William Dugard, appointed headmaster of the Merchant Taylors' School, London

Jan — John Taylor, the Water-Poet, *Mercurius Aquaticus; Or, The Water-Poets Answer to All that Hath or shall be Writ by Mercurius Britanicus*, attacking Marchamont Needham and the *Mercurius Britanicus*

Jan 3 — Thomas Goodwin, Philip Nye, Sidrach Simpson, Jeremiah Burroughs, and William Bridge, *An Apologeticall Narration, Humbly Submitted to the Honourable House of Parliament*, defense of Independency against Presbyterianism

Jan 11 — Charles I assembles a Royalist Parliament at Oxford, on the advice of Edward Hyde, Lord Chancellor and in the face of invasion by a Scots army allied with the Long Parliament

Jan 15 — Sir Dudley Digges, *The Unlawfulness of Subjects taking up Armes*, expanded version of *Answer to a Printed Book*, response to Henry Parker

Jan 18 — Scots Army crosses the Tweed River into England

Jan 19 — Richard Overton, *Mans Mortallitie or a Treatise wherein 'tis proved both Theologically and Phylosophically, that whole Man, (as a rationall Creature) is a Compound wholly mortall, contrary to that common distinction of Soule and Body*, argument for the mortalist heresy that the soul dies (re-issue, 1644, 1655)

Jan 24 — Scottish commissioners to the Westminster Assembly, *Reformation of Church Government in Scotland Cleered*, response to *The Apologeticall Narration*

Jan 30 — John Maxwell, *Sacro-sanctum Regum Majestas: Or, The Sacred and Royall Prerogative of Christian Kings*, tract

Jan 31 — Henry Parker, *The Contra-Replicant*, response to his multiple attackers

Feb — William Prynne, *A Check on Britanicus*, pamphlet, attack on Marchamont Needham

Feb 2 — **John Milton, *The Doctrine and Discipline of Divorce. Now the second time revis'd and much augmented*, published; 2nd enlarged edition; includes Milton's initials on title page and full name at the conclusion of the preface**

Feb 5 — Roger Williams, *Mr. Cottons Letter Lately Printed, Examined and Answered*, defense of himself against the Massachusetts Bay Colony

Mid-Feb — Marchamont Needham, *A Checke to the Checker of Britanicus*, 30-page response to William Prynne; Needham's first pamphlet publication, defending Independents and the Army

Feb 16 — The Committee of Both Kingdoms appointed by

Parliament to conduct the war against Charles I[384]

Feb 28 — Thomas Young, Milton's former tutor, warns listeners at Westminster against legalizing "digamy," possibly a reference to Milton's tracts[385]

— Robert Baillie, *Satan the Leader in Chief to All Who Resist the Reparation of Sion*, sermon

Feb 29 — Adam Steuart, *Some Observations and annotations*

Mar 12 — Archbishop William Laud brought to trial after three years in the Tower

Mar 21 — Lady Eleanor Davies, *The Humble Petition of Eleanor Davies*

Mar 24 — Henry Robinson, *Liberty of Conscience: or the Sole Means to Obtain Peace and Truth. Not onely reconciling His Majesty with His Subjects, but all Christian States and Princes to one another, with the freest passage of the Gospel. Very seasonable and necessary in these distracted times, when most men are weary of War, and cannot finde the way to Peace*, tract

Mar 26 — Philip Hunton, *Vindication of the Treatise of Monarchy*, response to his detractors, including Henry Ferne

Apr — Henrietta Maria leaves the court at Oxford

Apr 11 — John Smith, Fellow of Queen's College, Cambridge

Apr 23 — Richard Vines, *The Impostures of Seducing Teachers*, anti-toleration sermon

Apr 24 — Thomas Hill, *The Good Old Way, Gods Way*, anti-toleration sermon

May — Milton discusses education theory with Samuel

---

384. Although only granted an official life of three months, this committee is seen as one of the foundations of modern cabinet government. The members included all of the key military leaders for Parliament: Robert Devereux, 3rd Earl of Essex; Edward Montagu, 2nd Earl of Manchester; Robert Rich, 2nd Earl of Warwick; and General Sir William Waller. Much of the work in establishing the Committee was completed by Sir Henry Vane, the Younger

385. *Complete Prose*, II, 140.

Hartlib and reads tracts on divorce by Martin Bucer, a German theologian
— Ann Harrison m. Sir Richard Fanshawe, Secretary of War to Charles, Prince of Wales[386]
Jun 5 — **John Milton, *Of Education To Master Samuel Hartlib*, published**
Jun 14 — Alexander Forbes, *An Anatomy of Independency*, anti-toleration pamphlet
Jun 16 — Princess Henrietta Anna (Minette), b. (afterward Duchess of Orléans)
— Henrietta Maria gives birth to her final child, Henrietta Anna, in Exeter, and leaves England for exile in Paris; she will never see Charles I again
Jun 19 — Sir John Denham's moveable goods sold in London by order of Parliament
Jun 21 — Thomas Bakewell, *Confutation of Anabaptists*
Jun 22 — Sir Edward Dering, d. (b. 1598)
Jun 28 — Sidrach Simpson, *The Anatomist Anatomis'd*, pro-toleration pamphlet
Jun 30 — Prince Rupert forces Parliamentary troops to retreat from the siege of York to Marston Moor
Jun/Jul — [William Walwyn], *The Compassionate Samaritane*, pamphlet urging freedom and toleration, printed anonymously and unlicensed; dedicated to the House of Commons (2nd edition shortly thereafter)
Jul 2 — Battle of Marston Moor; Parliamentarian Lord General Thomas Fairfax defeats the Royalist Prince Rupert's army and subsequently recaptures York; Oliver Cromwell's troops now supreme in the North
Jul 13 — Thomas Edwards, *Antapologia*, pamphlet opposing toleration
Jul 15 — **John Milton, *The Judgement of Martin Bucer,***

---

386. Ann Harrison was seventeen; Fanshawe, never married, was thirty-five—roughly the age differential in Milton's first marriage. See also Antonia Fraser, *The Weaker Vessel*, pp. 61ff., for Ann Harrison Fanshawe's experiences as wife and mother.

Concerning Divorce, **SR by Matthew Simmons**
— Roger Williams, *The Bloudy Tenent of Persecution for Cause of Conscience, discussed, in a Conference betweene Truth and Peace*, addressed to Parliament but actually continuing Williams' debate with John Cotton[387]

Jul 29 — William Walwyn, *Good Counsell to All*, pamphlet

Aug 6 — **John Milton,** ***The Judgment of Martin Bucer, Concerning Divorce now English't. Wherein a late book restoring the doctrine and discipline of divorce is heer confirm'd*, published**

Aug 13 — **Herbert Palmer condemns Milton and the Divorce tracts while preaching against toleration in a sermon delivered before Parliament,** ***The Glass of God's Providence toward His Faithful Ones***

— Thomas Hill, *The Season for Englands Self-Reflection*, anti-toleration sermon

Aug 15 — John Dury, *An Epistolary Discourse*, tract addressed to Thomas Goodwin, Phillip Nye, and Samuel Hartlib, attempting reconciliation between Presbyterians and their opponents

Aug 17 — *An Answer to Mr. John Dury*, published anonymously by an Independent

Aug 24 — **The Stationer's Company petitions Parliament against Milton's divorce tracts, specifically mentioning "Pamphlets against the Immortality of the Soul and concerning divorce"[388], references to Richard Overton and John Milton**

---

387. William Heller notes that the *Bloudy Tenent of Persecution* was "one of the most widely condemned works of the time. Baillie, Gillespie, Pagitt, Prynne and Edwards, all called anathema upon it...," continuing to suggest that its central importance lay in its "single assertion that God intended Jews, Pagans, Turks, and unchristian consciences in general to be opposed by no sword save that of the spirit.... *The Bloudy Tenent* was perhaps the most extreme statement of the theory of natural rights which had yet appeared" (*Tracts*, p. 60)

388. Sirluck, *Complete Prose*, Vol. II, p. 142.

Aug 31 — Robert Devereux, 3rd Earl of Essex, attempts to break through Royalist lines surrounding his army at Lostwithiel, Cornwall

Sep — **Milton notices the first indications of his oncoming blindness**

— Edward Herbert, Lord Herbert of Cherbury, surrenders Montgomery Castle to Parliamentarian forces in order to preserve his library

— Thereafter: Royalist forces besiege the Castle and "Treacherous Lord Herbert"

— Roger Williams leaves London for New England

Sep 1 — Battle of Tibbermore, between Royalist troops and Covenanters

— Robert Devereux, 3rd Earl of Essex, forced to abandon his infantry and return by ship, discredited as a commander, to London

Sep 10 — George Walker, *A Brotherly Censure of the Errour of a Dear Friend*, an answer to Palmer's sermon of August 13

Sep 16 — **William Prynne, *Twelve Considerable Serious Questions...*, attack on Milton and others, particularly divorce tracts and the mortalist heresy, and a defense of authority**

Sep 18 — Herbert Palmer, *A Full Answer to a Printed Paper by William Prynne*

Sep 23 — Lady Eleanor Davies, *From the Lady Eleanor, Her Blessing to her Beloved Daughter, the Right Honorable Lucy, Countesse of Huntingdon*, published, interpreting Daniel, Chapter 7

Sep 26 — William Prynne, *Independency Examined*, anti-toleration pamphlet

Oct — John Merryweather's Latin translation of Sir Thomas Browne, *Religio Medici*, appears in Paris, to general enthusiastic responses and solid critical judgments by Guy Patin

Oct 3 — William Prynne, *A Vindication of Foure Serious Questions*, response to Palmer's tract of September 18

Oct 4 — *Certain Briefe Observations*, pamphlet, response to

William Prynne's tracts by members of John Goodwin's circle

Oct 7 — John Goodwin, *Theomachia; Or the Grand Imprudence of Men running the hazard of Fighting against God, In suppressing any Way, Doctrine, or Practice, concerning which they know not certainly whether it be from God or no...*, pro-toleration pamphlet (2nd issue 1644), defining the Independents' point of view

— Samuel Rutherford, *Lex-Rex: the Law and the Prince*, 466-page treatise; answer to John Maxwell

Oct 14 — Edward, Lord Herbert of Cherbury, leaves Montgomery Castle under Parliamentary control and retires to London

— William Penn[389] b. (d. 1718)

Oct 16 — Henry Parker, *Jus Populi*, response to his multiple attackers

Oct 19 — John Geree, *Vindiciae Ecclesiae Anglicanae*, anti-toleration pamphlet

— William Prynne, *Full Reply*, response to *Certain Briefe Observations* and to John Goodwin, *Theomachia*

Oct 26 — John Goodwin, *Innocencies Triumph*, defense of *Theomachia* against William Prynne

Oct 27 — Second Battle of Newbury; Parliamentary forces fail to establish a decisive victory

Nov — Sir Roger L'Estrange apprehended as part of a Royalist military action; incarcerated in Newgate Prison (until 1648)

Nov 1 — Henry Robinson, *An Answer to Mr. William Prynne's Twelve Questions*

Nov 5 — Henry Robinson, *Some Few Considerations*, response to John Dury, *Epistolary Discourse*

Nov 6 — Edmund Waller released from imprisonment and ordered to leave England

Nov 7 (?) — **Herbert Palmer, *The Glass of God's Providence toward His Faithful Ones*, published; attack on Milton**

---

389. Penn is credited with writing nearly 120 works in English, Dutch, German, and Latin, a record exceeded among the Quakers only by the even more prolific George Fox.

Nov 8 — Commons orders that Sir John Denham be removed as a counselor to Charles I and restrained from approaching the Court

Nov 14 — ***An Answer to a Book, Intituled, The Doctrine and Discipline of Divorce*, licensed by Joseph Caryl**

Nov 15 — Calibut Downing, *The Cleer Antithesis or Diametriall Opposition Betweene Presbytery and Prelacy*

Nov 19 — ***An Answer to a Book, Intituled, The Doctrine and Discipline of Divorce*, published, with laudatory preface by the censor, Joseph Caryl**[390]

Nov 22 — Lady Eleanor Davies, *A Prayer or Petition for Peace*, dated

Nov 23/24 — **John Milton, *Areopagitica* appears; signed with Milton's full name, but unlicensed, unregistered, without publisher or printer's imprint**[391]**; the pamphlets sold for 4d each, and appear to have had almost no immediate influence on political events**

Nov 24 — The Propositions of the Houses, presented to Charles I at Oxford, and discussed at the Treaty of Uxbridge; further limitations on monarchical power and privilege declared; comprehensive list of Royalists whose actions against Parliament will not receive pardons

---

390. While the anonymous author seems to have read Milton's book, he knows little about Milton personally, one of the intriguing characteristics of Milton's participation in the pamphlet wars. In spite of the personal nature of attacks and counter-attacks in pamphlet after pamphlet by others, Milton's pamphlets appear to have gone almost unnoticed, and none of his few adversaries bothered to unearth any useful gossip about him—not even relating to his own marital difficulties, which would surely have been considered fair game by the controversialists of the time.

391. Sirluck notes that this is the single edition of the *Areopagitica* until 1697, when it appeared in collected editions; yet the pamphlet remains among the most influential than Milton wrote and is most likely the most frequently reprinted of his prose works today. (*Complete Prose*, Vol. II, p. 480). Jonathan Green adds that the full text was not available in a second separate edition until 1738, nearly a century after the treatise first appeared (*Encyclopedia*, p. 247).

— Ephraim Pagitt, *The Mysticall Wolfe*, anti-toleration pamphlet

Dec — **Milton mentioned along with Hezekiah Woodward as an author of a scandalous book**

Dec 9 — Commons proposes a bill forbidding sitting members of Parliament to hold military commands

Dec 19 — Christmas celebrations forbidden by an Act of Parliament as pagan ceremonials

— The House of Lords, having failed to gain an exception for Robert Devereux, 3rd Earl of Essex, receives the bill forbidding members of Parliament to hold military commands, but defers acting on it[392]

Dec 28 — **Milton called before the House of Lords to answer charges of libel**

---

392. In some ways, the bill was a clear attempt to oust Essex from his command. Commons commanders—including Oliver Cromwell, Sir Arthur Haselrig, and others could resign their seats in Parliament and keep their commands; as a peer, Essex could not resign his seat in Lords, and would therefore be forced to resign his command instead.

1645

According to his nephew Edward Philips, Milton considers (a bigamous?) marriage to a daughter of Dr. Davis, "a very Handsome and Witty Gentlewoman"[393]

Elizabeth of Bohemia receives a complete set of Milton's tracts, 1641-1645 (after 1645)

Richard Barry, fifteen-year-old 2nd Earl of Barrymore, begins studies with Milton (continuing until as late as 1647)

Jacobus Arminius and Stephanus Curcellaeus, *Examen Thesium F. Gomare de Prædestinat, cum St. Curcellaei Vindicus, Quibus Suam et Arminii Sententiam de Jure Dei Increaturas, Adversus Mosis Amyraldi Criminationes, Defendit,* published in Amsterdam

John Ball, *A Treatise of the Covenant of Grace; Wherein... Divers errours of Arminians and Others are Confuted*

Sir John Berkenhead, *The true character of Mercurius Aulicus*

Lucius Cary, 2nd Viscount Falkland, *Of the Infallibility of the Church of Rome*

Lady Eleanor Davies, *Great Brittains Visitation*, published, enumerating conditions in England that signify the imminent Second Coming; *For Whitson Tyds Last Feast*, response to the last Whitsuntide (Penecost) before the Second Coming

Sir Kenelm Digby, *The Nature of Mans Soule*, Cartesian treatise

Thomas Fuller, *Good Thoughts in Bad Times*

---

393. Helen Darbishire, ed. *The Early Lives of Milton*, p. 66.

Edward Herbert, Lord Herbert of Cherbury, *Autobiography*, written but left incomplete; *Religio Laici; De Causis Errorum*, published

William Lilly, *A Collection of Ancient and Modern Prophecy*

William Prynne, *Hidden Workes of Darkenes Brought to Publicke Light*, published, further attacks on William Laud

Alexander Ross, *Medicus Medicatus: or the Physician's Religion cur'd by a lentine or gentle potion*, harsh critique of Sir Thomas Browne, *Religio Medici*

John Saltmarsh, *Free Grace, or the Flowing of Christ's Blood*, treatise on universal salvation

Edmund Waller, *Poems, Etc.*, published by Humphrey Moseley[394]

Westminster Assembly, *Director for the Publique Worship of God*, defining appropriate worship in England

Jacob Boehme d. (b. 1575)

William Browne of Tavistock d. (?; b. 1585?-91?)

Hugo Grotius d. (b. 1583)

William Strode d.

Mary Ward d. (b. 1585); advocate of education for women and founder of the Catholic educational Institute of the Blessed Virgin Mary

Giles Widdowes d. (b. ca. 1588)

William Cavendish (b. 1593) m. Margaret Lucas[395], at Queen Henrietta Maria's court-in-exile, France

Richard Crashaw converts to Catholicism

Inigo Jones, described as "Contriver of *Scenes* for the Queens *Dancing-Barne*," is "captured, stripped, and carried away in a blanket by Parliamentary troops."[396]

---

394. This first appearance of Waller's poems may have been unauthorized. See Bush, *English Literature*, p. 602. Waller's poems received a much stronger public reception than Milton's; they went through three editions in 1645, while Milton's *Poems* was "still being offered for sale fifteen years later" (Ricks, *English Poetry and Prose*, p. 246).

395. Cavendish was fifty-two, Margaret Lucas about twenty.

396. James Anderson Winn, *John Dryden*, p. 25.

Edmund Waller begins period of exile on the continent

By the beginning of 1645, abolition of the Star Chamber and of all licensing ordinances result in over 722 individual political newspapers being published

Jan — Sir Thomas Fairfax appointed Commander-in-chief of the New Model Army

Jan 2 — William Prynne, *Truth Triumphing over Falsehood, antiquity over Novelty*, pamphlet, response to John Goodwin, *Innocencies Triumph*

Jan 4 — Westminster Assembly of Divines abolishes the *Book of Common Prayer* in favor of the *Directory for Worship*

— Westminster Assembly of Divines determines that William Laud is to be executed

— John Saltmarsh, *Dawnings of Light*

Jan 5 — **William Walwyn, *The Compassionate Samaritane*, revised 2nd edition, echoing Milton's arguments in** *Areopagitica*

Jan 6 — Katherine Chidley, *A New Yeares Gift, or a Briefe Exhortation to Mr Thomas Edwards*

Jan 7 — **John Lilburne, *A Copie of a Letter…to Mr. William Prynne Esq.*, tract urging toleration; echoes Milton's** *Areopagitica*

Jan 8 — George Gillespie, *Wholesome Severitie*, Presbyterian attack on Independents (with no mention of Milton or *Areopagitica*)

— John Goodwin, *Innocency and Truth Triumphing*, response to William Prynne, *Truth Triumphing*

Jan 10 — *England and Irelands Sad Theater*, published, political tract, with engravings, "Prynne, Burton, and Bastwick in the Pillory" and "Lilburne Whipt at the Cart's Tail"

— Archbishop William Laud attainted and beheaded after a nine-month trial fails to prove treason (b. 7 Oct 1573)

— Immediately thereafter: *The Archbishop of Canterbury's Speech; or, His Funeral Sermon, Preacht by Himself on the Scaffold on Tower-Hill, on Friday, the 10. Of Januarie 1644,*

published
— Thereafter: Peter Heylen, *A Brief Relation of the Death and Suffering of the Most Reverend and Renowned Prelate, the Lord Archbishop of Canterbury*, published at Oxford

Jan 17 — Marchamont Nedham, *Britanicus his Blessing. Britanicus his Welcome*, printed by Roger Daniel, printer to Cambridge University

Jan 29 — Scots insist on peace negotiations with Charles I

Jan 31 — John Goodwin, *Calumny Arraign'd and Cast*, response to William Prynne, *Truth Triumphing*

Feb — [George Wither?], *The Great Assises Holden in PARNASSUS by APOLLO and His Assessours*, published, anonymous assessment of literary figures including Bacon, Davenant, Sylvester, and Shakespeare

Feb 6 — [William Walwyn], *A Helpe to the Right Understanding of a Discourse Concerning Independency, Lately published by William Prynn of Lincolnes Inne, Esquire*, pamphlet, anonymous, unlicensed, without printer's imprint

Feb 7 — Daniel Featley, *The Dippers Dipt. Or, the Anabaptists duck'd and plung'd Over Head and Eares*, attack on divorce pamphlets and other controversialist writings

Feb 28 — Thomas Young, *Hope's Encouragement*, Fast-day Sermon preached before the House of Commons

Mar 4 — John Milton, *Tetrachordon*, published; so named for the four 'chords' of scripture that form the foundation of Milton's argument; published under Milton's initials but with his full name at the conclusion of the preface; unlicensed, unregistered, with no printer's imprint as required by law[397]

---

397. Sirluck notes that there were no further editions during Milton's lifetime. (*Complete Prose*, II, p. 571) The four chords are: Genesis 1: 27-28, 2:18, 23-24; Deuteronomy 24: 1-2; Matthew 5: 31-32, 19: 3-11; I Corinthians 7: 10-16. Milton was aware of the inherent difficulty of the names he chose for these pamphlets, as his rhyming use of the word *Tetrachordon* in Sonnet XI indicates—he is forced to such straining rhymes as 'por'd on,' 'word on,' and 'Gordon,' all of which further indict the pitiable ignorance of his detractors in the face of the poet's easy use of sophisticated and elevated

— John Milton, *Colasterion, a reply to a namless answer against "The Doctrine and Discipline of Divorce."* By the former author, J. M., published with no printer's imprint; "Colasterion" means "something close to 'cat-o-nine-tails'" [398]

— **Following the publication of *Colasterion*, Milton ceases to participate in the pamphlet wars until *The Tenure of Kings and Magistrates* in 1649**

— Parliament, with representatives of the Scots, Commons, and Lords, requests a loan from London to carry on the war

Mar 5 — Charles, Prince of Wales, and Edward Hyde bid farewell to Charles I for the last time

Mar 15 — John Vicars, *Picture of Independency*, Presbyterian attack on Independents (no mention of Milton or *Areopagitica*)

Mar 21 — Lady Eleanor Davies, *As not Unknowne*, published, reprinting her 1633 condemnation of Archbishop William Laud

Apr 1 — Self-Denying Ordinance, passed; all Members of Parliament holding army commissions must resign from the army, leaving Oliver Cromwell and Sir Thomas Fairfax as ranking officers; New Model Army develops

Apr 3 — Amelia Lanier buried (chr. January 27, 1569)

Apr 4 — John Cotton, *The Way of the Churches of Christ in New England*

Apr 8 — [Richard Overton], *The Arraignement of Mr. Persecution ..., by Yongue Mr. Martin Mar-Priest, Son to old Martin the Metrapolitane*, pamphlet[399]

---

language.

398. Flannagan, *Riverside Milton*, p. 1025. *Colasterion* is perhaps most noteworthy to modern readers for its telling example of Milton's willingness to descend beyond colloquialism into personal attack: "I mean not to dispute philosophy with this pork, who never read any."

399. In addition to the by-line, connecting this text with the Elizabethan Martin Mar-Prelate tracts, Overton further indicates his hostility to government policies by adding the imprimatur: "This is Licensed, and

Apr 10 — Thomas Haynes, *Christs Kingdome on Earth, Opened According to Scriptures*, pamphlet, attacks literal interpretation of scripture

Apr 11 — **Milton signs as witness to the will of William Blackborow**

May — John Taylor, the Water-Poet, *Rebels Anathematized and Anatomized*, verse-pamphlet attacking *Mercurius Britanicus*

— *Mercurius Anti-Britanicus or the Second Part of the King's Cabinet Vindicated*, etc.

May 8 — William Dell, *Power from on High, Or the Power of the Holy Ghost*

— Ephraim Pagitt, *Heresio-graphy...*, blunt attack on the "Divorcer" along with other controversial sects

May 21 — John Bastwick, *Independency not Gods Ordinance*, pamphlet

May 31 — 'Martin Mar-priest' [Richard Overton], *A Sacred Decretal*

Jun 4 — Common Council of London request that Oliver Cromwell command new forces to be raise

Jun 10 — John Bastwick, *Independency not Gods Ordinance*, 2nd part, pamphlet

— Joshua Sprigge, *The Ancient Bounds, or Liberty of Conscience*, tract defining Independent limits to toleration

Jun 14 — Battle of Naseby; Cromwell's forces under General Sir Thomas Fairfax defeat the Royalists; capture of King Charles' state papers

— *The King's Cabinet Opened*, Charles I's state papers published by Parliament, under the direction of John Sadler, Thomas May, and Henry Parker; reveals Charles' secret dealings with the Irish and private correspondence with Henrietta Maria

---

printed according to Holy Order, but not Entered into the Stationers Monopole." The imprint reads: "Printed by Martin Claw Clergie, Printer to the Reverend Assembly of Divines and are to be sould at his Shop in Toleration Street, at the Signe of the Subjects Liberty, right opposite to Persecution Court. 1645." (William Heller, *Tracts*, Vol. III, p. 205)

Jul 21-28 — Marchamont Needham, *Mercurius Britanicus*, quotes extensively from captured papers written by Charles I

Jun 27 — 'Martin Mar-Priest' [Richard Overton], *Martins Eccho*

Jun 28 — Sir Simonds D'Ewes, *The Primitive Practise for Preserving Truth*, tract

Summer (Jul or Aug?) — Mary Powell Milton returns to London for a reconciliation with Milton

Jul 2 — 'Martin Mar-Priest' [Richard Overton], *The Nativity of Sir John Presbyter*

Jul 24 — William Prynne, *A Fresh Discovery of some Prodigious New Wandring-Blasing-Stars, & Firebrands*

Jul 24-31 — *A Diary or an Exact Journall*, Royalist journal, notes the frequency of witchcraft accusations in pro-Parliamentary counties

Jul 26 — By this date, twenty executions for witchcraft in Norfolk county, based on evidence collected by Matthew Hopkins

Jul 29 — Witchcraft trials begins at Chelmsford, Essex, presided over by Robert Rich, 2nd Earl of Warwick; 28 or 29 individuals accused, 18 executed

— Thereafter: John Stearne, *True and exact Relation of the severall Informations, Examinations and Confessions of the Late Witches...at Chelmesford...*

Aug 4 — Marchamont Needham, final issue of *Mercurius Britanicus* before its printer, Robert White, is sentenced to Fleet Prison

Aug 11 — Robert White released

— Marchamont Needham, *Mercurius Britanicus* resumes after missing only one issue

Aug 13 — *Aulicus His Hue and Cry Sent Forth after Britanicus*, pamphlet attacking Marchamont Needham

Aug 15 — Great Yarmouth, Norfolkshire, invites Matthew Hopkins to come there and search out witches; Hopkins visits in September and again in December; five women subsequently executed

Aug 27 — Witchcraft trials commence in Suffolk, presided over by Samuel Fairclough and Edmund Calamy; sixteen women and two men hanged

— Thereafter: *A True Relation of the Araignment of eighteene Witches at St. Edmundsbury....27th August 1645... As also a List of the names of those that were executed*

— Thereafter: *Signs and Wonders from Heaven.... Likewise a New Discovery of Witches in Stepney Parish. And how 20. Witches more were executed in Suffolk this last Assise. Also how the Divell came to Soffarn to a Farmers house in the habit of a Gentlewoman on horse back*

Aug 30 — John Bastwick, *Just Defense...*, pamphlet against Lilburne

Sep — *Mercurius Aulicus* ceases publication; succeeded by *Mercurius Academicus*

Sep 4-11 — *Moderate Intelligencer*, editorial critical of the increasing number of accusations of witchcraft directed primarily against "poore old women"

Sep 9 — Mother Lakeland burned in Ipswich as a witch, probably on evidence gathered by Matthew Hopkins

— Thereafter: *The Lawes against Witches and Conjuration, and Some brief Notes and Observations for the Discovery of Witches. Being very Usefull for these Times wherein the Devil reignes and prevailes.... Also The Confession of Mother Lakeland, who was arraigned and condemned for a Witch at Ipswich in Suffolke... By authority*

Sep 11 — Prince Rupert surrenders Bristol to Parliamentary forces

Sep 13 — Battle of Philiphaugh, parliamentarians defeated by General Leslie and his Scots army

Sep 19 — John Lilburne, *England's Miserie, And Remedie*, Leveller tract, published following Lilburne's imprisonment during the summer

Sep/Oct — **Milton and family move to Barbican, Cripplegate, London**

Oct — William Lawes d., at the Siege of Chester

Oct 8 — [John Lilburne], *Englands Birth-Right Justified*, pamphlet, anonymous, unlicensed, without imprint or title-page

Oct 11 — [William Walwyn], *Englands Lamentable Slavery*, pamphlet, published anonymously, without license, imprint, or title-page

Oct 15 — William Prynne, *The Lyar Confounded*, pamphlet

— Ralph Cudworth, Regius Professor of Hebrew, Cambridge

Oct 18 — William Faithorne taken at the surrender of Basing House; subsequently imprisoned and released on condition that he leave England

Nov — **William Marshall engraves a notoriously inept portrait of Milton for *Poems of Mr. John Milton***

Nov 24 — Robert Baillie, *A Dissvasive from the Errours of the Time*, attacks divorce tracts

Dec — First opera produced in France, *La Finta pazza*, sponsored by Cardinal Mazarin

— John Saltmarsh, *Free Grace*, published

Dec 8 — *The Perfect Diurnal* reports the fall of Lathom House to Parliamentary forces; the event recorded in *A Journal of the Seige of Lathom House* (1644)

Dec 29 — 'Martin Mar-Priest' [Richard Overton], *The Ordinance of Tythes Dismounted*

(?)— **John Milton, *Poems of Mr. John Milton*, title page dated, published by Humphrey Moseley, with engraved frontispiece by William Marshall; Milton's first published collection of poetry, both English and Latin**

— **John Milton, Sonnet IX: "Lady That in the Prime"**

— **John Milton, Sonnet X: "To the Lady Margaret Ley"**

— **John Milton, *In Effigiei eius sculptorem*, Greek epigram responding to Marshall's engraving; Hughes translates the original as: 'Looking at the form of its original, you might say, mayhap, that this likeness had been drawn by a tyro's hand; but, friends, since you do not recognize what is modelled here, have a laugh at a caricature by a

good-for-nothing artist.'[400]
— John Milton, Sonnet XI: "On the Detraction which followed...," written after *Tetrachordon* and *Colasterion* appeared
— John Milton, Sonnet XII: "On the Same"

---

400. Part of the joke, of course, is that Marshall, who presumably could not read Greek, ended up engraving his own disparagement unawares.

1646

John Milton, early work on *Samson Agonistes* (?)
William Bradford, *History of the Plimouth Plantation* (through 1651
Sir Thomas Browne, *Pseudo-doxia Epidemica* (Vulgar Errors
Walter Charlton, *Physiologia Epicuro-Gassendo-Charltonia, Or a Fabrick of Science Natural, Upon the Hypothesis of Atoms, Founded by Epicurus, Repaired by Petrus Gassendus, Augmented by Walter Charlton*, published, English scientific treatise
Samuel Clarke, *Mirror or Looking-Glasse both for saints and sinners*, Non-conformist treatise on God's judgments and mercies(4th edition. two volumes, folio, 1671)
Richard Crashaw, *Steps to the Temple; Delights of the Muses*
Nathanael Culverwel, *A Discourse of the Light of Nature*
Lady Eleanor Davies, *The Lady Eleanor her Appeal*, tract outlining her history as a prophet; subscribed with the anagram "Reveale O Daniel" (Eleanor Audeley); *Je Le Tien: The General Restitution*, published, with anagrams "Le Elen: Ti:," "Je Le Tien," and "I Ele(a)n(or) Ti(cher)," or Touchet
John Davies of Hereford, *Writing Schoolemaster*
John Donne, *Biathanatos*, treatise on suicide
John Dury, *Education of Nobles and Gentlemen* (?)
John Gaule, *Select Cases of Conscience Touching Witches and Witchcraft*
John Geree, *The Character of an Old English Puritane, or Non-Conformist*, pro-Puritan tract; *Astrologo-Mastix*, anti-

Catholic tract, including list of popes who had been conjurors and astrologers

John Hall, *Horae Vacivae*, essays, published in London

Samuel Hartlib, *The Parliaments Reformation*

Thomas Hobbes, *Of Liberty and Necessity*, published

Sir Francis Kynaston, *Leoline and Sydanis*, reprinted

John Lilburne, *The Freemans Freedom Vindicated*, published; *A true relation of the material passages of Lieut. Col. John Lilburnes sufferings*, published

Nicholas of Cusa, *The Vision of God*, translated by John Everard

William Prynne, *Canterburies Doome*, published, further attacks on William Laud

Bruno Ryves, *Mercurius Rusticus: or, The Countries Complaint of the Sacriledges, Prophanations, and Plunderings, Committed by the Schimastiques on the Cathedrall Churches of this Kingdome*, published at Oxford

John Saltmarsh, *Some Drops of the Vail*, names the Smectymnuuans for the first time

James Shirley, *Poems &c.*, including the epyllion, *"Narcissus or the Self-Lover"*

Sir John Suckling, *Fragmentum Aurea. A Collection of All the Incomparable Peeces, Written by Sir John Suckling. And Published by a Friend to Perpetuate his Memory*; including *The Goblins: A Comedy, presented at the Private House in Black Fryers, by his Majesties Servants*; and *Brennoralt: A Tragedy, presented at the Private House in Black Fryers by His Majesties Servants*; published by Humphrey Moseley (reprinted 1648, 1658)

Jeremy Taylor, *An Apology for Authorized and Set Forms of Liturgy*, defending the *Book of Common Prayer* against the *Directory of Worship*

Bishop John Wilkins, *Ars Predicandi*, published

William Dobson d.

Henry Hawkins d. (b. 1571?)

Roger Boyle, Lord Broghill (later 2nd Earl of Orrery) b.

First Civil War essentially over

Abraham Cowley joins Henrietta Maria's Court-in-Exile in France

Thomas May appointed secretary to the House of Commons

Sir Christopher Milton in active service as a Royalist

John Locke attends Westminster school

George Wither, pamphlets including *Mercurius Elenchus, Mercurius Pragmaticus,* and *Justicarius Justificatus,* burned

Jan 1 — *A Letter of the Ministers...against Toleration*, presented to the Westminster Assembly

Jan 2 — **John Milton, *Poems of Mr. John Milton both English and Latin, compos'd at several times. Printed by his true copy,* and *Joannis Miltoni Londinensis Poemata* (separately paged edition of Latin poems), registered for publication by Humphrey Moseley; other than *Lycidas*, *Comus*, "On Shakespeare" and the Hobson poem pirated for *A Banquet of Jests*, this constitutes Milton's first public appearance as a serious poet, his first collected edition, and his first work bearing his full name.**[401]

Jan 6 — John Lilburne, *Innocency and Truth*, reply to William Prynne

Jan 7 — By this date, seven executions for witchcraft in Aldeburgh, on evidence gathered by Matthew Hopkins between September and December

Jan 15 — Charles I, letter to Parliament asking for peace; answered by Sir Henry Vane and others with an ultimatum

Jan 16 — John Saltmarsh, *The Smoke in the Temple*, tract dealing with reconciling English congregations

---

401. Even more significantly, *Lycidas* had appeared only under the initials J.M., while *Comus* was first published anonymously; at the time *Poems* appeared, Milton would perhaps have been far better known as a pamphleteer and controversialist than as a poet, in spite of his life-long claim to a poetic calling. Nor, for that matter, would he publish substantially more poetry until the appearance of *Paradise Lost* over two decades later.

Jan 22 — **Robert Baillie, *A Disuasive from the Errours of the Time*, published (reprint?), with mention of Milton's advocacy for divorce-at-pleasure but little awareness of other information about him, certainly no reference to the *Poems***

Jan 24 — Richard Overton, *Divine Observations*, pro-toleration pamphlet responding to the *Letter of the Ministers*...

Jan 29 — William Walwyn, *Tolleration Justified*, pro-toleration pamphlet responding to the *Letter of the Ministers*...

Feb — Francesco Cavalli, *Egisto*, opera, performed in Paris, sponsored by Cardinal Mazarin

— John Hall admitted to St. John's College, Cambridge

Feb 9 — **John Milton, Sonnet XIII: "To My Friend, Mr. Henry Lawes"**

Feb 17 — John Goodwin, *Twelve Considerable Cautions*, pamphlet

Feb 26 — **Thomas Edwards, *Gangræna: Or, A Catalogue and Discovery of Many of the Errours, Heresies, Blasphmeies and Pernicious Practices of the Sectaries of This Time Vented and Acted in England in These Last Four Years, Part I*, attack on the divorce tracts, among others; Milton's was error 154 of 180**

Mar-Apr — Matthew Hopkins identifies witches in Cambridgeshire and Northamptonshire; thereafter in Huntingdonshire, with at ten examined and several executed

— Thereafter: *The Witches of Huntingdon, their Examinations and Confessions...*, pamphlet

Mar 10 — John Saltmarsh, *Groanes for Liberty*, tract

Mar 13 — [William Walwyn], *A Whisper in the Eare of Mr. Thomas Edwards Minister...Occasioned by his mentioning of him reproachfully, in his later pernitious booke, justly entituled the Gangræna*, pamphlet

Mar 18 — Edward Hyde, Earl of Clarendon, *History of the Rebellion*, begun (published 1702-4)

Mar 19 — John Goodwin, *Cretensis*, pamphlet, attack on Thomas Edwards

— William Walwyn, *A Word more to Mr. Thomas Edwards*, response to *Gangræna*

Mar 20 — Richard Overton, *The Last Warning to all the Inhabitants of London*, pro-toleration, anti-monarchical tract

Apr 13 — David Buchanan, *Truth's Manifest*, burned

Apr 25 — Leonard Busher, Anabaptist, *Religious Peace* (reprint from 1614), plea for toleration

Apr 27 — Charles I escapes from Oxford disguised a servant

May 5 — Charles I surrenders his person to the Scots army at Newark, infuriating Parliamentarians further

May 6 — Henry Lawrence, *Of Our Communion and Warre with Angels*

May 7 — Humphrey Moseley acquires the rights to Sir William Davenant, *The Unfortunate Lovers*

May 11-18 — Marchamont Needham, final issue of *Mercurius Britanicus*, No. 130, attacks Charles I

May 13 — The Scots army moves north to Newcastle to avoid attack by the New Model Army

May 23 — Marchamont Needham imprisoned in Fleet Prison for publishing the final, unlicensed issue of *Mercurius Britanicus*

May 25 — Lady Eleanor Davies, *The Day of Judgements Modell*, published, tract correlating Noah's experiences with England's in the first Civil War

May 26 — Common Council of the City of London, *Humble Remonstrance and Petition* submitted to Commons, demanding that heresy be suppressed

May 28 — Thomas Edwards, *The Second Part of Gangræna*

Jun 4 — Marchamont Needham released from Fleet Prison, on condition that he publish no further political tracts; Needham complies, taking up the practice of medicine

Jun 10 — William Walwyn, *An Antidote Against Master Edwards His old and New Poyson*, pamphlet-response to Thomas Edwards, *The Second Part of Gangræna*

— Charles sends orders from Newcastle for all of his commanders

to surrender cities and castles under their control
Jun 11 — Joseph Hunscott, representing the Stationer's Company, *Petition and information...to Parliament against diverse scandalous Libels and treasonous Pamphlets*, published
Jun 17 — John Saltmarsh, *Reasons for Unitie*, tract
Jun 22 — John Vicars, *Schismatick Sifted*, Presbyterian attack on Independents (no mention of Milton or *Areopagitica*)
Jun 24 — Surrender of Oxford, King Charles' headquarters
Jun 26 — Prince Charles arrives at St. Malo to begin his exile in France during the Interregnum
Jun 27 — **Richard Powell, Milton's father-in-law, given a pass to leave Oxford; his entire family moves in with Milton in London**
Jun 30 — William Walwyn, *A Pearle in a Dounghill*, pamphlet-response to John Lilburne's imprisonment in Newgate
Jul — Marchamont Needham, *Independencie No Schisme*, pamphlet, anti-Presbyterian plea for religious toleration
— Parliament finally approves the Nineteen Proposals to be sent to Charles I
Jul (?) — **John Milton, "On the New Forcers of Conscience"**
Jul 1 — Gottfried Wilhelm, Baron von Leibnitz b. (d. 1716)
Jul 7 — [Richard Overton], *A Remonstrance of Many Thousand Citizens, and other Free-Born People of England, to their owne House of Commons. Occasioned through the Illegall and Barbarous Imprisonment of that Famous and Worthy Sufferer for his Countries Freedoms, Lieutenant Col. John Lilburne...*, pamphlet, with modified engraving showing John Lilburne imprisoned[402]
Jul 13 — The Propositions of the Houses, delivered to Charles at Newcastle
Jul 22 — Worcester surrenders

---

402. "...Lilburne behind bars, as Overton made haste to depict him in the frontispiece to *A Remonstrance of Many Thousand* (July 7), was precisely what was needed to convert revolutionary sentiment into a coherent movement" (William Haller, *Puritan Tracts*, p. 101).

Jul 24 — John Price, *The City-Remonstrance Remonstrate*
Jul 29 — **Milton's daughter Anne b.**
Jul 31 — Richard Overton, *An Alarum to the House of Lords*, tract
Aug 1 — Charles I, *The King's First Answer to the Propositions presented at Newcastle*
Aug 8 — Sir Godfrey Kneller b. (d. 1723), as Gottfried Kniller, at Lübeck, Germany
Aug 11 — William Walwyn, *A Prediction of Mr. Edwards His Conversion, and Recantation*, pamphlet-response to Thomas Edwards
— Richard Overton arrested on order of the House of Lords; imprisoned in Newgate
Aug 17 — Pendennis Castle, Cornwall, surrenders
Aug 27 — John Goodwin, *Anapologesiates Antapologias*, response to Thomas Edwards
— Hugh Peters, *Mr. Peters Last Report of the English Wars*, pamphlet
Sep — Robert Devereux, 3rd Earl of Essex, d. without issue (b. 1591), buried in Westminster Abbey; earldom of Essex extinct in the Devereux family
Sep 2 — Presbyterians in Commons propose an ordinance to control blasphemy[403]
Sep 4 — Sir William Davenant, *Love and Honour*, *The Distresses*, *The Fair Favorite*, and *News from Plimouth*, SR entries by Humphrey Moseley
Sep 9 — Richard Overton, *A Defiance against all Arbitrary Usurpations or Encroachments, either of the House of Lords, or any other, upon the Soveraignty of the Supreme House of Commons...or upon the Rights, Properties and Freedoms of the People in General*, published while Overton is in prison
Sep 15 — Henry Vaughan, *Poems, with the Tenth Satire of*

---

403. Among other stipulations, denial of the Trinity or Incarnation would be punishable by death; denial of infant baptism or other Presbyterian views would be punishable by life imprisonment.

Juvenal, registered[404]

Sep 24 — Bathsua Makin, *The Malady and...Remedy of Vexations and Unjust Arrests and Actions*, pamphlet; Makin's first publication

Oct — Elias Ashmole, admitted into a Masonic Lodge

Oct 10 — Richard Overton, *An Arrow Against All Tyrants and Tyranny, shot from the Prison of New-gate into the Prerogative Bowels of the Arbitrary House of Lords.* published while Overton imprisoned in Newgate

Oct 29 — [William Walwyn], *Parable, or Consultation of Physitians upon Master Edwards*, allegorical tract. Published anonymously

Nov 4 — Dr. Nathan Paget becomes a fellow of the College of Physicians

Nov 30 — Richard Overton, *An Unhappy Game at Scotch and English*, tract; accuses Charles I of being the primary instigator of Civil War

Dec 2 — *An Unhappy Game...*, ordered to be burned by Parliament

Dec 10 — Samuel Richardson, *Certain Questions propounded to the Assembly whether corporall punishments may be inflicted upon such as hold Errours in Religion*

Dec 12 — Catherine Thomason, wife of George Thomason, buried

Dec 13 — **Milton signs as witness to the will of Richard Powell**

Dec 16 (?) — **John Milton, Sonnet XIV: "On the Religious Memory of Mrs. Catharine Thomason," in memory of the wife of George Thomason**

Dec 20 — Charles I, *The King's Second Answer to the Propositions presented at Newcastle*

Dec 28 — Thomas Edwards, *The Third Part of Gangræna*

---

404. Neither the poems nor the satires were particularly well received, in part perhaps because the Jonsonian, classical echoes of Vaughan's first poems clashed with the discordance of the times and with seemingly more critical historical events.

1647

Lancelot Andrewes, Bishop of Winchester, *The Private Devotions of...Lancelot Andrewes*, published

Robert Baillie, *Anabaptism*

Francis Beaumont and John Fletcher, *Comedies and Tragedies*, collected edition, published by Humphrey Moseley, with prefatory poem by Sir John Denham

A Call to All the Soldiers of the Army, pamphlet; accuses the Army of making an idol of King Charles

Laurence Clarkson, *A Generall Charge or Impeachment of High Treason, in the name of Justice Equity, against the Communality of England*, Leveller tract

John Cleveland, *The Character of a London-diurnall, with severall select poems: by the same author*, published, reissued between eight and sixteen times during the next two years[405]

Richard Corbett, *Certain Elegant Poems, written by Dr. Corbett, Bishop of Norwich*

Abraham Cowley, *The Mistress*, Petrarchan lyrics

The (D)Ivell in Kent, or His strange Delusions at Sandwich

Sir Richard Fanshawe, translation of Battista Guarini, *Il Pastor Fide*

Thomas Fuller, *Good Thoughts in Worse Times*

John Goodwin, *Independencie Gods Veritie*

---

405. As the numbers of re-issues suggests, John Cleveland was arguably the most popular poet of the mid-century, his books going through many editions and his poetry accepted as the standard for excellence among most readers.

Wenceslas Hollar, "Long Bird's-Eye View of London", engraved, including depictions of the Globe

Matthew Hopkins, *The Discovery of Witches: in answer to severall Queries, lately Delivered to the Judges of Assize for the County of Norfolk. And now published by Matthew Hopkins, Witch-finder. For the Benefit of the Whole Kingdome...*

John Lilburne, *Jonah's Cry out of the Whale's Belly*

William Lilly, *Christian Astrology*, published (2nd edition 1659)

Thomas May, *History of the Parliament of England*[406]

Henry More, *Philosophical Poems*, published at Cambridge, including *Psychozoia, Psychathanasia, Antipsychopannychia, Antimonopsychia, Democritus platonissans,* and *The Præxistency of the Soul*

Henry Neville, *The Ladies Parliament*, satire

Francis Quarles, *Hosanna*

[Joshua Sprigge], *Anglia Rediviva; England's Recovery; Being the History of the Motions, Actions, and Successes of the Army under the Immediate Conduct of His Excellency Sir Thomas Fairfax...*, published

Thomas Stanley, *Poems and Translations*, published

John Saltmarsh, *Sparkles of Glory, or some Beams of the Morning Star*, with discussion of progressive revelation

Robert Stapleton, translation of Juvenal, *Satires*, all sixteen satires included

Thomas Habington of Hindlip, d. (b. 1560)

Daniel Mytens d. (b. 1590?), painter, trained at The Hague but influential at the courts of James I and Charles I[407]

Gilbert Mabbot appointed official licenser of the press (to 1649)

Philosophical Club organized, Oxford University

---

406. May's *History* has been identified as an influence on Milton's *Eikonoklastes*. See Bush, *English Literature*, p. 565.

407. Mytens was the most important painter in England until the arrival of Sir Anthony Van Dyck. The finest painting in England during the period is executed by continental-trained artists.

Jan 1 — **John Milton's father-in-law, Richard Powell, d.**

Jan 6 — John Hall, *Poems*, dedicatory epistle to Thomas Stanley dated, thereafter published at Cambridge

— John Lilburne, *Regall Tyrannie Discovered*, tract; presents justifications for regicide

Jan 10 — **Broadsheet[408] satirizes Milton as a "divorcer"**

Jan 19 — *A Catalogue of the severall Sects and Opinions in England*, broadside, including woodcuts of the "Divorcer and the "Soul-sleeper"

Jan 23 — **John Milton, *Ad Ioannem Rousium, Oxoniensis Academiæ Bibliotecarium* (To John Rouse, Librarian of Oxford University)**

Jan 30 — Scots army surrenders Charles I at Newcastle; Charles held at Holmby House, Northamptonshire, by Parliamentary forces

Feb — Robert Boyle, letter to Francis Tallents, referring to the founding of the "invisible or…the philosophical college," a possible precursor to the Royal Society[409]

Robert Boyle, letter from London, noting the rapid increase of Independency in religion and politics[410]

— Lady Eleanor Davies, *The Gatehouse Salutation from the Lady Eleanor*, tract written during her imprisonment in the Gatehouse at Westminster, in rhyming prose, "To the Tune of *Magnificat*"

---

408. "Broadsheeets," also known as "broad-sides," were large, single-page publications, often crudely printed on illegal presses and distributed on the London streets, affixed to doors and walls. They served an important function in the continuing struggles, particularly religious.

409. Frances Yates sees the "invisible college" as strongly associated with Rosicrucianism, hermetism, and alchemy as well.

410. "There are few days pass here, that may not justly be accused of brewing or broaching some new opinion. Nay, some are so studiously changling in that particular, they esteem an opinion as a diurnal, after a day or two scarce worth the keeping. If any man have lost his religion, let him repair to London, and I'll warrant him he shall find it: I had almost said too, if any man has a religion, let him but come hither now, and he shall go near to losing it" (cited in Henry Thomas Buckle, *History*, Vol. 1, 347n.)

Feb 3 — James Howell, letter, noting that within the past two years, nearly 200 witches had been indicted in Essex and Suffolk alone, and half of those had been executed; a year later, he raises the number to 300 indicted[411]

Feb 5 — John Goodwin, *Hagio-mastix, or the Scourge of the Saints Displayed in His Colours of Ignorance and Blood*, published, attempting to expand the limits of toleration

Feb 10 — [Richard Overton], *The Commoners Complaint: or A Dreadful Warning from Newgate to the Commons of England...*, pamphlet, without license or imprint

Feb 18 — John Goodwin, *A Candle to See the Sunne*, pamphlet, continuation of the arguments in *Hagiomastix*

Feb 19 — Commons narrowly votes to disband the New Model Army

Mar — Luigi Rossi, *Orfeo*, opera, produced in Paris, sponsored by Cardinal Mazarin

Mar 9 — William Prynne, *The Sword of Christian Magistracy*, panicky diatribe against change

Mar 13 (?)— **John Milton, Sr., d., leaving Milton the Bread Street property**

Mar 15 — **John Milton, Sr., buried, St. Giles, Cripplegate, London**

Apr — Sir Roger L'Estrange, *L'Estrange his Appeal from the Court Martial to Parliament*

— Robert Boyle, first extant letter to Samuel Hartlib

Apr 2 — Lady Eleanor Davies undergoes a vision of Ezekiel while in the Gatehouse

— Lady Eleanor Davies, *Ezekiel the Prophet*, tract, dated

— John Goodwin, *A Postscript or Appendix*, pamphlet, completing the arguments begun in *Hagiomastix*

Apr 10 — John Wilmot, b. (afterward 2nd Earl of Rochester)

Apr 21 — **John Milton, Letter to Carlo Dati, entrusted for delivery to George Thomason, Milton's "very familiar acquaintance"**

---

411. Wallace Notestein, *History of Witchcraft*, p. 195.

Apr 26 — *These Tradesmen are Preachers*, broadside, attacking the doctrines of "mechanic preachers," with illustrations

Apr 27 — John Bastwick, *The Storming of the Anabaptists Garrisons*, pamphlet, attack on sectarianism

May — Samuel Hartlib, *Considerations tending to the Happy Accomplishment of Englands Reformation in Church and State*

May 12 — Charles I, *The King's Third Answer to the Propositions presented at Newcastle*

May 15 — John Cotton, *The Bloudy Tenent washed and made white in the bloud of the Lambe*, reply to Roger Williams, *The Bloudy Tenent of Persecution*

May 16 — Declaration of the Army, petition signed by 223 commissioned officers, presented to Parliament

May 18 — Charles I's peace proposals accepted by Parliamentary Presbyterians and Scots commissioners[412]

May 26 — Anthony Wood matriculates at Merton College, Oxford

May 27 — John Saltmarsh, *Sparkles of Glory*, tract, attack on all forms of organized ministry in favor of inner spiritual experience

May 31 — Parliamentary commissioners attempt to disband Sir Thomas Fairfax's regiment; the regiment mutinies and begins a march toward London

Early Jun — Marchamont Needham, *The Case of the Kingdom Stated, According to the Proper Interest of the severall Parties Engaged*, published, 18-page anti-Presbyterian pamphlet urging Royalists to merge with Independents (re-issued twice, summer 1647)

Jun 1 — Parliamentary deadline for all army regiments to disband

Jun 3 — Cornet George Joyce, of General Fairfax's lifeguards but acting on orders from Cromwell, accompanied by 500

---

412. "Thus was born an alliance between Scotland and the English Presbyterians that would lead to a second civil war" (J. H. Adamson and H. F. Holland, *Sir Harry Vane*, p. 252).

troops, removes Charles I from Holmby House[413]

Jun 5 — A Solemn Engagement of the Army, presented by the military to the Presbyterian Commons

Jun 6 — John Lilburne, *The Just Mans Justification* published, denies the House of Lords' jurisdiction over commoners; written while Lilburne is in Newgate Prison

Jun 14 — [William Walwyn?], *Gold Tried in the Fire*, pamphlet

Jun 23 — William Walwyn, *A Pearle in a Dounghill*, tract, attacks the House of Lords for tyranny; written during Walwyn's imprisonment

Jun 28 — Jeremy Taylor, *A Discourse on the Liberty of Prophesying with its just limits and temper; shewing the unreasonableness of prescribing to other men's Faith, and the iniquity of persecuting differing opinions*, 250-page treatise on liberty of conscience

Jul — Paul Best, *Mysteries Discovered, or a Mercurial Picture pointing out the way from Babylon to the Holy City...*, pamphlet, burned on three separate days in three places

Early Jul — Marchamont Needham, *The Lawyer of Lincolnes-Inn Reformed: Or, An Apology for the Army*, pamphlet rebutting William Prynne's *Nine Queries*

Jul 17 — Richard Overton, *An Appeale from the Degenerate Representative Body the Commons of England Assembled at Westminster: To the Body Represented, the Free People in General*

— Lady Eleanor Davies confined to Debtors' Prison by Thomas Paine, a printer

Jul 21 — London apprentices and others meet at Skinner's Hall, draw up a Solemn Engagement, supporting the Covenant and the King

Aug — Beginning of Cromwell's dictatorship

— Lady Eleanor Davies, *The Excommunication our of Paradice*,

---

413. What was essentially an organized kidnapping occurred primarily because of fears that the Scots were about to seize the King's person (a fairly common occurrence in the history of Scottish monarchs) and remove Charles I to Scotland; Cornet Joyce simply acted first.

tract, addressed to Oliver Cromwell as source of regeneration for England; with numerological calculations on 666

Aug 1 — The Heads of the Proposals agreed upon by his Excellency Sir Thomas Fairfax and the Council of the Army, to be tendered to the Commissioners of Parliament residing with the Army: containing the particulars of their desires…, presented

Aug 2 — [Henry Neville], *The Ladies, a Second Time, Assembled in Parliament. A Continuation of the Parliament of the Ladies*, satire

Aug 6 — Sir Thomas Fairfax's regiment enters Westminster

— Restored Parliament considers the Heads of the Proposals, over fifty proposals demanded by the Army

Aug 12 — Matthew Hopkins buried, Mistley-cum-Manningtree[414]

Aug-Sep — **John Milton, Mary Powell Milton, and Anne remove from the Barbican house to a smaller house in High Holborn, where there is no longer room for him to house his scholars or his in-laws**

Aug 20 — Levellers begin to break away from Independents and emerge as a separate political influence

Sep — Edward, Lord Herbert of Cherbury, visits Pierre Gassendi in Paris

Sep 4 — *Mercurius Melancholicus*, begins publication; contributions by Matthew Parker, the balladeer

Sep 21 — Marchamont Needham, first publication of *Mercurius Pragmaticus*, a Royalist newspaper supporting Charles I

Sep 29 — Thomas Collier preaches in a sermon that Christ will reign "in and by his saints"[415]

Sep 30 — Long Parliament reaffirms the 1643 Licensing Orders

Oct — *The Case of the Army Truly Stated* published; formal definition of Leveller beliefs and principles

---

414. He died of consumption.

415. Christopher Hill, *The Experience of Defeat*, p. 53

— Hugh Peter, *Word for the Army*, millenarian tract

Oct 26 — Richard Lovelace and Peter Lely admitted to the Freedom of the Painters' Company

Oct 29 — *An Agreement of the People for a firm and present peace upon grounds of common right*, a new Leveller-inspired constitution for England, debated by the General Council of the Army

Nov 1 — **Carlo Dati replies to Milton's earlier letter, requesting that Milton write commendatory verses for a recently deceased Florentine poet, Francesco Rovai**

Nov 6 — Parliament resolves that the King must henceforth assent to all laws tendered him by Commons and Lords—a step toward establishing Parliamentary sovereignty over monarchy

Nov 11 — Charles I escapes from confinement at Hampton Court and seeks asylum on the Isle of Wight, whose governor imprisons him at Carisbrook Castle prior to returning him to Parliamentary jurisdiction

— Thereafter: *The kings Majesties most gratious message, with a perfect narrative of the manner of his Majesties going from Hampton Court*, published

Dec — 'Pragmaticus' [Marchamont Needham?], *The Levellers Levell'd. Or, The Independent Conspiracie to root out Monarchie*

Dec 14 — Sion College ministers, *A Testimony to the Truth ...*, attack on divorce tracts

Dec 17 — Henry Vaughan, *Olor Iscanus* (Swan of Usk), prepared, dedicatory epistle dated; not published for over three years

Dec 18 — John Goodwin, *The Divine Authority of the Scriptures Asserted*, attack on the doctrine of predestination, in support of toleration

Dec 26 — Charles enters into a secret treaty with the Scottish Commissioners, agreeing to abolish Episcopacy and establish Presbyterianism in Scotland

Dec 29 — John Saltmarsh, *Wonderful Predictions*, tract

1648

John Milton, Sonnet to Henry Lawes, in George Sandys, *Choice Psalms Put into Musick for Three Voices*; **musical settings by Henry and William Lawes**
John Milton, *Character of the Long Parliament*, **written**
John Milton, *The History of Britain*, **begun (?)**
Richard Allen, *An Antidote against Heresy: or, A Preservation for Protestants against the Poyson of Papists, Anabaptists, Arrians, Arminians, etc. And Their Pestilent Errours*
Bishop Lancelot Andrewes, *Manual for the Sick* and *Manual of Private Devotions*, published, translations from Greek and Latin
Joseph Beaumont, *Psyche: or Loves Mysterie In XX. Canto's: Displaying the Intercourse Betwixt CHRIST, and the SOULE*
John Bulwer, *Philocophus: Or, the Deafe and Dumbe Mans Friend*, published, treatise on education for deaf-mutes
Mary Cary, *The Resurrection of the Witnesses*, Fifth-Monarchist tract
George Cockayne, *Flesh Expiring, and the Spirit Inspiring ... or God Himself...Inheriting all Nations*, Fifth Monarchist tract
Richard Corbett, Bishop of Oxford and Norwich, *Poëtica stromata or a collection of sundry pieces in poetry: drawne by the known and approved hand of R. C.*, published in Holland or France (?)
Abraham Cowley, *The Four Ages of England*; and *A Satyre against Separatists*, published

Richard Crashaw, *Steps to the temple, sacred poems. With the delights of the muses. The second edition wherein are added divers pieces not before extant*, published

Sir William Davenant, *Madagascar, with Other Poems*, printed by Humphrey Moseley

Thomas Deloney, *The Gentle Craft. A Discourse containing many matters of Delight ... shewing what famous men have been Shoomakers in times past in this Land...*, reprinted, prose and verse fiction (1st edition, SR 1597)

Sir John Denham, *Cato Major*

Mildmay Fane, 2nd Earl of Westmorland, *Otia Sacra* (Sacred Peace), poems, including emblems and typographical verse

Sir Richard Fanshawe, *Il Pastor Fido: The faithfull shepheard with an addition of divers other poems*, published

Robert Herrick, *Hesperides and His Noble Numbers*

William Lilly, *Whether His Majesty Shall Suffer Death*, published

Edward Johnson (?), *Good News from New-England*, poem, published

William Petty, *The Advice of W. P. to Mr. Samuel Hartlib*, treatise on educational reform and blueprint for a teaching hospital

Sir Edward Sherbourne, translation of Seneca, *Medea*

'*Pseudo*-Spenser', *The Faerie Leveller: or King Charles his Leveller descried, and deciphered in Queene Elizabeth's Dayes. By her Poet Laureate, Edmond Spenser, in his unparaleled Poeme, entituled, The Faerie Queene, A lively representation of our times*, published

John Stearne, *A Confirmation and Discovery of Witchcraft ... together with the Confessions of many of those executed since May 1645*, published

Jeremy Taylor, *The Great Exemplar*, 700-page life of Christ, published[416]

---

[416]. Hugh Ross Williamson describes the book as a history specifically designed for the romance-reading audience of the time, heavily based on French secular models (50).

William Walwyn, *The Bloody*

John Wilkins, *Mathematicall Magick, or, The Wonders that may be Performed by Mechanical Geometry*

Thomas Edwards d. (b. 1599)

George Jeffries b.

John Sheffield (afterward 3rd Earl of Mulgrave) b. (d. 1721)

George Fox initiates his public ministry, eventually leading to the formation nof the Society of Friends (Quakers

Richard Lovelace, in prison after being captured by Commonwealth forces, prepares his poems for publication

The Peace of Munster concludes the Thirty Years War on the Continent; Prince Charles Louis, son of Frederick V, restored as Elector Palatine

Dorothy Osborne meets Sir William Temple

Jan 3 — Army leaders, disillusioned by attempted negotiations with the King, decide that no one shall treat with Charles I unless by the express permission of Parliament

Jan 10 — *Loyalty Speaks Truth: or a conference of the Grand Mercuries*, Pragmaticus, *Melancholicus and Elenticus concerning the present condition of his Majesty and this blessed Parliament*, published

Jan 17 — *The resulting Vote of No More Addresses*, published

Jan 18 — **Attack on Milton by Sion College ministers published**

Feb 1 — John Goodwin, *Sion Colledg Visited*, pamphlet

— Elkanah Settle b.(d. 1724)

Feb 9 — John Cotton, *The Way of the Congregational Churches Cleared*, anti-toleration tract

— Elkanah Settle, baptized

Feb 11 — *Declaration of the Commons...Touching No Farther Address to be Made to the King*, published, foreshadowing many of the charges that would be brought against Charles within the next year

Feb 22 — Humphrey Moseley acquires the rights to Sir William Davenant, *Madagascar, with Other Poems*; thereafter, a new edition issued

Mar 13 — **The Long Parliament reaffirms the 1643 Licensing Orders; under this Order, Milton acts as censor for *Mercurius Politicus* through 1651**

Mar 21 — John Vicars, *Coleman-Street Conclave Visited*, satirical treatment of John Goodwin

Mar 30 — William Jenkyn, *The Busie Bishop*, attack on John Goodwin

Spring — Sir Roger L'Estrange escapes from Newgate and establishes himself in Holland

Apr — **John Milton, Psalm 80-88 paraphrased**

Apr 4 — John Lilburne, *The Prisoners Plea for a Habeas Corpus*, pamphlet

Apr 9 — Several thousand London apprentices 'tumultuate'; the mob is put down by Cromwell's forces

Apr 19 — Sir Robert Filmer, *Anarchy of a Limited or Mixed Monarchy*, pro-Royalist tract

Apr 21 — James, Duke of York, escapes from St. James Palace, assisted by Sir John Denham

May-Jun — As many as seventeen pro-Royalist newspapers flourish, including *Mercurius Bellicus, Mercurius Aulicus, Mercurius Melancholicus, Mercurius Elencticus,* and *Mercurius Pragmaticus*

May — Resolution to bring Charles I to death

May 1 — Wales raises arms against the Army; Sir Thomas Fairfax dispatches Oliver Cromwell's forces

May 2 — Ordinance against Heresy and Blasphemy passed by the Presbyterian Parliament; heresy and blasphemy, especially against the Trinity, made felonies punishable by death

May 8 — Oliver Cromwell's forces victorious at St. Fagan's, Wales

— Thomas Stanley m. Dorothy Enyon

May 20 — Gerrard Winstanley, *The Breaking of the Day of God, Wherein, Four things are manifested*, published, address to

"The despised sons and daughters of Zion" dated[417]

May 22 — Matthew Parker, *Mistris Parliament presented in her bed after sore travaile in the birth of her monstrous offspring the Childe of Deformation. By Mercurius Melancholicus*

May 27 — News reaches London of mutiny in six naval vessels; the Parliamentarian commander, Admiral Thomas Rainsborough, not allowed to board his own ships

Jun 2 — Sir Thomas Fairfax defeats Royalist forces at Maidstone

Jun 8 — Sir Henry Vane, the Younger, dispatched to treat with the mutinous sailors; the ships subsequently sail to Holland and join Prince Charles and Prince Rupert

Jun 13 — Sir Thomas Fairfax begins the siege of Colchester

Jul — **Samuel Hartlib notes in his diary that "Milton is not only writing a Vniv. History of Engl. But also an Epitome of all Purchas Volumes. Haack."[418]**

— Gerrard Winstanley, *The Saints Paradice*, published

— Sir John Denham escapes England, joins Henrietta Maria's court-in-exile in France

Jul 13 — *The Mad Dog Rebellion, worm'd and muzzl'd*, published; Royalist tract depicting Cromwell's forces as mad dogs

Jul 14 — House of Lords refuses to act against English soldiers invading England with the Scots Army

Jun 15 — William Jenkyn, *The Blinde Guide*, attack on John Goodwin

Jul 29 — T. C., *A Glasse for Our Times*, attack on divorce tracts

— **John Milton, Sonnet XV: "On the Lord General Fairfax," commemorating the victory at Colchester**

Aug — Robert Boyle, *Some Motives and Incentives to the Love of God (Seraphic Love)*, written

— Richard Lovelace imprisoned for his Royalist loyalties

---

417. Giles Calvert, a publisher and bookseller at the sign of the black spread eagle, at the west end of St. Paul's, has also been identified as the author of this volume.

418. Maurice Kelley, ed., *Complete Prose*, VIII, p. 459.

Aug 17 — Battle of Preston; Cromwell defeats Hamilton's Scots army

Aug 20 — Edward Herbert, Lord Herbert of Cherbury, d. (b. Mar 3, 1582/3)

Aug 23 — Marriage intention filed for James Philips and Katherine Fowler[419]

Aug 25 — James Hamilton, 1st Duke of Hamilton surrenders the Scots Army in Staffordshire

Aug 27 — General Thomas Fairfax's army takes the Royalist stronghold at Colchester

Aug 28 — Charles I's army surrenders to Parliamentary forces

Sep — Lady Eleanor Davies, *Given to the Elector*, reprinted, with additional verses demonstrating parallels between Belshazzar's feast and recent English history and politics; concludes with an anagram on Eleanor Audeley, "Reveal O Daniel

— Clement Walker, *History of Independency*, published, an attack on Presbyterianism and Parliament

Sep 13 — Parliamentary commissioners try to negotiate a peace with Charles I; the attempt lasts through the end of November

Sep 19 — Large petition of the Levellers, *To the Right Honourable and Supreme Authority of This Nation, the Commons in Parliament Assembled. 1647*, dated by George Thomason in his collection

— *Some Observations on the Late Dangerous Petition*, response to the Levellers' petition

Oct — Commons denies a petition for Richard Lovelace's release from prison

Oct 16 — Gerrard Winstanley, *To all the scholars of Oxford and Cambridge, and to all that Call Themselves Ministers of the Gospel, in City and Country*, first epistle in *Truth Lifting Up Its Head*, dated; full volume published, 1649

---

419. James Philips (b. 1594) was a widower of fifty-four; Katherine Fowler was not quite seventeen. Following the marriage Katherine removed from London to the small Welsh town of Cardigan.

Oct 25 — **Milton's daughter Mary b.**

Winter — Gerrard Winstanley, *The Saints Paradise, or, The Fathers Teaching the only satisfaction to waiting Souls, wherein Many experiences are Recorded, for the comfort of such as are under spiritual Burning*, published by Giles Calvert

Nov 7 — Milton's daughter Mary baptized

Nov 17 — Charles I, *His Majesty's Declaration of November 17th from the Isle of Wight*, response to the Army demands

Nov 20 — *A Remonstrance of His Excellency Thomas Lord Fairfax*, published, pro-army tract; foreshadows principles guiding Pride's Purge and the trial and execution of King Charles I

Nov 21-25 — Main points from the *Remonstrance* reported and reprinted in news weeklies, including:

— Gilbert Mabbott, editor, *The Moderate* (Nov 21)[420]

— *Packets of Letters* (Nov 22)

— Daniel Border, editor, *The Perfect Weekly Account* (Nov 22)

— John Dillingham, editor, *The Moderate Intelligencer* (Nov 23)

— Henry Walker, editor, *Perfect Occurrences*, strongly anti-Royalist weekly (Nov 24)

— Richard Collings, editor, *The Kingdom's Weekly Intelligencer* (Nov 25)

— Samuel Pecke, editor, *A Perfect Diurnall* (Nov 25)

Nov 29/30 (?)— 'Pragmaticus' [Marchamont Needham], *A Plea for the King and Kingdome*, published; response to the *Remonstrance*

Dec 2 — Sir Henry Vane addresses Commons in defense of republicanism and against the Monarchy

Dec 4 — William Prynne renounces the *Remonstrance* in a speech before Commons, possibly providing Milton with the

---

420. As the official government censor, Mabbott was able to pursue a coherent course of reporting without fear of external pressures.

impetus to write *Tenure of Kings and Magistrates*[421]

— **Carlo Dati writes to Milton, sending greetings from a number of Milton's Italian friends and acquaintances**

— Military moves Charles I from the Isle of Wight to a more secure location at Hurst Castle, in the mainland

Dec 5 — Presbyterian-controlled Commons accepts Charles' concessions as sufficient to begin peace negotiations

Dec 6 — Pride's Purge; all Presbyterian members expelled from the House of Commons by "authority of the sword"[422]; the sitting Parliament, wholly antagonistic to Charles I, is henceforth called the Rump Parliament[423]

Dec 7 — Henry More, first of four letters to René Descartes, praising the latter's philosophical system

Dec 19 — Charles I departs from confinement at Hurst Castle for his final journey to London

Dec 23 — The Rump appoints a committee to discuss judicial means of dealing with the King

— Robert Barclay b., Quaker

---

421. Merritt Y. Hughes, *Complete Prose*, Volume III, pp. 39-41.

422. Many were offered restoration to Commons if they would rescind their vote of the previous day to treat with Charles I for a restoration of monarchy; none accepted. Following the Purge, perhaps fifty or sixty men remained in Parliament to carry on the business of state under the direct control of the Army.

423. When this Parliament was formally dissolved after the Restoration of Charles II, Londoners celebrated by roasting rumps of beef over bonfires.

1649

Clement Walker describes Milton as a "libertine ... tied to no obligation to God or Man"[424]
Blindness begins to develop in Milton's right eye
Thomas Banaster, *An Alarum to the World, of the Appearing of Sions King*, Fifth-Monarchist tract
John Bulwer, *Pathomyotomia: Or, a Dissection of the Significative Muscles of the Affections of the Minde*, treatise on the relation between musculature of the head and emotions
Charles I, *Biblioteca Regia* (The King's Library), published at The Hague
Abiezer Coppe, "Preface" to *John the Divines Divinity*, Ranter tract, advocates abolishing all ordinances in the Church
Lady Eleanor Davies, *Strange and Wonderful Prophesies*, published; *The Crying Charge. To the High Court of Justice, appointed for the Tryal of Charles Stuart, King of England, by the Lady Eleanor Douglas*, pamphlet, defense of her brother, the executed Mervin Touchet, 2nd Earl of Castlehaven, and attack on King Charles I
John Donne, *Fifty Sermons*
John Everard, *The Divine Pymander of Hermes Mercurius Trismegistus*, published, English translation of Hermetic text
John Goodwin, *Obstructours of Justice*
Edward Herbert, Lord Herbert of Cherbury, *The Life and Reign*

---

424. Cited in Christopher Hill, *Milton and the English Revolution*, p. 109.

of King Henry the Eighth

Richard Lovelace, *Lucasta: Epodes, Odes and Sonnets*, with commendatory poem by Andrew Marvell

William Lilly, *Merlinus Anglicus*[425], almanac, published

John Lilburne, *England's New Chains Discovered*[426]

Andrew Marvell, "To His Noble Friend Mr Richard Lovelace, upon His Poems"

Christopher Morris, editor, *The Journeys of Celia Fiennes*

Thomas Newcombe, *A Discourse of Method*, translation of René Descartes

Robert Parker, *The Exposition of the Powring out of the Fourth Vial*

Joseph Salmon, *A Rout, A Rout, or Some Part of the Armies quarters Beaten Up*, published

Jeremy Taylor, *An Apology for Authorised and Set Forms of Liturgies*

William Chappell, Milton's first tutor at Cambridge, d. (b. 1582)

Giovanni Diodati d. (b. 1576; Swiss theologian)

John Geree d.

George Hakewell d. (b. 1578)

Nathaniel Lee b. (?; as late as 1653?)

Ballad-singing officially prohibited by the Commonwealth Government (through 1659); offenders subject to public flogging

Jan — Lady Eleanor Davies, *Her Appeal from the Court to the Camp. The word of the Most high: To the Lord General, Lord Fairfax, From the Lady Eleanor*, dated and published

Jan 2 — John Goodwin, *Right and Might Well Met*, pamphlet, supporting the Army's assumption of power

---

425. Part almanac, part astrological guide to the conjunction of stars, the book sold some 18,500 copies within the year (B. S. Capp, *Fifth Monarchy Men*, p. 17).

426. The Council of State instructed Milton to respond to this pamphlet but there is no indication that he completed the task.

— House of Lords rejects the bill to bring Charles I to trial; Commons determines to proceed

Jan 4 — Commons asserts its right to govern without Lords or King

— Commons passes a resolution asserting that all justice emanates from the people[427]

— Commons establishes a commission of 135 members to act as judge and jury against Charles Stuart

Jan 6 — Commission within Commons is appointed by Act of Parliament to bring Charles I to trial; Sir Thomas Fairfax, Henry Ireton, and Oliver Cromwell are prominent members

Jan 8 — Sir Francis Nethersole, *The Self-Condemned*, critique of John Goodwin, *Right and Might Well Met*

Jan 9 — New Great Seal engraved: "In the First Year of Freedom by God's blessing restored, 1648"

Jan 15 — *An Agreement of the People of England, and the places therewith incorporated, for a secure and present peace, upon grounds of common right, freedom and safety*, approved by the Army's Council of Officers

Jan 17 — James Butler, 12th Earl of Ormond, signs the "Articles of Peace" with Ireland, a pro-Royalist strategy

Jan 19 — William Prynne and Clement Walker, *A Declaration and Protestation of William Prynne and Clement Walker against the present proceedings of the Army*, tract

Jan 20 — *An Agreement of the People of England, and the places therewith incorporated, for a secure and present peace, upon grounds of common right, freedom and safety, presented with its accompanying petition to Commons*

— *The Charge against the King*, formally stated

— Trial of King Charles I begins in Westminster, with 68 of 135 commissioners present

Jan 21 — Charles I, *The King's Reasons for Declining the Jurisdiction of the High Court of Justice*

— Independents Hugh Peters and Joshua Sprigge preach

---

427. This was a critical move in preparing to try a King, from whom, traditionally, all justice was seen to flow.

anti-monarchical sermons before Commons, essentially demanding the King's execution
— Presbyterian ministers preach in London on behalf of the King
Jan 22 — Charles I returns to the court at Westminster Hall, again repudiating the authority of the court
Jan 23 — Third session of the King's trial ends inconclusively
Jan 25 — John Goodwin, *The Unrighteous Judge*, response to Sir Francis Nethersole, *The Self-Condemned*
Jan 26 — Gerrard Winstanley, *The New Law of Righteousness Budding forth, in restoring the whole Creation from the bondage of the curse*, pamphlet, announcing his plan to cultivate waste and common land under divine commission
Jan 27 — Trial of Charles I concludes; Judge Bradshaw decrees: "This Court doth adjudge that he the said Charles Stuart, as a Tyrant, Traitor, murderer, and Public Enemy, shall be put to death by the severing of his head from his body"[428]
Jan 29 — Death warrant for Charles I signed by John Bradshaw, Thomas Grey, Oliver Cromwell, and others
Jan 30 — Charles I beheaded outside King James' Banqueting Hall, an area surrounded by Army headquarters
— **Milton probably attends the execution**
— Immediately thereafter: Charles I, *King Charles his Speech made upon the scaffold*, published
— Thereafter: Henry King, Bishop of Chichester, *Elegy upon K. Charles I*
— Thereafter: Henry King, Bishop of Chichester, *A Groane at the Funerall of Charles the First*, published
— Thereafter: Henry King, Bishop of Chichester, *A Deepe Groane*
Jan 31 — John Owen, *Sermon..., With a Discourse about Toleration*, published, arguing penal restraints on disruptive opinions
Feb — John Cook, *King Charles His Case or an Appeal to all*

---

428. Cited in Wolfe, *Milton and His England*, #83.

Rational Men concerning his Tryall, published
— Lady Eleanor Davies, *The New Jerusalem at Hand. By the Lady Eleanor Douglas*, pamphlet dated and published
— Gilbert Mabbott, *A Perfect Narrative*, account of the trial of Charles I, licensed
— Sir Henry Vane, the Younger, appointed to the Council of State

Feb 5 — Charles II proclaimed King of Great Britain, France, and Ireland, at Mercat Cross, Edinburgh, Scotland; the Scottish Parliament acts in outrage at the English Parliament's failure to protect the person of the king, Charles I

Feb 6 — House of Lords, with six peers present, adjourn until 10:00 the next day; the House will not meet again until 1660[429]

Feb 7 — Charles I interred at Windsor
— Commons adopts a resolution abolishing the office of King

Feb 9 — 'Charles I' [pseudonym for John Gauden, afterward Bishop of Exeter and Worcester under Charles II], *Eikon Basilike, The Portraiture of His Sacred Majestie in His Solitude and Sufferings*,[430] appears, licensed by Joseph Caryl. The effect of the book is reflected in a subsequent publication, *A Miracle of Miracles wrought by the Blood of King Charles the First* (1649), which proclaimed Charles a martyr and a near-divinity whose very blood could heal

Feb 13 — **John Milton *The Tenure of Kings and Magistrates...*, published; under the initials J.M., with printer's imprint (Matthew Simmons at the Gilded Lyon in Aldersgate**

---

429. Henry Hallam, *Constitutional History*, II, p. 174.

430. The title means "the King's image." The book was an enormous success, with thirty-five editions in London and twenty-five additional editions in Ireland and abroad—all within the first year. The book was a political time-bomb hurled at the Commonwealth government at a time when the first shock of Charles' execution had begun to wear off and many in England were beginning to regret the action. It was a necessity for the Commonwealth government to find some way to counteract the book's popularity. For a discussion of the iconographic imagery of the frontispiece, see Ernest B. Gilman, *Iconoclasm and Poetry in the English Reformation*, p. 154ff.

Street)
— *The Charge against the King Discharged*, tract, published
— Act appointing a Council of State passed by Parliament[431]
Feb 19 — *Certain Quares*, first petition by the Fifth Monarchists, signed by saints in Norfolk, published
Mar 10 — John Bradshaw, President of the Council of State
By Mar 13 — **Council of State request Milton to leave private life and enter government service.**
— **John Milton, resumes work on his *History of Britain***
Mar 15 — **John Milton, appointment to the Council of State as Secretary for Foreign Tongues, at an annual salary of £288**
— **John Milton, numerous State Papers written over the next several years**
— **John Milton, eventually ordered by the Council to answer the *Eikon Basilike***
— William Dugard prints an edition of *Eikon Basilike* with four prayers, purported to be by Charles I, inserted
Mar 17 — An Act of Parliament formally abolishes the office of King; argues that the former monarch's power had in fact derived from Parliament itself
Mar 19 — An Act of Parliament formally abolishes the House of Lords and declares England a "Commonwealth, or a Free State"
Mar 20 — **Milton inducted into office**
Mar 26 — John Winthrop, Governor of Massachusetts Colony, d. (b. 1588)
Mar 28 — John Lilburne, William Walwyn, Thomas Prince, and committed to the Tower following their publication of *England's New Chains Part II*, attacking the Army Council of Officers

---

431. The initial act required members of the Council to take an oath approving of the execution of Charles I. When only fourteen of the forty-one members appeared, the oath was modified; finally, on February 22, all members appointed to the Council were required to attend without, however, taking any oath.

Apr — Marchamont Needham, *Digitus Dei: Or, God's Justice upon Treachery and Treason; Exemplified in the Life and Death of the Late James Duke of Hamilton. Being an exact Relation of his Traiterous practices since the Year 1630. Together with a true and full Discovery of the mysteries of his last Engagement for the destruction of the King and his Royall Posterity. Whereto is added an Epitaph*, 32-page pamphlet, published a month after Hamilton's execution

Apr 1 — The True Levellers or Diggers—under the leadership of William Everard and Gerrard Winstanley—establish a colony, St. George's Hill, Surrey, claiming that waste lands and commons belong to the people; within a year ten other such colonies begin

Apr 3 — Peter Chamberlain, *The Poore Mans Advocate, or England's Samaritan*, treatise urging economic reformation to aid the poor, dated

— John Lilburne, *The Picture of the Council of State*

Apr 5 — **Christopher Wasse, *Electra of Sophocles*, published at The Hague, Netherlands; includes attacks on Milton's divorce views**

Apr 9 — **Bishop Joseph Hall, *Resolutions and Decisions...*, attack on Milton's divorce views**

— Charles II, in exile in the Netherlands, becomes father to James Scott, afterward 1st Duke of Monmouth, the first of many illegitimate children

Apr 10 — Richard Lovelace released from prison

Apr 16 — John Crouch, *The Man in the Moon*, first issue, Royalist newspaper directed toward middle- to lower-class audiences, designed to reveal "a world of knavery under the sun, both in the Parliament, the Council of State, the Army, the City, and the Country

— Henry Sanders of Walton-upon-Thames lodges an official complaint to the Council of State against the Diggers at St. George's Hill

Apr 18 — Isaac Dorislaus, Commonwealth Ambassador, assassinated at The Hague by an English Royalist

Apr 19 — John Owen, *The Shaking and Translating of Heaven and Earth*

Apr 20 — Gerrard Winstanley, John Taylor, William Everard, and others, *A Declaration to the Powers of England, and to all the Powers of the World, shewing the cause why the common people of England have begun, and gives consent to digge up, manure, and sowe corn upon George-Hill in Surrey; by those that have subscribed, and thousands more that give consent*, address to the reader by John Taylor, dated

— William Everard and Gerrard Winstanley appear at Whitehall to defend their actions at St. George's Hill before Sir Thomas Fairfax

Apr 23 — William Everard, *The Declaration and Standard of the Levellers of England delivered in a Speech ... by Mr. Everard*, published

— Women petitioners attempt to address the House of Commons on behalf of John Lilburne and others; they are told that the House is too busy to receive them

— The Digger Colony at St. George's Hill, Surrey numbers some fifty people, with preparations being made for 5,000

Apr 24 — The women petitioners again dismissed by the Sergeant at Arms, this time as being incapable of understanding the complexities of matters under consideration by the House

Apr 25 — Twenty women present *The Humble Petition of divers well-affected Women inhabiting the City of London, Westminster, the Borough of Southwark, Hamblets and places adjacent, to Commons*; addressing taxation, employment, and arbitrary government[432]

— Peter Chamberlen, *The Poore Mans Advocate*, published

— [Gerrard Winstanley], *The True Levellers Standard Advanced, or, the State of the Community opened and Presented to the Sons of Men*, published, first Leveller/Digger manifesto,

---

432. Antonia Fraser, *The Weaker Vessel*, pp. 238-239.

with fifteen signators

— Robert Lockier, Leveller mutineer, sentenced to death

Apr 17-24 — Marchamont Needham, *Mercurius Pragmaticus (For King Charles II)*, begins publication

— Marchamont Needham, *Most Pithy Exhortation Delivered in an Eloquent Oration to the Watry Generation Aboard Their Admirall at Graves-End. By the Right Reverend, Mr. Hugh Peters, Doctor of the Chair for the Famous University of Whitehall, and Chaplain in ordinary to the High and Mighty K. Oliver, the first of that name, as it was took, verbatim, in short hand when he delivered it*, published, parodic satire on Peters, using Peter's prose style

Apr 26 — Marchamont Needham ordered arrested for his pro-Royalist sympathies in *Mercurius Pragmaticus*

— Sir Thomas Fairfax visits the Digger colony at St. George's Hill, Surrey

May — Oliver Cromwell invades Ireland

— Two additional petitions presented by women on behalf of Lilburne and others

May 11 — Claudius Salmasius [Claude de Saumais], *Defensio Regia pro Carolo I* (Defense of Kingship), appears in England[433]

May 14 — John Hall hired to assist Milton

May 16 — **John Milton, *Observations upon the Articles of Peace with the Irish Rebels*, published**

May 17 — William Lenthall, Speaker of the Parliament of England, formally criticizes the Scottish Parliament for acknowledging Charles II as King

---

433. Claude de Saumaise, whose names was Latinized to Claudius Salmasius, a Frenchman by birth, was generally acknowledged the most learned continental scholar of his generation. He was highly mobile, residing at a number of courts whose princes vied for the honor of his presence, including those of France, Sweden, and Holland. Given Salmasius' stature in the continental academic and scholarly world, the fledgling Commonwealth government felt pressured to supply an answer to his indictments prepared by an English scholar of corresponding reputation—and selected John Milton.

May 19 — An Act of Parliament formally declares England to be a Commonwealth

May 22 — **Gilbert Mabbot resigns as official licenser for the Commonwealth government; Milton largely—but unofficially—replaces him**

May 28 — Henry Brooke, *The Charity of churchmen*, rebuttal to John Goodwin, *Right and Might Well Met*

May 30 — **Milton ordered to examine the papers of John Lee, recently arrested for opposition to the commonwealth government**

— Act abolishing Kingship officially proclaimed in England

May 31 — Sir Thomas Fairfax, *The Speeches of the Lord Generall Fairfax ... to the Diggers at St. Georges Hill*, news sheet report published

Jun — Lady Eleanor Davies, *A Prayer or Letter for the Peoples Conversion and Deliverance from their Distraction*, written

Jun 1 — Gerrard Winstanley and others, *A Declaration from the Poor Oppressed People of England*, the Levellers' second manifesto, issued with forty-five signators

Jun 9 — Gerrard Winstanley, *A Letter to the Lord Fairfax and His Councell of War*, delivered to Fairfax, defense of the Diggers' activities at George-Hill

Jun 11 — A mob of men dressed in women's garments attack and beat four Diggers

— Immediately thereafter: [Gerrard Winstanley], *A Declaration of the Bloudie and Unchristian Acting of William Star and John Taylor of Walton*, published, pamphlet, condemning the beatings[434]

Jun 18 — Marchamont Needham arrested; imprisoned in Newgate for five months before accepting editorship of pro-Commonwealth publications

Jun 23 — **Milton ordered to examine issues of Marchamont**

---

434. Both T. Wilson Hayes and David Underdown devote a good deal of space to studying the implications of men assuming women's clothing during the period, particularly as a manifestation of social, political, religious, and legal fears.

Needham's *Mercurius Pragmaticus*

— Four legal actions for trespass begun against the Diggers

Jun 24 — Death of Henry, Lord Hastings on his wedding evening

— Thereafter: John Dryden, "Upon the Death of the Lord Hastings," an exercise in Donnian metaphysical poetry, later published in *Lachrymal Musarum*

— Thereafter: Andrew Marvell, "Upon the Death of the Lord Hastings"

— Thereafter: Sir John Denham, "Elegie upon the Death of the Lord Hastings"

— Thereafter: Nearly 100 published elegies in memory of Lord Hastings

After Jun 24 — *Lachrymæ Musarum* (Tears of the Muses), edited by Richard Brome, published; memorial volume to Henry, Lord Hastings; includes John Dryden's first published poem as well as poetry by Sir John Denham, Robert Herrick, Andrew Marvell, and others[435]

Jul — Peter Sterry appointed Chaplain to Oliver Cromwell

After Jul 4 — Lady Eleanor Davies *Sion's Lamentation, Lord Henry Hastings, HIS Funeral blessings by his Grandmother, the Lady Eleanor*, published; concludes with a reference to the funeral cortege

Jul 11 — Gerrard Winstanley, *An Appeal to the House of Commons, Desiring their Answer; Whether the Common-People shall have the quiet enjoyment of the Commons and Waste Lands: Or whether they shall be under the will of lords of Mannors still*, response to legal actions against the Diggers[436]

Jul 20 — John Earl, Bishop of Salisbury, translation of *Eikon*

---

435. Dryden's first appearance in print is now notorious for its use—and at times unconscious abuse—of the images and conventions of metaphysical poetry, a form distinctly uncongenial to Dryden's imagination. His subsequent poetry reflects more appropriately his neo-classical bent.

436. The address may have been presented to the House of Commons as late as July 24.

Basilike into Latin

Aug — Sir John Denham appointed ambassador to Poland by King Charles II

Aug 1 — Marchamont Needham, *Certain Considerations Tendered in all humility, to an honorable Member of the Council of State*, published as a signed pamphlet; shortly thereafter, Needham escapes from Newgate prison for two weeks before recapture

By Aug 16 — *Eikon Alethine, The Pourtraiture of Truths Most Sacred Majesty*, refutation of *Eikon Basilike*

Aug 20 — **Clement Walker, *Anarchia Anglicana...*, attack on Milton's divorce views**

— Endymion Porter, buried (b. 1587)

Aug 21 — Richard Crashaw d.

Aug 26 — Gerrard Winstanley, *A Watch-Word to the City of London and the Armie*, published, Leveller

Aug 28 — Parliament passes an Act "Prohibiting the Importing of any wines, Wooll or Silk from the Kingdom of France into the Commonwealth of England or Ireland..."

Sep — Oliver Cromwell initiates the massacre at Drogheda, Ireland

Sep 3 — Samuel Hartlib, *London's Charitie stilling the Poore Orphan's Cry*, pamphlet, urging increase in employment and aid to the poor

Sep 11 — *Eikon Episte. Or, the Faithfull Pourtraicture of a Loyall Subject, in Vindication of Eikon Basilike*

Oct — Engagement ordered by Committee for Regulating Universities

— Licenses for publications suspended, except official government organs, until June 1650

Oct 5 — **Milton leases his Bread Street property for twenty years**

Oct 6 (?)— **John Milton, *Eikonoklastes in Answer to a Book Intitl'd Eikon Basilike, The Portrature of his Sacred Majesty in his Solitudes and Sufferings*, by I. M., published; the** name means 'breaker of images' or 'breaker of icons'[437]

— John Milton, begins writing *History of Muscovia* (to 1660?)

Oct 10 — Council of State orders General Thomas Fairfax to dispatch troops to support the Justices of the Peace against the Diggers

Oct 16 — *A Brief Relation*, news sheet report of the Diggers' refusal to disperse

Nov — Claudius Salmasius, *Defenso Regia pro Carolo I*, appears in Leiden

Nov 14 — Marchamont Needham released from Newgate prison

Nov 19 — **Milton given official lodgings in Scotland Yard, Whitehall, London**

Nov 29 — Council of State prevents importation of Salmasius' tract into England

Dec — Lady Eleanor Davies, *The Everlasting Gospel. The Holy Gospel, According to the Evangelist, by the Lady Eleanor*, pamphlet condemning Charles I, issued as "The New-Years-Gift to all Nations and People, Jubile"

Dec 4 — William Drummond of Hawthornden d. (b. 1585)

— John Egerton, 1st Earl of Bridgewater, d. (b. 1579)

Dec 10 — Richard Lovelace released from prison at Peterborough

Dec 16 — **John Milton acts as licenser for *Histoire...du Process de Charles Stuart***

Dec 21-28 — Salmasius' tract confiscated in Holland

---

437. The *Eikonoklastes* is a chapter-by-chapter refutation of claims and arguments purportedly made by Charles on the eve of his execution. Christopher Hil notes that Milton had already suggested as a possible topic for a tragedy 'Gideon Iconoclastes' (*Milton and the English Revolution*, p. 173-174).

Decade Six: 1650-1659
The Commonwealth—
Enlightenment and Darkenings

1650

Milton completely blind in his left eye

Milton reputedly instrumental in having Sir William Davenant released from a Commonwealth prison; Davenant will later repay the favor by working in Milton's behalf after the Restoration

Richard Baxter, *The Saints Everlasting Rest*, published, his most popular volume, quoting several poems by George Herbert

John Bulwer, *Anthropometamorphosis, Man Tranform'd: Or, the Artificiall Changling*, treatise condemning cultures that believe in altering the human form (re-issued, 1653, 1654)

Laurence Clarkson, *A Single Eye All Light, No Darkness; or light and darkness one*, published, Ranter tract; burned by the public hangman

Abraham Cowley, *The Guardian*, drama, published

John Dury, *The Reformed School*, educational treatise

George Foster, *The Pouring Forth of the Seventh and Last Viall*, published; *The Sounding of the Last Trumpet*, published

Godfrey Goodman, Bishop of Gloucester, *An Account of his sufferings*

Joseph Hall, Bishop of Norwich *The Revelation Unrevealed*, published, asserts the imminent Last Judgment

John Hoddesdon, *Sion and Parnassus, or Epigrams...*, published with commendatory poem by John Dryden, "To His Friends the Authour, on his divine Epigrams

Henry Isaacson, *An Exact Narration of the Life and Death of the Late reverend and learned Prelate, and painfull Divine,*

 Lanceot Andrewes, late Bishop of Winchester..., published

Sir William Mure, *The Cry of Blood, and of a Broken Covenant*, published

Henry Neville, *Newes from the New Exchange, or the Commonwealth of Ladies, Drawn to the Life, in their severall Characters and Concernment*, satire

Henry Parker, *The True Portraiture of the Kings of England; Drawn from their Titles, Successons, Raigns and Ends. Or, a Short and exact Historical description of every King, with the Right they have had to the Crown, and the manner of their wearing of it; especially from WILLIAM the Conqueror. Wherein is Demonstrated, that there hath been no direct succession in the line to create an heriditary right, for six or seven hundred yeers; faithfully collected out of our best histories, and humbly presented to the Parliament of England*, published

Isaac Penington, *Light or Darknes*

Scottish Psalter

John Tatham, *Ostella: Or, The Faction of Love and Beauty Reconcil'd*, poetry

Jeremy Taylor, *The Rule and Exercise of Holy Living*, published[438]

Henry Vaughan, *Silex Scintillans (The Sparkling Flint), Part I*

Thomas Vaughan, *Four Treatises on Hermetic Philosophy*

Sir A. W. [Anthony Weldon], *The Court and Character of King James, Written and Taken by Sir A. W., Being an Eye and Ear Witness*

René Descartes d. (b. 1596)

John Everard d. (b. c. 1575)

Phineas Fletcher d. (b. 1582)

John Williams, Archbishop of York, d. (b. 1582)

Elizabeth, daughter of Charles I and Henrietta Maria, d., in Carisbrook Castle

---

438. Both *Holy Living* and *Holy Dying* proved to be highly influential and popular, seeing some twenty authorized editions by 1700.

John Banks b. (?)[439]
John Churchill (afterward Earl of Marlborough) b. (d. 1722)
Jeremy Collier b. (d. 1726)
William Faithorne returns from exile in France
Jacob's Coffee House established in Oxford, the first in England

Jan — Sir Thomas Browne practicing as a physician in Norwich

Jan 1 — Gerrard Winstanley, *A New-Yeers Gift for the Parliament and Army*, published, Winstanley's longest pamphlet since the formation of the Digger colony, representing the Digger movement as the core of the cause for which Parliament and Army have struggled

Jan 2 — Sir William Davenant, *Preface to Gondibert*, dated, addressed to Thomas Hobbes; later published in Paris, with Hobbes' reply

— *Engagement to be taken by all men of the age of Eighteen*, approved: "I do declare and promise, that I will be true and faithful to the Commonwealth of England, as it is now established, without a King or House of Lords"[440]

— **Thereafter: Milton ordered to write a defense of the oath, to be sent to Hamburg, Germany; Milton's first State Paper for the Commonwealth**

Jan 4 — Abiezer Coppe, *A Flying Fiery Roll: A Word from the Lord to the Great Ones* and *A Second Fiery Flying Roule: To all the Inhabitants of the Earth*, published, Ranter tracts; the two pamphlets subsequently ordered burned by Parliament; Coppe imprisoned

Jan 8 — **Milton ordered by the Council of State to respond to Claudius Salmasius, *Defensio Regia***

Jan 10 — Thomas Hobbes, "The Answer to Davenant's *Preface Before Gondibert*" dated

Jan 21 — Sir John Denham, *Coopers Hill*, republished in

---

439. There are no definitive dates for Banks' birth or death; he was probably born somewhere near 1650 and was composing dramas well into the mid-1690s.

440. Samuel R. Gardiner, *Constitutional Documents*, p. 391.

London by Humphrey Moseley (1647 version), with verses to Fanshaw and the prologue and epilogue to *The Sophy*

Jan 22-29 — **Mercurius Pragmaticus, attack on Milton's divorce views and *Eikonoklastes***

Jan 30 — Lady Eleanor Davies, *The Bill of Excommunication, for abolishing henceforth the SABBATH Call'd Sunday or First day. By the Leady Eleanor*, tract, in which Davies formally abolishes (excommunicates) Sunday as Sabbath, supplanting it with Monday (Moonday)

Feb — Thomas Hobbes, *On Human Nature*, published; Hobbes becomes a significant contributor to the political controversies

Feb 1 — Abiezer Coppe, *The Fiery Flying Roll...*, all copies located seized and burned

— William Dugard ordered imprisoned for trying to publish Claudius Salmasius, *Defensio Regia*

Feb 2 — Eleanor [Nell] Gwynn b. (afterward, Mistress to Charles II, by whom she had two sons)

Feb 4 — Sir John Denham, *The Sophy*, SR by Humphrey Moseley

Feb 8 — Sir William Davenant, *A Discourse upon Gondibert .... With an Answer to it by Mr. Hobbes*, SR for English publication

Feb 15 — **John Milton, *The Tenure of Kings and Magistrates*, 2nd edition**

Feb 16 — **Milton signs a receipt for payment from Rodolph Warcupp**

— Sir William Davenant appointed Governor of Maryland by Charles II, acting as King of the Scots

Feb 18 — **Milton re-appointed Secretary for Foreign Tongues**

Feb 20 — Gerrard Winstanley, *A Vindication of those Whose Endeavors is Only to Make the Earth a Common Treasury, called Diggers*, dated

— William Dugard in Newgate Prison for his attempt to print Royalist materials; released as headmaster of the Merchant

Taylors' School

Feb 26 — Papists ordered to Leave London by March 20; they are not to be allowed within five miles of the parish in which they register

Feb-Mar — Gerrard Winstanley, *Englands Spirit Unfoulded, or, an Incouragement to Take the Engagement*, published

Mar 5 — Samuel Pepys, admitted to residence at Magdalene College, Cambridge University

Mar 18 — James Okeford, *Doctrine of the Fourth Commandment, deformed by Popery, reformed and restored to its primitive purity*, all copies burned Mar 19

— Gerrard Winstanley, *Fire in the Bush: The Spirit Burning, not Consuming but purging Mankinde, or, the great Battell of God Almighty, between Michaell the Seed of Life, and the great red Dragon, the Curse fought within the Spirit or Man*, published but unfinished[441]

Mar 26 — Gerrard Winstanley, *An Appeale to all Englishmen, to judge between Bondage and Freedome, sent from those that began to digge upon George Hill in Surrey, but now are carrying on, that publick work upon the little Heath in the Parish of Cobham, neare unto George hill, wherein it appears, that the work of Digging upon the Commons, is not onely warranted by Scripture but by the Law of the Commonwealth of England likewise*, published

Mar 28 — *Truths Conflict with Error...In three Publike Disputations. The first between Mr. John Goodwin and M. Vavasour Powell... The other two between M. John Goodwin, and M. John Simpson*, published

Apr —William Dugard released and his press allowed to

---

441. This tract "is neither a desperate attempt to save the colony, an admission of defeat, nor a return to pre-Digger positions; it is the culmination of Winstanley's visionary, which is to say poetic, experience. Like Milton's Paradise Lost and Blake's Jerusalem, it sets out to explain how the bond between man and nature was destroyed, what that destruction means in modern life, and how it may be repaired..." (T. Wilson Hayes, *Winstanley the Digger*, p. 175).

publish
— Giles Calvert, *An Humble Request to the Ministers of both Universities and to all Lawyers in every Inns-a-Court*, published; final pamphlet supporting the Digger movement, reproducing a dialogue between "Parson Plat Lord of the Mannor of Cobham, and Gerrard Winstanley"
— Gerrard Winstanley notes that the Diggers have eleven acres under cultivation and have constructed a number of houses
— Thereafter: Digger colonies abandoned in Surrey and elsewhere in England, and the Digger/Leveller movement collapses

Apr 9 — Gerrard Winstanley, *An Humble Request*, his final pamphlet defending the Digger movement

Apr 15 — Samuel Hartlib, *London's Charitie inlarged*, economics pamphlet

Apr 18 — Sir Simonds D'Ewes d.

Apr 24 — Witch-trial concluded at Alnwick

— Thereafter: *Wonderfull News from the North, Or a True Relation of the Sad and Grievous Torments Inflicted upon the Bodies of three Children of Mr. George Muschamp, late of the County of Northumberland, by Witchcraft .... As also the Prosecution of the sayd Witches, as by Oaths, and their own confessions will appear and by the Indictment found by the Jury against one of them, at the Sessions of the Peace held at Alnwick, the 24 day of April 1650*

— Thomas Hobbes, *De Corpore Politico*, published (written as early as 1640)

May 1 — Charles II signs a treaty at Breda, acknowledging the Scottish National Covenant and the Solemn League and Covenant

May 8 — Marchamont Needham, *The Case of the Common-Wealth of England Stated*, defending the Commonwealth, published; he receives £50 and a £100 pension from the government (May 24)

May 11/18 — John Dryden admitted as a pensioner to Trinity College, Cambridge

May 24 — Abraham Cowley, letter to Henry Bennet, noting Sir William Davenant's capture at sea by Parliamentary forces; Davenant thereafter imprisoned in Cowes Castle

Jun — John Crouch, *The Man in the Moon*, final issue appears

— John Crouch imprisoned (released by 1652)

Jun 1 — Hamon L'Estrange, *An Answer to the Marquis of Worcester... with Smectymnuo-Mastix: or, Short Animadversions upon Smectymnuus Their Answer, and Vindication of that Answer, to the Humble Remonstrance in the Cause of Liturgie*

Jun 8 — **Prospectus for *Mercurius Politicus*, which Milton later licenses and censors**

Jun 13 — Marchamont Needham, first issue of the pro-Commonwealth newspaper, *Mercurius Politicus*

Jun 14 — **Milton assigned Council lodgings in Whitehall**

After June 19 — **John Milton, *Eikonoklastes Publish'd now a second time and much enlarg'd*, published, 2nd edition**

Jun 23 — Charles II arrives in Scotland and again subscribes to the required Covenants

Jun 25 — **Milton ordered to search William Prynne's house**

— **Robert Baron, *Pocula Castalia*, plagiarizing from Milton's *Poems***

Jun 26 — **Milton ordered to translate the *Declaration of the Causes of War with the Scots* into Latin; Theodore Haak to translate it into Dutch. Milton's assignment later transferred to Thomas May**

— General Thomas Fairfax resigns as commander of the Commonwealth forces

Summer — Andrew Marvell accompanies General Fairfax in his retirement to Nun Appleton House; serves as tutor to Fairfax's daughter, Maria

Jul — Oliver Cromwell invades Ireland

— Thereafter: Andrew Marvel, "An Horatian Ode upon Cromwell's Return from Ireland," written

Jul 1 — Anne Bradstreet, *The Tenth Muse Lately Sprung up in America*, published by her brother-in-law, John Woodbridge, in London without Bradstreet's knowledge; first book of poetry produced in the English American colony

Jul 6 — John Dryden matriculated at Trinity College, Cambridge

Jul 20 — John Bunyan's first daughter, Mary, born blind

Aug — Fourteen women and one man tried and executed for witchcraft in Newcastle

Aug 9 — Act against blasphemy passed

Aug 14 — John Clieveland, *The Character of Mercurius Politicus*

Sep — Laurence Clarkson, *A Single Eye All Light, No Darkness* (1650), burned; Clarkson subsequently jailed, then exiled from England

Sep 2 — Lady Eleanor Davies, *Before the Lord's Second Coming, of the Last Days to be Visited, signed with the Tyrant Pharaohs Overthrow. (by) The Most Mighty his Messenger, Eleanor Douglas, Dowager; Daughter of Lo: Audeley, Lo: Touchet, E: of Castlehaven*, tract confirming the signs of the imminent Second Coming; written in prison

Sep 3 — Battle of Dunbar; Charles II's Scots forces under General Leslie defeated by Cromwell[442]

Sep 8 — Princess Elizabeth, d., at Carisbrooke Castle

Sep 25 — William Dugard reappointed headmaster of the Merchant Taylors' School

Sep 27 — An Act of Parliament repeals all penalties for non-attendance at Anglican services

Oct — Lady Eleanor Davies, *Elijah the Tishbite's Supplication when Presented the likeness of Hand, &c.*, pamphlet, published

— Sir John Denham, *Coopers Hill*, re-issued by Humphrey Moseley

— Marchamont Needham, *The Case of the Common-Wealth of*

---

[442]. Under Cromwell's command, the English army routed the Scots. The Scots reportedly lost 3,000 men, with 10,000 captured, while English losses (according to Cromwell) amounted to less than 20 (Wolfe, *Milton and His England*, 87).

England Stated, 2nd edition

Oct 28 — G. W. [George Wither], *Respublica Anglicana or the History of the Parliament and Army...Wherein the Parliament and Army are Vindicated from the Calumnies Cast upon Them in that Libellous History of Independency*, response to Clement Walker

Nov 6 — William II, Stadtholder of Orange, d. of smallpox

Nov 7 — Sir William Davenant, *Gondibert. An Heroick Poem*, SR by Thomas Newcomb

Nov 13 — Thomas May d. (b. 1595), the occasion noted in Andrew Marvell, "Tom May's Death," a poem critical of Parliament

Nov 14 — William III, Stadtholder of Orange b. (d. Mar 9, 1702) eight days after his father dies

Dec — Lady Eleanor Davies, *The Lady Eleanor Douglas, Dowager, Her Jubilee Plea or Appeal...*, pamphlet, urging that the 50th year of the Century become a Biblical *Jubilee*

Before Dec 4 — **Joseph Jane, Eikon Aklastos. The Image Unbroaken..., written, refutation of *Eikonoklastes***

Mid-Dec — Sir William Davenant, *Gondibert*, available from booksellers

Dec 23 — Milton authorized to publish his now-completed response to Claudius Salmasius

— *Perfect Diurnall* reports the publication of Sir William Davenant, *Gondibert. An Heroick Poem*[443]

Dec 26 — *Mercurius Politicus* reports the publication of Sir William Davenant, *Gondibert. An Heroick Poem*

Dec 31 — John Milton, *Johannis Miltoni, Angli, pro Populo Anglicano Defensio contra Claudii Salmasii Defensionem Regiam* (Defense of the English People), SR

— John Spittlehouse, *Rome ruin'd by Whitehall* ***

---

443. "The first Heroick Poem in the English Tongue written by Sir William Davenant, a Booke much commended by the learned Mr. Hobs, and long expected, is now published in Print." (A. N. Nethercot, *Sir William Davenant*, p. 271)

1651

Milton's illness and near-blindness continues; his sight in his right eye noticeably diminished
Milton's bust sculpted by Simon or Pierce
Milton visited by a number of continental ambassadors
Anglia Liberata, or, the Rights of the people of England maintained against the pretenses of the Scotish King [444]
Noah Biggs, *The Vanity of the Crafte of Physick*, critique of the Royal College of Physicians and on the inadequacy of English medicinal education
Roger Boyle, Earl of Orrery, *Parthenissa*, published; first of five parts appearing through 1656
Alexander Brome, *The Cunning Lovers*, performed
Robert Burton, *The Anatomy of Melancholy*, posthumous 6th edition, containing Burton's final revisions and amendments
Thomas Carew, *Poems. With a Maske, by Thomas Carew Esquire...*, 3rd edition revised and enlarged, published by Humphrey Moseley
William Cartwright, *Comedies, Tragi-Comedies, with other Poems...The Ayres and Songs set by Mr Henry Lawes*, published by Humphrey Moseley; prefatory poem by Katherine Philips (20 years of age)
John Cleveland, *Poems by J. C., with Additions*

---

444. The "Scotish King" being Charles II; in the title one may readily see the need felt during the period for England to divest itself of monarchical pretensions, even to denying Charles (or any Stuarts, for that matter) monarchical rights in England because of his hereditary rights in Scotland.

Abiezer Coppe, *Coppe's Return to the Ways of Truth*, recantation of earlier radical beliefs

John Cotton, John Wilson, and Richard Mather, *The Psalms Hymns and Spiritual Songs of the Old and New Testament, Faithfully Translated into English Metre* (New England Psalm Book), published in Massachusetts

Nathaniel Culverwel, *Spiritual Optics*, sermons, published posthumously

Sir William Davenant, *Gondibert: an heroick poem* and *Preface to Gondibert*, published in London[445]

John Dee, "Mathematical Preface" to Euclid's *Elements of Geometry*, edited by Thomas Rudd

Sir John Denham, *The Anatomy of Play*

John Donne, *Essays in Divinity*

William Gilbert, *On our Sublunary World*, published

Bishop Joseph Hall, *Soliloquies*

George Herbert, *Jacula Prudentum*, 2nd edition of *Outlandish Proverbs*, increased to 1190 proverbs

Thomas Hobbes, *Leviathan; or, the Matter, Forms and Power of a Commonwealth, Ecclesiasticall and Civill*, published in Paris and London (no further English editions in the century); *Philosophical Rudiments Concerning Government and Society*, English translation of *De Cive*, published

Henry King, *from the New Translation of the Bible turned into Meter*, published

Harmon L'Estrange, *Smectymnuo-Mastix*

William Lilly, *Monarchy or No Monarchy in England*, published; astrological forecasts for England during the 1650s and 1660s; *Several Observations upon the Life and Death of King Charles*, published

Henry More [as: 'Alazonomastic Philalethes'], *The Second Lash*

---

445. "Despite its incompleteness, unevenness, and obscurity, *Gondibert* is a formidable piece of work, arguably the most significant attempt at epic between *The Faerie Queene* and *Paradise Lost*, certainly the most important long poem of the 1650s in its influence on Dryden" (James Anderson Winn, *John Dryden*, p. 72-73).

of Alazonomastix; Conteining a solid and serious Reply to a very uncivill Anser to certain Observations, published at Cambridge
Robert Parker, *The Mystery of the Vialls Opened*
Sir Edward Sherbourne, *Poems and Translation*
Thomas Stanley, *Poems*
Elizabeth Talbot, Countess of Kent,[446] *A Choice Manuall of Rare and Select Secrets in Physick and Chirurgery*, posthumous publication, with several subsequent editions
Jeremy Taylor, *The Rule and Exercise of Holy Dying*, published; *Sermons*
Henry Vaughan, *Olor Iscanus. A collection of some select poems, and translations, formerly written by Mr. Henry Vaughan Silurist*
Mrs A. W. [Anna Weamys], *A Continuation of Sir Philip Sidney's Arcadia: Wherein is handled the Loves of Amphialus and Helena..., Written by a young Gentlewoman, Mris A. W.*, published
Sir Anthony Weldon, *The Court and Character of Charles I*
Sir Henry Wotton, *Reliquiæ Wottonianæ*, first of four editions
Nathaniel Culverwel d
Aurelian Townshend d. (?, b. 1583?)
Daniel Skinner b. (?)
Alice Wandesford m. William Thornton
First Anglo-Dutch naval war begins
George Monck, commander of Commonwealth forces in Scotland

Jan 1 — Charles II formally crowned King at Scone, Scotland, Edinburgh being occupied by Cromwell's forces
Jan 17 — Henry Parker, *Scotlands Holy War*, published, defense of the Commonwealth[447]

---

446. Granddaughter of the redoubtable Bess of Hardwick, Countess of Shrewsbury, Talbot earns literary respect in her own right as well in her role as patron to Samuel Butler and John Selden.

447. Don M. Wolfe notes of Parker that he was "a paid writer for the

Jan 23 — **John Milton censors the weekly *Mercurius Politicus*, the official Commonwealth newspaper, edited by his friend Marchamont Needham**

Feb (?)— **Milton takes residence in Petty-France, Westminster**

Feb 3, 4, 5 — John Reeve receives his prophetic calling from the mouth of Jesus

Feb 6 — **Milton licenses issue 36 of *Mercurius Politicus*, the first issue for which he is responsible**

Feb 9 — John Donne, *Letters to Severall Persons of Honour*, published

Feb 18 — *A Declaration of Lord Willoughby and the Legislature of the Island of Barbados against the British Parliament*, response to Parliamentary Act opposing home rule and free trade in the colonies

Feb 19 — **Milton re-appointed Secretary for Foreign Tongues despite his increasing blindness**

Feb 21 — John Fry, *The Accuser Shamed* (1648) and *Clergy in their True Colors* (1650), burned; Fry ejected from his place in Commons

Feb 24 — **John Milton, *Joannis Miltoni Angli pro Populo Anglicano Defensio Contra Claudii Anonymi, aliàs Salmasii Defensionem Regiam* published, by William Dugard[448]; a triumph for Milton, it appears in seventeen editions, including five in the Netherlands, with transla-**

Council of State; but no party could buy his convictions, which were as sturdy as those of Harrison or Cromwell, or his flow of rhetoric, which was far more persuasive than that of Milton or Needham. Parker's polemical method was the most enlightened of his day, a method that refrained from epithets like those of Milton or fiery maledictions like those of Prynne" (*Complete Prose*, IV, 90).

448. Dugard's career over the previous year is of interest, not because of his inherent importance as a printer, but rather as a paradigm of the political shifting forced upon many from 1649 to 1651. Imprisoned for his association with one of the greatest dangers to the Commonwealth, the *Eikon Basilike*, a year later he produces one of its opposite numbers, Milton's widely respected defense of the regicide and the Commonwealth.

tions into Dutch and French; at least three issues in 1651
— Thereafter (before December): John Rowland, *Pro Rege et Populi Anglicano Apologia, contra Johannis Polypragmatici (alias Miltoni Angli) Defensionem Destructivam Regis et Populi Anglicani (An Apology for the King and the People of England. Against the 'Defence', Destructive of King and People of England, of John Meddler (alias 'Milton Englishman')*, **published anonymously at The Hague**
Feb 25 — **Milton signs and notes a petition concerning land owned by the Powell family**
— **Milton signs a schedule of income the Powell land**
Feb 27 — *The True Manner of the Crowning of Charles the Second King of Scotland*, appears, satirical treatment of Charles' coronation
Feb 28 — **Milton signs affidavit attesting to Richard Powell's debt to him**
Mar 16 — **Milton's only son, John, b.**
Mar 17 — **Milton continues as licenser for *Mercurius Politicus***
Apr — **Joseph Jane, *Eikon Aklastos* published, attack on *Eikonoklastes***
— Isaac Vossius writes to Nicolaas Heinsius, concerning the *Defensio*, "I had expected nothing of such quality from an Englishman."[449]
Apr 9—Easter — Lady Eleanor Davies, *Hells Destruction. By the Lady Eleanor Douglas*, published, account of her imprisonment for debt in 1647
— **Queen Christina of Sweden praises the *Defensio***
Apr 16 — Two country women have a vision of a battle in the sky, followed by a vision of angels; the experience is taken as an omen or portent
Apr 17 — **Milton licenses *Mercurius Politicus* (continues to do so for some time**

---

449. Cited in Christopher Hill, *Milton and the English Revolution*, p. 182.

— Mary (Rande) Cary, *The Little Horns Doom & Downfall: or a Scripture Prophesie of King James, and King Charles*, Fifth-monarchist tract

May-Jun — Sir John Denham returns from Poland to the Court of Charles II at The Hague

May 5 — **Salmasius, in Stockholm, infuriated by Milton's *Defensio***

Jun — *Old Sayings and Predictions verified and fulfilled touching the Young King of Scotland*, published, poem, showing the "Scots holding their young Kinges nose to the grindstone

Jun 18 — **Milton officially thanked by the Council of State for his response to Salmasius**

Jun 19 — John Amos Comenius, *Naturall Philosophy Reformed by Divine light*, published, scientific treatise

Jun 21 — Anne Finch, letter to Henry More, her former teacher, concerning More's poem on the pre-existence of the Soul

— Thereafter: Henry More, 19-page letter in response to Anne Finch's questions

Jun 25 — **John Milton, *Defensio* publicly burned in Toulouse, France**

Jun 26 — **John Milton, *Defensio* publicly burned in Paris**

Jul 26 — **A German traveler, Christopher Arnold, writes concerning the distinguished men he has met in England, including John Selden, Archbishop James Ussher, and John Milton**

Aug — **William Lilly, *Monarchy or No Monarchy*, praise for John Milton, *Eikonoklastes***

Aug 23 — Charles II proclaimed King at Worcester

Sep 3 — The Battle of Worcester, fought on the anniversary of the Battle of Dunbar; Cromwell's victory ends the possibility of a Scots invasion of England

— End of fighting in England

— Charles II escapes from England

Sep 4-11 — ***Mercurius Politicus* shows evidence not only of Milton as censor but also of Milton's writing**

Oct 16 — **Milton receives letter from Herman Mylius, their earliest extant correspondence**

Oct 28 — Lady Eleanor Davies, *The Benediction. From the A:lmighty O:mnipotent*, pamphlet, on the prophetic symbolism of Oliver Cromwell's initials

Nov-Dec — Thomas Hobbes returns to England from the Continent

Nov 5 — Peter Sterry, sermon of thanksgiving for victory at Worcester, delivered at Westminster before Parliament

— Gerrard Winstanley, dedicatory letter to Oliver Cromwell in *The Law of Freedom in a Platform: Or, True Magistracy Restored*, dated (full text published before February 20, 1652)[450]

Nov 7 — **John Milton, Letter to Herman Mylius, concerning Mylius' request for safe passage (a 'safeguard') through English territories in his mission on behalf of the Count of Oldenburg**

Nov 19 — **Milton signs the** *Album Amicorum* **(Album of Friends) of Christopher Arnold, later Professor of History at Nuremberg; Milton retains sufficient eye-sight to sign his name, although the rest of the inscription is in another's hand**

Nov 27 — Edmund Waller formally pardoned by Parliament for his participation in "Waller's Plot"

Dec — Fifth Monarchists meet in Allhallows the Great, London, to pray for a new Parliament more attuned to their political beliefs

Dec (?) — **John Phillips [and probably John Milton],** *Johannis Phillipi Angli Responsio ad Apologiam Anonymi Cujusdam*

---

450. T. Wilson Hayes connects Winstanley's ideas in the New Freedom to those expressed in Sir Thomas More's *Utopia*, Sir Francis Bacon's *New Atlantis*, Gabriel Plattes' *Marcaria*, James Harrington's *Oceana*, John Milton's *Readie and Easie Way to Establish a Free Commonwealth* (*Winstanley the Digger*, p. 210). Of Winstanley's life after this pamphlet appeared in 1652, almost nothing is known for certain; he may have been the Gerrard Winstanley, corn-dealer, who died on 10 September 1676 (*Winstanley the Digger*, p. 218).

Tenebrionis pro Rege et Populo Anglicano Infantissimam **(The Response of John Philips Englishman, to the Most Puerile 'Apology for the King and People of England,' by Some Anonymous Sneak), published**

Dec 17 — **Siege of illness begins; Milton's blindness increasing**

Dec 28 — Katherine Philips, "To the Excellent Mrs. Anne Owen, upon her receiving the Name Lucasia, and Adoption into our Society, December 28, 1651," written, cementing the relationship between 'Orinda' and 'Lucasia'

Dec 29 — **Milton re-appointed Secretary for Foreign Tongues**

Dec 31 — **John Milton, Letter to Herman Mylius**

1652

Milton begins residence in Petty France, Westminster (to 1660)

Milton gives a presentation copy of the *Second Defense* to John Fowler, eldest uncle of Katherine Philips

John Milton, *Joannis Miltoni Angli pro Populo Anglicano Defensio Contra Claudii Anonymi, aliàs Salmasii Defensionem Regiam*, 2nd edition

John Milton, *A Brief history of Moscovia*, completed but not published; begun as early as 1633-38?

Elias Ashmole, ed., *Theatrum Chemicum Britannicum;* includes John Dee, *Testimentum Johannis Dee Philosophi Summi ad Johannem Gwynn, transmissum 1568*

Eliza's Babes: or the virgins-offering. Being divine poems, and meditations. Written by a Lady, who onely desires to advance the glory of God, and not her own, published

E. B. [Edward Benlowes], *Theophila, or Loves Sacrifice. A Divine Poem, in Thirteen Cantos*, with music by J. Jenkins, published

William Cartwright, *An Off-Spring of Mercy*

John Clarke, *Ill News from New-England*

Richard Crashaw, *Delights of the Muses, Carmen Deo Nostro*

Nathaniel Culverwel, *An Elegant and Learned Discourse of the Light of Nature*, edited by William Dillingham

Thomas Gataker, *Antinomianism Discovered and Confuted*

Fulke Greville, 1st Lord Brooke, *The Life of the Renowned Sir Philip Sidney*, published

George Herbert, *Herbert's Remains*, including *A Priest to the Temple* (*The Country Parson*) edited by Barnabas Oley[451]
Peter Heylyn, *Cosmographie*, published
William Lilly, *Dark Year*
Levin Nicholas Moltke, *Annotations* to Sir Thomas Browne, *Religio Medici*, drawing scorn from Guy Patin, who argues that the text requires no outside hand to make it intelligible
John Playford, editor, *Select Musicall Ayres and Dialogues*, published; including music by Henry Lawes, verses by Robert Herrick, and others
John Reeve, *A Transcendent Spirituall Treatise*, published, possibily co-authored by Lodowick Muggleton
Jacobus Typotius, *Symbola divina & humana pontificum imperator regum*, published in Frankfurt, emblem collection
Sir Roger Twysden, *Historiæ Anglicanæ Scriptores Decem*, later a source text for portions of Milton's *History of Britain*
Henry Vaughan, *The Mount of Olives*
Gerard Winstanley, *The Law of Freedom*, pamphlet; dedicated to Oliver Cromwell, urging government establishment of a communist state
John Cotton d. (b. 1584)
Martin Parker d., balladeer
John Rous d. (b. 1574)
Arthur Wilson d. (b. 1595)
Lady Mary Sidney Wroth d. (?)
Sir Richard Blackmore b. (d. 1729)
Nahum Tate b. (d. 1715)
Edmund Waller pardoned by an Act of Parliament and allowed to return to England
John Reeve and Lodowick Muggleton, his cousin, declare that they have been called by God to be the Last Two Witnesses

---

451. "In his preface to *Herbert's Remains* Oley saw the triumph of the Commonwealth as the just punishment for the sins of the clergy; King and Church would triumph if the clergy imitated Herbert's life and his writings" (Joseph Summers, *George Herbert*, p. 13); thus Herbert was, after his death, enlisted in the Royalist cause during the controversies of the Civil War.

prophesied in Revelations, Chapter 11[452]
John Locke enrolls at Christ Church, Oxford

Jan — **John Milton resumes duties following his illness**
Jan 2—CANDLEMAS DAY—Lady Eleanor Davies, *The Restitution of Prophecy; That Buried Talent to Be Revived*, completed (begun on Christmas Day, 1651); written while imprisoned in the Fleet
Jan 8 — **John Milton, Letter to Herman Mylius, accompanying a copy of the proposed safeguard**
— As a result of the Battle of Worchester, Cromwell's forces take control of Scotland; his Commissioners arrive at Dalkeith Palace and annul the coronation of Charles II
Jan 20 — **John Milton, Letter to Herman Mylius**
Jan 22 — **John Milton ceases his active involvement as licenser for *Mercurius Politicus***
Late Jan (?)— Thomas Manley, *Veni; Vidi; Vici. The Triumphs of the most Excellent and Illustrious OLIVER CROMWELL*, including "Gratulatory Song of Peace," a 1,647-line heroic poem, published as panegyric to Oliver Cromwell
Feb 10 — **John Milton, Letter to Herman Mylius**
Feb 12 — **John Milton, Letter to Bulstrode Whitelock, former president of the Council, concerning a Latin transcription of the Oldenburg safeguard**
Feb 13 — **John Milton, Letter to Herman Mylius**
Feb 17 — **Milton retains enough sight to sign the Oldenburg safeguard, his last documented signature**
Feb 18 — **Sir Robert Filmer, *Observations upon the Originall of Government*, attack on Milton and others**
Feb 21 — **John Milton, Letter to Herman Mylius**

---

452. "I tried once to list those sects and radical groups which shared any of Milton's radical views: anti-clericism, millenarianism, antinomianism, anti-Trinitarianism, mortalism, materialism, hell internal. I was a little startled by the result: the group closest to Milton was the Muggletonians" (Christopher Hill, *Milton and the English Revolution*, p. 111; see also his World of the Muggletonians and related studies).

Feb 25 — Leo van Aitzema presents Commons his credentials as Resident from Hamburg, Lubeck and Bremen
Feb 28 — **Milton's blindness becomes complete**
Mar 3 — Thomas Otway b., Sussex
Mar 6 — **Herman Mylius notes in his diary that Milton is completely blind**
Mar 11 — **George Wekherlin appointed Milton's assistant**
Apr 11 — Joan Peterson executed for witchcraft
Thereafter: *The Witch of Wapping: or an Exact and Perfect Relation of the Life and Devilish Practices of Joan Peterson, who dwelt in Spruce Island, near Wapping; Who was condemned for practising Witchcraft, and sentenced to be Hanged at Tyburn on Munday the 11th of April, 1652*
— Thereafter: *A Declaration in Answer to Severall lying Pamphlets concerning the Witch of Wapping,... shewing the Bloudy Plot and wicked Conspiracy of one Abraham Vandenhemde, Thomas Crompton, and others*
Apr 19 — Joseph Glanvill matriculated at Exeter College, Oxford
Apr 28 — Roger Williams, *The Bloudy Tenent yet More Bloudy*, continued attack on John Cotton
May 2 — **Milton's daughter Deborah b.**
May 5 (?) — **Mary Powell Milton d., probably from complications of childbirth**
May — **John Milton, Sonnet XVI: "To the Lord General Cromwell"**
— **John Lilburne, *As You Were...*, includes praise for Milton**
Jun — **John Milton, Letter to Leonard Philaras, Ambassador from Parma to the King of France**
— Lady Eleanor Davies, *Bethlehem Signifying the House of Bread: or War...*, signed "Elea: Aud: Touch: Castleh: Da: & Do:" [Eleanor Audeley Touchet Castlehaven Davies and Douglas], her last published pamphlet
— Anglo-Dutch War begins (through 1654)
Jun 10/16 (?) — **Milton's son John d.**

Jun 21 — Inigo Jones d. (b. 1573)

Early Jul — Lady Eleanor (Audeley Touchet Castlehaven) Davies (and Douglas) d. (b. 1590)

Jul 3 — **John Milton, Sonnet XVII "To Sir Henry Vane"; presented to Sir Henry Vane on July 8**

Jul 30 — Six women executed as witches at Maidstone, Kent

— Thereafter: *A Prodigious and Tragicall History of the Arraignment, Tryall, and Condemnation of six Witches at Maidstone, in Kent, at the Assizes held there in July, Friday 30, this present year, 1652*

Jul 30-Aug 7 — *The Faithful Scout* (news weekly) reports six witches tried and condemned in Kent

Aug (?)— **Pierre Du Moulin, *Regii Sanguinis Clamor ad Coelum Adversus Parricidas Anglicanos* (The Cry of the Royal Blood to Heaven against the English Parricides), appears anonymously; Milton attributes it to Alexander More in spite of arguments against More's authorship by Samuel Hartlib and others**

— William Erbery declares in a sermon that from this day on he will preach only the New Jerusalem's "coming down from God out of heaven[453]

— **Thereafter: John Milton ordered to respond to *Regii Sanguinis Clamor...*, even though he is ill**

Aug 7 — John Smith, Cambridge Platonist, d. (b. 1616?)

Sep — *Mercurius Politicus* includes one of the earliest references to Quakers; four prisoners held to scorn for *thou*-ing their judge

Oct 7 — Sir William Davenant, still imprisoned, granted the freedom of the Tower through the influence of Bulstrode Whitelock; Davenant released shortly thereafter

Oct 18 — George Fox, Quaker, arrested and imprisoned

Nov 20 (?)— **John Milton, *Eikonoklastes*, translated into French by John Dury**

---

453. Cited in Jonathan Post, *Henry Vaughan*, p. 188; an example of the sense of imminence felt by preachers and religious writers during the decade.

Dec 1 — **Milton re-appointed Secretary for Foreign Tongues**

Dec 13 — **John Milton, Letter to Richard Heath; Milton addresses Heath as a "foster son" and gives him permission to write in English rather than Latin**

Dec 24 — **John Phillips,** *Responsio ad Apologiam Anonymi cujusdam tenebrionis pro Rege & Populo Anglicano infantissimam,* **reply to John Rowland's** *Apologia* **(with Milton's aid)**

— **Milton's nephew John Phillips acts as his amanuensis**

1653

John Milton composes some 300 letters of state (1653-1659)[454]

Zachary Bogen, *A View of the Threats and Punishments recorded in the Scriptures alphabetically composed*, published at Oxford, theological treatise of 600 pages, alphabetically tabulating sins and their appropriate punishments

Margaret Lucas Cavendish, Duchess of Newcastle, *Poems and Fancies*, containing *An Epistle to Souldiers*

J. C. [John Cleveland], *Poems..., with Additions, never before Printed*

Anne Collins, *Divine Songs and Meditacions composed by An Collins*

Richard Crashaw, *A letter from Mr. Crashaw to the Countess of Denbigh, against irresolution and delay in matters of religion*, poem, published

Sir John Denham, *Coopers Hill... Now Printed from a perfect Copy; And a Corrected Impression*, published

[Sir John Denham and others], *Certain Verses Written by Severall of the Authors friends, To Be Re-printed with the Second Edition of Gondibert*, published

John Dury, *Some Proposals upon the Advancement of Learning*, educational treatise

William Erbery, *The Babe of Glory*

---

454. These letters are reproduced, and discussed, in French Fogle, ed. *Complete Prose*, V, Part II, with preface and notes by J. Max Patrick. Because of their number, I have not included references to individual letters in this time-line.

Arise [Rhys] Evans, *The Bloudy Vision of John Farley, Interpreted by Arise Evans...*, published; identifies the mystical number 666 in the name "Will Laud" and the year 1666 in "William Laud"[455]

Sir Robert Filmer, *Advertisement to the Jurymen of England*, critique of witch-hunters and the witch-panics

Godfrey Goodman, Bishop of Gloucester, *The two mysteries of the Christian Religion the Trinity and the Incarnation, explicated*, published

Nicholas Hookes, *Amanda*, collection of Cavalier poems

Henry Lawes, *Ayres and Dialogues, for One, Two, or Three Voyces*, published, with commendatory verses by John and Edward Philips

Henry More, *An Antidote against Atheisme, or an Appeal to the Natural Faculties of the Minde of Man, whether there be not a GOD*; and *Conjectura Cabbalistica. Or, A conjectural Essay of interpreting the Minde of Moses, according to a Threefold Cabbala: Viz. Literal, Philosophical, Mystical, or Divinely Moral*, dedicated to Ralph Cudworth

John Rowlands, *Polemica*, attacks Milton

[Madeleine de Scudéry], *Artamènes, or the Grand Cyrus: An Excellent New Romance. Written by that Famous Wit of France, Monsieur de Scudéry, and now Englished by F. G. Gent*

James Shirley, *Cupid and Death*, masque, privately performed

Edmund Spenser, *Calendarium Pastorale... Latino carmine donatae a Theodoro Bathurst* (Shepherds Calendar translated by Theodore Bathurst), Latin version with English text

Izaak Walton, *The Compleat Angler*

Arthur Wilson, *The History of Great Britain, Being the Life and Reign of King James I...from his first Access to the Crown, till his Death*, published

John Taylor, the Water-Poet, d. (b. 1580)

Thomas D'Urfey b. (?; d. 26 Feb 1723)

---

455. Michael McKeon, *Politics and Poetry*, p. 242.

John Oldham b.

Jan 7 — Rump Parliament revives the Licensing Orders

Jan 8 — William Erbery, *The Bishop of London*, Fifth-Monarchist tract

— George Fox brought before the Justices for blasphemy in asserting himself equal with God

Jan 17 — John Evelyn begins building the gardens at Sayes Court, using recent innovations in agricultural technology

Feb 20 — **John Milton requests that Andrew Marvell serve as his assistant**

Feb 21 — **John Milton, Letter to John Bradshaw, indicating that Andrew Marvell—which name Milton spells 'Marvile'—has left the service of Lord General Thomas Fairfax and had earlier spent four years abroad "to very good purpose"**

Feb 27 — Dorothy Laugharne Owen d., age seventy (Lucasia's mother-in-law)

— Thereafter: Katherine Philips, "In Memory of the most justly Honoured, Mrs. Owen of Orielton," written

Mar 1 — Thomas Traherne enrolls as a Commoner of Brasenose College, Oxfordrecords give his age as fifteen

Mar 18 — George Fox appears before the assizes at Lancaster

— Thereafter: George Fox and James Nayler [attributed authors], *Saul's Errand to Damascus*, tract, answering Puritan objections to Quakerism

— Thereafter: Francis Higginson, *A Brief Relation of the Irreligion of the Northern Quakers*, anti-Quaker tract, responding to Fox's and Nayler's *Saul's Errand*

Apr 1 — Thomas Traherne matriculated at Brasenose College

Apr 20 — Oliver Cromwell forcibly dismisses the Rump of the Long Parliament

— Londoners publicly burn rumps of beef as a signal of their contempt for the former Parliament

Apr 22 — *A Justification of the Lord General and His Council of Officers*, published, defends the dissolution of the Long

Parliament

Apr 24 — John Spittlehouse, *The Army Vindicated in Their Late Dissolution of the Parliament*, pamphlet

Apr 25 — John Rogers addresses a congregation of hundreds in London, praising Oliver Cromwell as England's Great Deliverer

May 8 — **John Milton, *A Letter Written to a Gentleman in the Country, touching the dissolution of the late Parliament, and the Reasons thereof*** [456]

May 19 — John Spittlehouse, *Army Vindicated*, Fifth Monarchist tract, hails Cromwell as a second Moses for England

June 6 — Praise-God Barebone and other Independents summoned directly by Oliver Cromwell to appear at Whitehall and serve as a member of Parliament ("Barebones Parliament")

Jun 14 — John Lilburne returns to England after being exiled by the Rump Parliament

— John Lilburne, *The Banished Mans Suit*

Jul 4 — The Barebone Parliament, its members appointed by the Commonwealth government from among the Independents, assembles at Whitehall; in response to Cromwell's opening address, Parliament published a strongly millenarian declaration

Jul 5 — John Spittlehouse, *First Addresses*, Fifth Monarchist tract

Jul 7 — Mary Cary, *Twelve (New) Proposals to the Supreme Governours*, dated, Fifth-Monarchist tract

Jul 13 — John Lilburne brought to trial

Jul 15 — Radicals in Parliament propose abolishing all tithes

Jul 27 — John Carew proposes to Parliament a radical bill insuring complete freedom of preaching in all public places

Aug — **John Milton, Psalm I translated**

— John Lilburne, *The Upright Man's Vindication*, published; *The Just Defense of John Lilburne against Such as charge*

---

456. Cited in John P. Anderson, *Bibliography*, p. xiii.

him with *Turbulency of Spirit*

— *The Tryall of John Lilburne*, published in three parts

Aug 1 — William Aspinwall, *A Brief Description of the Fifth Monarchy, or Kingdome*, pamphlet

Aug 4 — Justices from Kent petition Parliament against Tithes, anticipating the imminent return of Christ to Earth

Aug 8 — **John Milton, Psalm II translated**

Aug 9 — **John Milton, Psalm III translated**

Aug 10 — **John Milton, Psalm IV translated**

Aug 12 — **John Milton, Psalm V translated**

Aug 13 — **John Milton, Psalm VI translated**

Aug 14 — **John Milton, Psalm VII translated**

— **John Milton, Psalm VIII translated**

Sep 3 — Claudius Salmasius d. (b. 1588), in Holland[457]

Sep 8 — **Philip Meadows, Secretary of State for Foreign Tongues, to assist Milton**[458]

Sep 9 — John Fletcher and William Shakespeare, *Cardenio* (a lost play), SR by Humphrey Moseley

Sep 28 — While radical members are absent, Parliament reconstitutes a High Court of Justice, a vital step toward religious control and repression

Oct — Robert Boyle in residence in Oxford, now the center of experimental philosophy and modern "science"; others in his circle include John Wilkins, Christopher Wren, Seth Ward, John Wallis, Jonathan Goddard, and William Petty

Oct 3 — John Brayne, *The New Earth, or the True Magna Charta of the...World to come: Called the Jews Commonweal*, Fifth-Monarchist tract

---

457. The story circulated throughout England and Europe that the great scholar, then in residence at the Court of Queen Christina of Sweden, was so chagrined at the enthusiastic responses Milton's pamphlet received that he returned to Holland in despair and there died. Having once chided Milton for his blindness, Salmasius is now in turn chided for having recognized his equal in controversy, given up in despair, and died. His unfinished reply to Milton was published posthumously.

458. Fallon, *Milton in Government* 14.

Oct 12 — John Webster, *The picture of Mercurius Politicus; or some of his falsities and mistakes mentioned in his intelligence of 12 Oct. concerning the dispute in Lumbard St. detected and disproved*

Oct 17 — **John Milton and Meadows confirmed as assistants to John Thurloe, Secretary of State**

Nov — John Canne, *John Lilb. Tryed and Cast*

Nov (?) — Sir William Davenant imprisoned for debt, shortly after his second marriage

Nov 3 — **John Milton re-appointed Secretary for Foreign tongues**

Nov 7 — John Rogers, *Ohel or Beth-shemesh. A Tabernacle for the Sun, published; Sagrir. Or doomes-Day drawing nigh, with Thunder and Lightning to Lawyers*, Fifth Monarchist tract, arguing the imminent collapse of all kingship worldwide

Nov 14 — Mary Cary, *The Resurrection of the Witnesses*, 2nd edition, enlarged, Fifth-Monarchist tract

Nov 19 — Christopher Feake and Vavasor Powell, both Fifth Monarchists, condemn Praise-God Barebones (and the Barebones Parliament) as villainous and perjured

Nov 20 — Christopher Feake, sermon on the Little Horn of Daniel 7:8, identifying the enemy of God as Oliver Cromwell

Nov 21 — Christopher Feake and Vavasor Powell arrested, their meetings forbidden

Nov 24-Dec 2 — *Mercurius Politicus* reports the discovery of fifteen witches in Lands-end

Dec 1 — Oliver Cromwell offered—and rejects—the Crown of England

Dec 12 — The Barebones Parliament forcibly dissolved by Oliver Cromwell

Dec 16 — *Instrument of Government*; Oliver Cromwell proclaimed Lord Protector

Dec 18 — **John Milton's books ordered confiscated in Ratisbon, Bavaria**

1654

1654 — The first of two dates calculated by Joseph Mede (and widely accepted by Puritan and Independent divines) for the end of the world, with Christ literally the "shortly-expected King"

John Milton, *An Apology for Smectymnuus With the Reason of Church-Government. By John Meltom, Gent., published* (reissue of both tracts)

Alexander Brome, *The Cunning Lovers*, printed

William Burden, *Christ's Personal Reign on Earth*, published, millenarian tract

Tommaso Campanella, *A Discourse Touching the Spanish Monarchy*, published[459]

John Collinges, *Responsoria Bipartita*

Thomas Goodwin, *A Sermon of the Fifth Monarchy*

The Harmony of the Muses: or the Gentlemans and Ladies Choisest Recreation, including the first printing of John Donne's elegy, "On His Mistress Going to Bed

Samuel Hartlib, *The True and Ready Way to Learn the Latin Tongue*

Edward Johnson, *Wonder-Working Providence of Sions Saviour in New England,* verse and prose description of New England, published in London

---

459. By this point, Campanella had concluded that the Spanish Monarchy represented the Universal Monarchy prophesied in Scripture and so eagerly sought by the English Fifth Monarchists.

Thomas Killigrew, *Thomaso*, drama[460]

Henry King, Bishop of Chichester, *The Psalmes of David... Unto which are newly added the Lord's Prayer, the Creed, the ten Commandements*, published

Jeremy Taylor, *The Real Presence and Spiritual of Christ in the Blessed Sacrament*, controversialist tract written

Anna Trapnel, *Strange and Wonderful Newes from White-Hall*, *The Cry of a Stone*, *A Legacy for Saints*, and *Anna Trapnel's Report and Plea*

Henry Vaughan, *Flores Solitudinis*, translations

Dr. John Bastwick d. (b. 1593)

William Habington d.

Thomas Hobbes, *De Cive*, placed on the Vatican's *Index Librorum Prohibitorum*

First of several Anglo-Dutch naval wars concludes

Jan — Anna Trapnel, *The Cry of a Stone: or a relation of something spoken in Whitehall, by Anna Trapnel, being in the visions of God. Relating to the governors, army, churches, ministry, universities: and the whole nation*, prophetic Fifth-Monarchist tract

Jan 18 — Johannes Cornubiensis [John Carew?], *The Grand Catastrophe, or the Change of Government*, Fifth-Monarchist tract

— John Hall, *Confusion Confounded:... Wherein is Considered the Reasons of the late Parliament*, published

Jan 24 — John More, *A Lost Ordinance Restored; or...the Laying on of Hands*, published

Jan 28 — Christopher Feake and John Simpson, Fifth Monarchists, ordered confined at Windsor

Jan 29 — J. N., *Proh Tempora! Proh Mores! Or an unfained Caveat to all True Protestants, Not in any case to touch ... Mr. Christopher Feakes Exhortations*

— James Naylor, *Lamentations...over the Ruines of This*

---

460. Aphra Behn would later borrow extensively from this play in writing her *The Rovers*.

Oppressed Nacion, Quaker tract
— George Fox, *Warning to the Rulers of England*, Quaker tract
Mar — John Dryden receives B.A., Cambridge University
— Samuel Pepys receives B. A., Cambridge University
Mar 15 — John Evelyn hears Dr. Jeremy Taylor preach at St Gregory's, the only Anglican Church officially allowed in London by Oliver Cromwell
Mar 20 — William Aspinwall, *An Explication and Application of the Seventh Chapter of Daniel, wherein is briefly shewed... the Beheading of Charles Stuart, who is proved to be the Little Horn*, pamphlet
Mar 24 — Oliver Cromwell declares a national day of fasting and humiliation
Mar 30 — *Vavasoris Examen, et Purgamen: or, Mr. Vavasor Powells Impartiall Triall: Who...is found Not Guilty*
Apr — Anna Trapnel, Fifth monarchist, arrested by the government
Apr 4 — **Milton writing response to *Regii Sanguinis Clamor ad Coelum*, incorrectly attributing it to Alexander More**
Apr 5 — Peace treaty signed between England and the Dutch
Apr 12 — *An Ordinance by the Protector for the Union of England and Scotland*
May — **Alexander More's friends try to dissuade Milton from publishing his tract**
— John Lilburne, *A Declaration to the Free-Born People of England concerning the Government of its Commonwealth*, published
May 1 — *Severall Proceedings* (news weekly) notes with displeasure the number of Londoners who persist in "going a-maying" and following other old celebrations
May 18 — Sir William Temple, only surviving love letter to Dorothy Osborne, written
May 30 — **John Milton, *Joannis Miltoni Angli pro populo Anglicano Defensio Secunda Contra infamem libellum anonymum cui titulus, Regii sanguinis clamor ad coelum adversus parricidas Anglicanos* (Second Defense of the**

English People), **published**
Jun — *Musarum Oxoniensum Elaiophoria*, poems published by members of Oxford University dealing with the Dutch Treaty; includes a poem by John Locke
— Charles X, King of Sweden, ascends to the throne
Jun-Jul — Anna Trapnel incarcerated in Bridewell Prison
Jun 2 — **Andrew Marvell writes to John Milton the only letter surviving from a friendship lasting from 1653 through Milton's death in 1674**
Jun 18 — John Dryden's father buried at Titchmarsh
Jul 6 — **John Milton, first letter to Henry Oldenburg**
Jul 13 — John Simpson, released from prison, ordered not to approach within ten miles of London
Jul 24 — **Rumor circulates that Alexander More is purchasing copies of the *Defensio* to keep them out of circulation**
Aug 3-10 — *Severall Proceedings* for the week reports "wrastlings" at Lincolns Inn Fields ordered suppressed by the government and crowds dispersed
Aug 4 — Sir William Davenant finally freed from imprisonment by Parliament
Aug 14 — John More, *A Trumpet Sounded*
Sep 1 — John Spittlehouse, *Certaine Queries*, Fifth-Monarchist tract, published; accuses Oliver Cromwell of treason against the 1649 Act forbidding government by one person
Sep 2 — *A Declaration of several of the Churches of Christ ... concerning the Kingly Interest of Christ*, tract
Sep 3 — First Parliament of the Protectorate convenes, with members representing England, Scotland, and Ireland
Sep 9 — Oliver Cromwell orders the arrest of Captain Thomas Harrison
Sep 11 — Thomas Flatman admitted to New College, Oxford
Sep 12 — Imposition of Recognition excludes radical members of Parliament who refuse to take an oath of loyalty to the government
Sep 28 — **John Milton, Letter to Leonard Philaras; describes symptoms of Milton's blindness**

Oct (?)— **Alexander More, *Alexandri Mori Ecclesiastæ Sacarumque Literarum Professoris Fides Publica, Contra Calumnias Joannis Miltoni Scurrae* (Alexander More's Public faith, against the Calumnies of John Milton), response to *Defensio Secunda*, published at The Hague**

Oct — Ralph Cudworth elected Master of Christ's College, Cambridge

Nov 30 — William Aspinwall, *A Premonition of Sundry Sad Calamities Yet to Come*, Fifth-Monarchist tract

— John Selden d. (b. 1584)

Dec — Christopher Feake, *Oppressed Close Prisoner*, Fifth-Monarchist tract accepting Cromwell as ruler in fact but not in law, published

— Thereafter: Christopher Feake and ten Fifth Monarchists ordered to appear before Parliament; Feake remains in custody

Dec 25 — Sir William Temple m. Dorothy Osborne

1655

Milton begins compiling Latin dictionary, Greek thesaurus (?)
Milton begins *De Doctrina Christiana* (?)
John Milton, Sonnet XIX: "When I Consider" (written as early as 1652?)
John Milton, Sonnet XX: "Lawrence of Virtuous Father..."
John Milton, Sonnet XXI: "Cyriack, Whose Grandsire"
John Milton, Sonnet XXII: "To Mr Cyriack Skinner"
Meric Casaubon, *Treatise Concerning Enthusiasm*, rationalist treatise on the causation of ecstatic states[461]
Margaret Lucas Cavendish, Duchess of Newcastle, *The Worlds Olio*
Chymical, Medicinal, and Chyrurgical Addresses made to S. Hartlib, published, including Robert Boyle, "An Epistolical Discourse of Philaretus to Empericus, inviting all true lovers of Vertue and Mankind, to a free and generous Communication of their Secrets and Receipts in Physick, Boyle's first (anonymous) publication
Sir John Denham, *Cooper's Hill...obtained from the Author's owne papers*, (Draft IV) enlarged edition; 1st authorized edition
[Sir John Denham and others?], *The Incomparable Poem Gondibert, Vindicated from the Wit-Combats of Four*

---

461. By the eighteenth century, the term *enthusiasm* will have assumed distinctly negative overtones, consonant with its connections to fanaticism, extremism, emotionalism, and irrationalism.

Esquires, Clinias, Dametas, Sancho, and Jack Pudding

William Dewsbury, *A True Prophecy of the Mighty Day of the Lord*, Quaker tract

Sir Richard Fanshawe, English translation of Luis de Camões' epic, *Os Lusiads*

Richard Farnsworth, *Witchcraft Cast out from the Religious Seed and Israel of God*, Quaker pamphlet, assumes the reality of magic and witchcraft

Thomas Fuller, *The Church-History of Britain; from the Birth of Jesus Christ untill the Year 1648*, published; with *The History of the University of Cambridge since the conquest*, and *The History of Waltham Abbey*

Thomas Goodwin, *The World to Come, or, the Kingdom of Christ asserted*

Thomas Hobbes, *De Corpore Politico; Art of Rhetoric*

Henry Lawes, *The Second Booke of Ayres and Dialogues, etc.*, printed by John Playford; with prefatory poems by Katherine Philips and others; lyrics by Edmund Waller, Robert Herrick, and Ben Jonson

M., *The Queens Closet Opened. Incomparable secrets in Physick, Churugery, Preserving, Candying and Cookery, As they were presented to the Queen. Never before published. Transcribed from the true Copies of her Majesties own recipe books, by W. M., one of her late Servants*[462]

John Phillips, *Satyr Against Hypocrites*

Katherine Philips, "Orinda upon little Hector Philips," and "Epitaph on her son H. P., at St. Syth's church, where her body also lies Interred," elegy and epitaph for the birth and death of her first child

Vavasor Powell, *A Word for God*; petition accusing the Commonwealth government of betraying the cause

---

462. In spite of the exigencies of life under the Commonwealth, household chores had to be completed; and the reference to the Queen, then in exile in France, seems nevertheless to have helped the popularity (and presumably the sales) of this handbook. See Antonia Fraser, *The Weaker Vessel*, p. 45-46

Thomas Stanley, *History of Philosophy*, first volume published (fourth volume, 1662)

John Sanders, *An Iron Rod Put into the Lord Protectors Hand, to break all Antichristian Powers inn pieces*

Henry Vaughan, *Silex Scintillans*, 2nd edition, with new introductory materials and a second part; *Hermetical Physic*

Thomas Vaughan completes series of alchemical and mystical treatises

Edmund Waller, "A Panegyric to My Lord Protector"

Isaak Walton, *The Compleat Angler*, revised and extensively altered

Pierre Gassendi d. (b. 1592)

Stephen Marshall d. (b. 1594)

Sir Theodore Turquet de Mayerne d. (b. 1573); physician to James I and Charles I

Sir Henry Vane, the Elder, d. (b.1589)

Edward Winslow d. (b. 1595)

Jan — Andrew Marvell, *The First Anniversary of the Government under His Highness the Lord Protector*

— Jeremy Taylor, *A Golden Grove*, miscellany of prayers, published

— First Parliament of the Protectorate dissolved

Feb — William Prynne, *The Quakers Unmasked*, published

Feb 5 — **John Milton, Letter to Leo van Aitzema with reference to Aitzema's visits to Milton and Milton's books on divorce**

Feb 13 — Oliver Cromwell informed of a plot against him by Christopher Feake, Thomas Harrison, and John Rogers, all Fifth Monarchists

Mid-Feb — Oliver Cromwell urges Parliament to accept limited religious toleration, particularly of Anglicans

Mar 5 — Anne Cademan, second wife to Sir William Davenant, d.

Mar 24 — **John Milton, Letter to Ezekiel Spanheim, mentioning Milton's willingness to receive letters from** foreigners and strangers, though he counts "no good man foreigner or stranger"[463]

Apr — Sir Henry Vane, *The Retired Man's Meditations, or the Mysterie and Power of Godliness*, published, religious treatise

Apr (?) — **Alexander More, *Suppletmenum Fidei Publicæ, Contra Calumnias Joannis Miltoni*, attacking Milton, published at The Hague**

Apr 17 — **John Milton's responsibilities limited and his salary reduced nearly by half (to £150), but he receives a life pension from the Commonwealth government**

Apr 20 — Richard Baxter, *The Quakers' Catechism, or the Quakers Questioned*, Puritan tract addressed to Separatists and Anabaptists, answering Quaker challenges, dated

— Thereafter: James Nayler, *An Answer to a Book Called the Quakers' Catechism put out by Richard Baxter, wherein the slanderer is searched, his questions, answered, and his deceit discovered...*, published

Apr 23 — John Dryden leaves Trinity College, Cambridge

Apr 24 — **Piedmontese massacre of 150 Waldensians, occasioning Milton's subsequent heroic sonnet**

May — Sir Henry Vane, the Elder, d

May 3 — Jeremy Taylor, *Unum Necessarium; or, The doctrine and Practice of Repentance, Describing the Necessities and Measures of a Strict, a Holy, and a Christian Life, and Rescued from Popular Errors*, SR, treatise on moral theology

May 25-Jun 29 — **John Milton, Letters of State protesting the Piedmont massacre**

Jun — Sir John Denham and other Royalists arrested in London

Jun 11 — **James Howell, *Epistolæ Ho-Elianæ*, 3rd edition, with references to Milton's views on divorce; last edition published during Howell's lifetime**

---

463. *Complete Prose*, IV, ii, p. 873.

(?)— **John Milton, Sonnet XVIII "On the Late Massacre in Piedmont"**

Jul 25 — Thomas Tillam, *The Fourth Principle of Christian Religion; or...Laying on of Hands asserted*

— Thomas Flatman matriculated, New College, Oxford University

Jul 28 — Cyrano de Bergerac d.

Aug — *A Short Discovery of His Highness's Intentions concerning Anabaptists in the Army*, circulates among the Army, accuses Cromwell of planning to purge the Army of Baptists and other radicals

— The Council of State refuses Bathsua Makin 's petition for a pension based on her position as governess to Princess Elizabeth

Aug 8 — **John Milton, *Pro Se Defensio contra Alexandrum Morum ecclesiasten Libelli famosi, cui titulus, Regii sanguinis clamor ad coelum adversus parricidas Anglicanos, authorem recte dictum* (Defense of Himself...), published**

Aug 17 — **John Phillips (Milton's nephew), *Satyr Against Hypocrites***

Aug 28 — Oliver Cromwell promulgates a severe Licensing Order, allowing only two newspapers, both licensed by John Thurloe, Secretary of State

Oct — Jeremy Taylor, *Unum Necessarium*, published to some controversy, while Taylor is imprisoned in Cheapstow[464]

Oct 10 — Samuel Pepys m. Elizabeth St. Michel, in a church ceremony; marriage repeated before a civil magistrate, Dec 1[465]

Oct 11 — Joseph Glanvill, B.S., Exeter College, Oxford University

Oct 24 — Treaty of Westminster, establishes friendly relations

---

464. The 'one thing necessary' (unum necessarium) for salvation being repentance for sin.

465. In this instance the age difference was minimal for the period, Pepys being twenty-two and his bride fifteen.

between England and France; Charles II and James, Duke of York, no longer allowed to remain in France

Nov 28 — **Thomas Young, Milton's former tutor and Smectymnuan, d. (b. 1588?)**

Dec 1 — Vavasor Powell, *A Word for God*, Fifth Monarchist petition bearing 322 signatures[466]

Dec 3 — Vavasor Powell's *A Word of God* read aloud to a mass meeting of 500 Londoners

Dec 17 — Anthony Wood admitted M.A., Oxford University

Dec 21 — John Owen d., age twenty-one

— Thereafter: Katherine Philips, "To my dearest Friend Mrs. A. Owen, upon her greatest loss," written in honor of Lucasia's husband, 'Charistus'

Dec 28 — Six players, performing in Newcastle in spite of the Commonwealth ban on theaters, are arrested and publicly whipped and their costumes hung from the gallows

---

466. Powell had claimed the support of some 20,000 Fifth Monarchists in Wales; slightly more than 300 actually signed the petition.

1656

1656 — Since 1656 years had passed between the Creation and the Great Flood, this 1656th year since the Crucifixion was seen as portentous of great happenings.

John Milton, *Apographum literarum serenissimi protectoris, etc.*, published in Leiden(?)[467]

Thomas Ady, *Candle in the Darkness*, critique of witch-hunters and of the witch panics

Thomas Baker, *Gods Providence Asserted*

John Bunyan, *Some Gospel-Truths Opened according to the Scriptures...*, published, 200-page duodecimo anti-Quaker tract; Bunyan's first publication

Margaret Lucas Cavendish, Duchess of Newcastle, *Natures Pictures Drawn by Fancies Pencil to the Life*, with an autobiographical section, "A True Relation of my Birth, Breeding, and Life"

Abraham Cowley, *Poems—Miscellanies, Pindarique Odes, Davideis*[468]

William Drummond of Hawthornden, *Poems*, edited by Edward Phillips

William Dugdale, *Antiquities of Warwickshire*, published, Anthony Wood's inspiration for his own antiquarian work

---

467. Cited in John P. Anderson, *Bibliography*, p. ix.

468. The unfinished *Davideis* provides an excellent example of the century's concern for (if not obsession with) writing Christian epic—a concern fulfilled in Milton's *Paradise Lost*, perhaps already in progress when Cowley's poem appeared.

in Oxfordshire

Thomas Fuller, *The Church History of England*

William Guild, *The Sealed Book Opened*, published[469]

Sir John Mennis and Dr. James Smith, *Musarum Deliciæ: or, The Muses Recreation...*, includes satirical references to Sir William Davenant's nose

Henry More ['Philophilus Parresiastes'], *Enthusiasmus Triumphatus, or, A Discourse of the Nature, Causes, Kings, and Cure, of Enthusiasme*

Francis Osborn, *Political Reflections upon the Government of the Turks*, including approval of polygamy; *Advice to a Son*

John Parkinson, *Paradisi in Sole Paradisus Terrestris. A Garden of All sorts of pleasant Flowers which our English ayre will permitt to be nourished up...*, 2nd edition, agricultural/horticultural treatise

Blaise Pascal, *Lettres Provinciales*

John Reeve and Lodowick Muggleton, *A Divine Looking-Glass*, proclaiming the imminent millennium; dedicated to Oliver Cromwell

Edward Reynolds, *A Treatise of the Passions and Faculties of the Soul of Man*, published

Thomas Stanley, *Psalterium Carolinum*, verse adaptation of *Eikon Basilike*

Jeremy Taylor, *Deus Justificatus or A vindication of the Glory of the Divine Attributes in the question of Original Sin*, published to defend *Unum Necessarium*

Charles Davenant b. (d. Nov 6, 1714

Jacob Tonson b. (?; d. 1736)

Edward Archer, bookseller, includes *The Puritan: or, The widow of Watling Street*, in his listing of plays by William Shakespeare

Jan 19 — Godfrey Goodman, Bishop of Gloucester, d. (b.

---

[469]. Guild's book identifies Samson with one of the angels of the Apocalypse, suggesting one level of understanding Samson prevalent during the period. Wittreich, *Interpreting Samson Agonistes*, p. 361.

1582/3)

Jan 30 — Sir J. M., Ja: S, Sir W. D., J. D. [Sir John Mennes, James Smith, Sir William Davenant, John Donne[470] and others], *Wit and Drollery, Jovial Poems. Never before Printed*, SR; includes Sir William Davenant, *The Long Vacation in London*, burlesque or mock-verse

Feb 5 — Sir John Denham, *The Destruction of Troye, being a translation of the second booke of Virgill's Eniods*, SR by Humphrey Moseley; published by late April/early May

Feb 26 — Charles II removes from Cologne to court-in-exile in The Netherlands

Mar 12 — Representatives of twelve churches in Suffolk and Norfolk meet to discuss the imminent millennium

Mar 14 — Oliver Cromwell proclaims a national day of fast and humiliation

Mar 21 — James Ussher, Archbishop of Armagh, d. (b. 1581, in Dublin)

Early Apr — *Sportive Wit*, edited and prefaced by Milton's nephew John Phillips, includes satires on Sir William Davenant

Apr 25 — Council of State orders *Sportive Wit*, edited and prefaced by John Milton's nephew John Phillips, burned; Phillips arrested and fined

May 12 — Sir Henry Vane, the Elder, *A Healing Question*, treatise dealing with reconciliation and harmony in government and religion

May 23 — Playbills announce the opening of the *Rutland House Theater*, managed by Sir William Davenant; *The First Dayes Entertainment at Rutland-House, by Declamations and Musick: after the manner of the Ancients*, produced[471]

May 29 — Joseph Hall, Bishop of Exeter, under the care of Dr. Thomas Browne of Norwich (later Sir Thomas Browne

---

470. The somewhat disreputable son of the earlier poet.

471. By referring to his production as an opera and by incorporating music, Davenant successfully circumvented Commonwealth laws against plays and play-going

May-Jun — **John Milton, first surviving letter to Richard Jones, afterward Earl of Ranelagh, possibly one of Milton's pupils, 1647-1649**

Jun 25 — **John Milton, Letter to Henry Oldenburg**

Jun 26 — Abraham Cowley, *Poems*, special edition presented to the Bodleian Library, with holograph "Pindarique Ode" appended

— Oliver Cromwell agrees to call a new Parliament

Jun 29 — Marchamont Needham, *The Excellencie of a Free State*, political treatise, published

Jul — Joseph Granvill attends Lincoln College

Aug — John Hall d.

Aug 19 — Mary Lee b. (afterward, Mary, Lady Chudleigh; d. 1710)[472]

Aug 20 — William Aspinwall, *The Legislative Power is Christ's Peculiar Prerogative*, published

— Sir Henry Vane summoned to London to appear before Cromwell's Council of State

— Thereafter, Sir Henry Vane committed by the Council to confinement at Carisbrooke Castle[473]

Aug 27 — Sir William Davenant, *Siege of Rhodes Made a Representation by the Art of Prospective in Scenes and the Story Sung in Recitative Musick*, SR

Sep — Sir William Davenant, *Siege of Rhodes*, performed, including a woman, Mrs. Coleman, singing one of the roles

— Second Protectorate Parliament sits

Sep 3 — Sir William Davenant, letter to Bulstrode Whitelock,

---

472. Lady Mary Chudleigh died 15 Dec 1710 after years of struggle against a crippling rheumatism. Her poems and prose, all published after 1700, were in large measure composed during the final two decades of the century.

473. By this time, Vane's commitment to the Long Parliament as the only viable authority in England and his radical belief in religious toleration had made him seem threatening to Cromwell's increasingly conservative regime; once friendly, the two men now realized the gulfs that separated them.

Lord Commissioner of the Treasury, requesting permission to perform an 'opera,' *The Siege of Rhodes*[474]; the play is presented shortly thereafter

Sep 8 — Joseph Hall, Bishop of Exeter and Norwich, and Milton's erstwhile antagonist in the pamphlet wars, first English satirist and early advocate of Senecanism in prose style, d. (b. 1574)

Sep 9 — Sir William Davenant, *The First Days Entertainment at Rutland-House, by Declamations and Musick: after the Manner of the Ancients*, SR

Sep 21 — **John Milton, Letter to Richard Jones**

Sep 24 — *The Banner of Truth Displayed ... Being the Substance of Severall Consultations, ...kept by a Certain Number of Christians, who are waiting for the visible appearance of Christ's Kingdome*, published

Oct — James Harrington, *The Common-wealth of Oceana* published, utopian treatise outlining a limited monarchy, dedicated to Oliver Cromwell

Oct 13 — Thomas Traherne, B.A. from Oxford

Nov — **John Milton, Letter to Peter Heimbach**

— **Sir William Davenant, *Epithalamium*, for the marriage of Martha Lawrence, to Richard Barry, 2nd Earl of Barrymore, John Milton's former pupil**[475]

---

474. "*The Siege of Rhodes* has been called the most epoch-making play in the English language. Dryden saw in it the 'first light' of the Restoration heroic plays, and others date from it the beginning of opera in England. It was presented with the accoutrements of proscenium arch, curtain, and moveable scenes, and in its limited cast was the first English woman to act upon the public stage. This was Mrs. Coleman, the wife of one of the Court musicians whom Davenant cautiously selected as his actors. The music was composed by Henry Lawes…and the scenes were designed by John Webb, the protégé of Inigo Jones" (Alfred Harbage, *Sir William Davenant*, p. 124-125).

475. The event—and the poem—provide interesting links to Milton. Martha Lawrence was the daughter of Henry Lawrence, Lord President of Cromwell's Council of State, to whose son Edward Milton addressed his Sonnet XX. Richard Barry, 1st Earl of Barrymore, had been Milton's pupil

Nov 12 — **John Milton m. Katherine Woodcock, by Sir John Dethicke, J.P., at St. Mary's Aldermanbury, London**
Nov 13 — Mary Trevor Lloyd d.(Lucasia's maternal grandmother)
— Thereafter: Katherine Philips, "In Memory of that excellent Person Mrs. Mary Lloyd of Bodidrist in Denbigh-shire, who died Nov. 13, 1656
Dec 17 — Thomas Shadwell admitted to Caius College, Cambridge

---

during Milton's brief career as schoolmaster. These connections—and an implicit connection thereby to Davenant—might lend greater credence to the stories of Milton's having rescued the poet-playwrite from prison earlier.

1657

Lancelot Andrewes, Bishop of Winchester, *A Collection of posthumous and orphan lectures; delivered at St Pauls and St Giles his Church by...Lancelot Andrewes*, published

Jacobus Arminius, *The Just Mans Defence; or, The Declaration of the Judgment of James Arminius...before the States of Holland, and Westfriezland*, English translation by Tobias Conyers

Daniel Baker, *God's Plea for Ninevah*, tract[476]

A Banquet of Jests, published, now attributed directly to "Archee"

Edward Benlowes, *The Summary of Wisedome*, published by Humphrey Moseley

Robert Boyle, *Mechanica Hydraulica-Pneumatica*, treatise on the properties of gases

Edward Burrough, *The True Faith of the Gospel of Peace, contended for in the spirit of meekness...against the secret opposition of John Bunyan, a professed minister in Bedfordshire*, published, Quaker response to Bunyan

Thereafter: John Bunyan, *A Vindication of Gospel Truths Opened*, published a few weeks after Burrough's response

Thereafter: Edward Burrough, *Reply unto his second book called 'A Vindication,' &c., &c. And this to clear the Truth*

---

476. Baker's tract, published some eight years before the Great Plague and the Great Fire, predicted disaster for London: "Methinks I see you bringing pick-axes to dig downe your owne walls, and kindling sparks that will set all in a flame from one end of the City to the other" (cited in James Leaser, *The Plague*, p. 11).

from above 100 of John Bunion's foule dirty lyes and slanders: By a friend of the Truth; and not as it is in mens carnall apprehensions, published

Abraham Cowley, *Poems*, including Pindaric odes and the incomplete *Davideis*

Edward Farnham, publisher, *Nature's Cabinet Unlock'd*, attributed to "Tho. Brown D. of Physic," an attempt to capitalize on the popularity of Sir Thomas Browne's *Vulgar Errors*

Bishop Francis Godwin, *The Man in the Moone: or, A Discourse of a Voyage thither*, satirical fiction (imaginary-voyage narrative), 2nd edition

Thomas Hall, *Chiliasto-Mastix redivivus...A confutation of the Millenarian Opinion*

Lady Ann Harcourt Halkett, *A Mothers Instructions*, written before the birth of her first child[477]

Thomas Hobbes, *Questions Concerning Liberty, Necessity, and Chance*

Henry King, Bishop of Chichester, *Poems, Elegies, Paradoxes, and Sonnets*, published in a pirated edition

Marchamont Needham, *The Excellencies of a Free State*, republican treatise

Bernardino Ochino, *Dialogue of Polygamy*, translated into English by Francis Osburn (?)

Joshua Poole, compiler, *The English Parnassus; Or, a Helpe to English Poesie. Containing a Collection of all Rhyming Monosyllables, the Choicest Epithets and Phrases: with Some General Forms upon All Occasions, Subjects, and Theams...*, includes extensive quotations from Milton, Davenant, Denham, and others

Sir Francis Vere, *Commentaries...Being Diverse Pieces of Service, wherein he had command...*, published, with William Dillingham, *Continuation of the Siege of Ormond*

---

[477]. Fully aware of the dangers of childbirth, Halkett wrote careful instructions before the birth of each of her children; unlike so many of her contemporaries, she survived the dangers and lived well into her seventies. Antonia Fraser, *The Weaker Vessel*, p. 70.

Paul Best d.
William Bradford d., in New England (b. 1590)
Edward Lawrence d.
Richard Lovelace d. (?)
Sir William Mure d. (b. 1594)
Herman Mylius d., in Oldenburg
John Dennis b. (d. 1734)
The Protectorate has become in essence monarchical; Oliver Cromwell functioning as an uncrowned "King"[478]
George Villiers, 2nd Duke of Buckingham and a Royalist, m. the daughter of General Thomas Fairfax and is restored to his ownership of York House

Jan — Plot to assassinate Oliver Cromwell discovered and foiled
Jan 13 — Katherine Philips, "Parting with Lucasia," dated
Feb — Anne Finch, m. Edward Lord Conway (later 1st Earl of Conway)[479]
Mar — *English Liberty and Property Asserted*, published
Mar 24 — **John Milton, Letter to Emeric Bigot, with references to Milton's "peace of mind in this severe loss of sight and in (his) willingness to receive foreign guests"**[480]
Mar 20 — *The Downfall of the Fifth Monarchy*, published
Apr 2 — Ferdinand III, Holy Roman Emperor, d.
Apr 7 — An abortive Fifth Monarchist insurrection in Epping

---

478. Henry Hallam, *Constitutional History*, II. P. 191: "...from 1657 (English government) had become substantially a monarchy, and ought to be placed in that class, notwithstanding the unimportant difference in the style of its sovereign."

479. Edward Lord Conway not only gave Henry More the freedom of his estate at Ragley, but was also an important patron of Jeremy Taylor.

480. *Complete Prose*, Volume VII, p. 497. Milton continues: "Why should I not quietly bear a loss of light which I expect is not so much lost as recalled and drawn inward to sharpen rather than dull the eye of the mind? For that reason I am not angry at written words nor do I entirely cease studying them, severely though they have punish me...."

Forest, attributed to Thomas Venner

May — John Goodwin, *The Triers Tried*, attack on Cromwell's arrangement for Church governance

— John Sturgeon arrested for trying to smuggle into London copies of *Killing No Murder*, tract by edward Sexby and Silius Titus (?) urging that Cromwell be assassinated

May 16 — William Medley, *A Standard Set Up; Whereunto the true Seed and Saints of the most High may be gathered together*

May 25 — *To his Highness the Lord Protector of the Commonwealth of England, Scotland and Ireland, and the dominions thereto belonging; the Humble Petition and Advice of the Knights, Citizens and Burgesses now assembled in the Parliament of the Commonwealth*

Jun — **Edward Sexby and Silius Titus (?), *Killing no Murder*, urging that Cromwell be assassinated; complimentary references to Milton**

— Parliament adjourns

Jun 3 — William Harvey d. (b. 1578)

Jun 26 — *To his Highness the Lord Protector of the Commonwealth of England, Scotland and Ireland, and the dominions and territories thereunto belonging; the humble additional and explanatory Petition and Advice of the knights, citizens and burgesses now assembled in the Parliament of this Commonwealth*

Jul — Marchamont Needham, *The Great Accuser Cast Down; Or, A Public Trial of Mr. John Goodwin...At the Bar of Religion & Right Reason*, pamphlet, attacking Goodwin and answering *The Triers Tried*

— Richard Cromwell, appointed Chancellor of Oxford University

Jul 15 — **John Milton, Letter to Henry de Bras**[481]

Aug — Jeremy Taylor, epistolary debate with Henry Jeanes, a Calvinist, over *Deus Justificatus*

---

481. Nothing more is known concerning De Bras, a continental scholar, than is contained in Milton's two letters.

Aug 1 — **John Milton, Letter to Henry Oldenburg, in Saumur, France; discusses the reception in France of Milton's *Pro Se Defensio***

— **John Milton, Letter to Richard Jones, now being tutored by Henry Oldenburg**

Aug 21 — **John Milton, Letter to Henry Oldenburg, who has distributed copies of Milton's *Pro Se Defensio***

Aug 29 — John Lilburne d.

Sep 2 (?) — **Andrew Marvell appointed Milton's assistant as Latin Secretary**

Sep 5 — Richard Baxter, *One Sheet against the Quakers*, Puritan tract

— Thereafter: Richard Baxter, *A Second Sheet against the Quakers*, published

Sep 8 — **Nathaniel (?) Sterry appointed to assist Milton in duties of Secretary for Foreign Tongues**[482]

Sep 26 — **Using an amanuensis, Milton signs the autograph book of John Zollikofer of Switzerland**

Fall — A cache of forty or fifty funeral urns discovered in a field at Old Walsingham and brought to the attention of Thomas Browne

Oct 19 — **John Milton's daughter Katherine b.**

— John Dryden signs a receipt for funds received from John Thurloe, Secretary of State to Cromwell[483]

Nov 11 — Oliver Cromwell's daughter, Mary, m. Viscount Fauconberg, a member of the nobility

Nov 19 — Oliver Cromwell's daughter Frances m. Robert Rich, heir of the Earl of Warwick

Dec — Sir Edward Herbert, former Attorney-General, Lord Keeper of the Seal for Charles II, d., with the court-in-exile in France (b. 1597)

---

482. There is some uncertainty over whether it was Nathaniel or his brother Peter; Fallon presents the case for Nathaniel in Milton in Government, pp. 14-15.

483. John Thurloe is also frequently referred to as a master spy and one of the most competent bureaucrats serving the Commonwealth.

— Thomas Traherne ordained and appointed to a living at Credenhill, through the patronage of Amabella, Dowager Countess of Kent

Dec 2 — Abraham Cowley, created M.D. at Oxford by order of the government

Dec 7 — Sir William Davenant, *An Essay for the New Theatre representing the Preparacion of the Athenians for the Reception of Phocion after Hee Had Gained a victory*, SR for a play intended for Sir William Davenant's *Rutland House Theater* (?)

— Sir William Davenant, *Epithalamium upon the Marriage of the Lady Marriage, Daughter to His Highnesse, with the Lord Viscount Ffalconbridge*, SR; *Poem to My Lord Broghill*, SR

Dec 10 — Oliver Cromwell summons Richard Cromwell—"our trusty and beloved son, Lord Richard Cromwell"—to attend the upcoming Parliamentary session in January

Dec 16 — **John Milton, Letter to Henry de Bras**

Dec 18 — **John Milton, Letter to Peter Heimbach, in The Hague**

Dec 20 — **John Milton, Letter to Henry Oldenburg, in response to a letter dated Dec 2, containing news from Paris**

1658

John Milton, *De Doctrina Christiana The Englishman John Milton's Two Books of Investigations into Christian Doctrine drawn from the Sacred Scriptures Alone*, completed in ms (?-1660?)

John Milton, Hobson poems reprinted in *Wit Restor'd*

Richard Allestree, *The Practice of Christian Graces: The Whole Duty of Man*, published

Anglia Rediviva, or, England Revived. An Heroick Poem, pro-Cromwellian anonymous poem in four Cantos, urging Cromwell to assume the Crown[484]

Pietro Aretino (1492-1556), *The Crafty Whore: the mystery and iniquity of the Bawdy Houses laid open...*, published, translation from the Italian

William Chamberlayne, *Love's Victory*, tragi-comedy, published

Sir Aston Cockayne, *Trappolin, A Supposed Prince*, drama; *Small Poems of Divers Sorts*, with several re-issues under various titles

Sir Kenelm Digby, *A Late Discourse...Touching the Cure of Wounds by the Power of Sympathy*, translated from the French; treatise on alchemical or sympathetic magic

William Erbery, *The Testimony of William Erbery*

James Harrington, *An essay upon two of Virgil's Eclogues, and two books of his Æneis (if this be not enough) towards the*

---

484. Compare the tenor of this poem with the 1660 poem under the same title (but with substantially different subtitle)

translation of the whole
John Heydon, *Advice to a Daughter in opposition to the Advice to a Son*, published
Peter Heylin, *A Short View of the Life and Reign of King Charles*
James Nayler, *The Lamb's War against the Man of Sin*, Quaker tract, published
John Reeve, *Joyful News from Heaven*, includes *The Baptists Commission Counterfeited*
William Sanderson, *Graphice. The use of the Pen and Pencil. Or, the Most Excellent Art of Painting*
Jeremy Taylor, *A Collection of Offices or Forms of Prayer, in cases ordinary and extraordinary, taken out of the Scriptures and the ancient liturgies of several churches, especially the Greek*, published
Anna Trapnel, *Voice for the king of saints and nations*, prophecies
Wit Restored, miscellany, including William Strode, "An Opposite to Melancholy"
Nathaniel Tovey, Milton's second tutor at Cambridge, d. (b. 1597?)
John Reeve d.

Jan — **John Milton, Letter to Christopher Milton (?)**
Jan 13 — Edward Hyde, Chancellor of the Exchequer to Charles II, appointed Lord Chancellor of England by Charles at Bruges, Belgium
Jan 20 — Oliver Cromwell, the Lord Protector, convenes Parliament at Westminster
Jan 28 — John Evelyn, letter to Thomas Browne concerning gardens and grottos; written on the day after the death of Evelyn's son
Jan 30 — John Tillinghast, *Elijah's Mantle*
Feb 3 — **Katherine Woodcock Milton d**.
Feb 9 — John Wilmot becomes 2nd Earl of Rochester at age eleven

Mar 17 — **Milton's daughter Katherine d.**

Mar 26 — Jane Brooks, executed for witchcraft

— Samuel Pepys undergoes operation, "cutting of the stone," and survives

Spring — Edmund Waller *Upon a War with Spain*, anonymous broadside, published

Apr 29 — John Cleveland d., Gray's Inn

May — **Milton begins work on *Paradise Lost* (as reported by his nephew, Edward Phillips)**

— **John Milton, *The Cabinet-Council containing the Chief Arts of Empire, and Mysteries of State Discabineted*, by Sir Walter Raleigh, published by Milton**

May 1 — Sir Thomas Browne, *Hydriotaphia, or Urn-Burial and The Garden of Cyrus, or, the Quincuncial, Lozenge or Net-Work Plantations of the Ancients, articifially, naturally, and mystically considered*, dated and thereafter published

May 20 — Sir William Davenant, *Satirical Declamations*, performed

Jun 3 — A whale killed in the Thames near Greenwich; John Dryden will incorporate the event as a portent of Cromwell's death in "A Poem upon the Death of His Late Highness..."

Jun 29 — Joseph Glanvill, M.A., Oxford University

(?)— **John Milton, Sonnet XXIII: "Methought I Saw..."**

Jul 7 — Edward Ashton and John Betteley of London hanged, drawn, and quartered for complicity in the City Plot against Cromwell's government

Jul 9 — John Sumner, Edward Stacy, and Oliver Allen to be executed for complicity in the City Plot; Sumner and Allen pardoned on the gallows

Jul 25 — Sir William Davenant, *The Cruelty of the Spaniards in Peru. Exprest by Instrumentall and Vocall Musick, and by Art of Perspective in Scenes, etc.*, pro-government propaganda play, performed daily at the Cock-Pit Theater in Drury Lane; text published shortly after the performance

Aug — Oliver Cromwell ill, confined to bed

Aug 13 — *Mercurius Politicus* reports Cromwell as merely

indisposed

Aug 20 — Cromwell reported by George Fox as looking like a dead man[485]

Aug 28 — *Order for the Control of the Press* re-establishes official censorship

Aug 30 — England experiences violent storms; later taken as a portent of Cromwell's death

Late Aug — John Bunyan, *A Few Sighs from Hell, or the Groans of a Damned Soul...*, published

Sep — **Andrew Marvell identified in state papers as "Latin Secretary," working with Milton**

— **John Milton, writes last Letters of State for Oliver Cromwell**

Sep 2-9 — *Commonwealth's Mercury*, black-edged notice of Cromwell's death, followed by an advertisement for John Bunyan, *A Few Sighs from Hell*

Sep 3 — Oliver Cromwell d. (b. 1599), on the Anniversary of Parliamentarian military victories at Dunbar and Worcester[486]

— Richard Cromwell appointed Protector within hours of his father's death; his appointment is initially widely approved

— Thereafter: Edmund Waller, *Upon the Late Storm, and of the Death of His Highness Ensueing the Same*

Sep 4 — Richard Cromwell proclaimed Lord Protector at Temple Bar, with all of the pomp of the proclamation of a king

Sep 5 — **John Milton, first Letter of State for Richard Cromwell**

Sep 6 — Richard Cromwell proclaimed Lord Protector at Oxford; students pelt the officials with "carret and turnip-tops" (Anthony à Wood)

Sep 20 — John, Lord Culpepper, letter to Edward Hyde, Earl of

---

485, Don M. Wolfe, *Milton and His Time*, #96.

486. Cromwell died on the day of the most violent storm to strike London in living memory, an appropriate emblem for his death.

Clarendon, declaring that "the devil is dead

Oct — **John Milton, *Defensio Prima*, 2nd edition**

Mid-Oct — Wax effigy of Oliver Cromwell lies in state at Somerset House, clothed in regal splendor and surrounded by the trappings of royalty

Oct 15 — Reference in a contemporary letter to Sir William Davenant producing "Stage-plaies"

Nov 10 — Oliver Cromwell's body interred

Nov 23 — Funeral ceremony for Oliver Cromwell, Lord Protector (represented by the wax effigy), rivals the magnificence and expense of a royal funeral

— **Milton participates in the funeral processional for Oliver Cromwell, accompanied by Andrew Marvell and John Dryden**

1659

An Account of the Last Hours of the late Renowned Oliver Cromwell Lord Protector...Drawn up and published by one who was an Eye- and Ear-Witness of the most part of it, published

Humphrey Bache, *A Few Words in True Love written to the Old Long Sitting Parliament*, Fifth-Monarchist tract

Clement Barksdale, *The learned Maid, or Whether a Maid May be a Scholar?: a logick exercise*, translation of *De Ingeniis Muliebis*, by Anna Maria van Schurman[487] (1641)

Richard Baxter, *A Key for Catholicks*, published; identifies most dissenting groups as "masked Papists"[488]

[Samuel Butler], *Mola Asinaria*, Royalist pamphlet, anonymous; Butler's first publication; assigned on the title page to 'William Prynne'

Samuel Carrington, *History of the Life and Death of Oliver... Late Lord Protector*, published, includes a revised and expanded version of Edmund Waller, *Upon a War with Spain*, an "Incomparable Poem of the English *Vergil* of our time

William Chamberlayne, *Pharonnida: A Heroick Poem*, in Five Books, 14,000 lines

Laurence Claxton [Laurence Clarkson], *Look About You...or,*

---

487. Schurman had corresponded with Basua Makins since 1640—both of them writing in Greek—and had attained a eminent continental reputation as a scholar (Katharina Wilson and Frank J. Warnke, *Women Writers*, p. 290).

488. Michael McKeon, *Politics and Poetry*, p. 133.

The Right Devil Unfolded, tract, an attempt to supersede John Reeve's status as prophet among the Muggletonians

John Cleaveland [Cleveland], *J. Cleaveland Revived: Poems, Orations, Epistles, and other of his Genuine Incomparable Pieces, never before publisht*

Pierre Corneille, *Oedipus*

John Dee, *A True & Faithful Relation of what passed for many Yeers Between Dr: John Dee...and Some Spirits, etc.*, edited by Meric Casaubon[489]

John Dryden, *Heroic Stanzas*, published[490]; *A Poem upon the Death of His Late Highness Oliver...*, published in a separate edition

John Eliot, *The Christian Commonwealth: or the Civil Policy of the Rising Kingdom of Jesus Christ*, Fifth-Monarchist tract

John Evelyn, letter to Robert Boyle, proposing that new colleges be established near London and elsewhere; educational reform

George Fox, *The Great Mystery of the Great Whore Unfolded*, 420-page Quaker treatise responding to Richard Baxter, *The Quakers' Catechism*

S. Hammond, *Gods Judgements upon Drunkards, Swearers and Sabbath-breakers, in a Collection of the Most Remarkable Examples*

Edward Johnson, *An Examination of the Essay; or, an Answer to the Fifth Monarchy*

Giovanno Francesco Loredano, *The Life of Adam*, translated into English

Richard Lovelace, *Lucasta: Posthume Poems*[491]

---

489. Casaubon (the son of Isaac Casaubon, the distinguished scholar who demonstrated that the Hermetic materials so central to Renaissance Neo-Platonism dated from well within the Christian era) largely established Dee's subsequent dubious reputation as magician, charlatan, and dupe through a judicious editing of Dee's journals.

490. Published in *Three Poems*, which included poems by Edmund Waller and Thomas Sprat.

491. The posthumous collection, edited by Lovelace's brother, is dated

Henry More, *The Immortality of the Soul, so farre forth as it is demonstrable from the Knowledge of Nature, and the Light of Reason*

James Shirley, *Honoria and Mammon. Whereunto is added the contention of Ajax and Ulisses, for the armour of Achilles*, published, play (written about 1645)

Sir John Suckling, *The Last Remains of Sir John Suckling. Being a Full Collection of All His Poems and Letters Which Have Been So Long Expected and Never Till Now Published*, including *The Sad One: A Tragedy*, an incomplete play; printed by Humphrey Moseley

Henry Stubbe, *Malice Rebuked: A Vindication of Sir Henry Vane*

Obadiah Walker, *Art of Oratory*

Edmund Waller, John Dryden, and Mr. Sprat of Oxford, *Three Poems upon the Death of his late Highnesse Oliver Lord Protector...*, published

Bulstrode Whitelock [Whitlock], *Memorials of the English Affairs*, published

Mary Frith ['Moll Cutpurse'] d.

John Dunton, b. (d. 1733)

Jean Baptiste Medina b. (d. 1710)

Henry Purcell b.

Thomas Southerne b. (d. 1746)

Anne Wharton b.

James Harrington and his Commonwealth-oriented Rota Club become fashionable and influential

Andrew Marvell elected Member of Parliament for Hull, serves until 1678

Jan 20 — Sir William Davenant, *The History of Sr Francis Drake. Expresst by Instrumental and Vocall Musick, and the Art of Perspective in Scenes, &c. The First Part...*, SR for libretto, opera; performances thereafter

---

1659 but appeared in 1660.

Feb 14/16 (?)— **John Milton, *A Treatise of Civil Power in Ecclesiastical Causes: shewing that it is not lawfull for any power on earth to compell in matters of Religion. The author J. M.*, published; printed by Thomas Newcomb**

Mar 3 — John Rogers, *The Plain Case of the Common-weal... stated*

April 21 — **John Milton, Letter to Jean Labadie, a French Protestant minister**

Apr 22 — Richard Cromwell forced to dissolve Parliament; conflict between Richard Cromwell's supporters and the Army shows that the Army has gained control

May — John Bunyan, *The Doctrine of the Law and Grace unfolded*, published

— John Canne, Fifth Monarchist, appointed editor of the government periodicals, *Mercurius Politicus* and *The Poublick Intelligencer* (through August 1659)

— Peter Chamberlen, *The Declaration and Proclamation of the Army of God*, tract

— John Rogers, *Mr. Pryn's Good Old Cause Stated and Stunted 10. Years ago*

May 7 — Restoration of the Rump Parliament by the Army; survivors are not sufficient to establish a quorum, so several new members are appointed

— Thereafter: Marchamont Needham removed as editor of *Mercurius Politicus*

May 13 — **William Prynne, *The Re-Publicans*, attack on Milton**

May 15 — **John Milton, first Letters of State for the restored Parliamentary Government**

May 18 — **William Prynne, *A True and Perfect Narrative...*, attack on Milton and others**

May 25 — Richard Cromwell abdicates (deposed by the Council of State), allowed to return to private life

May 20 — Sir John Denham, *News from Colchester or, A Proper New Ballad of Certain Carnal Passages betwixt a Quaker and a Colt, at Horsly near Colchester in Essex, to the tune of Tom of Bedlam*, broadsheet ballad

May 30 — Sir William Davenant, *The Second Part of the Siege of Rhodes*, SR by Henry Herringman (published posthumously); performances thereafter

Jun 6 — Broadsheets in London declare the Fifth Monarchists armed and ready to burn the city and massacre opponents

Jun 7 — [John Rogers], *a Vindication of that Prudent and Honourable Knight, Sir Henry Vane*

Jun 9 — [Charles Harvey], *A Collection of Several Passages Concerning His Late Highness Oliver Cromwell in he Time of His Sickness. Wherein is Related Many of his Expressions upon His Deathbed, together with His Prayer within Two or Three Days before His death. Written by One that was then Groom of his Bed-chamber*, published

Aug — **John Milton, *Considerations Touching the Likeliest Means to Remove Hirelings out of the church. Wherein is also discourc'd of Tithes, Church-Fees, Church-Revenues, and whether any maintenance of ministers can be settl'd by law. The author J.M.*, published**

Aug 15 — *The Londoners Last Warning*, published

Aug 16 — Sir William Davenant released from a brief imprisonment as a Royalist

Aug 21 — **James Harrington, *Aphorisms Political*, echoing portions of Milton's *The Likeliest Means*, pamphlet**

Aug 23 — *The Fifth Monarchy or Kingdom of Christ, in opposition to the Beast's, Asserted*, published

Sep 22 — John Rogers, *Mr. Harrington's Parallel Unparallel'd*

Oct — William Bray, *A Plea for the Peoples Good Old Cause*, published; *A Plea for the Peoples Fundamental Liberties*, published

Oct 15 — The Army refuses to allow the Speaker to enter the Houses of Parliament; Parliament is again forcibly dissolved

Oct 18 — James Harrington, *A Parallel of the Spirit of the People, with the Spirit of Mr. Rogers*

Oct 25 — **Milton and Andrew Marvell receive a portion of their annual salaries as Latin Secretary on the day**

Parliament adjourns

— John Milton, *Letter to a Friend Concerning the Ruptures of the Commonwealth*, written; first published in John Toland's complete edition, 1698

— Council of State formally dissolved

Oct 26-Dec 26 — **John Milton, *Proposalls of Certaine Expedients for the Preventing of a Civill War now Feard, & the Settling of a Firme Government*, written**

(?)— **John Milton, *Collected Letters of State and other Writings* (Columbia Ms.)**

Oct 27 — John Evelyn, *Apology for the Royal Party,* calling for restoration of the monarchy

Oct 31 — **John Bradshaw, Judge at the trial of Charles I, d.; John Milton receives a bequest of £10**

Nov 9 — *A Guild-Hall Elegie,* **Broadsheet, attacks John Milton as the author of *Eikonoklastes***

Nov 24 — James, Duke of York seals marriage contract at Breda with Anne Hyde[492]

Nov 29 — **John Milton's signs a document releasing Richard Powell's bond for the long-standing debt**

Dec 13 — *Remonstrance of London*, petition, circulated and gains 23,500 signatures, details the wrongs Londoners have suffered under the Army

— *A Faithfull Searching Home Word, Intended for the view of the remaining Members of the former Old Parliament, shewing the Reasonableness...of their first Dissolution*

Dec 17 — Committee of Safety in London orders all Royalists, former Royalist soldiers, Papist priests, and Jesuits out of London on penalty of treason

Dec 20 — **John Milton, Letter to Henry Oldenburg**

— **John Milton, Letter to Richard Jones, traveling with**

---

492. Anne Hyde's father, Edward, later Earl of Clarendon, was so appalled by the relationship between his daughter and the Duke of York, that he offered to carry personally a message to Parliament requesting that she be imprisoned in the Tower and beheaded (after the manner, he suggested, of Anne Boleyn).

Oldenburg

Dec 26 — The Rump Parliament, with fewer than fifty surviving original members, again restored by the Army; it immediately allies itself with General George Monck

Decade Seven: 1660-1669
Monarchy Regain'd and Paradise Lost

1660

Milton loses position as Secretary for Foreign Tongues
Milton referred to as a "Christian libertine"
The Age of Wonders, or Miracles are not ceased, published
Anglia Rediviva, or, A Poem on His Majesties most joyfull Reception into England, Royalist panegyric
Edward Bagshaw, *Saintship No ground of Sovereignty*, Fifth-Monarchist tract
Robert Boyle, *New Experiments, Physico-Mechanical, Touching the Spring of the Air*, treatise on respiration, Boyle's first signed published study; *The Christian Virtuoso*, arguing that there is no conflict between religion and science, published
William Chamberlayne, *England's Jubilee*, on the restoration of Charles II
A Choice Banquet of Jests, imitation of *A Banquet of Jests*, jest-book
L. Claxton [Laurence Clarkson]. *The Lost Sheep Found*, tract, second attempt to assume John Reeve's authority among the Muggletonians
Abraham Cowley, *Upon His Majesties Restoration and Return*
Sir William Davenant, *Satirical Declamations at the Opera*
John Donne, *XXVI Sermons*
John Dryden, *Astraea Redux*
The Famous Tragedie of the Life and Death of Mris Rump. Shewing How She was brought to bed of a monster With her terrible Pangs, bitter Teeming, hard Labour, and lamentable Travell from Portsmouth to Westminster, and the great

misery she hath endured by her ugly, deformed, ill-shapen, base-begotten Brat of Imp of Reformation, pamphlet[493]

Richard Flecknoe, *Portraits*

[Henry Fletcher], *The Perfect Politician: or, A Full View of the Life and Actions (Military and Civil) of O. Cromwell. Whereunto is Added His Character; and Complete Catalogue of All Honors Conferred by Him on Severall Persons*, published

Thomas Forde, "Upon His Sacred Majesties most happy Return," published in *Virtus Rediviva. A Panegyric on King Charles I, with several other peeces from the same pen*, published; reprinted in 1661

George Fox, *A Battle-Door for Teachers and Professors to Learn Singular and Plural*

Thomas Fuller, *An Alarum to the Counties of England and Wales*

Grampious, *Congratulations in plain Scots Language To His Majesties Trise Happy Return*, published in Edinburgh (?)

Joseph Hall, *The Remaining Works of ...*

Charles Hoole, *A New Discovery of the Old Art of Teaching*, published

Henry More, *An Explanation of the Grand Mystery of Godliness*

Isaac Penington, *The Consideration of a Point Concerning the Book of Common Prayer*

J. P. (John Philipot), *A Perfect Collection of all Knight Bachelors made by King James...*, published

William Sedgwick, *Inquisition for the Blood of our Late Soveraign*, allegorical prose poem comparing the English Revolution to Biblical history

---

493. The publication purports to print the text of a play presented on the day of Charles' entry into London: "presented on a burning stage at Westminster the 29th of May, 1660." Gerald MacLean doubts that claim but does discuss the rather scurrilous poem in the context of more elegant tributes to Charles, including John Dryden's *Astraea Redux* (*Time's Witness*, pp. 257-259)

John Smith, *Select Discourses*, edited by John Worthington

Robert Stapleton, *Mores Hominum*, folio edition, translation of Juvenal's *Satires*[494]

Jeremy Taylor, *Ductor Dubitantium*, Taylor's 1300-page *magnum opus* theological treatise, published; *The Worthy Communicant*, published

Joost van den Vondel, *Samson, von Heilige Wraeck: Treurspel* (Samson, of Holy Revenge: A Tragedy)[495], published, Amsterdam

Edmund Waller, *To the King upon His Majesty's Happy Return*

[Thomas Widdowes], *The Just Devil of Woodstock, or a true narrative of the severall apparitions, the frights and punishments inflicted upon the Rumpish commissioners sent thither to survey the manors and houses belonging to His majesty*[496]

Robert Wild, *Iter Boreale*, poem

Robert Chamberlain d.

Jacob Cats, Dutch emblemist and poet, d. (b. 1577)

James Nayler, d.

Thomas Creech b.

Daniel Defoe b. (d. 1731)

Robert Gould b. (?; d. 1709?)

Anne Killigrew b.

Sir Hans Sloane b. (d. 1753)[497]

William Juxon, Bishop of London, appointed Archbishop of Canterbury

The Rota Club disbanded after the Restoration

494, Stapleton's translations of Juvenal remained among the most popular of the period.

495. Harold Skulsky, *Justice in the Dock*, considers similarities and differences between Vondel's drama and Milton's Samson Agonistes.

496. Sir Walter Scott notes that this pamphlet provided the background for his novel, Woodstock.

497. Sloane's bequest of books and manuscripts provided the foundation for the British Museum. The materials were purchased by a special act of Parliament for a minimal £20,000.

More than eighty coffeehouses established in London alone[498]

Jan 1—SUNDAY — W. Kilbourne, *A New Years-Gift for Mercurius Politicus*, attack on Marchamont Needham
— Samuel Pepys begins his *Diary* (to 1669[499])
Jan 9 — Sir Henry Vane summoned to appear before the Rump and is dismissed from his seat in Commons and ordered to leave London
Jan 16 — **The Outcry of the London Prentices for Justice..., satirizes Milton for his blindness**
Jan 21 — Brabazon Aylmer apprenticed to Luke Fawne, a publisher
Jan 23 — John Wilmot, 2nd Earl of Rochester, admitted a commoner at Wadham College, Oxford
Jan 28 — *KLEIS PROPHETEIAS or, The Key of Prophecie: whereby The Mysteries of all the Prophecies from the Birth of Christ until the Present, and so forward, are unlocked and opened ... and the speedy Resurrection of King Charles II. Out of Banishment into Advancement, is certainly foreshewn*
Feb 3 — General George Monck camps near London with his army, an act that will—after a fair amount of hedging and outright deceit concerning Monck's intentions—facilitate the return of Charles II
Feb 11 — Burning of the Rumps in London
Feb 13 — Oxford celebrates the announcement of a "free Parliament" with bonfires, bells, and the roasting of rumps
Feb 18 — Peter Anthony Motteux b., Rouen (d. 1718)
Feb 21 — Parliament consents to restore excluded members to their seats
— John Thurloe re-appointed Secretary of State, even though he continues to oppose the Restoration

---

498. By the eighteenth century, the number will reach 2,000.

499. Fear that his eyesight might be failing caused him to cease writing. During the latter part of the century, the principal diarist is John Evelyn.

Feb 23-29 — **John Milton, *The Ready & Easy Way to Establish a Free Commonwealth, and the Excellence thereof, Compar'd with The inconveniences and dangers of readmitting kingship in this nation.* The author J. M., published**

Feb 23-Mar 4 — **John Milton, *The Present Means and Brief Delineation of a Free Commonwealth,* written to General Monck; first published in John Toland's complete edition, 1698**

Mar — General George Monck occupies London

— Thereafter: Sir William Davenant, *A Panegyrick to His Excellency the Lord Generall Monck*, published

Mar 10 — *Newes from Brussels; in a letter from a neer attendant on his Majesties person, 10 March 1660*

Mar 17 — ***The Character of the Rump,* attack on Milton's *Ready and Easy Way***

— Sir William Davenant receives pass to Calais, from whence he rejoins Charles II's court in exile

Mar 23 — Samuel Pepys begins career in the Admiralty, serving under his cousin, Edward Montagu, recently appointed "general at sea"

Mar 24 — **William Collinne, *The Spirit of the Phanatiques Dissected,* attack on Milton**

Mar 25 — **Matthew Griffith, *The Fear of God and the King,* preached in Mercers' Chapel, attack on all who opposed Charles I, including Milton**

— Oliver Cromwell's head buried at Sidney Sussex College, Cambridge

Mar 28 — "A Dialogue betwixt Tom and Dick, The former a Country-man The other a Citizen, Presented to his Excellency and the Council of State, at Drapers-Hall, London," a theatrical *jig* or *droll*

Mar 30 — **James Harrington, *Censure of the Rota,* published by "Paul Giddy, Printer to the Rota, at the Sign of the Windmill in Turn-Again Lane," pamphlet; satirical** answer to Milton[500]

Mar 31 — Matthew Griffith, *The Fear of God and the King and The Samaritan Revived; and the course he then took to cure the wounded Traveller, by pouring in Wine and Oyl; Historically applied to the sound and speedy healing of our present dangerous Distractions*, SR; dedicated to General George Monck

Apr — **Sir Roger L'Estrange, *Treason Arraigned in Answer to Plain English*, attack on Milton's *The Ready and Easy Way***

— **George Starkey (?), *The Dignity of Kingship Asserted*, answering *The Ready and Easy Way***

Apr 1-10 — **John Milton, *The Ready and Easy Way...*, 2nd edition; one of the last significant attempts to forestall monarchy**

Apr 4 — Charles II, *The Declaration of Breda*, declaring liberty of conscience without a return to Laudian High-Church practices

Apr 5 — Matthew Griffith imprisoned in Newgate for publishing sedition and libel

Apr 9 — Marchamont Needham removed as editor of *Mercurius Politicus* and other journals

— *The Downfall of Mercurius Britannicus, Pragmaticus, Politicus, that three headed Cerberus. Printed in the year that the Saints are disappointed*

Apr 10-15 — **John Milton, *Brief Notes Upon a Late Sermon titl'd, The Fear of God and the King; Preachd, and since Publishd, by Matthew Griffith, D. D. and Chaplain to the late king. Wherein many notorious Wrestings of Scriptures, and other Falsities are observed by J. M.*, written**

Apr 14 — Charles II, *Declaration of Breda*, announcing pardons and indemnities for all, saving only those explicitly

---

500. Harrington's parody of the typical publisher's imprint makes his attitude quite clear.

exempted by Parliament[501]
Apr 16 — Marchamont Needham flees to Holland
— Only one printer remains committed to the Commonwealth, Livewell Chapman
Apr 20 — **Sir Roger L'Estrange, *No Blinde Guides...*, response to Milton's *Brief Notes*[502]**
Apr 22 — Margaret Fell presents a petition to Charles II signed by George Fox and other Quakers, defining Quaker beliefs
Apr 23 — Sir Roger L'Estrange, *Physician, Cure Thyself*
— Parliament meets to consider the restoration of Charles II
Apr 25 — Commons meets and elects a moderate, Harbottle Grimstone, Speaker
— The House of Lords re-convenes after its 21-year hiatus, with ten members present[503]
May — **Milton goes into hiding**
— General George Monck occupies London with his forces; declares a free parliament
— John Thurloe arrested and charged with treason
— Humphrey Smith, Quaker, receives a prophecy of London in flames
— Thereafter: *The Vision of Humphrey Smith Which he saw concerning London in the 5th Month, in the Year 1660, being not long after the King came in*, Quaker tract and predictive prophecy concerning the burning of London
May 1 — The Commonwealth is formally abolished and Monarchy restored

---

501. Initially General George Monck urged Charles to except no more than four names from the general amnesty; after much debate, Parliaments agreed upon some twenty individuals to whom the King's proposed act of indemnity would not apply. Milton's name was not included in the initial twenty (Henry Hallam, *Constitutional History*, II, p. 225).

502. Milton's blindness "was well merited, L'Estrange believed, since Milton had stared too long and too maliciously upon the portrait of the King" (Dora Raymond, *Oliver's Secretary*, p. 218).

503. The same ten that had adjourned for the day at the last meeting of the House of Lords

— Anthony Wood reports May-poles erected in Oxford, 'set up on purpose to vex the Presbyterians and Independents'; by the end of the month, twelve erected over objections of Puritans

May 7 — **Milton goes into hiding in Bartholomew's Close, London**

— **Milton makes over a bond to Cyriack Skinner for £400, since £2000 he had deposited with the Excise were not available to him**

May 8 — King Charles II, proclaimed King by Parliament in London

May 10 — *O. Cromwell's Thankes to the Lord Generall (Monk)....Together with a Hue and Cry after Politicus*, broadside, published

May 14 — **George Starkey,** ***Britain's Triumph for her unparalleled deliverance and her joyful celebrating of her most gracious, incomparable King Charles II***, **published, ridicules Milton as blind and a divorcer**

May 15 — John Danvers, *The Royal Oak; or an Historical Description of the Royal Progress, Wonderful Travels...of his Sacred Majesty, Charles the Second... I. H. M's Strange and Wonderful Escape from Worcheste...II.The Pursuing of His Royal Person by Oliver Cromwell and His Bloodhounds*, published

May 16 — George Fox, the Younger, *A Noble Salutation and a Faithful Greeting unto Thee, Charles Stuart, Who art now Proclaimed King of England, Scotland, France, & Ireland*, Quaker tract written from Essex prison, dated

May 17 — ***A Third Conference**,* **mentions Milton satirically**

May 25 — Charles II met by General George Monck at Dover

May 26 — Charles II disembarks at Dover, to the acclaim of the crowds

— General George Monck knighted at Canterbury

May 29 — King Charles II enters London on the anniversary of his birthday

May 30 — Sir Edmund Waller, panegyric ode for the King's

Restoration printed and available in the bookstalls
May 31 — Abraham Cowley, panegyric ode for the King's Restoration printed and available in the bookstalls
Jun — **John Heyden, *The Idea of Law Charactered*, rebukes Milton**
— Sir John Denham appointed Surveyor-General of Works[504]
Jun 2 — Mary Barret Dyer, hanged as a Quaker, Boston Common, Massachusetts
Jun 6 — **Sir Roger L'Estrange, *His Apology*, repeats his attacks on Milton**
Jun 12 — Henry More, dates chapters from *Grand Mystery of Godliness* attacking Quakerism as the greatest of all heresies for denying the divinity of Christ
Jun 16 — **Parliament resolves an arrest order for Milton, and orders the *Defensio* (First Defense) and *Eikonoklastes* burned, along with John Goodwin's *The Obstructors of Justice***
Jun 17 — Samuel Pepys, *Diary*, records the first organ music performed in Whitehall Chapel
Jun 20 — Petition to Parliament, claiming that, among other infractions, a minister had given his pulpit to an unlearned country tinker, named John Bunyan, from which to preach (Petition denied on July 25)
Jun 29 — John Thurloe, Cromwell's Secretary of State, freed; no specific charged were brought against him[505]
Jul 1 — Sir Henry Vane ordered arrested by Charles II, subse-

---

504. Denham's only major 20th century biographer, Brendan O Hehir, notes that while Denham filled the post adequately as a competent if uninspired architect, he had the signal misfortune to succeed to the post after it had been held by Inigo Jones, the outstanding architectural genius of the first half of the century. Worse, his own successor (although at Denham's own instigation) was Sir Christopher Wren, arguably the greatest architect England has produced.

505. It might be instructive to compare the Restoration Parliament's relatively bland responses to Thurloe, often referred to as Cromwell's "Spy-chief," with their initial animosity toward Milton. Following the Restoration, Thurloe continued to advise the government.

quently taken to the Tower[506]

Jul 7 — General George Monck, created Baron Monck of Potheridge, Beauchamp, Teyes, Earl of Torrington, and 1st Duke of Albemarle by Charles II

— Edward Montagu created Earl of Sandwich

Jul 9 — Thomas Killigrew receives royal warrant to organize the King's Company of players and build a theater

Jul 3/13 — **George Starkey, *Royal and Other Innocent Blood, Crying Aloud to Heaven for due Vengeance*, published, attacks Milton**

Jul 14 — *The Picture of the Good Old Cause Drawn to the Life in the Effigies of Master Praise God Barebones with several examples of God's Judgments on some eminent engagers against Kingly Government*, **broadsheet, satirizes Milton for blindness and his attacks on monarchy**[507]

Aug — Sir William Davenant, *Poem, upon His Sacred Majesties Most Happy Return to His Dominions*, panegyric ode, published

Aug 3 — General George Monck, Duke of Albemarle, made Captain-General of the Army for life

Aug 6 — Jeremy Taylor nominated to the vacant Irish Bishopric of Down and Connor; subsequently appointed vice-chancellor of Dublin University

Aug 13 — **Royal Proclamation issued for Milton's arrest; the suppression of two of his books, the *Defensio* and *Eikonoklastes*; and the arrest of John Goodwin and the suppression of his *The Obstructors of Justice***

Aug 14 — Henry Jessey, *The Lords Loud Call to England*, Dissenting tract outlining God's disastrous judgments on

---

506. Vane would remain imprisoned for two years without a trial, then, in express contravention of Charles' assertion at the Restoration, would be executed for past offenses even though he was not a regicide.

507. Item #3 on the broadside: "Milton that writ two Books against the Kings, and *Salmasius* his Defence of Kings, struck totally blind, he being not much above 40. years old" (reproduced in Wolfe, *Milton and His England*, #104)

England since the Restoration of Charles II

Aug 17 — ***The Blazing Star,* satirical poem, accuses Milton of defending "Noll's Red Nose"**[508]

Aug 18 — Samuel Pepys, *Diary*, records Pepys attending his first post-Restoration play, John Fletchers' *The Loyal Subject*, at the Cockpit in Drury Lane

Aug 25 — **Indemnity Bill passed by Commons; Milton and several others no longer in danger of execution, but the Arrest Warrant remains in effect**

Aug 27 — **Copies of Milton's books publicly burned by the common hangman in London**

Aug 29 — **Milton escapes the death penalty, in part through the influence of Andrew Marvell and others**

— Act of Indemnity and Oblivion introduced by Charles II and passed by Parliament[509]

Sep (?) — **Milton taken into custody while living in Holborn**

Sep 2 — Hugh Peters arrested and confined in the Tower

Sep 3 — ***The London Printer...,* ridicules Milton**

— James, Duke of York, officially m. Anne Hyde[510], by the Bishop of Worchester in a private ceremony

Sep 3-10 — **Copies of Milton's books burned by the common hangman in London**

Sep 10 — Sir Roger L'Estrange, *A Rope for Pol, or, A hue and Cry after Marchemont Nedham. The Late Scurrilous Newswriter. Being a collection of his Blasphemies and Revilings*

---

508. "Noll" being a slighting—or familiar—nickname for Oliver Cromwell.

509. The Bill provided a general pardon for all participants in the Interregnum, excepting only the Regicides (i.e., those who had signed the Death Warrant for Charles I) and a handful of specifically named individuals—including John Milton and his publisher. Disappointed supporters of the restored King later observed that it was an act of indemnity for his enemies and oblivion for his friends.

510. James seduced Anne Hyde; when she became pregnant he promised to marry her, much to the chagrin of his brother, the King; his mother, Henrietta Maria (known for the vigor of her rages); and his future father-in-law, Edward Hyde

against the King's Majesty, published in his weekly Politicus
Sep 19 — Claudius Salmasius, *Salmasius Posthumus*
Sep 20 — Henry, 1st Duke of Gloucester, d., of smallpox; youngest son of Charles I and Henrietta Marie
Oct (?)— **Arrest order for Milton issued; Milton sent to prison**
— London Theaters reopen
Oct 9 — Twenty-nine individuals indicted for treason as Regicides during the Interregnum[511]
Oct 10 — The accused Regicides arraigned in batches, without being allowed to speak or to confer with counsel
Oct 11 — Trials of the Regicides begin, including Major General Thomas Harrison
Oct 13-19 — Regicides executed
Oct 13 — Major-General Thomas Harrison hanged, drawn, and quartered, at Charing Cross
— Hugh Peters tried and condemned
— Samuel Pepys, *Diary*, notes that he had seen Charles I executed and now has seen the first blood spilled by the Regicides
Oct 14 — Evelyn records: "Axtall, Carew, Clement, Hacker, Hewson, and Peters, were executed"
Oct 16 — Hugh Peters executed[512]
Oct 17 — Evelyn records: "Scot, Scroop, Cook and Jones, suffered for reward of their iniquities at Charing Cross, in sight of the place where they put to death their natural prince, and in the presence of the King his son, whom they also sought to kill"[513]

---

511. Technically, according to Charles' act of Pardon, these were the only individuals susceptible to the death penalty for their actions during the Commonwealth; Sir Henry Vane was not among those indicted.

512. Derek Wilson, *The Tower*, p. 181

513. John Evelyn, *Diary*, p. 337. The passage continues: "I saw not their execution, but met their quarters, mangled, and cut, and reeking, as they were brought from the gallows in baskets on the hurdle. Oh, the miraculous providence of God!"

Oct 22 — Charles, Duke of Cambridge, b. to James, Duke of York and Anne Hyde

Oct 23 — John Feak (pseudonyn). *A Funeral Sermon Thundered forth ... for the Loss of ... Harison*, published

Oct 25 — Philip Skippon, Parliamentary major-general, member of Cromwell's House of Lords, and Katherine Philips' second step-father; will proved

— Thereafter: Katherine Philips, "Epitaph on my truly honored Publius Scipio" written in his memory

Oct 28 — Joseph Glanvill ordained in the Church of England

Nov — John Fletcher and Philip Massinger, *The Beggars' Bush*, performed with a male cast

Nov 5 — Sir William Davenant, completes contracts for the Duke of York's Company of players

Nov 13 — John Bunyan arrested in Bedfordshire for preaching without credentials or academic degrees (i.e., as a Non-Conformist); remains in the Bedford jail for twelve years (to 1672, during which time he wrote *The Pilgrim's Progress*)

Nov 19 — Ben Jonson, *Epicoene, or The Silent Woman*, revived by Thomas Killigrew, first official dramatic presentation of the Restoration, with prologue to the King by Sir William Davenant (or Sir John Denham), as part of an entertainment offered the King by George Monck, Duke of Albemarle

— Thereafter: Sir William Davenant, *The Prologue to His Majesty at the First Play Presented at the Cock-pit in Whitehall...*, published anonymously

Nov 25 — **Christopher Milton called to the bench of the Inner Temple as a lawyer**

Nov 26 — *Observations Upon the Last Actions and Words of... Harrison*

Nov 28 — The bodies of Oliver Cromwell, Henry Ireton (Cromwell's son-in-law), John Bradshaw, and Thomas Pryde disinterred, hanged at Tyburn, and burned beneath the gallows

— Founding of the Royal Society under the leadership of

Christopher Wren

Dec — **Claudius Salmasius, *Opus Posthumum*, reply to Milton's *Defensio***

Dec 8 — Thomas Killigrew produces *The Moor of Venice*, with a woman portraying Desdemona[514]

Dec 12 — Sir William Davenant gains exclusive production rights to William Shakespeare's *The Tempest, Measure for Measure, Much Ado about Nothing, Romeo and Juliet, Twelfth Night, Henry VIII, King Lear, Hamlet,* and *MacBeth,* John Webster's *The Duchess of Malfi,* and plays by Beaumont and Fletcher

Dec 15 — **Parliament orders Milton released from custody of Serjeant at Arms, James Norfolke**

— Andrew Newport, letter, noting the presence of actresses on the stage in England, as had appeared earlier on the Continent

Dec 17 — **Milton complains to Commons of excessive fees charged by the Sergeant at Arms; both are required to appear before Commons. Andrew Marvell works to have the fees reduced**[515]

Dec 24 — Mary Henrietta, Princess Royal, eldest daughter of Charles I and mother of William III, d., in London of smallpox

---

514. This date is frequently cited as marking the appearance of women as professional actors on the English stage.

515. "Milton was ordered to be prosecuted separately from the twenty.... He was put in custody of the Serjeant-at-Arms, and released, December 17. Andrew Marvell, his friend, soon afterwards complained that fees to the amount of £150 had been extorted from him; but Finch answered that Milton had been Cromwell's secretary, and deserved hanging" (Henry Hallam, *Constitutional History*, II, p. 226n.).

1661

Milton moves to Jewin Street
John Milton, edition of Sir Walter Ralegh, *The Cabinet-Council*, appears as an anonymous reprint, *Aphorisms of State*[516]
John Batchilder, *The Virgins Pattern*, biography of Susanna Perwick
George Bate, *The Lives, Actions, and Execution of the prime Actors...of that horrid Murder of...King Charles*, published
Robert Boyle, *The Sceptical Chymist*
Alexander Brome, *Songs and Other Poems*, 1st edition (rpt. 1664, 1668)
Robert Codrington, *Youth's Behaviour or Decency in Conversation Amongst Women*, published
Abraham Cowley, *Propositions for the Advancement of Experimental Philosophy*, treatise on educational practices and theory, foreshadowing the Royal Society; *Vision, concerning his late pretended Highness, Cromwell the Wicked*, published; *Ode to the Royal Society*
John Dee, "Mathematical Preface" to *Euclid's Elements of Geometry*, edited by John Leeke and George Serle
Owen Feltham, *Lusoria, or Occasional Pieces*, revision of *Resolves...*
Joseph Glanville, *The Vanity of Dogmatizing* (revised 1665)
Richard Hooker, *The Works of Mr. Richard Hooker....:In Eight*

---

516. Milton's notoriety as a Republican would have made his name on the title-page of any work anathema in 1661

Books of Ecclesiastical Polity, published

The Life of That Reverend Divine, and Learned Historian, Dr. Thomas Fuller, published anonymously

Mundorum Explicatio...A Sacred Poem, published

Ephraim Paget, *Heresiography, Or a Description of the Hereticks and Sectaries Sprung Up in These Latter Times*, published

Percy Herbert, *The Princess Cloria*

Mirabilis Annus, or, the year of Prodigies and Wonders Part I, Dissenting tract listing divine signs against the Restoration and the Anglican Church (3 parts by 1662)

William Secgwick, *Animadversions Upon a Book Entituled Inquisition for the Blood of Our Late Soveraign*, prose, analysis of the English Revolution

Clement Walker, *The Complete History of Independency*, reprinted

Humphrey Moseley, d.

Susanna Perwick d.

John Cutts b. (d. 1707; afterward Baron Cutts of Gowran

Sir Samuel Garth b. (d. 1719)

Nicholas Hawksmoor b. (d. Mar 25, 1736), architect; clerk and associate to Sir Christopher Wren

Charles Montagu, afterward Earl of Halifax, b. (d. 1715)

Sir John Denham knighted, Order of the Bath

Sir Richard Fanshawe, appointed Ambassador to Portugal

Jan — **George Bate, *Elenchi Motuum*, attacks Milton**

Jan 3 — Samuel Pepys, *Diary*, records a performance of John Fletcher and Philip Massinger, *The Beggars' Bush*, with a woman in the cast

Jan 4 — Samuel Pepys attends Francis Beaumont and John Fletcher's *The Scornful Lady*, with a male cast; within weeks the title-role is performed by a woman

Jan 6 — Thomas Venner and about 50 Fifth Monarchists march on St. Paul's Cathedral with a petition, *A Door of Hope*, and a slogan, "King Jesus, and the heads upon the gate"

Jan 9 — Fifth Monarchists revolt in London on behalf of "King Jesus," led by Thomas Venner, attempted and defeated, with the death of about sixty soldiers and revolutionaries; the attempt promotes increased persecution of that group and of Quakers

— Thereafter: *A Last Farewel to the Rebellious Sect Called the Fifth Monarchy Men on Wednesday January the Ninth*

Jan 10 — "By the King," royal proclamation prohibiting "seditious meetings of '*Quakers, Anabaptists*, and *Fifth-Monarchy-men*'"[517]

Jan 16 — *The last farewel to the Rebellious Sect Called the Fifth Monarchy-Men...with the total dispersing, defeating, and utter ruining of that Damnable and Seditious Sect in general*, tract

Jan 17 — *A Judgment and Condemnation of the Fifth-Monarchy-Men, their Late Insurrection...*, tract

Jan 20 — "Royal Proclamation," further limiting actions by Quakers and other Non-Conformists

Jan 21 — John Gauden acknowledges his authorship of the *Eikon Basilike*, in a letter to Edward Hyde, 1st Earl of Clarendon[518]

Jan 23 — Samuel Pepys attends his first meeting of the Royal Society

Jan 25 — *Londons Glory, or the Riot and Ruine of the Fifth Monarchy Men*, published

Jan 28 — *An Advertisement as touching the Fanaticks Late Conspiracy*, pamphlet

[James Howell], *The Humble apology of some commonly called Anabaptists...with their Protestation against the late wicked and most horrid treasonable Insurrection and Rebellion*

---

517. Michael McKeon, *Politics and Poetry*, p. 86.

518. Neither Hyde nor Charles II was particularly pleased to received written confirmation of the authorship of the most important tract of the Royalist campaign against the Commonwealth; Gauden's subsequent appointment to the bishopric he requested has been seen by some as thinly disguised blackmail, by others as an appropriate reward for services well rendered.

acted in the City of London

Jan 30 — The bodies of Oliver Cromwell and two followers disinterred, hanged at Tyburn until sundown, then decapitated; the bodies were reburied beneath the scaffold, while the heads were "set up on poles at the top of Westminster Hall" where they remained—presumably in ever-advancing states of decay—until well into the 1680s[519]

Feb 10 — Sir Christopher Wren appointed astronomer at Oxford University

Feb 21 — George Fox, and others, *A Declaration from the Harmless & Innocent People of God called Quakers. Against all Plotters and Fighters in the World...in Answer to that Clause of the Kings late Proclamation, which mentions the Quakers...*, published

Feb 25 — Anne Palmer [Fitzroy] (later Countess of Sussex), illegitimate daughter of Charles II and Barbara Villiers Palmer (Duchess of Cleveland), b. (d. 1722)

Mar 1 — Joseph Glanvill, *The Vanity of Dogmatizing; or Confidence in Opinions Manifested in a Discourse of the Shortness and Uncertainty of our Knowledge, And its Causes; with some Reflexions on Peripateticism; and An Apology for Philosophy*, dedicatory epistle dated, Glanvill's first published work

Mar 9 — Cardinal Mazarin d.; nineteen-year-old Louis XIV assumes control of the government of France

Apr — Marchamont Needham, *The Cities Feast to the Lord Protector*, signed broadside, anti-Cromwellian verse

— Jeremy Taylor appointed Bishop of Down and Connor and Dromore, Ireland

Apr 5 — Edmund Waller, *A Poem in St. James Park*, SR for book publication of "On St. James's Park, as lately improv'd by his Majesty"[520]

---

519. Liza Picard, *Restoration London*, p. 212.

520. Perhaps Waller's best contribution to the topographical, or loco-descriptive poem. Cf. Ben Jonson, "To Penshurst," Amelia Lanier, "The Description of Cooke-ham," Andrew Marvell, "Upon Nun Appleton

Apr 17 — *A true Discovery of a Bloody Plot*

Apr 20 — **Arthur Annesley, Milton's friend, created 1st Earl of Anglesey; Annesley remained a frequent visitor after the Restoration**

Apr 23 — ST. GEORGE'S DAY — Coronation of King Charles II in Westminster Abbey; a crowd of 10,000 assembles for the occasion

— John Dryden, *To His Sacred Majesty: A Panegyric on His Coronation*

— Between May 1660 and the Coronation less than a year later, over 100 individual poems had appeared celebrating the King's Restoration, with even more broadsheets, pamphlets, sermons, proclamations, ballads, and songs, including:

— Henry Bold, *St. George's Day Sacred to the Coronation of his Most Excellent Majesty and ever Glorious Prince, Charles the II*

May 5 — Charles, Duke of Cambridge, d.; first son of James, Duke of York and Anne Hyde

May 8 — Cavalier Parliament sits (to 1679)

Jun — [George Rust?] *Letter of Resolution concerning Origen*, including a defense of the Preexistence of the Soul

Jun 22 — Ben Jonson, *The Alchemist*, revived at Gibbon's Tennis Court, performed by Thomas Killigrew's players (additional performances on 14 Aug and 16 Dec)

Jun 28 — Lisle's Tennis Court Theater opens, managed by Sir William Davenant[521]

— Sir William Davenant, *The Siege of Rhodes*, revived and performed

Jul 2 — Sir William Davenant, *The Second Part of the Siege of Rhodes*, revived and performed

Aug 15 — Sir William Davenant, *The Witts*, opera, performed

Aug 15/16 — Thomas Fuller d.

Sep 7 — Samuel Pepys reports seeing *Bartholomew Fair*, with

House," Sir John Denham, "Cooper's Hill," and others.

521. The manager lived on-site with his family until his death.

puppet-show, "acted today, which has not been these forty years (it being so satyricall against Puritanism, they durst not till now)..."[522]

Sep 9 — John Wilmot, 2nd Earl of Rochester, created M.A., Oxford, at age 14

Sep 13 — John Evelyn, *Fumigium*, pamphlet, attack on coal-smoke pollution in London[523]; presented by Evelyn to Charles II

— Thomas Traherne, receives M.A. at Oxford

Oct 21 — Sir William Davenant, *Love and Honour*, revived and performed

Nov 9 — Thomas Flatman, *Miscellanies*, autograph ms. of twenty-three poems, dated

Nov 21 — John Wilmot, 2nd Earl of Rochester, begins his Grand Tour of France and Italy, in company with Sir Andrew Balfour

Dec — Alexander More ['Morus'] returns to England

Dec 16 — Abraham Cowley, *Cutter of Coleman Street*, comedy, performed at Lincoln's Inn Fields (revision of *The Guardian*)

---

522. *Diary*, cited in James Hanford, *A Restoration Reader*, p. 167.

523. The primary source of the pollution was the low-grade coal used to stoke the thousands of householders hearths throughout the city, a problem compounded by the invention of relatively inexpensive bricks for chimneys in the sixteenth century and the rapid increase in population in the seventeenth. Later, in the aftermath of the Great Fire of 1666, Evelyn noted in his *Diary* that many who had read the pamphlet now considered it prophetic.

1662

Milton begins tutoring a young Quaker, Thomas Ellwood, a friend of Milton's friend Dr. Nathan Paget[524]

Milton's sonnet to Sir Henry Vane, appears in George Sykes, *The Life and Death of Sir Henry Vane*

Robert Boyle, *New Experiments Physico-Mechanicall*, published, includes first statement of Boyle's Law[525]

Margaret Lucas Cavendish, Duchess of Newcastle, *Playes; Orations of Divers Sorts, Accommodated to Diverse Places*

Christ and Antichrist: or, 666. Multiplied by 2½. Whereby the true Number of Antichrists Reign is Discovered, published[526]

John Dryden, *To My Lord Chancellor* (Edward Hyde, Earl of Clarendon)

John Dryden and Sir Robert Howard, *The Indian Queen*, performed at the Theatre Royal

William Faithorne, *The Art of Graveing and Etching*, published

Henry Foulis, *The History of the Wicked Plots*

Thomas Fuller, *The History of the Worthies of England*

John Gauden, *Life of Hooker*, published; *The Strange and Wonderfull Visions and Predictions of William Juniper of*

---

524. Ellwood's account of his connections with Milton were published in *The History of the Life of Thomas Ellwood...Written by His Own Hand*, first published in 1714. In 1712, Ellwood, following Milton's model, published his own Biblical poem, *Davideis*.

525. The pressure of a gas varies in an inverse proportion to its volume.

526. Michael McKeon, *Politics and Poetry*, p. 291. The title, while perhaps not in itself significant, may stand for the number of like-minded (and like-titled) pamphlets and tracts that proliferated during the 1650s and 1660s.

Gosfield in Essex, relating to the Troubles in England, pro-Royalist revisionist text[527]

John Graunt, with Sir William Petty, *Natural and Political Observations mentioned in a following index and made upon the bills or mortality*

George Herbert, *Musæ responsoriæ* (Responses of the Muses), published[528]

Elizabeth Jocelyn, *Treatise of Education*

Francis Kirkman, printer, *The Birth of Merlin; or, the Child hath found his Father*, published, attributed to William Shakespeare and William Rowley

The Life and Death of Mistress Mary Frith, biography, published

Mirabilis Annus Secundus; or the Second Year of Prodigies

Mirabilis Annus Secundus; or, the Second Part of the Second Years Prodigies

Owen Lloyd, *The Panther-Prophecy*

Richard Perrinchief, *The Works of King Charles the Martyr*, describing Milton as a "base scribe"

William Petty, *Treatise of Taxes and Contributions*, published

Robert Sanford, *Surinam Justice*

Thomas Stanley, *History of Philosophy*, 4th volume published

John Taylor, *The Traitor's Perspective Glass*, with references to Milton's blindness

W. Turner, *The Common cries of London Town, Some go up street, some go down. With Turners dish of stuff, or a gallymaufery*, broadside ballad

Rowland Watkyns, *Flamma sine Fumo*, poems

Michael Wigglesworth, *The Day of Doom*, published in New England[529]; *God's Controversy with New England*,

---

527. Gerald M. MacLean refers to Gauden's book as "another instance of the continuing need to erase the memory of revolution by historicizing the Restoration" (*Time's Witness*, p. 262).

528. Apparently his first completed work of poetry, this book was also the last of his works published during the seventeenth century.

529 Selling 1800 copies during its first year of publication in New

published
William Dugard d.
Samuel Hartlib d. (b. 1596-1600)[530]
Peter Heylyn d. (b. 1600)
Henry Lawes d. (b. 1595)
Richard Bentley b. (d. 1742)[531]
Samuel Wesley, the Elder, b. (d. 1735)
Henrietta Maria returns to England as Queen Mother
Act of Settlement expels over 2,000 Puritan clergy from their livings
Act of Uniformity suspends free worship for Congregationalists and other Non-Conformists
Quaker Act causes 15,000 non-conformists to be punished for their religious beliefs
John Lambert, parliamentarian general and commander of the forces in the north, tried for treason; imprisoned in Guernsey
Sir Roger L'Estrange appointed Surveyor of the Imprimery (i.e., official censor)[532]
Anglican persecution of Dissenters, Non-Conformists, and Catholics continues unabated

---

England, then immediately reprinted in both England and America, *The Day of Doom* became, after the Bible, the most widely read book available to 17th century New Englanders.

530. Hartlib had been born in Polish Prussia, to an anglophile father and an English mother. His early education was at Cambridge; he returned to Germany during the Thirty Years' War.

531. Bentley's chief connection with Milton studies was his 1732 edition of *Paradise Lost* which, on the basis of a hypothesized ignorant editor who had tampered with blind Milton's text, provided extensive emendations and notes to the poem, often "correcting" lines to bring them into focus with prevailing eighteenth-century attitudes. For his work, Bentley was roundly attacked in Alexander Pope's *Dunciad*

532. D. I. B. Smith notes, however, that between 1662 and 1679, probably fewer than half of the pamphlets published were officially licensed (Andrew Marvell, p. xx)..

Jan 20 — Joseph Glanvill, letter concerning Origen and the doctrine of Pre-existence

Feb 13 — Elizabeth Stuart, Winter-Queen of Bohemia, d. (b. 1596), in London; buried in Westminster Abbey

Apr 19 — Colonel John Okey, Barkstead, and Corbet hanged, drawn, and quartered at Tyburn Gallows as regicides

Apr 25 — Thomas Killigrew, issued a patent to perform plays, with women playing women's roles

Apr 30 — Mary (later Queen Mary II) b., to James, Duke of York, and Anne Hyde

May 21 — Charles II m. Catherine of Braganza, daughter of King John IV of Portugal (no issue)

May 23 — John Gauden, Bishop of Exeter and Worcester d.

Jun 14 — Sir Henry Vane executed on Tower Hill as a regicide

— Thereafter: George Sikes, *The Life and Death of Sir Henry Vane*

— Sir William Petty, knighted

Jun 18 — Charles Fitzroy (afterward Duke of Southampton), illegitimate son of Charles II and Barbara Villiers Palmer, baptized (d. 1730)

Jul 15 — The Royal Society for the Improvement of Natural Knowledge by Experiment chartered and incorporated by Charles II

Aug — Non-Conforming ministers refusing to use the new Prayer Book removed from their positions

Aug 19 — Blaise Pascal d.

Aug 29 — Henry More refers to a recently published "good ingenious book on the preexistence,"[533] Joseph Glanvill, *Lux Orientalis*

Oct — The Theatre Royal, in Smock Alley, opens in Dublin

Oct 19 — Katherine Philips, letter to Roger Boyle, Earl of Orrery, reports her translation of Pierre Corneille, *Pompey*, completeNov

— Ensign Tong and others arrested for a plot to overthrow

---

533. Jackson I. Cope, *Joseph Glanvill*, p. 11.

Charles

Nov 11 — Samuel Butler, *Hudibras*, Part I, licensed

Nov 12 — John Dryden proposed as member of the Royal Society; elected November 19, admitted November 26

Dec — [Samuel Butler], *Hudibras*, appears anonymously in bookstalls

Mid-Dec — Katherine Philips reports seeing *Othello* performed at the Theatre Royal, Dublin

Dec 26 — Charles II, *Declaration of Indulgence*, proposed; offers limited toleration for Dissenters and Catholics

— Samuel Pepys sells back his copy of Samuel Butler's *Hudibras*, disliking the poem sufficiently to take a loss on the transaction

Late 1662 — **Milton reaches the midpoint in composing *Paradise Lost***

1663

Robert Boyle, *Usefulness of Experimental Natural Philosophy, Parts I & II*, published (written c. 1650-1658)
Samuel Butler, *A Proposal Humbly Offered for the Farming of Liberty of Conscience*, prose tract
Abraham Cowley, *Cutter of Coleman Street*, drama, published
Sir William Davenant, *Poem to the King's Most Sacred Majesty*, laureate-poem, published
Fair Warning: or, XXV. Reasons Against Toleration and indulgence of Popery With an Answer to the Roman-Catholicks Reasons for Indulgence, tract
Fair Warning: The Second Part. Or XX. Prophesies Concerning the Return of Popery...with the Several Plots laid...for Restoring Popery, Now Discovered...., tract
Edward Herbert, Lord Herbert of Cherbury, *De Religione Gentilium*, published in Amsterdam
Sir Roger L'Estrange, *News* and *Intelligencer* commence, weekly newspapers
Lodowick Muggleton, *The Neck of the Quakers Broken*
News of a New World, or the Mystical Prison-Door Opened, published, announcing 1666 as a Year of Vengeance and Redemption, tract...
Thomas White, *Sciri, sive sceptices & scepticorum a jure disputationis exclusio*, attack on Joseph Glanvill, *The Vanity of Dogmatizing*
James, Duke of Cambridge b. and d.; son of James, Duke of York and Anne Hyde

John Bramhall, Bishop of Derry, d. (b. 1594)
Robert Chamberlain d.
Humphrey Smith, Quaker, d., in prison
Tom Brown b. (d. 1704)
George Stepney b. (d. 1707)
William Walsh b. (d. 1708)
Five-Mile Act forbids Non-Conformists from participating in local government
Number of physicians in London allowed by the Royal College is raised to forty (fewer than 1 for each 5,000 inhabitants)
Aphra Behn travels to Surinam, the scene of her subsequent romance, *Oroonoko*
Henry Oldenburg appointed Secretary to the Royal Society

Jan 1 — Katherine Philips, "An Epitaph on my Honoured Mother-in-Law, Mrs. Phillips of Portheynon in Cardiganshire, who dyed Jan. 1. Anno 1662/3," panegyric
Jan 15 — Sir William Davenant received a patent to manage the Duke of York's Players
Jan 30 — **Robert South attacks John Milton in Court sermon**
Feb 5 — John Dryden, *The Wild Gallant*, produced, published 1669
Feb 10 — Katherine Phillips, *Pompey*, translation from Corneille, performed at the Theatre Royal, Dublin; thereafter, published in London and in Dublin
Feb 11 — **Milton's signature appears on an allegation of his intent to marry Elizabeth Minshull**
Feb 24 — **Milton m. Elizabeth Minshull, introduced to him earlier by Dr. Nathan Paget, Milton's friend and her second cousin**
— **Milton moves with his family to Bunhill Fields**
Mar 14 — Richard Eadlyn, *Præ-Nuncius Syderius: an Astrological Treatise of the effects of the great conjunction of the two superior Planets, Saturn & Jupiter, October Xth. 1663*, licensed for publication by Sir Roger L'Estrange

Apr 8 — Katherine Phillips, *Pompey. A Tragedy*, translation from Corneille, published by John Crooke in Dublin; and thereafter in London

May — Marchamont Needham, *A Discourse Concerning Schools and Schoolmasters*, published

— John Aubrey elected to the Royal Society

— Theater Royal opens in Drury Lane

May 20 — Sir John Denham elected to the Royal Society

Jun 3 — **Sir Roger L'Estrange, *Considerations and Proposals in order to the Regulation of the Press: Together with Diverse Instances of Treasonous, and Seditious Pamphlets, Proving the Necessity Thereof*; declares Milton's *The Tenure of Kings and Magistrates* treasonous**

Jun 4 — William Juxon, Archbishop of Canterbury since the Restoration, d. (b. 1582)

— Thereafter: Gilbert Sheldon consecrated Archbishop of Canterbury

Jul — Charles II promises to bring bills to Parliament to curtail activities of fanatics and papists

— Katherine Philips, "Lucasia, Rosania, and Orinda parting at a Fountain," written, marking the separation of Philips, Anne Owen, and Mary Aubrey[534]

Jul 10 — The Earl of Bristol speaks before the House of Lords and impeaches the Lord Chancellor, Edward Hyde, as responsible for England's troubles; Clarendon successfully defends himself; the Earl of Bristol is ordered arrested and censured[535]

Jul 17 (old style: 17th day of the 4th month) — John Bunyan, *Christian Behaviour*, final page dated

Jul 31 — Rowland Wogan d.

— Thereafter: Katherine Philips, "To Mrs. Wogan, my

---

534. A mutual friend of all three women, probably known under the pseudonym Thersis, was Henry Lawes, Milton's composer for *Arcades* and *Comus*

535. The event clearly indicated, however, the rise in opposition to Clarendon that would result in his exile within a decade.

Honoured Friend on the Death of her Husband," panegyric

Aug 15 — Sir Roger L'Estrange appointed surveyor of printing presses

Sep 20 — Henry Fitzroy (afterward Duke of Grafton), illegitimate son of Charles II and Barbara Villiers Palmer b.

Sep 17 — Katherine Philips, letter, indicating that she has returned from Dublin to Cardigan, Wales

Oct 12 — Yorkshire Plot by Dissenters to overthrow Charles II scheduled

Oct 24 — **Edward Phillips appointed tutor to John Evelyn's son (to 1665), providing a personal link for Evelyn's subsequent biography of Milton**[536]

Nov 5 — Samuel Butler, *Hudibras, Part II*, licensed

Dec 1 — John Dryden m. Lady Elizabeth Howard

Late-Dec — Samuel Butler, *Hudibras*, nine editions (four pirated)

---

536. Evelyn, a Royalist, notes in his *Diary*, concerning his new preceptor: "This gentleman was nephew to Milton who wrote against Salmasius's *Defensio*; but was not at all infected with his principles, though brought up by him" (*Diary*, p. 3710. *The Milton Encyclopedia* alters the final phrase to, "and though brought up by him, yet no way tainted" (III, p. 85)

1664

John Milton, "On Shakespeare," in William Shakespeare, *Third Folio*
Robert Boyle, *Usefulness of Experimental Natural Philosophy*, 2nd edition
Alexander Brome, *Poems*, enlarged 2nd edition
Samuel Butler, *Hudibras, Part 2*
Margaret Lucas Cavendish, Duchess of Newcastle, *CCXI Sociable Letters; Philosophical Letters: or, Modest Reflections Upon some Opinions in Natural Philosophy, maintained By several Famous and Learned Authors of this Age, Expressed by way of Letters*, published, responses to Thomas Hobbes, René Descartes, Henry More, and others; *Poems and Fancies*, 2nd revised edition
Robert Codrington, *The second part of Youth's Behaviour; or, Decency in Conversation Amongst Women*, published
John Amos Comenius, *Orbis Sensualium Pictus*, published; first illustrated textbook intended for children
Charles Cotton, *Scarronides*, burlesque of Virgil, *Aeneid*, Book I
The Court and Kitchin of Elizabeth, Commonly Called Joan Cromwell, the wife of the late Usurper, Truly Described and Represented And now Made Publick for general satisfaction, published
Sir George Etherege, *The Comical Revenge; or, Love in a Tub*, comedy, published (reprint 1667)
John Evelyn, *Sylva*, horticultural treatise, first book published

by the Royal Society

Richard Flecknoe, *Love's Kingdom, with a short treatise of the English Stage*, published

Lucy Apsley Hutchinson, begins *Memoirs of Colonel Hutchinson* after his death; memoirs first published in 1806

Thomas Jordan, *A Royal Arbor of Loyal, Poesie*, including "The Cheaters Cheated. A Representation in four parts to be Sung by Nim, Filcher, Wat, and Moll, made for the Sheriffs of London," published, a theatrical jig.

Thomas Killigrew, *The Parson's Wedding*, comedy[537]; *Comedies and Tragedies*, published

Henry King, *Poems, Elegies, Paradoxes, and Sonnets*, reissued with a new title-page and additional elegies

Henry More, *A Modest Enquiry into the Mystery of Iniquity, with The Apology of Dr. Henry More*

William Shakespeare, *Third Folio*, published[538]

Edmund Waller, *Poems, etc.*, "Never till now corrected and published with the approbation of the author"[539]

Dukes of Kendal and Cambridge, twin sons, b. to James, Duke of York, and Anne Hyde

Matthew Prior b. (d. 1721)

Sir John Vanbrugh b. (d. 1726)

Sir Richard Fanshawe, Ambassador to Spain

Jan — John Dryden and Sir Robert Howard, *The Indian Queen*, performed

---

537. Along with Sir William Davenant, Thomas Killigrew received one of the two monopolies on theater companies following the Restoration. This comedy is generally regarded as among the most obscene productions of the Restoration Stage, embarrassing even Samuel Pepys.

538. Among other changes, the *Third Folio* included seven plays that had not appeared in Heminges and Condell's *Folio*: *A Yorkshire Tragedy, Pericles, Sir John Oldcastle, The London Prodigal, Locrine, Thomas Lord Cromwell*, and *The Puritan*, the latter four having previously been published with the attribution to "W. S." on their title-pages.

539. Cited in Jack G. Gilbert, *Edmund Waller*, p. 14.

Jan 14 — Katharine Philips, *Poems* (pirated edition published by Richard Marriot[540])

Jan 18 — Richard Marriot, announcement of his intent to withdraw from sale Katharine Philips, *Poems*

Feb 15 — Katherine Philips, *Pompey*, SR by Henry Herringman but never printed

Mar 10 — Judge Sir Matthew Hale condemns Amy Duny and Rose Cullender to death for witchcraft at Bury St. Edmunds; Dr. Thomas Browne testifies for the prosecution; both women hanged

Mar 20 — Anne Bradstreet, *Meditations Divine and moral*, prefatory epistle dated, ms. collection intended for her son, Simon

Late Mar — Katherine Philips arrives in London

Mar 26 — John Evelyn, *Diary*: "It pleased God to take away my son, Richard, now a month old, yet without any sickness of danger perceivably, being to all appearances a most likely child; we suspected much the nurse had overlain him; to our extreme sorrow, being now again reduced to one; but God's will be done."

Mar 29 — John Evelyn, *Diary*: "After evening prayers, was my child buried near the rest of his brothers—my very dear children."

May — John Dryden, *The Rival Ladies*, performed, tragicomedy

— Aphra Behn returns to London from Surinam

May 2 — Bathsua Makin, *Elegy*, for Elizabeth, daughter of Lucy, Countess of Huntington, written[541]

May 16 — Charles Rich d., son of Charles Rich, Earl of Warwick and Mary Boyle Rich, age nineteen, of smallpox

— Thereafter: Katherine Philips, "On the Death of my Lord Rich, only Son to the Earl of Warwick, who dyed of the

---

540. Philips worked to have the edition withdrawn, and the publisher's announcement a few days later indicated that he would do so. Her subsequent death shortly thereafter makes the matter problematical

541. Makin had taught both the Countess and her daughter.

small Pox, 1664

Jun 5 — John Dryden, *The Rival Ladies*, SR; thereafter performed and published, 1664

Jul 10 — Katherine Philips, "To his Grace, Gilbert, Lord Arch-Bishop of Canterbury,[542] July 10, 1664," written

Jul 22 — Katharine Philips (The 'Matchless Orinda') d., of smallpox[543]

— Thereafter: C. J., "An Elegy upon the Death of the most Incomparable Katherine Philips," published

Aug 20 — John Evelyn, dedication dated for *A Parallel of Antient Architecture with the Modern*, translation from the French of Roland Freart; with commendatory comments on Sir John Denham's activities as Surveyor General

Sep — 'M. N. Med. Londineus' [Marchamont Needham], *Medala Medicinæ: A Plea for the Free Profession, and a Renovation of the Art of Physick...*, published, 500-page medical treatise, attacks the College of Physicians and supports experimentation in medicine

Sep 5 — Charlotte Fitzroy (afterward Countess of Litchfield), illegitimate daughter of Charles II and Barbara Villiers, b. (d. 1718)

Oct 11 — Colonel John Hutchinson d.

Oct 18 — Joseph Glanvill, *Scepsis scientifica: or, Confest ignorance the way to science* (The Vanity of Dogmatizing, revised), with "Address to the Royal Society," *Sciri tuum nihil est: or, The Author's Defense of The Vanity of Dogmatizing, and A Letter to a Friend concerning Aristotle*, registered, partial response to Thomas White's *Sciri, sive sceptices...*

Winter — A comet appears north of London, resulting in books and pamphlets foretelling plague and doom[544]

---

542. Gilbert Sheldon, who donated the Sheldonian Theatre to Oxford University

543. As a matter of collateral interest—and as an indication of how richly and complexly interrelated many of the writers of the century were, Katherine Philip's stepfather was the brother to John Dryden's aunt.

544. A number of such prognostications pointed to 1665/1666 as years

Dec — Dr. Thomas Browne admitted an honorary fellow of the College of Physicians

Dec 10 — Joseph Glanvill, *Scepsis scientifica: or, Confest ignorance the way to science* presented to the Royal Society, reported in a letter from Henry Oldenburg to Robert Boyle

Dec 14 — Joseph Glanvill elected to the Royal Society

Dec 16 — Anthony à Wood records the appearance of a comet over Oxford, accompanied the following year by "a great plague in England, prodigious births, great inundations and frosts, warr with the Dutch, sudden deaths, particularly in Oxon &c"[545]

Dec 23 — John Wilmot, 2nd Earl of Rochester, returns to Court in England

Late Dec — Dr. Nathaniel Hodges treats a plague victim during the Christmas Holidays; first documented case in what becomes the Great Plague

— John Gadbury associates the recent comet with his own case of plague at Christmas-time; he survives

— Reports indicate that 290 people die in London's 130 parishes[546]

---

of unusual portent; and, since the pamphlets in question were published before the Great Plague, the Great Fire, and the Anglo-Dutch naval war, they were seen as part of the quasi-prophetic, frequently millenarian tenor of the times.

545. Llewelyn Powys, *Life & Times*, p. 119.

546. The average annual death rate for London at the time was reported as about 17,000 from all causes.

1665

Henry Adis, *A Letter Sent from Surinam*

Sir Richard Baker, *A Chronicle of the Kings of England, from the Time of the Romans Government unto the Death of King James .... Whereunto is Added, the Reign of King Charles the First. With a Continuation of the Chronicle, in This Fourth Edition, to the Coronation of His Sacred Majesty King Charles the Second...*, continuation by Edward Phillips

Sir William Davenant, *Two Excellent Plays: The Wits, a Comedie: The Platonick Lovers, a Tragi-Comedie*, printed

[William Drage], *Daimonomageia: a small Treatise of Sicknesses and Diseases from Witchcraft and Supernatural Causes .... Being useful to others besides Physicians, in that it confutes Atheistical, Sadducistical, and Skeptical Principles and Imaginations...*[547]

John Dryden, *Four New Plays*, published

Sir Thomas Fairfax, Lord Fairfax, *Short Memorials of some things to be cleared during my Command in the Army (1645 to 1650 A.D.)*, written (?); *A Short Memorial of the Northern Actions, during the War there, from the year 1642 till the year 1644*, written (?)

Simon Ford, *A Christian's Acquiescence*, memorial volume containing an elegy by Bathsua Makin and other verse

Robert Hooke, *Micrographia*, published, first treatise on the microscope

---

547. Drage refers to himself as William Drage, D. P. (Doctor of Physic) of Hitchin, a medical practitioner

Sir Robert Howard, *Four New Plays*
François La Rouchefoucauld, *Maximes*
Andrew Marvell, *Character of Holland*
Mene Tekel to the Fifthy Monarchy, published
Simon Patrick, *Parable of a Pilgrim*
Royal Society, *Philosophical Transactions*, begin publication
Edmund Waller, *Upon Her Majesty's New Buildings*
John Earle, d.
James Goodwin d. (b. 1594?)
Nicholas Poussin d. (b. 1593)
Charles Gildon b. (d. 1724)
Henrietta Maria, the Queen Mother, makes a final visit to France
Samuel Parker, elected fellow of the Royal Society
Edward Phillips, Milton's nephew, appointed tutor to Philip Herbert, son of the Earl of Pembroke and Montgomery (to 1667?)

Jan 2 — John Evelyn, *The Mystery of Jesuitism*, translated and collected, published anonymously
— Charles II verbally commits himself to a naval war against the Dutch
Feb 6 — Anne (afterward Queen Anne) b., to James, Duke of York and Anne Hyde
Feb 22 — Second Anglo-Dutch Naval War declared (to 1667)
Feb 24 — John Evelyn's *Diary*: "Dr. Fell, Canon of Christ Church, preached before the King...a very formal discourse *and in blank verse, according to his manner*"[548]
— John Evelyn's *Diary*: "Mr. Philips, preceptor to my son, went to be with the Earl of Pembroke's son, my Lord Herbert"[549]
Mar 15 — War with the Netherlands officially begins
Mar 18 — Edward Herbert, Lord Herbert of Cherbury, *Occa-*

---

548. John Evelyn, *Diary*, Vol. II, p. 3. Italics added for emphasis.

549. John Evelyn, *Diary*, Vol. II, p. 3. The 'Mr. Philips' mentioned is Milton's nephew, Edward Philips.

sional Verses of Edward Lord Herbert, Baron of Cherbury, dedication page dated

Apr — John Dryden, *The Indian Emperour*, performed; published 1667

— St. Giles parish admits to two plague cases; The Great Plague strikes in London

Apr 6 — John Evelyn records a performance of Roger Boyle, Earl of Orrery, *Mustapha*, tragedy

May — Reports of 43 deaths from plague in London

May 25 — John Dryden, *The Indian Emperor*, SR; sequel to *The Indian Queen*, by Sir Robert Howard with Dryden's assistance

— Sir John Denham m. Margaret Brooke[550]

May 26 — John Wilmot, 2nd Earl of Rochester, attempts to 'kidnap' Elizabeth Mallet, a prominent heiress, as part of his suit to marry her; the next day a warrant is sent to the Tower for his arrest and incarceration

June — Official reports of 600 plague deaths in London

— London theaters ordered closed due to the plague

Jun 3 — First maritime engagement between English and Dutch ships; the English are victorious under former General George Monck, now 1st Duke of Albemarle

Jun 5 — Sir Roger L'Estrange first acknowledges the Plague in his quasi-official newspaper, *The Intelligencer*; he reports only 43 plague-related deaths during May[551]

Jun 11 — Sir Kenelm Digby d.

Jun—SECOND WEEK — Mortality Bills report 112 deaths in 12 parishes; other reports indicate 168

Jun 15 — Samuel Pepys comments on the effects the growing Plague has on London

Jun 19 — John Wilmot, 2nd Earl of Rochester, release from the

---

550. Denham was fifty; his bride, twenty-three. In this instance, however, the age disparity would have noticeable results on their marriage...and subsequently on Denham's reputation.

551. James Leasor, *The Plague*, p. 40. The actual number of deaths in London was nearer 1,500, extraordinarily high under any circumstances.

Tower, where he had been held during the first weeks of the Great Plague

Jun 20 — Thanksgiving Day declared to celebrate an English naval victory over the Dutch

Jun—THIRD WEEK — 267 plague deaths

Jun 29 — Key Whitehall personnel, including Charles II and his Queen, evacuate the city[552]

Jun—FOURTH WEEK — 470 plague deaths

Jul — **With the help of the young Quaker, Thomas Ellwood, Milton moves to Chalfont St. Giles, Buckinghamshire, to avoid the plague in London; during the same summer, John Dryden removes his family to Charlton, Wiltshire**

Jul—FIRST WEEK — 725 plague deaths reported

— Total deaths in London from the plague now number in the thousands

Jul 4 — 1,004 deaths from all causes, with only 470 attributed to plague

Jul 5 — London's Aldermen order additional "rakers" to rid the streets of dead dogs and cats, ordered killed to prevent the Plague[553]

Jul 7 — Nathaniel Lee admitted to Trinity College, Cambridge

Jul 11 — 1,268 deaths admitted during the past week, 725 from plague

Mid-Jul — Over 1,000 plague deaths reported in one week; the actual number is probably considerably higher

— By mid-July, 10,000 homes abandoned; over 200,000 people

---

552. James Leasor, *The Plague*, p. 55: "Charles was by no means a physical coward, nor was he completely indifferent to his people. But in those times, no one thought it a monarch's duty to expose himself to the hazards and horrors of a full-scale epidemic, least of all the monarchs themselves." Data concerning the Bills of Mortality on the following pages are drawn from Leasor.

553. The irony of the order was, of course, that with fewer cats, the rats which actually disseminated the plague-fleas increased dramatically in number.

have fled London[554]

Jul 14 — Because of the Plague, Scotland prohibits all trade between Scotland and England

Jul 15 — John Wilmot, 2nd Earl of Rochester, joins the fleet against the Dutch, under the command of the Earl of Sandwich (father of Rochester's chief rival for the hand of Elizabeth Mallet

Jul 18 — 1,761 deaths reported, 1089 from plague

Jul 25 — 2,785 deaths reported, 1,843 attributed to plague

Jul 26 — Edward Lord Conway invites Valentine Greatrakes to attend his wife, Anne Finch, Lady Conway, and 'touch' her for her chronic pain; Henry More and George Rust, both resident at Ragley, agree with the request

Jul 27 — The Court moves from Hampton Court to Salisbury to escape the plague; then to Wilton, and finally to Oxford

Aug 1 — Deaths reported for the previous week reach 3,104, with 2,020 attributed to plague; actual figures are probably much higher

Aug 2 — John Evelyn: "A solemn fast through England to deprecate God's displeasure against the land by pestilence and war"[555]

— English fleet defeated in an engagement with the Dutch at Bergen

Aug 8 — Deaths the previous week, 4,018; 2,817 attributed to plague

Aug 15 — Deaths the previous week, 5,319; 3,880 attributed to plague

Aug—LAST WEEK — Mortality Bill for the last week in August indicates 7,496 deaths; 6,102 admitted to be from plague

— Samuel Pepys estimates the figure at nearer 10,000; another administration official raises the estimate to 14,000 in one week

---

554. In an effort to control the disease, Charles II ordered stray dogs and cats killed; up to 40,000 dogs and 200,000 cats died.

555. Vol. II, p. 8.

Sep — **Thomas Ellwood reads ms. of *Paradise Lost* in X Books; later claims to have given Milton at the time the idea for *Paradise Regain'd*[556]**

— Plague arrives in Norwich; over 3,000 die over the next year

Sep 5 — Fires set throughout London and kept burning for three days to "purify" the air

— Henry Danvers' Plot to assassinate Charles II, establish a republic, and redistribute wealth planned (discovered and foiled before it could occur, leaders, including Colonel Rathbone, arrested and executed)

Sep 7 — John Evelyn's *Diary*: "Came home (from Chatham), there perishing near 10,000 poor creatures weekly; however, I went all along the city and suburbs from Kent Street to St. James's, a dismal passage, and dangerous to see so many coffins exposed in the streets, now thin of people; the shops shut up, and all in mournful silence, not knowing whose turn might be next"[557]

Sep 8 — Unexpected rains douse the fires, but in that single night, more than 4,000 people die

Sep 11 — Plague mortalities drop for the first time, by over 500 deaths

Sep 16 — The Court resides at Oxford because of the Plague

Sep 17 — Philip IV, King of Spain, d.; succeeded by Charles II, an infant[558]

Sep 18 — Deaths the previous week rise to 8,297, with 7,165 from plague; the French ambassador puts the number at more than 14,000

Sep 25 — Deaths the previous week number 6,460, with 5,553 from plague; from this point on the numbers drop continu-

---

556. "Thou hast said much here of Paradise Lost; but what has thou to say on Paradise Found?" According to Ellwood, Milton said nothing in response but sat for a while lost in thought.

557. Vol. II, p. 9.

558. The infant king's sister, Maria Theresa, was the wife of Louis XIV, the energetic and ambitious young King of France, which allowed Louis an excuse to begin his military incursions upon Spanish Territory.

ously until the end of the Great Plague

Oct 1 — Bill of Mortality for the last week of September shows 5,720 deaths, 4,929 from plague

Oct 8 — Deaths the previous week, 5,068; 4,327 from plague

Oct 10 — Rathbone's Plot revealed to Parliament

Oct 14 — Matthew Griffith d. (b. 1599?); suffers a ruptured blood vessel during a sermon

Oct 15 — Deaths the previous week, 3,219; from plague, 2,665

Oct 22 — Deaths the previous week, 1,802; from plague, 1,421

Nov — New outbreaks of plague are reported in outlying areas of greater London

— Twice-weekly *Oxford Gazette*, begins publication

Nov 9 — Deaths the previous week, 1,787; from plague, more than 1,400

Nov 16 — Deaths the previous week, 1,359; from plague, 1,050

Nov 23 — Deaths the previous week, more than 900; from plague, over 600

Dec 1 — Samuel Pepys m. Elizabeth St. Michel

Dec—FIRST WEEK — Deaths, 428; from plague, 210

Dec—SECOND WEEK — Deaths, 442; from plague, 243

Dec—THIRD WEEK — Deaths, 525; from plague, 281

Dec—FOURTH WEEK — Deaths, 350; from plague, 152

— Small shops begin to open in London for the first time in months

Dec 28 — George Fitzroy (later Earl and Duke of Northumberland), illegitimate son of Charles II and Barbara Villiers, b. (d. 1716)

— By end of the year, Bills of Mortality officially indicate over 97,306 dead, 68,596 from plague—most probably an underestimation[559]

---

559. Palmer, *Charles II*, p. 87f. The mortality rate for London was one in seven; in some particularly crowded parishes, it rose to one in two. Among pregnant women who contracted the plague, the mortality rate was virtually one hundred percent.

1666

1666—A year that had taken on intense eschatological significance during the previous several decades[560]

John Bunyan, *Grace Abounding to the Chief of Sinners: or a brief and faithful Relation of the exceeding mercy of God in Christ to his poore servant, John Bunyan*

Nicholas Boileau, *Satire*

Margaret Lucas Cavendish, Duchess of Newcastle, *Observations upon Experimental Philosophy, To which is added, The Description of a New World, Called The Blazing World*, critique of Robert Hooke, *Micrographia* and imitation of Lucan

Margaret Askew Fell, *Womens Speaking, Justified, Proved and Allowed of by the Scriptures, All such as speak by the Spirit and Power of the Lord Jesus*

R.G., *MDCLXVI. A Prognostick on this Famous Year 1666. Or, The Number of the Beast, so much talked of, Dialogue-wise, Chronogrammatically Explained*

Valentin Greatrakes, *A Brief Account of Mr Valentine Greatraks, and divers of the Strange Cures By him lately Performed...*

Dr. Nathaniel Hodges, *An Account of the first Rise, Progress,*

---

560. Michael McKeon, *Politics and Poetry*, pp. 190ff. As early as 1597, T. Lupton had declared in *Babylon is Fallen* that the year 1666 would mark the fall of the Anti-Christ in Rome, a revelation that received widespread acceptance during the next decades. By 1641 John Archer would confidently verify 1666 as the year of the Fall of Rome, a requisite precursor to Christ's return, in *The Personal Reigne of Christ upon Earth* (B. S. Capp, *Fifth Monarchy Men*, p. 26, 30-31)

Symptoms, and Cure of the Plague, being the Substance of a Letter from Dr. Hodges to a Person of Quality, published

Molière, *Le Misanthrope*

Henry More, *Enchiridium Ethicum, præcipua moralis philosophiæ rudimenta complectens*, in Latin (several reprints, also in Latin)

Samuel Parker, *A Free and Impartial Censure of the Platonick Philosophy*, published; *An Account of the Nature and Extent of the Divine Dominion and Goodnesse*, published

[George Wither], *Ecchoes from the Sixth Trumpet.... Imprinted in the Year chronogrammatically expressed in this Seasonable Prayer LorD haVe MerCIe Vpon Vs*, published[561]

Edward Calamy d.

Mildmay Fane, 2nd Earl of Westmorland, d.

James Howell d. (b. 1593/4)

Matthew Newcomen d.

George Thomason d.

Thomas Vaughan d.

Mary Astell b.

Thomas Flatman, M.A. at Cambridge University at the King's request

Jan 26 — Louis XIV of France declares war on England, in accordance with a treaty with the Dutch

Feb (?) — During the previous month, 253 deaths in London, only 70 from plague

— The Court returns to London as the plague diminishes

— **Milton returns to his house in Artillery Walk, London, from Chalfont St. Giles following the Great Plague**

— The *Oxford Gazette* becomes the *London Gazette*, following the Court's return to London after the Great Plague; the government's official newspaper to the present

Feb 6 — Edward, Lord Conway, letter indicating that after a

---

[561]. One of the many tracts that noted the significance of the sequential Roman numerals composing 1666. See Michael McKeon, *Politics and Poetry*, pp. 220ff.

fortnight, Valentine Greatrake's 'touching' has had no effect on Lady Conway's illness

Mar 1 — John Evelyn, *The Pernicious Consequences of the new Heresy of the Jesuits against Kings and States*, presented by Evelyn to Charles II

— Edmund Waller, *Instructions to a Painter for the Drawing of the Posture and Progress of His Maties forces at Sea under the Command of his Highness Royal. Together with the Battel and Victory obtained over the Dutch, June 3, 1665*, SR, verse eulogizing the Duke of York's activities in the war,

Apr — The plague severe in outlying counties, although nearly disappeared from London

— Sir John Denham suffers briefly from an attack of madness, recovers

May 14 — R. F., *St. Leonard's Hill. A Poem*, licensed by Sir Roger L'Estrange; imitation of Sir John Denham, *Coopers Hill*[562]

May 27/Jun 6 — **Peter Heimbach,[563] letter to Milton; last known letter received by Milton, expressing pleasure that reports of Milton's death from Plague were unfounded**

Jun — Lady Denham becomes mistress to James, Duke of York (afterward James II)

Jun 1-4 — Four Days Battle of the English fleet against the Dutch at Foreland[564]; narrow victory claimed by English

Jun 26 — Sir Richard Fanshawe d., in Madrid, Spain

— Thereafter, Lady Anne Harrison Fanshawe, *Memoir*, commemorating her husband, Sir Richard Fanshawe,

---

562. While among the first imitations of Coopers Hill, this anonymous poem is by no means the last. Theodora Banks notes that some 46 'hill' poems are published in the two centuries following the first appearance of Denham's poem.

563. Birth and death dates for Peter Heimbach are not known.

564. This has been called the bloodiest sea battle of the century. The English fleet lost 17 ships, with 5000 seamen killed and 3000 captured. The Dutch fleet lost four ships, with three admirals and 400 men killed. (Van der Zee, *William and Mary*, p. 41)

(published 1979)

Jun 30 — Alexander Brome d.

Jul 4 — Charles, Duke of Kendal, b., son of James, Duke of York and Anne Hyde

Summer — Joseph Glanvill *A Philosophical endeavour towards the defense of the Being of Witches as Apparitions*, completed; most copies of the first edition destroyed in the Great Fire

Jul — Aphra Behn sails to Antwerp as a spy for Charles II

Jul 13 — Elkanah Settle matriculates at Trinity College, Oxford; withdraws without receiving a degree

Jul 25 — St. James Day Fight; English fleet defeats the Dutch

Aug 4 — — English fleet defeats the Dutch fleet at Dunkirk

Aug 15 — **John Milton, letter to Peter Heimbach, his last known correspondence**

Aug 18 — English fleet destroys 140 Dutch merchant ships at Terschelling

Aug 27 — Committee composed of Sir Christopher Wren, Thomas Chicheley, John Evelyn, and others, survey St. Paul's Cathedral to formulate plans to refurbish and where necessary rebuild the structure, including plans to replace the long-burned steeple with a cupola, "a form of church-building not as yet known in England, but of wonderful grace" (Evelyn, II: 20)

Fall — Aphra Behn, recently widowed (in the Great Plague?), a spy in the Netherlands

Sep 1 — Shortly before midnight, a small fire erupts at the home of Thomas Farynor, baker to Charles I in Pudding Lane

Sep 2-6 — The Great Fire of London

— All of the old City and a portion beyond the city wall to the west (436 acres) demolished

— Over 13,200 homes lost; only 8,000 eventually rebuilt

— Eighty-seven churches destroyed, including Old St. Paul's Cathedral[565]

---

565. Sir Christopher Wren had recently begun surveying Old St. Paul's to determine the extent of restoration needed to preserve it.

— Some 200,000 "burnt Londoners" left homeless for several days, until permanent shelter could be found
— Many printers and booksellers burned out, and their stocks of paper and books destroyed when the leading in the roof of St. Paul's melted and flowed into the crypts that were being used as storage facilities.[566]
— Losses to the Great Fire estimated at some £10,000,000

Sep 3—Monday night — **Milton's house in Bread Street (the only property he owned) destroyed in the Great Fire**

Sep 4 — John Evelyn's *Diary*: "...the stones of St. Paul's flew like grenados, the melting lead running down the streets in a stream, and the very pavements glowing with fiery redness, so as no horse, nor man, was able to tread on them, and the demolition had stopped all the passages, so that no help could be applied" (II: 21-22)

Sep 6 — John Dryden's son, Charles, b.

Sep 7 — John Evelyn's *Diary* graphically reports the devastation of London[567]

---

566. Liza Picard, *Restoration London*, pp. 25-35.

567. "At my return (from a tour of devastated London), I was infinitely concerned to find that goodly Church, St. Paul's—now a sad ruin, and that beautiful portico (for structure comparable to any in Europe, as not long before repaired by the late King*) now rent in pieces, flakes of large stones split asunder, and nothing remaining entire but the inscription in the architrave showing by whom it was built, which had not one letter of it defaced! It was astonishing to see what immense stones the heat had in a manner calcined, so that all the ornaments, columns, friezes, capitals, and projectures of massy Portland stone, flew off, even to the very roof, where a sheet of lead covering a great space (no less than six acres by measurement) was totally melted. The ruins of the vaulted roof falling, broke into St. Faith's, which being filled with the magazines of books belonging to the Stationers, and carried thither for safety, they were all consumed, burning for a week following. It is also observable that the lead over the altar at the east end was untouched, and among the divers monuments the body of one bishop remained entire. Thus lay in ashes that most venerable church, one of the most ancient pieces of early piety in the Christian world, besides near one hundred more. The lead, ironwork, bells, plate, etc., melted, the exquisitely wrought Mercers' Chapel, the sumptuous Exchange, the august

— An alarm is raised among the people in London, fearful that the Dutch and the French (suspected of setting the fire) would invade, were invading, or had already invaded London

Sep 13 — John Evelyn presents Charles II with annotated plans for rebuilding London

Sep 17 — Anthony à Wood reports that "the devil appeared at Westminster at Whitehall and frighted the gards out of their wits"[568]

Oct — Thomas Hobbes censured by Parliament for *Leviathan*; accused of atheistic leanings

— London theaters re-open following the Great Plague

Oct 10 — General Fast ordered throughout England, to urge humility in the face of the plague, the fire, and the Dutch war

Oct 11 — Parliament orders stricter control of Dissenters and Papists

Oct 16 — John Dryden loans Charles II £500

Oct 25 — William Lilly examined by a parliamentary committee investigating the Great Fire; he is asked to explain engravings accompanying his 1651 tract, *Monarchy or No Monarchy for England*[569]

Oct 29 — James Shirley buried[570] (b. Sep 1596)

---

fabric of Christ Church, all the rest of the Companies' Halls, splendid buildings, arches, entries, all in dust; the fountains dried up and ruined, while the very waters remained boiling; the voragos of subterranean cellars, wells, and dungeons, formerly warehouses, still burning in stench and dark clouds of smoke; so that in five or six miles traversing about I did not see one load of timber unconsumed, nor many stones but what were calcined white as snow" (II: 24). The portico he mentions had been constructed by Inigo Jones during the reign of Charles I.

568. Llewelyn Powys, *Life and Times*, p. 132.

569. Since the engraving showed a city under siege from warships on the nearby river (suggesting the incursions of the Dutch warship up the Thames during the recent war), and the city in flames (further suggesting the Great Fire), Lilly was held to have been either a prophet or a saboteur in collusion with the Papists assumed responsible for starting the Great Fire.

570. Shirley is said to have died as a result of exposure and terror,

Nov 10 — John Dryden sends copy of *Annus Mirabilis* to Sir Robert Howard

Nov 22 — John Dryden, *Annus Mirabilis*, licensed

Dec — George (afterward Duke of Northumberland) b., illegitimate son of Charles II and Barbara Castlemaine

---

consequences of the Great Fire.

1667

Margaret Lucas Cavendish, Duchess of Newcastle, *Life of the thrice Noble born, High and Puissant Prince William Cavendishe, Duke, Marquis, and Earl of Newcastle*
William Dell, *The Increase of Popery in England* published but all copies confiscated by the government
John Dryden, *Annus Mirabilis The Year of Wonders, 1666 An Historical Poem Containing...*
John Dryden and Sir William Davenant, revision of William Shakespeare, *The Tempest*
Thomas Ellwood, *Speculum Seculi, or a Looking-Glass for the Times*, Quaker verse-tract
[Simon Ford], *The Conflagration of London: Poetically Delineated*
J.G. ([oseph Guillim], *Akamaton Pur. Or, the Dreadful Burning of London: Described in a Poem*
Thomas Hobbes, *Leviathan*, Dutch edition published in Amsterdam
William Lilly, *Mr. Lillyes Prognostications*[571]
Andrew Marvell, "The Last Instructions to a Painter," written and circulated in manuscript (published, 1689)
Molière, *Tartuffe*
Henry More, *Divine Dialogues*
Katherine Phillips, *Poems by Mrs Katherine Philips the*

---

571. In light of the similarities between his writings during the 1650s and the occurrences of 1665/1666, Lilly seems to have 'edited' a number of his prognostications to make him seem even more attuned to reading future events.

Matchless Orinda, authorized and enlarged edition

Henry Purcell, "Sweet Tyranness," composed, at the age of eight

Pyrotechnica Loyolana, Ignatian Fire-works Or, the Fiery Jesuits Temper....Exposed to Publick view for the sake of London, charges complex Papist conspiracy in the Great Fire and other disasters

Jean Baptiste Racine, *Andromaque*

Elkanah Settle, *An Elegie on the late Fire And Ruines of London*

Thomas Sprat, *History of the Royal Society*

T. V. [Thomas Vincent], *God's Terrible Voice in the City: wherein you have I. The Sound of the Voice, in the narration of the two late dreadful judgments of plague and fire... II. The interpretation of the Voice*, published[572]

George Warren, *An Impartial Description of Surinam*

Samuel Woodford, *A Paraphrase Upon the Psalms of David*

Laurence Clarkson d., while in prison for debt

Charles Hoole d.

William Spurstowe d.

George Wither d. (b. 1588)

Abel Boyer b. (d. 1729), French Huguenot refugee

John Reynolds b. (d. 1727), dissenting minister and poet

Jonathan Swift b., in Dublin (d. 1745)

Thomas Traherne, serving as Chaplain to Sir Orlando Bridgeman, Lord Keeper of the Seal; Traherne is in residence in London

Nathaniel Lee, BA from Trinity College, Cambridge

Early 1667 — Joseph Glanvill, *A Philosophical Endeavour towards the defense of the Being of Witches as Apparitions*, reprinted

---

572. The Great Plague and the Great Fire were "National judgments," because "London was the Metropolis of the land" and God chose to express his displeasure with England by punishing the metropolis (cited in Michael McKeon, *Politics and Poetry*, p. 48f).

Jan 6 — Lady Margaret Denham dies, after complaining of poisoning; an autopsy shows no evidence of poison[573]; Sir John Denham, convalesced from a fit of madness, returns to writing poetry

Jan 29 — John Wilmot, 2nd Earl of Rochester, m. Elizabeth Mallet, against the expectations of her family and friends, but with the support of Charles II

Feb — Catherine of Braganza miscarries

Feb 15 — John Evelyn, *Public Employment, and an Active Life with its Appanages, preferred to Solitude*, published, response to Sir George Mackenzie

Mar — [Sir John Denham?], *The Second Advice to a Painter, for Drawing the History of our Navall Business; In Imitation of Mr. Waller. Being the last Work of Sir John Denham*, published, the first of five mock eulogies concerning the Duke of York

— George Villiers, 2nd Duke of Buckingham, implicated in treason against Charles II

Mar 2 — Samuel Pepys records seeing *Secret-Love, or, The Maiden Queen*, a new play by John Dryden (published 1668)

Spring — Aphra Behn returns from Antwerp

Before Apr 24 — **Milton having troubles in finding a publisher for *Paradise Lost***

Apr 26 — Samuel Pepys writes in his *Diary* that "all the town-talk nowadays" is of the "extravagancies" of Margaret Cavendish, Duchess of Newcastle[574]

Apr 27 — **Contract signed with Samuel Simmons to publish**

---

573. Lady Denham had requested herself that her body be opened. Later rumor suggested that she had been poisoned by the Duchess of York. No attempt was made at the time to implicate Denham in her death, and o Hehir suggests that the most probably cause of death was appendicitis.

574. Elsewhere in the diary Pepys writes that "The whole story of this Lady is a romance...and all she doth is romantic"; and of seeing "100 boys and girls running looking upon her" (*Diary*, 10 May 1667, 11 April 1667; cited in Paul Salzman, *English Prose Fiction*, p. 293).

Paradise Lost; the contract is the oldest author's contract still existing. Milton is to be paid £5; Simmons is to publish 1,300 copies of the poem[575]

May — Louis XIV of France sends armed forces into the Spanish Netherlands

May 9 — Colonel Thomas Blood makes his attempt to steal the Crown Jewels from the Tower of London

May 12 — Colonel Blood interviewed personally by Charles II and James, Duke of York

Jun 11 — Ships from the Dutch fleet sail into King's Channel on the Thames, burning and looting

Jun 20 — Charles, Duke of Kendal d. (?), son of James, Duke of York and Anne Hyde

Jun-Jul — Theaters closed in London

Jul — Treaty of Breda concludes the second naval war with the Netherlands; the conflict is inconclusive

Jul 18 — Colonel Thomas Blood officially released from custody

Jul 28 — Abraham Cowley d.

Aug 1 — Colonel Thomas Blood pardoned, his lands confiscated in 1660 restored, and he is granted a pension of £500[576]

---

575. The poem sold over 1,500 copies during Milton's lifetime. Milton was to receive £5 for the first 1,300 copies sold; an additional £5 for the second and each subsequent 1,300 sold. Milton thus received £10 but died before the third issue of 1,300 sold. After his death, his widow attempted to collect another £10 from the publisher but ultimately sold her rights to the poem for £8. Within twenty-five years, John Dryden would receive a substantial sum for his translation of Virgil's *Aeneid*, sold by subscription (Incidentally, Dryden's theatrical income for 1667, the year in which *Paradise Lost* earned Milton £5, was in the neighborhood of £700); and within twenty-five years after that, Alexander Pope would see a profit of some £5,000 for his translation of Homer's *Iliad*, and another £5,000 for the *Odyssey*—these being the only poems consistently held up as equal or superior to Milton's achievement.

576. Derek Wilson suggests that Blood's bizarre attempt to steal the jewels, especially in light of his subsequent treatment by Charles II and several key Court favorites, was essentially a demonstration of his abilities at espionage and conspiracy; Wilson notes that for the remaining nine years of his life,

Aug 3 — Abraham Cowley buried, Westminster Abbey

Aug 7 — John Dryden, *An Essay of Dramatic Poesy*, *Secret Love*, *The Wild Gallant*, and *The Maiden Queen*, SR

Aug 13 — Jeremy Taylor, Chaplain to Charles I, Bishop of Downe and Connor (and Dromore) d., in Ireland

Aug 15 — John Dryden, *Sir Martin Mar-All*, performed; written with William Cavendish, Duke of Newcastle; epilogue includes caustic comments on William Lilly's predictions for 1665-66; published 1668

Aug 17 — Frances Aylesbury buried, Westminster Abbey

Aug 20 — **John Milton, *Paradise Lost. A Poem Written in Ten Books by John Milton*, SR**

Aug 26 — James, Duke of York, sent to demand the Great Seal of Office from the Lord Chancellor, Edward Hyde, 1st Earl of Clarendon

Aug 30 — Edward Hyde, 1st Earl of Clarendon and Lord Chancellor, dismissed from office

— Sir Orlando Bridgeman dispatched by Charles II to demand the seal from Clarendon

(?)— **John Milton, *Paradise Lost. A Poem Written in Ten Books by John Milton*, published**

Sep 14 — Edgar, Duke of Cambridge, b., son of James, Duke of York, and Anne Hyde

Oct 5 — John Wilmot, 2nd Earl of Rochester, called to the House of Lords by Charles II, before the age of 21

Oct 10 — Parliament assembles; Charles II speaks to the dismissal of Edward Hyde, 1st Earl of Clarendon

Oct 25 — John Evelyn commended by Oxford University for acquiring the Arundel Marbles for the University; the classical sculptures placed around the new Sheldonian Theater

Nov 7 — John Dryden, *The Tempest*, performed, an adaptation of William Shakespeare, *The Tempest*; written with Sir William Davenan

Nov 20 — John Wilmot, 2nd Earl of Rochester, signs the

Blood was involved as a government agent (*The Tower*, p. 191)

Petition approving Commons' impeachment of the Earl of Clarendon

Nov 29 — Edward Hyde, 1st Earl of Clarendon, exiled from England

Late 1667 — Joseph Glanvill, *Some Philosophical Considerations Touching the Being of Witches*, 3rd reprint, as *A Blow at Modern Sadducism*

1668

John Milton, *Paradise Lost*, praised by John Dryden and the Earl of Dorset

John Milton, Two additional issues of *Paradise Lost* published; Simmons begins inserting the prose "Arguments" for each Book with these issues

Meric Casaubon, *Of Credulity and Incredulity in Things Natural, Civil, and Divine*, published, admits the plausibility of denying the existence of witches

Margaret Lucas Cavendish, Duchess of Newcastle, *Plays, Never Before Printed; De Vita et Rebus Gestis Nobilissime Ilustrissimique Principis, Guililemis Ducis Novo-castrensis, commentarii; Poems and Fancies*, 3rd revised edition

Abraham Cowley, *Davideis; The Works of Mr Abraham Cowley*, with *Several Discourses by way of Essays in Prose and Verse*, edited by Thomas Sprat, with biography of Cowley

John Dryden, *Essay of Dramatic Poesy*

Joseph Glanvil, *Plus Ultra*, advocating the experimental method

David Lloyd, *Memoirs of the Lives, Actions, Sufferings, and Deaths of those Noble, Reverend and Excellent Personages that Suffered ... for the Protestant Religion*

Molière, *Amphitryon*

Sir Charles Sedley, *The Mulberry Garden*, drama

Thomas Sprat, *An Account of the Life and Writings of Mr Abraham Cowley*

Edmund Waller, *Poems, Etc.*, 3rd edition

John Wilkins, *An Essay Towards a Real Character, And a Philosophical Language*[577]
Owen Feltham d.
Geffray Mynshul d. (b. 1594?)

Jan — Triple Alliance signed—England, Sweden, and Holland against France
Nathaniel Lee, B.A., Cambridge University
Jan 10 — Sir John Suckling, *Aglaura*, performed at the King's House; the play disparaged in Samuel Pepys' diary for this date
Jan 13 — John Dryden, special court performance of *The Indian Emperour*; Duke and Duchess of Monmouth participate as actors
Feb 4 — Katherine Philips, *Horace*, translation from Pierre Corneille, completed by Sir John Denham, performed; account entered in John Evelyn's *Diary*
Feb 6 — Sir George Etherege, *She Wou'd if She Cou'd*
Feb 21 — John Thurloe, Secretary of State to Oliver Cromwell, d.
Mar 2 — Conventicle Act, limiting non-conformist religious worship, expires; Parliament fails to renew the Act before adjournment
Mar 26 — Samuel Pepys records seeing Sir William Davenant's final play, *The Man is the Master*

---

577. One of the most interesting results of the century's concern for language, science, and reason, the *Essay* attempts nothing less than to create a purely rational language in which the signs (verbal and visual) used to indicate words would have an inherent, logical relation to the idea—or 'notion'—signified. At something over 350 pages, the "essay" is essentially an attempt to codify all human knowledge into a sequence of 10,000 notions, accompanied with modes of writing and pronouncing each. While eminently logical, and at times admirable in its scope and ambition, Wilkins' system had one overriding flaw: there is no indication that anyone, not even Wilkins himself, could ever have mastered it sufficiently to communicate. (Later in the next century, Jonathan Swift would ridicule such 'notional' ideas toward communication in *Gulliver's Travels*).

Mar 31 — Jean de La Fontaine, *Fables Choisies, I*, collection of 124 fables

Spring — Sir John Denham, *Poems and Translations*, published, with revised edition of the 1655 *Coopers Hill*

Apr-May — In two months, Samuel Pepys attends the two licensed theaters thirty times

Apr — Thomas Flatman, miniaturist and poet, inducted as a Fellow of the Royal Society

Apr 7 — Sir William Davenant d.

Apr 9 — Sir William Davenant buried in Westminster

— Thereafter: Richard Flecknoe, *Sr William D'avenant's Voyage to the Other World: With His Adventures in the Poets Elizium. A Poetical Fiction*, published

Apr 13 — John Dryden appointed Poet Laureate, succeeding Sir William Davenant

May 2 — Thomas Shadwell, *The Sullen Lovers*, performed (published 1668)

May 9 — Parliament adjourns at the King's desire

Jun — John Dryden, *An Evening's Love: or, The Mock Astrologer*, performed (published 1671)

Jun 17 — John Dryden granted M.A. by Gilbert Sheldon, Archbishop of Canterbury, at the request of Charles II

Jun 18 — Joseph Glanvill, *Plus Ultra: or, The Progress and Advancement of Knowledge Since the Days of Aristotle*, presented by Henry Oldenburg to the Royal Society

Jun 24 — John Dryden, *Sir Martin Mar-All*, SR; published anonymously later in the year

Jul 23 — Edward Hyde, 1st Earl of Clarendon, *Life*, begun (completed 1672)

Jul 24 — Edward Hyde, 1st Earl of Clarendon, *A Discourse, by Way of Vindication of my self*, begun

Aug — Sir William Temple, Ambassador to the Hague

Oct 8 — John Bunyan's church at Bedford resumes worship services after a five-and-one-half year lapse due to the Conventicle Act

1669

John Milton, two additional issues of *Paradise Lost*
John Aubrey, *The Idea of Education*, begun; with references to John Milton, *Of Education*
Edward Bagshaw, *The Doctrine of the Kingdom and Personal Reign of Christ*, Fifth-Monarchist tract
Roger Boyle, Earl of Orrery, *Parthenissa, Part Six*, published[578]
Gilbert Burnet, *Modest and Free Conference between a Conformist and a Nonconformist*, pro-toleration treatise
Meric Casaubon, *A Letter... to Peter du Moulin...concerning Natural Experimental Philosophy and some Books lately set out about it*, pamphlet critical of atheism in Glanvill and the Royal Society, published at Cambridge
Abraham Cowley, *Collected Works*
[D. Coxe], *A Discourse wherein the Interest of the Patient in Reference to Physick and Physicians is Soberly Debated*, treatise condemning many authorized and unauthorized medical practices of the time
John Donne, *Poems*
Edward Howard, *The British Princes*, heroick (epic) poem
Henry Lawes, *Select Ayres and Dialogues to Sing to the Theorbo-Lute or Basse Viol. The Second Book*, published by John Playford; *Select Ayres and Dialogues to Sing to the Theorbo-Lute or Basse Viol. The Third Book*, published by John Playford; *The Treasury of Music, containing Ayres and*

---

578. Even after six parts, the romance remained incomplete (an occupational hazard for writers of Renaissance romances and epics)

Dialogues. Book I, edited by John Playford

Guy Miège, *A relation of three embassies from his Sacred Majestie Charles Ii, to the Great Duke of Muscovie, the King of Sweden, and the King of Denmark. Performed by the Right Honorable Earl of Carlisle, in the years 1663-1664. Written by an attendant on the embassies*, published

Lodowick Muggleton, *A True Interpretation of the Witch of Endor*, rationalist tract denying witchcraft

John Owen, *Truth and Innocence Vindicated*, response to Samuel Parker, *Discourse of Ecclesiastical Politie...*

Samuel Parker, *A Discourse of Ecclesiastical Politie, wherein the authority of the Civil Magistrate over the Consciences of Subjects in matters of Religion is asserted; the Mischiefs and Inconveniences of Toleration are represented, and all Pretenses pleaded in behalf of Liberty of Conscience are fully answered*

Christoph Peter d., hymnist

Leo van Aitzema d.

Gilbert Burnet, offered and declines two bishoprics while Professor of Divinity at Glasgow University, before he turns thirty

Sir Isaac Newton appointed Lucasian Professor of Mathematics, Cambridge University (until 1701)

Oxford University Press housed in the Sheldonian Theatre

Jan 13 — Henriette, d., daughter of James, Duke of York, and Anne Hyde

Jan 19 — Katherine Philips, *Horace*, translation from Pierre Corneille and completed by Sir John Denham, again performed; account entered in John Evelyn's *Diary*

Feb — Thomas Shadwell, *The Royal Shepherdess*, performed (published 1669)

Feb 15 — John Evelyn records attending yet another performance of Katherine Philips, *Horace*

Feb 17 — Samuel Pepys records an incident of the previous day, in which John Wilmot, 2nd Earl of Rochester, while drunk, boxed the ears of Thomas Killigrew, in the King's presence; Rochester subsequently barred from Court.

Mar — Sir John Denham d.

Mar 23 — Sir John Denham buried, Westminster Abbey

Apr 26 — **Milton receives an additional £5 for sales of *Paradise Lost***

May 2 — John Dryden's son, Erasmus-Henry, b.

May 27 — Thomas Otway enters a commoner at Christ Church, Oxford; withdrew without taking a degree, 1672

May 31 — Samuel Pepys concludes his *Diary*, largely from the fear (unfounded) that he is going blind

Jun 24 — John Dryden, *Tyrannic Love,* performed (published 1670)

Jun 26 — Anthony à Wood notes of himself in his journal that he is "exceeding melancholy and more retir'd, was also at great charge in taking physick and slops, *to drive noises out of his ears*"

Jun 28 (?) — **John Milton, *Accedence Commenc't Grammar, supply'd with sufficient rules, for the use of such as are desirous to attain the Latin tongue with little teaching and their own industry*, announced in the *Mercurius Librarius*; published shortly thereafter**[579]

— Sir William Davenant, *The Man's the Master*, published

Jul 14 — John Dryden, *Tyrannic Love*, SR

Aug 18 — John Dryden appointed Historiographer Royal, succeeding James Howell[580]

Aug 31 — Anne Bradstreet, "As weary pilgrim," composed;

---

579. David P. French assesses the influence of Milton's treatise: "Insofar as I can tell, the *Accedence* had no effect whatever upon either the schoolmasters of the day or the reading public at large....it was apparently never used in schools or even discussed by other grammarians"; the two references identified by William Riley Parker are used solely as means of satirizing Milton "the schoolmaster" (Maurice Kelley, ed. *Complete Prose*, VIII, p. 33).

580. While the appointment augmented Dryden's salary as Poet Laureate, there is no evidence that he wrote anything specifically as Historiographer Royal.

only ms. poetry of Bradstreet's to survive
— Henrietta Maria, Queen Mother, d., in France, of an overdose of sleeping pills
Sep 30 — Henry King, Bishop of Chichester, d. (b. 1592)
Oct 4 — Rembrandt van Rijn d., Amsterdam, Netherlands
Oct 6 — Henry Stubbe, *Legends No History: or, a Specimen of some Animadversions upon the History of the Royal Society ... together with The Plus Ultra reduced to a Non Plus*, preface dated (published 1670), pamphlet; attack on experimental science and on Joseph Glanvill
Oct 9 — Frances Boothby, *Marcelia: or, The Treacherous Friend*, play, licensed for publication (performed earlier in the year?)
Oct 24 — William Prynne d.
Nov 10 — Elizabeth Pepys d., age twenty-nine
Nov 15 — Edgar, Duke of Cambridge, d., son of James, Duke of York, and Anne Hyde
Nov 23 — John Wilmot, 2nd Earl of Rochester, participates in an abortive duel with John Sheffield, Earl of Mulgrave (also known as "Monster All-Pride"); Rochester's subsequent writing becomes increasingly cynical and satirical
Dec 11 — Thomas Traherne, bachelor of divinity, Oxford
Dec 16 — Nathaniel Fiennes, d.

Decade Eight: 1670-1679
The End of the Renaissance in a Decade of Deaths

1670

1670—Second date calculated by Joseph Mede for the end of the world

William Faithorne portrait executed for the first edition of Milton's *History of Britain*

H. C. [Henry Carey], *Female Pre-Eminence or the Dignity and Excellency of that Sex, above the Male, Done into English*, translation of Henry Cornelius Agrippa

Meric Casaubon, *Of Credulity and Incredulity in Things Divine and Spiritual: wherein ... the business of Witches and Witchcraft, against a late Writer, (is) fully argued and Disputed*

Charles Cotton, *A Voyage to Ireland in Burlesque*

John Dryden, *Tyrannic Love* published

John Eachard, *The Grounds and Occasions of the Contempt of the Clergy...Enquired into*, published, advocates reforms in educating the Clergy, while attacking the outmoded language of earlier decades, including George Herbert's

Phineas Fletcher, *A Fathers Testament. Written long since for the benefit of the particular relations of the author*, prose tract with interspersed poetry

Joseph Glanvill, *A Seasonable Recommendation, and Defense of Reason; in the Affairs of Religion*, sermon, philosophical attack on Puritan Enthusiasm

Fulke Greville, 1st Baron Brooke, *The Remains: Poems of Monarchy and Religion*, published

Thomas Hobbes, *Leviathan*, Latin translation, published in

Amsterdam
Molière, *Le Bourgeois Gentilhomme*
Samuel Parker, *Discourse of Ecclesiastical Policy*
Blaise Pascal, *Pensées*
Jean Baptiste Racine, *Bérenice*
John Reynolds, *The Triumphs of Gods Revenge against the Crying and Execrable Sinne of (Wilful and Premeditated) Murther...*, published, "Fifth and Last Edition," prose fiction
Izaak Walton, *Life of George Herbert*
John Amos Comenius d. (b. 1592)
Sir John Mennes d. (b. 1598)
Alexander More d.
Vavasour Powell d.
William Congreve b. (d. 1729)
John Toland b. (d. 1722)
Anglican persecution of Dissenters again grows strong
Hudson's Bay Company, chartered with Prince Rupert as its First Governor
Robert Boyle, living with his sister Lady Ranelagh in London, suffers stroke but continues scientific experimentation in spite of paralysis
Brabazon Aylmer, bookseller at the Three Pigeons, near the Royal Exchange (d. 1709)

Jan 3 — General George Monck, 1st Duke of Albemarle, d.
— Thereafter: *Threnodia*, published, memorial verses by Cambridge students, including Nathaniel Lee
Feb 16 — Henry Stubbe, *A Censure upon Certaine Passages Contained in the history of the Royal Society as being Destructive to the Established Religion and Church of England*, preface dated, pamphlet; published in Oxford
Apr 6 — Leonora Baroni d.
Apr 11 — New Conventicles Act passed with the approval of Charles II, severely limiting rights of non-Conformists to public and private worship

May — Unsuccessful war against the Dutch declared
— Secret Treaty of Dover signed with France[581]

May 8 — Charles Beauclerk b., illegitimate son of Nell Gwyn and Charles II (afterward Duke of St. Albans)

May 16 — Henry Stubbe, *Campanella Revived. Or an Enquiry into the History of the royal Society, Whether the Virtuosi there do not pursue the Projects of Campanella for the reducing of England unto Popery*, preface dated, pamphlet

Jun — Samuel Parker, appointed arch-deacon of Canterbury

Jun 12 — Henrietta ('Minette'), favorite sister of Charles II, leaves England with Charles' signature on a Secret Treaty with Louis XIV of France

Jun 19 — Henrietta ('Minette') d., in Versailles

Jul 1 — Daniel Skinner enrolled at Trinity College, Cambridge; Junior Fellow on Oct 2

Jul 2 — **John Milton, *Paradise Regained*, licensed by Thomas Tomkyns**

— **John Milton, *Samson Agonistes*, licensed by Thomas Tomkyns**

Jul 25 — Izaak Walton presents Anthony à Wood with copies of his lives of John Donne, Sir Henry Wotton, Richard Hooker, and George Herbert

Aug 1 — Edward Hyde, 1st Earl of Clarendon, *Life*, completed through 1660[582]

Aug 8 — Robert Boyle, "New Pneumatical Experiments about Respiration," published, in *Philosophical Transactions of the Royal Society*.

Aug 18 — John Dryden appointed Historiographer Royal and confirmed as Poet Laureate

Aug 30 — Barbara Villiers Palmer, Countess of Castlemaine,

---

581. The treaty included provisions that Charles II would ameliorate the condition of English Catholics and publicly announce his own Catholicism.

582. At approximately 600,000 words, the *Life* was the most ambitious attempt at autobiography in English to that date.

created Duchess of Cleveland[583] by Charles II

Sep 1 — Sir William Temple recalled as Ambassador to The Hague, strengthening rumors of a secret treaty between Charles II and Louis XIV

Sep 10 (or 20) — **John Milton, *Paradise Regained. A Poem in IV Books....The Author John Milton. To wch is added Samson Agonistes, A drammadic Poem, by the same Author John Milton*, SR by Thomas Tomkyns**

Sep 20 — Aphra Behn, *The Forced Marriage; or, The Jealous Bridegroom,* performed at Lincoln's Inn Fields, with Thomas Betterton; Behn's first production

Oct 2 — Daniel Skinner Junior Fellow, Cambridge

Nov (?)— **John Milton, *The History of Britain that part especially now call'd England, from the first traditional beginning continu'd to the Norman conquest. Collected out of the antientest and best authors by John Milton*, published**

— Joseph Glanvill, *A Prefaetory Answer to Mr. Henry Stubbe, the Doctor of Warwick*, pamphlet, published (dated 1671)

— Samuel Parker, installed prebendary of Canterbury

Nov 30 — Henry Stubbe, *A Reply to a Letter of Dr. Henry More (printed in Mr. Ecebolius Glanvill's Praefatory Answer to Hen. Stubbe.) With a Censure upon the Pythagorico-Cabbalistic Philosophy promoted by him. With a Preface against Ecebolius Glanvil; Fellow of the Royal society, and Chaplain to Mr. Rouse of Eaton, late Member of the Rump Parliament*, pamphlet, preface dated (published 1671)

Dec — John Dryden, *The Conquest of Granada by the Spaniards*, Part I, performed, published 1672

— Thomas Shadwell, *The Humorists*, performed (published 1671)

— Charles II signs the public version of the Secret Treaty, without the pro-Catholic clauses

---

583. John Harold Wilson (and other historians and scholars) add the unofficial title of "Mistress Emeritus" (*Court Satires*, p. 20).

1671

William Dolle, copy of Faithorne portrait of Milton executed
John Milton, *History of Britain*, re-issue
Edward Bagshaw, *The Life and Death of Mr. Vavasour Powell*
William Cartwright, *November, or, Signal Days*
Samuel Collins, *The Present State of Russia, in a letter to a friend at London; written by an eminent person residing at the great Tsars court at Mosco for the space of nine years*, published, report of the English physician to Tsar Alexis (1660-1669)
John Crowne, *Juliana*, performed
Joseph Glanvill *Philosophia Pia: or, a Discourse of the religious Temper and Tendencies of the Experimental Philosophy, which is profest by the Royal Society*, links experimental science with Christianity
George Herbert, *A Priest to the Temple*, 2nd edition, by Barnabas Oley
William Hicks, *Oxford Jests*, jestbook, so popular as to remain in print until 1740
Henry King, Bishop of Chichester, *The Psalms of David, from the New Translation of the Bible Turned into Meter*, published
Henry More, *Enchiridion metaphysicum: sive, de rebus incorporeis succincta & lucenta dissertatio. Pars prima: de exsistentia & natura rerum, incorporearum, in genere*, published (portions later translated as part of Joseph Glanvil,

Saducismus Triumphatus)
Samuel Parker, *A Defense and Continuation of the Ecclesiastical Politie*, published
John Playford, *Playford's Psalter*
Elizabeth Polwhele, *The Frolicks, or the Lawyer Cheated*
William Sermon, *The Ladies Companion, or The English Midwife*, manual for housekeeping, etc.
Thomas Shadwell, *The Humorists*, published
Meric Casauson d. (b. 1599)

Jan — John Dryden, *The Conquest of Granada by the Spaniards*, Part II, performed (published 1672)
— Elkanah Settle, *Cambises*, first play produced (published 1671)
Feb 9 — John Evelyn records attending a performance of John Dryden, *The Siege (Conquest) of Granada*
— Catherine, b. to James, Duke of York, and Anne Hyde; the tenth child born to the couple and fourth still living
Feb 13 — John Dryden, *An Evening's Love: or, The Mock Astrologer*, published
Feb 14 — Joseph Glanvill, *A Further Discovery of Mr. Stubbe, in a Brief Reply to His Last Pamphlet against Joseph Glanvill*, pamphlet dated, including references to Sir Francis Bacon as authority
— Thereafter: Henry Stubbe, *The Lord Bacons Relation to the Sweating-Sickness Examined, in Reply to George Thompson, Pretender in Physick and Chymystry. Together with a Defence of Phlebotomy .... And a Reply, by way of Preface to the Calumnies of Ecebolius Glanvile*, pamphlet; alternate title: *A Bacon-face No Beauty: or, a reply to George Thompson*, etc.
Feb 20 — John Dryden, *The Conquest of Granada by the Spaniards*, SR
Feb 24 — Aphra Behn, *The Amorous Prince*, performed at Lincoln's Inn Fields (published 1671
Mar — Edward Howard, *The Six Days' Adventure; or The New*

Utopia, performed; prologues by Aphra Behn and Edward Ravenscroft

— William Wycherley, *Love in a Wood*, produced; Wycherley's first play

Mar 31 — Anne Hyde, Duchess of York, d., after receiving Catholic Last Rites

May — Deadline for expulsion of all Jesuits and priests from England as demanded by Parliament, approved by Charles II

Jul 13 — Anthony à Wood, printers begin setting type for *Historia Et Antiquitates Universitatis Oxoniensis*

Aug 1 — Anthony à Wood, first completed sheets of his book printed and prepared for proofreading

Sep 4 — Edward Southwell b.

Sep 29 — Sir Thomas Browne knighted by Charles II during a Royal progress to Norwich; the Mayor, Thomas Thacker, declined the knighthood in lieu of the most eminent person in the city, the author of *Religio Medici*

Oct 18 — John Evelyn, *Diary*, records his meeting with an old friend and correspondent in Norwich, Sir Thomas Browne; Evelyn examines many of Browne's collections of rarities and curiosities

Nov 6 — Colley Cibber b. (d. 1757)

Nov 12 — Sir Thomas Fairfax d.

By Nov 22 — **John Milton, *Paradise Regained* and *Samson Agonistes*, published**

Dec 5 — Catherine d., daughter of James, Duke of York and Anne Hyde

Dec 7 — George Villiers, 2nd Duke of Buckingham, *The Rehearsal*, dramatic farce, performed; attacks John Dryden in the character of Mr. *Bayes*

Dec 25 — James Beauclerk b., illegitimage son of Charles II and Nell Gwynn

1672

A. B. [Aphra Behn?], *The Covent Garden Drollery; or a Collection of all the Choice Songs, Poems, Prologues, and Epilogues, (Sung and Spoken at Courts and Theaters) never in print before. Written by the refined'st Witts of the Age. And Collected by A. B.*, published

Robert Boyle, *New Experiments about the Relation between Air and the Flamma Vitalis of Animals*

John Bramhall, Bishop of Derry, *Vindication of himself and the Episcopal Clergy from the Presbyterian Charge of Popery*, published, with Samuel Parker, *A Preface Shewing what grounds there are of Fears and Jealousies of Popery* prefixed

Sir Thomas Browne, *Pseudo-doxia Epidemica*, 6th edition, the last corrected and augmented by Browne

John Crowne, *The History of Charles the Eighth of France*, performed

Henry Danvers, *Theopolis, or the City of God*

John Gale, *Theophile*

Joseph Glanvill, *Earnest Invitation to the Sacrament of the Lords Supper*, published (10 editions by 1695

Dr. Nathaniel Hodges, *Loimologia, or an Historical Account of the Plague in London in 1665*, published

Sir William Temple, *An Essay upon the Original and Nature of Government*, written

William Wycherley, *The Country Wife* (possibly written as late as 1674)

Archee Armstrong d., former jester to James I and Charles I
Abiezel Coppe d.
Edward Johnson d. (b. 1598)
Sir Roger Twysdend d. (b. 1597)
Sir Richard Steele b. (d. 1729)
John Bunyan released from prison after sixteen years

Early — William Wycherley, *The Gentleman Dancing Master*, produced, with a six-day stage run

Jan — Thomas Shadwell, *The Miser*, drama, adapted from Molière, performed (published 1672)

Jan 18 — Sir Isaac Newton, letter to Henry Oldenburg, announcing Newton's discovery of the nature of light

Jan 21 — John Bunyan elected Pastor (Elder) of the Bedford Church

Jan 25 — The Theatre Royal in Drury Lane destroyed by fire

Feb 6 — Sir Isaac Newton, *The New Theory about Light and Colors*, presented before the Royal Society

Feb 7 — John Dryden, *The Conquest of Granada* in print; with preface, *Of Heroic Plays*

Feb 19 — Sir Isaac Newton, *The New Theory about Light and Colors*, published in the *Philosophical Transactions of the Royal Society*

Mar 15 — Charles II, Declaration of Indulgences, issued, suspending penal laws regarding religion, offering licenses for worship in public to Protestant Nonconformists, and granting Catholics the right to worship in private homes.

— New Conventicles Act suspended by the passage of the Declaration of Indulgences

Mar 27 — John Bunyan, *A Defense of the Doctrine of Justification by Faith in Jesus Christ...*, dated

Apr 6 — Charles II declares war on the Dutch United Provinces; Third Anglo-Dutch War

— William of Orange emerges as key continental Protestant leader

Apr 7 — Louis XIV of France declares war on the United

Provinces, the opening movement of his Grand Design

Apr/May — John Dryden, *Marriage A-la-Mode*, performed (published 1673)

May (?)— **John Milton, *Joannis Miltoni Angli, Artis Logicæ Plenior Institutio, ad Petri Rami Methodum concinata. Adjects est Praxis Analytica and P. Rami vita* (A Fuller Course in the Art of Logic Conformed to the Method of Peter Ramus), published; presumably composed much earlier**[584]

May 1 — Joseph Addison b. (d. 1719)

May 8—Charles Beauclerk b., illegitimate son of Charles II and Nell Gwynn (afterwards 1st Duke of St.Albans; d. 1726)

— John Bunyan and others petition the King for consideration of their imprisonment

May 9 — John Bunyan granted a licence to preach under the Declaration of Indulgences

May 29 — First encounter of the English fleet under Lord High Admiral James, Duke of York (afterward James II) with the Dutch fleet

Jun — The Exchequer halts payments, leading to bankruptcies and financial crises

Jul — John Dryden, special performance of *Secret Love*, performed by women only

— Edward Ravenscroft, *The Citizen Turned Gentleman*, performed at Dorset Garden Theater, his first play (reissued 1675 as *Mamamouchi*)

— Charles, illegitimate son of Louise de Kéroualle and Charles II b. (afterward Duke of Richmond)

Jul 8 — William III, Stadtholder of Orange, proclaimed Captain-

---

584. Walter J. Ong writes: "Milton's *Logic* was read by some students at Harvard in the late seventeenth and early eighteenth century and was used in England at Rathmell Academy, founded in 1669. I know of no other indications of its academic use, and the fact that after its first edition of 1672 (1673) it was never reprinted except as part of a collection of Milton's works makes it unlikely that it had any widespread effective currency" (Maurice Kelley, ed., *Complete Prose*, VIII, p. 169).

and Admiral-General of the United Provinces for life

Jul 11 — Sir Isaac Newton, letter to Henry Oldenburg, outlining the experimental method of science and the science of colors

Aug — Henry Neville, *The Fatal Jealousy*, performed

Aug 19 — Johann and Cornelius de Witt, chief opponents of William III's rule in the United Provinces, assassinated by a mob

Sep — Andrew Marvell, *The Rehearsal Transpros'd: Or Animadversions upon a late Book intituled A Preface Shewing what Grounds there are of Fears and Jealousies of Popery*, 500-page treatise, unlicensed, anonymous; defense of toleration and attack on Samuel Parker, *Discourse of Ecclesiastical Policy*

— Thereafter: Henry Stubbe, *Rosemary & Bayes: or, An Animadversion upon a Treatise Called the Rehearsal Transpros'd*, response to Marvell's anonymous treatise

Sep 10 — *Dirt Wip'd Off: or a manifest Discovery of the Gross Ignorance, Erroneousness, and most Unchristian and Wicked Spirit of one John Bunyan, Lay-Preacher in Bedford*, response to Bunyan's *Doctrine of justification by Faith...* and personal attack on Bunyan

Sep 13 — John Bunyan officially pardoned (although probably released from jail some months earlier)

Sep 16 — Anne Dudley Bradstreet d., North Andover, Massachusetts

Nov — John Dryden, *The Assignation*, performed (published 1673)

— Benjamin Woodroffe, letter to Theophilus Hastings, 7th Earl of Huntingdon, indicating that attempts to restrict publication and sales of *The Rehearsal Transpros'd* have failed

— Sir Orlando Bridgeman removed from office; Thomas Traherne accompanies the family to Teddington

— Anthony Ashley Cooper, Earl of Shaftesbury, succeeds Bridgeman as Lord Keeper

Nov 1 — Peter Sterry, Cambridge Platonist, d.

Nov 19 — John Wilkins, Bishop of Chester, d.

Nov 21 — Sir William Davenant, *The Works of Sr William D'avenant, K^t Consisting of Those Which Were Formerly Printed, and Those Which He Design'd for the Press: Now Published Out of the Authors Original Copies*, in folio, publication overseen by Lady Mary Davenant, frontispiece engraved by William Faithorne

Nov 30 — John Evelyn elected Secretary of the Royal Society

Dec — **Thomas Shadwell, *Epson Wells*, comedy; includes a Miltonic argument for divorce based on incompatibility**[585]

Dec 12 — John Wilkins, Bishop of Chester and founding member of the Royal Society, buried; funeral sermon preached by William Lloyd

---

585. Christopher Hill, *Milton and the English Revolution*, p. 132.

1673

Daniel Skinner, acts as Milton's amanuensis (as early as 1670?)
John Milton, *Art of Logic* **re-issued**
[Richard Allestree?], *The Ladies' Calling*
Robert Barclay, *A Catechism and Confession of Faith*
A Common Place-Book Out of the Rehearsal Transpros'd, published, attacking Marvell
[Joseph Glanvill?], *The Character of a Coffee-House, with the Symptoms of a Town-Wit*, satirical pamphlet, anonymous
Susanna Hopton, *Daily Devotions*, anthology, with materials by Thomas Traherne (see below)
Richard Leigh, *The Transproser Rehears'd*, satire of Marvel's style and argument
Bathsua Makin, *An Essay to Revive the Antient Education of Gentle women*, in conjunction with which Makin opened one of the first schools for women[586]
Molière, *Malade Imaginaire*
S. N. *The Loyal garland, containing choice songs and sonnets of our late unhappy revolutions*, anthology of lyrics and ballads, published
Jean Baptiste Racine, *Mithridate*
Sir William Temple, *Observations upon the United Provinces of the Netherlands*

---

586. Frances Teague notes that the *Essay* served in part as an advertisement to potential students and their parents for Makin's school (Katharina Wilson and Frank J. Warnke, *Women Writers*, p. 291).

Thomas Traherne, *Daily Devotions, Consisting of Thanksgivings, Confessions and Prayers*, by "an Humble Penitent," prepared by Susanna Hopton (see above)

William Wycherley, *The Country Wife*, produced

Joseph Caryl d.

Sir Henry Herbert d.; brother to Edward Herbert and George Herbert, and Master of Revels under James I and Charles II[587]

Francis Higginson d.

Leonard Philaras d.

Moll Davis bears Charles II an illegitimate daughter, Mary, who later marries the Earl of Derwentwater

Feb — Aphra Behn, *The Dutch Lover*, comedy, performed at Dorset Garden Theater; Behn's third play

— Elizabeth Hooten d., Port Royal, Jamaica

Feb 4 — Charles II announces to Parliament his intent to stand by the Declaration of Indulgences

Feb 10 — Commons resolves that no penal statutes may be lifted except by an Act of Parliament, contravening Charles' Declaration

Feb 17 — Molière d.[588]

Feb 24 — Robert Boyle, "A New Experiment concerning an Effect of the Varying Weight of the Atmosphere upon some Bodies in the Water; Suggesting a Conjecture, that the very Alterations of the Air, in point of Weight, may have Considerable Operations, even upon Men's Sickness or Health," published, in *Philosophical Transactions of the*

---

587. His post was abolished during the Commonwealth, but he was restored to it at the Restoration.

588. Abel Boyer's *The Wise and Ingenious Companion*, a jestbook published in 1700, includes the following on the death of Molière: "The famous Molière being dead, many Poetasters writ Epitaphs upon him. One of them went one Day and presented one of his own making to a Prince much renowned for his Wit. 'Would to God,' said the Prince, receiving the Epitaph, 'that Molière presented me yours" (Zall, *Nest*, p. 258-259).

Royal Society

Mar — Edward Ravenscroft, *The Careless Lovers*, performed (published 1673)

Mar 8 — Charles II officially withdraws the Declaration of Indulgences

Mar 29 — Test Act ("An Act for preventing dangers that may happen by Popish Recusants") passed, making it impossible for Catholics and Puritan extremists or Dissenters to hold public office

Spring — John Dryden, *Marriage A-la-Mode*, and *The Assignation*, published

— **Samuel Parker, Bishop of Oxford, *A Reproof to the Rehearsal Transpros'd*, abusive attack on Andrew Marvell and John Milton**

May/Jun — John Dryden, *Amboyna*, anti-Dutch tragedy, performed (published 1673)

Between Mar 13 and May 6 — **John Milton, *Of True Religion, Hæresie, Schism, Toleration; and what best means may be used against the Growth of Popery, The Author J. M.*, written; Milton's final religious tract, which denies toleration to Papists on the grounds that they represent a political, not a religious, movement; all other religious movements must be tolerated**

May 1 — Andrew Marvell, *The Rehearsal Transpros'd: The Second Part*, licensed[589]

May 3 — Andrew Marvell, letter to Sir Edward Harley, indicating his intention to answer attacks on *The Rehearsal Transpros'd*

Jun — Thomas Duffett (formerly a milliner), *The Spanish Rogue*, performed at Lincoln Inn's Fields (published 1674)

— James, Duke of York, a Catholic, resigns his public offices, including his position as Lord High Admiral, because of the Test Act

---

589. The continuation of *The Rehearsal Transpros'd* was licensed but was not registered with the Stationers' Company or entered in the Term Catalogue.

— Thereafter: Samuel Pepys appointed to the post of Secretary to the Office of the Lord High Admiral of England, head of naval administration

Jun 15 — Henry Vaughan, letter to his cousin, John Aubrey, noting that *Thalia Rediviva* is ready for printing; the book will not appear until 1678

Jul — Elkanah Settle, *The Empress of Morocco*, drama, performed; published with a dedication attacking John Dryden[590]

— Thereafter: John Dryden, Thomas Shadwell, and John Crowne, *Notes and Observations upon the Empress of Morocco*

Jul 22 — Sir William Temple, *An Essay upon the Advancement of Trade in Ireland*, written to the Earl of Essex, Lord Lieutenant of Ireland

Jul 23 — Louise Keroualle, mistress to Charles II, created Duchess of Portsmouth

Sep 20 — James, Duke of York, m. by proxy, in Modina, Mary Beatrice d'Este of Modina, a Catholic, alienating many of his English supporters

Nov — Thomas Traherne, *Roman Forgeries*, published; dedicated to Sir Orlando Bridgeman; published anonymously "by a Faithful Son of the Church of England"

— Samuel Pepys elected M.P. for Castle Rising, Norfolk

Nov 1 — **Thomas Agar, Milton's brother-in-law, d. (b. 1597?)**

Nov 3 — J. G. [Joseph Glanvill?], letter to Andrew Marvel: "If thou darest publish any lie or libel against Dr. Parker, by the Eternal God I will cut thy throat"[591]

— Thereafter: Andrew Marvel, *The Rehearsal Transpros'd: The Second Part. Occasioned by Two Letters: The First Printed, by a nameless Author, Intituled, A Reproof, &c. The*

---

590. *The Empress of Morocco* also has the distinction of being regarded as the first play published with engraved illustrations, an indication of the increasing importance of drama as literature.

591. Jackson I. Cope, *Joseph Glanvill*, p. 34.

Second Letter left for me at a Friends House, Dated Nov. 3. 1673. Subscribed J. G. and concluding with the words; If thou darest to Print or Publish any Lie or Libel against Doctor Parker, By the Eternal God I will cut thy Throat, published

— Thereafter: Joseph Glanvill, *An Apology and Advice for Some of the Clergy, Who Suffer Under False, and Scandalous Reports Written on the Occasion of the Second Part of the Rehearsal Transpros'd"*

Nov 21 — James, Duke of York, m. Mary Beatrice d'Este of Modena, adopted daughter of the King of France; in London

Before Nov 24 — **John Milton, *Poems, &c., upon Several Occasions, both English and Latin, etc., composed at several times. With a small Tractate of Education to Mr. Hartlib*, published (even though all copies of the 1645 edition have not yet sold.)**

Dec — Elkanah Settle, *The Empress of Morocco*, performed at Drury Lane Theater, with elaborate prologue and epilogue

Dec 15 — Margaret Lucas Cavendish, Duchess of Newcastle d.

1674

Milton referred to as a "great agent of libertinism"[592]
Christopher Milton serves as a M.P. (also 1676 and 1679)
Robert Barclay, *The Anarchy of the Ranters*, Quaker treatise
Nicholas Boileau, *Le Lutrin; Art Poétique*
Robert Boyle, *Suspicions about some hidden Qualities in the Air*
Thomas Flatman, *Poems*, published (4 augmented editions by 1688)
Elkanah Settle, *Notes and Observations on the Empress of Morocco Revised*, response to John Dryden, Thomas Shadwell, and John Crowne
Samuel Vincent, *The Young Gallants' Academy*
William Wycherley, *The Plain Dealer*, stages at Lincoln's Inn
Nicholas Rowe b. (d. 1718), Poet-Laureate and first biographer of William Shakespeare
Elizabeth Singer b.
Isaac Watts b. (d. 1748), hymnist
Marriage proposed between William of Orange and Princess Mary, first cousins and grandchildren of King James I

Jan 7 — Margaret Lucas Cavendish, Duchess of Newcastle, buried
Jan 29 — Sir William Temple, *Upon the Excesses of Grief*, written to the Countess of Essex
Feb 9/19 — Peace of Westminster signed, concluding the Anglo-

---

592. Cited in Christopher Hill, *Milton and the English Revolution*, p. 109.

Dutch War, Parliament having refused to vote Charles II further monies to continue hostilities

Feb 28 — Elkanah Settle m. Mary Warner

Mar 25 — The King's Company opens new theater in Drury Lane

— Mary Lee m. George Chudleigh (later 3rd Baron Chudleigh)[593]

Spring — Mary Beatrice of Modena suffers her first of eight miscarriages

Apr — Thomas Shadwell, *The Tempest*, performed (published 1674)

Apr 17 — **John Dryden's dramatization in rhymed couplets of *Paradise Lost*, *The State of Innocence and the Fall of Man*, registered**[594]

Apr 23 — John Dryden, revival of *Marriage a la Mode*

May — Nathaniel Lee, *The Tragedy of Nero*, produced

May 26 (?)— **John Milton, *Joannis Miltoni Angli Epistolarum Familiarium liber unus: quibus accesserunt ejusdem jam olim in collegio adolescentis prolusiones quaedam oratoriæ* (Familiar Letters), identified as being by *Joannes Miltonus, Anglus*, echoing his quarter-century old controversy with Salmasius and reminding his readership of his identity; published by Brabazon Aylmer**

— **John Milton, *Prolusions* (College exercises—see issue above)**

Jul (?)— **John Milton, *A Declaration, or Letters Patents of the Election of this present King of Poland, John the Third (John Sobieski, King of Poland), Elected on the 22ᵈ of May last past, Anno Dom. 1674....*, translated by Milton, published anonymously by Brabazon Aylmer; Milton's**

---

593. Four of the six children of the marriage died in infancy.

594. Dryden apparently undertook the adaptation with Milton's foreknowledge and, if not blessing, at least tacit permission. Winn finds the unstaged opera among Dryden's most interesting works: "The very idea was bold, not because Paradise Lost had achieved the status of a classic in the seven years since its first publication, but because Dryden was claiming such status for it by basing an opera upon it." (*John Dryden*, p. 265)

last publication during his lifetime
Jun 25 — Sir Orlando Bridgeman, former lord Keeper of the Seal, d., in retirement in Teddington
Jul 3 — Sir Orlando Bridgeman buried, in Teddington
Jul 6 (?)— **John Milton, *Paradise Lost. A Poem in Twelve Books. The Author John Milton. The Second Edition Revised and Augmented by the Same Author*, with dedicatory poem by Andrew Marvell**
Jul 14 — James Scott, Duke of Monmouth, appointed Chancellor of Cambridge University
Jul 20 (?)— **Milton makes oral will; his health declining seriously**
Jul 27 — Anthony à Wood, *Historia et Antiquitates Universitatis Oxoniensis* (History and Antiquities of Oxford University), published, Latin rendition of Wood's history of the university: "My book published at Oxon. Full of base things put in by Dr. John Fell to please his partial humor and undo the author...."[595]
Sep 27 — Thomas Traherne makes his will
Oct 10 — Thomas Traherne buried beneath the reading desk, Teddington Church
Oct 15 — Robert Herrick buried (b. 1591), at Dean Prior
Nov — Elkanah Settle, *Love and Revenge,* drama, performed (published 1675)
Nov 8 — **John Milton, poet, d., in Bunhill, London**
Nov 12 — **Milton buried near his father at St. Giles, Cripplegate, London**
Dec — *Calysto*, masque, performed at Court by ladies only, with Princess Mary taking the title role
Dec 19 — Edward Hyde, 1st Earl of Clarendon, former Lord Chancellor of England, d. in Rouen, still an exile from England[596]

---

595. Lwellyn Powys, *Life & Times*, p. 178.

596. Hyde, the grandfather of Queen Mary II and Queen Anne, was buried in Westminster Abbey.

1675

Bishop Lancelot Andrewes, *Rev. Patris Lanc. Andrewes episc. Winton: Preces privatæ, Graece & Latine*, published (complete)

John Bunyan, *Light for Them that Sit in Darkness...*, published

Margaret Lucas Cavendish, Duchess of Newcastle, *Life of the thrice Noble born, High and Puissant Prince William Cavendishe, Duke, Marquis, and Earl of Newcastle*, 2nd edition

John Crowne, *Andromache*, performed; *The Countrey Wit*, performed and published

Sir Francis Fane, *Love in the Dark*, published

Robert Ferguson, *The Interest of Reason in Religion; with the Import & Use of Scripture-Metaphor*, counters attacks by Joseph Glanvill and others on Non-Conformists

René Le Bossu, *Traité du poème épique*, French publication, treatise on Epic theory

Andrew Marvell, *The mock Speech from the Throne*, satire, published anonymously

Nathaniel Lee, *The Tragedy of Nero*, tragedy in heroic couplets, published

Stopford, J., *Pagano-Papismus: or, an exact parallel between Rome-Pagan and Rome-Christian in their Doctrines and Ceremonies*, anti-Papist treatise

Peter Sterry, *A Discourse of the Freedom of the Will*

Thomas Traherne, *Christian Ethicks*

Hannah Woolley, *The Gentlewomans Companion, or a Guide*

to the Female Sex...With Letters and Discourses upon all occasions, Whereunto is added, a Guide for Cook-maids, Dairy-maids, Chamber-maids, and all others that go to service*, published

William Wycherley, *The Country Wife*, performed and published

Jan Vermeer d.

Charles II announces to Parliament that he is £4,000,000 in debt for public and private expenses

Parliament attempts to close all coffeehouses; the order rescinded within weeks[597]

Jan — Catherine Laura b., to James, Duke of York and Mary of Modena

Jan 25 — Sir Isaac Newton, letter to Henry Oldenburg, *An Hypothesis Explaining the Properties of Light Discoursed of in My Several Papers*

Feb — Thomas Shadwell, *Psyche*, performed (published 1675)

Apr — Nathaniel Lee, *Sophonisba*, performed (published 1676)

Apr 3 — William III, Prince of Orange, ill with smallpox, the same disease that killed his parents

Apr 22 — Sir Robert Southwell, *On Water*, lecture before the Royal Society

Apr 29 — John Evelyn, *Of Earth and Vegetation*, lecture before the Royal Society

May — **Edward Philips, *Theatrum Poetarum: or, a Complete Collection of the Poets*, with some material possibly by Milton**

— Elkanah Settle, *The Conquest of China*, drama, produced (published 1676)

May 18 — **John Aubrey, letter to Anthony Wood, with infor-**

---

[597]/ Initially, the government feared that the gossip endemic to the coffee houses, especially false reports of military actions, might work against the war with the Netherlands; gradually the government realized that it could in fact use the houses and manipulate the gossip for its own advantage.

mation concerning Milton's biography

Jun — Thomas Shadwell, *The Libertine*, performed (published 1676)

Jun 19 — John Crowne, Prologue to *Calisto*, entered in the Term Catalogue; thereafter, *Calisto*, performed

June 25 — The cornerstone is laid for Sir Christopher Wren's new St. Paul's Cathedral, nearly nine years after the older edifice was destroyed in The Great Fire

Jul — Ben Jonson, revival of *Every Man out of his Humour*

Jul 28 — Bulstrode Whitelock d.

(?)— **Daniel Skinner gives Symon Heere the manuscript copy of *De Doctrina Christiana* and Milton's Letters of State; Heere delivers them to Daniel Elsevier in the Netherlands. The manuscript eventually reaches Phillipus van Limborch, a scholar in Amsterdam**

Sep — Thomas Otway, *Alcibiades*, produced, Otway's first play (published 1675)[598]

Oct — Catherine, daughter of James, Duke of York, and Mary of Modina, d.

Nov 29 — John Dryden, *Aureng-Zebe*, SR; Dryden's last rhymed play

Dec 9 — Sir Isaac Newton, *An Hypothesis Touching on the Theory of Light and Color*, presented to the Royal Society

---

598. Otway first attempted a career as an actor, following his acquaintance with Aphra Behn, who promised him a role in one of her plays. His acting skills left much to be desired—"he fluffed his lines and ruined the play"—so he turned to writing instead (Urdang, *Lives of the Stuart Age*).

1676

William Cavendish, Duke of Newcastle, compiler, *Letters and Poems in Honour of the Incomparable Princess Margaret, Dutchess of Newcastle*, published; memorial volume

Lady Anne Clifford, *Diary* (published 1923)

Charles Cotton, *The Compleat Angler, Part II*, written in ten days

John Dryden, *Mac Flecknoe*, written and circulating in manuscript but not published

Joseph Glanvill, *Essays on Several Important Subjects in Philosophy and Religion; and thereafter, Seasonable Reflections and Discourses In Order to the Conviction, & Cure of the Scoffing, & Infidelity of a Degenerate Age*, four sermons, published

Great News from the Barbadoes, or, A True and faithful account of the grand conspiracy of the Negroes against the English and the happy discovery of the same, pamphlet

Thomas Hobbes, *Thucydides*, 2nd edition[599]; *Leviathan*, Latin edition published in London

Hortense Mancini, Duchess of Mazarin, *Memoirs*, published

Andrew Marvell, *Mr. Smirke, or the Divine in Mode*, prose satire

William Sewell, translator, *The Doctrine of Devils proved to be the grand apostacy of these later Times*, treatise attacking belief in witchcraft

Benjamin Thompson, *New Englands Crisis*, verse history,

---

599. The third edition, "Corrected and Amended," appeared in 1723.

published in London as *Sad and Deplorable Newes from New England*

Richard Wiseman, *Severall Chiururgicall Treatises*[600]

Lady Anne Clifford d. (b. 1590)[601]

Carlo Dati d.

Gerard Winstanley d.

Isabella, daughter of James, Duke of York, b. (d. 1681)

Sir James Thornhill b. (d. 1721), English Baroque painter

Judge Rainsford regrets not being able to sentence Lodowick Muggleton to death by burning[602]

Sir Godfrey Kneller, trained in Amsterdam by a pupil of Rembrandt, arrives in England and begins a career as the leading Court portrait painter after Sir Peter Lely

Leibnitz develops differential calculus

Lodowick Muggleton, *A Looking Glass for George Fox, the Quaker, and other Quakers, wherein they may See Themselves to be Right Devils* (written during the Interregnum), burned

---

600. Thomas Keith notes that the reputation of physicians and surgeons was—justifiably—so low during the century that Wiseman's book was commonly referred to as *Wiseman's Book of Martyrs* (*Religion*, 9). Throughout the seventeenth-century, medical knowledge amounted to little more than attempts to treat symptoms, most frequently through applications of humoral theories of physiology, with a consequent emphasis on bleeding, purging, examination of urine, and other largely useless (when not overtly dangerous) treatments.

601. Lady Ann Clifford, Amelia Lanyer's patron, first married Richard Sackville, Earl of Dorset, in 1609; then Philip, Earl of Montgomery and Pembroke, in 1630. Following his death in 1649, she remained a widow and enjoyed her accumulated wealth as Clifford heiress and dowager countess of Dorset, Montgomery and Pembroke by becoming one of the key patrons of literature and books. Antonia Fraser, *The Weaker Vessel*, pp. 95-97.

602. A suggestion as to how serious Milton's situation might have been in his final years, particularly considering his radical religious views. See Christopher Hill, *Milton and the English Revolution*, p. 217. The issue of how extensively radical Milton's beliefs were, and the relationship of *Paradise Lost* and *De Doctrina Christiana* to Seventeenth-Century radical movements is still hotly debated among critics.

Jan — Elizabeth Carey, Viscountess Mordaunt, records the posthumous birth of George Mordaunt in her *Diary* (published 1856)

— Nathaniel Lee, *Gloriana* performed (published 1676)

Feb — **Sir Peter Wentworth's will clears probate, leaving £50 to Marchamont Needham and £100 to John Milton**

Feb 17 — John Dryden, *Aureng-Zebe*, advertised in the *Gazette*

Mar 11 — Sir George Etherege, *The Man of Mode; or, Sir Fopling Flutter*, acted before Charles II at the Duke's Theater; subsequently published

Mar 30 — James, Duke of York, attends Anglican chapel for the last time; thereafter his Catholic leanings become increasingly apparent

May — Thomas Shadwell, *The Virtuoso*, performed, attack on Dryden included in the preface (published 1676)

May 29 — John Dryden, *Aureng-Zebe*, performed at Court

Jun — Elkanah Settle, *Ibrahim*, drama, produced (published 1677)

Jun 8 — Thomas Otway, *Don Carlos*, tragedy in rhymed couplets, published (1676)

Jun 27 — John Wilmot, 2nd Earl of Rochester, said to be about to stand trial for implication in a murder; Rochester 'absconds' and is pardoned by Charles II when he returns to Court

Jul — Aphra Behn, *Abdelazer*, performed at Dorset Garden Theater, tragedy (published 1677)[603]

Aug 26 — Samuel Pepys and John Evelyn dine with Captain Baker, who discusses his attempts to discover a Northwest Passage

Sep — Aphra Behn, *The Town Fopp; or Sir Timothy Tawdrey*, performed (published 1677)

— Thomas D'Urfey, *The Siege of Memphis*, produced, first play (published 1676)

---

603. Adapted by Behn from an earlier, anonymous play, *Lust's Dominion, or, the Lacivious Queen*. As a brief glance at titles will suggest, one staple of the Restoration stage was adaptation of older plays, occasionally laying the authors open to charges of plagiarism.

— Edward Ravenscroft, *The Wrangling Lovers*, performed (published 1677)

Before Oct 18 — **John Milton, *Letters of State* published as *Literæ Pseudo-Senatus Anglicani, Cromwellii*; 136 documents published in Amsterdam**

Nov — Tom D'Urfey, *Madam Fickle*, produced, comedy (published 1677); D'Urfey becomes a favorite entertainer and companion to Charles II[604]

— Thomas D'Urfey, *The Fool Turn'd Critick*, performed (published 1678)

Dec — Thomas Otway, *Titus and Berenice*, performed (published 1677)

— Elkanah Settle, *Pastor Fido*, drama, produced (published 1677)

— Edward Benlowes d.

Dec 11 — William Wycherley, *The Plain Dealer*

Dec 25 — William Cavendish, 1st Duke of Newcastle d.

---

604. A collection of his songs, popular with the Court and with the common people, appeared in 1719 as *Wit and Mirth: or Pills to Purge Melancholy*.

1677

John Milton, *The History of Britain*, re-issue
John Banks, *The Rival Kings*, published, Banks' first play
John Cleveland, *Clievelandi Vindiciæ; or, Clieveland's Genuine Poems, Orations, Epistles, &c. Purged from the many False & Spurious Ones Which had usurped his Name...*, edited by Bishop Lake and S. Drake
John Crowne, *The Destruction of Jerusalem, Parts I and II*, performed
John Dryden, *All for Love; The State of Innocence and the Fall of Man* published; *Heads of an Answer to Rymer* (unpublished)
William Hickes, *Coffee-House Jests*, published
Andrew Marvell, *Account of the Growth of Popery and Arbitrary Government in England*, published anonymously, reiterating Milton's arguments
John Oldham, *A Dityrambic*
Jean Baptiste Racine, *Phèdre*
Thomas Rymer, *Tragedies of the Last Age Consider'd*
Sir Charles Sedley, *Anthony and Cleopatra*, drama; *Bellamira*, drama
Thomas Scott, *The Unhappy Kindness*, performed, with epilogue by Joseph Haynes, spoken by an actor seated on an ass[605]

---

605. Haynes' epilogue began: "Wherefore by th' Example of Fam'd Doggett, my Brother,/To shew our Stage has Asses on't as well as t'other; / Thus mounted I'm come..." Autrey Wiley notes that the applause was so great that it took the actor speaking the Epilogue almost an hour to

Benedict [Baruch] Spinoza, *Ethics*
Nahum Tate, *Poems*, first publications
John Webster, *The Displaying of Supposed Witchcraft*[606]
Henry Oldenburg d. (?)
Gilbert Sheldon, Archbishop of Canterbury, d.
William Sancroft consecrated Archbishop of Canterbury
Jacob Tonson begins his career as a publisher
Edward Phillips serves as tutor to Elizabeth Bennett, daughter of Henry Bennet, 1st Earl of Arlington (to 1679?)

Feb (?)— [Aphra Behn], *The Debauchee*, performed, published
— **John Dryden, *The State of Innocence and the Fall of Man*, based on John Milton, *Paradise Lost*, published; never produced**
— John Dryden, *The Author's Apology for Heroic Poetry and Poetic License*, preface to *The State of Innocence*
— Anthony Ashley Cooper, Earl of Shaftesbury, committed to the Tower of London for a year
Feb 21 — Baruch [Benedict] Spinoza d.
Mar — Aphra Behn, *The Rover, or the Banished Cavaliers*, performed; published anonymously, two issues, 1677; third issue, with Behn's name on the title-page
Mar 17 — Nathaniel Lee, *The Rival Queens, or the Death of Alexander the Great*, performed
Mar 28 — Wenceslas Hollar buried, in St. Margaret's, Westminster; engraver, and drawing instructor to Charles II
May — Edward Ravenscroft, *Scaramouch a Philosopher*, performed, published
Jun 18 — Sir William Temple, *An Essay upon the Cure of the Gout, by Moxa*, written at Nijmegen for Monsieur de Zulichem

---

complete it.

606. Webster's work accuses Meric Casaubon of misrepresenting John Dee and asserts Dee's status as the "greatest and ablest Philosopher, Mathematician, and Chymist" of his time (cited in Peter French, *John Dee*, p. 12)

Aug 22 — Samuel Butler, *Hudibras, Part III*, licensed

Sep — [Aphra Behn], *The Counterfeit Bridegroom*, performed

Sep 16 — **John Evelyn recommends Edward Phillips as tutor for Henry Bennet, 1st Earl of Arlington; Evelyn's connections with Milton's family still close**

Sep 11 — James Harrington d.

Oct 9 — William III, Prince of Orange, arrives in England

Nov — Samuel Butler receives a gift and pension from Charles II

Nov 4 — Princess Mary (afterward Queen Mary II), daughter of James, Duke of York, and Anne Hyde, m. William III of Orange (afterward King William III of England), Stadtholder of the United Provinces and her first cousin; both grandchildren of King James I

— Princess Anne, absent from the wedding, ill with smallpox

— Edmund Waller, *Epithalamium* in celebration of the wedding

Nov 7 — Samuel Butler, *Hudibras, Part III*, available at bookstalls

— Charles, Duke of Cambridge, b. to James, Duke of York and Mary of Modena; dies of smallpox within a month

Nov 19 — The Prince and Princess of Orange depart for the United Provinces

Dec — John Dryden, *All for Love*, performed (published 1678)

— Edward Ravenscroft, *King Edgar and Alfreda*, performed, published; *The English Lawyer*, performed (published 1678

1678

John Milton, *Paradise Lost*, reissue
John Milton, *The History of Britain*, 2nd edition
Richard Baxter, *A Christian Directory*
Anne Bradstreet, *Several Poems*, published in Boston
John Bunyan, *Pilgrim's Progress, Part I*
Samuel Butler, *Hudibras, Part III*, title-page dated
Ralph Cudworth, *The True Intellectual System of the Universe: the First Part; wherein, all the Reason and Philosophy of Atheism is Confuted; and its Impossibility Demonstrated*
Henry Dickinson, translation of Richard Simon, *Histoire Critique du Vieux Testament*, published, elicits a response from John Dryden in *Religio Laici*
John Dryden, *Mac Flecknoe*, written (?)
Thomas Herbert, *Memoirs of the last years of the reign of King Charles*
Roger L'Estrange, translation of Seneca, *Morals*
Jean Gailhard, *The Compleat Gentleman: or, Directions for the Education of Youth*, educational treatise
Thomas Hobbes, *Leviathan*, Latin edition published in London
Andrew Marvell, *Remarks upon a Late Disengenuous Discourse*, criticizing theological arguments concerning free will and predestination
Henry More, *Divine Dialogues*, 2nd edition, rescinding his indictment of Quakerism
Thomas Rymer, *The Tragedies of the Last Age*
John Smith, *Select Discourses*, 2nd edition

Nahum Tate, *Brutus of Alba; or the Enchanted Lovers*, produced, Tate's first play[607]

Ezrael Tongue, *The Jesuits Unmasked*; *Jesuitical Aphorisms*, translation from French

Henry Vaughan, *Thalia Rediviva*

Nathaniel Wanley, *The Wonders of the Little World*, including a version of the Pied Piper of Hamelin

Cardinal Francesco Barberini d. (b. 1597)

Richard Flecknoe d. (?)

George Farquhar b. (d. 1707)

William Croft b. (d. 1727), hymnist

Mary of Modena, Duchess of York, suffers another miscarriage

William Wycherley seriously ill; Charles II gives him £500 to convalesce, but the playwright never completely recovers

Jan — Aphra Behn, *Sir Patient Fancy*, produced

— Thomas Shadwell, *The History of Timon of Athens*, performed, adaptation of William Shakespeare, *Timon of Athens*; published

Jan 10 — Anglo-Dutch Treaty signed

Jan 21 — John Dryden, *All for Love*, SR

Jan 27 (?) — William Sancroft consecrated Archbishop of Canterbury

Mar — Thomas D'Urfey, *Trick for Trick*, performed, published

— Thomas Shadwell, *A True Widow*, performed (published 1679

Mar 11 — John Dryden, *The Kind Keeper*, premier performance (published 1680)

Mar 28 — Nathaniel Lee, *Mithridates, King of Pontus*, licensed for publication, tragedy

Apr — Thomas Otway, *Friendship in Fashion*, performed,

---

607. While popular during his own time, Tate's primary reputation as a dramatists stems from his adaptations of Shakespeare's plays, including a *King Lear* in which everyone lives 'happily ever after'—the most frequently produced version of the play through the mid-nineteenth century.

published

Apr 12 — Thomas Stanley d.

Apr 28 — John Wilmot, 2nd Earl of Rochester, erroneously reported dead by Anthony à Wood, suggesting how seriously ill Rochester was

Jun — Thomas D'Urfey, *Squire Oldsapp*, performed (published 1679)

Jul — Nahum Tate, *Brutus of Alba*, performed, published

— Treaty of Nymegen concludes war with the Dutch

Aug — John Dryden and Nathaniel Lee, *Oedipus*

Aug 1 — Act for burying the dead in woolens takes effect

Aug 13 — Charles II informed of a plot among Jesuits to assassinate him; beginnings of the "Popish Plot

Aug 18 — Andrew Marvell d.; buried in St. Giles-in-the-Fields

Aug 24 — John Evelyn inspects a papermill and describes the processes used in making paper from cast-off linen

Aug 28 — Titus Oates reveals the "Popish Plot" before the Council

Aug 29 — John Evelyn procures the Arundelian Library for the Royal Society, a gift from Henry Howard, Duke of Norfolk

Sep 25 — Izrael Tongue reveals the Popish Plot to Charles II, "having been first told it by Titus Oates"[608]

Sep 27 — Titus Oates, Deposition given to Sir Edmund Berry Godfrey; later (1823) found on top of the packet containing the manuscript for John Milton's *De Doctrina Christiana*

Oct 1 — John Evelyn records consternation throughout England caused by the reports of Popish Plot as disclosed by Titus Oates and Ezrael Tongue

Oct 17 — Sir Edmund Berry Godfrey found murdered, final stimulus to pursue the "Popish Plot"

Oct 30 — Proclamation issued, ordering all Papists to leave London

Nov — John Banks, *Destruction of Troy*, performed (?)

---

608. Llewelyn Powys, *Life & Times*, p. 195.

(published 1679)
— Marchamont Needham, *Christianissimus Christianandus. Or, Reason for the Reduction of France to a More Christian State in Europ*, 80-page tract advocating immediate war with France
— Proposal to exclude James, Duke of York, from succeeding his brother
Nov 4 — Parliamentary order to stop all funeral professions and search coffins for secreted weapons, for fear of an armed Catholic uprising
— Dr. John Tillotson, sermon accusing Papists of impudence in denying the historicity of the Gunpowder Plot
Nov 5 — Anti-Papist sermons preached in London; bonfires and pope-burnings along with the burning of Richard Langhorne and Edward Coleman, two "plotters"
Nov 15 — The Queen's Birthday; Titus Oates accuses the Queen of attempting to poison Charles II
Nov 19 — Marchamont Needham buried

1679

John Bancroft, *The Tragedy of Sertorius*, published
Richard Baxter, *Which is the True Church?*
William Bedloe, *A Narrative and Impartial Discovery of the Horrid Popish Plot*, published
Charles Blount (?), *An Appeal from the country to the city, for the preservation of his Majesty's person, liberty, property, and the Protestant religion*, viciously anti-Papist pamphlet
Gilbert Burnet, *History of the Reformation in England, Volume I* published[609]
John Crowne, *The Ambitious Statesman*, performed
"Ephelia," *Female Poems on Several Occasions*[610]
Joseph Hall, *Contemplations upon the Remarkable Passages in the Life of the Holy Jesus*, published
Thomas Hobbes, *Behemoth: The History of the Civil Wars of England*, published
Henry More, *Opera Omnia*
Titus Oates, *A True Narrative of the Horrid Plot*, published
John Oldham, "A Satire against Virtue," satire on Rochester; *Satires Upon the Jesuits* begin (until 1681)
William Penn, *One Project for the Good of England: That is, Our Civil Union is Our Civil Safety...*, pamphlet attempting to unite English Protestants

---

609. Appearing as it did during the furor over the "Popish Plot," Burnet's treatise stirred a great deal of controversy

610. Nothing is known concerning the identity or life of "Ephelia" except the publication data of her book of poems.

Sir Edward Sherbourne, translation of Seneca, *Troades or the Royal Captives*

Edmund Spenser, *The Works of that Famous English Poet, Mr. Edmond Spenser*, with "Life"

Henry Vaughan, *Olor Iscanus*, reprinted[611]

Edmund Waller, *Upon the Lady Mary*

Lady Ann Harrison Fanshawe d.

Henry Lawrence d.

Isaac Penington d.

Robert Wild d.

William Wycherley becomes tutor to the Duke of Richmond, illegitimate son of Charles II, at £1500 per year

Jan — Dr. Nathan Paget d., leaving Milton's widow a bequest of £20 S

Jan 11 — William Chamberlayne

Jan 25 — Cavalier Parliament (Long Parliament) dissolved after 18 years

Feb 23 — Anne Finch, Lady Conway, d., after appealing to Quaker leader George Fox for spiritual and physical healing

Feb 28 — Sir Isaac Newton, letter to Robert Boyle, discussion of Gravity and Ether

Mar — Aphra Behn, *The Feign'd Curtizans*, performed, Dorset Garden Theater; published

— Catherine Darnley b., illegitimate daughter of Catherine Sedley and James, Duke of York

Apr 14 — John Dryden, *Troilus and Cressida, or, Truth Found too Late*, performed, published thereafter[612]

— John Dryden, *The Grounds of Criticism in Tragedy*, preface to Troilus and Cressida

---

611. Douglas Bush notes that this was the only reprint of Vaughan's books during the century. *English Literature*, p. 600.

612. An adaptation of Shakespeare's play to the sensibilities of a Restoration audience; Cresside is transformed into a faithful and falsely accused maiden. See George Noyes, *Dryden*, p. 84.

Apr 17 — Anne Finch, Lady Conway, buried[613]

Apr 24 — James, Duke of York, travels to Flanders in the face of charges of recusancy

May — Nathaniel Lee, *Caesar Borgia*, performed; published 1680

— Licensing Act of 1662 expires; replaced by royal proclamations until 1685

— First bill presented to exclude James, Duke of York, from the succession

— *Habeas Corpus* Act passed

May 23 — Daniel Skinner, Fellow of Trinity College, Cambridge

Jun 4 — Samuel Pepys briefly imprisoned in the Tower on charges of malfeasance at the Admiralty

Jun 22 — John Evelyn, *Diary*: "There were now divers Jesuits executed about the plot, and a rebellion in Scotland of the fanatics, so that there was a sad prospect of public affairs" (II, 133)

Sep — Aphra Behn, *The Young King*, performed[614] (published 1683)

— Thomas D'Urfey, *The Virtuous Wife*, performed (published 1680)

— Thomas Otway, *The History and Fall of Caius Marius*, performed (published 1680)

— Elkanah Settle, *The Female Prelate*, performed (published 1680)

— Thomas Shadwell, *The Woman-Captain*, performed (published 1680)

---

613. "The reason for so unusual a delay was this—'Her husband was absent in Ireland at the time of her decease, but in order that he might have a last look at her features, Van Helmont preserved the body in spirits of wine and placed it in a coffin with a glass over the face" (Frederick J. Powicke, *The Cambridge Platonists*, p. 168).

614. This and the previous seven of Behn's plays were performed at Dorset Garden Theatre by the Duke's Company; of the eight, only this last title failed to attain even a moderate success.

- James, Duke of York, and James Scott, Duke of Monmouth, exiled
- Pope Innocent XI cautions James, Duke of York, against zealousness in pushing Catholicism in England

Sep 11 — *Colin*, anonymous satirical poem attacking mistresses of Charles II, circulating in London

Sep 12 — James, Duke of York, returns from Flanders to visit with Charles II, who is ill; James subsequently travels to Scotland

Oct — Meal Tub Plot engineered by Catholics

- John Wilmot, 2nd Earl of Rochester, requests Gilbert Burnet to wait on him during his illness; Burnet later reports details their conversations and of Rochester's 'conversion'

Nov — John Sheffield, 3rd Earl of Mulgrave, *An Essay upon Satire*, circulating in London, popularly attributed to John Dryden and possible cause of the attack on Dryden, Dec 18

Nov 17 — Accession Day of Elizabeth I, celebrated with "Pope-burnings"[615]

- *Londons Defiance to Rome: A Perfect Narrative of the Magnificent Processions and Solemn Burnings of the Pope at Temple Bar, Nov. 17th 1679*, tract

Dec — Nahum Tate, *The Loyal General*, performed (published 1680)

Dec 4 — Sir John Berkenhead d. (possibly Katherine Philips' 'Cratander')

- Thomas Hobbes d., at Hardwick (b. Apr 15, 1588)

Dec 18 — John Dryden beaten by hired thugs in Rose Alley (with the possible complicity of Louise Keroualle, Duchess of Portsmouth, and/or John Wilmot, 2nd Earl of Rochester)

---

615. "Pope-burnings" frequently coincided with Guy Fawkes Day celebrations following the Great Fire of 1666, during which effigies of the Pope, often shown consorting with various devils, replacing those of Fawkes. Historians have noted that none of the Popes reigning during the second half of the century attempted to interfere with England's internal affairs, yet fear and hatred of all things Papist increased in intensity, culminating (in some senses) in the Glorious Revolution of 1688. Between 1685 and 1688, during the reign of James II "Pope-burnings" were officially outlawed.

Decade Nine: 1680-1689
Three Kings and One Queen—
But "Long Live the Parliament"

1680

John Milton, ***Paradise Regained and Samson Agonistes*,** **2nd edition**
John Bunyan, *The Life and Death of Mr. Badman*
Mrs. Elizabeth Marshall Cellier, *Malice Defeated, or a Brief Relation of the Accusation and Deliverance of Elizabeth Cellier, etc.*
Sir James Chamberlayne, *A Sacred Poem*
John Crowne, *The Misery of the Civil War*, performed
Thomas Dangerfield, *Don Tomazo*
Wentworth Dillon, Earl of Roscommon, translation of Horace, *Art of Poetry*, into blank verse
John Dryden, *Ovid's Epistles translated by Several Hands*, published, with contributions by Nahum Tate, Aphra Behn, Thomas Rymer, Thomas Otway, Elkanah Settle, and others
Sir Robert Filmer, *Patriarcha: or the Natural Power of Kings*, pro-Royalist treatise
Sir Roger L'Estrange, *Citt and Bumpkin, in a Dialogue*
The Merry Jests and Witty Shifts of Scogin, published (abridgement of 1626 edition), jest-book
The Midwife Unmask'd: or, The Popish Design of Mrs Cellier's Meal-Tub plainly made known: being a Second Answer to her Scandalous Libel, in short Remarques upon the same-
Michel Millot (?), *The School of Venus*, prose pornography, translated from French into English[616]

---

616. Samuel Pepys credited the volume with being the "most bawdy, lewd book I ever saw" (Jonathan Green, *Encyclopedia*, p. 171-172).

Henry More, *Apocalypsis Apocalypseos; or the Revelation ... unveiled*
Lodowick Muggleton, *Letter to Robert Pierce, Concerning the Holy Ghost*, tract
Thomas Otway, *Epistle of Phaedra to Hippolytus*, translation from Ovid; *The Poet's Complaint of the Muses*, published
John Phillips, *Dr. Oates' Narrative of the Popish Plot Vindicated; Mr. L'Estrange Refuted*
Henry Purcell, *A Song to Welcome home the King from Windsor*, composed, first of twenty-nine state odes
Nahum Tate, *The History of King Richard the Second*, drama
Sir William Temple, *Miscellanea, the First Part*
John Wilmot, 2nd Earl of Rochester, *Poems on Several Occasions*
Gianlorenzo Bernini d. (b. 1594); continental artist and sculptor[617]
Nathaniel Wanley d.
Henry Purcell, appointed organist at Westminster Abbey

Jan 11 — Sir Peter Lely knighted
Jan 29 — Gilbert Burnet, *Plain Speech to Royalty*
Feb — Aphra Behn, *The Rover*, performed at Court
Feb 18 — Denzil Hollis, d., last of the "Five Members"
Mar — Aphra Behn, *The Feigned Curtezans*, performed at Court
— John Dryden, *The Spanish Fryar*, performed (published 1681)
— Thomas Otway, *The Soldiers Fortune*, performed (published 1681); *The Orphan*, tragedy in blank verse, performed, published
May 31 — Elkanah Settle, *The Female Prelate: Being the History of the Life and Death of Pope Joan* premiered, anti-Catholic drama
Jun — [Aphra Behn], *The Revenge; or, A Match in Newgate*,

---

617. Esmor Jones asserts that Milton "almost certainly met him in Rome" (*Milton*, p. 41).

performed at Dorset Garden Theater; published thereafter[618]
— John Wilmot, 2nd Earl of Rochester, and Elizabeth, Countess of Rochester (formerly a Catholic), take Sacraments according to the Anglican rite

Jun 19 — John Wilmot, 2nd Earl of Rochester, *Remonstrance*, dictated and signed, formally adjuring the "whole course of my wicked life"

Jul 26 — John Wilmot, 2nd Earl of Rochester, d., aged thirty-three

After Jul 26 — Gilbert Burnet, *Some Passages in the Life and Death of John, Earl of Rochester*

Sep — James Beauclerk, Lord Beauclerk, d. (illegitimate son of Charles II and Eleanor [Nell] Gwynn)

— Nathaniel Lee, *Theodosius*, performed, with incidental music by Henry Purcell; published

— Elkanah Settle, *Fatal Love*, drama, produced; published

Sep 25 — Samuel Butler d., of consumption

Sep 26 — John Dury d. (b. 1596)

Oct — Whig Parliament sits

Oct 27 — **Samuel Simmons sells his rights to *Paradise Lost* to Brabazon Aylmer**

Nov — Exclusion Bill killed in the House of Lords

Nov 1 — John Dryden, *The Spanish Fryar*

Nov 4 — Second Exclusion bill read before the House of Commons

— Joseph Glanvill, d.

Nov 30 — Robert Boyle elected President of the Royal Society

Nov/Dec (?)— Aphra Behn, *The Second Part of the Rover*, produced (published 1681)

Dec — Nathaniel Lee, *Lucius Junius Brutus*, performed (published 1681)

— Nahum Tate, *The History of King Richard the Second*, performed (published 1681)

---

618. The play was performed and published anonymously, but a contemporary reference assigns authorship to Mrs. Ann Behn.

Dec 7 — Sir Peter Lely d.[619]

Dec 29 — William Stafford, Lord Viscount Stafford, brother to Henry Howard, Duke of Norfolk, beheaded on Tower Hill for treason, his conviction based in part of Titus Oates deposition

---

619. As is typical during the century, Lely was an immigrant from The Hague to London, who emphasized paintings of the Commonwealth courts

1681

John Milton, *History of Britain* re-issued, with previously suppressed passages restored

Theodore Haak, translation of *Paradise Lost* into Dutch or German[620]

Richard Baxter, *Poetical Fragments*[621]

Sir James Chamberlayne, *Manuductio ad Coelum*, religious verse

John Crowne, *Henry the Sixth*, performed; *Thyestes*, performed

T. Frankland, *Annals of King James and King Charles the First*

Joseph Glanvill, *The Zealous, and Impartial Protestant*, pamphlet; *Saducismus Triumphatus*

Robert Hooke, *Some Discourses, Sermons and Remains of the Reverend M. Jos. Glanvill*, published

Nathaniel Lee, *The Princess of Cleves*, performed (published, 1689)

John Locke, *Treatises on Government*, written

---

620. The first attempt to translate Milton's poetry into another language. Although German and Latin translations of the major poems begin appearing by the end of the seventeenth century, translations in other important languages (Greek, French, Italian, Spanish, Portuguese, Hebrew, Japanese, Korean, and a number of others) do not begin until the early eighteenth century. Translations continue to the present; recently, a student presented me with an Internet printout of *Paradise Lost, Book I* rendered in Ebonics.

621. Included in the preface is the following evaluation of George Herbert: "Herbert speaks to God like one that really believeth a God, and whose business in the world is most with God. Heart-work and Heaven-work make up his Books" (cited in Joseph Summers, *George Herbert*, p. 16).

Andrew Marvell, *Miscellaneous Poems*
John Oldham, *Satyrs upon the Jesuits: Written in the Year 1679*, published
John Phillips, *The Character of a Popish Successor, Part the Second*
Edward Ravenscroft, *The London Cuckolds*
Elkanah Settle, *Character of a Popish Successor*, political tract
Thomas Shadwell, *The Lancashire Witches*
Francis Smith, *An Account of the Injurious Proceedings of Sir George Jeffreys...against Francis Smith Bookseller*, critique of abuses by the Stationers Company
Nahum Tate, *A History of King Lear*, drama[622]
Nicolaas Heinsius d.

Jan — Aphra Behn, *The Rover, Part Two*, performed
Jan 10 — Charles II prorogues Parliament
Mar — John Dryden, *The Spanish Friar* published
— Nahum Tate, *The History of King Lear*, performed, published
— Third Whig Parliament summoned by Charles II; sits at Oxford
— Louis XIV of France begins secretly financing Charles II
Mar 28 — Charles II dissolves Parliament; thereafter relies on subsidies from Louis XIV of France
Apr (?)— John Milton, Character of the Long Parliament, published
Jun 9 — William Lilly d., astrologer[623]
Jun 18 — Sir Christopher Wren's monument commemorating the Great Fire receives a plaque blaming Papists for causing the fire[624]

---

622. Tate's version of *Lear*, complete with happy ending in which both Lear and Cordelia survive and prosper, was popular throughout the Eighteenth century.

623. Lilly, who constructed an almanac every year from 1644 to 1681, appeared in Samuel Butler's *Hudibras*, as 'Sidrophel'

624. The plaque was removed in 1685, restored in 1689, and finally

Jul 1 — Execution of Oliver Plunket, Archbishop of Armagh and final victim of the "Popish Plot"

Aug — Stephen College hanged, drawn and quartered for publishing libelous verses

Aug 2 — William III, Prince of Orange arrives in London; Mary remains in Holland, reportedly pregnant; departs Aug 15

Sep — John Banks, *The Unhappy Favourite: or, The Earl of Essex*, performed (published 1682)

— Thomas D'Urfey, *Sir Barnaby Whigg*, performed, published

— Thomas Shadwell, *The Lancashire Witches*, performed (published 1682)

Oct — Charlotte Mary b., to James, Duke of York, and Mary of Modena[625]

Nov — Aphra Behn, *The False Count*, performed[626]

— Edward Ravenscroft, *The London Cuckolds*, performed (published 1682)

— Anthony Ashley Cooper, Earl of Shaftesbury, brought before London grand jury on charges of high treason; the jury rejects the charges

Nov 17 — John Dryden, *Absalom and Achitophil*, published

Nov 30 — Sir Christopher Wren elected President of the Royal Society

Dec — Aphra Behn, *the Roundheads*, produced

— Nahum Tate, *The Ingratitude of a common-wealth*, drama based on William Shakespeare, *Coriolanus*, performed (published 1682)

---

removed permanently in 1830.

625. Charlotte Mary was "born prematurely and died prematurely" (Maurice Ashley, *The Stuarts in Love*, p 189). By this time, James already had four illegitimate children by his mistress, Arabella Churchill, sister to John Churchill.

626. Behn notes that she completed this play in five days (Angeline Goreau, *Aphra Behn*, p. 247).

1682

John Milton, Letters of State, loosely translated into English as *Milton's Republican-Letters*
John Milton, *Defence of the People of England*, plagiarized from Milton and published in Julian the Apostate
Ernst Gottlieb von Berge, translation of *Paradise Lost* into German, as *Das Verlustigte Paradeis*[627]
John Bunyan, *The Holy War*
Sir Thomas Browne, *Religio Medici*, 8th edition (so-called; in actuality at least the 14th), the last presumably corrected by Browne
T. Comber, *The Nature and Usefulness of Solemn Judicial Swearing*, treatise on the use of required oaths
Matthew Coppinger, *Poems, Songs, and Love-Verses*, published[628]
Sir Simonds D'Ewes, *The Journals of All the Parliaments during the Reign of Queen Elizabeth*, published
Thomas Dangerfield, *The Grand Imposter Defeated*, pamphlet in response to Elizabeth Cellier
"Ephelia," *Female Poems on Several Occasions*, enlarged re-issue
Joseph Glanvill, *Lux Orientalis*, 2nd edition

---

627. The first partial translation of the poem was by Theodore Haak; his work on the first four books of *Paradise Lost* was incorporated into von Berge's edition (*Milton Encyclopedia*, VIII, p.78)

628. Coppinger represents a large but often undernoticed category of seventeenth-century poets: he published a single book, and nothing more is known about him, his life, or his writings.

Robert Gould, *Love Given O'er; a Satyr against Women*

John Nalson, *An Impartial Collection of the Great Affairs of State*, 2 volumes (through 1683)

Alexander Oldys, *The Fair Extravagant*, published, novel

William Petty, *Essay in Political Arithmetick, concerning the people, housing, hospitals, etc. of London and Paris*, published; *An Essay Concerning the Multiplication of Mankind, together with an Essay on the Growth of London*, published; *Quantulumcunque Concerning Money*, economics treatise

George Rust, Bishop of Dromore, *Discourse of Truth*, edited and published by Joseph Glanvill

Southerne, Thomas, *The Loyal Brother*, drama, published, Southerne's first play

A Tryal of Witches at the Assizes held at Bury St. Edmonds for the County of Suffolk; on the tenth day of March, 1664, published, detailed account of procedures for such a trial

Edmund Waller, *Poems, Etc.*, 4th edition

Bulstrode Whitelock, *Memorials of the English Affairs*

Edmund Halley observes the comet later named after him

Sir Edward Sherbourne, knighted

Jan — Thomas D'Urfey, *The Royalist*, performed, published

Feb (?)— **John Milton, *A Brief History of Moscovia and other less-known Countries lying eastward of Russia as far as Cathay. Gather'd from the Writings of several Eye-witnesses, by John Milton*, published by Brabazon Aylmer (completed before 1652?).**

Feb — Thomas Otway, *Venice Preserv'd*, tragedy in blank verse; produced, published

Mar — Aphra Behn, *Like Father, Like Son*, performed (never published)[629]

— Thomas D'Urfey, *The Injured Princess*, performed, published

1682

---

629. Only the published Prologue and Epilogue survive of the play.

Mar 11 — Elkanah Settle, *The Heir of Morocco*, performed, published thereafter

Mar 16 — John Dryden, *The Medall*, published

Mar 17 — Edmund Hickeringill, *The Mushroom*, attack on Dryden's *The Medall* written overnight

Apr — John Banks, *Vertue Betray'd: or, Anna Bullen*, performed, published

Apr 21 — Thomas Otway, *Venice Preserv'd, or a Plot Discover'd*, special performance for James, Duke of York, following the Duke's return from Scotland

May — Aphra Behn, *The City-Heiress; or, Sir Timothy Treatall*, produced; published

— Elkanah Settle, *Absalom Senior; or, Achitophel Transposed*, Whig attack on John Dryden

— Thomas Shadwell, *The Medall of John Bayes*, satirical attack on Dryden

Jun 15 — John Crowne, *The City Politicks*, licensed for performance

Jun 18 — John Webster, Puritan preacher, d.

Jun 26 — John Crowne, *The City Politicks*, license for performance revoked by the Lord Chamberlain

Aug — Aphra Behn, *Epilogue* to *Romulus and Hersilla*, an anonymous play

Aug 12 — Aphra Behn and Lady Mary Slingsby ordered taken in custody for the *Epilogue* to *Romulus*, written by Behn, spoken by Slingsby, and attacking the Duke of Monmouth

Aug 25 — Temperance Lloyd, Mary Trembles, and Susanna Edwards executed as witches at Exeter

— Thereafter: *The Tryal, Condemnation, and Execution of Three Witches, viz. Temperance Floyd, Mary Floyd, and Susanna Edwards. Who were Arraigned at Exeter on the 18th of August 1682*

— Thereafter: at least four separate published accounts of the trial and executions, including: *Witchcraft Discovered and Punished. Or the Tryals and Condemnation of three Notorious Witches, who were Tried at the last Assizes, holden at the Castle of Exeter ... where they received sentence of Death, for bewitching severall Persons, destroying Ships at Sea, and Cattel by Land. To the Tune of Doctor Faustus; or Fortune my Foe*, broadside ballad of 17 quatrains

Sep — Aphra Behn, *The False Count*, performed; published 1682

— Tories take control of London

Sep 7 — Dr. Edward Browne, son of Sir Thomas Browne, appointed physician to St. Bartholomew's Hospital by command of Charles II

Oct 4 — John Dryden, *MacFlecknoe: A Satyr upon the True-Blew-Protestant Poet, T. S.*, published by D. Green

Oct 19 — Sir Thomas Browne d., on his seventy-seventh birthday

Nov — The King's company and the Duke's Company merge as the United Company of players

— Anthony Ashley Cooper, Earl of Shaftesbury, flees

Nov 10 — John Dryden, *The Second Part of Absalom and Achitophel*, with Nahum Tate

Nov 18 — John Crowne, *The City Politicks*, licensed for performance; published 1683[630]

Late Nov — John Dryden, *Religio Laici*

Nov 29 — Prince Rupert of the Rhine, Duke of Bavaria, d.

About Nov 30 — John Dryden and Nathaniel Lee, *The Duke of Guise*, performed, published 1683

Dec 18 — Heneage Finch, Lord Chancellor and 1st Earl of Nottingham, d.

---

630. The play's satirical attacks on the Earl of Shaftesbury may have caused the delay in its production.

1683

Aphra Behn, *Love Letters Between a Nobleman and His Sister, Part I*, published, one of the earliest epistolary novels in English

Nicholas Boileau, *The Art of Poetry*; translated by Sir William Soame and John Dryde

Sir Thomas Browne, *Certain Miscellany Tracts*, edited by Thomas Tenison

Gilbert Burnet, *History of His Own Time*, begun (published 1724)

John Chalkhill, *Thealma and Clearchus. A Pastoral History... written long since by John Chalkhill, Esq; An Acquaintance and Friend of Edmund Spenser*, published with preface by Isaak Walton (preface dated 7 May 1673)

Samuel Crossman, *The last testimony & declaration of the Reverend Samuel Crossman, D.D. and Dean of Bristoll setting forth his dutiful and true affection to the Church of England as by law established*, published (?)

John Crowne, *City Politiques*

Thomas Creech, translation of Lucretius, *De Rerum Natura*, published

John Dryden, *Life of Plutarch*, published

Robert Gould, *Love Given O're*, published, satire against women

William Lilly, *Lilly's Hieroglyphics*, published, prophecies

John Oldham, *Poems and Translations*

Thomas Otway, *The Atheist; or, the Second Part of the Soldiers*

Fortune

Henry Purcell, *Sonatas of III Parts: two violins and bass: to the organ or harpsichord*, published; *The Art of Descant*, published; two *Odes to St. Cecilia*, performed

Elkanah Settle, *A Narrative of the Popish Plot*, political tract; and *A Panegyrick upon Sir George Jeffries*, political writing

Thomas Shadwell and Thomas Hunt, *Reflections upon the Pretended Parallel in the play called the Duke of Guise*, published, attack on John Dryden

Thomas Tanner, *Primordia, or, the Rise and Growth of the First Church of God Described*

John Owen d.

Roger Williams d.

Edmund Curll b. (d. 1747)

George Jeffreys appointed Lord Chief Justice

Jan 21 — Anthony Ashley Cooper, Earl of Shaftesbury, d., age sixty-two, in exile on the Continent

Feb 4 — Samuel Crossman d., hymnist

Mar — John Lambert d., still imprisoned on St. Nicholas Island, off Plymouth, for treason as a parliamentary general

Mar 19 — Thomas Killigrew d.

May 24 — Benjamin Whichcote buried

— Thereafter: John Tillotson, Archbishop of Canterbury, *A Sermon Preached at the Funeral of the Reverend Benjamin Whichcote*, published

Jun 12 — Rye House Plot exposed to assassinate Charles II and James, Duke of York; Fifth Monarchists involved

Jun 18 — The City of London, disenfranchised because of administrative abuses, remaining under the King's control until the accession of William III

Jun 26 — Algernon Sidney, brother to Dorothy Sidney Spenser, countess of Sunderland, arrested for complicity in the Rye House Plot

Jul 10 — Arthur Capel, Earl of Essex, arrested for complicity in the Rye House Plot

Jul 13 — Arthur Capel, Earl of Essex, found in his closet in the Tower with his throat cut, apparently a suicide

Jul 19 — George, Prince of Denmark, arrives for his wedding to Princess Anne

Jul 21 — Executions continue for the Rye Plot, including Lord Russell and others

— **In the aftermath of the Rye House Plot, Oxford burns several of Milton's political books, while preserving the presentation copy of *Eikonoklastes* in the Bodleian Library**

Other books and tracts burned include:

— Richard Baxter, *The Holy Commonwealth*
— Cardinal Bellarmine, *De Potestate Papae; De Conciliis et Ecclesia Militante*
— George Buchanan, *De Jure Regni apud Scotos*
— Dolman, *Succession*
— John Goodwin, *The Obstructours of Justice*
— Thomas Hobbes, *De Cive*; *Leviathan*
— Samuel Rutherford, *Lex Rex*

Jul 23 — **Brabazon Aylmer registers Milton's *Paradise Lost* in his own name**

Jul 28 — Princess Anne (afterward Queen Anne) m. Prince George of Denmark, in St. James Chapel[631]

Aug 17 — **Brabazon Aylmer sells half his ownership of *Paradise Lost* to Jacob Tonson**[632]

Sep — Thomas Otway, *The Atheist*, produced (published 1684); comedy, Otway's last play

— Edward Ravenscroft, *Dame Dobson*, performed (published

---

631. Anne endured eighteen pregnancies, including 13 stillborn children. She outlived her husband and all of her surviving children; at her death, the throne of England reverted to the House of Hanover, descendants of James I through Elizabeth of Bohemia.

632. Throughout a long career that included publishing works by Dryden and Rowe's edition of Shakespeare, Tonson realized more profit from *Paradise Lost*, once he attained full rights to the poem, than any other endeavor.

    1684)

Nov 7 — Algernon Sidney brought to trial before Judge Jeffreys and condemned on the evidence of Lord Howard of Escrick; thereafter executed[633]

Dec — Nathaniel Lee, *Constantine the Great*, performed (published 1684)

Dec 7 — Algernon Sidney beheaded on Tower Hill

c. Dec 20 — John Oldham d.

Dec 25 — Izaak Walton d. (b. 1593)

---

633. Julia Cartwright adds that Sidney's nephew, the 4th Baron Sunderland, then Secretary of State to Charles II, refused to help his uncle (*Sacharissa*, p. 304).

1684

Edward Phillips publishes Latin dictionaries that incorporate Milton's notes

John Banks, *The Island Queens: or, The Death of Mary, Queen of Scotland*, tragedy, written and published, but not performed[634]

Aphra Behn, *Love Letters between a Nobleman and His Sister*, published; *Poems upon Several Occasions*, published; *The Adventures of the Black Lady*, fiction

Robert Boyle, *Memoirs for the Natural History of the Human Blood*, medical treatise, written without the benefit of dissection

John Bunyan, *Pilgrim's Progress, Part II*

Wentworth Dillon, Earl of Roscommon, *Essay on Translated Verse*

John Dryden, "To the Earl of Roscommon," "To the Memory of Mr. Oldham"

Charles Goodall, *The Royal College of Physicians*, including appendix, "An Historical Account of the College's Proceedings against empirics"

Elizabeth Brooke Josceline, *The Mothers Legacy to her Unborn Child*, unaltered re-issue of 1622 edition

Increase Mather, *Essay for the Recording of Illustrious Providences*, published in Boston

John Nalson, *A True Copy of the Journal of the High Court of*

---

634. An edition of the play, under the title *The Albion Queens*, appeared in 1704

Justice for the Trial of King Charles I, published from minutes by John Phelps, Clerk of the Court and other sources

John Oldham, *Remains of Mr. John Oldham*; includes poem by John Dryden

'Philotheos Physiologue', *Friendly Advice to the Gentlemen-Planters of the East and West Indies*

John Struys, *The voyages and travels of John Struys through Italy, Greece, Muscovy, Tartary, Media, Persia, E. India, Japan and other countries in Europe, Africa and Asia*, report of a Dutch trader

Jacob Tonson, editor, *Miscellany Poems* (First Miscellany), with poetry by John Dryden, Anne Wharton, published

Hannah Woolley, *The Queen-Like Closet*

Sir Aston Cockayne d.

Peter du Moulin d.

Records indicate duty charged on 6,318,000 barrels of beer (averaging 25 gallons per barrel) for England and Wales, or nearly a pint a day[635]

James, Duke of York, re-appointed Lord High Admiral

Thomas Sprat, appointed Bishop of Rochester

Samuel Pepys appointed President of the Royal Society

Feb — John Wilmot, Earl of Rochester, *Valentinian*, performed, with prologue by Aphra Behn

Feb 25 — Dorothy Sidney, Countess of Sunderland, buried, near Althorp (Edmund Waller's 'Sacharissa')

Apr — Princess Anne (later Queen Anne), first daughter stillborn

Apr 4 — James Scott, Duke of Monmouth, removed as Chancellor of Cambridge University by Charles II

Apr 5 — Thomas Southerne, *The Disappointment*, performed

May 10 — Titus Oates arrested for slander against James, Duke

---

635. Keith Thomas reminds readers that these figures account only for *official* production; perhaps as much as a two-third again of the amount might have been produced privately and hence not taxed, for a much higher per capita consumption than in modern times. (*Religion*, p. 18)

of York; subsequently tried by Judge George Jeffreys, the "Hanging Judge"

May 25 — **John Aubrey, letter to Anthony Wood with references to several of Milton's sonnets**

Sep — James Darnley b., illegitimate son of James, Duke of York, and Catherine Sedley

Oct 1 — Pierre Corneille d.

Nov — Nahum Tate, *A Duke and No Duke*, performed (published 1685)

Nov 11 — Nathaniel Lee confined to Bethlehem (Bedlam) Hospital for mental illness, where he remains for five years

1685

John Milton, "On Shakespeare," in William Shakespeare, *Fourth Folio*
Aphra Behn, *Love Letters Between a Nobleman and His Sister, Part II*, published, novel
Charles Cotton, *Essays of Michael Seigneur de Montaigne*, translation
Jacob Tonson, editor, *Sylvae (Second Miscellany)*, published with poems by John Dryden
Thomas Sprat, *A True Account...of the Horrid Conspiracy Against the King*
Thomas Traherne, *The Soul's Communion with her Saviour*, edited and published by Philip Traherne
Edmund Waller, *Divine Poems*
Samuel Wesley, *Maggots: or, Poems on Several Subjects Never Before Handled*, published by John Dunton[636]
Wentworth Dillon, Earl of Roscommon, d.[637]
John Pell d.
Anne Wharton d.
Johann Sebastian Bach b. (d. 1750)
John Gay b. (d. 1732)
Georg Frederic Handel b. (d. 1750)
Mary, daughter of Princess Anne (later Queen Anne), b.

---

636. The volume included such remarkable titles as "A Pindarique on the Grunting of a Hog," "To My Gingerbread Mistress," " and "An Anacreontique on a Pair of Breeches" (Gilbert McEwen, *Oracle*, p. 7)

637. Roscommon's *Poems* were first published in 1717.

Feb 2 — Charles II awakens with convulsions

Feb 5/6 — Charles II d.

— Accession of King James II officially proclaimed in London

— Thereafter, theaters closed for an official period of mourning for Charles II

About Mar 14 — John Dryden, *Threnodia Augustalis: A Funeral-Pindaric Poem, Sacred to the Happy Memory of King Charles II*

About Mar 25 — John Dryden, *Threnodia Augustalis...*, 2nd edition

Apr — Aphra Behn, *Miscellaneous Poems and Translations*, published

— Thomas Otway d.[638]

Apr 16 — Thomas Otway buried, St. Clement Danes

Apr 20 — Theaters allowed to re-open following mourning for Charles II

Apr 23 — Coronation of James II, Westminster Abbey; Mary of Modena adorned with jewels worth £50,000

— Thereafter: Elkanah Settle, *Heroick Poem*, on the coronation of James II, published

— Thereafter: Aphra Behn, *A Pindaric Poem on the Happy Coronation*, published

— James Darnley, illegitimate son of James II, d.

Apr 27 — John Dryden confirmed as Poet Laureate and Historiographer

May — John Crowne, *Sir Courtly Nice*, performed

— Nahum Tate, *Cuckolds-Haven*, performed, published 1685

May 8-9 — Titus Oates tried and convicted of perjury; subsequently whipped, pilloried, and returned to jail

May 19 — *The Humble Address*, published, satirical poem focusing on James II as Catholic

May 24 — James Scott, Duke of Monmouth, sets sail from Holland with four armed ships, to invade England

Jun 6 — John Dryden, *Albion and Albanius*, his first opera, with

---

638. The first collected edition of Otway's dramas was published in 1713.

music by Louis Grabu[639] and a preface on theory of opera, published thereafter

Jun 11 — James Scott, Duke of Monmouth, lands at Lyme, Dorset; publishes a declaration announcing himself legitimate heir and King

Jun 15 — James Scott, Duke of Monmouth, marches from Lyme with an army of 3,000

Jun 16 — James Scott, Duke of Monmouth, stripped of his titles and condemned a traitor by a Bill of Attainder

— Anne Killigrew d. of smallpox

Jun 17 — Plaque blaming Papists for the Great Fire is removed from Sir Christopher Wren's memorial to the fire

Jul 3 — Officials at Cambridge University publicly burn Sir Thomas Lely's portrait of James Scott, Duke of Monmouth

Jul 6 — Battle of Sedgemoor (last battle on English soil prior to World War II); the rebellion of James Scott, Duke of Monmouth, defeated

— Daniel Defoe, partisan and pamphleteer on behalf of Monmouth

Jul 8 — James Scott, Duke of Monmouth, captured by Royalist forces

Jul 15 — James Scott, Duke of Monmouth, beheaded on Tower Hill

— Thereafter: Matthew Prior, *Advice to the Painter: On the Happy Defeat of the Rebels in the West and the Execution of the Late Duke of Monmouth*, published, satirical poem

Jul 25 — James II reviews his forces at Hounslow Heath

Jul 26 — Official day of Thanksgiving following Monmouth's Rebellion

Jul 28 — Henry Bennet, 1st Earl of Arlington, d.

Sep — Thomas D'Urfey, *A Common-Wealth of Women*, performed (published 1686)

— Alice Lisle, widow of a regicide and over 70 years old, executed for complicity in Monmouth's rebellion; first offi-

---

639. Credited as being the first English opera.

cial victim of Judge Jeffreys' Bloody Assizes
— Thereafter: More than 300 Dorsetshire peasants hanged, 800 deported to the West Indies
Sep 28 — George Jeffreys appointed Lord Chancellor and receives care of the Great Seal of England
Sep 30 — Anne Killigrew, *Poems*, licensed
Oct 4 — Louis XIV of France revokes the Edict of Nantes, eliminating freedom of worship for French Protestants
Nov 9 — James II assembles Parliament; subsequently prorogues Parliament until February 1686
Nov 30 — Anne Killigrew, *Poems*, published (dated 1686)
— John Dryden, "To the Pious Memory of the Accomplish'd Young Lady, Mrs. Anne Killigrew…an Ode," published with Killigrew's Poems

1686

J. C., *Paradisus Amissa,* **Latin translation of** *Paradise Lost,* ***Book I,* published in London**
Aphra Behn, *La Montre, or The Lover's Watch*, translation from the French by Balthazar Bonnecorse, published
Sir Thomas Browne, *Collected Works*, edited by Thomas Tenison
Thomas Flatman, *Poems and Songs…, With Additions and Amendments,* 4th edition
William Mountfort, *The Life and Death of Doctor Faustus*, performed (published 1697)
Edmund Waller, *Poems, Etc.*, 5th edition, final issue published under Waller's direct supervision
Anne Sophia b. to Princess Anne (later Queen Anne)

Jan — Charles II, private letters printed, which suggest that Charles had died a Catholic
Jan 19 — John Evelyn records the Court's dismay at learning that James II has created Catherine Sedley, his mistress, Countess of Dorchester
Feb — Thomas D'Urfey, *The Banditti*, performed, published
— James II prorogues Parliament until August 1686
Apr — Aphra Behn, *The Luckey Chance*, performed at the Theatre Royal, Drury Lane (published 1687)
— Edward Ravenscroft, *Titus Andronicus*, performed (published 1687)
Apr 3 — Roger Palmer, Earl of Castlemaine (husband of

Barbara Villiers, mistress to Charles II), arrives in Rome as Emissary of James II

Apr 16 — Arthur Annesley, Earl of Anglesey, d.

Apr 18 — Riots break out at the opening of a Catholic Chapel in London

Apr 20 — *To Mr. Bays*, satirical poem, copied into a letter from John Newton, establishing a terminus date for John Dryden's conversion to Catholicism

Apr 26 — **Christopher Milton elevated to a knighthood by James II**

May 8 — Sir Isaac Newton, *Philosophia Naturalis Principia Mathematica*, preface dated; text published thereafter

Jun 16 — James II successfully manipulates the courts in a test case—Godden vs. Hales—allowing him to appoint Catholics to public positions

Summer — James II again musters his forces on Hounslow Heath as a show of strength against his opponents

July — James II attempts to control the Church by appointing a High Commission

— Catholics openly appointed to positions at Court and in the army, increasing fears of and antagonism toward Papists

Jul 10 — Dr. John Fell, Bishop of Oxford and dean of Christ Church College, d.

Sep 6 — Henry Compton, Bishop of London, tried for treason; suspended from office during James' pleasure

Nov 16 — Arthur Annesley, Earl of Anglesey, library auctioned; contains documents relating to the authorship of *Eikon Basilica*

1687

Anonymous Life of Milton published
Charles I, *The Works of Charles I*, published
Philip Ayres, *Lyric Poems, Made in Imitation of the Italians. Of which, many are Translations from Other Languages*, including *Endymion and Diana: An Heroic Poem*, published
Aphra Behn, *Love Letters Between a Nobleman and His Sister, Part III—The Amours of Philander and Silvia*, published
Mrs. Elizabeth Marshall Cellier, *A Scheme for the Foundation of a Royal Hospital, and Raising a Revenue of Five or Six-Thousand Pounds a year, by, and for the Maintenance of a Corporation of skillful Midwives, and such Foundlings or exposed Children, as shall be admitted therein, etc*
John Cleveland, *The Works of Mr. John Cleveland*
John Cutts, Baron Cutts of Gowran, *Poetical Exercises*
Sir Isaac Newton, *Principia Mathematica* (Mathematical Principles of Natural Philosophy)
Sir William Petty, *Five Essay in Political Arithmetick*, published; *Observations upon the Cities of London and Rome*, published
Sir Charles Sedley, *Bellamira*, produced
Elkanah Settle, *Reflections on Several of Mr. Dryden's Plays*, published
Anne Wharton, *Vinculum Societatis*, poetry
William Winstanley, *The Lives of the Most Famous English Poets...*, published[640]

---

640. Winstanley concludes of Milton that, although he must be credited

Royal College of Physicians orders members to dispense free advice and medications at cost to the poor

Joseph Addison enrolls at Queen's College, Oxford University

William Wycherley receives a pension of £200 from James II, who is impressed with *The Plain Dealer*

Feb — Mary and Anne Sophie, daughters of Princess Anne (later Queen Anne) and Prince George of Denmark, both d.

Feb 12 — James II issues a partial act of religious toleration in Scotland, apparently to probe Anglican reactions

Feb 15 — James II orders that Alban Francis, a Catholic priest, be made M.A. at Cambridge; the university refuses

Feb 18 — Charles Cotton d.

Mar — Aphra Behn, *The Emperor of the Moon*, performed; published 1687

Mar 18 — James II informs the Privy Council that he intends to declare full religious toleration in England

Apr — Nahum Tate, *The Island Princess*, performed, published thereafter

Apr 4 — James II, *Declaration of Indulgences*; full text subsequently published in the *London Gazette*

Apr 11 — John Dryden, *The Hind and the Panther*, licensed

Apr 16 — **Sir Christopher Milton appointed justice of common pleas**

— George Villiers, 2nd and last Duke of Buckingham d.[641]

Apr 27 — James II declares general religious and releases Dissenters from prison

May 27 — John Dryden, *The Hind and the Panther*, SR, poem, supporting Catholicism

---

with writing an epic poem, "...his fame is gone out like a Candle in a Snuff, and his Memory will always stink, which might have ever lived in honorable Repute, had not he been a notorious Traitor, and most impiously and villainously bely'd that blessed Martyr King Charles the First" (Miller, *Critical Response*, p. 31).

641. Buckingham's collected works, including poetry, were first published in 1704.

- Thereafter: Tom Brown, *Reflections on the Hind and the Panther*, satirical attack on John Dryden
- Summer — James II musters his army for a third time on Hounslow Heath, increasing fears of a Papist threat to England
- Princess Anne (later Queen Anne), pregnant, after having had five miscarriages; this pregnancy ends in a miscarriage also
- Jul 2 — James II dissolves his original Parliament
- July 19 — Matthew Prior and Charles Montagu, *The Hind and the Panther Transvers'd to the Story of the Country-Mouse and the City-Mouse*, satirical attack on Dryden
- Sep 1 — Henry More d.
- Oct 21 — Edmund Waller d., buried in Beaconsfield churchyard
- Thereafter: Aphra Behn, commemorative verses on Edmund Waller
- Nov 11 — Father Petre formally admitted to the Privy council, thus antagonizing Protestants and moderate Catholics
- Nov 14— Eleanor [Nell] Gwynn, former mistress of Charles II, d.
- Nov 22 — John Dryden, *A Song for St. Cecilia's Day*, musical setting by Giovanni Baptista Draghi
- Dec 16 — William Petty d., anatomist and mathematician
- Dec 31 — Samuel Parker, president of Magdalen College, Oxford, required to appoint twelve new fellows, at least six to be known Roman Catholics

1688

John Milton, *Paradise Lost***, 4th edition; with illustrations by Jean Baptiste Medina (Milton's first illustrator), and an epigram by John Dryden**[642]**; subscription edition by Jacob Tonson, marking Tonson's first involvement with Milton's works**

John Milton, *Paradise Regained***, 3rd edition, published by Randall Taylor**

Jane Baker, *Poetical Recreations Consisting of Original Poems, Odes, etc.*, published in two parts

Aphra Behn, *A Congratulatory Poem to Her Most Sacred Majesty*; *The Fair Jilt*, published, novel; *Oroonoko: or, the Royal Slave. A True History*, published, romance-novel; *Agnes de Castro*, fiction, published; *Lycidus, or the Lover in Fashion*, fiction; *A Poem to Sir Roger L'Estrange on his Third Part of the History of the Times; relating to the death of Edmund Berry Godfrey*, published

Robert Boyle, *Receipts sent to a Friend in America*, collection of medical remedies

Tom Brown, *Reasons of Mr. Bays Changing His Religion*, Anglican critique of John Dryden, *The Hind and the Panther*

Sir Thomas Browne, *Collected Works*, translated into Dutch

Nicholas Chorier, *A Dialogue between a married lady and a*

---

642. Dryden's "Lines on Milton" were among the earliest poetic tributes to Milton's power: Three Poets, in three distant ages born, / Greece, Italy, and England did adorn. / The First in loftiness of thought Surpass'd; / The Next in Majesty; in both the Last. / The Force of Nature cou'd no farther goe: / To make a Third she joynd the former two.

maid, published, translation from the Latin original, earliest surviving work of English prose pornography

John Crowne, *Darius King of Persia*, performed

Samuel Johnson[643], *Of Magistracy*

Sir Roger L'Estrange, *Brief History of the Times*, published (1687-1688)

Henry More, *Divine Dialogues, containing sundry Disquisitions & Instructions concerning the Attributes of God and his Providence in the World*, 2 volumes

Henry Playford, editor, *Harmonia Sacra*, music collection; includes, among others, music by Henry Purcell and texts by George Herbert

Poems to the Memory of that Incomparable Poet Edmond Waller, memorial volume

Sylvia's Revenge; or, A Satyr against Man

Sylvia's Complaint of her sex's Unhappiness, being the second part of Sylvia's Revenge, or a Satyr against Man

Ralph Cudworth d.

Francis Leach, bookseller, arrested for publishing John Wilmot, 2nd Earl of Rochester, *Poems on Several Occasions*; Leach charged with "promoting the lasciviousness and vicious qualities of Rochester's work".[644]

Jan 16 — Mrs. Elizabeth Marshall Cellier, *To Dr —— An Answer to His Queries, Concerning the Colledg of Midwives*

Feb — [Charles Sackville, Earl of Dorset?], *A Faithful Catalogue of Our Most Eminent Ninnies*, satirical poem

— James II issues Declaration of Liberty of Conscience in Scotland

Mar — William Mountfort, *The Injur'd Lovers*, performed, published 1688

Mar 20 — Princess Anne (later Queen Anne), letter to Mary, Princess of Orange (later Queen Mary II), expressing doubts

---

643. Samuel Johnson (1649-1703), Rector of Corringham.

644. Jonathan Green, *Encyclopedia*, p. 237.

that Queen Mary is in fact pregnant
Apr — Thomas D'Urfey, *A Fool's Preferment*, performed, published 1688
— Lewis Theobald b. (possibly on All Fools Day)[645]
Apr 4 — James II issues *Declaration of Indulgence* in England
Apr 27 — James II issues *Second Declaration of Indulgences*
May — Thomas Shadwell, *The Squire of Alsatia*, comedy, performed; published 1688[646]
May 5 — James II orders that the second *Declaration of Indulgences* be read on two consecutive Sundays from every pulpit in England
— In London, only 4 out of 100 parish churches obey the order
May 11 — William Sancroft, Archbishop of Canterbury, and six other Bishops petition to be excused from reading the Declaration
May 21 — Alexander Pope b., in Lombard Street, London
Jun 8 — William Sancroft, Archbishop of Canterbury; Francis Turner, Bishop of Ely; John Lake, Bishop of Chichester; Thomas White, Bishop of Peterborough; William Lloyd, Bishop of St. Asaph; Jonathan Trelawney, Bishop of Bristow; Thomas Ken, Bishop of Bath and Wells—committed to the Tower by James II and his council
Jun 10 — James Francis Edward Stuart,[647] Prince of Wales and Chevalier St. George, b. a month prematurely to Mary Beatrice D'Este of Modena, following five previous miscar-

---

645. Mack suggests that, given the future rivalry between Theobald and Pope, Pope might have relished the though of Theobald actually being born on All-Fools Day. "There is something touching as well as funny in the thought of these two, each (according to the theories of their time) a blank sheet of paper awaiting the inscriptions of experience, yet each blindly strengthening day by day toward a confrontation that would initiate the last great English poem in the Renaissance tradition" (*Alexander Pope*, p. 13).

646. The play was an enormous success. It ran for thirteen days, and Shadwell's third-day profits exceeded £130.

647. Later known in England as the "Old Pretender" to distinguish him from his son, the "Young Pretender," Bonnie Prince Charles.

riages[648]

Jun 11 — John Dryden, *Britannia Rediviva, A Poem on the Prince, Born on the Tenth of June 1688*, laureate poem in honor of Prince James, licensed; published late June

Jun 15 — The imprisoned Bishops released, to "great joy by the (true sons of the church of England)"[649]

Jun 30 — Arthur Herbert, former Admiral and Master of the Robes, sails to Holland in disguise, with a document signed by three leading Whigs, three leading Tories, and Dr. Henry Compton for the Church[650]

— William III, Prince of Orange invited to England to assume throne as co-monarch with Mary II, Protestant daughter of James II

Jul 6 — Sir Christopher Milton retires as Justice

Jul 24 — Princess Anne (later Queen Anne), letter to her sister Mary, Princess of Orange (later Queen Mary II), describing the birth of the Prince of Wales

— Mary increasingly convinced of a conspiracy and of the baby's illegitimacy as Heir

Late Aug — England anticipates a probable invasion by William of Orange

Aug 14 — John Bunyan delivers his final sermon, at Whitehall[651]

Aug 31 — John Bunyan d.

---

648. So great was the concern over the new prince's religion that rumors almost immediately began circulating that the true prince had died or been stillborn and that a substitute had been smuggled in to secure a Catholic succession. Mack notes that the future Queen Anne had grave reservations about the child's birth, while the future Queen Mary "continued to believe in her father's perfidy as a way of justifying what she knew to be her husband's treacherous intention 'to dethrone him by force'" (*Alexander Pope*, p. 11f).

649. Llewelyn Powys, Life & Times, p. 264.

650. The signators were: William Cavendish, Earl of Devonshire, Edward Russell, and Charles Talbot; Earl of Shrewsbury for the Whigs; Thomas Osborne, Earl of Danby, Richard Lumley, and Henry Sidney for the Tories.

651. Bunyan's own funeral sermon is the only one of his sermons to be preserved.

Oct 15 — James Edward Francis Stuart, Prince of Wales, baptized

Oct 22 — James II convenes a special council with forty-one witnesses to verify James Francis Edward's legitimacy and birth to the Lords at Whitehall

Nov — **Elizabeth Foster, Milton's granddaughter, b., in Ireland**

Nov 5 — Samuel Pepys learns at the Admiralty that William of Orange had passed through the straits of Dover the previous day; invasion is imminent; William of Orange lands his forces as Torbay in Devonshire

Nov 6 — News arrives in London that William of Orange has landed in Devon

Nov 27 — William III marches his forces into Dorset; then continues slowly and peacefully toward London

Dec 8 — Thomas Flatman d.

Dec 10 — Queen Mary Beatrice of Modena leaves Whitehall with James, Prince of Wales (at 3 AM)

Dec 11 — James II leaves Whitehall, travelling incognito (at 3 AM)

— George Jeffreys, Lord Chancellor and "most hated man in England," captured at Wapping while attempting to escape England[652]

Dec 12 — William III receives news of James' flight, prepares to move directly toward London

— London mobilizes to rumors that Irish Papists are invading the city and slaughtering Protestants

Dec 16 — Sir Roger L'Estrange imprisoned because of his opposition to William of Orange

Dec 18 — William of Orange enters St. James Palace

---

652. Derek Wilson grants Jeffreys this distinction, noting as well that at the time of his capture, the Lord Chancellor was carrying some £37,000 in cash (*The Tower*, p. 199). Even Wilson, a less than sympathetic biographer of Jeffreys, notes, however, that the Lord Chancellor was the only major advisor to James II to remain with him until the end; only after James deserted London did Jeffreys seek his own safety.

Dec 19 — William of Orange enters London; summons Samuel Pepys to an audience and allowing him to continue in office at the Admiralty

Dec 25 — James II arrives in France, near Calais, before continuing to his exile in Paris (d. 1701)

1689

John Milton, *Pro Populo adversus Tyrannus*, reprint of *Tenure of Kings and Magistrates*
Aphra Behn *The History of the Nun: Or, The Fair Vow-Breaker*, published, novel; *The Lucky Mistake*, published; *Of Plants*, paraphrase of Latin original by Abraham Cowley, *Sex libri plantarum*, Book VI, published
Sligsby Bethel, *The World's Mistake in Oliver Cromwell*, published
Charles Cotton, *Poems on Several Occasions*
Sir Francis Fane, *The Sacrifice*, drama, published but not performed; commendatory verses by Aphra Behn
Robert Gould, *Poems, Chiefly consisting of Satyrs and Satyrical Epistles*, published[653]
[Edward Littleton], *The Groans of the Plantations*, pamphlet
Cotton Mather, *Right Thoughts for Sad Hours*, published in London, with stanzas by Edward Taylor
Poems on Affairs of State, collected (through 1716)
Henry Purcell, *Dido and Aeneas*, opera
Thomas Shadwell, *A Congratulatory Poem on His Highness the Prince of Orange's coming into England*, published; *a Congratulatory Poem to the Most Illustrious Queen Mary*, published
Emeric Bigot d.
William Chamberlayne d.

---

653. Gould was the author of a diatribe against the stage, *The Play-House*, published here and reprinted in 1709.

Isaac Vossius d.

Samuel Richardson b. (d. 1761)

Jonathan Swift leaves Sir William Temple's house at Moor Park

Nathaniel Lee released from Bedlam Hospital

In the preceding two decades (1670-1689), some 30,000 people die of smallpox in London

Jan — Titus Oates released from imprisonment

Jan 22 — Convention assembles to determine a successor to the departed James II

Feb 13 — Accession of William III and Mary II as co-sovereigns

— William Bentinck serves as Groom of the Stole to William III[654]

— All public servants to leave their posts until either reconfirmed or replaced; Samuel Pepys resigns from the Admiralty

Feb 23 — Sir Isaac Newton, Letter, discussion of a telescope Newton has constructed: "I have seen with it Jupiter distinctly round and his satellites, and Venus horned"[655])

Mar 1 — James II, letter to the Scottish Parliament, threatening revenge and retribution if they treat with the usurping Prince of Orange and asking them to aid him in recovering his throne

Mar 9 — Thomas Shadwell appointed Poet Laureate

Mar 24 — James II arrives in Dublin with his forces

Apr — Thomas Shadwell, *Bury Fair* performed; published

---

654. Bentinck's appointment is included to suggest one level of court intricacy throughout the century, although the extremes of etiquette are never developed in England to quite the extent later characterized by the Court of Louis XIV of France. By the time of William, "The sovereign," writes David Durant, "was usually waited upon by gentlemen who deemed the most intimate task an honour. The office of Groom of the Stole...was held in 1689 by William Bentinck, at a salary of £5,000 a year for doing no more than emptying William III's close-stool" (*What Queen Elizabeth*, p. 79.)

655. Thayer, *Newton*, p. 190

1689

Apr 4 — Scottish Parliament declares James II to have abandoned his throne and his claim thereunto forfeit

Apr 11 — Joint coronation of William III and Mary II, in Westminster Abbey

— Scots Estates formally offer the Crown of Scotland to William and Mary

— News arrives of James II's invasion of Ireland

Apr 16 — Aphra Behn d.; buried in The Cloisters, Westminster Abbey

Apr 19 — Queen Christina of Sweden d., a Catholic convert in Rome

— Sir George Jeffreys, Lord Chancellor, d. in prison of kidney failure before he could be brought to trial, at age forty-three

Thereafter:

— *The Protestant Martyrs: or, the Bloody Assizes. Giving an Account of the Lives, Tryals, and Dying Speeches of all those Eminent Protestants that suffered in the West of England, by the Sentence of that Bloody and Cruel Judge Jeffries; being in all 251 Persons...*, pamphlet, published

— *The Dying Speeches, letters and prayers of those eminent Protestants who suffered in the West of England*, pamphlet

— *The Second and Last Collection of the Dying Speeches; etc.*, pamphlet

— *The Bloody Assizes, or a complete history of the life of George Jefferies etc.*, omnibus collection of pamphlets

— *The New Martyrology*, published, establishing the Whig version of Jeffrey's character, actions, and reputation as "The Hanging Judge"[656]

May 26 — Lady Mary Pierrepont b. (later Lady Mary Wortley Montague; d. 1762)

---

656. The final version, published in 1705 as *The Western Martyrology, or the Bloody Assizes...*, was largely written by John Dunton, John Tutchin, and Titus Oates. Both Whigs and Tories accepted the distorted view of events presented, since it allowed the onus of ten year's of unrest and rebellion to rest on a single man, safely dead.

Apr 1 — Oath of Allegiance in effect

Jul 24 — Princess Anne (afterward queen Anne) gives birth to a son, William Henry, Duke of Gloucester, named in honor of William III

Aug — William III pardons Titus Oates

Aug 21 — Battle of Dunkeld; Mary II's forces defeat Scots Jacobite Highlanders under Cameron leadership

Oct — Nathaniel Lee, *The Massacre of Paris*, performed; published 1690

Nov — Aphra Behn, *The Widdow-Ranter, or The History of Bacon in Virginia*, Behn's last play, produced, Drury Lane Theatre, published 1690

Nov 20 — John Dryden, *Prologue and Epilogue* to Aphra Behn's *The History of Bacon in Virginia*, SR by Jacob Tonson

Dec — John Dryden, *Don Sebastian*, performed, published 1690

— Thomas D'Urfey, *Love for Money*, performed, published 1691

Dec 16 — Bill of Rights promulgated

Dec 18 — George Jeffreys and others hanged in effigy on the anniversary of William's arrival at Whitehall

Dec 29 — Dr. Thomas Sydenham, the "English Hippocrates" and the greatest physician of the period, d.

Decade Ten: 1690-1700
"Descending to Its Close"

1690

John Milton, *Eikonoklastes in Answer to a Book intitled Eikon Basilikon, the portraiture of his sacred majesty in his solitudes and sufferings*, reprinted; published in Amsterdam; influential in re-opening the controversy concerning the authorship of *Eikon Basilike*

William Hog, *Paradise Lost* (1667 version), *Paradise Regained*, and *Samson Agonistes*, translated into Latin as *Paraphrasis Poetica in Tria ata, viz. Paradisum Amissum, Paradisum Recuperatum, et Samson Agonisten*; published in London by John Darby

John Milton, Letters of State published in Germany as *Literæ nomine Senatus Anglicani, Cromwellii Richardique*, edited by Johann Georg Pritius

Robert Boyle, *Medicina Hydrostatica*, published, pharmacological study

Sir Thomas Browne, *A Letter to a Friend, Upon occasion of the Death of his Intimate Friend*, edited by Archbishop Thomas Tenison, under the direction of Dr. Edward Browne, Browne's son

John Crowne, *The English Frier*, performed

Mary Evelyn, *Mundus Muliebris: or, The Ladies Dressing-Room Unlock'd and her Toilette spread in Burlesque*

John Locke, *Essay Concerning Human Understanding*, published; *Two Treatises of Government*, published; *An Essay Concerning the True Origin, Extent and End of Government*, published

John Norris of Bremerton, *Christian Blessedness: or, Discourses upon the Beatitudes*, published

Francis Osborne, *The Secret History of King James I and King Charles I*

Samuel Pepys, *Memoires Relating to the State of the Royal Navy of England, For Ten years, Determin'd December 1688*, published, Pepys' only publication during his lifetime

Thomas Southerne, *Sir Anthony Love*, comedy

Sir William Temple, *Miscellanea, the Second Part*, dedicated to Cambridge University

Edmund Waller, *The Second Part of Mr. Waller's Poems*, including his revisions to Beaumont and Fletcher's *The Maid's Tragedy* as *The Maid's Tragedy, Alter'd*

Theodore Haak d.

Cyriack Skinner d.[657]

David Teniers II d.

Christopher Wase d.

Mary, daughter to Princess Anne (later Queen Anne) b.; lives two hours

Jan — John Dryden, *Don Sebastian*, printed

Mar — Thomas Shadwell, *the Amorous Bigotte*, performed; published 1690

Apr — John Dryden, *Amphitryon*, performed

May — Mris A. W. [Anna Weamys]. *A Continuation of Sir Philip Sidney's Arcadia*, 2nd edition, registered in the Term Catalogue

Jun — A number of men, including Samuel Pepys, imprisoned for conspiring against William III

Jun 4 — William III leaves London to lead his forces into Ireland

Jul 1 — William III defeats his father-in-law, James II, at Battle of the Boyne in Ireland

Jul 8 — Bonfires in Oxford to celebrate William III's victory

---

657. John Cary states that Skinner died in the year 1700 (*John Milton: Complete Shorter Works*, p. 410).

over James II in Ireland

Aug 11 — Siege of Limerick by forces of William III begins

Sep — Colley Cibber contracts as an actor at the Theatre Royal, Drury Lane

Sep 5 — William III raises the siege, having lost 1200 men, and departs for England

Oct — John Dryden, *Amphitryon*, published

— Henry More, *An Account of Virtue: or, Dr. Henry More's Abridgement of Morals, put into English*, translated by Edward Southwell,[658] (reprinted 1701)

— Elkanah Settle, *Distress'd Innocence*, performed, published 1691

Oct 9 — Henry Fitzroy, Duke of Grafton, illegitimate son of Charles II and Barbara Villiers, d. at the Battle of Cork

Nov 7 — William Petty, *Political Arithmetick, or A Discourse concerning the extent and value of Lands, People, Buildings; Husbandry, Manufacture(s), Commerce, Fishery, Artizans, Seamen, Soldiers; Public Revenues, Interest, Taxes, Superlucration, Registries, Banks; Valuation of Men, Increasing of Seamen; of Militias, harbours, Situation, Shipping, Power at sea, &c...*, dated, published by Petty's son, now Lord Shelburne (pirated edition, 1683)

Dec — Thomas Shadwell, *The Scowers*

Dec 3 — Robert Barclay d.

Dec 31 — Three Jacobite emissaries, carrying secret documents to James II in France, arrested and imprisoned in the Tower

---

658. At the time the translation was published, Edward Southwell was not yet twenty years of age.

1691

Anthony à Wood, *Life of Milton*, published
Sir Newton Puckering presents his collections to the Trinity College Library, including loose pages by Milton bound (1736) as the Trinity Manuscript
T. P. [Thomas Powers], *Paradisi Amissi*, Latin translation of *Paradise Lost*, Book I, published in Canterbury
Richard Baxter, *Certainty of the World of Spirits*, published
John Dryden, *Sir Martin Mar-All*, published under Dryden's name
John Dunton, *Voyage Around the World*
[Robert Gould], *A Satyrical Epistle to the Female Author of a Poem Called 'Sylvia's Revenge'*
John Locke, *Some Considerations of the Consequences of the Lowering of Interest and Raising the Value of Money*
Gerard Langbaine, *Account of the English Dramatick Poets*, published at Oxford, hostile to Dryden
Elkanah Settle, *Triumphs of London*, pageant[659]
William Walsh, *A Dialogue Concerning Women, being a Defense of the Sex*; with a preface by John Dryden
Anthony Wood, *Athenae Oxonienses*, 2nd volume, 1692
Sir George Etherege d.
William Faithorne, the Elder, d.
Elkanah Settle made City Poet of London

---

659. In his capacity as City Poet, Settle produced four additional pageants under this title, 1692-1695.

Jan 13 — George Fox d.; founder of the Society of Friends

Feb 1 — Archbishop William Sancroft ordered to leave Lambeth Palace

Feb 9 — John Dryden, *Satyrs from Juvenal*, registered by Jacob Tonson

Feb 18 — Anthony à Wood, "Mr. Arthur Charlet shew'd me at his chamber a pamphlet newly extant printed in double columns in half a sheet of paper in quart entit. 'The tribe of Levi,' written by John Dryden; satyricall against the clergy for their perjuryes and baseness—a bitter thing in verse"[660]

Mar — Thomas D'Urfey, *Bussy d'Ambois*, performed, published 1691

Mar 17 — John Dunton, Richard Sault, and Samuel Wesley, editors, *The Athenian Gazette, or Casuistical Mercury, Resolving all the most Nice and Curious Questions proposed by the Ingenious*, begins weekly—then semi-weekly—publication

Mar 24 — **Jacob Tonson obtains full copyright to *Paradise Lost* and retains it until the copyright period expires**

Apr — John Tillotson elected Archbishop of Canterbury

Apr 9 — Whitehall Palace burns; Queen Mary barely escapes the flames

May — John Dryden, *King Arthur*, acted; opera, with music by Henry Purcell, published thereafter

May 31 — Eleanora, Countess of Abingdon, d.[661]

Jun — William Mountfort, *The Successful Strangers*, performed

Jun 18 — Anthony à Wood, *Athenae Oxonienses*, published

Jun 19 — Anthony à Wood, *Athenae Oxonienses*, copies arrive by wagon in Oxford

Jun 22 — Anthony à Wood, *Athenae Oxonienses,* presentation copy to the Vice-Chancellor and the Library

---

660. Llewelyn Powys, *Life & Times*, p. 285.

661. Dryden's memorial ode to the Countess of Abingdon illustrates the duties placed upon him as Poet Laureate; the poet knew neither the Countess nor the Earl of Abingdon, who commissioned the poem.

Jun 23 — Archbishop William Sancroft expelled from Lambeth Palace by force; retires to Suffolk; Archbishop John Tillotson subsequently appointed in his place

Jul — English forces victorious in Ireland

Sep 18 — Battle of Leuze; French forces defeat English and Dutch armies

Oct 3 — Treaty of limerick; concludes conflict in Ireland

Dec 8 — Richard Baxter d.

About Dec 23 — Katherine Boyle, Lady Ranelagh, d.[662]

Dec 30 — Robert Boyle d., a week after his sister, Lady Ranelagh

---

662. According to Antonia Fraser, Lady Ranelagh "incarnated the masculine ideal of a good woman. Her leaning therefore, far from being a disturbing quality, became an added grace. As a result she had the distinction, perhaps a slightly dubious one, of being the one woman of whom Milton actually approved" (*Weaker Vessel*, p. 132). The distinction, while less than dubious, was well deserved; on the other hand, Fraser's assessment of Milton's attitudes toward women seems somewhat narrow. J. E. Stephens adds that Lady Ranelagh was "one of the most talented women of her age and advocate of educational reform" *Aubrey on Education*, p. 189).

1692

John Milton, *A Defense of the People of England in answer to Salmasius' Defense of the King,* translation of the *Defensio* into English by Joseph Washington

The Arts of Empire and Mysteries of State discabineted. **By Sir Walter Raleigh, published by John Milton**

Charles Gildon, *Miscellany Poems upon Various Occasions: Consisting of Original Poems, By the Late Duke of Buckingham, Mr. Cowley, Mr. Milton...,* with several incorrect ascriptions to Milton

Robert Boyle, *General History of the Air,* published; *Medicinal Experiments, or a Collection of Choice and Safe Remedies, for the most Part Simple, and Easily Prepared: Very Useful in Families, and fitted for the Service of Country People,* published, vernacular self-help medical book

John Bunyan, *Works*

Gilbert Burnet, Bishop of Salisbury, *A Discourse on Pastoral Care*

William Congreve, *Incognita: or, Love and Duty Reconcil'd,* novel, published anonymously

John Crowne, *Daeneids,* poem, published

John Dennis, *Poems in Burlesque; The Passions of Byblis,* with preface commending Milton's blank verse

Sir Roger L'Estrange, *The Fables of Aesop and Other Eminent Mythologists, Part I,* translated[663]

---

663. L'Estrange was among the first professional translators, an occupation that would serve both Dryden and Pope well.

John Hoyle, *Bibliotheca Hoyleana*, published

Ben Jonson, *Second Folio*

Henry More, *Discourses on Several Texts of Scripture*, edited by John Worthington

Alexander Oldys, *The Female Gallant*, published, novel

Henry Purcell, *The Fairy Queen*, opera

William Walsh, *Letters and Poems. Amorous and Gallant*, published anonymously

John Byrom b. (d. 1763), hymnist

England at war with France; loses Namur; France plans an invasion of England

Society for the Reformation of Manners formed

Sir Godfrey Kneller knighted by William III for his services as Court painter; later (1715), elevated to baronet by King George I

Daniel Defoe appointed Accountant to the Commissioner of the Glass Duty (until 1697) as a reward for his political pamphlets; declares bankruptcy

Jan — Thomas D'Urfey, *The Marriage-Hater Match'd*, performed, published 1692

— William III orders John Churchill, the Duke of Marlborough, to resign from all offices

Feb — William III orders the massacre at Glencoe, Scotland

— Princess Anne (afterward Queen Anne) gives birth to her last child, a son, who lives only a few minutes

Mar — John Dryden, *Eleanora, A Panegyrical Poem Dedicated to the Memory of the Late Countess of Abingdon*

Apr — Elkanah Settle, The Fairy-Queen, performed, published thereafter

Apr 1 (?)—ALL FOOLS DAY — Jonathan Swift, "Ode" to the Athenian Society, published by John Dunton; Swift's first poem published in England

Apr/May — John Dryden, *Cleomenes*, performed, published thereafter

May 5 — John Churchill, 1st Duke of Marlborough, imprisoned

on Queen Mary's orders

May 6 — Nathaniel Lee buried, St. Clement Danes[664]

May 18 — Elias Ashmole d.

May 29-Jun 4 —War of the Grand Alliance; battles of Barfleur and La Hogue remove the threat of French invation

Jul 19 — Anthony à Wood, *Athenae Oxonienses*, 2nd volume, published at London

Jul 19 — Copies of the book arrive at Oxford

Jul 31 — Copies of *Athenae Oxonienses* burned in the Theater yard at Oxford

Aug 3 — War of the Grand Alliance; English and Dutch forces defeated at the Battle of Steenkerque

Aug 8 — John Dryden, "Discourse Concerning the Origin and Progress of Satire"

Oct — John Dryden, *The Satires of Decimus Junius Juvenalis, translated into English Verse by Mr. John Dryden and Several Other Hands*

Nov — Thomas Shadwell, *The Volunteers*, comedy, performed; published 1693

Nov 19/20 — Thomas Shadwell, Poet Laureate and arch-rival of John Dryden, d.[665]

— Thomas Rymer, subsequently appointed Historiographer Royal

Nov 24 — Thomas Shadwell, buried, at Chelsea

Dec — Thomas Rymer, *A Short View of Tragedy*, antagonistic toward Dryden's poetics

Dec 9 — William Mountfort stabbed to death at his own door[666]

---

664. The first collected edition of Lee's plays appeared in 1713.

665. Of an overdose of opium.

666. "On 9 Dec. 1692 Mountfort was stabbed before his door in Howard Street, Strand, by Captain Richard Hill, assisted by Lord Mohun. Mountfort was buried in St. Clement Danes. His murderers went unpunished, Hill escaping, and Mohun winning an acquittal at his trial" (*Autrey Wiley*, p. 253). It is an interesting coincidence (and certainly nothing more) that two playwrights best known for their treatments of the Faustus legend—Christopher Marlowe and William Mountfort—were both stabbed to death

Dec 10 — Sir Isaac Newton, letter to Richard Bentley, arguments for the existence of God from scientific observation
Dec 24 — Nahum Tate, appointed Poet Laureate (to 1715)

---

under suspicious circumstances, and that their deaths occurred almost precisely a century apart.

1693

Joseph Addison, *An Account of the Greatest English Poets*
Richard Bentley, *Unreasonableness of Atheism* (Eight Sermons against Atheism)
Thomas Brown, *Lives of All the Princes of Orange*
William Congreve, *The Old Bachelor*
Abraham Cowley, *Works*
John Dryden, *A Discourse concerning Satire*
John Hacket, *Scrinia Reserata: A memorial offered to the great deserving of John Williams D.D. ... containing a series of the most remarkable occurrences and transactions of his life*, 2 vols.
John Locke, *Thoughts Concerning Education*
Cotton Mather, *The Wonders of the Invisible World: being an Account of the Tryals of...Witches...in New England*
Increase Mather, *A Further Account of the Tryals of the New-England Witches*
Thomas Phillips, *A Journal of a Voyage Made in the Hannibal of London*, diary of an English slaver (published 1732)
George Story, *An Impartial History of the War in Ireland*
Samuel Wesley, the Elder *The Life of our Blessed Lord and Savior Jesus Christ, an Heroic Poem*, published; with references to John Milton
Anne Wharton, *A Collection of Poems*
James Wright, *The Humours and Conversations of the Town*, published, includes a discussion of the value of theaters[667]

---

667. Wright was a friend of Aphra Behn, contributing a song to one of her

Joseph Addison receives MA from Magdalen College, Oxford University

Elizabeth Latham fined and imprisoned for selling John Wilmot, 2nd Earl of Rochester, *Poems on Several Occasions*

Jan 17 — Sir Isaac Newton, letter to Richard Bentley, discussion of planetary motion as evidences of God's existence

Feb. — **John Milton, *Latin Dictionary***

— Thomas D'Urfey, *The Richmond Heiress*, performed, published 1693

Feb 11 — Sir Isaac Newton, letter to Richard Bentley, further scientific evidence for the existence of God

Mar — William Congreve, *The Old Bachelor*, performed at the Theater Royal, Drury Lane; Congreve's first play

Mar 22 — **Sir Christopher Milton buried, St. Nicholas, Ipswich**

May 9 — Colley Cibber m. Katharine Shore

Summer — Jacob Tonson, ed., *Examen Poeticum* (*The Third Miscellany*), including translations by John Dryden

June 27 — War of the Grand Alliance, English and Dutch forces defeated by the French at the Battle of Lagos

Jul 29 — War of the Grand Alliance; English and Dutch forces defeated by the French at the Battle of Landen

Nov — William Congreve, *The Double-Dealer*, performed

Dec — John Dryden, *Love Triumphant*, performed, published 1694

---

plays.

1694

John Milton, *Letters of State, Written by Mr. John Milton, To most of the Sovereign Princes and Republicks of Europe. From the Year 1649 Till the Year 1659. To which is added, An Account of His Life*, edited by Edward Phillips

John Milton, *Letters of State*, placed on the Papal Index (*Paradise Lost* added in 1732)

T. P. [Thomas Powers]), further selections from *Paradise Lost*, translated into Latin

Charles Blake, Latin translation of *Paradise Lost, Book V*, published in *Lusus Amatorius*

William Hog, Latin translation of *Lycidas*; published with a Latin translation of John Cleveland's elegy on Edward King, as *Paraphrasis Latina in duo Poemata*

Mary Astell, *A Serious Proposal to the Ladies for the Advancement of their true and greatest interests*, advocating a women's seminary for studying philosophy and languages; re-issue, 1697

John Banks, *The Innocent Usurper; or, The Death of the Lady Jane Gray*, written and published, but not performed

Abel Boyer, *The Complete French Master*, French grammar and rhetoric, including bilingual segments of fables and jests

Richard Burthogge, *An Essay upon Reason and the Nature of Spirits*, with considerations of witchcraft

William Congreve, *The Double Dealer*, published

John Crowne, *Regulus*, performed; *The Married Beau*, performed

John Dryden, "To My Dear Friend, Mr Congreve"; "To Sir Godfrey Kneller

George Fox, *Journal*, edited and published by Thomas Ellwood

Charles Gildon, editor, *Chorus Poetarum*, anthology, with poetry by Aphra Behn

The Ladies Dictionary being a General Entertainment for the Fair-Sex. A Work never attempted before in English, printed for John Dunton

Lady Damaris Masham, *Occasional Thoughts in reference to a Vertuous or Christian Life*

Peter Anthony Motteux, English translation of Rabelais (Books I-III)

William Penn, *Rise and Progress of...Quakers*, published

Thomas Southerne, *The Fatal Marriage*, adapted from Aphra Behn's novel

Henry Vaughan, last surviving writing, a letter to his cousin, John Aubrey[668]

William Wotton, *Reflections upon Ancient and Modern Learning*

Richard Barry, 2nd Earl of Barrymore, d.

Voltaire [François Marie Arouet] b.

Thomas Tenison, late friend of Sir Thomas Browne, appointed Archbishop of Canterbury (to 1714)

All official attempts at maintaining a press-licensing system end

Jan — John Dryden, *Love Triumphant*, published; Dryden's last play

Jan 11 — John Evelyn's diary records John Dryden's intention to give over the theater and translate Virgil

Feb — Elkanah Settle, *The Ambitious Slave*, performed published thereafter

Feb 27 — John Aubrey, letter to Anthony Henley concerning *The Idea of Education*; introduction completed, although the

---

668. Cited in Jonathan F. S. Post, *Henry Vaughan*, p. xv.

work remains unfinished (published 1972)

Apr — **Peter Motteux, *The Gentleman's Journal: or, The Monthly Magazine*, includes an advertisement for Thomas Powers, Latin translation of *Paradise Lost***

Apr 3 — **Joseph Addison, "An Account of the Greatest English Poets" (poem), including Addison's first statements about Milton**

May — **Thomas Powers, selections from *Paradise Lost*, Book III, Latin translation, in Peter Motteux, *The Gentleman's Journal*, etc.**

— Thomas D'Urfey, *The Comical History of Don Quixote; The Comical History of Don Quixote, Part II*, performed, published 1694

Jun — **Thomas Powers, selections from *Paradise Lost*, Book IV, Latin translation, in Peter Motteux, *The Gentleman's Journal*, etc.**

Jun 15 — John Dryden contracts with Jacob Tonson for translations of Virgil's *Pastorals, Georgics*, and *Aeneid*

Jul — **Thomas Powers, selections from *Paradise Lost*, Book V, Latin translation, in Peter Motteux, *The Gentleman's Journal*, etc.**

Jul 25 — Bank of England founded by William Patterson

Aug 8 — Francis Hutchinson b. (d. 1746), philosopher and teacher of Adam Smith

Sep — Edward Ravenscroft, *The Canterbury Guests*, performed, published 1695

Nov — Thomas D'Urfey, *The Comical History of Don Quixote, Part III*, performed, published 1696; epilogue spoken by Doggett, seated on an ass

Nov 20 — William III bed-ridden with a chill

Nov 22 — John Tillotson, Archbishop of Canterbury, d.

Dec — Triennial Act passes, defining Parliament's superiority over the Sovereign

Dec 21 — Mary II awakens feeling ill; she is diagnosed as having contracted smallpox

Dec 28 — Mary II d., of smallpox, at age thirty-three, leaving

William III as sole monarch

1695

John Milton, *The Poetical Works of John Milton. Containing Paradise Lost, Paradise Regained, Samson Agonistes, and His Poems on Several Occasions*, edited by P. H. [Patrick Hume], in five volumes, with notes on each book of *Paradise Lost*, published by Jacob Tonson

John Milton, *The History of Britain*, reissue

John Milton, four sonnets, translations of Letters of State, and a brief biography published by his nephew Edward Phillips

Mary Astell and John Norris, *Letters concerning the Love of God*

Gilbert Burnet, *An Essay on the Memory of the Late Queen*

Charles Davenant, *A Memorial Concerning the Coyn of England*, economics treatise

Daniel Dring, *Life of that Incomparable Princess Mary*

John Dryden, "Parallel of Painting and Poetry" published

George Granville, Lord Lansdowne, *The She-Gallants*

P. H. [Patrick Hume], *Annotations on Milton's "Paradise Lost." Wherein the Texts of Sacred Writ, relating to the Poem, are Quoted...*, published

William Laud, Archbishop of Canterbury, *The History of the Troubles and Tryal of the Most Reverend Father in God, and Blessed Martyr William Laud, Lord Arch-Bishop of Canterbury. Wrote by Himself, during his Imprisonment in the Tower. To which is prefixed the diary of his own Life...*, edited by H. Wharton

René Le Bossu, *Traité du poème épique*, English translation, treatise on Epic theory

John Locke, *The Reasonableness of Christianity; and Further Considerations*

Thomas Southerne, *Oroonoko, or The Royal Slave*, produced, adapted from Aphra Behn's novel[669]

Anne Wharton, *The Temple of Death*, published

Richard Busby, Headmaster at Westminster School, d., ending a fifty-seven-year tenure

Elizabeth Legge d. (b. 1580); Legge figures prominently, primarily for her advanced age, in George Ballard, *Memoirs of Several Ladies of Great Britain who have been celebrated for their writings or skill in the learned languages, arts and sciences*, published 1752

Dorothy Osborne, Lady Temple, d.

George Savile, Marquis of Halifax, d.

Thomas Tenison elected Archbishop of Canterbury

The *Flying Post* and the *Post Boy*, rival weekly newspapers, begin publication[670]

Actors and actresses receive equal shares in a newly formed theatrical company

Jonathan Swift ordained; appointed to Prebendery of Kilroot, in Ireland

Feb — **Richard Blackmore, *Prince Arthur*, published, epic poem, imitating Milton's use of blank verse**

Mar 5 — Mary II buried in Westminster Abbey, the procession moving through a heavy snowstorm

— Thereafter: Thomas Tenison, *A Sermon Preached at the Funeral of Her Late Majesty Queen Mary*, published

Mar 26 — Charles Doe, *The Heavenly Footman*, including a

---

669. For most of the early eighteenth century, Southerne's adaptation of Behn's romance remained the most frequently produced post-Shakespearean drama in England.

670. The *Daily Courant*, the first English daily newspaper, would not begin publication until 1702.

complete bibliography of works to date by John Bunyan

Apr — John Banks, *Cyrus the Great; or, The Tragedy of Love*, performed, published 1696

— Licensing Act expires and is not renewed

Apr 5 — George Savil, 1st Marquis of Halifax, d.

Apr 13 — Jean de La Fontaine d.

Apr 23 — Henry Vaughan d.

Apr 30 — William Congreve, *Love for Love* performed at Thomas Betterton's Lincoln's Inn Fields theater

Jun — Colley Cibber, *An Ode upon the Death of our Late sovereign Lady Queen Mary*, one of many memorial verses published

Aug — William III recovers territories lost to the French; other victories

Winter — Aphra Behn, *The Younger Brother*, produced (written during the early 1680s?); published 1696

Sep 1 — War of the Grand Alliance; William III captures Namur

Nov 12 — Anthony à Wood, final entry, reporting the death of Nathaniel Wilson, Bishop of Limbrick

Nov 21 — Henry Purcell d.

Nov 26 — Henry Purcell buried in Westminster Abbey; funeral accompanied by the music Purcell wrote for the funeral of Queen Mary II

Nov 29 — Anthony Wood [Anthony à Wood] d., in the same house in which he had been born

1696

John Aubrey, *Miscellanies upon Various Subjects*[671]
Richard Baxter, *Reliquiae Baxterianae: or Mr Richard Baxter's Narrative of the Most Memorable Passages of his Life and Times, Parts I, II, and III*, folio
Aphra Behn, *All the Histories and Novels of the Late Ingenious Mrs. Behn. In One Volume*, with "History of the Life and Memoirs of Mrs. Behn, by One of the Fair Sex," collected by Charles Gildon
Sir Robert Cotton, *Catalogus Librorum Manuscriptorum Bibliothecae Cottonianae*, edited by T. Smith
Charles Davenant, *A Memorial Concerning Creditt*, economics treatise
John Dennis, *Remarks on a Book, Entitled Prince Arthur, An Heroick Poem*, defending Milton against his imitators
Judith Drake (?), *An Essay in Defense of the Female Sex*
Gregory King, *Natural and Political Observations upon the State and Condition of England*, written (published 1801)
Letters on Several Occasions: Written By and Between Mr. Dryden, Mr. Wycherley, Mr. _____, Mr. Congreve, and Mr. Dennis, published
Peter Anthony Motteux, *Love's a Jest*
Mary Pix, *Ibrahim*, drama
Elizabeth Singer, *Poems on Several Occasions by Philomela*,

---

671. Aubrey's *Miscellanies* contains an account of a ghostly apparition appearing to Thomas Traherne (Gladys Wade, *Thomas Traherne*, p. 28). It was the only volume Aubrey published during his lifetime, his famous *Lives* not appearing in a complete edition until the nineteenth century.

    edited by John Dunton
Thomas Southerne, *Oroonoko: A Tragedy*, published
Sir John Suckling, *Works*
Nahum Tate and Nicholas Brady, *New Version*, psalm-hymns for Anglican services
Zachary Taylor, *The Devil Turned Casuist, or the Cheats of Rome Laid open in the Exorcism of a Despairing Devil*
John Toland, *Christianity not Mysterious*, rationalist treatise on religion
Sir John Vanbrugh, *The Relapse, or Virtue in Danger*, presented
Edward Philips d. (?)
Persecution of Catholics continues
John Arbuthnot, receives M.D., St. Andrews College, Oxford University[672]
Alexander Pope attends school at Twyford (perhaps 1697), a refuge for Catholics
Jonathan Swift returns to Moor Park at the behest of Sir William Temple

Jan — Colley Cibber, *Love's Last Shift, or The Fool in Fashion*, performed, with Cibber playing Sir Novelty Fashion, Cibber's first play[673]; published 1696, 2nd edition 1696
Feb — Aphra Behn, *The Younger Brother*, performed, Drury Lane Theatre
Feb 25 — Anti-Williamite, pro-Jacobite uprising revealed
Jul — John Dryden, "Ode on the Death of Mr. Henry Purcell"
— John Dryden, the Younger, *The Husband His Own Cuckold*, published; preface by John Dryden
Jul 25 — William Henry, Duke of Gloucester, installed Garter Knight at age seven
Nov — Aphra Behn, *The Younger Brother*, performed; there-

---

  672. In 1704, Arbuthnot would be elected a Fellow of the Royal Society; in 1705, he would be appointed Physician-Extraordinary to Queen Anne

  673. Helene Koon argues that the performance of this play marks the shift from Restoration comedy of wit to 18th century sentimental comedy, along with a re-orientation of attitudes toward the stage (*Colley Cibber*).

after published, 1696

Dec (?)— Colley Cibber, *Women's Wit; or, The Lady in Fashion*, completed; performed and published, 1697

1697

John Milton, *The Works of Mr. John Milton*, collected prose in English
Mary Astell, *A Serious Proposal to the Ladies, Part 2*
Daniel Baker, *On Mr. George Herbert's Sacred Poems Called, The Temple*, published, poem in honor of Herbert
Roger Coke, *A Detection of the Court and State of England during the Last Four Reigns and the Inter-regnum...*, in two volumes
William Congreve, *The Mourning Bride*
Charles Davenant, *An Essay on the East India Trade*
Daniel Defoe, *Essay upon Projects*, with discussions of banking, bankruptcy, education, etc
Familiar Letters. *Written by the Right Honourable John, late Earl of Rochester, and several other Persons of Honour and quality. With letters written by Thomas Otway and Mrs. K. Philips ...*, published
Peter Anthony Motteux, *The Loves of Mars and Venus*, performed; *The Musical Play of Mars and Venus*, published
Edward Ravenscroft, *The Italian Husband*, performed, published 1698
The Surrey Demoniack,... or, an Account of Satan's...Actings, In and about the Body of Richard Dugdale, published, based on events in April 1689
Jonathan Swift, *A Tale of a Tub and The Battle of the Books*, written (1696-1698)
Zachary Taylor, *The Surrey Imposter, being an answer to a ...*

Pamphlet, Entituled The Surrey Demoniac

William Turner, *A Compleat history of the most remarkable Providences, both of Judgment and Mercy, which have hapned in this present age, last compilation during the century intended to demonstrate God's working in human history*

Sir John Vanbrugh, *The Provok'd Wife*; *Relapse*

Charles Wagstaffe, *A Vindication of King Charles the Martyr*

Jan 28 — Sir John Fenwick beheaded on Tower Hill for complicity in a Jacobite plot to assassinate William III

Feb — Thomas D'Urfey, *The Intrigues of Versailles*, performed, published 1697

Mar — Edward Ravenscroft, *The Anatomist*, performed, published 1697

May — Elkanah Settle, *The World in the Moon*, performed, published 1697

Jun — John Aubrey d.

Jun 14 — John Dunton, *The Athenian Gazette* ceases publication; over twenty volumes, Dunton answered more than 6,000 questions

Jun 28 — John Dryden, *The Works of Virgil...*, advertised

Aug — John Dryden, *The Works of Virgil: Containing His Pastorals, Georgics and Aeneis*, published by subscription[674]

Sep — Thomas D'Urfey, *Cinthia and Endimion*, performed, published 1697

Sep 10 — Treaty of Ryswick signed

Sep 11 — William III meets Peter I the Great, Tsar of Russia, in Utrecht

---

674. Publication by subscription—that is, selling a specific quantity of books before their publication—became a method by which authors might actually realize a profit from their works. Dryden demonstrated that the process could succeed; Pope accumulated a fortune through his subscription sales of *Homer*. In contrast, Milton and his estate received less than £20 total for *Paradise Lost*.

Sep 14 — Matthew Prior presents the Treaty of Ryswijk to the House of Lord in London

Sep 20 — Treaty of Ryswick concludes the war against France, with England taking the advantage

Oct 5 — Peace of Ryswijk ratified, concluding hostilities between England and France

Oct 28 — Thomas Brown, *A Satyr upon the French King*, satirical verse response to the Treaty of Ryswick, published

Oct 30 — Thomas Brown arrested, along with his publisher, Abel Roper, for violating the Treaty of Ryswick with his satire

Nov 10 — William Hogarth b. (d. 1764)

Nov 13 — "Mr. Stacy," *An Answer to the Satyr upon the French King*, pro-Jacobite response to Thomas Brown[675]

Nov 22 — John Dryden, *Alexander's Feast* performed

Nov 23-25 — *The Flying Post* publishes the *Petition of Tom Brown, who was taken up on account of the Satyr upon the French King* (by Charles Sackville, 6th Earl of Dorset?), in defense of Brown

Dec 2 — William III announces a day of Thanksgiving to celebrate the Peace of Rijswijk; to be held in the nearly completed and newly consecrated St. Paul's Cathedral

Dec 11-16 — [William Shippen?], *Advice to a Painter*, anonymous satirical verse, Tory response to the Treaty of Ryswick, published

---

675. Brown responded to his respondent, this time in a prose pamphlet included in Brown's posthumous *Works* (1711) and there titled *Mr. Brown's Characters of the Jacobite Clergy*, found among his private Papers, and suppos'd to be writ upon the Occasion of Mr. Stacy's Answer to the Satyr against the French King,

1698

John Milton, *A Complete Collection of the Historical, Political, and Miscellaneous Works of John Milton. With some papers never before publish'd. To which is prefixed a life of the Author, Containing, Besides the history of his Works, Several Extraordinary Characters of Men and Books, Sects, Parties, and Opinions*, published in London and Amsterdam; includes John Toland's biography, with assistance from John Phillips

John Milton, *The Poetical Remains of Mr. Milton, etc.*, edited by Charles Gildon

William Hog, Latin translation of *Comus*, as *Commoedia Joannis Miltoni*

Joseph Addison, *Examen Poeticum Duplex*, including five of Milton's Latin Poems

Philippi Avril, *Travels into divers parts of Europe and Asia, undertaken by the French king's order to discover a new way by land into China, containing many curious remarks in Natural Philosophy, Geography, Hydrography, and History. Together with a description of Great Tartary and of the different people who inhabit there*

Aphra Behn, *The Adventure of the Black Lady; The Court of the King of Bantam; The Nun: Or, Perjur'd Beauty; The Unfortunate Happy Lady; The Unfortunate Bride: Or, The Blind Lady a Beauty; The Wandering Beauty; The Unhappy Mistake: Or, The Impious Vow Punish'd*, published (novels); *All the Histories and Novels written by the Late Ingenious*

Mrs. Behn. Entire in One Volume, published
Gilbert Burnet, *Exposition of the Thirty-nine Articles of the Church of England*, latitudinarian treatise
John Crowne, *Caligula*, performed
Charles Davenant, *Discourses on the Public Revenues and of the Trade in England*
John Dryden, "To Mr Granville"; "To My Friend," published
George Fox, *Epistles*, edited by Thomas Ellwood
Charles Gildon, *Poetical Remains*, including poetry by Aphra Behn
Thomas Hearne, *Ductor historicus: or, A Short System of Universal History*
[Charles Leslie], *The History of Sin and Heresie Attempted, From the First "War" that they Rais'd in "Heaven"...*, published, with references to *Paradise Lost*
Luke Milbourn, *Notes on Dryden's Virgil*, attack on Dryden
Peter Anthony Motteux, *Beauty in Distress*, performed
[Matthew Prior?], *Money Masters all Things; or, Satyricall Poems*, published
Algernon Sidney, *Discourses concerning Government*
C. T., *The new Atlas; or Travels and voyages in Europe, Asia, Africa and America, thro' the most renowned parts of the world*, published
Zachary Taylor, *Popery, Superstition, Ignorance and Knavery... very fully proved...in the Surrey Imposture*, attack on Papists and belief in witchcraft
Benjamin Whichcote, *Select Sermons*
[William Wycherley], *A Vindication of the Stage*
Sir Robert Howard d.
William III concludes a secret treaty with France concerning the division of Spain at the death of the current Spanish King
Joseph Addison made a Fellow of Magdalen College, Oxford University
John Wilmot, 2nd Earl of Rochester, *Poems on Several Occasions*, the publisher reissuing the book is charged with obscene libel before the King's Bench

Jan — George Granville, *Heroic Love* acted, tragedy

Jan 4 — Whitehall Palace, with the exception of Inigo Jones' Banquet Hall, destroyed by fire

Jan 10 — Peter the Great of Russia arrives in England on his 'incognito' tour of western Europe

Mar 14 — Lodowick Muggleton d.

Spring — Jeremy Collier, *A Short View of the Immorality and Profaneness of the English Stage*

Apr — First free out-patient clinic in London opens

Apr 23 — Peter the Great departs England

June — John Dennis, *The Usefulness of the Stage*, first full response to Jeremy Collier's critique

— John Dryden, translation of Tacitus

Aug 20 — Amabella, Dowager Countess of Kent and patroness to Thomas Traherne, d., at age 92

Nov — Thomas D'Urfey, *The Campaigners*, performed, published 1698

— George Farquhar, *Love and a Bottle*, performed, Farquhar's first play

— Peter Motteux, *The Island Princess*, opera, based on John Fletcher

Dec 6 — The fourth Parliament of William III opens

Dec 15 — **John Toland, biography of Milton SR**

1699

Rev. Offspring Blackall, *Remarks on the Life of Mr. Milton, As Publish'd by J. T. With a Character of the Author and His Party*
Amyntor: or, a Defense of Milton's Life, **response to Blackall**
Rev. Offspring Blackall, *Mr. Blackall's Reasons for not Replying to a Book Lately Published, Entituled Amyntor. In a Letter to a Friend*
William Hog, *Paradise Lost* **(1667 version),** *Paradise Regained*, **and** *Samson Agonistes*, **translated into Latin as** *Paraphrasis Poetica in Tria*; **reprinted in Amsterdam**
John Hopkins, *Milton's Paradise Lost Imitated in Rhyme. In the Fourth Sixth and Ninth Books; Containing the Primitive Loves. The Battel of the Angels. The Fall of Man*
Thomas Allison, *An Account of a voyage from Archangel in Russia in the year 1697*
Sir Richard Blackmore, *A Satyr against Wit*, published
Abel Boyer, *Dictionary*, French-English dictionary; standard work for over a century
John Cleveland, *Poems*[676]
Charles Davenant, *An Essay upon the probable methods of making the people gainers in the Balance of Trade*
John Deane, *A letter from Moscow to the Marquess of Carmarthen relating to the Czar of Muscovy's forwardness*

---

676. The final of some twenty editions (more or less) published of his works during the century, an indication of his enormous popularity

in his great navy, report on naval preparations by Peter the Great John Dunton, *Some Account of my conversation in Ireland ..., with The Dublin Scuffle: Being a Challenge sent by John Dunton, Citizen of London*, published

John Evelyn, *Acetaria: A Discourse of Sallats*, i.e., 'Salads,' with quotations from *Paradise Lost*

George Farquhar, *The Constant Couple*

Charles Gildon, *Longbaine's Lives of the English Dramatic Poets*, published

Walter Harris, *A Brief Description of the King's Royal Palace and Gardens at Loo*

Foy de La Neuville [pseudonym for Adrian Baillet], *An account of Muscovy, as it was in the year 1689...*, report from the Envoy of the King of Poland, describes accession of Peter the Great

Peter Anthony Motteux, *The Island Princess*, performed; *The Four Seasons*, performed

Lodowick Muggleton, *The Acts of the Witnesses of the Spirit*

Sir William Temple, *Letters Written by Sir William Temple During His Being Ambassador at The Hague*

Thomas Traherne, *A Serious and Pathetical Contemplation of the Mercies of God, in several most Devout and Sublime Thanksgivings for the Same*, published anonymously by George Hickes

Joseph Wright, *Historica Histrionica*, published

Christopher Pitt b., future translator of Vida's *Art of Poetry*

Joseph Beaumont d.

Sir James Chamberlayne, d.

Lady Anne Harcourt Halkett d. (*Memoirs* published 1979)

Joseph Addison receives a pension from the Crown of £300

Samuel Pepys granted the freedom of the City of London

Jonathan Swift returns to Ireland as chaplain to the Lord Justice, the Earl of Berkeley

Early 1699 (?)— Joseph Addison, *The Play-House. A Satyr*, verse satire against the stage, written

Jan-Feb — Arthur Mainwaring (?), *An Excellent New Ballad, call'd, The Brawny bishop's Complaint. To the Tune of Packington's Pound*, verse satire attacking Gilbert Burnet, Bishop of Salisbury

Jan 27 — Sir William Temple d.

Feb — Colley Cibber, *Xerxes*, tragedy, performed at Lincoln's Inn Fields; published April 1699

May — Thomas D'Urfey, *The Famous History of the Rise and Fall of Massaniello, Parts I & II*, performed, published 1700

May 4 — The fourth Parliament of William III closes

— Thereafter: Daniel Defoe, *An Encomium upon a Parliament*, verse satire

May 6-8 — Samuel Garth, *The Dispensary*, satirical verse, published

May 10-17 — Edward Ward, *An Answer to An Encomium on a Parliament*, published in the *Weekly Comedy*

Nov 30 — Dated preface to John Toland, ed., *The Oceana of James Harrington, and His Other Works*, published, renewing the debate with Blackall over Toland's earlier biography of Milton

Dec — Colley Cibber, *The Tragical History of Richard III*, adaptation from William Shakespeare

1700

John Milton, *Letters of State* published as *Oliver Cromwell's Letters to Foreign Princes and States*, printed in London by John Nutt

John Asgill, *An Argument proving that According to the Covenant of Eternal Life, revealed in the Scriptures, Man May be Translated from Hence into that Eternal Life without Passing through Death, although the Human Nature of Christ Himself could not be Thus Translated till He had Passed Through Death*, pamphlet, afterward ordered burned by two sessions of Parliament

Mary Astell, *Some Reflections upon Marriage*

Aphra Behn, *Histories, The Dumb Virgin: Or, The Force of Imagination*, novel

Sir Richard Blackmore, *A Satire against Wit*

Abel Boyer, *The Wise and Ingenious Companion*, jest-book

Miguel de Cervantes, *Don Quixote*, translation into English by Motteux

Colley Cibber, *Love Makes a Man*, performed; published 1701

Jeremy Collier, *A Second Defense of the Short View*, published[677]

William Congreve, *The Way of the World*, performed and published David Crawford, *Courtship à-la-mode*, published

Thomas Creech, *Catalogue of His Library*, published

Daniel Defoe, *An Inquiry into Occasional Conformity*

---

677. Collier's additional attacks on the stage continued with *A Dissuasive from the Playhouse* (1703) and *A Farther Vindication of the Short View* (1707).

John Dennis, *Iphigenia. A Tragedy. Acted at the Theatre in Little Lincoln-Inn-Fields*

Charles Doe, *A Collection of Experience*, published, includes a discussion of how Doe came to be instrumental in publishing John Bunyan's posthumous works

Henry King, *Ben Johnson's Poems, Elegies, Paradoxes, and Sonnets*, reissued, attributed by the printer to Ben Jonson

William Laud, *Second Volume of the Remains*, edited by H. Wharton

John Pomfret, *The Choice*

George Savile, Marquis of Halifax, *The Ladies' New Year Gift, or, Advice to a Daughter*, published

Thomas Southerne, *The Fate of Capua*, produced

Nahum Tate, *Panacea: A Poem upon Tea: In Two Canto's*[678]

Sir William Temple, *Letters Written by Sir William Temple, Bart, and other Ministers of State (1665-1672)*, published posthumously by Jonathan Swift; *Memoirs*, written

John Toland, editor, *The Oceana of James Harrington, and His Other Works*, continues Toland's debate with Blackall concerning Milton's biography

John Tutchin, *The Foreigners*

Samuel Wesley, *An Epistle to a Friend Concerning Poetry*, ranking Milton superior as a moral poet

John Dyer b.

James Thomson b. (d. 1748)

The population of England and Wales has increased from approximately 4,500,000 in 1600 to approximately 5,300,000, in spite of incursions made by war, disease (particularly the Plague) and other causes

Tobacco consumption has risen from 140,000 pounds a year (1614-1621) to 11,300,000 pounds a year (1699-1709)

Monument to Edmund Waller erected in Beaconsfield, emphasizing his service to Parliament rather than his poetry

Alexander Pope the Elder moves with his family to Whitehill

---

678. In its use of mock-epic conventions, Tate's poem prefigures Pope's brilliant *Rape of the Lock*.

House at Binfield, near Windsor[679]

Sir John Cotton donates to the nation the collection of books and manuscripts amassed by his antiquarian great-grandfather, Sir Robert Cotton; they form part of the core collection for the British Museum, formally opened in 1759

Feb 15 — **Daniel Defoe, *The Pacificator*, with references to Milton as among the "Giants...of wit and sense"**

Mar — John Dryden, *Fables, Ancient and Modern Translated into Verse from Homer, Ovid, Boccace & Chaucer: with Original Poems*, advertised; *A Secular Masque*, published; with critical preface

Apr (?) — John Vanbrugh, *The Pilgrim*, performed

May 1 — John Dryden d.[680]

May 2 — John Dryden buried in St. Anne's, Soho; London's theaters closed in his honor

May 13 — John Dryden exhumed and re-buried in Chaucer's grave in Westminster Abbey

Mid-May — Alexander Pope, a short "Ode on Solitude," written just before his twelfth birthday[681]

Jun — [William Shippen?], *A Conference*, published

Jul 25 — William Henry, Duke of Gloucester, ill following his birthday party, possibly of smallpox

Jul 30 — William Henry, Duke of Gloucester, d.; between his birth and his death, Princess Anne (afterward Queen Anne) suffers six more miscarriages

Aug — Tutchin, *The Foreigners*, published, attack on William III and the Dutch

— Thereafter (Jan 1701): Daniel Defoe, *The True-Born Englishman: A Satyr*, verse response to Tutchin (eventually

---

679. The move was required by increasingly stringent anti-Papist laws, one of which forbade Papists and "reputed Papists" from living within ten miles of the cities of London and Westminster.

680. Earl Miner adds that Dryden died at 3 a.m. of degenerative diseases, his mind clear and functioning

681. Identified as such by Pope in a letter dated 11 July 1709.

nine editions by Defoe, twelve pirated editions)

Oct — William III meets in Holland with the Electress Sophia and her daughter Sophie Charlotte, to discuss the Electress' possible succession to the throne, following the now-childless Princess Anne

Nov — Charles II, King of Spain, d., making the political balance in Europe increasingly fragile

— Louis XIV thereafter claims Spain in the name of his grandson, Philippe d'Anjou, alienating the Holy Roman Emperor

And Beyond....
Some Eighteenth-Twentieth Century Contributions To a Milton Timeline

1711 — Phillipus van Limborch notes in a letter that he had advised against publishing Milton's *De Doctrina Christiana* because of its Arian leanings

1727 — Milton's daughter Deborah d.

1731 — "Onslow" portrait in the collection of Arthur Onslow, Speaker of the House of Commons

1732 — Richard Meadowcourt (1695-1760), *A Critique of Milton's Paradise Regain'd*, the first book-length study of one of Milton's works

1734 — Jonathan Richards, *Life* (of Milton)

1737 — Monument to Milton, Westminster Abbey, by John Michael Rysbrack

1738 — Feb 10 — John Ward visits Elizabeth Foster, Milton's granddaughter
Feb 11 — Thomas Birch visits Elizabeth Foster
Mar 1 — Thomas Birch, *A Complete Collection of the...Works of John Milton* (with biography)
Mar 4 — First theatrical performance of *Comus* at the Theater

in Drury Lane

1743 — Publication of State Letters and other documents

1749 — Thomas Newton, *Paradise Lost*, with a Life of Milton

1750 — Jan 6 — Thomas Birch interviews Elizabeth Foster
Apr 5 — Performance of *Comus* as a benefit for Milton's granddaughter Elizabeth Foster, earning just over £130
— Samuel Johnson, *A New Prologue Spoken by Mr. Garrick, Thursday, April 5, 1750. At the Representation of Comus, for the Benefit of Mrs. Elizabeth Foster, Milton's Grand-Daughter, and Only Surviving Descendant*
Nov 13 — Thomas Birch interviews Elizabeth Foster, incorporating information received into a revision of Milton's collected prose, published in 1753

1754 — May 9 — Milton's last lineal descendent, Elizabeth Foster, d., age 66.

1804 — William Blake, *Milton*, begun

1809 — William Blake, engravings for Milton, *Nativity Ode*

1818 — William Blake, *Milton*, completed

1825 — Manuscript, *De Doctrina Christiana* discovered by Robert Lemon, Deputy Keeper of His Majesty's State Papers in a cupboard in the Old State Office, Whitehall
— Publication of *Joannis Miltoni Angli de Doctrina Christiana libri duo posthumi, quos ex schedis manuscriptis depromisit, et typis mandari primus curavit* (The Christian Doctrine), edited by Charles Sumner

1859 — David Masson begins publishing his monumental *The Life of John Milton, narrated in Connexion with the Political,*

Ecclesiastical, and Literary History of his Times, 7 volumes (issued through 1894; rev. ed., Vols. I-III, 1881-1896)

1874 — David Masson, *The Poetical Works of John Milton* (reprinted 1890)

1876 — Photographic facsimile of Milton's *Commonplace Book* published by A. J. Horwood

1968 — William Riley Parker, *Biography*, 2 vol.; 2nd edition, 1997

APPENDIX ONE:
Genealogical Tables

Section I:
Ancestry Charts

MILTON, JOHN, poet
born: 9 Dec 1608, London, England
chr 20 Dec 1609, All Hallows, Bread Street, London
died 8 Nov 1674, London, England
buried 12 Nov 1674, St. Giles, Cripplegate, London
married
1. Jun 1642 — Mary (Marie) Powell
2. 12 Nov 1656 — Katherine Woodstock
3. 24 Feb 1663 — Elizabeth Minshull

I. Parents

John Milton, scrivener
born 1562/63, Stanton St. Johns, Oxfordshire[682]
died 13 Mar (?) 1647, London
buried 15 Mar 1647, St. Giles Cripplegate, London
married 1590-1600 Sara Jefferays (Jefferay, Jeffreys, Jeffrey)

---

682. According to Elizabeth Foster (Milton's granddaughter), John Milton, Sr., was born in France; this might simply mean that he was born in Petty-France, a section of London.

she born about 1572[683]
died 3 Apr 1637, Horton
buried 6 Apr 1637, Horton parish church, Horton

IIA. PATERNAL GRANDPARENTS

Richard Milton, yeoman[684]
born Stanton St. Johns, Oxfordshire
died after Oct 1601
married Elizabeth Haughton

IIB. MATERNAL GRANDPARENTS

Paul Jeffrey
born about 1537
died 1583, of Stanton St. Johns, Oxfordshire
married Helen/ Ellen
buried 26 Feb 1610/11, All Hallows, London,

IIIA. PATERNAL GREAT-GRANDPARENTS

Henry Milton
died before 5 Mar 1558/59, Stanton St. Johns, Oxford
married Agnes
died before 14 Jun 1561, Stanton St. Johns, Oxford

IIIB. MATERNAL GREAT-GRANDPARENTS

John Jeffrey
died after 22 Feb 1551, Essex
married Joan/Johan
died after 9 Mar 1572, Essex

---

683. Sara Jefferay is mentioned in John Jeffrey's will, dated 1572/73.

684. Milton's grandfather was Catholic, an under-ranger at Shotover. He was excommunicated in May 1582, along with John White.

IV. Maternal Great-Great-Grandparents

Mr. Jeffrey
married Julian

POWELL, MARY, Milton's 1st wife
born 24 Jan 1624/25, Forest Hill, Oxfordshire
died about May 1652

I. Parents

Richard Powell, tax-collector
died 1 Jan 1647, in Milton's home, Barbican, London
married Anne (Archdale?)[685]
died before 6 Nov 1682, London
Children:
Mary Powell, married John Milton
Richard Powell, married Anne
died before 3 Feb 1696; will proved 29 Dec 1693
Anne Powell, married Thomas Kingston, merchant
Sarah Powell, married. Richard Pierson, Gentleman
died after 1678
Elizabeth Powell, married Thomas Howell, Gentleman
Elizabeth Powell, married Christmas Holloway, Gentleman
William Powell, Captain Lieutenant
died before Dec 1652, in battle in Scotland

II. Maternal Grandparents

Richard Archdale (Merchant)
Richard had a brother, Bernard Archdale, of Oxford

---

685. Anne refers in her will to her son's "grandmother Archdale"

WOODCOCK (WOODSTOCK) KATHERINE, Milton's 2nd wife
died 3 Feb 1657/58, Petty France, Westminster
buried 10 Feb 1658, St. Margaret's, Westminster
married 12 Nov 1656, St. Mary Virgin, Aldermanbury London

I. Parents

William Woodcock, Captain
died before 1644

MINSHULL, ELIZABETH, Milton's 3rd wife
born about 1638, in Cheshire
died about 23-26 Aug 1727, Nantwich, Cheshire[686]

I. Parents

Randle/ Randall Minshull
born 1605
died 1660, Wistaston, Cheshire
married Anne Boote
died about 1676

II. Paternal Grandparents

Richard Minshull
born 1575
died 1658
married Ellen Goldsmith
born 1583
died 1624

---

686. Masson refers to Elizabeth Minshull as moving to her "native" Cheshire in about 1681. She is noted as being alive on Aug 22, 1712, and therefore must have died between August 23 and August 26. (Masson, *Life of Milton*, VI, p. 745)

III. Great-Grandparents

Thomas Minshull
married 1592
died 1606
Alice

Nicholas Goldsmith
died 1617
married Dorothy
Children:
Margery Goldsmith, m. 1613, Rev. Thomas Paget
born 1579
Ellen Goldsmith, m. Richard Minshull

IV. Great-Great-Grandparents

Randall Minshull of Wistaston
died 1595
married Margery Rawlinson of Crewe
died 1592

Randle Goldsmith of Wistaston
died 1577
Margery

PHILLIPS, EDWARD, m. Anne, Milton's sister
born about Dec 1597
chr 11 Dec 1597, St. Julian's, Shrewsbury
died about 22 Aug 1631, London
buried 25 Aug 1631, St. Martin-in-the-Fields, London

I. Parents

Edward Phillips
married 7 Feb 1597, St. Julian's, Shrewsbury

buried 20 Oct 1618, St. Julian's, Shrewsbury
married Katherine Prowde
born about 1569
chr 31 Jul 1569, St. Julian's, Shrewsbury
buried 3 Aug 1650, St. Julian's, Shrewsbury
Children:
Edward Phillips, married Anne Milton
Mary Phillips
born Apr 1600
chr 13 Apr 1600, St. Julian's, Shrewsbury
buried 8 Jan 1632, St. Julian's, Shrewsbury
Andrew Phillips
born May 1602
chr 6 May 1602, St. Julian's, Shrewsbury
John Phillips
born Apr 1696
chr 10 Apr 1606
Martha Phillips
born Mar 1609
chr 20 Mar 1609, St. Julian's, Shrewsbury
George Phillips
born Jul 1612
chr 9 Jul 1612, St. Julian's, Shrewsbury

IIA. PATERNAL GRANDPARENTS

Hugo Phillips, of Shrewsbury and Caresws, Montgomeryshire, Wales

IIB. MATERNAL GRANDPARENTS

George Prowde, draper
buried 1 Jan 1592, Shrewsbury
married Ellen Lewis

Section II:
Descendants Charts

MILTON, JOHN, scrivener (Milton's father), m. SARA JEFFERAY
married:about 1590/1600

CHILDREN

1. (Child) Milton[687]
born about 1601, London
buried May 12, 1601, All Hallows, Bread Street, London
2. Anne Milton[688]
born about 1604
married Nov 22, 1623, Edward Phillips, London
about 1634, to Thomas Agar
3. John Milton (poet)
born 9 Dec 1608, The Spread Eagle, Bread Street, London
chr 20 Dec 1608, All Hallows, Bread Street, London
died 8 Nov 1674, London
buried 12 Nov 1674, St. Giles Cripplegate, London
4. Sara Milton
chr 15 Jun 1612, All Hallows, Bread Street, London
buried 6 Aug 1612, All Hallows, Bread Street, London
5. Tabitha Milton
chr 30 Jan 1613, All Hallows, Bread Street, London
buried 3 Aug 1615, All Hallows, Bread Street, London
6. Christopher Milton

687/ Parker notes that the child probably died before being baptized or christened, since it is referred to as a "chrisom" child, that is, one who died before the white cloth or 'chrisom' of baptism could be placed over the face. (I, p. 5)

688. Details of Anne Milton's birth have not been discovered. Parker speculated that she might have been born while Sara Jefferay Milton was visiting family in Essex.

born about 24 Nov 1615, Spread Eagle, Bread Street[689]
chr 3 Dec 1615, All-Hallows, Bread Street, London
died about 20 Mar 1693, Rushmere, Suffolk,
buried 22 Mar 1693, St. Nicholas, Ipswich
married about Mar 1638 — to Thomasine Webber
(baptized 18 Oct 1618; died after 1656)

MILTON, JOHN, poet, m. (1) MARY POWELL

married about Jun 1642

CHILDREN

1. Anne Milton[690]
born 29 Oct 1645, Barbican Street, London
died before 24 Oct 1678, London
married 1675-78 (name of husband unknown)
2. Mary Milton
born 25 Oct 1648, High Holborn, Cripplegate, London
chr St. Giles Cripplegate, London
died 1681-1694
unmarried
3. John Milton
born 16 Mar 1651, Scotland Yard, Whitehall, London
died about 16 Jun 1652, Petty-France, Westminster
4. Deborah Milton
born 2 May 1652, Petty-France, Westminster
died 24 Aug 1727, of Pelham Street, Spitalfields
married I Jun 1674, St. Kevin's, Ireland, to Abraham Clarke

---

689. The birth-entry for Christopher Milton, in the family bible and in John Milton, Jr., specifies that the younger brother was born on Friday, about a month before Christmas, but does not give a precise date; The Friday one month before Christmas in 1615 would have fallen on 24 November.

690. Anne Milton died during the birth of her first child; the child died also.

MILTON, JOHN, poet, m. (2) KATHERINE WOODCOCK

married 12 Nov 1656

CHILDREN

1. Katherine Milton
born 19 Oct 1656, London
died 17 Mar 1657, London

MILTON, ANNE, Milton's sister, m. (1) EDWARD PHILLIPS

married 22 Nov 1623

CHILDREN

1. John Phillips
chr 6 Jan 1624, St. Martin-in-the-Fields, London
died 15 Mar 1629
2. Anne Phillips
bornJan 1626, London
chr 12 Jan 1626, St. Martin-in-the-Fields, London
died Jan 1628, London
buried 22 Jan 1628, St. Martin-in-the-Fields, London
3. Elizabeth Phillips
chr 9 Apr 1628, St. Martin-in-the-Fields, London
buried 19 Feb, 1631, St. Martin-in-the-Fields, London
4. Edward Phillips
born about Aug 1630, Strand, Charing Cross, London
died about 1696
married about 1679-1680, a widow
5. John Phillips
born Aug 1630
died 1706
married date and name unknown

MILTON, ANNE, Milton's sister, M. (2) THOMAS AGAR

married about 1634
Thomas Agar born 1597(?)
died 1 Nov 1673

Children:

1. Mary Agar
died child
2. Anne Agar
married 1662, David Moore

MILTON, DEBORAH, Milton's daughter, m. ABRAHAM CLARKE of Dublin, Ireland; weaver in Spitalfields, London

married 1 Jun 1674, St. Kevin's, Dublin, Ireland
Abraham Clarke died 1678-1702

CHILDREN (Milton's grandchildren):

Abraham Clarke and Deborah Milton had ten children—seven sons and three daughters; of these, the names of four are known, and only two of those married and in turn had children. References to the family disappear around 1750.

1. Deborah Clarke
born Nov 1688, Dublin, Ireland
2. Caleb Clarke
died about 1719, Madras, India
buried 26 Oct 1719, St. George Cathedral, Madras, India
Caleb Clarke had moved to Madras before 2 June 1703, when
    his son was baptized
3. Elizabeth Clarke
born Nov 1688, Ireland
died 9 May 1754, Sugar Loaf, Islington

buried 14 May 1754, Tindalls, Pelham Fields, London
married 1719, Thomas Foster, weaver in Spitalfields, London

Elizabeth Clarke was the last surviving known descendant of John Milton; the families of his sister, Anne, and his brother, Christopher, continue into the twentieth century

4. Urban Clarke, weaver
died before 1749

CLARKE, CALEB, Milton's grandson, m. MARY

Mary buried 26 Jan 1715/16

CHILDREN (Milton's great-grandchildren)

1. Abraham Clarke
chr 2 Jun 1703, St. George Cathedral, Madras, India
buried 5 Oct 1743, St. George Cathedral, Madras, India
married 22 Sep 1725, Anna
2. Mary Clarke
chr 17 Mar 1707/9, St. George Cathedral, Madras, India
buried 15/16 Dec 1716, St. George Cathedral, Madras, India
3. Isaac Clarke
chr 13 Feb 1711, St. George Cathedral, Madras, India
died 1746-1749, Madras, India

William Riley Parker and Gordon Campbell both note that nothing more is known of Isaac Clarke; he may have married and had children, perpetuating the family name.

CLARKE, ABRAHAM, Milton's great-grandson, m. ANNA CLARK[691]

married 22 Sep 1725, St. George Cathedral, Madras, India

By 1738, this branch of the family had completely lost contact with the Clarkes in England and Ireland

CHILDREN

1. Mary Clarke
chr 5 Apr 1727, Madras, India
buried about 4 Oct, St. George Cathedral, Madras, India

CLARKE, ELIZABETh, Milton's granddaughter, m. THOMAS FOSTER

married 1719

CHILDREN (Milton's great-grandchildren)

Elizabeth Clarke and Thomas Foster had seven children, all of whom died before 1738

POWELL, RICHARD m. ANNE ARCHDALE—Milton's father- and mother-in-law

CHILDREN

1. Mary Powell
chr 24 Jan 1625, Forest Hill, Oxford
died about 5 May 1652, Petty France, Westminster
married about June 1642, John Milton
2. Richard Powell

---

691. Anna Clark's maiden name was the same as her married name.

died before 3 Feb 1696
married Anne
3. Anne Powell
married Thomas Kingston, merchant
4. Sarah Powell
died after 1678
married Richard Peirson, Gentleman
5. Elizabeth Powell
married Thomas Howell, Gentleman
6. Elizabeth Powell
married Christmas Holloway, Gentleman
7. William Powell, Captain-Lieutenant
died before 1652, in battle in Scotland

Sources and Resources

Adams, Robert M., ed. *Ben Jonson's Plays and Masques*. New York: Norton, 1979.

Adamson, J. H., and H. F. Holland. *Sir Harry Vane: His Life and Times (1613-1662)*. Boston: Gambit, 1973.

Aitken, George A., intro. *Later Stuart Tracts: An English Garner*. Westminster, England: Archibald Constable, 1903.

Anderson, John P. *Bibliography*. In Richard Garnet, *Life of John Milton*. London: Walter Scott, 1890. Separately paginated at the end of the biography.

Andrews, Charles, ed. *Ideal Empires and Republics: Rousseau's Social contract; More's Utopia, Bacon's New Atlantis; Campanella's City of the Sun*. Washington and London: M. Walter Dunne, 1901.

Ashley, Maurice. *The Stuarts in Love, with Some Reflections on Love and Marriage in the Sixteenth and Seventeenth Centuries*. London: Hodder and Stoughton, 1963.

Aubrey, John. *Aubrey on Education: A Hitherto Unpublished Manuscript by the Author of BRIEF LIVES*. Ed. J. E. Stephens. London: Routledge & Kegan Paul, 1972.

Ayers, Robert, ed. *Complete Prose Works of John Milton, Volume VII, 1559-1660*. New Haven: Yale University Press, 1974.

Bacon, Sir Francis. *Bacon's Advancement of Learning and The New Atlantis*, preface by Thomas Case. London: Oxford University Press, 1907.

Bacon, Sir Francis. *The Advancement of Learning*. Ed. by

William Aldis Wright. Oxford at the Clarendon Press, 1873.

Barbour, Hugh, and Arthur O. Roberts, eds. *Early Quaker Writings 1650-1700.* Grand Rapids MI: William B. Eerdmans, 1973.

Barbour, Hugh, and J. William Frost. *The Quakers.* New York: Greenwood Press, 1988.

Baugh, Albert C. *A Literary History of England.* New York: Appleton-Century-Crofts, 1948

Beaurline, L. A. *The Works of Sir John Suckling: The Plays.* Oxford at the Clarendon Press, 1971.

Bedford, R. D. *Dialogues with Convention: Readings in Renaissance Poetry.* Ann Arbor: University of Michigan Press, 1989.

Behrendt, Stephen C. *The Moment of Explosion: Blake and the Illustration of Milton.* Lincoln NB: University of Nebraska Press, 1983.

Berman, Ronald. *Henry King and the Seventeenth Century.* London: Chatto & Windus, 1964.

Bloom, Harold, ed. *Christopher Marlowe.* New York: Chelsea House, 1986.

Bloom, Harold, ed. *Andrew Marvell.* New York: Chelsea House, 1989.

Bloom, Harold, ed. *Elizabethan Dramatists.* New York: Chelsea House, 1986.

Bowen, Catherine Drinker. *Francis Bacon: The Temper of a Man.* Boston: Little, Brown, 1963.

Bowen, Elizabeth, and others. *The Heritage of British Literature.* New York: Thames and Hudson, 1983.

Boyce, Benjamin. *The Theophrastan Character in England to 1642.* London: Frank Cass, 1971.

Brooke, John L *The Refiner's Fire: The Making of Mormon Cosmology, 1644-1844.* 1994. New York: Cambridge University Press, 1996.

Brown, John. *John Bunyan (1628-1688): His Life, Times, and Work.* London: Hulbert, 1928.

Buckle, Henry Thomas. *History of Civilization in England.* 3

Vols. London: Longmans, Green, 1903.

Bulwer, John. *Chirologia: or the Natural Language of the Hand, and Chironomia: or the Art of Manual Rhetoric.* Carbondale and Edwardsville IL: Southern Illinois University Press, 1974.

Bush, Douglas. *English Literature in the Earlier Seventeenth Century, 1600-1660.* Oxford at the Clarendon Press, 1945.

Campbell, Gordon, Thomas N. Corns, and others. "The Provenance of *De Doctrina Christiana*," in *Milton Quarterly* 31:3 (1997): pp. 67-109

Campbell, Gordon. "Milton in Madras." *Milton Quarterly* Vol. 31, no. 2 (1997).

Campbell, Lily B. *Shakespeare's "Histories": Mirrors of Elizabethan Policy.* San Marino CA: Huntington Library, 1965.

Campbell, Oscar James, intro. *Shakespeare's Hamlet: The Second Quarto, 1604—Reproduced in facsimile from the Copy in the Huntington Library.* San Marino CA: Huntington Library, 1964.

Carey, Frank, ed. *John Donne.* New York: Oxford University Press, 1990.

Carlton, Charles. *Archbishop William Laud.* London: Routledge & Kegan Paul, 1987.

Carlton, Charles. *Charles I: The Personal Monarch.* London: Routledge & Kegan Paul, 1983. London: Ark Paperbacks, 1984.

Capp, B. S. *The Fifth Monarchy Men: A Study in Seventeenth-Century Millenarianism.* Totowa NJ: Rowman and Littlefield, 1972.

Carpenter, Frederic Ives. *A Reference Guide to Edmund Spenser.* Chicago: University of Chicago Press, 1923. Rpt. New York: Kraus, 1969.

Cartwright, Julia [Mrs. Henry Ady]. *Sacharissa: Some Account of Dorothy Sidney, Countess of Sunderland, Her Family and Friends, 1617-1684.* 3rd edition. London: Seeley and Co., 1901.

Cary, John, ed. *John Milton: Complete Shorter Poems.* London: Longman, 1968, 1971.

Carlton, Charles, *Charles I: The Personal Monarch.* 1983. London: Ark/Routledge & Kegan Paul, 1984.

Cavendish, Margaret Lucas, Duchess of Newcastle. *The Life of William Cavendish, Duke of Newcastle, to which is added The True Relation of my Birth, Breeding, and Life.* New York: Scribner & Welford, 1886.

Charles, Amy M. *A Life of George Herbert.* Ithaca NY: Cornell University Press, 1977.

Clayton, Thomas, ed. *The Works of Sir John Suckling: The Non-Dramatic Works.* Oxford at the Clarendon Press, 1971

Clegg, Cyndia Susan. *Press Censorship in Elizabethan England.* Cambridge University Press, 1997.

Clegg, Cyndia Susan. *Stationers' Register.* Unpublished research data-base.

Coffin, Robert P. Tristram. *The Dukes of Buckingham: Playboys of the Stuart World.* New York: Brentano's, 1931.

Cook, Albert S., ed. *The Art of Poetry: The Poetical Treatises of Horace, Vida, and Boileau, with the Translations by Howes, Pitt, and Soame.* Boston MA: Ginn & Company, 1892.

Cope, Esther S., ed. *The Prophetic Writings of Lady Eleanor Davies.* New York: Oxford University Press, 1995.

Cope, Jackson I. *Joseph Glanvill: Anglican Apologist.* St. Louis: Washington University Studies, 1956.

Cowan, Samuel. *The Royal House of Stewart: From its Origin to the Accession of the House of Hanover.* London: Greening & Co., 1908.

Croft, P. J., ed. and comp. *Autograph Poetry in the English Language: Facsimiles of original manuscripts from the Fourteenth to the Twentieth Century.* 2 vols. London: Cassell, 1973.

Crump, Galbraith M., ed. *Poems on Affairs of State: Augustan Satirical Verse, 1660-1714. Vol. IV: 1685-1688.* New Haven CT: Yale University Press, 1968.

Cullen, Patrick Colborn, ed. *Anna Weamys: A Continuation of Sir Philip Sidney's* Arcadia. New York: Oxford University Press, 1994.

Daiches, David, and John Flower. *Literary Landscapes of the*

British Isles: A Narrative Atlas. New York: Paddington Press, 1979.

Danielson, Dennis Richard. *Milton's Good God: A Study in Literary Theodicy.* Cambridge: Cambridge University Press, 1982.

Darbishire, Helen, ed. *The Early Lives of Milton.* New York: Barnes & Noble, 1965.

De Santillana, Giorgio. *The Crime of Galileo.* Chicago: University of Chicago Press, 1955; New York: Time, 1962.

Delany, Paul, *British Autobiography in the Seventeenth Century.* London: Routledge & Kegan Paul, 1969.

Dell, Floyd, and Paul Jordan-Smith, eds. *The Anatomy of Melancholy by Robert Burton.* 1927. New York: Tudor, 1941.

Di Cesare, Mario A, ed. *George Herbert and the Seventeenth-Century Religious Poets.* New York: Norton, 1978.

Di Cesare, Mario. *George Herbert: The Temple. A Diplomatic Edition of the Bodleian Manuscript (Tanner 307).* Binghamton NY: Medieval and Renaissance Tests and Studies, 1995.

Donno, Elizabeth Story, ed. *Elizabethan Minor Epics.* New York: Columbia UP, 1963.

Duncan-Jones, A. S. *Archbishop Laud.* London: Macmillan, 1927.

Duncan-Jones, Katherine. *Sir Philip Sidney: Courtier Poet.* New Haven: Yale University Press, 1991.

Dunlap, Rhodes. *The Poems of Thomas Carew with his Masque* Coelum Britannicum. Oxford at the Clarendon Press, 1949, 1964.

Durant, David N. *Where Queen Elizabeth Slept & What the Butler Saw: Historical Terms from the Sixteenth Century to the Present.* New York: St. Martin's, 1996.

Durant, Will and Ariel. *The Age of Louis XIV: A History of European civilization in the Period of Pascal, Molière, Cromwell, Milton, Peter the Great, Newton, and Spinoza: 1648-1715.* New York: Simon and Schuster, 1963.

Ellis, Frank H. *Poems on Affairs of State: Augustan Satirical Verse: 1660-1714. Vol. 6: 12697-1704.* New Haven CT: Yale

University Press, 1970.

Endicott, Norman, ed. *The Prose of Sir Thomas Browne*. New York: New York University Press, 1968.

Evans, G. Blakemore, and others. *The Riverside Shakespeare*. Boston: Houghton Mifflin, 1974.

Evelyn, John. *The Diary of John Evelyn*. 2 volumes. Washington and London: M. Walter Dunne, 1901.

Ezell, Mary J. M., ed. *The Poems and Prose of Mary, Lady Chudleigh*. New York: Oxford University Press, 1993.

Faber, Richard. *The Brave Courtier: Sir William Temple*. London: Faber and Faber, 1983.

Falco, Raphael. *Conceived Presences: Literary Genealogy in Renaissance England*. Amherst: University of Massachusetts Press, 1994.

Fallon, Robert Thomas. *Milton in Government*. University Park PA: Pennsylvania State University Press, 1993.

Firth, Charles Harding. *Oliver Cromwell and the Rule of the Puritans in England*. New York and London: G. P. Putnam's Sons/The Knickerbocker Press, 1900.

Firth, Charles Harding, ed. *Stuart Tracts 1603-1693*. Westminster: Archibald Constable, 1903.

Flannagan, Roy. *The Riverside Milton*. Boston: Houghton Mifflin, 1998.

Fogle, French, ed. *Complete Prose Works of John Milton, Volume V, 1648?-1671, Parts I and II*. New Haven: Yale University Press, 1971.

Frank, Joseph. *Cromwell's Press Agent: A Critical Biography of Marchamont Nedham, 1620-1678*. Lanham MD: University Press of America, 1980.

Frank, Joseph. *The Levellers: A History of the Writings of Three Seventeenth-Century Social Democrats: John Lilburne, Richard Overton, William Walwyn*. New York: Russell & Russell, 1955.

Fraser, Antonia. *Faith and Treason: The Story of the Gunpowder Plot*. New York: Nan A. Talese/Doubleday, 1996.

Fraser, Antonia. *King James VI of Scotland and I of England*.

New York: Alfred A. Knopf, 1975.

Frazier, Antonia. *The Weaker Vessel.* New York: Knopf, 1984.

French, J. Milton, ed. *The Life Records of John Milton.* 5 vols. 1948-1958. New York: Gordian 1966.

French, Peter. *John Dee: The World of an Elizabethan Magus.* 1972. London and New York: Ark/Routledge & Kegan Paul, 1987.

Frye, Roland Mushat. *Milton's Imagery and the Visual Arts: Iconographic Tradition in the Epic poems.* Princeton NJ: Princeton University Press, 1978.

Gardiner, Samuel Rawson, ed. *The Constitutional Documents of the Puritan Revolution 1625-1660.* 1889. 3rd edition. Oxford at the Clarendon Press, 1906, 1936.

Gardiner, Samuel R. *History of England from the Accession of James I to the Outbreak of the Civil War, 1603-1642.* 10 volumes. London: Longmans, Green, 1883.

Garnett, Richard. *Life of John Milton.* London: Walter Scott, 1890.

Gilbert, Jack G. *Edmund Waller.* Boston: Twayne, 1979.

Gilman, Ernest B. *Iconoclasm and Poetry in the English Reformation: Down Went Dagon.* Chicago: University of Chicago Press, 1986.

Glanvil, Joseph. *The Vanity of Dogmatizing.* London, 1661. New York: Facsimile Text Society/Columbia University Press, 1931.

Godfrey, Elizabeth [Jessie Bedford]. *Social Life Under the Stuarts.* New York: E. P. Dutton, 1904; London: Grant Richards, 1904.

Goldberg, Jonathan. *Writing Matters: From the Hands of the English Renaissance.* Stanford CA: Stanford University Press, 1990.

Goreau, Angeline. *Reconstructing Aphra: A Social Biography of Aphra Behn.* New York: The Dial Press, 1980.

Gosse, Edmund. *Sir Thomas Browne.* 1905. London: Macmillan, 1924.

Green, Jonathan. *The Encyclopedia of Censorship.* New York: Facts on File, 1990.

Greene, Graham. *Lord Rochester's Monkey, Being the Life of John Wilmot, Second Earl of Rochester.* New York: Studio/Viking, 1974.

Greer, Germaine, and others, eds. *Kissing the Rod: An Anthology of Seventeenth-Century Women's Verse.* New York: Noonday/ Farrar Straus Giroux, 1989.

Gregg, Pauline. *King Charles I.* Berkeley CA: University of California Press, 1981.

Hallam, Henry. *The Constitutional History of England from the Accession of Henry VII to the Death of George II.* Vol. II. 5th ed. Paris: A. and W. Galignani, 1841.

Haller, William, ed., *Tracts on Liberty in the Puritan Revolution 1638-1647.* 3 vols. New York: Columbia University Press, 1934.

Halsband, Robert. *The Life of Lady Mary Wortley Montagu.* 1956. New York: Oxford UP/Galaxy, 1960.

Hanford, James Holly. *John Milton: Englishman.* New York: Crown, 1949.

Hanford, James Holly, ed. *A Restoration Reader.* New York: Grove, 1954, 1960.

Hannay, Margaret P. *Philip's Phoenix: Mary Sidney, Countess of Pembroke.* New York: Oxford University Press, 1990.

Harbage, Alfred. *Sir William Davenant: Poet Venturer 1606-1668.* 1935. New York: Octagon, 1971.

Hause, Earl Malcolm. *Tumble-Down Dick: The Fall of the House of Cromwell.* New York: Exposition Press, 1972.

Hay, Millicent V. *The Life of Robert Sidney, Earl of Leicester (1563-1626).* Washington CD: Folger Shakespeare Library, 1984.

Hayes, T. Wilson. *Winstanley the Digger: A Literary Analysis of Radical Ideas in the English Revolution.* Cambridge MA: Harvard University Press, 1979.

Haynes, Alan. *The Gunpowder Plot: Faith in Rebellion.* London: Grange, 1994.

Helm, P. J. *Jeffries: A New Portrait of England's 'Hanging*

Judge.' New York: Crowell, 1966

Hibbert, Christopher. *The Virgin Queen: Elizabeth I, Genius of the Golden Age.* Reading MA: Addison-Wesley, 1991.

Hill, Christopher, Barry Reay, and William Lamont. *The World of the Muggletonians.* London: Temple Smith, 1983.

Hill, Christopher. *Change and Continuity in Seventeenth-Century England.* Cambridge MA: Harvard University Press, 1975.

Hill, Christopher. *A Nation of Change & Novelty: Radical Politics, Religion and Literature in Seventeenth-Century England.* London and New York: Routledge, 1990.

Hill, Christopher. *God's Englishman: Oliver Cromwell and the English Revolution.* New York: Dial, 1970. Rpt. New York: Harper & Row, 1972.

Hill, Christopher. *Milton and the English Revolution.* New York: Viking, 1977.

Hill, Christopher. *The Century of Revolution, 1603-1714.* Edinburgh: Thomas Nelson and Sons, 1961. New York: W. W. Norton, 1982.

Hill, Christopher. *The English Bible and the Seventeenth-Century Revolution.* 1993. New York: Penguin Books, 1994.

Hill, Christopher. *The Experience of Defeat: Milton and Some Contemporaries.* New York: Viking, 1984.

Hill, Christopher. *The World Turned Upside Down: Radical Ideas during the English Revolution* 1972. New York: Penguin, 1991.

Hinchman, Walter S. *A History of English Literature.* 1915. New York: Century, 1917.

Hotson, Leslie, *The Death of Christopher Marlowe.* London: Nonesuch, 1925; Cambridge MA: Harvard University Press, 1925.

Hotson, Leslie. *Mr. W. H.* New York: Knopf, 1964.

Hubbard, Elbert. *John Milton.* East Aurora NY: Roycrofters, 1901.

Hughes, Merritt Y., ed. *John Milton: Complete Poems and Major Prose.* New York: Macmillan, 1957.

Hughes, Merritt Y., ed., *Complete Prose Works of John Milton, Volume III, 1648-1649.* New Haven CT: Yale University Press, 1962.

Hunter, William B., Jr., C. A. Patrides, and J. H. Adamson. *Bright Essence: Studies in Milton's Theology.* Salt Lake City UT: University of Utah Press, 1971.

Hunter, William B., Jr., ed. *The English Spenserians: The Poetry of Giles Fletcher, George Wither, Michael Drayton, Phineas Fletcher, and Henry More.* Salt Lake City: University of Utah Press, 1977.

Hunter, William B., Jr., general editor. *A Milton Encyclopedia.* 9 vols. Lewisburg: Bucknell University Press, 1978-1983.

Huntley, Frank Livingstone. *Bishop Joseph Hall (1574-1656): A Biographical and Critical Study.*, Cambridge: D. S. Brewer, 1979.

Huntley, Frank Livingstone. *Essays in Persuasion: On Seventeenth-Century Literature.* Chicago: University of Chicago Press, 1981.

Huntley, Frank Livingstone. *Jeremy Taylor and the Great Rebellion: A Study of His Mind and Temper in Controversy.* Ann Arbor MI: University of Michigan Press, 1970.

Hutchinson, Lucy. *Memoirs of the Life of Colonel Hutchinson..., to Which is Prefixed The life of Mrs. Hutchinson... to which is now first added an account of The Siege of Latham House.* 5th edition. London: Henry G. Bohn, 1846.

Hyde, Edward, Earl of Clarendon. *The Life of Edward Earl of Clarendon, Lord High Chancellor of England, and Chancellor of the University of Oxford, in which is included a Continuation of the History of the Grand Rebellion. Written by Himself.* Vol. I. Oxford at the Clarendon Press, 1827.

Hyman, Lawrence W. *Andrew Marvell.* New York: Twayne. 1964.

Jarrett, Derek. *England in the Age of Hogarth.* New Haven: Yale UP, 1974, 1992.

Jones, Esmor. *Milton.* Glasgow: Blackie, 1977.

Jorgens, Elise Bickford. *The Well-Tun'd Word: Musical*

Interpretations of English Poetry, 1597-1651. Minneapolis: University of Minnesota Press, 1982.

Kaplan, Barbara Beigun. *Divulging of Useful Truths in Physick": The Medical Agenda of Robert Boyle.* Baltimore and London: Johns Hopkins University Press, 1993.

Kelley, Maurice, ed. *Complete Prose Works of John Milton, Volume VI, ca. 1658-ca. 1660.* New Haven CT: Yale University Press, 1973.

Kelley, Maurice, ed. *Complete Prose Works of John Milton, Volume VIII, 1666-1682.* New Haven CT: Yale University Press, 1982.

Kent, William. *London for the Literary Pilgrim.* London: Salisbury Square, 1949.

King, Bruce. *Seventeenth-Century English Literature.* New York: Schocken, 1982.

Knoll, Robert E. *Christopher Marlowe.* New York: Twayne, 1969.

Koon, Helene. *Colley Cibber: A Biography.* Lexington: University Press of Kentucky, 1986.

Kozlenko, William, ed. *Disputed Plays of William Shakespeare.* New York: Hawthorn, 1974.

Lamson, Roy, and Hallett Smith, eds. *The Golden Hind: An Anthology of Elizabethan Prose and Poetry.* New York: Norton, 1942.

Lane, Jane [pseud. Elaine Dakars], *Puritan Rake and Squire.* London: Evans, 1950.

Le Comte, Edward. *A Milton Dictionary.* New York: Philosophical Library, 1961.

Le Comte, Edward. *Grace to a Witty Sinner: A Life of Donne.* New York: Walker and Company, 1965.

Leason, James. *The Plague and the Fire.* New York: McGraw-Hill, 1961.

Lewalski, Barbara Kiefer. "Lucy, Countess of Bedford: Images of a Jacobean Courtier and Patroness." *Politics of Discourse: The Literature and History of Seventeenth-Century England.* Ed. Kevin Sharpe and Steven N. Zwicker. Berkeley and Los Angeles: University of California Press, 1987. 52-77.

Lewalski, Barbara Kiefer, ed. *The Polemics and Poems of Rachel Speght.* New York: Oxford University Press, 1996.

Lindley, David, ed. *Court Masques: Jacobean and Caroline Entertainments 1605-1640.* Oxford: Oxford University Press, 1995.

Lipking, Joanna, ed. *Aphra Behn: Oroonoko.* New York: W. W. Norton, 1997.

Lockyer, Roger. *Buckingham: The Life and Political Career of George Villiers, First Duke of Buckingham, 1592-1628.* London: Longman, 1981.

Lonsdale, Roger, ed. *Dryden to Johnson.* London: Sphere, 1971, 1986.

Lossky, Nicholas. *Lancelot Andrewes, The Preacher (1555-1626): The Origins of the Mystical Theology of the Church of England.* Trans. Andrew Louth. Oxford. Clarendon Press, 1991.

Macaulay, Rose. *Milton: Great Lives.* London: Duckworth, 1934.

Mack, Maynard. *Alexander Pope: A Life.* New Haven: Yale University Press, 1985. New York: Norton, 1988.

MacKeller, Walter. *A Variorum Commentary on The Poems of John Milton: Volume Four. Paradise Regained..* New York: Columbia University Press, 1975.

MacLean, Gerald M. *Time's Witness: Historical Representation in English Poetry, 1603-1660.* Madison: University of Wisconsin Press, 1990.

Maclean, Hugh, ed. *Ben Jonson and the Cavalier Poets.* New York: Norton, 1974.

MacLure, Millar. *George Chapman: A Critical Study.* University of Toronto Press, 1966.

Mann, Francis Oscar. *The Works of Thomas Deloney.* Oxford at the Clarendon Press, 1912.

Martz, Louis L. *The Meditative Poem.* New York: Doubleday, 1963.

Martz, Louis L. *The Poetry of Meditation: A Study in English Religious Literature of the Seventeenth.* New Haven CT: Yale

University Press, 1954.

Mathew, David. *James I.* London: Billing & Sons, 1976; University AL: University of Alabama Press, 1968.

McColley, Diane Kelsey. *Milton's Eve.* Urbana IL: University of Illinois Press, 1983.

McElwee, William. *The Wisest Fool in Christendom: The Reign of James I and VI.* London: Faber and Faber, 1958.

McEwen, Gilbert D. *The Oracle of the Coffee House: John Dunton's* ATHENIAN MERCURY. San Marino CA: Huntington Library, 1972.

McKeon, Michael. *Politics and Poetry in Restoration England: The Case of Dryden's* Annus Mirabilis. Cambridge: Harvard University Press, 1975.

McMillin, Scott, ed. *Restoration and Eighteenth-Century Comedy.* 1973. 2nd ed. New York: Norton, 1997.

Mead, Lucia Ames. *Milton's England.* Boston: L. C. Page, 1908.

Miller, Timothy C., ed. *The Critical Response to John Milton's* Paradise Lost. Westport CT: Greenwood, 1997.

Milton Encyclopedia, A. See: Hunter, William B., Jr.

Michell, John. *Who Wrote Shakespeare?* Great Britain: Thames & Hudson, 1996.

Milton, John. *Britain under Trojan, Roman, Saxon Rule.* London: Alex. Murray, 1870.

Milton, John. *Complete Prose Works of John Milton.* New Haven: Yale University Press, 1953-1974. See also entries under editors for individual volumes.

Miner, Earl, ed. *John Dryden.* Writers and their Backgrounds. Athens OH: Ohio University Press, 1972, 1975.

Mitchell, John. *Who Wrote Shakespeare?* London: Thames and Hudson, 1996.

Mish, Charles C., ed. *Short Fiction of the Seventeenth Century.* New York: New York University Press, 1963.

Moore Smith, G. C., ed. *The Poems English & Latin of Edward, Lord Herbert of Cherbury.* Oxford at the Clarendon Press, 1923.

More, Henry. *Enchiridion Ethicum: The English Translation of 1690.* New York: Facsimile Text society, 1930.

Muir, Kenneth, ed. *King Lear.* Cambridge MA: Harvard University Press, 1952.

Nerhood, Harry W., comp. *To Russia and Return: An Annotated Bibliography of Travelers' English-Language accounts to Russia from the Ninth Century to the Present.* Ohio State University Press, 1968.

Nethercot, Arthur. H. *Sir William D'Avenant: Poet Laureate and Playwright-Manager.* 1938. New York: Russell & Russell, 1967.

Nichol, John. "Introduction" in *The Poetical Works of George Herbert.* Ed. Charles Cowden Clarke. London: Bickers and Bush, 1863.

Nicholl, Charles, *The Reckoning: The Murder of Christopher Marlowe.* New York: Harcourt, 1992.

Notestein, Wallace. *A History of Witchcraft in England from 1558 to 1718.* 1911. New York: Thomas Y. Crowell, 1968.

Noyes, Alfred. *Tales of the Mermaid Tavern.* New York: Frederick A. Stokes, 1913.

Noyes, George R. *The Poetical Works of John Dryden—Cambridge Edition.* Boston: Houghton Mifflin, 1909.

O Hehir, Brendan. *Expans'd Hieroglyphicks: A Critical Edition of Sir John Denham's Coopers Hill.* Berkeley and Los Angeles: University of California Press, 1969.

Oakeshott, Walter. *The Queen and the Poet.* New York: Barnes & Noble, 1961.

Palmer, Tony. *Charles II: Portrait of an Age.* London: Book Club Associates, 1979

Parfitt, George. *English Poetry of the Seventeenth Century.* New York: Longman, 1985.

Parker, William Riley. "The Date of *Samson Agonistes* Again." *Calm of Mind: Tercentenary Essays on Paradise Regained and Samson Agonistes in Honor of John S. Diekhoff,* ed. Joseph Anthony Wittreich, Jr. Cleveland and London: Case Western Reserve University Press, 1971. 161-174.

Parker, William Riley. *Milton: A Biography.* 2 vols. Oxford at the Clarendon Press, 1968.

Patrick, J. Max, ed. *The Complete Poetry of Robert Herrick.* New York: New York University Press, 1963.

Patrides, C. A., ed. *The Cambridge Platonists.* 1969. Cambridge: Cambridge University Press, 1980.

Pepys, Samuel. *The Diary and Correspondence of Samuel Pepys, F. R. S., Secretary to the Admiralty in the Reign of Charles II and James II.* Life and Notes by Richard, Lord Braybrooke. 2 vols. Boston and New York: C. T. Brainard, 1900.

Pepys, Samuel. *The Diary of Samuel Pepys, Esquire, F. R. S.* Ed. Lord Braybrook. London: Simpkin, Marshall, Hamilton, Kent, [1908]. New York: Scribner's [1908]

Pepys, Samuel. *The Diary of Samuel Pepys, 1660-1669.* Abridged and Edited by Isabel Ely Lord. Eu Claire WI: E. M. Hale, [n.d.]

Picard, Liza. *Restoration London: From Poverty to Pets, from Medicine to Magic, from Slang to Sex, from Wallpaper to Women's Rights.* New York: St. Martin's, 1997.

Post, Jonathan F. S. *Henry Vaughan: The Unfolding Vision.* Princeton NJ: Princeton University Press, 1982.

Powicke, Frederick J. *The Cambridge Platonists: A Study.* 1926. Rpt. Westport CT: Greenwood Press, 1970.

Quennell, Peter. *Alexander Pope: The Education of Genius, 1688-1728.* London: Weidenfeld and Nicolson, 1968.

Raymond, Dora Neil. *Oliver's Secretary: John Milton in an Era of Revolt.* New York: Minton, Balch & Company, 1932.

Raymond, Joad. "The Cracking of the Republican Spokes." *Prose Studies: History, Theory, Criticism* Vol. 19, no. 3 (December 1996): 255-274.

Ricks, Christopher, ed. *English Poetry and Prose, 1540-1674.* London: Sphere, 1970.

Riddell, Edwin, ed. *Lives of the Stuart Age 1603-1714.* New York: Barnes and Noble, 1976

Riggs, David. *Ben Jonson: A Life.* Cambridge MA: Harvard University Press, 1989.

Rogow, Arnold A. *Thomas Hobbes: Radical in the Service of Reaction.* New York: W. W. Norton, 1986.

Rowse, A. L. *The English Spirit: Essays in History and Literature.* New York: Macmillan, 1945.

Rollins, Hyder E., ed. *A Pepysian Garland: Black-Letter Broadside Ballads of the Years 1595-1639, Chiefly from the Collection of Samuel Pepys.* Cambridge: Harvard University Press, 1922, 1971.

Sabine, George H., ed. *The Works of Gerrard Winstanley, with an Appendix of Documents Relating to the Digger Movement.* New York: Russell & Russell, 1965.

Saintsbury, George, ed. *Minor Poets of the Caroline Period.* 3 vols. Oxford at the Clarendon Press, 1905, 1906, 1921.

Salzman, Paul, ed. *An Anthology of Seventeenth-Century Fiction.* New York: Oxford University Press, 1991.

Salzman, Paul. *English Prose Fiction 1558-1700: A Critical History.* Oxford: Clarendon Press, 1985.

Sasek, Lawrence A., ed. *Images of English Puritanism: A Collection of Contemporary Sources 1589-1646.* Baton Rouge LA: Louisiana State University Press, 19889.

Schoenbaum, S. *Shakespeare: The Globe & the World.* New York: Folger Shakespeare Library/Oxford University Press, 1979.

Schulman, Lydia Dittler. *Paradise Lost and the Rise of the American Republic.* Boston MA: Northeastern University Press, 1992.

Scott, A. F. *The Poet's Craft: A Course in the Critical Appreciation of Poetry....* Cambridge at the University Press, 1957.

Sirluck, Ernest, ed. *Complete Prose Works of John Milton, Vol. II, 1643-1648.* New Haven, Yale University Press, 1959.

Skelton, Robin, ed. *The Cavalier Poets.* New York: Oxford University Press, 1970.

Skulsky, Harold. *Justice in the Dock: Milton's Experimental Tragedy.* Newark: University of Delaware Press, 1995.

Skulsky, Harold. *Language Recreated: Seventeenth-Century*

Metaphorists and the Act of Metaphor. Athens GA: University of Georgia Press, 1992.

Smith, D. I. B., ed. *Andrew Marvell: The Rehearsal Transpros'd and The Rehearsal Transpros'd The Second Part.* Oxford at the Clarendon Press, 1971.

Smith, David Nichol, ed. *Characters from the Histories & Memoirs of the Seventeenth Century, with an Essay on the Character and Notes by David Nichol Smith.* Oxford at the Clarendon Press, 1918.

Smith, G. C. Moore, ed. *The Poems English & Latin of Edward, Lord Herbert of Cherbury.* Oxford at the Clarendon Press, 1923.

Smith, Nigel. Literature and Revolution in England, 1640-1660. New Haven: Yale University Press, 1994.

Souers, Philip Webster. *The Matchless Orinda.* Cambridge MA: Harvard University Press, 1931.

Squier, Charles L. *Sir John Suckling.* Boston: G. K. Hall, 1978.

Stauffer, Donald Barlow. *A Short History of American Poetry.* New York: E. P. Dutton & Co., 1974.

Stavely, Keith W. F. *Puritan Legacies: Paradise Lost and the New England Tradition, 1630-1890.* Ithaca NY: Cornell University Press, 1987.

Steadman, John M. *The Lamb and the Elephant: Ideal Imitation and the Context of Renaissance Allegory.* San Marino CA: Huntington Library, 1974.

Steadman, John. M. *Milton and the Paradoxes of Renaissance Humanism.* Baton Rouge: Louisiana State University Press, 1987.

Stewart, Stanley. *The King James Version.* New York: Random House, 1977.

Strommer, Diane Weltner. *Time's Distractions: A Play from the Time of Charles I.* College Station TX: Texas A&M University Press, 1976.

Sullivan, Ernest W., II. *The Influence of John Donne: His Uncollected Seventeenth-Century Verse.* Columbia MO, and

London: University of Missouri Press, 1993.

Summers, Joseph H. *George Herbert: His Religion and Art.* 1954. Binghamton NY: Medieval & Renaissance Texts and Studies, Center for Medieval and Early Renaissance Studies, 1981.

Summers, Claude J., and Ted-Larry Pebworth, eds. *"Too Rich to Clothe the Sun": Essays on George Herbert.* Pittsburgh PA: University of Pittsburgh Press, 1980.

Tayler, Edward W., ed. *Literary Criticism of 17th Century England.* New York: Alfred A. Knopf, 1967.

Thayer, H. S., ed. *Newton's Philosophy of Nature: Selections from His Writings.* New York: Hafner, 1953.

Thomas, Keith. *Religion and the Decline of Magic.* New York: Charles Scribner's Sons, 1971.

Thomas, P. W. *Sir John Berkenhead, 1617-1679: A Royalist Career in Politics and Polemics.* Oxford at the Clarendon Press, 1969.

Tillyard, E. M. W. *Milton.* London: Chatto and Windus, 1930.

Traditional Hymns. New York: Henry Holt, 1996.

Trease, Geoffrey. *Portrait of a Cavalier: William Cavendish, First Duke of Newcastle.* New York: Taplinger, 1979.

Trease, Geoffrey. *Samuel Pepys and His World.* New York: G. P. Putnam's Sons, 1972.

Tuve, Rosemond. *Elizabethan and Metaphysical Imagery: Renaissance Poetic and Twentieth-Century Critics.* Chicago IL: University of Chicago Press, 1961.

Underdown, David. *A Freeborn People: Politics and the Nation in Seventeenth-Century England.* Oxford: Clarendon Press, 1996.

Urry, William. *Christopher Marlowe and Canterbury.* London: Faber & Faber, 1988.

Van der Zee, Henri, and Barbara van der Zee. *William and Mary.* London: Macmillan, 1973.

Wade, Gladys I. *Thomas Traherne.* 1944. New York: Octagon, 1969.

Wakefield, Gordon. *John Bunyan: The Christian.* 1992.

London: Fount, 1994.

Wasserman, George R. *Samuel "Hudibras" Butler.* Boston: G. K. Hall/Twayne, 1976.

Wedgwood, C. V. *A Coffin for King Charles: The Trial and Execution of Charles I.* 1964. New York: Book-of-the-Month, 1991.

Weidhorn, Manfred. *Richard Lovelace.* Boston: Twayne, 1970.

White, Beatrice. *Cast of Ravens: The Strange Case of Sir Thomas Overbury.* New York: George Braziller, 1965.

Wiley, Autrey Nell, ed. *Rare Prologues and Epilogues 1642-1700.* London: George Allen and Unwin, 1940.

Williamson, George Charles. *Milton Tercentenary: The Portraits, Prints and Writings of John Milton. Exhibited at Christ's College, Cambridge, 1908.* Cambridge: Cambridge University Press, 1908. Rpt. Norwood Editions, 1976.

Williamson, Hugh Ross. *Four Stuart Portraits.* London: Evans Brothers, 1949.

Williamson, Hugh Ross. *Jeremy Taylor.* London: Dennis Dobson, 1952.

Wilson, A. N. *The Life of John Milton.* New York: Oxford University Press, 1983.

Wilson, Derek. *The Tower: The Tumultuous History of the Tower of London from 1078.* 1978. New York: Charles Scribner's Sons, 1979.

Wilson, John Harold. *Court Satires of the restoration.* Columbus OH: Ohio State University Press, 1976.

Wilson, Katharina M. and Frank J. Warnke. *Women Writers of the Seventeenth Century.* Athens GA: University of Georgia Press, 1989.

Winn, James Anderson. *John Dryden and His World.* New Haven CT: Yale University Press, 1987.

Winton, John [pseudonym]. *Sir Walter Raleigh* New York: Coward, McCann & Geohegan, 1975.

Witherspoon, Alexander M., and Frank J. Warnke, eds. *Seventeenth-Century Prose and Poetry.* 2 ed. New York:

Harcourt, Brace & World, 1963.

Wittreich, Joseph Anthony. *Interpreting Samson Agonistes*. Princeton NJ: Princeton University Press, 1986.

Wolfe, Don M. *Milton and His England*. Princeton NJ: Princeton UP, 1971

Wolfe, Don M., ed. *Complete Prose Works of John Milton, Volume IV, 1650-1655, Parts I and II*. New Haven: Yale University Press, 1966.

Wolfe, Don M., ed., *Complete Prose Works of John Milton, Volume I, 1624-1642*. New Haven: Yale University Press, 1953.

Woudhuysen, H. R., ed. *The Penguin Book of Renaissance Verse*. Selected by David Norbrook. New York: Penguin, 1993.

Wright, William Aldis, ed. *Bacon: The Advancement of Learning*. Oxford at the Clarendon Press, 1873.

Wynne-Davies, Marion, ed. *Prentice Hall Guide to English Literature*. New York: Prentice Hall/Simon & Schuster, 1990.

Yates, Frances A. *Giordano Bruno and the Hermetic Tradition*. 1964. Chicago: University of Chicago Press, 1979, 1991.

Yates, Frances A. *The Art of Memory*. Chicago: The University of Chicago Press, 1966.

Yates, Frances A. *The Rosicrucian Enlightenment*. 1972. London: Routledge, 1993, 1996.

Yates, Nigel. *Buildings, Faith, and Worship: The Liturgical Arrangement of Anglican Churches 1600-1900*. Oxford: Clarendon Press, 1991.

Zack, Naomi. *Bachelors of Science: Seventeenth-Century Identity, Then and Now*. Themes in the History of Philosophy, ed. Edith Wyschogrod. Philadelphia PA: Temple University Press, 1996.

Zall, P. M., ed. *A Nest of Ninnies and Other English Jestbooks of the Seventeenth Century*. Lincoln NB: University of Nebraska Press, 1970.

About the Author

MICHAEL R. COLLINGS is a Professor Emeritus of English at Seaver College, Pepperdine University, where he directed the Creative Writing Program for over two decades and taught, among other things, courses in Milton and Renaissance Literature. His dissertation, completed under the direction of a world-renowned Milton scholar, has been recently published in a substantially revised version as *In Endless Morn of Light: Moral Agency in Milton's Universe* (2010). His long-time interest in Seventeenth-Century literature and society is reflected in key essays in *Toward Other Worlds: Perspectives on John Milton, C. S. Lewis, Stephen King, Orson Scott Card, and Others* (2010), several of which use Renaissance epic theory as a scaffold for discussions of contemporary Science Fiction, Fantasy, and Horror. His fascination with *Paradise Lost* and the Epic resulted in a Book-of-Mormon Miltonic epic, *TheNephiad* (1996, 2010).

In addition to these books, has published over 100 volumes of poetry, novels, short fiction, and scholarly studies of such contemporary writers as Stephen King, Orson Scott Card, Dean R. Koontz, and Piers Anthony. Recent works include *The Art and Craft of Poetry (1996, 2009)*; *In the Void: Poems of Science Fiction, Myth and Fantasy, and Horror (2009)*; *Matrix: Growing Up West—Autobiographical Poems (2010)*. His fiction, also published through Wildside, includes: *The House Beyond the Hill: A Novel of Fear (2007)*; *Wordsmith, Volume One: The Thousand Eyes of Flame (2009)* and *Wordsmith, Volume Two: The Veil of Heaven (2009)*; *Singer of Lies: A Science-Fantasy*

Novel (2009); Wer *Means* Man *and Other Tales of Wonder and Terror (2010)*; *Three Tales of Omne: A Companion to* Wordsmith (2010); *Devil's Plague: A Mystery Novel (2011)*; and *The Slab (2010)*, the story of a haunted tract house in Southern California…that consumes people.

With his wife Judi he recently published *Whole Wheat for Food Storage: Recipes for Unground Wheat*. He is now retired and lives in his native state of Idaho.

www.ingramcontent.com/pod-product-compliance
Lightning Source LLC
Chambersburg PA
CBHW032026150426
43194CB00006B/175